# A·N·N·U·A·L E·D·I·T·I·O·N·S

# Comparative Politics 99/00

*Seventeenth Edition*

**EDITOR**

**Christian Søe**
*California State University, Long Beach*

Christian Søe was born in Denmark, studied in Canada and the United States, and received his doctoral degree in political science from the Free University in Berlin. He is a political science professor at California State University, Long Beach. Dr. Søe teaches a wide range of courses in comparative politics and contemporary political theory, and he actively participates in professional symposiums in the United States and abroad. His research deals primarily with developments in contemporary German politics, and he has been a regular observer of party politics and elections in that country, which he visits annually to conduct interviews and gather research materials. At present Dr. Søe is observing the shifts in the balance of power within the German party system, with particular attention to their implications for the formation of new government coalitions and changes in policy directions. As the Bonn Republic prepares to become the Berlin Republic, he is completing work as coeditor with Mary N. Hampton on a forthcoming book, *Between Bonn and Berlin: German Politics Adrift?* He also plans to contribute as coeditor and chapter author to a book on the 1998 Bundestag election. Three of his most recent publications are a biographical essay on Hans-Dietrich Genscher, Germany's foreign minister from 1974 to 1992, in *Political Leaders of Contemporary Western Europe;* a chapter on the Free Democratic Party in *Germany's New Politics;* and another chapter on the Danish-German relationship in *The Germans and Their Neighbors.* Dr. Søe is also coeditor of the latter two books. He has been editor of *Annual Editions: Comparative Politics* since its beginning in 1983.

*Dushkin/McGraw-Hill*
Sluice Dock, Guilford, Connecticut 06437

**Visit us on the Internet**
*http://www.dushkin.com/annualeditions/*

D0082278

# World Map

This map has been developed to give you a graphic picture of where the countries of the world are located, the relationship they have with their region and neighbors, and their positions relative to the superpowers and power blocs. We have focused on certain areas to more clearly illustrate these crowded regions.

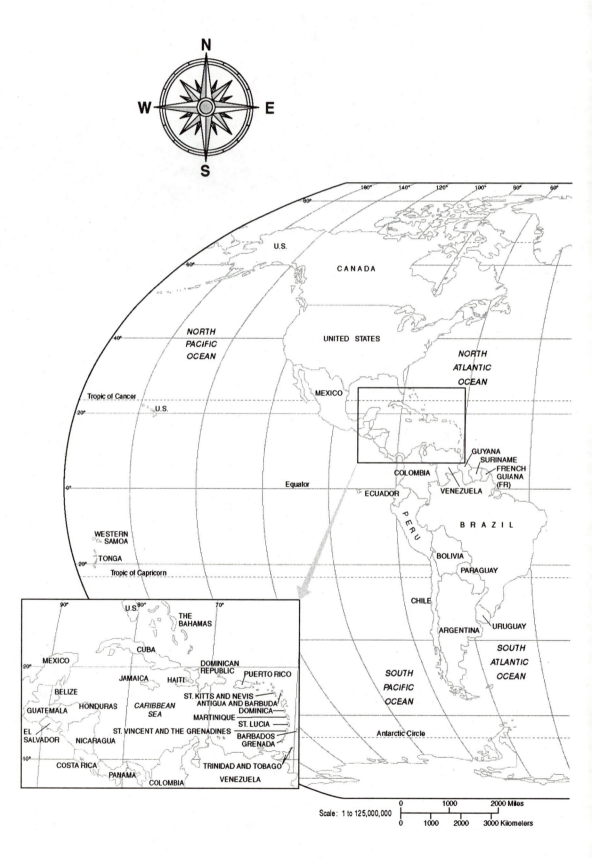

Scale: 1 to 125,000,000

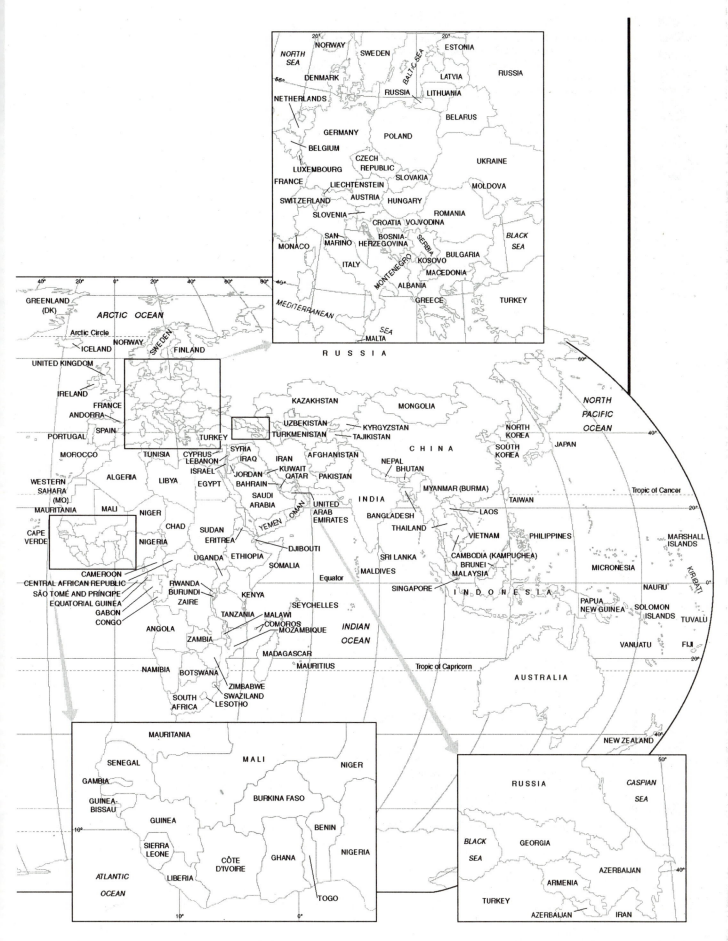

# Credits

**1. Pluralist Democracies: Country Studies**
Unit photo—Christian Science Monitor photo by R. Norman Matheny.
**2. Pluralist Democracies: Factors in the Political Process**
Unit photo—AP/Wide World photo by Michael Euler.
**3. Europe—West, Center, and East: The Politics of Integration, Transformation, and Disintegration**
Unit photo—United Nations photo.
**4. Political Diversity in the Developing World**
Unit photo—United Nations photo.
**5. Comparative Politics: Some Major Trends, Issues, and Prospects**
Unit photo—United Nations photo by J. Isaac.

Cataloging in Publication Data
Main entry under title: Annual Editions: Comparative politics. 1999/2000.
1. World politics—Periodicals. 2. Politics, Practical—Periodicals.
I. Søe, Christian, *comp.* II. Title: Comparative politics.
ISBN 0–07–034949–5     909'.05     83–647654     ISSN 0741–7233

Seventeenth Edition

Cover image © 1999 PhotoDisc, Inc.

Printed in the United States of America     1234567890BAHBAH5432109     Printed on Recycled Paper

# To the Reader

In publishing ANNUAL EDITIONS we recognize the enormous role played by the magazines, newspapers, and journals of the public press in providing current, first-rate educational information in a broad spectrum of interest areas. Many of these articles are appropriate for students, researchers, and professionals seeking accurate, current material to help bridge the gap between principles and theories and the real world. These articles, however, become more useful for study when those of lasting value are carefully collected, organized, indexed, and reproduced in a low-cost format, which provides easy and permanent access when the material is needed. That is the role played by ANNUAL EDITIONS.

New to ANNUAL EDITIONS is the inclusion of related World Wide Web sites. These sites have been selected by our editorial staff to represent some of the best resources found on the World Wide Web today. Through our carefully developed topic guide, we have linked these Web resources to the articles covered in this ANNUAL EDITIONS reader. We think that you will find this volume useful, and we hope that you will take a moment to visit us on the Web at **http://www.dushkin.com** to tell us what you think.

This collection of readings brings together current articles that will help you understand the politics of foreign countries from a comparative perspective. Such a study not only opens up a fascinating world beyond our borders; it will also lead to greater insights into the American political process.

The articles in unit 1 cover Britain, Germany, France, Italy, and Japan in a serial manner. Each of these modern societies has developed its own political framework and agenda, and each has sought to find its own appropriate dynamic balance of continuity and change. Nevertheless, as the readings of unit 2 show, it is possible to point to some common denominators and make useful cross-national comparisons among these and other representative democracies. Unit 3 goes one step further by discussing the impact of two major changes that are rapidly transforming the political map of Europe. One of them is the irregular, sometimes halting, but nevertheless impressive growth of the European Union (EU). The other is the difficult political and economic reconstruction of Central and Eastern Europe after the collapse of this region's Communist regimes. The continuing political importance of Europe has been underscored by these two developments.

Unit 4 looks at some of the developing countries, with articles on Mexico and Latin America as a whole, Nigeria and the Union of South Africa, China, and India. A careful reader will come away with a better understanding of the diversity of social and political conditions in these countries. Additional readings cover the newly industrialized countries of Eastern and Southeastern Asia—the so-called small "dragons," which have managed to generate an impressive, but also fragile, process of rapid economic modernization. Here the central question concerns the combination of factors that have made such a take-off possible and sustainable. Perhaps the answer will point toward a more promising strategy of development for other developing countries.

Unit 5 considers three major trends in contemporary politics from a comparative perspective. The "third wave" of democratization may already have crested, but it is nevertheless important in having changed the politics of many countries. The widespread shifts toward a greater reliance on markets, in place of centralized planning and heavy governmental regulation, is also of great significance. The move is frequently toward some form of a market-oriented "mixed economy," and it should not be misunderstood for a sweeping victory of doctrinaire "laissez-faire." Finally, the surge of what has been called "identity politics," with particular emphasis on exclusive cultural or ethnic group assertion, is a development that bears careful watching.

There has rarely been so interesting and important a time for the study of comparative politics as now. We have an increasingly clear view of how the political earthquake of 1989–1991 has altered the landscape with consequences for many years to come. The aftershocks continue to remind us that we are unlikely to ever experience a "post-historical" condition of political equilibrium. Even in a time of political transformation, however, there are important patterns of continuity as well as change. We must be careful to look for both as we seek to gain a comparative understanding of the politics of other countries and peoples as well as of our own condition.

This is the seventeeth edition of *Annual Editions: Comparative Politics.* It is a sobering reminder that the first edition appeared just as the Brezhnev era had come to a close in what was then a powerful Soviet Union. Over the years, the new editions have tried to reflect the developments that eventually brought about the post–cold war world of today. In a similar way, this present edition tries to present information and analysis that will be useful in understanding today's political world and its role in setting the parameters for tomorrow's developments.

A special word of thanks goes to my own past and present students at California State University, Long Beach. They are wonderfully inquisitive and help keep me posted on matters that this anthology must address. Several of my past graduate students have come back to help gather material for this year's collection. I am particularly grateful to Susan B. Mason. She received her master's degree in political science several years ago, but continues to volunteer as a superb research assistant. Another graduate of our M.A. program, Erika Reinhardt, has provided me with some very useful articles from her own collection. Once again I also wish to thank some other past and present students, Linda Wohlman, Jon Nakagawa, Perry Oliver, Mike Petri, Rich Sherman and Ali Taghavi. For his many contributions I am also indebted to Darell Ten Eyck, who suddenly passed away last year. Like so many others, these individuals first encountered this anthology in my comparative politics courses. It is a great joy to have worked with all these present and former students, whose enthusiasm for the project is contagious.

I am very grateful to members of the advisory board and Dushkin/McGraw Hill as well as to the many readers who have made useful comments on past selections and suggested new ones. I ask you all to help me improve future editions by keeping me informed of your reactions and suggestions for change. Please complete and return the article rating form in the back of the book.

Christian Søe
*Editor*

# Contents

To the Reader     vi
Topic Guide     4
◎ Selected World Wide Web Sites     6

Overview     8

**UNIT 1**

## Pluralist Democracies: Country Studies

Seventeen selections examine
the current state of politics
in the United Kingdom, Germany,
France, Italy, and Japan.

### A. THE UNITED KINGDOM

**1. Tony Blair Rides Triumphant as a Visionary and a Promoter,** Warren Hoge, *New York Times*, February 2, 1999.     15
In *a recent assessment of Tony Blair* and his cabinet, Warren Hoge examines both the substance and style of their governance. The list of achievements is impressive. There are further "centrist" reforms on the agenda, and so far New Labour has deflected the impact of several scandals by imposing damage control.

**2. Unwritten Rules: Britain's Constitutional Revolution,** Donley Studlar, *Harvard International Review*, Spring 1999.     18
An American scholar surveys *the British constitutional order* and provides an up-to-date review of Labour's constitutional reform agenda.

**3. There Will Always Be an England,** Andrew Sullivan, *New York Times Magazine*, February 21, 1999.     22
On his return to Britain after 15 years away, Andrew Sullivan concludes that the United Kingdom is in the process of a social and cultural transformation. Socioeconomic and institutional reform have proven to be of major consequence for the British and their relationships with European neighbors and the United States.

**4. Perspectives on "New" Labour's "Third Way"**     30
First, *Tony Blair* identifies a "third way" with pragmatic *"social democratic" politics* of the center-left that embrace rights and responsibilities, recognition of social compassion, and individual ambition. Thomas Edsall puts this approach into a broader trans-Atlantic perspective. Finally, *The Economist* examines the vague concept of a middle way.

   **a. Third Way, Better Way,** Tony Blair, *Washington Post National Weekly Edition*, October 5, 1998.

   **b. Neither Left Nor Right: Bill Clinton and Tony Blair Are Looking to Internationalize Their 'Third Way' Philosophy,** Thomas B. Edsall, *Washington Post National Weekly Edition*, July 6, 1998.

   **c. Goldilocks Politics,** *The Economist*, December 19, 1998

### B. GERMANY

**5. From the Bonn to the Berlin Republic: Can a Stable Democracy Continue?** Lewis J. Edinger and Brigitte L. Nacos, *Political Science Quarterly*, Volume 113, Number 2, 1998.     37
Writing a few months before the September 1998 election, which brought a *major change of government to Germany,* the authors give an informed assessment of the familiar Bonn Republic. They stress its major political achievements and expect that the new Berlin Republic will continue much of that tradition.

**6. Gerhard Schröder's Government**     44
The September 1998 election brought *a major power shift to Germany* with Gerhard Schröder forming a majority center-left government of Social Democrats (SPD) and Greens that replaced Helmut Kohl's center-right coalition of Christian Democrats (CDU/CSU) and Free Democrats (FDP). These articles look at the election outcome and the somewhat rocky start of the new "red-Green" movement.

   **a. Gerhard Schröder's Task,** *The Economist*, October 3, 1998.
   **b. Where Is It Going?** *The Economist*, December 5, 1998.

**7. Birth of the Berlin Republic,** Peter Norman, *Financial Times,* November 10, 1998.   **51**

The move of **Germany's political center** to Berlin coincides with the transfer of power to a new generation. As Peter Norman emphasizes, the new German government is confronted with the need for social and economic reforms, but some of its strategies are at odds with the conventional wisdom of market economics.

**8. Goodbye to All That,** Ralph Atkins, *Financial Times,* December 30, 1998.   **53**

**Germany now has its first completely left-of-center government** at the national level, and the first one led by politicians who have no first-hand memories of the Nazi period. It is a government that seems ready to be more self-confident in pursuing a German agenda.

**9. Perspectives on the German Model**   **55**

**Germany's social-market system,** traditionally a model for delivering stability and prosperity, is currently in worse shape than it looks. Germany is faced with new worker-manager reforms. Unknown still is whether future reforms will produce a new model that is defined differently. Some argue that Germany's political system itself promotes gridlock.

**a. Is the Model Broken?** *The Economist,* May 4, 1996.

**b. The German Welfare Model That Still Is,** Peter Ross Range and Robert Gerald Livingston, *Washington Post,* August 11, 1996.

**c. Germans Cut Labor Costs with a Harsh Export: Jobs,** Edmund L. Andrews, *New York Times,* March 21, 1998.

**C. FRANCE**

**10. Field Victory Colors French View of Themselves,** John-Thor Dahlburg, *Los Angeles Times,* July 25, 1998.   **62**

In a stunning upset victory, France won the World Cup in soccer in 1998. The event triggered a national exuberance, but it also served as a powerful reminder that the winning team ("Les Bleus") represented an ethnic harmony-in-diversity that is far from realized in the country's daily life. The event may **promote integration of French citizens of North African, sub-Saharan, or Asian descent.**

**11. Resisting Reform to de Gaulle's Old Constitution,** Robert Graham, *Financial Times,* October 14, 1998.   **64**

The constitution of the Fifth Republic attracts much criticism for being outdated. A central issue is a change in the balance of presidential and prime ministerial power in favor of the latter. A change in regional elections is also being seriously discussed as a way of **reducing the influence of the National Front.**

**12. Right and Left in France: Two Recent Reports,**   **66**

These articles report on **the condition of the French right and left.** The right remains deeply fragmented by the issues of Europe, the National Front, domestic policy questions, and policy rivalries. The French left is in far better condition and shows an almost "Blairite" pragmatism in office.

**a. France's Right: An Utter Mess,** *The Economist,* September 19, 1998.

**b. The French Left Begins to Falter,** *The Economist,* January 9, 1999.

**13. Perspectives on the French Model**   **69**

France and the United States appear to offer **two very different models of capitalism.** Roger Cohen believes that the differences may be smaller than rhetoric or caricature would have it. Daniel Sanger contends that France may pursue a more determinedly left-wing alternative to U.S.–style market capitalism. Meanwhile, *The Economist* reports that Prime Minister Lionel Jospin has had second thoughts about the French stereotype of the "American model."

**a. France vs. U.S.: Warring Views of Capitalism,** Roger Cohen, *New York Times,* October 20, 1997.

The concepts in bold italics are developed in the article. For further expansion please refer to the Topic Guide and the Index.

**b. Is There a French Alternative?** Daniel Singer, *The Nation*, October 27, 1997.

**c. Jospin Discovers America,** *The Economist*, June 27, 1998.

### D. ITALY

14. **Tocqueville in Italy,** David L. Kirp, *The Nation*, November 8, 1993.      **74**
    David Kirp reviews Robert Putnam's highly praised work on the role of different **civic traditions** in the varying economic and political development of Italy's regions. The findings stress the importance of a community's "stock of **social capital.**"

15. **Former Communist Installed in Italy,** Alessandra Stanley, *New York Times*, October 22, 1998.      **76**
    **Italy's new coalition government** is headed by Massimo D'Alema, the leader of the former Communist Party. It spans a wide political spectrum from far left to moderate right.

### E. JAPAN

16. **The July 1998 Election: Two Reports**      **78**
    Japan has recently experienced its worst economic crisis in more than half a century. Politically the country is going through some significant changes as **the ruling Liberal Democratic Party is being challenged.**
    **a. Japanese Rebuke Governing Party in National Vote: Stage Set for Premier's Resignation—More Disarray Expected,** Nicholas D. Kristof, *New York Times*, July 13, 1998.
    **b. Election as Reproof: Japan Challenges the System,** Stephanie Strom, *New York Times*, July 26, 1998.

17. **Japan's Search for a New Path,** T. J. Pempel, *Current History*, December 1998.      **83**
    Japan is in the middle of a struggle over how to deliver the country's familiar mix of economic dynamism and social equity. It is still unclear how the struggle will play out, but **the pressures for a major economic and political redirection** have become immense.

**Overview**      **88**

### A. POLITICAL IDEAS, MOVEMENTS, PARTIES

18. **Europe: A Continental Drift—to the Left,** *The Economist*, October 3, 1998.      **93**
    Parties of the left now either control or share power in **13 of the EU's 15 national governments.** That does not mean that they agree on what "the left" stands for. But the left has a useful pan-Europan party network and some shared priorities. Soon after this article was published, Massimo D'Alema replaced Romano Prodi as head of a broad coalition government of the center-left in Italy.

19. **Europe's Right: Displaced, Defeated and Not Sure What to Do Next,** *The Economist*, January 23, 1999.      **95**
    **Within the EU,** parties of the right-of-center have experienced electoral decline in recent years.

### B. WOMEN AND POLITICS

20. **Women in Power: From Tokenism to Critical Mass,** Jane S. Jaquette, *Foreign Policy*, Fall 1997.      **98**
    Worldwide there are more **women in elected national office** than ever before, and their presence is achieving critical mass in some countries. This article gives a historical overview of women's representation and suggests reasons for the recent breakthroughs.

**UNIT 2**

## Pluralist Democracies: Factors in the Political Process

Seven selections examine the functioning of Western European democracies with regard to political ideas and participation, ethnic politics, the role of women in politics, and the institutional framework of representative government.

The concepts in bold italics are developed in the article. For further expansion please refer to the Topic Guide and the Index.

**C. THE INSTITUTIONAL FRAMEWORK OF REPRESENTATIVE GOVERNMENT**

21. **What Democracy Is . . . and Is Not,** Philippe C. Schmitter and Terry Lynn Karl, *Journal of Democracy,* Summer 1991. **105**

   The authors point out that **modern representative democracies** vary considerably in their institutions, practices, and values, depending upon their different socioeconomic, historical, and cultural settings.

22. **Devolution Can Be Salvation,** *The Economist,* September 20, 1997. **112**

   A regional parliament in Scotland will link Britain to a wider European experience with political devolution. This short article looks at some of **the continent's regional trends** and problems.

23. **Parliament and Congress: Is the Grass Greener on the Other Side?** Gregory S. Mahler, *Canadian Parliamentary Review,* Winter 1985–1986. **114**

   Gregory Mahler examines the arguments advanced by supporters of both the **parliamentary and the congressional systems of government.**

24. **Campaign and Party Finance: What Americans Might Learn from Abroad,** Arthur B. Gunlicks, *Party Line,* Spring/Summer 1993. **118**

   Arthur Gunlicks looks at **campaign and party finance** in several Western democracies, with an eye on some possible lessons for the United States.

**Overview** **120**

**A. THE EUROPEAN UNION**

25. **The Untied States of Europe,** Tyler Marshall, *Los Angeles Times,* May 20, 1996. **125**

   After 20 years of reporting from Europe, a top U.S. reporter reflects on its fitful **efforts at integration.** He stresses that cultural diversity remains important, even though it tends to be officially ignored.

26. **What Is Europe? The Changing Idea of a Continent,** Richard Rose, *Politics Review,* January 1997. **127**

   Any attempt to reduce Europe to a single idea is bound to fail. It is marked by diversity and complexity. The author explores some **politically relevant differences among the countries of Europe.**

27. **The Institutional Framework of the EU** **132**

   In a series of short articles, *The Economist* presents the major **EU institutions** and emphasizes the need for reform if the EU is to be successful in its project of eastward expansion.

   a. **Looking for Legitimacy,** *The Economist,* January 11, 1997.

   b. **The Big Squeeze,** *The Economist,* February 8, 1997.

   c. **Doing the Splits,** *The Economist,* March 8, 1997.

   d. **Biased Referee?** *The Economist,* May 17, 1997.

   e. **Coreper, Europe's Managing Board,** *The Economist,* August 8, 1998.

28. **Europe's Censure Motion,** Quentin Peel and Peter Norman, *Financial Times,* January 15, 1999. **138**

   In an unprecedented move, the European Parliament voted on a motion of censure of the European Commission. Although the motion was defeated, it could represent a major step toward establishing **parliamentary responsibility in the EU.**

**UNIT 3**

## Europe—West, Center, and East: The Politics of Integration, Transformation, and Disintegration

Nine selections examine the European continent: the European Union, Western European society, post-communist Central and Eastern Europe, and Russia and the other post-Soviet Republics.

The concepts in bold italics are developed in the article. For further expansion please refer to the Topic Guide and the Index.

## B.  THE INTRODUCTION OF THE EURO

**29. Europe's New Currency: Gambling on the Euro,** 139
*The Economist,* January 2, 1999.
At the beginning of 1999, the EU countries launched *a common currency, the euro,* which will more closely tie them together. This article emphasizes that Europe's monetary union is neither bound to succeed nor to fail. Political leadership and circumstances will decide the outcome of this historic move.

## C.  POST-COMMUNIST CENTRAL AND EASTERN EUROPE

**30. Eastern Europe a Decade Later: The Postcommunist** 144
**Divide,** Jacques Rupnik, *Journal of Democracy,* January 1999.
*Post-communist countries in Central and Eastern Europe* have taken very different paths of political development. The author offers a multifactor analysis that helps explain the uneven transition in the region.

## D.  RUSSIA AND THE OTHER POST–SOVIET REPUBLICS

**31. What Now for Russia?** John-Thor Dahlburg, *Los* 147
*Angeles Times,* November 8, 1998.
Economic collapse and political paralysis have eroded post-Soviet optimism. This article gives a realistic picture of the miserable *living conditions of most Russians* along with the attendant political dangers of this situation.

**32. Russia's Summer of Discontent,** Michael McFaul, 149
*Current History,* October 1998.
Completed soon after President Yeltsin named Yevgeni Primakov as new prime minister in September 1998, this article emphasizes that no matter who rules the country, there can be *no quick solutions to Russia's economic problems.*

**33. Can Russia Change?** David Remnick, *Foreign Affairs,* 154
January/February 1997.
An American with a deep understanding of *Russia* gives a relatively *hopeful assessment* of the country's long-term prospects. He acknowledges its present disarray in leadership and societal morale, but warns against ignoring the scattered evidence of an embryonic cultural transformation.

**Overview** 160

## A.  POLITICS OF DEVELOPMENT

**34. Let's Abolish the Third World,** *Newsweek,* April 27, 1992. 165
Now that we know much more about the *economic and social problems* of the former "second," or communist, world, there is less reason for clinging to the categories of *"three worlds."*

**35. The 'Third World' Is Dead, but Spirits Linger,** Bar- 166
bara Crossette, *New York Times,* November 13, 1994.
In 1955 the Bandung Conference promoted an *image of a fraternal "third world"* of developing nations, which shared similar problems, interests, and goals in opposition to the West and the developed world. Over the years, some of these countries have forged ahead while many others are mired in economic and social stagnation.

## B.  LATIN AMERICA

**36. Latin Economies Soar, Stumble with Reforms,** Chris Kraul 168
and Sebastian Rotella, *Los Angeles Times,* January 10, 1999.
Over the last decade, *Latin America has experimented as never before with free-market reforms.* This article takes stock of the consequences, both positive and negative. The authors stress the political need to combine overdue changes with a more visible concern for the victims of economic dislocation.

UNIT 4

# Political Diversity in the Developing World

Eleven selections review the developing world's economic and political development in Latin America, Africa, China, India, and newly industrialized countries.

The concepts in bold italics are developed in the article. For further expansion please refer to the Topic Guide and the Index.

**37. Mexico: Sweeping Changes of Last Decade 172 Translate into a Tale of 2 Economies,** James F. Smith, *Los Angeles Times,* January 10, 1999.
Seen through a macroeconomic lens, Mexico looks "more competitive, more productive, leaner and healthier" than a decade ago. But personal income has fallen sharply. This article explores *Mexico's "two economies" and their political ramifications.*

**C. AFRICA**

**38. After Mandela's Miracle in South Africa,** Michael 175 Bratton, *Current History,* May 1998.
"A miracle is a hard act to follow," as the author of this article on South Africa points out. He reminds us of the amazingly peaceful passage *from racial oligarchy to a liberal multiracial governance,* and then reviews the political, social, and economic landscape of this new democracy.

**39. Nigeria's Long Road Back to Democracy,** *The* 181 *Economist,* December 12, 1998.
After 15 years of repressive military rule, *Nigeria is once again on a difficult path toward democratic governance.*

**D. CHINA**

**40. Jiang Zemin Takes Command,** Joseph Fewsmith, *Current History,* September 1998. 182
As political leader of China, *Jiang Zemin has surprised observers with his political strength,* flexibility, and even vision. The author examines the political transition since the death of Deng Xiaoping in 1997, and surveys some risks ahead.

**41. In March toward Capitalism, China Has Avoided 188 Russia's Path,** Henry Chu, *Los Angeles Times,* September 16, 1998.
In remarkable contrast to its former Russian or Soviet role model, as this article points out, *China has managed so far to avoid economic collapse* as it moves from a centrally planned to a more market-oriented economy.

**E. INDIA**

**42. What a Difference a Year Can Make,** Mark Nichol- 191 son, *Financial Times,* October 26, 1998.
*The Hindu-led nationalist government,* in power since early 1998, takes special pride in the country's status as a nuclear power. This article reviews some of its nonmilitary accomplishments.

**F. NEWLY INDUSTRIALIZED COUNTRIES**

**43. Asian Values Revisited: What Would Confucius 193 Say Now?** *The Economist,* July 25, 1998.
Only a few years ago, it was widely argued that so-called Asian values helped explain East Asia's remarkable economic success. Some critics, however, have attributed the last couple of years of economic turbulence to the very same values. This article questions the assumptions that underlie *the whole debate about Asian values.*

**44. Asia and the "Magic" of the Marketplace,** Jeffrey 197 A. Winters, *Current History,* December 1998.
The author emphasizes *the crucial role of mobile global capital in destabilizing Asian economies.* He raises the crucial political question of whether people will want their lives to be determined "so thoroughly, randomly, suddenly, and irrationally" by the wielders of such uncontrolled power.

The concepts in bold italics are developed in the article. For further expansion please refer to the Topic Guide and the Index.

**Overview**                                                    **204**

*A. THE DEMOCRATIC TREND: HOW STRONG,*
*   THOROUGH, AND LASTING?*

**45. Is the Third Wave Over?** Larry Diamond, *Journal of*    **208**
*Democracy,* July 1996.
Larry Diamond reviews Samuel Huntington's seminal thesis about
the "third wave" of democratization which, beginning in 1974,
has brought **a major political transformation to many
countries.** He asks whether a "reverse wave" is now setting in.

*B. THE TURN TOWARD MARKETS: WHAT ROLE FOR THE*
*   STATE?*

**46. Serial Utopia,** Christian Tyler, *Financial Times,* March   **217**
21/22, 1998.
The author points out that economic models, like their fashion
equivalents, come and go. He concludes that there is **no economic model or size "that fits all."** Pragmatic pluralism
would seem to more sensible than the pursuit of "serial utopias."

**47. Capitalism and Democracy,** Gabriel A. Almond, *PS:*      **219**
*Political Science and Politics,* September 1991.
Gabriel Almond, a leading political scientist, examines the ambiguous **relationship between capitalism and democracy,** ex-
ploring how capitalism supports and subverts democracy as well
as how democracy subverts and fosters capitalism.

*C. ETHNIC AND CULTURAL CONFLICT: THE POLITICAL*
*   ASSERTION OF GROUP IDENTITIES*

**48. Cultural Explanations: The Man in the Baghdad**          **229**
**Café,** *The Economist,* November 9, 1996.
This essay critically reviews several recent scholarly attempts to
explain **economics and politics in terms of cultural differences,** including the views advanced by Samuel Huntington
and Benjamin Barber in the articles that follow.

**49. A Debate on Cultural Conflicts**                         **231**
Harvard professor Samuel Huntington argues that we are entering
a **new political stage** in which the **fundamental source of
conflict** will be neither ideological nor economic but cultural. Josef
Joffe, a foreign affairs specialist, argues that there are other important sources of conflict rooted in **military buildups, extreme
poverty, and global migrations.** Then, political scientist Chandra Muzaffar maintains that **Western dominance** is still the major factor in world politics.

**a. The Coming Clash of Civilizations—Or, the West
against the Rest,** Samuel Huntington, *New York Times,* June 6,
1993.

**b. A Clash between Civilizations—or within Them?** Josef
Joffe, *World Press Review,* February 1994.

**c. The West's Hidden Agenda,** Chandra Muzaffar, *World
Press Review,* February 1994.

**50. Jihad vs. McWorld,** Benjamin R. Barber, *The Atlantic*  **236**
*Monthly,* March 1992.
Benjamin Barber sees two major tendencies that are shaping much
of the political world today. One is a form of **tribalism,** which
pits cultural, ethnic, religious, and national groups against one
another. This orientation clashes with **globalism,** brought about
by modern technology, communications, and commerce.

**Index**                                                      **241**
**Article Review Form**                                        **244**
**Article Rating Form**                                        **245**

# Comparative Politics: Some Major Trends, Issues, and Prospects

Six selections discuss the rise of
democracy, how capitalism impacts
on political development, and the
political assertion of group identity
in contemporary politics.

**UNIT 5**

The concepts in bold italics are developed in the article. For further expansion please refer to the Topic Guide and the Index.

# Topic Guide

This topic guide suggests how the selections and World Wide Web sites found in the next section of this book relate to topics of traditional concern to students and professionals involved with the study of comparative politics. It is useful for locating interrelated articles and Web sites for reading and research. The guide is arranged alphabetically according to topic.

The relevant Web sites, which are numbered and annotated on pages 6 and 7, are easily identified by the Web icon ( ◎ ) under the topic articles. By linking the articles and the Web sites by topic, this ANNUAL EDITIONS reader becomes a powerful learning and research tool.

| TOPIC AREA | TREATED IN | TOPIC AREA | TREATED IN |
|---|---|---|---|
| **Africa's Politics** | 34. Let's Abolish the Third World<br>35. 'Third World' Is Dead<br>38. After Mandela's Miracle<br>39. Nigeria's Long Road Back<br>◎ **1, 2, 3, 18, 25, 26** | | 29. Europe's New Currency<br>36. Latin Economies<br>37. Mexico<br>38. After Mandela's Miracle<br>41. March toward Capitalism<br>44. Asia and the "Magic" of the Marketplace<br>46. Serial Utopias<br>47. Capitalism and Democracy<br>50. Jihad vs. McWorld<br>◎ **1, 5, 6, 7, 8, 13, 14, 17, 18, 20, 22, 27, 34** |
| **Britain's Government and Politics** | 1. Tony Blair Rides Triumphant<br>2. Unwritten Rules<br>3. There Will Always Be an England<br>4. "New" Labour's "Third Way"<br>20. Women in Power<br>22. Devolution Can Be Salvaged<br>23. Parliament and Congress<br>24. Campaign and Party Finance<br>25. Untied States of Europe<br>26. What Is Europe?<br>◎ **1, 3, 5** | **Elections and Parties** | 2. Unwritten Rules<br>3. There Will Always Be an England<br>4. "New" Labour's "Third Way"<br>5. Bonn to the Berlin Republic<br>6. Gerhard Schröder's Task<br>8. Goodbye to All That<br>11. Resisting Reform<br>12. Right and Left in France<br>15. Former Communist Installed in Italy<br>16. July 1998 Elections<br>17. Japan's Search for a New Path<br>18. Europe<br>20. Women in Power<br>21. What Democracy Is . . . and Is Not<br>24. Campaign and Party Finance<br>45. Is the Third Wave Over?<br>◎ **1, 4, 5, 6, 7, 8, 9, 12, 14, 16, 17, 18, 20** |
| **Central and Eastern Europe** | 30. Eastern Europe a Decade Later<br>33. Can Russia Change?<br>45. Is the Third Wave Over?<br>47. Capitalism and Democracy<br>49. Debate on Cultural Conflicts<br>◎ **1, 2, 3, 9, 17, 26, 30, 32** | | |
| **China's Government and Politics** | 40. Jiang Zemin Takes Command<br>41. March toward Capitalism<br>43. Asian Values Revisited<br>45. Is the Third Wave Over?<br>47. Capitalism and Democracy<br>48. Cultural Explanations<br>49. Debate on Cultural Conflicts<br>◎ **1, 2, 3, 22, 26** | **Ethnicity and Politics** | 9. Perspectives on the German Model<br>10. Field Victory Colors French View<br>26. What Is Europe?<br>33. Can Russia Change?<br>48. Cultural Explanations<br>49. Debate on Cultural Conflicts<br>50. Jihad vs. McWorld<br>◎ **1, 5, 6, 7, 9, 14, 16, 17, 30, 34** |
| **Conservatives and Conservative Parties** | 2. Unwritten Rules<br>3. There Will Always Be an England<br>4. "New" Labour's "Third Way"<br>10. Field Victory Colors French View<br>11. Resisting Reform<br>12. Right and Left in France<br>19. Europe's Right<br>◎ **1, 5, 6, 7, 8** | | |
| **Developing Countries** | 34. Let's Abolish the Third World<br>35. 'Third World' Is Dead<br>36. Latin Economies<br>37. Mexico<br>38. After Mandela's Miracle<br>39. Nigeria's Long Road Back<br>45. Is the Third Wave Over?<br>48. Cultural Explanations<br>49. Debate on Cultural Conflicts<br>50. Jihad vs. McWorld<br>◎ **1, 2, 18, 20, 22, 23, 24, 25, 27, 28, 30, 31, 33** | **European Union** | 5. Bonn to the Berlin Republic<br>6. Gerhard Schröder's Government<br>19. Europe's Right<br>25. Untied States of Europe<br>26. What Is Europe?<br>27. Institutional Framework of the EU<br>28. Europe's Censure Motion<br>29. Europe's New Currency<br>◎ **1, 5, 6, 7, 14** |
| **Economics and Politics** | 3. There Will Always be an England<br>9. Perspectives on the German Model<br>28. Europe's Censure Motion | **Federal and Unitary Systems** | 5. Bonn to the Berlin Republic<br>6. Gerhard Schröder's Government<br>14. Tocqueville in Italy<br>22. Devolution Can be Salvation<br>25. Untied States of Europe<br>26. What Is Europe?<br>33. Can Russia Change?<br>45. Is the Third Wave Over? |

4

| TOPIC AREA | TREATED IN | TOPIC AREA | TREATED IN |
|---|---|---|---|
| **Federal and Unitary Systems (continued)** | 50. Jihad vs. McWorld<br>◎ **1, 5, 6, 7, 14, 16, 17** | **Parliamentary Politics and Parliamentary Systems** | 1. Tony Blair Rides Triumphant<br>2. Unwritten Rules<br>3. There Will Always Be an England<br>4. "New" Labour's "Third Way"<br>14. Tocqueville in Italy<br>15. Former Communist Installed in Italy<br>16. July 1998 Elections<br>17. Japan's Search for a New Path<br>20. Women in Power<br>21. What Democracy Is . . . and Is Not<br>22. Devolution Can Be Salvation<br>23. Parliament and Congress<br>24. Campaign and Party Finance<br>27. Institutional Framework of the EU<br>28. Europe's Censure Motion<br>35. 'Third World' Is Dead, but Spirits Linger<br>45. Is the Third Wave Over?<br>◎ **1, 4, 5, 6, 7, 8, 17** |
| **France's Government and Politics** | 10. Field Victory Colors French View<br>11. Resisting Reform<br>12. Right and Left in France<br>13. Perspectives on the French Model<br>20. Women in Power<br>25. Untied States of Europe<br>26. What Is Europe?<br>◎ **1, 6, 14** | | |
| **Germany's Government and Politics** | 5. Bonn to the Berlin Republic<br>6. Gerhard Schröder's Government<br>7. Birth of the Berlin Republic<br>8. Goodbye to All That<br>9. Perspectives on the German Model<br>20. Women in Power<br>25. Untied States of Europe<br>26. What Is Europe?<br>◎ **1, 7, 14** | **Religion and Politics** | 48. Cultural Explanation<br>49. Debate on Cultural Conflicts<br>50. Jihad vs. McWorld<br>◎ **1, 2, 4, 18, 21, 30, 34** |
| **India's Government and Politics** | 35. 'Third World' Is Dead, but Spirits Linger<br>42. What a Difference a Year Can Make<br>45. Is the Third Wave Over?<br>48. Cultural Explanations<br>49. Debate on Cultural Conflicts<br>◎ **1, 30, 31, 33, 34** | **Russia and Other Post-Soviet Republics** | 30. Eastern Europe a Decade Later<br>31. What Now for Russia?<br>32. Russia's Summer of Discontent<br>33. Can Russia Change?<br>45. Is the Third World Over?<br>47. Capitalism and Democracy<br>48. Cultural Explanations<br>◎ **1, 9, 17, 30, 34** |
| **Italy's Government and Politics** | 14. Tocqueville in Italy<br>15. Former Communist Installed in Italy<br>20. Women in Power<br>25. Untied States of Europe<br>26. What Is Europe?<br>◎ **1, 14** | **Social Democrats and Democratic Socialists** | 3. There Will Always Be an England<br>4. "New" Labour's "Third Way"<br>5. Bonn to the Berlin Republic<br>6. Gerhard Schröder's Government<br>8. Goodbye to All That<br>9. Perspectives on the German Model<br>13. Perspectives on the French Model<br>47. Capitalism and Democracy<br>◎ **1, 5, 6, 7, 14, 34** |
| **Japan's Government and Politics** | 16. July 1998 Elections<br>17. Japan's Search for a New Path<br>48. Cultural Explanations<br>◎ **1, 8** | | |
| **Latin America** | 36. Latin Economies<br>37. Mexico<br>45. Is the Third Wave Over?<br>48. Cultural Explanations<br>◎ **1, 12, 13, 24** | **Women in Politics** | 20. Women in Power |
| **Mexico's Government and Politics** | 37. Mexico<br>◎ **1, 12, 13, 24** | | |

# AE: Comparative Politics

The following World Wide Web sites have been carefully researched and selected to support the articles found in this reader. If you are interested in learning more about specific topics found in this book, these Web sites are a good place to start. The sites are cross-referenced by number and appear in the topic guide on the previous two pages.  Also, you can link to these Web sites through our DUSHKIN ONLINE support site at *http://www.dushkin.com/online/*.

**The following sites were available at the time of publication. Visit our Web site—we update DUSHKIN ONLINE regularly to reflect any changes.**

## General Sources

**1. Central Intelligence Agency**
*http://www.odci.gov/cia/ciahome.html*
Use this official home page to get connections to other sites and resources, such as *The CIA Factbook*, which provides extensive statistical and political information about every country in the world.

**2. National Geographic Society**
*http://www.nationalgeographic.com*
This site provides links to National Geographic's huge archive of maps, articles, and other documents. There is a great deal of material related to political cultures around the world.

**3. U.S. Information Agency**
*http://www.usia.gov/usis.html*
This USIA page provides definition, related documentation, and discussion of topics on global issues. Many Web links are provided.

**4. World Wide Web Virtual Library: International Affairs Resources**
*http://www.etown.edu/home/selchewa/international_ studies/firstpag.htm*
Surf this site and its extensive links to learn about specific countries and regions, to research and international organizations, and to study such vital topics as international law, development, the international economy, and human rights.

## Pluralist Democracies: Country Studies

**5. British Information Service**
*http://britain-info.org*
This site of the British Information Service leads you to reams of material on Tony Blair and the Labour Party, the European Union, relations with Northern Ireland, and many other topics in the study of the British political system.

**6. France.com's Web Directory**
*http://www.france.com/cgi-bin/france/linkorama.cgi.test*
The links in this site will lead you to extensive information about the French government and politics.

**7. GermNews**
*http://www.mathematik.uni-ulm.de/de-news/*
Search this site for German political and economic news covering the years 1995 to the present.

**8. Japan Ministry of Foreign Affairs**
*http://www.mofa.go.jp*
Visit this official site for Japanese foreign policy statements and discussions of regional and global relations.

## Pluralist Democracies: Factors in the Political Process

**9. Carnegie Endowment for International Peace**
*http://www.ceip.org*

This organization's goal is to stimulate discussion and learning among both experts and the public at large on a wide range of international issues. The site provides links to the well-respected journal *Foreign Policy*, to the Moscow Center, to descriptions of various programs, and much more.

**10. Communications for a Sustainable Future**
*gopher://csf.colorado.edu*
This Gopher site will lead you to information on topics in international environmental sustainability. It pays particular attention to the political economics of protecting the environment.

**11. DiploNet**
*http://www.clark.net/pub/diplonet/DiploNet.html*
DiploNet is a network uniquely concerned with the needs of diplomats in the post–cold war era. It provides avenues of research into negotiation and diplomacy. It also addresses conflict management and resolution, peacemaking, and multilateral diplomacy.

**12. Inter-American Dialogue**
*http://www.iadialog.org*
This is the Web site for IAD, a premier U.S. center for policy analysis, communication, and exchange in Western Hemisphere affairs. The 100-member organization has helped to shape the agenda of issues and choices in hemispheric relations.

**13. The North American Institute**
*http://www.santafe.edu/~naminet/index.html*
NAMI, a trinational public-affairs organization concerned with the emerging "regional space" of Canada, the United States, and Mexico, provides links for study of trade, the environment, and institutional developments.

## Europe—West, Center, and East: The Politics of Integration, Transformation, and Disintegration

**14. Europa: European Union**
*http://europa.eu.int*
This server site of the European Union will lead you to the history of the EU; descriptions of EU policies, institutions, and goals; discussion of monetary union; and documentation of treaties and other materials.

**15. NATO Integrated Data Service**
*http://www.nato.int/structur/nids/nids.htm*
NIDS was created to bring information on security-related matters to the widest possible audience. Check out this Web site to review North Atlantic Treaty Organization documentation of all kinds, to read *NATO Review*, and to explore key issues in the field of European security.

**16. Research and Reference (Library of Congress)**
*http://lcweb.loc.gov/rr/*
This massive research and reference site of the Library of Congress will lead you to invaluable information on the former Soviet Union and other countries attempting the transition to democracy. It provides links to numerous publications, bibliographies, and guides in area studies.

**17. Russian and East European Network Information Center, University of Texas at Austin**
*http://reenic.utexas.edu/reenic.html*
This is *the* Web site for information on Russia and the former Soviet Union.

## Political Diversity in the Developing World

**18. Africa News Online**
*http://www.africanews.org*
Open this site for extensive, up-to-date information on all of Africa, with reports from Africa's leading newspapers, magazines, and news agencies. Coverage is country-by-country and regional. Background documents and Internet links are among the resource pages.

**19. ArabNet**
*http://www.arab.net*
This home page of ArabNet, the online resource for the Arab world in the Middle East and North Africa, presents links to 22 Arab countries. Each country Web page classifies information using a standardized system of categories.

**20. ASEAN Web**
*http://www.asean.or.id*
This official site of the Association of South East Asian Nations provides an overview of Asian Web resources, Asian summits, economic and world affairs, political foundations, regional cooperation, and publications.

**21. Human Rights Web**
*http://www.hrweb.org*
The history of the human-rights movement, text on seminal figures, landmark legal and political documents, and ideas on how individuals can get involved in helping to protect human rights around the world can be found in this valuable site.

**22. Inside China Today**
*http://www.insidechina.com*
Part of the European Internet Network, this site leads to information on China, including recent news, government, and related sites pertaining to mainland China, Hong Kong, Macao, and Taiwan.

**23. InterAction**
*http://www.interaction.org/advocacy/index.html*
InterAction encourages grassroots action and engages government bodies on various advocacy issues. The organization's Advocacy Committee provides this site to inform people on its initiatives to expand international humanitarian relief, refugee, and development-assistance programs.

**24. The North-South Institute**
*http://www.nsi-ins.ca/info.html*
Searching this site of the North-South Institute—which works to strengthen international development cooperation and enhance gender and social equity—will help you find information and debates on a variety of political issues.

**25. Organization for Economic Cooperation and Development/FDI Statistics**
*http://www.oecd.org/daf/cmis/fdi/statist.htm*
Explore world trade and investment trends on this OECD site. It provides links to many related topics and addresses global economic issues on a country-by-country basis.

**26. Penn Library: Resources by Subject**
*http://www.library.upenn.edu/resources/websitest.html*
This vast site is rich in links to information about global politics and economic development. Its extensive population and demog-

raphy resources address such concerns as migration, family planning, and health and nutrition in various world regions.

**27. SunSITE Singapore**
*http://sunsite.nus.sg/asiasvc.html*
These South East Asia Information pages provide information and point to other online resources about the region's 10 countries, including Vietnam, Indonesia, and Brunei.

**28. U.S. Agency for International Development**
*http://www.info.usaid.gov*
This Web site covers such broad and overlapping issues as democracy, population and health, economic growth, and development about different regions and countries.

**29. World Bank**
*http://www.worldbank.org*
News (e.g., press releases, summaries of new projects, speeches) and coverage of numerous topics regarding development, countries, and regions are provided at this site.

## Comparative Politics: Some Major Trends, Issues, and Prospects

**30. Commission on Global Governance**
*http://www.cgg.ch*
This site provides access to *The Report of the Commission on Global Governance*, produced by an international group of leaders who want to find ways in which the global community can better manage its affairs.

**31. IISDnet**
*http://iisd1.iisd.ca*
This site of the International Institute for Sustainable Development, a Canadian organization, presents information through links on business and sustainable development, developing ideas, and Hot Topics. Linkages is its multimedia resource for environment and development policymakers.

**32. ISN International Relations and Security Network**
*http://www.isn.ethz.ch*
This site, maintained by the Center for Security Studies and Conflict Research, is a clearinghouse for extensive information on international relations and security policy. Topics are listed by category (Traditional Dimensions of Security, New Dimensions of Security) and by major world regions.

**33. United Nations Environment Program**
*http://www.unep.ch*
Consult this home page of UNEP for links to critical topics about global issues, including desertification and the impact of trade on the environment. The site leads to useful databases and global resource information.

**34. Virtual Seminar in Global Political Economy/Global Cities & Social Movements**
*http://csf.colorado.edu/gpe/gpe95b/resources.html*
This site of Internet resources is rich in links to subjects of interest in regional studies, covering topics such as sustainable cities, megacities, and urban planning. Links to many international nongovernmental organizations are included.

**We highly recommend that you review our Web site for expanded information and our other product lines. We are continually updating and adding links to our Web site in order to offer you the most usable and useful information that will support and expand the value of your Annual Editions. You can reach us at:**
***http://www.dushkin.com/annualeditions/.***

## Unit Selections

*The United Kingdom*
1. **Tony Blair Rides Triumphant as a Visionary and a Promoter,** Warren Hoge
2. **Unwritten Rules: Britain's Constitutional Revolution,** Donley Studlar
3. **There'll Always Be an England,** Andrew Sullivan
4. **Perspectives on "New" Labour's "Third Way,"** Tony Blair; Thomas B. Edsall; *The Economist*

*Germany*
5. **From the Bonn to the Berlin Republic: Can a Stable Democracy Continue?** Lewis J. Edinger and Brigitte L. Nacos
6. **Gerhard Schröder's Government,** *The Economist*
7. **Birth of the Berlin Republic,** Peter Norman
8. **Goodbye to All That,** Ralph Atkins
9. **Perspectives on the German Model,** *The Economist*; Peter Ross Range and Robert Gerald Livingston; Edmund L. Andrews

*France*
10. **Field Victory Colors French View of Themselves,** John-Thor Dahlburg
11. **Resisting Reform to de Gaulle's Old Constitution,** Robert Graham
12. **Right and Left in France: Two Recent Reports,** *The Economist*
13. **Perspectives on the French Model,** Roger Cohen; Daniel Singer; *The Economist*

*Italy*
14. **Tocqueville in Italy,** David L. Kirp
15. **Former Communist Installed in Italy,** Alessandra Stanley

*Japan*
16. **The July 1998 Election: Two Reports,** Nicholas D. Kristof; Stephanie Strom
17. **Japan's Search for a New Path,** T. J. Pempel

## Key Points to Consider

❖ How has Tony Blair taken major steps to reform the image and program of his Labour Party? What are the main items on his party's constitutional reform agenda, and how are they being addressed by the new government?

❖ What are some major difficulties faced by the new German government headed by Gerhard Schröder? Explain how the Greens have become an alternative coalition party to the liberal Free Democrats. Is it politically possible or even desirable to scrap the "German model" of a generous social welfare state?

❖ Why did Jacques Chirac call an early parliamentary election in 1997, and how did the outcome bring about a new form of "cohabitation" in the Fifth Republic? What are the signs that French politics have become more centrist or middle-of-the-road for the main political parties?

❖ What is "tangentopoli"? Explain the recent shake-up in the Italian party system and the development of the PDS into the major reform party of the Left.

❖ Explain why the LDP is jokingly said to be "neither liberal, nor democratic, nor a party." What has been the role of this party in postwar Japanese politics?

**DUSHKIN**ONLINE **Links**          **www.dushkin.com/online/**

5. **British Information Service**
   *http://britain-info.org*

6. **France.com's Web Directory**
   *http://www.france.com/cgi-bin/france/ linkorama.cgi.test*

7. **GermNews**
   *http://www.mathematik.uni-ulm.de/de-news/*

8. **Japan Ministry of Foreign Affairs**
   *http://www.mofa.go.jp*

These sites are annotated on pages 6 and 7.

The United Kingdom, Germany, France, and Italy rank among the most prominent industrial societies in Western Europe. They have all developed into pluralist democracies with diversified and active citizenries, well-organized and competitive party systems and interest groups, and representative forms of governments. Japan appears to be considerably less pluralist as a society, but it occupies a similar position of primacy among the few representative democracies in Asia.

The articles in the first unit cover the political systems of these five countries. Each of them has found its own dynamic balance of continuity and change. Nevertheless, as later readings will show more fully, it is possible to find some common denominators and make useful cross-national comparisons among these and other representative democracies.

**The United Kingdom** has long been regarded as a model of parliamentary government and majoritarian party politics. In the 1960s and 1970s, however, serious observers spoke about the spread of a British sickness or "Englanditis," a condition characterized by such problems as economic stagnation, social malaise, political polarization, and a general incapacity of the elected government to deal effectively with such a situation of relative deterioration.

Some British political scientists defined their country's condition as one of "governmental overload." According to their diagnosis, British government had become so entangled by socioeconomic entitlements that the country had reached the threshold of a condition of political paralysis or ungovernability. In the United States, Mancur Olson developed a similar explanation of this political sclerosis, which he traced to the effects of a highly developed interest-group system making excessive demands on governments.

A second explanation of the British governing crisis focused on the unusually sharp adversarial character of the country's party politics. This approach emphasized that Britain's famed "Westminster Model" of government by a single majority party often had more polarizing and disruptive consequences than the power-sharing coalitions found in some other parliamentary systems in Western Europe. Still other interpreters explained Britain's relative decline in terms of socioeconomic and institutional inertia. Two of the most commonly cited problems were rooted in Britain's heritage as a class-divided society and a former colonial power. It was argued that the United Kingdom was hampered by a dysfunctional and outmoded social order at home, and an equally costly and unproductive legacy of overcommitment in foreign affairs. The latter thesis was advanced by the British-American historian, Paul Kennedy, in his widely discussed book on the rise and fall of the great powers.

As if to defy such pessimistic analyses, Britain by the mid-1980s began to pull ahead of other West European countries in its annual rate of economic growth. This apparent turnabout could be linked in part to the policies of Prime Minister Margaret Thatcher, who came to power in May 1979 and then introduced a drastic change in economic and social direction for the country.

In foreign affairs, Prime Minister Thatcher combined an assertive role for Britain in Europe and close cooperation with the United States under the leadership of Presidents Reagan and Bush. As a patriot and staunch defender of both market economics and national sovereignty, Thatcher distrusted the drive toward monetary and eventual political union in the European Community. She became known throughout the continent for her unusually sharp attacks on tendencies toward undemocratic statism or technocratic socialism in Brussels. Critics in her own party regarded her Eurocritical position as untenable, because it isolated Britain.

For the mass electorate, however, nothing seems to have been as upsetting as the introduction of the community charge, a tax on each adult resident that would replace the local property tax or "rates" as a means of financing local public services. Although this so-called poll tax was very unpopular, Thatcher resisted all pressure to abandon the project before its full national implementation in early 1990.

The politically disastrous result was that, as a revenue measure, the poll tax was anything but neutral in its impact. It created an unexpectedly large proportion of immediate losers, that is, people who had to pay considerably more in local taxes than previously, while the immediate winners were people who had previously paid high property taxes. Not surprisingly, the national and local governments disagreed about who was responsible for the high poll tax bills, but the voters seemed to have little difficulty in assigning blame to Margaret Thatcher and the Conservative Party. Some observers correctly anticipated that the tax rebellion would undermine Thatcher's position in her own party and become her political Waterloo.

The feisty prime minister had weathered many political challenges, but she was now confronted with increasing speculation that the Tories might try to replace her with a more attractive leader before the next general election. Indeed, a leadership challenge in the Conservative Party ended with Thatcher's resignation.

The transition in power was remarkably smooth. John Major, who was chosen to be Thatcher's successor as party leader and prime minister, had long been regarded as one of her closest cabinet supporters. He basically supported her tough economic strategy, which she often described as "dry." He combined a market approach in economics with a somewhat more compassionate or "wet" social policy. Not surprisingly, he abandoned the hated poll tax. His undramatic governing style was far less confrontational than that of his predecessor, and some nostalgic critics were quick to call him dull.

By the time of Thatcher's resignation, Labour appeared to be in a relatively good position to capitalize on the growing disenchantment with the Conservative government. The big political question had become whether Prime Minister Major could recapture some of the lost ground. Under its leader, Neil Kinnock, Labour had begun to move back toward its traditional center-left position, presenting itself as a politically moderate and socially caring reform party.

As the main opposition party, Labour was now troubled by a new version of the Social Democratic and Liberal alternatives that had fragmented the non-Conservative camp in the elections of 1983 and 1987. The two smaller parties, which had operated as an electoral coalition or alliance in those years, had concluded that their organizational separation was a hindrance to the political breakthrough they hoped for. After their defeat in 1987, they joined together as Liberal Democrats. Under the leadership of Paddy Ashdown, they have attempted to overcome the electoral system's bias against third parties by promoting themselves as a reasonable centrist alternative to the Conservatives on the right and Labour on the left. Their strategic goal has been to win the balance of power in a tightly fought election and then, as parliamentary majority-makers, enter a government coalition with one of the two big parties. One of their main demands would then be that the existing winner-take-all system, based on plurality or "first-past-the-post" elections in single-member districts, be replaced by some form of proportional representation (PR) in multimember districts. Such a system, which is used widely in Western Europe, would almost surely guarantee the Liberal Democrats not only a much larger and more solid base in the House of Commons but also a pivotal role in any future process of coalition politics in Britain. Given their considerable electoral support, the Liberal Democrats would then enjoy a strategic position at the fulcrum of party politics similar to that occupied for decades, until 1998, by their liberal counterparts in Germany, the Free Democrats (FDP).

The rise of this centrist "third force" in British electoral politics during the 1980s had been made possible by a temporary leftward trend of Labour and a simultaneous but longer-lasting rightward movement of the Conservatives a few years earlier. The challenge from the middle had the predictable result that the two main parties eventually sought to "recenter" themselves, as became evident in the general election called by Prime Minister Major for April 9, 1992. The timing seemed highly unattractive for the Conservatives as the governing party, for Britain was still suffering from its worst recession in years. Normally, a British government chooses not to stay in office for a full 5-year term, preferring to dissolve the House of Commons at an earlier and politically convenient time. It will procrastinate, however, when the electoral outlook appears to be dismal. By the spring of 1992 there was hardly any

time left for further delay, since an election had to come before the end of June under Britain's 5-year limit. At the time, many observers expected either a slim Labour victory or, more likely, a so-called hung Parliament, in which no single party would end up with a working majority. The latter result would have led either to a minority government, which could be expected to solve the political impasse by calling an early new election, or a coalition government, which would have included the Liberal Democrats as the majority-making junior partner.

The outcome of the 1992 general election confounded all those who had expected a change in government by giving the Conservatives an unprecedented fourth consecutive term of office. Despite the recession, they garnered the same overall percentage of the vote (about 43 percent) as in 1987, while Labour increased its total share only slightly, from 32 to 35 percent. The Liberal Democrats received only 18 percent, about 6 percent less than the share the Alliance had won in its two unsuccessful attempts to "break the mold" of the party system in 1983 and 1987. In the House of Commons, the electoral system's bias in favor of the front-runners showed up once again. The Conservatives lost 36 seats but ended up with 336 of the 651 members—a slim but sufficient "working" majority, unless a major issue fragmented the party or attrition eroded its parliamentary advantage. In 1992, Labour increased its number of seats from 229 to 271—a net gain of 42, but far short of an opportunity to threaten the majority party. The Liberal Democrats ended up with 20 seats, down from 22. A few remaining seats went to representatives of the small regional parties from Northern Ireland, Scotland, and Wales.

Soon after the 1992 election, John Major ran into considerable difficulties with a wing of his own party that followed Thatcher in opposing his European policy. In by-elections over the next years, the Tories gradually saw their parliamentary majority dwindle.

The Labour Party, with its newest leader, Tony Blair, made some tremendous advances in the regular opinion polls. It soon moved to an early, continuing, and commanding lead over the government party, and John Major thus had good reason to delay the next election as long as possible, until May 1997. This time there were no surprises, except for the parliamentary landslide of the victor. With about 44 percent of the total vote (only about 1.5 percent more than the Conservatives had won in 1992), the Labour Party won a commanding majority of 419 of the 659 seats in the House of Commons. The Liberal Democrats saw their share of the vote drop by 1 percent, but tactical voting in swing districts more than doubled their number of parliamentary seats to 46. They were not needed to form a majority government, however, and so they once again failed to reach their strategic goal of becoming pivotal partners in a coalition government. The outcome of the 1997 general election in Britain was a dramatic demonstration of the "disproportional" representation brought about by the country's "first-past-the-post" or "winner-take-all" electoral system. But it also reaffirmed that system's celebrated tendency to create strong single party majorities in parliament that produce effective governments, which in turn are held accountable by the opposition.

Labour's victory has given prominence to the growing demand for constitutional change in Britain. The Liberal Democrats had been in the vanguard of the constitutional reform movement from the beginning. But the growing importance of the issue was reflected in the fact that even Conservatives entered the fray. Labour's position has become crucial since it took office in May 1997. While he was still opposition leader, Tony Blair identified himself and his party with a constitutional reform agenda, with the notable exception of the electoral system that underpins the Westminster model of government by a single majority party.

One of the recurrent reform suggestions has been to set up special regional assemblies for Scotland and Wales within the United Kingdom. Soon after Labour took power, referendums resulted in majority approval of such assemblies—a fairly strong one (with powers of taxation) for Scotland, and a weaker one for Wales. The regional problems associated with Northern Ireland are far more divisive, but they have been vigorously addressed by Blair's government and in 1998 a resolution was finally reached that appeared to be acceptable to all sides. In addition to a new regional level of representative government, there are plans for a devolution of power to the existing local governments in reversal of the shift in the opposite direction that took place under Prime Minister Thatcher.

The articles on Britain cover various aspects of political change that have come with Labour's sweeping victory. Donley Studlar takes stock of Tony Blair's agenda of institutional reform, while Andrew Sullivan reflects on the social and economic as well as institutional transformation of Britain under its last three prime ministers. The new Labour government has a formidable majority, but some observers wonder if Blair can keep his center-left party "on track" without engaging in some major social reforms as well. There is at present no danger from the weakened and divided Conservatives under their new leader, William Hague. But behind its show of unity, Labour still harbors some of its own factional disputes. The major ideological and strategic cleavage runs between traditional socialists, who favor more emphasis on public social programs, and more pragmatic modernizers, who wish to continue the centrist reform policies of Tony Blair's "New Labour."

**Germany** was united in 1990, when the eastern German Democratic Republic, or GDR, was merged into the western Federal Republic of Germany. The two German states had been established in 1949, 4 years after the total defeat of the German Reich in World War II. During the next 40 years, their rival elites subscribed to the conflicting ideologies and interests of East and West in the cold war. When the two states were getting ready to celebrate their fortieth anniversaries in 1989, no leading politician was on record as having foreseen that the German division would come to end during the course of the following year.

Mass demonstrations in several East German cities and the westward flight of thousands of citizens brought the GDR government to make an increasing number of concessions in late 1989 and early 1990. The Berlin Wall ceased to be a hermetical seal after November 9, 1989, when East Germans began to stream over into West Berlin. Under new leadership, the ruling Communists of East Germany introduced a form of power-sharing with noncommunist groups and parties. It was agreed to seek democratic legitimation through a free East German election.

At first, the East German Communists only abandoned their claim to an exclusive control of power and positions, but by the time of the March 1990 election it was clear even to them that the pressure for national unification could no longer be stemmed. The issue was no longer whether the two German states would be joined together, but *how* and *when*. These questions were settled when an alliance of Christian Democrats, largely identified with and supported by Chancellor Kohl's party in West Germany, won a surprisingly decisive victory, with 48 percent of the vote throughout East Germany.

During the summer and fall of 1990, the governments of the two German states and the four former occupying powers completed their so-called two-plus-four negotiations that resulted in mutual agreement on the German unification process. A monetary union in July was followed by a political merger in October 1990. In advance of unification, Bonn was able to negotiate an agreement with Moscow in which the latter accepted the gradual withdrawal of Soviet troops from eastern Germany and the membership of the larger, united Germany in NATO, in return for considerable German economic support for the Soviet Union. The result was a major shift in both the domestic and international balance of power.

The moderately conservative Christian Democrats repeated their electoral success in the first Bundestag election in a reunited Germany, held in early December 1990. Under a special provision for the 1990 election only, the two parts of united Germany were regarded as separate electoral regions as far as the 5 percent threshold was concerned. That made it possible for two small eastern parties to get a foothold in the Bundestag. One was a coalition of dissidents and environmentalists (Alliance 90/Greens); the other was the communist-descended Party of Democratic Socialism. The PDS won about 10 percent of the vote in the East by appealing to a number of groups that feared social displacement and ideological alienation in a market economy.

The election results of December 1990 suggested that national unification could eventually modify the German party system significantly. By the time of the next national election, in October 1994, it became evident that a new east-west divide had emerged in German politics. This time, the far-left PDS was able to almost double its support and attract 20 percent of the vote in the East, where only one-fifth of Germany's total population lives. Despite a widespread unification malaise, the conservative-liberal government headed by Chancellor Helmut Kohl won reelection in 1994.

Between 1949 and 1999, the seat of government for the Federal Republic had been the small Rhineland town of Bonn. Reunification made possible the move of the government and parliament several hundred miles eastward to the old political center of Berlin. The transfer remains controversial in Germany, both because of the costs and the symbolism involved, but it was approved by the Bundestag in 1991, with a narrow parliamentary majority, and then delayed until 1999. Writing a year in advance of the geopolitical move, Lewis Edinger and Brigitte Nacos provide a superb assessment of the "Bonn Republic" and suggest that the Berlin Republic will continue the democratic tradition that has been firmly established in Germany.

Unlike their British counterparts, German governments are produced by the vagaries of coalition politics in a representative system based on the country's modified form of proportional representation. There is rarely a complete replacement of one government by another, since one of the parties in a coalition cabinet will frequently be needed as majority-maker in the next government.

In advance of the 1998 election, it had been widely expected that the outcome once again would be only a partial shift in power, resulting from a grand coalition of Social Democrats (SPD) and Christian Democrats (CDU/CSU), with the chancellorship going to the leader of the front-running party—most likely the SPD. The result would have been a considerable continuity and, as interpreted by rival scenarios, either considerable inertia or a newfound strength in dealing with Germany's backlog of social and economic reforms. Instead, the election made possible what Germans like to call a "Red-Green" coalition by giving the Social Democrats a sufficient margin (almost 6 percent) over the Christian Democrats to form a majority coalition with the small party of Greens. Thus the emergence of the Berlin Republic has come to coincide with a complete change in government leadership. In the federal chancellery, Social Democrat Gerhard Schröder, born in 1944, has replaced Christian Democrat Helmut Kohl, born in 1930.

A similar political and generational replacement has taken place elsewhere in the top level of German government shortly in advance of its transfer to Berlin. The new leaders have grown up in postwar Germany. In many cases they had their initial political experiences in youthful opposition to the societal establishment of the late 1960s. By now the "68ers" are themselves well into middle age, but they have ascended to power as successors to Kohl's generation, whose politically formative years coincided with the founding years of the Federal Republic. Unlike the latter, the new German leaders do not have youthful memories of the Third Reich, World War II or, in many cases, the immediate postwar years of military occupation. In that sense, they are Germany's first postwar generation in power.

Several articles on Germany examine the situation of the political parties and leaders after the milestone election of September 1998. For the time being, at least, Germany has a party system consisting of two major parties of the moderate center-left (SPD) and center-right (CDU/CSU), along with three small parties that each has a regional concentration either in the West (Greens and FDP) or almost exclusively in the East (PDS). One important result of the 1998 Bundestag election was the failure of the parties of the extreme right, with their authoritarian and xenophobic rhetoric, to mobilize a significant support in the German electorate.

The articles include evaluations of both Helmut Kohl, the veteran chancellor who served longer than any of his predecessors since Bismarck, and his successor, Gerhard Schröder. In the election, German voters in effect decided it was "time for a change" in their country, similar to the political turnabouts in Britain and France in 1997.

**France** must also cope with major political challenges within a rapidly changing Europe. The sharp ideological cleavages that marked French politics for so much of the past two centuries were losing significance. Instead, there was emerging a more pragmatic, pluralist form of accommodation in French public life. However, this deradicalization and depolarization of political discourse is by no means complete in France.

As widely expected, the Socialists suffered a major setback in the parliamentary elections of 1993. They and their close allies were among the losers in this largest electoral landslide in French democratic history. Receiving less than 20 percent of the popular vote, they plummeted from their previous share of 282 seats in 1988 to about one-quarter of that number. The Communists, with about half as many votes, were able to win 23 seats. With a similar share of the vote, the ultra-right National Front won no seats at all. The environmental alliance was doubly disappointed, winning a smaller share of the vote than expected and capturing no seats either.

Socialist President François Mitterrand's 7-year presidential term lasted until May 1995. After the parliamentary rout of the Socialists in March 1993, he was faced with the question of whether to resign early from the presidency or to begin a period of "cohabitation" with a conservative prime minister. Mitterrand opted once again for the latter solution, but he made sure to appoint a moderate Gaullist, Edouard Balladur, as the new prime minister. Balladur in turn appointed a new, compact government that included members from all main factions of the conservative alliance. For a time, Balladur enjoyed considerable popularity, and he decided to enter the presidential race in 1995. In declaring his own candidacy, Balladur in effect snubbed Jacques Chirac, the assertive Gaullist leader who had served as prime minister in the first period of cohabitation (1986-1988).

The presidential race in France tends to become highly individualized. Eventually the tough and outspoken Chirac pulled ahead of his more consensual and lackluster party colleague. In the first round of the presidential election, however, a surprising plurality of the vote went to the main socialist candidate, Lionel Jospin, a former education minister and party leader. In the run-off election, 2 weeks later, Chirac defeated Jospin and thereby ended 14 years of Socialist control of the presidency. He appointed another Gaullist, Alain Juppé, to replace the hapless Balladur as prime minister.

Some of the articles in this section give a perspective on what many observers insist on calling "the new France." In fact, contemporary French politics and society combine some traits that reflect continuity with the past and others that suggest considerable innovation. One recurrent theme among observers is the decline of the previously sharp ideological struggle between the Left and the Right, which has been replaced by a more moderate and seemingly more mundane party politics of competition among groups that cluster near the center of the political spectrum.

In the last months of 1995 and again in late 1996, French politics took on a dramatic form and immediacy when workers and students resorted to massive strikes and street demonstrations against a new austerity program introduced by the conservative government. The proposed cutbacks in social entitlements such as pension rights appeared to many as sudden, drastic, and unfair. They were difficult to explain to the public at large, and many observers saw the political confrontation in France as a major test for the welfare state or "social market economy" that is now being squeezed in the name of international "competitiveness" throughout Western Europe.

The loss of the grand ideological alternatives may help account for the mood of political malaise that many observers claim to discover in contemporary France. But the French search for political direction and identity in a changing Europe has another major origin as well. The sudden emergence of a larger and potentially more powerful Germany next door cannot but have a disquieting effect upon France. French elites now face the troubling question of redefining their country's role.

Since 1997, French governmental policy has been affected by a new version of "cohabitation" resulting from an electoral upset in that year. No parliamentary elections had been necessary in France until 1998, but President Chirac decided to hold them 10 months early while the conservative coalition still appeared to be ahead of the left. As it turned out, Chirac underestimated the collapse of public confidence in Juppé's government. The two-stage elections for the National Assembly took place in May and early June of 1997, and the result was a major setback for the neo-Gaullists (RPR) and their neoliberal allies (UDF). The Socialists and their non-Communist allies won 274 seats in the 577-seat National Assembly, making it necessary for them to form a coalition government that also included the small Communist Party, with its 38 seats. Lionel Jospin was appointed prime minister by President Chirac, who had defeated him in the presidential race barely 2 years earlier. It is France's third experiment at cohabitation, but the first time that the president has been a conservative serving with a socialist prime minister. In some ways, the new arrangement is also a test of how far the moderate Left and Right in France have really overcome their ideological differences. Jospin's government got off to a very good start in restoring some public confidence. Meanwhile, the French parties of both the moderate and extreme Right have been weakened by internal disagreements on policy and strategy as well as personal rivalries at the leadership level.

A persistent question is whether the long-run structural problems of France—similar to those of some of her neighbors—can be handled without a resort to the very market-oriented "therapy" that the voters seem so clearly to have rejected. Three articles in this section discuss both sides of that issue, with each emphasizing that French capitalism is very different from its British or American counterpart. On the other hand, careful observers have noted that Jospin has effectively managed to introduce some economic reforms that reduce the traditional interventionist role of the French state. Once again, the moderate Left appears to identify itself with a kind of "new centrism."

*Italy* is roughly comparable to France and Britain in population and gross economic output, but it has a different political tradition that includes a long period of fascist rule and a far more persistent and troubling element of north-south regionalism. The country became a republic after World War II and, using a system of proportional representation, developed a multiparty system in which the center-right Christian Democrats played a central role as the major coalition party. The Communists, as second major party, were persistently excluded from government at the national level. In 1993 and 1994, however, they experienced a political revival, as Italian voters abruptly turned away from the Christian Democrats and other corrupt establishment parties.

The corruption issue had come to the fore as the cold war ended. As middle class fears of Communism declined, many Italians were no longer willing to tolerate the self-serving manner in which the governing parties and their leaders had prospered from all manners of side-payments for political services and public contracts. Some vigorous prosecutors and judges played a major role in exposing the extent of what became known popularly as *tangentopoli* (kickback city) in public affairs.

In late March 1994 Italy held what was at the time heralded as the most important parliamentary elections in over four decades. Once again Italian voters demonstrated their disgust with the old government parties, but the end result provided at least as much confusion as previous contests. Using a new electoral system, in which three-quarters of the members of parliament are elected on a winner-take-all basis and the rest by proportional representation, Italian voters decimated the centrist alliance, which included the former Christian Democrats. On the left, an alliance led by the PDS (former Communists) won 213 of the 630 seats in the Chamber of Deputies, compared to the 46 seats for the main centrist group. But it was the Freedom Alliance of the right that triumphed by winning 366 seats. It consisted of an incongruous coalition of three main groups, of which the strongest was the *Forza Italia* (Go Italy) movement, led by the media magnate and multimillionaire, Silvio Berlusconi, whose campaign against both corruption (the centrists) and communism (the PDS), had catapulted him and his party to the front by a skillful of use of the electronic media. He faced the difficult task of creating a government based on a fractious coalition. Berlusconi's government soon lost its parliamentary majority and a new caretaker government of technocrats, headed by the banker Lamberto Dini, took over the reins in January 1995 and held on for a full year.

In April 1996, Italy finally went to the polls once again in an attempt to find a more stable parliamentary base for a new government. Using the hybrid electoral system that had resulted in such confusion 2 years earlier, the Italians voters managed this time to select a winning team. The victors were the left-of-center Olive Tree coalition, in which the PDS, under its new leader, Massimo D'Alema, remains by far the strongest parliamentary party. However, the new prime minister, Romano Prodi, was a banker who came from the moderate PPI. His minority government included the post-Communist PDS, but it was also dependent upon the pivotal support of the far-left party of refounded Communists for its parliamentary majority. When this party asserted its far-left identity in late 1997, it caused Prodi's government to step down. In a quick turnabout, the same government returned to office after offering some concessions to the refounded Communists. A year later, in October 1998, Prodi's

center-left government was finally toppled from power when the prime minister lost a parliamentary vote of confidence by a single vote. He was succeeded as prime minister by the PDS leader, Massimo D'Alema, who thus became the first former Communist to head the government of a major European country. The new cabinet, which is number 56 in Italy's postwar history, resembles the previous one, but it stretches further to the right by including some conservatives.

**Japan,** the fifth country in this study of representative governments of industrial societies, has long fascinated students of comparative politics and society. After World War II, a representative democracy was installed in Japan under American supervision. This political system soon acquired indigenous Japanese characteristics that set it off from the other major democracies examined here.

For almost four decades the Japanese parliamentary system was dominated by the Liberal Democratic Party, which is essentially a conservative political force, composed of the personal followers of political bosses. At periodic intervals the LDP's parliamentary hegemony has been threatened, but it was always able to recover. In 1993 several of its important politicians defected in protest against the LDP's reluctance to introduce political reforms. As a result, the government lost its parliamentary majority. A vote of no confidence was followed by early elections in July 1993, in which the LDP failed to recover its parliamentary majority. Seven different parties thereupon formed what turned out to be a very fragile coalition government.

By the summer of 1994, the LDP had managed to return to the cabinet in coalition with its major former rival, the Socialists. This peculiar alliance was possible because of the basically pragmatic orientation adopted by the leadership of both major parties at this point in Japan's history. By December 1995, the LDP had recaptured the prime ministership as the result of winning a parliamentary majority for its candidate, Ryutaro Hashimoto. He became the country's eighth prime minister in 7 years. In the parliamentary election of October 1996, his party made an advance but failed to win a clear majority. In the summer of 1998, the LDP had a disastrous performance, winning only 44 of 126 seats. Hashimoto took responsibility for the setback and resigned. His successor as prime minister was Keizo Obuchi of the LDP.

Observers differ about the significance of the political changes in Japan. There is a growing belief, however, that the entrenched bureaucratic elites have lost some of their invincibility and may now become the targets of reform geared at opening up a society that seems to be both overly regulated and sometimes poorly regulated. A setback for the entrenched bureaucrats could lead to long-term shifts in Japan's balance of power.

# Tony Blair Rides Triumphant As a Visionary and a Promoter

## By WARREN HOGE

LONDON, Jan. 31—He is youthful, articulate and visionary, leader of a nation in dramatic transition, with a compassionate vision and a ruthless dedication to seeing it through. His name is Tony Blair.

He is all style and fluff, a spiffy promoter with a preachy speaking manner and a trendy tendency to put the possessive "people's" before the mention of any British institution and the verb "modernize" in any sentence about his goals for the country. His name is also Tony Blair.

Twenty months after he led Britain's "new" Labor Party to power, it is the first image of Britain's attention-getting 45 year-old Prime Minister that is prevailing—much to the consternation of his Conservative opponents who have failed to put across the second.

But while he is the most popular Prime Minister in British history and no one questions his extraordinary public appeal, people are asking what is actually inside the enticingly wrapped package he is offering.

Mr. Blair says he is leading a "radical" 10-year project that will free Britain from the grip of class consciousness, energize the individual parts of the United Kingdom by yielding much of London's authority over them, liberate British business from restrictions that discourage enterprise and punish risk-taking, reduce the poor's dependency on the state and end Britain's estrangement from the Continent and make it a leader in Europe.

Still, the Blair Government's emphasis on presentation, or "spin," has left it vulnerable to criticism that all this may represent slick talk of accomplishment, and not solid accomplishment itself.

"A gravity-defying victory of style over substance," is the verdict of one critic, Boris Johnson, columnist for the conservative Daily Telegraph. Mr. Blair's Government, said Michael Gove, a columnist for The Times of London, "is about entrenching a clique's hold on power, not advancing policies for the nation."

The end-of-year list of achievements put out in December by 10 Downing Street included the peace settlement in Northern Ireland; decisions to move regional power out of the Parliament in London to newly created legislatures in Edinburgh, Cardiff and Belfast; reforming the House of Lords; setting a minimum wage; starting a welfare-to-work program; granting independence to the Bank of England in setting interest rates, and establishing Britain as a more positive presence in Europe while maintaining strong ties to the United States.

With a 179-seat majority in Parliament, ineffective opposition from the Conservatives and only rumblings of discontent from dissidents in his party, Mr. Blair has remarkable freedom of action, and his Presidential-style presence has become the most important factor in New Labor's performance.

As focus groups and opinion research become a growing force in Britain, political muscle is increasingly measured with the tape that shows the public popularity numbers. By this standard, Mr. Blair is an outstanding success: his approval ratings are persisting in mid-60's percentiles, the highest ever for a

British Prime Minister and 15 points higher than the ratings for his Government. This is occurring in spite of Cabinet scandals and disarray—including the resignation of his chief ally, Peter Mandelson—of the kind that contributed to the overwhelming rejection of his predecessor, John Major, in the 1997 election.

He has the support of 87 percent of the fractious Labor Party, and recent polls indicate that even the Tory rank and file prefer him to their own leader, William Hague. Although Mr. Blair heads the country that Europeans most love to loathe for its reluctance to join in their grand ventures like monetary union, he often comes first even on the Continent in polls measuring the popularity of individual leaders.

He has gained favorable international notice for a formless and airily defined theory about the divisions between individual and state responsibilities called simply the Third Way. It seems to maintain a following chiefly because he is the one who is peddling it.

At home, his Government's purpose, Mr. Blair said in a recent policy speech, is to serve a "new, larger, more meritocratic middle class," which now displays "greater tolerance of difference, ambition to succeed, greater opportunities to earn a decent living." His congeniality goes down easily in today's Britain, where attitudes are shaped more by consumerism than by class.

He put the Labor Party through a force-fed reformation in the 1990's, aimed at shedding the socialist ideology, tax and spending habits and tribal in-fighting that had scared off middle-class voters in past elections and given the Tories their dominance of British politics.

Outwardly, Mr. Blair has a glad-handing appeal. He is a shirt-sleeves boss, trading jocular banter with his aides in his back office at 10 Downing Street. But he is said to be steely when it comes to internal discipline. During the push to transform the party, insiders called his methods "Stalinist."

"The odd thing about him is that no one thinks of him as Machiavellian," said Robert Harris, the novelist, who is a fan of the Government. "I suppose that is what is so Machiavellian about him."

## A Favorite 'Project' Is Running Government

With an information management policy keeping Government spokesmen resolutely "on message," Mr. Blair holds to simple definitions and repeated slogans. One of his favorites is that he is not just running a Government but heading up a "project."

Projects need more than five years to fulfill, he and his ministers stress, and it is an article of faith among the Blairites that this Government must overcome the curse of Labor's nearly 100-year-old history of never having run Britain for two successive full five-year terms. The week after Labor's rout of the Tories on May 1, 1997, members of the new Government were already talking about the urgency of winning the next election.

The extent of the ambitiousness of the political project is seen in Mr. Blair's efforts to find areas of co-operation with the Liberal Democrats, Britain's third party, and end century-old divisions on Britain's left between the Labor and Liberal traditions.

Labor's preoccupation with becoming consistently electable has led critics to fault the Blair Government for being overly cautious and vague, more eager not to disaffect than to engage and lead. To a certain extent, New Labor's success can be measured by what has not happened as much as by what has.

"This is the first unfrightening Labor administration," said Anthony King, professor of government at Essex University. Past Labor Governments are notorious in Britons' memories for economic mismanagement, convulsive social clashes and raucous internal wrangling. A main reason for the Blair Government's suc-

cess so far, Mr. King said, is "its conspicuous failure" to make mistakes.

Perhaps Mr. Blair's boldest move was to seize on a problem first tackled by Prime Minister Major—the intractable conflict in Northern Ireland. While Mr. Major lacked the political clout to make much tangible progress, Mr. Blair committed his carefully rationed personal prestige to a successful outcome of the rancorous negotiations by joining the talks himself and staying up all night with the haggling negotiators last April to nail down the final terms.

Mr. Blair has created a "New Deal" program for getting jobs for youths that has placed 50,000 unemployed in jobs in seven months. But in other areas welfare reform has stalled, and steps to cut benefits for single mothers have caused widespread resentment in a country where "welfare state" is not a pejorative phrase.

## Searching for Money For Schools and Health

In education, Mr. Blair is meeting targets for reducing the class sizes of primary schools, and in health he has succeeded in lowering waiting lines. But he must find money to give teachers and nurses needed raises, and he is continually embarrassed by disclosures of failing schools and shortages of hospital beds.

To keep his erstwhile trade union supporters on board, he pushed through a minimum wage and moved to restore organizing rights, though in both cases the terms were not as generous as the Labor traditionalists had wished. Old Labor stalwarts are constantly unhappy with Mr. Blair, but their power is greatly diminished, and they have no other welcome port on the current map of British politics.

Mr. Blair has established close relations with the monarchy, offering needed political guidance as it passed through the trauma of the death of Diana, Princess of Wales, and reaching out to Prince Charles, whose social concerns are surprisingly harmonious with his own.

His personal diplomacy has made relations with Europe less frosty, even though Mr. Blair kept Britain out of the introduction of the euro. The Prime Minister stresses at every opportunity that Britain is a European country and increasingly hints that its future destiny is in monetary union.

The delicate task of educating a majority of Britons out of their traditional hostility and suspicion toward Europe has been made easier for him by the absolutist position of the Conservative leader, Mr. Hague. He favors declaring now that Britain will not consider entry into monetary union for at least eight years, a view that Mr. Blair is able to mock without having to make a commitment of his own.

Gordon Brown, the Chancellor of the Exchequer, who steers the economy and is the second most powerful man in the Government, is charged with navigating Britain past what currently looks to be the only threat to Mr. Blair's hold on British affections—a year of limited growth, or even mild recession. That could mark the end of the country's current economic good health, which

had its origins in the last years of the Conservatives.

The only bumps in the road that the purring New Labor machine has been gliding along have been in an area of potential vulnerability for this Government—the ethical conduct of its ministers and the unity of their commitment to the Prime Minister's program. These were two of the principal counts in the electoral indictment of the Conservatives by Mr. Blair.

In the last three months, four principals in his Government have walked the forced resignation plank that was a permanent feature of the Major years. Among them was Mr. Mandelson, Mr. Blair's closest confidant and as central an architect of New Labor as the Prime Minister himself. He quit on Dec. 23 when he was found not to have declared a $625,000 home loan from a colleague who was under investigation by his trade and industry department.

## Scandal Control: Quick Resignations

The departures and evidence that emerged of feuding within the Gov-

ernment posed a challenge to Mr. Blair's reputation for discipline and control, and the scandal-starved British press gave the subject ample coverage. But showing his bent for damage control, Mr. Blair obtained resignations rapidly, in marked contrast to Mr. Major's lingering response in similar situations.

Most of the criticisms directed at Mr. Blair have been accusations of lapses in style—that he is a "control freak," that he is surrounded by "cronies," that he is creating a "nanny state." His Foreign Secretary, Robin Cook, was portrayed recently as a womanizer and a heavy drinker in a vengeful book by the wife he left for a younger woman in 1997, and newspapers have also raised questions about the number of homosexuals in the Government.

"It's partly to ward off boredom of Labor's unbreakable domination that the politics of the personal holds such sway," commented Hugo Young, columnist for The Guardian.

A Gallup poll published in The Daily Telegraph this month showed what the consequences of personal politics were for Mr. Blair. His approval ratings went up a point to 66.

# Unwritten Rules: Britain's Constitutional Revolution

**Donley Studlar**

When the New Labor government led by Tony Blair took office in May 1997, one of its most distinctive policies was its program of constitutional reform. Indeed, few British parties have ever campaigned so consistently on constitutional issues. From its first days of power, Labor promoted its constitutional reform agenda: (1) devolution to Scotland and Wales, (2) an elected mayor and council for London and possibly other urban areas, (3) removal of the voting rights of hereditary peers in the House of Lords, (4) incorporation of the European Convention on Human Rights into British law, (5) a Freedom of Information Act, and (6) electoral reform at various levels of government, including a referendum on changing the electoral system for Members of Parliament. This article considers the nature of Labor's constitutional proposals, including their inspiration, implementation, and potential impact.

## British Constitutional Principles

The United Kingdom as a state in international law is made up of four constituent parts—England, Scotland, Wales, and Northern Ireland—all under the authority of the Queen in Parliament in London. The constitution is the structure of fundamental laws and customary practices that define the authority of state institutions and regulate their interrelationships, including those to citizens of the state. Although in principle very flexible, in practice the "unwritten" British constitution (no single document) is difficult to change. The socialization of political elites in a small country leads to a political culture in which custom and con-

vention make participants reluctant to change practices which brought them to power.

Even though Britain is under the rule of law, that law is subject to change through parliamentary sovereignty. Instead of a written constitution with a complicated amending process, a simple majority of the House of Commons can change any law, even over the objections of the House of Lords if necessary. Individual rights are protected by ordinary law and custom, not an entrenched Bill of Rights.

Although limited devolution has been utilized in the past, especially in Northern Ireland, 1921–1972, central government retains the authority to intervene in local affairs. A recent example was the change in local government taxation, a controversy which ultimately contributed to the downfall of Margaret Thatcher as Prime Minister in 1990. In this centralized, unitary system, the voters are asked once every four or five years to choose a team of politicians to rule them. Under the single member district, simple plurality electoral system, the outcome is usually a single-party government (prime minister and cabinet) chosen based on a cohesive majority in the House of Commons, a fusion of power between the legislature and the executive. Referendums have been few and are advisory only—parliament retains final authority. The judiciary seldom makes politically important decisions, and even then it can be overridden by a parliamentary majority. Thus, in the United Kingdom almost any alteration of the interrelationship of political institutions can be considered constitutional in nature.

Constitutional issues were one of the few on which there were major party differences during the 1997 General Election campaign. Labor and the third party, the Liberal Democrats, had an agreed agenda for constitutional change, developed in consultation over several years. The Conservatives under John Major upheld traditional British constitutional principles, including the unwritten constitution, no guarantees of civil liberties except through the laws of Parliament, maintenance of the unitary state, and a House of Lords composed of hereditary peers and some life peers, the latter appointed by the government.

Other features of the British constitution have also resisted change. Unauthorized communication of government information is punishable by law, making British government one of the most secretive among Western democracies. Urban areas do not elect their own mayors, or, since the mid-1980s, even their own metropolitan governing councils. The House of Commons is one of the few remaining legislatures elected by the single member district, simple plurality electoral system, which rewards a disproportionate shares of parliamentary seats to larger parties having geographically concentrated voting strength. Thus Britain continued to have an overwhelmingly two-party House of Commons despite having had a multiparty electorate since 1974, to the chagrin of the Liberal Democrats.

Even though the new Labor government proposed to change some of these procedures and to consider reform in others, there were good reasons to doubt its commitment. Traditionally, constitutional reform had been of little interest within the party; like the

Conservatives, it embraced the almost untrammeled formal power that the "elective dictatorship" of British parliamentary government provided for a single-party majority in the House of Commons. When in opposition, Labor sometimes voiced decentralist and reformist concerns; in government, however, it was usually as centralist as the Conservatives.

## Labor's Constitutional Promises

There was general agreement that the most radical aspect of Labor's election manifesto was constitutional reform. This program was designed to push the normally passive, relatively deferential British public into becoming more active citizens. In addition to choosing their rulers once every five years in a parliamentary election, they would vote for other levels of government with greater authority and to have enhanced individual rights. More electoral opportunities, both at different levels of government and within the voting process itself, would provide a wider range of choice for citizens.

Tony Blair, and his immediate predecessors as party leader, Neil Kinnock and John Smith, had for some years advocated an infusion of a more participatory citizenship into British constitutional practices. As Blair says in his book *New Britain* (Westview Press, 1997):

"The era of big, centralized government is over. . . . Any government which wants to change Britain for the better has to care about political renewal . . . It is essential to meeting the challenges of new times. . . . Britain is the most centralized government of any large state in the Western world. . . . The first right of a citizen in any mature democracy should be the right to information. It is time to sweep away the cobwebs of secrecy which hang over far too much government activity. . . . Perhaps the oddest and least defensible part of the British Constitution is the power wielded by hereditary peers in the House of Lords."

In other pre-election statements, Blair called Labor's constitutional program "democratic renewal," argued that there had been 80 years of erosion of consent, self-government, and respect for rights under governments of both Left and Right, and contended that the Left's mission is concerned with extension of political rights as well as economic and social equality.

## How and Why Labor Developed a Program for Constitutional Change

Several events and trends focused Labor's thinking on constitutional reform as never before. Labor suffered four consecutive general election losses (1979, 1983, 1987, 1992) even though the Conservatives never achieved above 43 percent of the popular vote. Eighteen years of being out of government led to fears that Labor might never get back into power by itself again.

Groups interested in constitutional reform were evident. The third party in Britain, the Liberal Democrats, have long been interested in changing the electoral system to have their voting strength better represented in Parliament and also have advocated decentralization and greater protections for civil liberties. Since 1988, a nonpartisan lobby group, Charter 88, has advocated not only most of the reforms that Labor eventually embraced but also others, such as a full-scale written constitution and bill of rights. Other influential thinkers on the moderate left argued that social and economic change in an increasingly middle-class Britain depended on greater popular participation and limiting central government authority. In Scotland, where the Conservatives had continuously declined as an electoral force, the Scottish Constitutional Convention encouraged devolution of power through cooperation across party and group lines. This experience eventually led Labor and the Liberal Democrats to form a pre-election commission on constitutional matters, which continued after the election in the form of a special cabinet committee on constitutional reform.

Skeptics have argued that public support for constitutional change is a mile wide and an inch deep. Surveys indicate that the public usually supports constitutional reform proposals in principle without understanding very much about them. Intense minorities, such as Charter 88 and the Electoral Reform Society, have fueled the discussion. During the 1997 election campaign constitutional issues featured prominently in elite discussions of party differences but did not emerge as a critical voting issue, except perhaps in Scotland.

New Labor had multiple incentives in developing an agenda for constitutional change. It provided a clear sense of Labor distinctiveness from the Conservatives, especially important when there were so few differences in social and economic policy between the two parties. It was designed to alleviate threats to Labor support by Scottish and Welsh nationalist parties arguing for more autonomy. There was also the longer-term prospect of realigning the party system by co-opting the Liberal Democrats and their issues into a more permanent government of the center, thereby reducing both the Conservatives and die-hard socialists of the Labor party left wing to permanent minority status. What is unusual is that, even with the large majority that Labor gained in the May,1997 election, they have not abandoned electoral reform.

## Constitutional Change after Two Years of Labor Rule

No British government since the early twentieth century has presided over such a large agenda of constitutional reform. There are new legislative assemblies in Northern Ireland, Scotland, and Wales, a report from the Independent Commission on the Voting System advocating a change in the electoral system, and legislation progressing to remove hereditary peers from the House of Lords. The incorporation into British law of the European Convention on Human Rights has been completed. Legislation on a Freedom of Information bill, however, has been delayed, suggesting forceful bureaucratic opposition. In May, 1998, London voters accepted a proposal for the city to be governed by a directly elected mayor and strategic authority; similar procedures are planned for other urban areas.

One indication of New Labor's commitment to elements of this constitutional reform agenda was the speed with which action was taken. White papers (intentions to legislate) on devolution to Scotland and Wales were published immediately after the election, and referendums were held shortly thereafter in each country. Support for devolution was shown to be stronger in Scotland than in Wales. Legislation was duly introduced into parliament to create the new legislatures. Elections will take place in May, 1999, for the new bodies.

Eighty percent of the population of the United Kingdom, however, lives in England, which has been treated as a residual consideration in the plans for decentralization. Tony Blair has stated that he would be willing to form devolved governments in "regions with strong identities of their own," but, not sensing any immediate demand for them, the government has postponed such plans.

Seventy-two percent of London voters approved plans for an elected mayor and statutory authority in the May, 1998, referendum, but only 34 percent turned out. The Mayor of London will be the first major directly elected executive in the United Kingdom, a constitutional innovation which may lead to a greater personalization of politics and institutionalized lobbying for urban concerns.

Britain signed the European Convention on Human Rights in 1951. Since 1966 it has allowed appeals to the European Court of Human Rights at Strasbourg, where it has lost more cases than any other country. During the first session of parliament under New Labor, a law was passed incorporating the European Convention on Human Rights into domestic law. Now British judges will make decisions about whether Britain is conforming to the Convention. As in the past, however, it is still up to parliament to decide whether the judges' decisions will be implemented.

Despite this flurry of activity during the Blair Government's first year in office, the tougher questions—electoral reform for Westminster elections, freedom of information, and House of Lords reform—were postponed. Currently the United Kingdom remains one of the most secretive democracies in the world, under the doctrine of executive prerogatives of Ministers of the Crown.

House of Lords reform appears simple on the surface since the House of Commons can eventually override any objections from the Lords. Politically, however, it is quite complicated. New Labor has pledged to abolish voting by hereditary peers, leaving only the appointed life peers, many of whom have substantial political experience, in place as a second chamber. Without a more comprehensive reform of the House of Lords, however, the power of the Commons over the Lords would continue and perhaps even be enhanced with an entirely patronage-based second chamber. Critics have suggested that a form of direct or indirect election, perhaps by regions, would be preferable. In response, Tony Blair has promised to appoint life peers in consultation with a special advisory commission and to appoint a Royal Commission to recommend the second stage of Lords reform. Furthermore, in late 1997 he compromised further by allowing 91 hereditary peers to remain until the second stage of Lords reform is completed.

Although Prime Minister Blair indicated that he was not "personally convinced" that a change in the electoral system was needed, he appointed an Independent Commission on the Voting System in December, 1997. Its charge was to recommend an alternative to the current electoral system for the House of Commons, backed by a government pledge to put any proposed change to a referendum. In October, 1998, the Commission recommended what is called "Alternative Vote Plus." The single-member district system would be retained, but instead of casting a vote for one person only, the electorate would rank candidates in order of preference, thus assuring a majority rather than a plurality vote for the winner. There would also be a second vote for a "preferred party." These votes would be put into a regional pool, with 15-20 percent of the total seats being awarded to parties based on their proportional share of these second votes, a favorable development for smaller parties.

Even such a relatively mild reform, however, has generated substantial political conflict, as expected when the very basis on which politicians hold their seats is challenged. Although Prime Minister Blair "warmly welcomed" the Commission report and invited a period of public debate on its recommendations, others were not so reticent. Conservative leader William Hague,

fearing that a change in the electoral system would realign the party system permanently against the Conservatives, promised Tony Blair "the fight of his life" if the latter tried to implement the report. Even within the Labor party, many cabinet ministers and members of parliament oppose any change in a system in which Labor retains the power to obtain a single-party parliamentary majority.

Some analysts, however, argue that the most significant constitutional change in United Kingdom has been brought about not by Labor but by three actions of Conservative governments—joining the European Community in 1972, approving the Single European Act (1986), and signing the Maastricht Treaty (1991). EU law supercedes British law in those areas where the two conflict; the European Court of Justice has judicial review over United Kingdom law. Already one-third of total legislation in the United Kingdom comes from the European Union.

## Conflicting Views on the Effects of Constitutional Change

Labor's program of constitutional change has already brought about some changes in Britain, but the larger impacts are yet to come. Instead of near-uniform use of the single member district, simple plurality electoral system, now there are several different systems: Single Transferable Vote (a form of proportional representation with candidate choice) in Northern Ireland, party list proportional representation for the June, 1999 European Parliament election, alternative member systems (combination of single member district and party list proportional) for the devolved legislatures in Scotland and Wales and the London Council, and a popularly elected executive for London. Plurality elections remain the norm only for the Westminster parliamentary and local government elections. Until 1997, there had been only four referendums in the history of the United Kingdom. Within nine months of taking power, Labor held four additional referendums (in Wales, Scotland, Northern Ireland, and London), with two others promised, on changing the Westminster electoral system and on joining the European single currency.

Broadly, four interpretations of these developments have been voiced by commentators, as outlined below. We might term these the (1) popular social liberalism, (2) lukewarm reform, (3) symbolic politics, and (4) doomsday scenarios. These contending explanations exist at least partially because Labor itself has never outlined a coherent theory of its constitutional reforms beyond Blair's pre-election formulations. There is to be no overall constitutional convention; instead there have been a series of ad hoc measures, to some degree dependent on demand.

The American analyst of Britain, Samuel H. Beer, has compared Blair's reforms to the popular social liberalism of the early twentieth century Liberal governments, who restricted the power of the House of Lords and attempted to devolve power to Ireland, among other things. In the wake of the First World War, even though government spending grew substantially, the Conservatives electorally came to dominate a political Left divided between an insurgent Labor Party and the remaining Liberals. Social and constitutional reform under Blair is a substitute for a more traditional Labor program of increased government spending and is aimed at establishing the long-term political dominance of a revitalized center-left, either with or without the Liberal Democrats.

Another constitutional scholar, Philip Norton, argues that New Labor's proposals are radical in concept but so far moderate in form and effects, e.g., lukewarm reform. Similarly, Anthony Barnett of Charter 88 says that the government practices *constitutus interruptus.* Another British academic, Patrick Dunleavy, has suggested that constitutional reform for New Labor represents continuous but financially cheap activity when the government is afraid of appearing to be another Labor "tax and spend" administration. This allows a sense of achievement based on a permissive consensus among the public but amounts to little substantive change, at least until electoral reform is confronted.

Finally, there is the doomsday scenario, as envisioned by the Conservative former editor of *The Times,* William Rees-Mogg. He argues that Labor's constitutional changes erode democracy in the United Kingdom. They will result in a semi-permanent Labor-Liberal coalition in the Westminster parliament, Scotland, and Wales, with a weakened patronage-based House of Lords. A further transfer of power to European Community institutions will lead to the United Kingdom losing its sovereignty within a bureaucratic European super-state.

## Unintended Consequences Over the Horizon?

Institutional rearrangements often have unanticipated consequences. Although New Labor legislation on constitutional matters claims to leave parliamentary sovereignty undisturbed, it is likely that this constitutional convention will be compromised even more than it already is under Britain's membership [in] the European Union. Devolution is likely to become entrenched de facto, as the process of decentralization has in other European countries. Although specific powers are granted to each devolved government, disputes over which level has authority over certain policies will inevitably arise. Some type of adjudication commission or court for such jurisdictional disputes may be formed. Even without a comprehensive Bill of Rights, incorporation of the European Convention on Human Rights may mean a stronger, more politically active judiciary. House of Lords reform, if it is not to be simply an appointed chamber reflecting the wishes of the government of the day, could also lead to a more symmetrical bicameralism.

Incorporation of the European Convention on Human Rights, as well as a limited form of joint authority with Ireland over Northern Ireland and possible membership [in] the European common currency and central bank, suggest that Britain may be moving into new patterns of international shared authority in certain areas heretofore considered exclusively within the realm of the sovereign state. Regional policies of the European Union even may be helping stimulate ethnonationalist demands. If the SNP, still committed to independence for Scotland, achieved a majority in the Scottish Parliament, the United Kingdom could be faced with a "Quebec scenario," whereby control of a level of government enhances rather than diminishes claims for independence.

The "third way" ideas of Anthony Giddens, influential in the New Labor government, advocate a restructuring of government to promote "subsidiarity" (the taking of decisions at the lowest level possible) and correcting the "democratic deficit" through constitutional reform, greater transparency, and more local democracy. In such a process, Britain would become a more complex polity institutionally. Habits of conciliation, cooperation, and consent would have to be developed rather than the usual reliance upon parliamentary laws and executive orders.

The electoral system, however, may be the lynchpin of the British parliamentary system as it currently exists. Thus even the relatively mild changes proposed might have the biggest impact by realigning the party system. Whatever one's view of the desirability and impact of the changes, New Labor under Tony Blair has pursued its campaign pledges on constitutional reform. Although tactical retreats have occurred on some issues, this agenda promises to be a major part of British politics for the foreseeable future.

---

*Donley T. Studlar is Eberly Family Distinguished Professor of Political Science at West Virginia University, Executive Secretary of the British Politics Group, and author of* Great Britain: Decline or Renewal? *(Westview Press 1996).*

**After four centuries, Great Britain is disappearing. Scotland and Wales are going their own ways, the House of Lords is under attack, the monarchy and the Constitution are being reinvented and the currency could soon be abandoned, but . . .**

# There Will Always Be an England

## By Andrew Sullivan

I didn't fully realize it growing up but, in its way, my hometown was a kind of ground zero for Englishness. Almost a national synonym for middle-class ennui, East Grinstead was the last stop on a railway line south of London, the first place outside the metropolis that wasn't actually metropolitan, a welter of disappointment and understatement and yet also of a kind of pride. The inhabitants of a small town in New Jersey will have an idea of what I mean, except East Grinstead had its roots in Anglo-Saxon times and always wore its modernity with a shrug.

When I grew up, it was a commuter-belt development of 20,000 but also, still, a place of its own. Its Victorian railway station and Elizabethan main street, its unique mix of local butchers, bakers, hardware stores and bookshops, the vegetable allotments and rugby pitches, the St. Swithun's church spire punctuating the skyline, the great swaths of bluebells that turned the neighboring woodlands into a shock of violet in the springtime—they made it a place in itself, a place to stay and grow up in, a place that knew itself and knew where it stood.

A British pop song of the 1980's expresses how I feel walking around the place today, 15 years after I left Britain for the United States: "This must be the place I waited years to leave." But it is a place I also almost fail to recognize. The meadows I played in as a boy are now covered with crowds of pseudocottages built for the burgeoning middle class. The old railway station has been dismantled and replaced by a concrete terminus. Its parking lot is now shared with the new de facto town center: a cavernous aircraft hangar of a supermarket, which has displaced almost every local shop in the town. The main street is now a ghostly assortment of real-estate offices and charity bookshops, banks and mortgage companies. The

main road now leads swiftly onto the new M25, the freeway that circles London. Trucks with Belgian and Italian license plates clog the artery on their way to Gatwick Airport, the Channel Tunnel or farther—to London, Oxford, Reading and, by train, to Paris and Brussels. The house I grew up in, after 34 years, is finally occupied by another family. My parents have built a grand new, American-style retirement home a mere hundred yards down the street. And in the long evening of an English winter, I click past dozens of German cable channels to watch "South Park" and "Larry King," before logging on to my parents' AOL account to check my E-mail. My sister has dubbed the house South Fork. And my toddler niece and nephew bring their Disney toys to play in it.

This wasn't quite the script I had imagined when I left in 1984. Every immigrant to America likes to think of his home country as a repository of the old and the quaint, of unchanging stability and backward thinking. It is the vanity of immigration, and in a deeper sense, the vanity of America itself. So it is somewhat of an adjustment to find the suburban England I had once seen as a rickety edifice of nostalgia, class and passivity become the kind of striving, anonymous exurb I once associated with America, and to feel the still-raw unease that such a transformation has clearly brought about.

By transformation, I don't mean merely the shift that has occurred everywhere the global economy has been allowed to do its work unchecked. And I don't mean the changes that happen with every hometown between remembered adolescence and adulthood. I mean something a little deeper, something alien to the American experience, which is why perhaps it has gone largely unnoticed in this country. I mean the loss of national identity itself, the unraveling of a sense of nationhood and settled way of life that was once almost definitional of the stolid British. For in a way perhaps invisible to outsiders and too gradual for insiders to fully acknowledge, the combined forces of globalization, political reform and the end of the

*Andrew Sullivan is a contributing writer for the magazine. His last article, "What We Look Up To Now," appeared in November.*

cold war have swept through Britain in the last two decades with a force unequaled in any other country in the Western world.

As the century ends, it is possible, I think, to talk about the abolition of Britain without the risk of hyperbole. The United Kingdom's cultural and social identity has been altered beyond any recent prediction. Its very geographical boundaries are being redrawn. Its basic Constitution is being gutted and reconceived. Its monarchy has been reinvented. Half its Parliament is under the ax. Its voting system is about to be altered. Its currency may well soon be abandoned. And its role in the world at large is in radical flux. The implications for Britain's closest ally, the United States, are far from trifling.

Some of this change was organic and inevitable. But much of it is also the legacy of three remarkable Prime Ministers, who have successively managed in very different ways and with very different styles to revolutionize Britain's economy, society and Constitution—in a way that promises to free the people of the island from the past that long threatened to strangle them.

I T IS PART OF THE GENIUS OF BRITAIN'S UNDEMOCRATIC DEMOCracy that this transformation has taken place with such speed and thoroughness. In the vastness of America, a single President can do only so much. He is hampered by the checks of the Constitution and the power of the states. He has a limited time in office. But a British Prime Minister commands a largely unitary state with almost unchecked power for an indefinite tenure. With a solid majority in Parliament, she can do almost anything, and come from almost anywhere. In retrospect, Margaret Thatcher showed both the power and the limits of that position.

The results of her reign of willful uplift are now familiar. Britain, unlike her European partners, was turned from a social democracy into a market economy just in time for the gale of globalization. Union power was decimated; Government-owned businesses were privatized in one of the largest shifts in property since the Reformation; corporate and personal income taxes were simplified and cut; exchange controls were lifted; unemployment was allowed temporarily to soar; whole industries, like coal and steel, were allowed to wither and die before re-emerging as efficient private enterprises; the public health and education services were subjected to a financial scrutiny they had previously avoided.

It is a myth that Thatcher ended the British welfare state. She merely restrained it and allowed an ebullient private sector to grow disproportionately alongside. But it is not a myth that she single-handedly imposed a new order upon an old society. She attacked the socialism of the working class and the Toryism of the upper. She promoted the market economy as not simply the only means of economic growth but also as the very fabric of the country she ruled. "There is no such thing as society," she once declared. And she acted as if there weren't.

But while Thatcher's revolution transformed the structure of society and the economy, it left the institutions of Government largely intact. Her political and constitutional instincts were as archaic as her economic and social policies were radical. She still curtsied to the Queen; she revered the military; her patriotism was forged by the experience of the Second World War, which lingered in her distrust of Germany and her idiosyncratic love affair with the United States. She was a stickler for parliamentary protocol and believed passionately in the union with Northern Ireland. She treated Scotland with thinly veiled contempt, an attitude the Scots were glad to return in equal measure. Despite a pledge to extend freedom, she amassed power in the central Government, stripping London of self-government and trying to impose a national poll tax. Her finest hour was sending battleships to reconquer a tiny outpost of Empire in the South Atlantic. Her suspicions of the European Union eventually grew to such an overwrought pitch that she was cruelly dispatched by a Tory cabal.

In social matters, she also seemed an anachronism. Uncomfortable with women, appalled by homosexuals, utterly without connection to Britain's racial minorities, she seemed increasingly divorced from the dynamic, multicultural country she helped spawn. She was, in other words, a strutting contradiction: a modernizing traditionalist, a radical reactionary. And her replacement was, as replacements often are, her opposite: a small man of singular coherence.

There can be few more reviled figures in British political history than John Major. He was selected as Thatcher's replacement because he was the least divisive figure in a Conservative Party that was swiftly degenerating into vicious, internecine warfare over the question of Britain's relations with the European Union. The working-class son of a manufacturer of concrete garden gnomes, he had no college education and made his first trip to the United States a year before he became Prime Minister. And he spent much of his six-year tenure in office trying to bridge the unbridgeable.

His assigned task was to pursue Thatcherite reform while softening its rough edges, to soothe relations with the European Union while appeasing his fellow Tory Europhobes and to boost public services while lowering taxes and stabilizing the currency in a steep recession. In all this, it has to be said, he failed spectacularly. The media hounded his indecision and ambivalence, while the Tory Party self-destructed in a mess of division and sleaze. In an early debacle, the pound sterling was bounced out of the European Union's exchange rate mechanism—in one trading session wrecking the Tory reputation for economic competence.

After a brief period of support, the public grew to wince almost instinctively at Major's fathomless grayness, his whiny lower-middle class accent and his often fractious, odious colleagues. An increasingly diverse and feisty country looked at him and saw a man of the colorless, passive English past: a British Calvin Coolidge of the 1990's. Thatcher had bequeathed him, as she later pointed out to friends, a Tory majority in the House of Commons

## Major's lightweight steeliness made it possible for Thatcherism to endure and, paradoxically, for the Labor Party to revive. He was the essential midwife to the revolution that is now taking place.

of 100. By the time Major resigned as Tory leader, Labor had a majority of 179.

And yet it is no exaggeration to say that without Major, the current transformation of Britain would never have occurred. He was the indispensable cementer of deep change, the mortar between the bricks of Thatcher and Blair. Thatcher, after all, had never been able to establish a deep acceptance of her economic reforms. She still summoned in her opponents the kind of visceral hatred that Bill Clinton does in his, and she never commanded even a fraction of Clinton's approval ratings.

But Major turned grudging respect for Thatcher's accomplishments into exhausted acceptance. For however one might squirm at Major or condescend to him, it was hard to hate him. He exuded the middle-English trait of "good blokeness." He had endurance. Previous Prime Ministers, like Harold Macmillan, had affected a pose of English absent-mindedness, conveying a sense that they would rather be reading a Jane Austen novel than dealing with social security reform. But Major needed no affectation to play the part. On the day of his horrendous defeat in 1997, he left No. 10 Downing Street at lunchtime and spent the afternoon watching cricket. It was not a photo opportunity and everyone knew it. In stark contrast to his successor, he was remarkably unspun. And in that modest, quiet posture, he made the Thatcher revolution irreversible.

Under Major, the economy grew steadily, inflation was subdued, public spending muted and the most difficult reforms of the public sector were accomplished. The patchy prosperity of the Thatcher era began to seep into a deeper *embourgeoisement* of Britain. The North caught up with the once-booming South; the middle class expanded from 30 percent of the British population in 1979 to more than 50 percent by the end of the 1990's. Major's reform of pensions insured that Britain remains among the better prepared among developed nations for the social security crisis of the next century. He started a national lottery that began funneling billions of pounds into the arts, sports and culture. Moreover, Major temporarily defused the nettlesome question of Britain's place in European integration. He did so by negotiating an opt-out for Britain from the new euro currency while retaining Britain's full trading relationship with its European partners. His fellow Tories were apoplectic at the fudge. History will be less severe.

But Major's most important legacy was surely Tony Blair. Without Major, no Blair—it's as simple as that. In 1992, with scarcely a year of premiership under his belt, John Major faced a general election. His Labor opponent, Neil Kinnock, was a man of the left who had put his party through cosmetic, but not fundamental, ideological sur-

gery. Almost no serious commentator gave Major a chance after 13 years of divisive Conservative rule. But by a combination of doggedness on Major's part and skepticism of Labor among Britain's new middle class, the Tories stunned the experts by winning a record fourth term.

Without that victory, it would have been far easier for an unreconstructed Labor Party to have chipped away at much of the Thatcher legacy. And without that victory, a Labor leader like Tony Blair, who carried through a complete overhaul of his party's principles, would have taken perhaps another generation to emerge, if at all. But Major's lightweight steeliness made it possible both for Thatcherism to endure and for Labor to revive. He was the midwife to the revolution that is now taking place, although it would embarrass both him and Blair to acknowledge it.

WALK THROUGH CENTRAL LONDON TODAY AND IT IS SOMETIMES HARD to believe it is the capital of Britain. Within a few blocks, you hear Arabic and Italian, French and Spanish, Urdu and German. Australian accents are almost as common as American ones. The distinct class dialects I remember from my youth—the high vowels of the aristocracy; the rough, broad edges of cockney; the awkward flatness of middle England—are far less distinct. Even the BBC is a cacophony of regional twang, with Scottish brogue and Welsh lilt more common than the plummy Queen's English of my teens.

Elsewhere, there is a kind of sonorous merging, the rise of a new accent that seems to have absorbed East End vowels with a Southern English blandness. I'd never heard the accent before. It is classless but at the same time fashionably down-market. Tony Blair's voice captures it: he swings in one sentence from solid English propriety to sudden proletarian slang. Call it lower Blair: the new England wired into the very vocal cords. It is best absorbed while listening to a black or Asian Briton. When I was young, most immigrants still retained a Caribbean lilt or Pakistani staccato. Now they reflect lower Blair or the English region they come from.

Britishness was once a universally recognizable characteristic: diffident, self-effacing, stoic, decent, white, male. It was bound up, as George Orwell put it less than 60 years ago, with "the to-and-fro of the lorries on the Great North Road, the queues outside the Labor Exchanges, the rattle of pintables in the Soho pubs, the old maids biking to Holy Communion through the mists of the autumn morning." It had something to do with "suet puddings and . . . red pillar-boxes."

Think of what Britain once meant and a handful of clichés come to mind. Bad food. Crooked teeth. Good

Walk through central London today and you hear Arabic and Italian, French and Spanish, Urdu and German. The distinct class dialects I remember from my youth are far less distinct. Even the BBC is a cacophony of regional twang.

manners. Pragmatism. Free speech. Theater. Class. Monarchy. Poor heating. Old couches with the stuffing coming out. Sexual awkwardness. Sentimentality toward animals. Stoicism. Marmite. Looking at this list today, only a handful survive: the theater, free speech and the pet fixation. Even the latest ad campaign for Marmite, the odious brown sauce made out of vegetable extract, ironizes: Love it or hate it. Indeed, a modern list of Britishness would look altogether different. Designer furniture. Misogyny. Public relations. Sarcasm. Excessive drinking. Fast driving. Celebrity. Beaujolais nouveau. Cell phones. Tabloids. Sexual ease.

The latter is perhaps the most surprising. Stroll through Soho, where as a teen-ager I peeked into dirty bookstores and video booths, titillated by the clammy desire that was inextricable from English sexual shame. Now, most of the cheap sex industry has gone, and the streets pulse with a throng of Italian and French immigrants and a freshly visible gay subculture. Outdoor cafes serve cappuccinos, and shaved homo-punks chatter with preppy young media types. Gay bars are everywhere, but then straight bars are everywhere, too. Night life begins at 2 A.M. and continues past dawn—every day of the week. Unlike those in America, after-hours gay bars allow, indeed facilitate, sexual activity on the premises.

To add to the tolerance, it was recently estimated that on an average weekend in Britain, some three million tablets of ecstasy are sold. The techno-rave culture of the British teen-ager in the 1990's is a product of a mass drug culture, which the authorities have only recently begun to constrain. There is an economic reason for this. The music this culture has spawned is a major export and money-earner, from Berlin to Los Angeles. But what's striking is not that this culture exists—it's a feature, to a lesser extent, of American youth culture as well. What is striking is how banal it now seems to the English, who appear to have abandoned in a single generation a habit of awkwardness for an assumption of hedonism.

Old britishness, of course, endures. while I was there, the morning-radio news show devoted 10 minutes to a new study about how best to dunk a biscuit in a cup of tea. Local television news led with a story not of the latest gang murder but of six decapitated cats found in a London suburb. A friend stopped me tipping in a pub, as if I had offended some inviolable social code: "Don't tip the barman, mate. It's not your fault if he's got a crap job." I ate fish and chips out of a newspaper at 2 A.M. and indulged my taste for suet pudding. It seemed psychologically impossible to

evoke a response to the question, "How are you?" that was more enthusiastic than, "Not too bad." But everywhere the new intercepted the old: the Seattle Coffee bar next to the pub, the gleaming new gym next to the tube station, the Millennium Dome near the old Docklands, the banks of female deputies behind Tony Blair in the House of Commons.

Perhaps most striking is the racial integration. When I left Britain, London was still reeling from race riots in Brixton and from a sense that the island could not possibly absorb all the immigrants who were arriving without a racial conflagration. But oddly enough that hasn't happened. There is still racism, of course, and evidence of unequal police treatment and employment discrimination. Parliament, the armed forces and the police force remain disturbingly white. But compared with the racial tension I feel every day in Washington, the ethnic mix in London seems remarkably at ease. Some of this is because of the still-tiny percentage of the British population that is non-white—roughly 5 percent (in some parts of London that proportion can rise to 45 percent, but a passive civility still seems to predominate). And part is because of the diversity of the racial mix. The wide cultural differences between South Asian and Caribbean immigrants, for example, has made it difficult for hostility to coalesce along crude racial stereotypes.

But none of this fully accounts for the racial calm. Perhaps it's because, unlike the situation in the 1970's, almost half of nonwhite Britons are now born in the country and are disproportionately young. Perhaps it's because urban Britain itself has become more generally cosmopolitan. For more than a decade, European Union nationals have had an automatic right to live and work in Britain. With economic growth in that period roughly twice the European average and with the British unemployment rate roughly half the European average, the influx has been palpable and continues. More foreign E.U. nationals live and work in London than in any other European city. "Welcome to Euroland!" an old friend guffawed, with only a trace of irony as he ordered a claret in a West End restaurant. London may not have adopted the euro, but it reflects a truly European culture more than any capital on the Continent.

There is no doubt that the free market has been the catalyst for this cosmopolitanism. To Margaret Thatcher's horror, the market she worshiped has unraveled the England she loved. By exposing Britain to the world economy, by deregulating the labor market and by lowering corporate taxation, the Tories also encouraged a massive influx of foreign capital and investment. Foreign companies based in Britain account for 40 percent of British exports. The automobile industry, pioneered by such British names as Rover, Morris and Leyland, has now become a manufacturing plant for Japanese and Korean multinationals producing for European markets. Rolls-Royce is now a German-owned company. American multinationals and media companies also saturate the British market, with all the cultural baggage that implies.

Or take a smaller example of the interaction between markets and culture. While the famous London black cabs still seem dominated by pasty-faced cockneys, hundreds of barely regulated minicabs ferry people across London through the night, staffed mainly by Asian and Caribbean immigrants. As Britain has grown at the whim of the market, its culture has inexorably changed.

A deregulated, deunionized media sector has also given the new Britain a means to express and understand itself better—and so accelerate the cultural change. When I left England in the early 1980's, there were four regulated television channels and five or six radio stations. The BBC held a virtual monopoly on the tone of Britishness: a sometimes soothing, often excellent, but also stifling echo chamber for the nation's elites. Now every house seems wired, and personal computer ownership is by far the highest in Europe.

As a boy, I walked home from school each night through a public housing project, where at election times I remember seeing red Labor Party posters in every window. Today every house is owner-occupied, and there's a Murdoch-subsidized satellite dish where the Labor poster used to be. Literally hundreds of channels are poured into these homes, from sources as diverse as Rome and New York.

Or take the national sport of soccer. When I left England, it was almost a tribal expression of regional loyalty, a cohort of white men on sacred ground surrounded by thousands of working-class supporters who were prone to sudden outbursts of stunning brutality. Now, football is a sprawling branch of the entertainment industry. The teams and even the leagues have corporate sponsorship, and iconic franchises like Manchester United and Arsenal are full of free-agent French, Italian and German players. Media moguls like Rupert Murdoch compete to buy teams, and niche cable television sells the package in slices to the European market. More than any other industry, perhaps, soccer shows the unique dynamic that has both Europeanized and Americanized Britain at the same time. In football, it was only the introduction of American-style sports economics that thoroughly Europeanized the sport.

In a couple of weeks, I met a handful of old college friends. One, from a Dutch family, used to be a chorister in my Oxford College choir. He now works for Deutsche Bank and lives in Soho; we ate lunch in his new London club and talked of our favorite "Simpsons" episodes. Another now edits nonfiction for Penguin books and has just returned from six years in New York. One more conducts

policy research at the Tory Party's central office, after spending several years in Chicago.

My best friend from college days, Niall Ferguson, is now a historian who wrote his dissertation on the German inflation of the 1920's and has just completed a massive history of the Rothschilds. A new friend, Julia Hobsbawm, is tired of being trotted out as an emblem of the new Britain, but she is one, so I'll trot her out. The daughter of the Marxist historian Eric Hobsbawm, she now runs one of the hottest young public relations companies in London, with close ties to New Labor. As she breastfed her newborn son in a North London snack bar, she spoke longingly of New York and Edinburgh and confided increasing sympathy with the Tories.

While in London, I also befriended a young Australian actor whose parents are Lebanese and who has just married an American. He strode the streets of the West End as if it were truly home. These people are not typical of anything, of course. They are merely my friends. But their eclectic internationalism is far more conspicuous than their Britishness. And they are as much a part of their England as bowler-hatted bankers and flat-voweled dockworkers once were of theirs.

In fact, I think it is only through this cosmopolitan prism that the phenomenon of Diana Spencer can in retrospect be understood. Under 18 years of Tory Government, this new society took shape and heft, but it could find no viable political symbol or expression. The Tories were as culturally inept as they were economically successful; they created the substance of the new country but they couldn't articulate it.

Diana, in contrast, reflected the new reality Like many of her English generation, she was an individualist trapped in an anachronism. She was a creature of the media, like her peers; she was at ease in a world of Hollywood movie culture, Mediterranean vacations and sexual honesty. She seemed genuinely able to communicate with women and gay men, with racial minorities and middle England. In her pursuit of pleasure, even to the point of having an Arab boyfriend, she saw no cultural boundaries and felt constrained by no traditional mores. She was, for a while, the only figure or institution truly reflective of a country that had changed beyond recognition but had still found no way to symbolize the change.

So her death prompted a shock wave of fear that this new cultural dawn could suddenly be a dusk. In the outpouring of their garish grief, the British were almost wantonly telling themselves and the world that they were different for good and that what Diana represented in their unconscious was something that they had no intention of losing with her. As indeed they haven't. Which is why their self-confidence is now secure enough that they can move on with scarcely a backward glance at the late, immortalized "people's princess."

Tony Blair came up with that phrase to describe Diana and, in a curious way, it was the moment he truly became Prime Minister. He got it. His semi-impromptu words on

Britain is still the most reliable, and often sole, ally of the United States. If it largely ceases to exist, the consequences could be substantial. But so far, Washington seems as insouciant about these changes as London.

that August morning when England woke to the news of the crash in Paris cemented his hold on the country as surely as Ronald Reagan's calm poetry after the shuttle Challenger disaster helped strengthen his bond with Americans.

Some Tories complained that he was trying to make political capital out of a tragedy, but that was simply an expression of their complete estrangement from the country they had ruled for so long. Their new young leader, William Hague, made such a stilted formal statement of regret that it probably guaranteed his failure to connect in any way with British voters for good. More than a year later, despite many mishaps, Labor's lead over the opposition in the opinion polls is still over 20 percentage points. And its hold is as much cultural as political.

When Blair's reconstructed Labor Party came to power in May 1997, all eyes searched for evidence that it would backtrack on Thatcherism's market economics. Blair himself had promised a sweeping end to alleged Tory neglect of the public services—particularly health and education—but he had also won election by convincing middle England that he would not return to the tax-and-spend policies of the Labor past. In this, of course, he echoed his mentor in Washington. And like Clinton's, his first moments in office presented him with a stark choice. Confronted by nervous bond markets, Clinton had junked his planned economic stimulus package in favor of deficit reduction and only a minor nudge upwards in taxation. Blair, with the benefit of hindsight, was able to be more proactive.

Within days of coming to power, he announced that the Bank of England, which had always been subject to direct political control, would now be granted independence along the same lines as the American Fed. Its mission would be to control inflation. He also announced that he would stick to the spending plans of the Major Government for the next two years. It would be hard to think of a more conservative overture to the New Labor symphony. For good measure, Blair cut corporation taxes even further than the Tories had. This year, Germany's combined income, corporate and social security taxes are some 40 percent higher than Britain's. France's tax burden is 80 percent greater. By sticking to this low-tax regime, indeed celebrating it, Blair declared that his was not going to be a backward Clintonite co-optation of the right. It was a declaration of a new kind of middle-class, left-of-center Government.

But in retrospect, this focus on economics missed the point. Blair rightly saw that the old left-right paradigm in economics was dead. He harbored no belief that govern-

ment knew better than industry how to invest or manage a business. He had long since lost faith in the sclerotic European social-democratic model, which had insured that the Continent had produced an average 11 percent unemployment rate, compared with Britain's 6 percent. And he knew that low tax rates were one of Britain's few competitive advantages in the world economy. To be sure, he made some small Clintonite changes: increasing the minimum wage, tinkering with welfare reform, setting up the equivalent of Clinton's earned income tax credit to benefit the working poor. All were worthy ameliorations of Thatcherism—but no reversal.

Blair's real radicalism turned out to be constitutional. He saw the decrepitude of Britain's constitutional order and embarked on perhaps the most farreaching series of reforms ever tried by a modern British Government. If Thatcher and Major had dissolved the economic and social glue that had made Britain Britain, Blair set out to dismantle its deepest constitutional identity. The Bank of England was the first sign.

Since then, the sheer scope of Blair's proposals is a little hard to absorb, let alone convey. In American terms, it is simply inconceivable. Imagine if a new President proposed independence for Texas and Florida, 300 new Senate seats, abandonment of the dollar as currency in favor of the peso, adoption of proportional representation in Congressional seats and the abolition of the President's ceremonial role as Commander in Chief. This is only a rough analogy, but it captures the fundamental reform Blair is pushing. In America, of course, the Constitution would prevent or drastically impede such radicalism. In Britain, where the Constitution is largely what the parliamentary majority says it is, anything can happen and probably will.

To begin with, Blair is proposing what amounts to the end of the unitary government of the United Kingdom. Scotland's new Parliament will be elected in May, a symbol of self-government not known since the 16th century. In the referendum that sanctioned it, 74 percent of Scots voted in favor. More significant, a full 64 percent supported the notion that such a Parliament should have tax-raising powers, essentially replacing Westminster.

Blair has allowed the Scottish Parliament the leeway to lower or raise the British rate of income tax by only 3 percentage points. But the direction is clear enough. Blair clearly believed that by devolving some power to Scotland he would defuse the independence movement. Instead, the opposite could happen. The latest polls suggest that in the new Edinburgh Parliament the largest single party may well be the Scottish Nationalists, who see the new

Parliament as a way station to full independence. Of the dozens of conversations I had in London about the future of the United Kingdom, literally no one I spoke with believed that Scotland would be a part of Britain in 10 years' time.

The Welsh, too, voted in favor of their own assembly, which they will also elect in May, although separatism there is not as intense. The Good Friday agreement in Northern Ireland presages a slow dissolution of London's rule in Ulster. The third de facto country in the island—greater London—will finally elect its own mayor. What Blair has ushered in, in other words, may well turn out to be a return to a political Constitution last seen in the late Middle Ages: an English state with an almost independent European metropolis on the Thames, a feisty neighbor to its north and a half-heartedly controlled province to its west.

The corollary to Welsh and Scottish nationalism, of course, is English nationalism. The neophyte Parliaments in Edinburgh and Cardiff beg the question of why there are is no English equivalent. There will still be Scottish M.P's in Westminster. Why should Scots have a say in how the English are taxed and the English have no say in the reverse? The paradox is made more acute by the prominence of Scots in the Labor Cabinet: if you include Blair, who was educated in Scotland, the three top Government officials are Scottish, in a country where the English outnumber the Scots by 10 to 1.

The Government has batted these objections away but the signs of the inevitable are everywhere. When I left for America, the clear, simple symbol of England was the Union Jack. It is now increasingly the bare emblem of St. George: a red cross on a white background. You see it in soccer stadiums and emblazoned into the skulls of East End skinheads. In 1995, the biggest greeting-card distributor introduced a card to celebrate St. George's Day on April 23. Within two years, as the journalist Jeremy Paxinan pointed out, the number of cards sold had grown to 50,000.

The repercussions of this are a little hard to envisage. They extend from the possibility of a bitter, if peaceful, internal split-up—a kind of Yugoslavia with cups of tea—to more far-reaching questions like Britain's place in the United Nations Security Council. Britain's seat even now is somewhat indefensible, given its economic weight compared with Germany and Japan's. But will England deserve a seat—with a population of merely 49 million, on barely two-thirds of a small island? No one seems to know.

To Americans, this might seem a somewhat recondite development, but of course it isn't. Britain, after all, is still the most reliable, and often sole, ally of the United States. From the cold war to the gulf war and Bosnia, Britain has been both an unsinkable aircraft carrier for American military reach in Europe and a vital echo in international debates. If Britain largely ceases to exist as it has in the past—either by being absorbed into the European Union or itself dissolving into smaller pieces of real estate—the consequences for America could be substantial. But so far Washington seems as blithely, insouciant about these changes as London.

Just as blithely, Blair is also set to change Britain's second chamber beyond recognition. In 1940, when George Orwell envisaged a future socialist government, he saw its first objective as the abolition of the House of Lords. Sixty years later, it's finally happening. This year, more than 600 of 752 hereditary peers—the descendants of royal mistresses and ancient landowners, among others—will be fired from the upper chamber. A parliamentary commission will report within the next 10 months on who will replace them, what the new chamber will be called and how its members will be elected or appointed. What the powers of the new chamber will be no one knows. A less radical Government might have proposed an actual alternative to a second chamber before essentially abolishing it. Or even invited a lengthy national debate. Not this one.

Blair, then, is just as much a paradox as Thatcher. Watching him in the Commons, you see a tousled, somewhat prissy figure, uncomfortably unable to control the rambunctious deputies around him. But you are also aware of his meticulous preparation, command of detail and desire to please. Outside, his merciless spin operation is often guilty of overkill, wary of even the smallest scandal, demanding in one instance that a minister publicly choose between his wife and his mistress in order to win the spin cycle for the nightly news. In a stroke of genius, the satirical magazine Private Eye portrays him as a trendy young vicar in a small suburban church, whose beaming self-righteousness is tempered by a ferocious control of the timing of choir practice. His zeal is only marginally undercut by his sincerity.

And there are many in London who see his liberal constitutionalism as a means not to lose control but to retain it. By abolishing the Lords, after all, Blair also abolishes a built-in Tory majority in the second chamber. And by changing the voting system, as Blair is now proposing, he goes one step further. Britain has always had the American system of single-member districts, awarded to the candidate who secures the most votes. This has often served to minimize the strength of small and third parties and allowed small electoral swings to generate large majorities in the House of Commons.

In 1997, for example, Labor won 43 percent of the vote but 63 percent of the seats in the House of Commons. Britain's third party, the left-of-center Liberal Democrats, won 17 percent of the vote but a mere 7 percent of the seats. The benefit is strong single-party government without the fractious parliamentarism of, say Israel, or the consensual torpor of Germany. But Blair's commission on electoral reform has already backed a shift to a European model, one that would essentially end one-party rule in Britain for good and shift power to exactly the moderate left-of-center politics Blair favors. In this way the electoral system would do for Blair what Major did for Thatcher. It would make his constitutional revolution irreversible. And it would permanently change Britain from an American-style democracy to a European one. The system that was able—however unfairly—to throw up a Disraeli, Churchill or Thatcher will in the future be reduced to consensus products like a Chamberlain or a Wilson.

Adoption of the euro has been the more contentious battle. It has almost destroyed the Conservative Party, as free trade did in the 19th century, and divides Britain's elites as deeply as the culture war divides America's. Adoption of the euro has come to symbolize the ambivalence with which the British, if that is still a meaningful term, have come to abandon their nationhood. The country, in any case, has already unraveled in more amorphous ways. But the adoption of a foreign currency, the abolition of the English "quid," the handing over of the power of money itself to a bank in Frankfurt, has stuck quite understandably in the collective English throat. It has become a rallying cry for all those suddenly fearful of the symbolic end of a nation that has, in truth, already ended. It is a symbol of a reality the English have accepted but not yet acknowledged. Blair, in a rare cautious mood, has promised a national referendum on the issue—after the next election. He is canny enough not to commit political capital to a policy that the elites war over, the tabloids loathe and middle England fears.

"HOME IS SO SAD," THE ENGLISH POET PHILIP LARKIN ONCE WROTE, and for the first 20 years of my life, I knew what he meant. Everyone did. Loss, after all, is the central theme of modern Britain: loss of empire, loss of power, loss of grandeur, loss of the comfort of the past. When Churchill rallied his countrymen to the immense task of 1940 by calling the Battle of Britain his nation's "finest hour," he was perhaps unaware of the burden that phrase would impose on future generations. How do you envisage a future in a country whose greatest moment has been indisputably centered in the past? For a while, the British tried the nirvana of socialism, a kind of anesthetic to Churchill's evocation of an imperial, capitalist past. But socialism failed, and other chimeras, like seeking new greatness in a united Europe, also waned as time went by. The European Union, of its very nature, will never be a British creation. Its central axis is inevitably Continental. Even the short-lived illusions of vicarious power, like Margaret Thatcher's intense alliance with Ronald Reagan, could not restore greatness to Britain, as greatness had always been understood.

The problem was, after all, insoluble. It was the problem of decline. And perhaps the new era is symptomatic of a simple, exhausted decision to drop the issue altogether, a mass letting go, a communal sigh of acceptance that because the problem cannot be solved it should be quietly abandoned. It is a silent statement that the people of the island simply do not care anymore if their national power is restored or lost. It is a recognition that for each successive generation, the question of national power that once dominated the country's politics has less and less

meaning or force. The British, it might be said, have finally stopped seeking a role and started getting a life.

It is a typically pragmatic improvisation. By quietly abolishing Britain, the islanders abolish the problem of Britain. For there is no problematic "Great" hovering in front of Scotland, England or Wales. These older, deeper entities come from a time before the loss of empire, before even the idea of empire. Britain, one forgets, is a relatively recent construct, cobbled together in the 17th century in the Act of Union with Scotland, overreaching in Ireland and America in the 18th and finally spreading as an organizing, colonial force across the globe in the 19th. Like the Soviet empire before it, although in an incomparably more benign way, this contrived nation experienced a cathartic defeat-in-victory in the Second World War, and after a desperate, painful attempt to reassert itself, has finally given up. Before very long, the words "United Kingdom" may seem as anachronistic as "Soviet Union," although they will surely be remembered more fondly.

But unlike Russia's future, Britain's is far from bleak. London is Europe's cultural and financial capital, as well as one of the world's truly international hubs. Scotland has returned to its oldest union—not with England but with England's rivals on the Continent. England itself remains as opaque as ever: undemonstrative yet restless, cantankerous yet docile, open to the world and yet oddly at ease with its isolation. The ruddy faces and warm beer may be receding, but the rowdy cosmopolitanism that was once typical of the islanders under the last Queen Elizabeth seems clearly on the rebound.

Perhaps England's future, then, will be as a Canada to the E.U.'s United States, with Scotland playing the role of Quebec. Or perhaps London and the South of England will become a kind of liberalized Hong Kong to Europe's *dirigiste* China. Or maybe Blair will lose his nerve, a backlash will occur and the dissolution of Britain may slow for a while. We cannot know for sure. The changes imposed by a free market in a free society with a fluid Constitution are inherently unpredictable, which is part, of course, of the attraction of the project.

What we can know, however, is that the English, for their part, seem to be enjoying the ride. Maybe they intuit that Orwell was wrong about the endurance of British nationalism but right about the tenacity of Englishness. It is hard to forget Orwell's elegiac hope, as German bombs were raining down on London, that even if every major institution in Britain were thrown onto the scrap heap, England would still somehow be England, "an everlasting animal stretching into the future and the past, and, like all living things, having the power to change out of recognition and yet remain the same." Or perhaps the islanders have merely sensed that there is only so long, even if you are English, that you can cling to a culture of loss. Sooner or later, you begin to feel the possibility of gain.

# Perspectives on "New" Labour's "Third Way"

## Third Way, Better Way

*Tony Blair*

The Third Way is the route to renewal and success for modern social democracy. It is not simply a compromise between left and right. It seeks to take the essential values of the center and center-left and apply them to a world of fundamental social and economic change, and to do so free from outdated ideology.

The challenge we face is formidable—global markets, continued poverty and social exclusion, rising crime, family breakdown, the changing role of women, a revolution in technology and the world of work, popular hostility to politics and demands for deeper democratic reform, and a host of environmental and security issues requiring international action.

People seek leadership. They want to know how to adapt and prosper, how to build stability and security in this changing world.

They embrace the center-left's traditional values of solidarity, social justice, responsibility and opportunity. But they know we must move decisively beyond outdated ways of thinking—beyond an old left preoccupied by state control, high taxation and producers' interests and a new laissez-faire right championing narrow individualism and a belief that free markets are the answer to every problem.

The 20th-century left has been dominated by two camps: a fundamentalist left, which saw state control as an end in itself; and a more moderate left, which accepted this essential direction but favored compromise. The Third Way is a serious reappraisal. It draws vitality from uniting the two great streams of left-of-center thought—democratic socialism and liberalism—whose divorce in this century did so much to weaken progressive politics across the West.

The old left and new right have taken—and continue to take—different forms across Europe. There is no single blueprint for the Third Way. But Europe's progressive parties share common values, and all of us are adapting to meet new challenges.

For many years in opposition, the British Labor Party was seen—however unfairly—as the party of big government, nationalization, anti-enterprise, soft on crime, unconcerned with family life, gripped by pressure groups and favoring more tax and public spending across the board. We were also regarded as poor managers of public services, under the thumb of trade unions and producers' interests and too little concerned with choice and quality. The right was able to turn privatization and free markets into universal panaceas.

A false opposition was set up between rights and responsibilities, between compassion and ambition, between the public and private sectors, between an enterprise economy and the attack on poverty and exclusion.

New Labor has sought to move ahead and apply its values in a different way. In the economy, our approach is neither laissez-faire nor one of state interference. The government's role is to promote macroeconomic stability; develop tax and welfare policies that encourage independence, not dependence; to equip people for work by improving education and infrastructure; and to promote enterprise. We are proud to be supported by business leaders as well as trade unions.

Education is a critical priority. Higher education standards are the key to international competitiveness and an inclusive society for the future. Significant new investment is driving radical school reform, backed by targets and strong intervention in the case of failing schools.

In welfare and employment policy, the Third Way means reforming welfare to make it a pathway into work where pos-

---

A false opposition was set up between rights and responsibilities, between compassion and ambition, between the public and private sectors.

---

sible. It promotes fair standards at work while making work pay by reducing the taxes and penalties that discourage work and the creation of jobs.

The Third Way strives for a new balance between rights and duties—not just in welfare but in a tough approach to youth crime and far greater emphasis on the duties of parenthood. A new approach to family support is being forged to meet the needs of children and to help families—particularly the most vulnerable—balance work and home more effectively.

The Third Way stands for democratic renewal and a restoration of faith in politics. New Labor has devolved power within the United Kingdom: Northern Ireland has an elected assembly; the first elections to a new Scottish Parliament and Welsh Assembly take place next year; and the election of a new mayor of London is one of many steps to renewing local government.

Governments in the course of this century have been well equipped to regulate money, send out benefit checks, build houses, even fight wars and put men on the moon. Now they need to learn new skills: to work in partnership with the private and voluntary sectors; to share responsibility and answer to a much more demanding public; and to cooperate internationally in new ways.

This is the Third Way. A new alliance between progress and justice.

With courage, we can revere our history without living in it and build dynamic social democratic societies for the 21st century.

_The writer is the British prime minister._

# Neither Left Nor Right

_Bill Clinton and Tony Blair are looking to internationalize their 'third way' philosophy_

## Thomas B. Edsall
Washington Post Staff Writer

President Clinton and British Prime Minister Tony Blair are seeking to take advantage of the unprecedented number of Western governments controlled by center-left parties to turn their "third way" political strategies in the United States and Great Britain into an international movement.

Their goal is to give formal direction to the general trend in which liberal, labor and socialist parties are abandoning government ownership of major industries and tax and spending programs that aggressively seek to redistribute income.

Blair and Clinton have met twice this year—once in this country and in May in England—to discuss the so-called third way strategy that is neither the traditional right or left approach to governing. Clinton also explored the subject at a May meeting with Romano Prodi, the Italian prime minister, and on June 7 at a Camp David meeting with Brazilian President Fernando Henrique Cardoso.

While playing down any immediate organizational plans, some of those involved in the discussions suggest that the long-range aim would be to set up a middle-ground counterpart to the Socialist International on the left or the International Democrat Union on the right.

Any formal efforts to set up such an organization or forum would begin after the German elections in September. If Gerhard Schroeder, the Social Democratic candidate, wins, the German leadership would help Clinton and Blair counter some quiet opposition in the French and Portuguese left.

**Many of the criticisms of Blair, from both the left and the right, are exactly similar to those of the president," says Clinton aide Sidney Blumenthal.**

In place of direct state intervention, Clinton and Blair have been promoting a version of liberal-left politics that calls for competitive, free-market strategies while using government to prevent the market from devastating those least prepared to live without the protections of the welfare state.

"For the first time in all human history," Clinton told the 50th anniversary celebration of the World Trade Organization in Geneva in May, "the argument over which is better, free enterprise or state socialism, has been won, when people on every continent seek to join the free market system."

⌗

CLINTON CONTENDS THAT THE OBLIGATION OF GOVernment is "to ensure that spirited economic competition among nations never becomes a race to the bottom, in environmental protections, consumer protections or labor standards. We should be leveling up, not leveling down."

Blair says the current political balance "is an historic opportunity, and we're seizing it. We are taking the historic values of the left—our long commitment to fairness, democracy and freedom—and we are applying them to our new world of dynamic markets."

Writing in London Independent, Blair declared: "It is the center-left which holds the intellectual advantage; it is our agenda which will reshape people's lives. . . . [T]he right-wing agenda turns out to be hollow at the core."

The steady growth in international economic competition—globalization—has posed a three-decade-long dilemma for the Democratic Party in the United States and socialist-social democratic parties in Europe and other parts of the world.

These parties have depended on national high wage, pro-union, welfare spending policies—and in some cases state ownership—to maintain the support of working-class and poor voters. Faced with competition from low-wage countries, the center-left political parties have encountered severe difficulties maintaining widespread support for policies that are seen as costly liabilities in the international struggle for market shares.

"The recent record of socialist, social democratic and labor parties around the world" shows "that none of them are socialist. . . . Not one of the important left parties advocates widespread public ownership or extensive redistributionist policies involving progressive income taxes and entitlements," Seymour Martin Lipset and Gary Marks wrote in "It Didn't Happen Here: The Failure of Socialism in America."

"The British election in May 1997, won overwhelmingly by the Labour Party after it had rejected its historic emphasis on public ownership, basically puts a period, an end to a century of socialist efforts in Europe to eliminate private ownership of the economy. The party's leader, Tony Blair, has been deliberately following the free market, smaller government policies of Bill Clinton," Lipset and Marks wrote.

The Clinton-Blair "third way" approach claims to balance the inescapable power of competitive markets with policies seeking to provide workers with access to job training, health care and some pension security.

The de facto Clinton-Blair alliance, which the two leaders are conducting at both a personal and staff level, is viewed by some conservatives as simply a response or accommodation to the ideological upheavals initiated by President Ronald Reagan and Prime Minister Margaret Thatcher.

"One of the ironies of history is that left-of-center governments are presiding over the privatizing of Social Security and the introduction of market forces into the public sector," says William Kristol, editor of the conservative magazine The Weekly Standard. "Reagan and Thatcher and [German chancellor Helmut] Kohl will remain the giant figures of the late 20th century, not Clinton, Blair and Schroeder."

"Blair in many ways represents the consolidation of Thatcherism; Clinton represents an accommodation to many conservative ideas," says Adam Meyerson, editor of the Heritage Foundation's magazine, Policy Review.

Meyerson is more open to the possibility that Clinton and Blair could substantially change politics on a large scale, but says

## Center-Left Governance

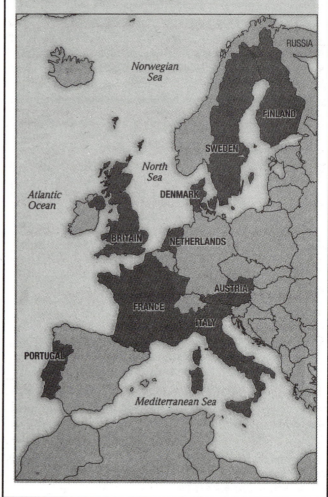

*An unprecedented number of Western governments are controlled by center-left parties. In the Americas, such countries as Canada, Brazil and the United States would be included as well.*

BY LOUIS SPIRITO—THE WASHINGTON POST

he has "not seen it yet. It's more talk than action." He contends that Clinton has "the potential to reshape politics much more so than he has done, while Blair has been much bolder on issues such as privatizing Social Security and school reform."

On the left, both in this country and in Europe, there are those who suspect that Blair, with Clinton's assistance, wants, in the words of one U.S. activist, "to put a knife into the heart of what remains of international socialism. There isn't much spirit in the Socialist International, and Blair is acting like he would like to see some kind of 'third way' organization replace it."

※

WHILE DISPUTING ANY GOAL OF UNDERMINING the Socialist International, Adrian McMenamin, spokesman for Blair's Labor Party, says Blair has argued "that the party needs to enter into a dialogue with other center-left parties which might not be socialist." He says the moment is not ripe for the actual formation of an international organization, but Blair is interested in setting up some kind of "framework" or "loose organization," where representatives of center-left parties could discuss varying approaches to governance.

In the United States, Sidney Blumenthal is the Clinton aide working most closely with the Blair government and with center-left parties in France, Germany, Italy and Brazil. "We are sharing our experiences on the issues that confront us in all advanced industrial nations," Blumenthal says, describing the discussions as informal.

"With Great Britain, we have forged a new special relationship, a 21st-century alliance, as the president called it, based not only on all our traditional mutual interests, but on our common conviction of the necessity for a new social

contract," Blumenthal said in a May speech at the World Policy Institute.

"Many of the criticisms of Blair," Blumenthal said, "from both the left and the right are exactly similar to those of the president. Blair is accused of spin and waffling, lacking conviction, offering up a blur, just conservatism in disguise. But the emergence of transatlantic, one-nation politics of a new third way makes it increasingly clear that far more than personality is at stake."

Within the feuding wings of the Democratic Party, the "third way" approach has won support from traditional adversaries. On the Democratic Party's right flank, Al From, head of the Democratic Leadership Council, and one of his long-term critics, Robert Kuttner, editor of the liberal, pro-labor American Prospect magazine, both agree that the "third way" offers mechanisms for the Democratic Party and other left parties to remain competitive in a global economy.

# Goldilocks politics

**The much-heralded "Third Way" in politics often seems to boil down to refusing porridge too hot for the voters without offering porridge that has actually gone cold. But though it lacks ideological rigour, Tony Blair's project has a serious purpose**

EVEN her detractors admit that Mrs Thatcher made Britain interesting to people overseas. Bits of the doctrine that came to be known as Thatcherism (a combination of privatisation, patriotism, hostility to trade unions and above all a belief in people taking responsibility for themselves instead of expecting the state to look after them) have been imitated in many countries. Now that her Conservative Party has been out of power for a year and a half, its New Labour successor says it is again turning Britain into a political trendsetter. This time the doctrine being tested for export is Tony Blair's celebrated "Third Way". But what is it?

The answers should be readily to hand. After all, Mr Blair and his ministers give frequent speeches on the Third Way. He crosses the Atlantic to discuss its marvels with Bill Clinton. Anthony Giddens, director of the London School of Economics, has written an impenetrable book on it, and Mr Blair himself has put his name to a Fabian society pamphlet. Clever young things huddle in Downing Street seminars delineating it ever more exquisitely. Gluttons for punishment can read the latest musings on it on the Internet. Following Gerhard Schröder's election as German chancellor, an Anglo-German working group has been set up to look at the *Neue Mitte*, the Third Way's German counterpart.

Clearly, something exciting is going on. But despite all the seminars, speeches and articles, its champions insist on describing the Third Way at an unhelpful level of generalisation. "My fellow Americans, we have found a Third Way: smaller government and a stronger nation" (Bill Clinton). Sometimes

> # Clever young things huddle in Downing Street seminars delineating it ever more exquisitely

it just seems to mean compromise. Peter Mandelson, Britain's trade secretary, says the Third Way in a European context means something in between the nation state (too small to cope with some problems) and a super-state (too big and too remote). All agree on what the Third Way isn't: neither the Old Left nor the New Right. But nor, say its visionaries, is it just splitting the difference. No, it is "about traditional values in a changed world" (Blair); a "very fundamental paradigm shift in politics" (Giddens).

Trying to pin down an exact meaning in all this is like wrestling an inflatable man. If you get a grip on one limb, all the hot air rushes to another. But it is worth persevering; it may be a poor ideology, but as a piece of politics the Third Way needs to be understood.

Despite the obfuscatory fog of generalities, one thing is reasonably obvious. For "a very fundamental paradigm shift in politics" the core ideas of the Third Way sound rather familiar. In Mr Clinton's vision of the Third Way, government does not just provide services: it is an "enabler and catalyst", "a partner with the private sector and community groups". The president wants government to be fiscally disciplined and less bureaucratic. It should not try to solve all of people's problems, but to create the conditions in which people solve their own. For his part, Mr Blair says that the Old Left championed indiscriminate and often ineffective public spending, but that the Third Way concentrates on making sure that the spending produces the desired result. He also says (something of a conceptual breakthrough for the Labour Party) that governments should be friendly to private enterprise (as the workers' class enemies are now known).

In short, these new politicians want to make government smaller and cleverer, fiscally sound, and friendly to business. It is hard to fault these commonsensical objectives. And in Britain's case they mark a clear departure from the big, stupid, overspending, business-hostile Labour governments of the 1960s and 1970s. But hang on. Aren't they precisely the objectives that Labour's Conservative foes tried to achieve before Mr Blair turfed them out of office in 1997?

Having demonised those Tory governments while opposing them Labour is understandably reluctant to admit that it is following the path they marked out. So a big part of the business of the Third Way consists of making up a story about what the Tories stand for which makes their Labour replacements look clearly different. In his Fabian pamphlet, for example, Mr Blair says that the New Right treats "public investment and often the very notions of 'society' and collective endeavour as evils to be undone"; and that it advocates the "wholesale dismantling of core state activity in the cause of 'freedom' ".

Maybe he has some other country's politicians in mind? The Conservatives tried to stop the state from growing, and to roll it back, but never in their wildest dreams to abolish it. Indeed, 18 years of Tory government left the state's overall share of the economy virtually undiminished: 44% of GDP in 1979 and 43% in 1996. Some things had been privatised, yes, but others had grown. Had there been any "wholesale dismantling of core state activity", you would expect New Labour to have entered office with plans for reconstruction, perhaps through the re-nationalisation of what the Tories privatised. It didn't.

The claim that the Conservatives rejected "the very notion of society" is no less preposterous. Mrs Thatcher did once say that "there is no such thing as society", a quotation New Labour politicians cite time and again to press home the idea that Conservatives see people as atomised economic actors rather than social beings bound together (another vaunted Third Way insight) by mutual rights and responsibilities. But the quotation, notoriously, is incomplete. What Mrs Thatcher actually said was that:

> Too many people have been given to understand that if they have a problem it's the government's job to cope with it. . . . They're casting their problem on society. And, you know, there is no such thing as society. There are individual men and women, and there are families. And no government can do anything except through people, and people must look to themselves first. It's our

duty to look after ourselves and then, also, to look after our neighbour. People have got the entitlements too much in mind, without the obligations. There's no such thing as entitlement, unless someone has first met an obligation.

You could slip that into any fashionable tract on the Third Way without it looking out of place. According to Jack Straw, Mr Blair's home secretary, the Third Way, too, has no need for such a thing as society, on the basis that "society is not a 'thing' external to our experiences and responsibilities. It is us, all of us."

## The big idea is that there is no big idea

Mrs Thatcher had more time for society than her critics allow; on some other matters, though, the portrait painted is, if exaggerated, at least basically accurate. She definitely saw government's tendency to grow, and to crowd out enterprise and private choice, as a problem. Her mission to halt and reverse what looked like an inexorable growth in the state's reach was clear to her departmental ministers and civil servants, even those whose instincts pulled in the opposite direction. Thatcherism was not a fully worked out theory when Mrs Thatcher entered office in 1979 (and critics of the Third Way may want to bear that in mind). But from the beginning it possessed one big idea—shrink the state so as to enlarge the space available for private choice and enterprise. It was all the more striking because it ran counter to the prevailing consensus.

In this area, Labour's Third-Way leaders and the Tories they replaced may genuinely disagree a bit. Third-Way propagandists are keen to contrast the right-wing assumption that governments almost always get things wrong with their own belief in the possibility, at least, of successful state intervention. Arguing that choice tends to be available only to those with the means to choose, and as such is too often a cover for privilege, they insist that the state really can get things right, provided it is managed better.

---

# The claim that the Conservatives rejected "the very notion of society" is preposterous

---

But how to manage it better? The Old Left answer would have been by spending more money on more public employees belonging to trade unions. The Third Way is against this. Mr Straw says that, apart from being the most expensive of options, "the statist approach—in housing, in policing, in education, in welfare—treated our citizens as passive recipients of services". Mr Blair says the Conservatives damaged health and education by showing "a visceral antipathy" towards the public services. But he refuses to equate the interests of the welfare state's consumers with the interests of its workers, whom he has already begun to antagonise by creating a regime of inspectors to weed out bad teachers, social workers and doctors.

In October, Mr Blair tried to explain his Third Way to senior civil servants by giving examples of ways in which it had helped the government find new ways to act. These included his government's use of a public-private partnership, rather than outright privatisation, to modernise the London Tube; government co-operation with the Wellcome Foundation, a charity, to invest in public research laboratories; and an invitation to private firms to help raise school standards in designated "education action zones".

However it is not plain what these disparate examples have in common. Public-private partnerships were pioneered by the Tories—and in many cases amount to little more than an ac-

| **Ways and words** | | |
|---|---|---|
| **Right** | **Left** | **Third Way** |
| Bosses | Workers | Consumers |
| Claret | Bitter | Sauvignon Blanc |
| Judgment | Analysis | Research |
| Crime | The causes of crime | Both |
| Feckless | Oppressed | Excluded |
| Competition | Planning | Teamwork |
| Small government | Big government | Clever government |
| Silent majorities | Vocal minorities | Focus groups |
| Wiltshire | South Yorkshire | Tuscany |
| Market | State | Community |
| Colleague | Comrade | Contact |
| Steak | Peas | Monkfish |

counting trick to take public spending off the balance sheet. And there is nothing radical about a government providing matching funds to encourage charitable spending, as in the case of the Wellcome Foundation. Perhaps the common theme is a willingness to blur the boundary between state and public provision? But if so, why the continued ritualistic hostility to private schools and private medicine?

Blurriness is certainly not something the Third Way fights shy of. Indeed, in as much as it airily dismisses the relevance of most of the "old-style dichotomies" which maintained certain clarities in political life, the Third Way is pro-blur. While Mr Blair does not want to continue Thatcherism's crusade against the state, nor does he seek to reverse it (which means it is likely to grow). He and his colleagues want people to be less selfish, but claim to have no problem with anyone becoming "filthy rich" (Mandelson). They want to promote equality, but not to restrict choice (except, perhaps, in the matter of schooling). They want the dynamic market of America but they also want the social cohesion of Western Europe. They want to be liberal and they also want to be social-democratic. And they want to believe that none of these wants clashes with any other.

Mr Straw has said that people need a "framework of belief", and as a result those who govern in their name need to have this framework marked out for them "so that there is some template for the scores of individual decisions which they have to make every day." But it is hard to see how any template could sort out these disparate goals and aspirations. To its de-

tractors, their very multiplicity shows the Third Way's fundamental hollowness: a doctrine that says you can have your cake and eat it too is a recipe for ducking every hard decision.

Enthusiasts see it differently. Some of these goals may be in tension, even incompatible, but they happen to be what the voters—who are seldom ideologues—want, whether they have fitted them into a "framework of belief" or not. In striving to do what the voters want, the Third Way frees policymakers from the need to place every decision on a left-right spectrum, or inside any other fixed ideological scheme. The Third Way, Mr Blair told the French National Assembly helpfully, is whatever works.

## What it's really for

Pragmatism has much to commend it. If nothing else, it frees a government to experiment. How else could Mr Blair have taken workfare, an idea that originated with America's Republicans, and made it into Britain's "new deal" for the unemployed, a flagship Third Way policy? But whatever the merits, this pragmatic approach means that the Third Way must by definition be several planks short of a framework of beliefs consistent enough to provide Mr Straw's "template" for the scores of decisions that a government has to make every day.

In the final analysis, though, as the comrades used to say, that was never what the Third Way was meant to do. Some political doctrines start with ideas. This one started with a predicament: the inability of the Labour Party to win an election by running on its traditional policies. A few years before the 1997 election, Philip Gould, a party strategist and pollster, summed it up by writing an internal memorandum with the succinct title: "Winning the Trust of the Centre without Betraying the Left". Although not an adequate description of what the Third Way is, this may not be too bad a description of what it is actually for.

New Labour has a strong sense of guilt about its move to the right. The constant complaints about Mr Blair being a

---

# He is convinced that you can do Tory things on the basis of Labour beliefs and be thanked for it

---

"control freak" arise from the long and still incomplete battle he has had to wage within the party against those on the left who think of themselves as "true Labour". He is exquisitely sensitive to the charge that he is merely a Tory in disguise. At his party's annual conference last September he made a point of rejecting this "nonsensical" allegation. And it is nonsensical, if you swallow the Third Way's nonsensical caricature of what Conservatism is.

The big gap in today's British politics is not between the Third Way and the policies of the Conservative governments that preceded Mr Blair. It is between the Third Way and what Labour used to stand for. That is why many politicians on Labour's left heap such scorn on the new idea. One such MP, Austin Mitchell, calls the Third Way "a convenient label for pragmatism, empiricism, eclecticism and a general approach of 'do nothing and ask your focus group'." He says that if the left is not to be swept hither and thither by every fad and fashion, it needs to be anchored in "redistribution, intervention, high public spending, full employment and equality". There's a template for you.

## Your policies, my values

Unfortunately for Mr Mitchell, reverting to such a platform would spell disaster for the party. But so would abandoning all of the feelings behind it. The strength of the Third Way is that by embracing a certain level of contradiction it helps Mr Blair to talk seriously about social justice—in some sort of which he believes—without having to say much about social-ism, a word deemed to have outlived its usefulness. His critics look at New Labour's theft of Tory clothes and say the prime minister has no convictions. But they are wrong. He is con-vinced that you can do Tory things on the basis of Labour beliefs and be thanked for it. He believes that while his policies have changed with the times he remains faithful to Labour's central values.

In 1995, as leader of the opposition, Mr Blair travelled to Hayman Island in Australia and told a meeting of News Corp executives:

> If—and I accept this is the real challenge—the left can liberate itself from outdated preconceptions, strip its essential values out from the means of their application relevant to another part of their history, then a modern left-of-centre is the best able to provide security amid change.

The idea that a party can reverse its policy ideas but cling to its underlying values is arresting. Policies that were base when they sprang from Tory values (greed, worship of the market) become suddenly precious when reprocessed through the al-chemy of Labour's higher purpose (altruism, community). La-bour may have mislaid a core value or two along the way (in Mr Blair's Fabian pamphlet equality becomes "equal worth", something rather different), but as long as not too many babies are lost in the torrent of bathwater the voters seem unfussed. As Lewis Namier, a historian, once said, what matters most in politics are the underlying emotions, "the music, to which ideas are a mere libretto often of very inferior quality". The music of the Third Way may well harmonise economic effi-ciency and social justice, a tune the Tories somehow forgot. But can the libretto be made to make any sense at all?

# From the Bonn to the Berlin Republic: Can a Stable Democracy Continue?

LEWIS J. EDINGER
BRIGITTE L. NACOS

German politics have not attracted much attention in the United States since the fall of the Berlin Wall and other spectacular events marking the end of the cold war. On occasion, there are sensational accounts harking back to the Nazi era, but reports of neo-Nazi activities and renewed religious persecution are misleading, because they tend to ignore that in this day and age politics in Germany are solidly rooted in democratic institutions, beliefs, and practices. Two upcoming events are, however, likely to get the attention of the American media. The first is Germany's national election on 27 September 1998 that could mark the end of Chancellor Helmut Kohl's and his government's long rule; the second follows a few months later on 1 January 1999, when Germans will start to move from the long comfortable certainties of a sound national currency to the uncertainties of the new untried one of the European Monetary Union (EU).

After the parliamentary election the German Bundestag will no longer meet in Bonn but in Berlin, once again the capital of the leading country in Europe. Its home will be the more than 100-year-old former Reichstag or parliament, torched when Hitler came to power, almost totally destroyed in World War II, and more recently restored and refurbished for a new era of German politics. Just before the job got under way, two American conceptual artists were allowed to briefly conceal the remaining shell of the massive nineteenth-century structure by draping it entirely in silken-colored fabric. The spectacle gave the crowds that flocked to see it no clues as to what the home of their legislature would be like in the future. For the transition from the politics of the Bonn Republic in a divided Germany to those of the Berlin Republic in a reunited Germany, however, emerging trends and patterns indicate quite a bit about how, if not where, the process is going.

Several developments seem particularly striking: first, as German politics are moving out of the distinctive shadows of the Nazi era, they are becoming less exceptional. Second, reunification has led to long-lasting socioeconomic cleavages between East and West Germans. Third, while the fundamental features of the political system remain in place, there are indications that changes in united Germany's party line-up, in the electorate, and in the mass media move the country toward an American-style television democracy. Fourth, with Germany's economic engine stalling, policy makers and the public are preoccupied with economic and social policy. Finally, military security and foreign policy issues are not as essential as they used to be.

## OUT OF THE SHADOWS

Politics in the Bonn Republic were from the start marked not only by decidedly negative memories of the Third Reich but of the failure of the democratic regime during the preceding Weimar Republic. The constitutional Basic Law of 1949 was designed to make sure that Bonn would not be Weimar. Its authors concluded from bitter personal experiences that under Weimar's constitution, democracy had gone too far. Too much direct democracy allowed its enemies to use presidential elections and plebescites for the mobilization of misguided

LEWIS J. EDINGER is professor of government emeritus and BRIGITTE L. NACOS is an adjunct professor of political science at Columbia University. This article is adapted from their new book, *From Bonn to Berlin: German Politics in Transition.*

From *Political Science Quarterly*, Vol. 113, No. 2, 1998, pp. 179-191. Excerpted from "From Bonn to Berlin: German Politics in Transition." © by Lewis J. Edinger and Brigitte L. Nacos. Reprinted by permission.

voters. A more restrictive form of representative democracy in the present constitution limits direct democracy to the election of parliamentary deputies.

The Basic Law denies "antidemocratic" elements the freedom of expression and organization they enjoyed in the Weimar era and lets public authorities limit their activities–or even outlaw them entirely. These and other restrictions–such as a ban on neo-Nazi publications and broadcasts–curtail liberties in ways that would be unacceptable to most Americans. Germans accept them in light of the Nazi past as safeguards against antidemocratic propaganda. Memories of Nazi control over the citizenry in the Third Reich made Germans reluctant to adopt curbs acceptable to Americans, such as government eavesdropping on suspected criminals. But in early 1998, the governing coalition of Chancellor Kohl and the leaders of the Social Democratic opposition managed jointly to get just enough votes in the parliament for a constitutional amendment allowing electronic surveillance of private homes for fighting crime–an overriding issue for voters in Germany as in the United States.

Weimar's fate and Hitler's rule left their imprint on the law and politics of the Bonn Republic for close to half a century and on occasion are still brought to mind. When a huge influx of refugees from former communist countries stirred popular opposition and acts of violence against foreigners in the early 1990s, horrified commentators reminded their fellow Germans of Nazi persecution. Later, when unemployment climbed to what it had been just before Hitler came to power, opinion leaders recalled the disastrous collapse of the Weimar democracy as they debated whether political stability and social peace would now be better served by reducing or preserving costly social benefits. The invocation of specters of the past by right-wing extremists set on violating prevailing anti-Nazi political norms capture more media attention at home and abroad than warranted by the circumstances.

Right-wing extremism is far less of a problem in Germany than in France, Austria, and other countries. Two to three generations of West Germans have been effectively immunized through formal schooling and mass media exposure against a recurrence of mass opposition to democracy and mass support for totalitarianism. But roughly one out of five Germans who did not live in the Federal Republic until the end of the cold war draw their experiences primarily from the dictatorial rule in East Germany or some other communist country. Whether these newcomers are as sensitive to the lessons of the past and as strong in their support of democracy as the old Federal Republicans–especially in the face of prolonged socioeconomic difficulties–remains to be seen.

## DISUNITY IN UNITY

Eight years after reunification, 3 October, the Day of German Unity marking the event, is still not a particularly festive national holiday like America's Fourth of July. Since the days of jubilation over the fall of the Berlin Wall, East as well as West Germans have found little to celebrate and much to complain about coming together. When both of them were asked by their political leaders in the mid-1990s to give up a work-free legal holiday to fund a new social insurance program, two out of three East Germans questioned by pollsters showed their disillusionment by nominating the Day of German Unity. West Germans, who used to wax sentimental about "our brothers and sisters in the East" before unification, now joke nastily that the communist wall builder, Erich Honecker, should have been given the Federal Republic's highest decoration "for keeping the East Germans off our neck for so long." And while East Germans had shouted "we are one people" in demonstrating for unification in 1989, their morning-after hangover sentiments point to economic and social consequences of political union that created a new wall between the old and the new members of the Federal Republic of Germany.

The West Germans of the Bonn Republic had learned to consider their country the only legitimate Germany and communist East Germany its missing part. Reunification accordingly brought lands and people back into the country from which they had been improperly separated. But the cost of the merger has taken a lot more money out of their pockets than West Germans had expected and has substantially dimmed their initial enthusiasm. The unavoidable restructuring of communist Germany's decrepit economy and the integration of some sixteen-million new citizens into the Federal Republic's extensive socioeconomic system requires vast transfers of public funds from old to new states.[1] This has proved politically a lot more difficult than it might have been if West Germany's own economy had not been forced to undergo a costly restructuring process that provides its policy makers with a lot less expendable income than before unification.

East Germans perceive the substitution of West German institutions for those of the communist regime as outright annexation, rather than gradual integration. Most consider themselves much better off politically but not socially and economically than under communism. Joining the Federal Republic did not, as East Germans had come to expect from watching the West's television before unification, instantly bring West German living standards. Catching up is likely to take a long time. For the foreseeable future, East Germans will have lower average income, suffer more unemployment, and lack the inherited capital available to West Germans for private investments in government–subsidized economic development projects in East Germany.

---

[1] From 1993 to 1997 such transfers amounted to 549 billion German Marks or about $322 billion according to "Excerpts of Current Accounts on Economic Recovery in the New States" put out by the German Federal Government in January 1997.

## NEW WINE IN OLD BOTTLES

The 1990 treaty that brought East Germany into the Federal Republic called for a thorough reconsideration of its Basic Law, if not an entirely new German constitution. Little came of that. The provisional structure established in 1949 for the Bonn Republic suited the ruling Western parties that had expanded into the East; in a specially formed constitutional reform commission, their representatives vetoed all proposals for significant changes. Thus, the basic features of the anatomical framework of German politics established half a century ago remain in place for the Berlin Republic. Such institutional continuity matters more in the German than in the American political system, as formal-legal arrangements for dealing with ordinary as well as extraordinary policy issues carry more weight, and informal ones are less common and more tenuous.

Germany's Basic Law is similar to the U.S. Constitution in that it establishes a complex and rather cumbersome system of checks and balances between executive, legislature, and judicial authorities. But there are significant differences. Germany's parliamentary form of government provides for much greater interdependence between executive and legislature, and its federalism has more extensive interaction between national and subnational authorities. The states are responsible for the uniform applications of national law, but they also play a substantial role in national policy making. Representatives of the state governments make up the upper house of the national legislature, which can block measures desired by the federal government in control of the directly elected lower house. Since most laws require the approval of the upper chamber, the federal government must negotiate and find common ground with recalcitrant state leaders—often members of the major opposition party. That has become more difficult in a reunified Germany beset by mounting socioeconomic problems. Conflicting economic interests of the old West German and the new East German

states cause differences between governmental representatives in the Council—and with the federal government—that override common party labels. Moreover, the constitutional separation of powers between national and subnational authorities is being undermined by the growing intrusion of the European Union in policy making.

Political parties are the principal elements within the anatomical structure of the German political system—its lifeblood, so to say—in the Berlin Republic as in the Bonn Republic. National parties are the leading players at every level of government, and it is not enough to be a nominal member to get ahead in politics. A most unusual constitutional provision specifically makes democratically constituted parties the only proper instruments for the selection and election of the German people's representatives in public offices. The parties not only choose the candidates for public office, but also finance and run their campaigns.

More than in the United States, that arrangement has and will continue to give individual lawmakers less freedom from their party but more from their constituents when it comes to unpopular decisions. Under the American form of representative democracy, legislators are more dependent on their popularity in particular districts than under the German system. American legislators tend to give more consideration to their popularity among the folks at home than among their party colleagues in Congress and state houses, even when they are elected for more than two-year terms. Members of the German federal parliament and state legislatures, in contrast, are all elected for four years and not only have more time between elections to live down unpopular legislative actions but fewer reasons to be concerned about their personal standing with the voters. German voters are accustomed to hold entire parties, rather than individual lawmakers, accountable for legislation they favor or oppose. But under the Federal Republic's special brand of cooperative federalism, meting out rewards or punishment to com-

peting parties in state and national elections is not so easy when governing and opposition parties have obscured the choices before the voters by overcoming their differences through compromise agreements.

In the American system of winner-takes-all, single-member elections, one of the two major parties is sure to win a majority in national and state legislatures; but that is nearly impossible under the German system of proportional representation in national elections and very difficult in state contests. Thus, the Christian Democrats (CDU/CSU) and the Social Democrats (SPD) have formal as well as informal legislative coalitions with each other and/or at least one minor party. For many years the only third party in the Bonn Republic, the Free Democratic Party (FDP), had a disproportionate amount of influence as coalition partner in federal and state governments. After winning representation in the national diet in the 1980s for the first time, the Green Party has strengthened its position in the 1990s—especially in the western states. The Party for Democratic Socialism (PDS), the successor party of East Germany's Communist party, is a force to be reckoned with in the eastern states, because East Germans perceive the PDS as the only genuine East German party and an outlet to voice their protest against West German dominance.

Christian and Social Democrats will most likely remain the leading players in German politics. But loyalties that once tied a majority of the electorate to these parties have diminished, a trend that parallels the increase in independent voters in the United States. About one out of two German voters is now an independent swing-voter. Young people, far more than the older generation, identify themselves as independents. And not surprisingly, East Germans, who have no direct experience with the Western parties that have expanded into their territory, show a particular inclination for swing-voting.

Strategies and tactics in election campaigns have been changing correspondingly. Parties and candidates can no longer aim at getting the party faithful to the polls but must try to win over the growing number of unaffiliated swing-voters. This cannot be accomplished by playing the party circuit but requires broader appeals through the mass media. Moreover, given the decline of party media in the last decades, even party members must be addressed increasingly through media outlets that claim to be non-partisan.

While German voters still cast their ballots primarily for parties and not for individual candidates, they are increasingly inclined to evaluate and compare the personal attributes of top contenders. The major parties' candidates for the chancellor's office have always more or less affected the outcome of elections, as Konrad Adenauer or Willy Brandt demonstrated. But the more recent changes in Germany's party line-up and in the electorate have forced candidates, especially those on top of the ticket, more than ever to compete personally for votes. This development has been magnified by the proliferation of private cable and satellite television channels. Commercial television–far more than the nonprofit public channels that enjoyed long years of a virtual broadcast monopoly–tends to focus on personalities rather than on issues. Moreover, the new abundance and competition of channels and programs offer politicians unprecedented opportunities to appeal to large audiences.

In the United States the decline of the political parties, the proliferation of binding primaries, and the concurrent rise of television have shifted important political functions from the parties to the mass media, namely those of informing citizens about political matters and politicians about the electorate's attitude. Moreover, the media have become instrumental in the recruitment of candidates and the strategies and tactics used in campaigns. In some respects, electoral politics in the Federal Republic seem to move in the same direction: while traditional campaign tools such as posters and personal appearances in party meetings are still used, they are less important than in the past. Mass-mediated activities are moving center-stage in national and state-wide campaigns. Even mass rallies and other personal encounters between candidates and voters are increasingly tailored to attract the greatest possible media attention.

Young and middle-aged politicians, who have grown up in the age of television, are comfortable with the electronic media and skillful in exploiting television and interactive communication technologies in ways that the party bosses of the past could not have imagined. While the road to public offices still goes through the political parties, one would expect that this will change in the foreseeable future. Dwindling party membership, weakening party loyalties, and the growing role of the mass media should favor the swift rise of media-savvy newcomers who understand the shift from programmatic to personality-centered politics.

Unlike U.S. presidents, German chancellors have not spent a great deal of time and effort to lead and shape public opinion; German leaders are not as obsessed with public opinion polls as American politicians. But as party membership and loyalty has declined and unity within and between parties has been harder to come by, leaders have looked increasingly to public opinion as a means to get their way with fellow-partisans and political foes. Even an old-style party politician like Chancellor Helmut Kohl, though not embracing opinion-leadership like Ronald Reagan and Bill Clinton, was eventually persuaded by his advisers to use regular question-and-answer sessions with friendly journalists on a private TV channel to go public.

Some observers of the German political scene deny that public opinion affects decision makers; they point to the differences between public opinion polls and the climate of opinion that entails a much broader spectrum of views. But just as public opinion polls have mushroomed and become influential in American politics, there has been a comparable proliferation of survey organizations and greater attention to poll results in Germany.

As in the United States, the leading newspapers, news magazines, and television channels in the Federal Republic have formed partnerships with survey organizations. Moreover, the political parties and/or their think-tanks commission opinion polls.

As the American example shows, a shift toward media-centered politics offers political elites and citizens ample opportunity to communicate with and sometimes even understand each other. But the mass media's reporting formats are more likely to trivialize politics and politicians and magnify the public's negative and cynical view of the governmental process and the political class.

In the coming years, as the Federal Republic must deal with the most formidable problems in its history, German decision makers are likely to use the mass media increasingly for opinion leadership in efforts to win support for reforming its socioeconomic system.

## PUTTING THE SYSTEM TO THE TEST

The Bonn Republic's democratic house rested for more than forty years on two pillars of strength: a broad consensus on the country's vital role within the West's anticommunist camp, and a robust economy that supported a generous social safety net and a comfortable, virtually riskfree standard of living for all. When the cold war ended, a robust economy was all the more important. But when the economic engine began to stall shortly after the two Germanys united, more than minor repairs were needed to get it moving again. Unemployment rose to and has remained at record levels, and the welfare state is under pressure to trim down. But many observers inside and outside the country doubt that Germany's brand of capitalism with a human face can cope with these problems.

The country's economy is by far the largest in Europe and the third largest in the world behind the United States and Japan. Although foreign trade has been and will continue to be imperative for Germany's economic well-being, business executives, labor union leaders, and public policy makers have been much slower than their counterparts in the United States in adjusting to the changes in the competitive global markets. While labor costs dropped in the United States during the 1980s, they rose in West Germany. And well before reunification in 1990, many manufacturing sectors in West Germany were rapidly pricing themselves out of global markets. Even in the face of record unemployment, Germany's labor force still earns higher hourly wages, works shorter hours, enjoys significantly longer vacations, and collects more contractual perks than their counterparts elsewhere in the industrialized world. The Federal Republic's industries are squeezed both by competitors in newly emerging markets with low labor costs and by highly industrialized countries like the United States, which have restructured old industries and moved swiftly into the high technology sector. In addition, there is now competitive pressure from former communist countries such as the Czech Republic and Poland.

Blaming the high labor costs in the Federal Republic for their competitive woes, most business leaders do not acknowledge that this is but one reason for their problems. During their prosperous decades, they failed to push ahead with innovation and rationalization at home and missed early opportunities to move into newly emerging markets.

The Federal Republic established early on and fine-tuned over the years an elaborate legal framework of rules, regulations, and processes for a capitalist system in which the various actors operate and, just as important, cooperate with each other. This dependence on law and order in the economic arena, what Germans call *Ordnungspolitik,* relies for most routine matters and conflict resolution on prescribed statutes, regulations, and standard operating procedures that leave little to chance. Thus, the whole area of labor relations is shaped by a complex system of legal precepts designed to foster cooperation between and among employers and employees and their respective top-level organizations. This particular feature made the Federal Republic for many years a most attractive site for industrial production. But many aspects of *Ordnungspolitik* also caused some serious problems and/or prevented early intervention to effectively solve them. Major restructuring measures and reforms would have been inevitable for West Germany's economic model, even if reunification had not taken place; but there is no doubt that the immense cost of rebuilding East Germany's debilitated economic base magnified these problems and hastened the need to deal with them.

Like other national governments, the Federal Republic cannot control an economy that is increasingly affected by global market forces. Moreover, as the policies and rulings of the European Union intrude more and more into economic, fiscal, and monetary matters, they constitute potent outside checks—even though representatives of the Federal Republic do have, of course, influence in the organs of the EU. But to the extent that Germany's domestic institutions and actors matter—and they still do—they have given some signals that they try to adapt to the new realities. Nowhere has that been more obvious than in what used to be a rather rigid system of collective bargaining. In the last few years, labor unions and/or works councils along with employer associations are showing considerable flexibility about agreeing on such matters as changes in wages, work hours, weekend-shifts, and the employment of part-time workers. Reforms of restrictive blue laws now allow retailers to stay open longer than before. And there have been some improvements in the cumbersome government regulations that delayed approval of genetic engineering research, the marketing of new drugs, or simply the construction of new plants.

In the 1990s and probably well beyond, the German economic model is tested as never before. There are encouraging signs along with business-as-usual tendencies regarding the outcome of this trial. New or more pronounced divisions within and between the major political parties, labor unions, and business groups interfere with the old consensus-oriented decision-making process and make for more adversarial relationships along the line of American capitalism. But the unchanged institutional arrangements, the formalized rules of the game, and the lingering legacy of the past continue to provide powerful impulses for continued cooperation and consensus-building—even when that means making substantial adjustments in what Germans call "social market economy."

The "social" component of German-style capitalism is under pressure as well. When Americans encounter the term "social security," they think of the government's old-age pension insurance that was adopted with the Social Security Act of 1935. For Germans, the quasi-public old-age pension insurance is merely one element in the nationally mandated social security package encompassing a wide range of social insurance, social assistance, and other benefits such as child allowance and educational assistance. Germany added a mandatory long-term care insurance at the same time the U.S. Congress rejected President Clinton's health-care reform plan. In contrast to the United States, the basic premises of the well developed German welfare state—including a social assistance program that is generous in comparison to American welfare benefits—have all along rested on a societal consensus that spans the ideological, partisan, and socioeconomic spectrum.

The challenges from the global markets, the costs of rebuilding East Germany, the extension of benefits to East Germans, millions of asylum seekers and refugees, and a demographic shift toward an aging society force Germans to seriously reexamine their social welfare system. By common agreement, the system is too costly and needs to be overhauled. To be sure, whose ox is to be gored, how and when benefits are to be cut and taxes for social programs to be increased are touchy political questions. But as the legislative approach leading to negotiated agreements of several cost-cutting measures in the mandatory health insurance system recently indicated, politicians in the party state can and do override even the most influential interest groups, when they convince the general public that those reforms will preserve the social security system. Ultimately, the political institutions and arrangements of the strong party state with their stress on conflict-resolution and consensus give the strongest assurance that the country can effectively reform its welfare state short of drastic surgery and keep the basic strand of its social security net intact.

## THE POLITICS OF FOREIGN POLICY

In Germany, as elsewhere, the politics of foreign policy are concerned with how people inside the country deal with matters on the outside. Contrary to the fears of some and the hopes of others on the outside, the people on the inside appear at this point neither ready nor willing to have the Federal Republic take a more active part in world politics than before unification. They still have to come to terms with their country's new geopolitical position in the midst of Europe, where it is second only to Russia in population and second to none in economic power. The capital of the new Berlin Republic is closer to the eastern borders with Poland than the capital of the old Bonn Republic to the western borders with Belgium. But West as well as East Germans, accustomed to parochial politics when they lived apart in separate states, have been slow to expand their vision beyond their borders since coming together in one state.

Since reunification, foreign policy issues have on the whole been neither particularly prominent nor controversial. Germans certainly do not want their country to engage in power politics as in the past. But few seem to have more than a vague idea of where they might be going in international re-

lations. Neither government nor opposition leaders have been keen to tackle a question for which they evidently have no clear answer—at least not for publication. Instead they have confined themselves to noncontroversial generalizations concerning the desirability of democracy, stability, and open markets for free trade throughout the world. The ideological cleavages and passions that once animated the politics of foreign policy in the Bonn Republic have given way to bland interparty consensus on the need for lasting military security arrangements with the United States in NATO, for more European economic integration, and for greater efforts to keep Germany at the top in world trade. But clearer and potentially more divisive definitions for distinctive German intercuts in these areas seem unavoidable in a world where "normal" countries like the United States have no inhibitions about promoting their own. The incoming generation of new leaders competing for policy-making positions in the Berlin Republic can be expected to be more specific, outspoken, and assertive on that score than the present leaders of the Bonn Republic.

The politics of the Bonn Republic in a divided Germany featured some bitter battles on particular aspects of the preeminently military American connection, especially over the potential use of American nuclear weapons on German soil. Those controversies are now meaningless. United Germany is not threatened by any country and threatens none. American forces remain in large numbers under NATO auspices with German blessings. The question facing German leaders in this connection concerns the mission, structure, and cost of their armed forces in the years ahead—more particularly, whether, when, and how the Federal Republic should use force or the threat of force in dealing with other countries. That it would do so on its own except in self-defense is politically out of the question. That it would do so under all circumstances to honor mutual defense commitments under the NATO and Western European Union treaties is more open to question. However, the

long avoided question of German participation in the international military operations outside the NATO area was answered in the affirmative by Germany's parliament in December 1995. With their lopsided vote to let German soldiers join NATO peace-keeping forces in Bosnia, government and opposition parties may have set a pathmark for the politics of German foreign policy on the road from Bonn to Berlin.

More economic integration with European countries and more competition with the United States in global markets diminish the value of the American connection for the Germans. The times are past when close personal ties between influential German and American proponents of a so-called Atlantic Community provided strong links. Future German policy makers are likely to be not so much against but rather not so much for their American partners in world affairs.

The constitution of the Federal Republic once called for a united Germany. Now it is the only one committed to "the realization of a united Europe." That, however, seems to be even less up to the Germans than the international treaties leading to the unification of their own country. The Bonn Republic of divided Germany was considered an economic giant but a political dwarf among European countries. The united Germany of the Berlin Republic is still the economic giant of Europe but certainly no longer its political dwarf.

While Germany was divided, what was then the European Economic Community afforded the Federal Republic its best opportunity for the gradual recovery of German influence on the continent. No wonder that West German governments consistently embraced Europeanization with a great deal more enthusiasm and public support than the French and especially the British governments did. Germans did not have to yield national independence in the bargain but could subscribe to limitation on national sovereignty then and now totally unacceptable to Americans.

Since unification and the full restoration of their political independence, the benefits of European integration have seemed less attractive to Germans. Thus far, however, neither the scheduled elimination of their valued Deutsche Mark through the currency of the European Monetary Union nor the existing and scheduled limitations by organs of the European Union on their domestic and foreign policies have aroused much controversy. Sustained mass unemployment might provoke more questions about whether a strong commitment to European integration continues to serve German interests. Most business and political leaders hold that the benefits remain much greater than the costs. As they have it, Germany's economy, which depends so heavily on foreign trade and investments, is sheltered by an umbrella providing unencumbered access to markets in other countries within the Union as well as protection against competition from countries on the outside, like the United States.

## THE ROAD AHEAD

Commenting on the Federal Republic's bright economic past and the present difficulties, one American observer noted recently that the Germany entering the year 2000 would be a very different place from the Germany of 1990. Others have suggested that nothing less than Germany's particular brand of democracy was on the test stand, since the successes of the Bonn Republic had strongly relied on its prosperity and generous social system.[2] But if the Federal Republic has arrived at a crossroads, as conventional wisdom has it, a fundamental change of direction is just as unlikely as the notion that the Berlin Republic will simply be a carbon copy of the Bonn Republic.

Today's foremost question is whether the predominantly old and

the limited, but not insignificant new features in the present system will help or hinder leaders in finding a balance between the continuity that most Germans cherish and the change that the country's immense socioeconomic problems demand. The verdict is not yet in. But it seems to us that the very features of Germany's political institutions and arrangements that work in favor of continuity and incremental change in normal times have at the same time the attributes needed for adopting major reforms in the face of extraordinary problems and looming crises. Some Germans believe that the magnitude of their socioeconomic problems call for bold solutions that only a grand coalition government of the two major parties can work out and adopt. Others prefer joint problem solving between government, opposition parties, and interest groups in case-by-case negotiations. Either way, the idea is that broad consensus is the best hope for meaningful reforms.

All of this is not to say that contemporary German politics are without bitter conflicts and confrontations. On the contrary, the enormity of the problems and the dimension of the needed reforms have led to more inter- and intraparty divisions between conservatives and liberals, friends of labor and friends of business, those

[2]Klaus Friedrich has concluded that the Germans "are running into severe problems with their much-praised system." See his "The End of Germany's Economic Model,"' *New York Times*, 10 June 1996. And George Melloan has predicted that "the Germany that enters the year 2000 is going to be very different from the Germany that began this decade with one of the most momentous events in its modern history." See his "German's 'Flagship' Casts Off as Kohl Fiddles," *Wall Street Journal*, 13 January 1997. See also, Kurt J. Lauk, "Germany at the Crossroads: On the Efficiency of the German Economy," *Daedalus* 123 (1) 1994.

emphasizing the social and others stressing the free market part of Germany's brand of capitalism. Moreover, as the projected demise of the German Mark as well as the waning influence of Germany's highly respected central bank, the *Bundesbank,* approach and the impact of the European Union's decision making on German affairs becomes more transparent, one wonders whether the deepening and widening of Europe's integration may not become a major issue in German politics.

Most Germans support meaningful change to preserve their socioeconomic arrangement, even if that means sacrifices. Of course, they have different views about specific measures and how they should affect various societal groups. This presents German politicians with a need for opinion leadership. While the privatization of broadcasting offers political leaders plenty of opportunities to go public, they are on the whole not yet as media-savvy as their American counterparts.

"Reform" was the most frequently used word in the headlines of German newspapers in 1997. As the nation warmed to the subject, one politician compared his country's politics with the disarray at a giant construction site in the heart of Berlin, where a multitude of monumental buildings rose for the relocation of the federal government from Bonn to Berlin. What looked like a wasteland for a while became eventually the new center of Berlin with new buildings and traditional structures side by side. The successful transformation of Berlin may be a good omen for Germany's struggle to cope with the challenge of today and tomorrow—although restructuring the economic and social system will be far more difficult than preparing Berlin for housing the federal government.

# Gerhard Schröder's New Government
## Gerhard Schröder's task

BONN

## Germany's much-needed reform will depend on who calls the shots within the new government

THE oddest thing about the German election result is the number of grins it has induced. You would expect the triumphant left to be euphoric, especially the Social Democratic chancellor-in-waiting, Gerhard Schröder, who has realised his dream of a lifetime. But why do so many members of Helmut Kohl's trounced centre-right coalition look far from glum too?

It is almost as though the stolid old Germans have had a fix. Once so angst-ridden at the prospect of any change, they now cannot, it seems, get enough of it. After regaining national unity eight years ago, then deciding to shift the capital from Bonn to Berlin and give up their hitherto-beloved D-mark for the euro, they voted to throw out an incumbent chancellor for the first time in a federal election since 1945.

That is not the only novelty. Before, when governments changed in post-war Germany, one partner from the previous coalition survived in office. In 1969 it was the Social Democrats, in 1982 the Free Democrats (often known simply as the liberals). This time all the government parties—Christian Democrats, Bavaria's Christian Social Union, and the Free Democrats—were bundled out to make way for a red-Green alliance, still under negotiation but nearly certain to emerge.

Thanks to their 40.9% of the vote, the Social Democrats have become the largest party in the Bundestag, Germany's lower house of parliament. The Greens, with 6.7%, enter national government for the first time. Together they have a workable majority over all other parties of 21 seats. But the dominance of the left is even more striking than these figures imply.

First, the Social Democrats already controlled the Bundesrat, parliament's second chamber, which groups representatives from the *Länder*, Germany's

states. With majorities in both houses, in principle a red-Green team can now shove through parliament almost any laws it wishes.

Second, the left will now hold a majority in the Federal Assembly, a joint Bundestag-*Länder* electoral college that will meet next May to choose a new federal president for five years. So the next head of state seems almost certain to be a Social Democrat—probably Johannes Rau, ex-premier of North Rhine-Westphalia, who lost in 1994 to Roman Herzog, the current conservative incumbent.

Third, the election result consolidates the strength of the ex-communist Party of Democratic Socialism, long expected to expire by many western Germans (and some eastern ones). True, the party wins backing almost only in the east. But this time it picked up so much support there (more than 19%) that it took 5.1% nationally, thus clearing the 5% minimum needed to enter parliament. At the last election, in 1994, the ex-communists won only 4.4%, but got into the Bundestag under a rule letting in parties that win at least three constituencies outright. Thanks to their latest boost, the ex-communists will probably play a growing role in governing the eastern states, though they are still shunned by all parties (so far) as a partner in the Bundestag.

A deeply depressing spectacle, one would think, for parties of the old centre-right coalition. But a lot of conservatives and liberals look as if a weight has been lifted off them—a weight called Helmut Kohl, chancellor for 16 years and Christian Democratic chairman for 25. Many Christian Democrats had long felt a change at the top would give them a better chance at the polls. But when the chancellor made clear he would stand again in 1998, no one in his party had enough clout or courage to talk him out of it. In the event, the Christian Democrats and their Bavarian friends together mustered only 35.2%, their worst post-war result.

Now the Christian Democrats are making a new start. On November 7th they will probably choose Wolfgang Schäuble, their popular parliamentary leader, as chairman to succeed Mr Kohl. And in Bavaria, Theo Waigel is making way as party leader for the state's ambitious premier, Edmund Stoiber. Mr Schäuble, Mr Stoiber and the outgoing defence minister, Volker Rühe, all in their 50s, are possible conservative candidates, one day, for chancellor.

The Free Democrats feel even more buoyant—at least many of them do. Guido Westerwelle, their abrasive general secretary, believes that further attachment to Mr Kohl would have

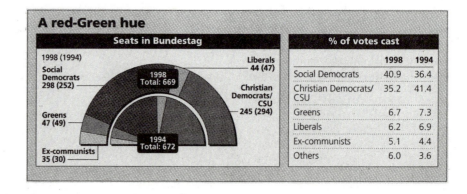

**A red-Green hue**

**Seats in Bundestag**

1998 (1994)
Social Democrats 298 (252)
1998 Total: 669
Greens 47 (49)
1994 Total: 672
Ex-communists 35 (30)
Liberals 44 (47)
Christian Democrats/CSU 245 (294)

| % of votes cast | | |
| --- | --- | --- |
| | 1998 | 1994 |
| Social Democrats | 40.9 | 36.4 |
| Christian Democrats/CSU | 35.2 | 41.4 |
| Greens | 6.7 | 7.3 |
| Liberals | 6.2 | 6.9 |
| Ex-communists | 5.1 | 4.4 |
| Others | 6.0 | 3.6 |

destroyed what was left of the party's liberal profile. After 13 years of coalition with Social Democrats and another 16 with Christian Democrats, the liberals in opposition can remind themselves and the world what they really stand for.

For both conservatives and liberals, part of the attraction of opposition is that it may not last long. Rightly or wrongly, it is argued that German voters are becoming more volatile and that a red-Green alliance will soon begin to split under the pressure of its contradictions. That is the main reason why on election night the conservatives ruled out a "grand coalition" with the Social Democrats—even before the latter did.

They may well be underestimating Mr Schröder. He ran a red-Green alliance smoothly enough for four years in his home state of Lower Saxony, before his Social Democrats won enough votes to rule alone. Negotiations for forming a national government will be tricky and may last all month. But since the Green leaders who count most have dropped maximum demands, like taking Germany out of NATO or tripling the price of petrol, they are unlikely to collapse. The Greens want four ministries but will probably end up with three.

The main challenge for Mr Schröder, as he publicly admits, is whether he can cut unemployment, now at 10.6% (4.1m people), by far Germans' biggest worry. What, though,

is he actually going to do? He aims to call together employers, trade unions—even the churches—in an "alliance for work" but the problem's roots have long looked plain enough: wages, taxes, social-security deductions and state subsidies are all too high, the labour market too inflexible. Jost Stollmann, the non-party computer entrepreneur who may become Mr Schröder's economics supremo, has already said just that—loud and clear.

But will the Social Democrats under their powerful chairman, Oskar Lafontaine, back the measures needed to curb these ills? The main challenge to Mr Schröder looks set to come, not from the Greens or the ousted opposition, but from the ranks of his own party.

---

## Germany and the European Union

# Welcome, whoever you are

BRUSSELS

## The European Union's other leaders are itching to see what Mr. Schröder is made of—and what he wants to make of Europe

THE ostensible reason for the European Union's heads of government to meet for two days next month in Austria is for an informal chat about "the future of Europe". How, among other things, can the Union make itself less disliked by its citizens? But the real draw for 14 of the 15 leaders will be the chance to fuss around Gerhard Schröder. Item one on the first day's agenda will consist of sizing him up. Item two, in a break with the past, will be to make him feel welcome. New boys used to get a fairly frosty reception at EU summits. They had to be taught the club rules; till they learnt them, they were liable to behave awkwardly.

Mr Schröder, though almost as preoccupied with the EU budget as Margaret Thatcher once was, can count on a much more sympathetic reception—for several reasons. For a start, he will be among political friends. His victory leaves Spain as the only large EU country still with a conservative government. Mr Schröder's fellow socialists see their own success reflected in his victory.

Another reason for courting him is that, as leader of by far the richest and most populous country in the Union, he will be its main paymaster—even if he can argue down Germany's contribution to the budget. Nothing in the

Union can be done without Germany's say-so, and Germany has been expressing itself more forcefully with each passing year, as lingering postwar inhibitions have fallen away.

Then there is the incentive for other countries to see if bilateral ties can be improved with the change of government. The stakes are highest for France (see box "Oil that Motor"). The cooling of Franco-German relations has led Britain, egged on by some merry words from Mr Schröder, to hope for a new spell of Anglo-German bonding. Britain hankers after something closer to a triumvirate at Europe's centre, with France—tant pis—as third member. But such hopes are sure to be dashed, at least so long as Britain remains outside Europe's single currency. The most urgent strategic questions within the EU concern the euro, and are therefore mainly for euro-insiders.

A final reason for EU leaders to welcome Mr Schröder is procedural. An alarmingly high proportion of Union business was hanging fire on a German election result. Now work can resume, nicely in time for Germany's assumption of the EU presidency on January 1st.

In particular, most EU countries hope Mr Schröder will be more sympathetic than Mr Kohl was to revamping the com-

mon agricultural policy (CAP). This would mean lowering EU prices for meat, grain and butter close to world levels. Mr Kohl resisted such cuts because his government relied on a big Bavarian farm vote. Mr Schröder's Social Democrats are much less beholden.

But CAP reform is only one part of a package of financial and institutional reforms on which EU governments are supposed to agree in the course of next year. New members from Eastern Europe can then be readied for admission. Mr Schröder will need to fight hard if he wants the final deal to include a serious reduction in Germany's huge budget bill. France, which does so well out of current budget arrangements that it makes almost no net contribution at all, will resist doggedly. Mr Schröder will also have to persuade Spain, and other big recipients of EU funds, to lower their claims in favour of new entrants from Central Europe whose need for EU cash will be much more urgent.

The countries waiting to join the Union accept that Mr Schröder faces much the same pressures and calculations as Mr Kohl did. In the long term Germany wants stable and prosperous neighbours to its east. But in the short term it fears an influx of cheap labour from Poland and Hungary. So, for a decade or more after they join, Mr Schröder will be wary of giving new entrants fully free movement of labour.

And Europe's common foreign and security policy? Quite a few European leaders hope Mr Schröder will be less cautious than Mr Kohl was in trying to create one. Later this year the EU is due to appoint a "high representative" for foreign policy—Monsieur PESC, to use the French acronym for the common foreign and security policy. Germany has favoured giving the job to a bureaucrat unlikely to mount much of a challenge to the prerogatives of national governments. Italy, the Netherlands and smaller EU countries are keen to have an experienced, big-shot politician to take the world stage in Europe's name.

None of these issues involves classic left-right divides. It remains to be seen whether Mr Schröder will press for more active social policies in Europe. His Green allies in government will demand more consumer protection and environmental legislation at the European

### A marked imbalance, frankly

| Country | Net contribution ecu bn | Net contribution per person | | GDP ecu bn | GDP per person ecu |
|---------|---|---|---|---|---|
| | | ecu | Rank | | |
| Germany | 10.0 | 121.6 | 2 | 1,910.3 | 23,225.5 |
| Netherlands | 2.4 | 152.9 | 1 | 334.5 | 21,316.6 |
| Britain | 2.3 | 38.9 | 4 | 1,248.7 | 21,102.9 |
| Italy | 1.3 | 22.6 | 6 | 1,049.0 | 18,209.0 |
| Sweden | 0.7 | 78.3 | 3 | 210.1 | 23,511.6 |
| France | 0.4 | 6.8 | 7 | 1,280.5 | 21,748.7 |
| Austria | 0.2 | 24.7 | 5 | 188.8 | 23,285.6 |
| Finland | -0.1 | -19.4 | 8 | 109.8 | 21,299.7 |
| Denmark | -0.2 | -37.8 | 9 | 149.9 | 28,293.7 |
| Luxembourg | -0.8 | -1,875.7 | 15 | 14.8 | 34,701.1 |
| Belgium | -1.8 | -176.3 | 11 | 221.0 | 21,649.7 |
| Ireland | -2.3 | -622.3 | 14 | 70.2 | 18,993.5 |
| Portugal | -2.8 | -283.2 | 12 | 89.4 | 9,043.1 |
| Greece | -4.1 | -387.9 | 13 | 104.6 | 9,895.9 |
| Spain | -6.1 | -154.9 | 10 | 492.2 | 12,501.6 |

Source: Centre for European Policy Studies, Eurostat

level—though these days even the European Commission, weary of criticism, wants Europe to regulate less intrusively. Ideology also permeates the argument about how far Europe's new central bank should submit to political control. Mr Kohl, the conservative, backed the central bankers' total independence. Mr. Schröder, the socialist, may be more sympathetic to political intervention.

Whatever he does, he will have to contend with the perception that he is a lesser leader than the man he replaces—that with Mr Kohl's going Europe has lost not only its doyen but also its wise man and institutional memory. Whereas Mr Kohl saw European integration as a historical imperative, his successors are liable to see it more as a series of tactical decisions, primarily economic in nature.

If the EU's capacity for strategic thinking does shrink, the loss will scarcely show in the next year or two. Countries that join the euro will be furiously busy, harmonising and integrating their economies in thousands of large and small ways. But the new currency's arrival and the approach of eastward expansion will put strategic issues back on the agenda soon enough. Then Mr Schröder will face the test of reconciling Germany's national and European destinies with the authority that was his predecessor's badge. Europe awaits.

# Oil that motor

PARIS

## The French fear that Gerhard Schröder may pay them too little attention

HELMUT KOHL is said once to have told France's late president, François Mitterrand, that he would be Germany's "last pro-European chancellor". That is exactly what many French now fear. Not that they have anything specific against Gerhard Schröder. But he is little known in France—and what is known about him, as a Protestant from Hanover, in Germany's north, and as a reputed Anglophile, makes him seem worryingly different from Mr Kohl, a Catholic Francophile from the nearby Rhineland.

Mr Schröder, they hear, belongs to a new generation of Germans wanting to put national interests before those of "Europe"—an ideal he mentioned remarkably seldom during his election campaign. He is the first post-war chancellor, notes the left-leaning Le Monde, no longer weighed down by the "burdens of the past". The newspaper describes his Germany as "décomplexé". He does not, it seems, share Mr Kohl's belief that furthering European unity is a "matter of war and peace in the 21st cen-

tury", or that nurturing friendship between France and Germany is the very bedrock of European harmony. Galling, too, was Mr Schröder's suggestion, at the end of last year, that the Franco-German couple could be extended into a ménage à trois with the British.

But it is not just the arrival of a less ardent European as Germany's new leader that has put a spanner in the Franco-German motor. Actually, it has been sputtering for several years. Remember, in 1995, Germany's lack of sympathy when France resumed nuclear tests in the Pacific? Or German annoyance when France—without informing Germany—said it would have an all-professional army? Or French irritation at German insistence on a "stability pact" to ensure strict adherence to the rules of Europe's single currency? Or France's reluctance to let a Dutchman head the new European Central Bank?

Naturally, on his first visit to France as chancellor-elect, on September 30th, Mr Schröder declared his loyal devotion to the German axis. But awkward questions have been nagging policy

makers in Paris for several years. Does a powerful, reunited Germany still need French friendship quite as much as before? Without it, could France go on moulding Europe in accordance with its own desires?

Now, with an unknown in charge in Bonn—and one who will soon move to the old imperial capital, Berlin, with its window on to the east—will Europe's leading duo happily oversee the continent's emerging new shape, not to mention the EU's finances? As an editorial in Le Figaro, the leading Gaullist newspaper put it, "the [Franco-German] couple is no longer the motor of European construction".

The first ugly moment, with Mr Schröder as chancellor, could occur in Vienna in December, when EU leaders will discuss the Union's budget for the seven years after 2000. France will be desperate to avoid a row—while still being reluctant to pay an extra few billion dollars into Europe's coffers. Even if that early problem is sorted out, a more pragmatic, less emotional, sort of relationship is likely to grow.

**CHARLEMAGNE**

# Oskar Lafontaine's commanding German presence

HE WAS not amused. Oskar Lafontaine, chairman of Germany's Social Democratic Party drummed his fingers on the table, then twice leaned over with whispers of advice to the speaker on his left answering journalists' questions. Nothing odd in that—except that the person being so peremptorily prompted was none other than Gerhard Schröder, fresh from his general-election triumph a day earlier. And surely a chancellor, even one in waiting, is well able to speak for himself.

Times change. No one dared on such occasions to interrupt Helmut Kohl, the outgoing chancellor; not even when he waffled, as he not infrequently did. Besides, Mr Kohl was (and for the moment still is) head of his party, the Christian Democratic Union, as well as government leader. He did not have to share the podium with even a potential niggler. But now Mr Kohl's 16-year solo is giving way to a Social Democratic duet, and Mr Lafontaine may well turn out to have the more powerful—at least persuasive—voice in it.

How so? Isn't Mr Lafontaine a chronic loser who badly wanted to become the Social Democrats' candidate for chancellor this year but was pipped by Mr Schröder? Did he not, when running against Mr Kohl in the election of 1990, German unity year, lead his party to its lowest share of votes—33.5%—since 1957? True, he has been a popular premier of the Saarland since 1985. But that is a pipsqueak state with a lot of debt, even less of a power base than unexciting Lower Saxony, run for the past eight years by Mr Schröder. To emerge from all that as arguably Germany's most influential politician needs some explaining.

All the more so since over the past two decades Mr Lafontaine has managed to upset one bigwig after another in his own party, as well as to infuriate conservatives. At the start of the 1980s his opposition to atomic power and NATO's missile strategy put him at odds with the Social Democrats' then chancellor, Helmut Schmidt. Mr Lafontaine had plenty of party backers on both issues; but even they were repelled

when he snapped that the qualities of staunchness and sense of duty which Mr Schmidt esteemed were "secondary" ones—useful, perhaps, for "running concentration camps". In 1987 Mr Lafontaine could have had the party chairmanship but he turned it down at that stage with near-contempt, temporarily losing himself still more allies. What he wanted was the chancellorship.

In 1990 he failed to get it and, thanks to his reservations about the rush to German unity, he also ran foul of the party's elder statesman, Willy Brandt, who was as much of a unity fan as Mr Kohl. The same year he narrowly escaped death when a demented woman slashed him with a knife during a campaign rally. Bouts of deep depression followed. The message from party colleagues, sometimes delivered with crocodile tears, was "Oskar has had it." Still, he is not nicknamed Napoleon just because of his stocky build, often imperious manner and love of France (which the Saarland adjoins), a love that extends to fine cuisine and the game of boules. He contrives to bounce back after often self-inflicted setbacks, he knows how to bide his time until the foe is weak, and he can rouse the rabble with speeches of a fury wholly at odds with his cherubic features and twinkling eyes. Ask Rudolf Scharping, whom Mr Lafontaine thrust from the party's chair in a brilliantly ruthless putsch at a congress in Mannheim three years ago. By this time Mr Lafontaine had decided he would like the leadership after all—so he grabbed it.

Much of that applies to Mr Schröder too. Both are rebels—in part, some claim, because they lost their fathers in the war and grew up without paternal discipline. Both have had private lives about as tumultuous as their public ones: Mr Lafontaine has been married three times, Mr Schröder four. But Mr Lafontaine is the niftier, more intellectually rigorous debater, perhaps because he was educated by Jesuits. At 55, he is only a year older than his colleague. But when the two appear together, as at that post-election press conference, Mr

Lafontaine manages to look the senior partner, and Mr Schröder tends to yield to him with at least as much respect as irritation. Oskar can get away with it. Others not.

Besides, Mr Schröder knows who he has to thank for smoothing his path to the chancellery, and who he will need to keep him there. It was Mr Lafontaine who helped convince the public that Mr Kohl was played out by organising a near-total blockade of the government's tax reforms in the Bundesrat, the second chamber of parliament. As Mr Kohl's grip on his Christian Democrats began to falter, so Mr Lafontaine tightened his hold on the Social Democrats. What price will Mr Schröder have to pay for all this?

For one thing, Mr Lafontaine can have any job he wants, as well as the party chair. He might just opt to lead the Social Democrats in parliament, but more likely he will go for the finance ministry—arguably now the weightiest job in government. In some ways it would suit him down to the ground. He has long been a fan of the euro (unlike the sceptical Mr Schröder) and urges a European initiative, led by Germany, France and Britain, to help bring greater international currency stability. Ironically, on this issue he sounds much like his old foe, Mr Schmidt, co-founder of the European monetary system.

Having Mr Lafontaine in the finance job might just pay off for Mr Schröder too. Only the party's chairman could curb demands by the faithful—and by Greens—for big spending. Mr Lafontaine has the clout. But the will, too? Unlike Jost Stollmann, Mr Schröder's would-be economics minister, he is all for reversing previous efforts to trim pensions and sick pay. He is keen to raise family allowances, wants wages up to boost domestic demand, and favours heavier petrol taxes (which Mr Schröder, a member of Volkswagen's supervisory board, fears could cost jobs). Putting Mr Lafontaine in charge of finance, his critics say, would be like setting a wolf to guard a sheep pen. Perhaps—except that he might just turn out to be a sheep in wolf's clothing.

# Where is it going?

BONN AND PARIS

## Germany's new leader needs to sort out a muddle over people, power and policy—and to tell the world what he means to do

EVEN Gerhard Schröder, Germany's chancellor, admits that not everything has been hunky-dory. The government coalition that he has led in Bonn since October 27th tried to do too much too soon, quality suffered and criticism is—he agrees—justified. But after all, the chancellor adds with his habitual vote-trapping grin, new administrations are usually given 100 days' grace to get their act together. Instead, something of an instant miracle is seemingly expected from his Social Democratic-Green alliance, the first such tie-up at national level in Germany's history.

Just teething troubles then—the coalition discord over everything from tax to immigration policy, the stand-up row with the Bundesbank and (indirectly) with the European Central Bank over interest rates, the questioning of NATO's nuclear doctrine? A lot of voters, who yearned for a new but competent team after 16 years of centre-right rule under Helmut Kohl, desperately hope so. So do many of Germany's allies. Government mayhem at the heart of Europe's most powerful economy would be a worry at any time. With Germany about to take over the presidency of the European Union as well as the chairmanship of the G8 club of the world's rich countries, both with daunting agendas of reform, it looks truly alarming.

Alas, few of the government's problems can be put down just to new boys (and girls) needing time to settle in. Most are more deeply rooted and were clearly heralded in the "twin-track" strategy pursued by the Social Democrats during the election campaign. Breezing down one track was media-star Schröder, a pal of industry bosses as well as (moderate) trade-union leaders, preaching about a "new centre" in politics and promising woolly but on the whole painless reform. "We will not do everything differently, but a lot better," he chanted time and again.

Not so Oskar Lafontaine, the Social Democrats' party chairman and former rival of Mr Schröder to become "chancellor candidate", who was grinding determinedly along the other track. Pledging that "we do not seek power so that things will stay the same," he kept the party faithful happy with promises to overturn the Kohl government's (modest) cuts in social welfare, to tax energy use and raise the incomes of the less well off. Wage restraint, he claimed, had been overdone. People needed more cash so that domestic demand could be boosted and the horrendous jobless total of close to 4m cut.

Did not Mr Schröder, well aware of the link between Germany's high costs and its soaring unemployment from his years on Volkswagen's supervisory board, realise he was heading for trouble? Perhaps, but to win the election he needed Mr Lafontaine's backing at least as much as the latter needed Mr Schröder's vote-catching charisma. Besides, Mr Schröder did not expect (and probably did not hope for) a majority big enough to form an alliance with the Greens. A "grand coalition" with the Christian Democrats, though without Mr Kohl, seemed more likely. Mr Lafontaine's influence would then be diluted, the Social Democratic left more easily checked.

Unhappily for Mr Schröder, reds and Greens together won a workable-looking majority of 21 in the Bundestag, the lower house of parliament. They already had a majority in the Bundesrat, the second chamber, where the federal states are represented and which has a veto on key matters including tax. It was mainly thanks to that veto that the bold (albeit belated) plan of the Kohl administration to simplify the tax system and slash rates came to naught. Now the new government can push through almost any legislation it wishes—once it has agreed what it wants.

Mr Lafontaine, who had rashly been promised by Mr Schröder any job he wanted, pounced on the already powerful finance ministry, and proceeded to make it stronger still, hiving off key departments from the economics ministry and adding them to his own realm. As party chairman too, he could well echo a notorious remark of the late Bavarian supremo Franz Josef Strauss: "I do not care who is chancellor under me." The confrontation between the Schröder and Lafontaine camps is widely dubbed a battle of "modernisers" against "traditionalists." But that is to oversimplify. On this or that point (repealing cuts in pensions and sick-pay made under Mr Kohl, for instance) the chancellor happily shares his party's sentiments. Mr Lafontaine, for his part, often startles with new ideas, or at least new twists to old ones.

## Divided they stand

It would be more accurate to call the struggle one between pragmatists and ideologists with a fair dash of opportunism thrown in on both sides. Mr Schröder, although a Marxist in much younger days, is no "ideas man" but a gifted improviser. He has managed to modify at least two of Mr Lafontaine's tax-increase schemes, on energy and low-paid jobs, because, although he favours the long-term aim of both, he sees decisive short-run drawbacks. Not surprisingly he inclines more to the practical approach of Tony Blair and New Labour than to the grand designs for state and society presented in France by Lionel Jospin and his governing Socialists.

Mr Lafontaine, educated by Jesuits and trained as a physicist, is much the opposite: a Francophile, ultra-wary of market forces, who reckons that faced with the challenge of globalisation governments badly need to assert more, not less, control. Hence his drive for an "ecological tax reform", raising energy prices and using the revenue to help cut the social-security charges that add to labour costs. Hence also his recent (abortive) bid to force the Bundesbank to drop interest rates, as well as his scheme to stabilise major world currencies inside target zones. And hence, too, his backing for tax harmonisation in the EU.

Has Mr Lafontaine been put off by the howls his actions have aroused in many places, with the notable exception of Paris? Not a bit. He is fired by enthusiasm for ideas whose time, he reckons, has nearly come. And he is egged on by fervent advisers like his economist wife, Christa Müller, and his powerful state secretary, Heiner Flassbeck, who for years have been preaching the doctrine he now advocates. If he has for now become a bit quieter, long-time Lafontaine-watchers claim, it is because he is gathering strength for a new advance. "*Reculer pour mieux sauter,*" as it were.

## Where's the boss, then?

Small wonder that with "Oskar" capturing so many headlines in the coalition's first tumultuous month, the cry went up "Where is Schröder?" Part of the answer is that he was too often abroad for his own domestic good. Paris, Washington, London, Brussels, Moscow, Warsaw; all are considered vital trips for a new chancellor and Mr Schröder dutifully made them.

Among other things he had to convince the French that he still considers them Germany's closest allies, despite his earlier talk of "a triangular relationship" including Britain. If you go by the smiles and back-slapping that ended Franco-German consultations in Potsdam on November 30th and December 1st, he may have succeeded. But do not take smiles and back-slaps too seriously.

The Franco-German relationship is no longer what it was. With German unification and the arrival in power of a new generation of leaders born after 1945, the French realise that Germany is shedding many of its former complexes, becoming more self-assured, assertive and nationalistic. Indeed, the French fear that Germany no longer needs them as it once did. This, insists Hubert Védrine, France's phlegmatic foreign minister, should be regarded as "neither shocking nor worrying". It is quite "normal" to him that Germany should seek to defend its own interests, just as Britain and France have always done.

Yet behind this reassuring tone lurks a long-held French worry that a united Germany may one day seek to punch its real European weight and no longer treat France as an equal—even as its sole playmate. During his election campaign, the French were upset

**Oskar's choice**
Labour costs in manufacturing
$ per hour worked, 1997

by Mr Schröder's suggestion that their hitherto exclusive partnership should be opened up to form a *ménage à trois* with the British. To France's relief, there has been no further mention of this distinctly touchy issue.

Was a political Viagra pill taken this week in Potsdam to give the ageing relationship a new fizz? Maybe, maybe not. Talk of a possible new Paris-Bonn-London triangle in Europe is nothing new: every time, over the past decade, that a new president or prime minister has taken over in France, he briefly—and in the end unsatisfactorily—flirts with the Eurosceptical British, only to fall back in relief on the old liaison with Germany. But now, for the first time since the second world war, there are centre-left governments in France, Britain and Germany. Tony Blair is certainly seeking ways for a more Euro-positive Britain to play a bigger role in Europe. Under Mr Schröder, who likes Britain, a punchier Germany may be claustrophobically anxious to escape from the French clasp. And France, nervous about being left out in the cold, has begun searching for alternative allies to help it keep its threatened diplomatic pre-eminence in Europe.

## Potsdamnation?

So, despite Mr Schröder's avowed reluctance to talk about "geometric constructions" in Europe, a new triangle may yet be emerging. Both France and Germany are ever keener to do business with Europe's other key player—either separately, as in planned Anglo-German arms mergers and stock-exchange link-ups, or together, as in defence. The triangle may not be

equilateral. For sure, France and Germany are likely to go on being each other's main partner. But that partnership, though still necessary for getting things done in Europe, no longer looks sufficient on its own.

And in Potsdam awkward Franco-German differences did stick out—over nuclear energy, ideas for joint arms-making and, above all, contributions to Europe's budget and France's farm subsidies. Though the leaders came closer to agreement on the pace of the EU's eastward expansion, Mr Schröder failed to squeeze out of the French a pledge that Europe's common farm policy be reformed double-quick, so that Germany's net payment into the Brussels budget can be cut. This spells trouble, however wide those Potsdam grins.

In any case, Mr Schröder wants to persuade the British, whom he sees as allies in many things, including the battle for farm reform, that his talk of a "triangle" was in fact no mere slip of the tongue; and he has sought to reassure the Poles that he wants them to join the EU as soon as possible, although he is not prepared to set a target date. Hardest of all, he has to convince the fidgety Americans that Germany is as staunch an alliance partner as ever, even though in Joschka Fischer it now has a Green foreign minister.

Mr Fischer made the right kind of statesmanlike noises, until he let slip a tricky fact that few outsiders (and not all insiders) had hitherto noticed: that, under the Bonn coalition accord reached in October, the government wants NATO to renounce the possible first use of nuclear weapons. Both Mr Schröder and his defence minister, Rudolf Scharping, have since sought to present this stand as "a contribution to alliance discussion"; but the Americans, the British and even the French are definitely not amused. The point was put into the accord at the insistence of the Greens; it will now be hard to get it out again.

## When the cat's away . . .

While Mr Schröder was on his travels his rivals were winning points at home. Now, though, he is fighting back, above all by greatly beefing up his chancellery team.

His chief of staff, Bodo Hombach, is a string-puller of legendary skill, one of whose priorities is to strengthen those links with Britain's New Labour. His economic adviser is Klaus Gretschmann, a respected professor whose views on international finance—pegging currencies

# Continuity, please—or else

WASHINGTON, DC

As THEY watch Germany descend into what looks to them like introspective confusion, American officials draw comfort from two main arguments. The first is that German-American relations are bound to improve, no matter what kind of coalition runs Germany. As Germany's economy becomes more open, so this argument goes, there will be more mergers between German and American firms like the recent Daimler-Chrysler marriage and the Deutsche Bank-Bankers Trust tie-up; these alliances will deepen cultural and intellectual links, binding the American and German world views more tightly together. The second argument is that Germany's coalition is not really worrying anyway. The new chancellor, Gerhard Schröder, has promised continuity in his country's foreign policy. "We plan to take him at his word," says one State Department official, a bit menacingly.

This hint of menace was evident in November, when Germany's defence secretary, Rudolf Scharping, visited Washington in the midst of a nasty spat over NATO's nuclear policy. On the eve of this trip Germany's Green foreign minister, Joschka Fischer, had suggested that NATO should promise not to use nuclear weapons before being attacked with them. This "no-first-use" policy is anathema to the Americans, who reckon that NATO needs the option of first use to deter chemical or biological attack. And so, when Mr Scharping appeared before the press with his American counterpart, William Cohen, something revealing happened.

At the press conference, Mr Scharping waffled about Germany's nuclear thinking. Nuclear forces, he said, played "a fundamental political role", but his government also cherished the vision of a world without nuclear weapons. But Mr Cohen put bolder words into his mouth. He declared that Mr Scharping had promised that Germany had "no intention" of questioning "core elements of NATO's strategy". Indeed, the American went on, "Germany remains prepared to contribute to the nuclear element of NATO". You promised continuity, Mr Cohen seemed to be saying; if you tell us anything different, we will refuse to hear you.

A similar tactic—arm-twisting by press conference—is likely to confront Germany's finance minister, Oskar Lafontaine, when he arrives in Washington on December 4th, and meets an array of American officials who want him to drop his Keynesian reflation talk in favour of deregulation. The close relationship Germany enjoyed with America during the Clinton years cannot be taken for granted. On the contrary, it must be earned—and there is strong competition from the British. President Clinton got along famously with Helmut Kohl, and did not much care for John Major. Mr Clinton likes Tony Blair a lot, but he has yet to strike up much of a relationship with Mr Schröder.

Conceivably, therefore, the diplomacy of "continuity, or else" may spur Germany to drop its wilder notions. But that, too, depends on who does end up in charge of German policy. In any case, such American tactics may backfire. Some wise heads in Washington reckon that too much arm-twisting could increase anti-Americanism in Germany: the Germans may not merely repair their old alliance with the French, they may actually become like them. Now that, in American eyes, really would be worrying.

for instance—are more pragmatic than Mr Lafontaine's. Mr Gretschmann—not Mr Flassbeck, as Mr Lafontaine wanted—will be the chancellor's "sherpa" to prepare the G8 summit meetings. Not least, Mr Schröder has appointed Michael Steiner, a shrewd former trouble-shooter in Bosnia, as his top foreign-affairs man. With him on the job, the traditional, latterly damaging, rivalry between chancellery and foreign ministry should be a lot less marked.

What Mr Schröder is trying to do is build a chancellor's fortress with the sturdiness and fire-power of the one run by the previous Social Democratic chancellor, Helmut Schmidt. In his era, the chancellery became the spot where most key government initiatives (like the European Monetary System) were hatched, and where dubious plans from elsewhere in Bonn tended to disappear as though into a black hole. Not a bad model for Mr Schröder: at last he is trying to emulate it.

But that alone may not be enough. Mr Schmidt has long believed that one main reason he fell from power in 1982 was that he did not become Social Democratic Party chairman as well as chancellor. Mr Kohl, too, led his party as well as the government, and survived as chancellor for 16 years. If Mr Schröder is going to stay on top he may eventually have to tip Mr Lafontaine out of the party chairmanship. But that is a task vastly easier proposed than done.

# Birth of the Berlin republic

The victory for Gerhard Schröder's red-green coalition, says
**Peter Norman**, signals the dawning of a new era as clearly as
the return of government to the country's historic capital

There are some months to go before the trucks move eastwards taking the paraphernalia of Germany's federal ministries, the diplomatic corps and the various government hangers-on from Bonn to Berlin.

But the September 27 election victory of Gerhard Schröeder and his coalition of Social Democrats and environmental Greens has marked such a break in Germany's postwar history that it already seems natural to talk of the "Berlin republic".

Admittedly, a casual visitor in these blustery autumn days could be forgiven for asking "What has changed?" Apart from some dancing in the streets on election night, there was none of the euphoria that gripped Bonn in 1969 when a SPD-led coalition last took power.

Helmut Kohl, now just an ordinary MP, still lives in the chancellery bungalow and is on hand to give Mr Schröder advice if he wants it. Exuding an air of business as usual, the coalition partners have quickly got down to agreeing their government programme.

That document contains elements of continuity with the policies of Mr Kohl's centrist coalition of Christian Democrats, the Bavarian Christian Social Union and the small market-oriented Free Democrat Party.

This is especially true in foreign affairs, where the incoming and outgoing governments co-operated on policy over Kosovo and where both Mr Schröder and Joschka Fischer, Germany's Green foreign minister, have hastened to reassure close allies and neighbours in France, the US, Britain and Poland that a red-green administration does not represent discontinuity.

But change there is and will be. When Germany next goes to the polls in a general election in 2002 it is likely to be a very different country to that created by 16 years of Mr Kohl's government.

In itself, Mr. Schröder's victory merits a place in the history books and not simply because it ended the political career of a chancellor who had become a living national monument.

It was confirmation of Germany's status as a mature democracy because, for the first time in the federal republic's 49-year history, a government changed through the ballot box rather than through a reshuffling of coalition parties between elections.

Although Mr. Schröder's coalition is postwar Germany's third SPD-led government, his is the first red-green government at national level and the first to be made up entirely of left-of-centre parties.

It has far more power to effect change than did Mr Kohl's last government because the coalition parties also control the Bundesrat, the second chamber of the Bonn parliament representing the states.

Mr Schröder gained an unexpected bonus when elected chancellor by MPs on October 27. He is the first federal chancellor to be elected by more than the combined strength of his coalition's MPs in the Bundestag, the lower house of parliament.

He may, therefore, be in a stronger position than Willy Brandt and Helmut Schmidt, the previous SPD chancellors, to deal with rivals and dissidents in his own party.

The new government has brought a new generation to power. Mr Schröder, born in 1944, is Germany's first post-war leader not to have had personal experience of the horrors of war.

Many of his cabinet colleagues are members of the generation that first became politically active in the student unrest of 30 years ago. Mr Fischer, now 50, is a veteran of student street battles and demonstrations.

Mr Schröder and Otto Schily, the interior minister, are former defence lawyers who represented Red Army Faction terrorists in the 1970s.

Not surprisingly, the red-green coalition agreement is according greater importance to civil rights, including reform of Germany's anachronistic and restrictive citizenship laws to permit more of Germany's 7m foreign residents to become integrated into society.

The move to Berlin from sleepy Bonn will also change German politics and the way the country is governed. The Rhenish, Catholic influence than permeated Mr Kohl's administration and earlier CDU-led governments in the 1950s and 1960s will decline.

Ministers and MPs will be in the midst of a big city with all its attendant problems. They will be surrounded by the former communist eastern German *Länder,* which are still struggling to catch up with the more affluent west, and only a short distance from the Polish border.

Finally, huge pressure for change will come from the introduction of the euro, the single European currency, on January 1.

German industry and commerce will be exposed to greater transparency and competition. European integration will increase pressure to restructure anti-competitive tax, social security and pension systems.

The euro might even herald a better deal for consumers in a society which bestows advantages disproportionately on producers.

A decisive change is already under way in economic and social policy. Oskar Lafontaine, in charge of a strengthened finance ministry and with the additional power base of the SPD chairmanship, is determined to tackle Germany's problem of 4m unemployed. He plans a Keynesian programme to boost consumption underpinned by greater economic and social policy co-ordination in the European Union.

Mr Lafontaine's plans to redistribute some of the tax burden from rich to poor and from big business to workers and families mark a significant break with the supply-side agenda of Mr Kohl and Theo Waigel, the former finance minister.

By urging interest rate cuts from the Bundesbank and the European Central Bank, which takes responsibility for monetary policy from January, Mr Lafontaine is cheerfully breaking one of the great taboos of Germany's post-war system of governance—that independent central banks should be left alone to conduct monetary policy with the overriding aim of securing stable prices.

The idea of greater social justice runs like a thread through the policies of the red-green coalition. One of its first promises was to draft legislation reversing the limited supply-side reforms of Mr Kohl's government which trimmed pension entitlements and sick pay to reduce the cripplingly high non-wage labour costs of German business.

It is a policy mix that, until recently, would have been dismissed as a prescription for disaster. And it has triggered a storm of protest from leaders of business and industry, including such traditional moderates as Dieter Hundt, leader of BDA, the German employers' association.

Mr Lafontaine's ideas appear to pay scant heed to the mobility of capital and foreign direct investment and the increasingly hard-nosed approach of German business towards boosting profits and shareholder value.

Mr Kohl was unable to cut unemployment partly because businesses judged his supply-side agenda too half-hearted to justify increased investment. How, therefore, can Mr Lafontaine expect that his policy, with its unmistakable echoes of the 1970s, will be a success?

The new government is pinning much hope on Germany's tradition of consensus. It attaches a high priority to an "alliance for jobs" in which government, trade unions and employers would create a framework for increasing employment.

It has also convinced itself that its policies are the correct response to international financial turmoil and the perceived threat of global deflation. Its analysis of the economic crises in Asia and Russia has strengthened its belief in the need for a strong welfare state in Germany's social market economy.

Opinion surveys conducted before election day suggested that a majority of Germany's 60.5m voters wanted "change without risk". Instead, there will be much that is experimental in the coming four year term of the red-green coalition.

Ultimately, however, the new government will be judged on whether it can deliver a significant cut in unemployment.

Mr Kohl's last government failed this crucial test. Mr Schröder, who will be spelling out his government's programme in the Bundestag today, knows that here he must succeed.

**IT WAS THE YEAR WHEN ... THE KOHL ERA ENDED**

# Goodbye to all that

**Ralph Atkins** asks whether the election of a left-of-centre government and the start of the Berlin republic signals a more assertive Germany

**1998** **NINETEEN NINETY EIGHT** Has Joschka Fischer, Germany's Green foreign minister, broken with the zeitgeist? For years, the former street revolutionary work black T-shirts under his jacket. Since taking office at the end of October, he has invariably worn a tie.

While continuity and conservatism may be the fashion at the foreign ministry, Gerhard Schröder, the new Social Democrat chancellor whose neckwear sometimes slips to half-mast, has ushered in an unstuffy style of government. After 16 years of Helmut Kohl, the Germany Mr Schröder seeks to create is more self-confident: and less formal, conscious of but not hamstrung by its history and determined to pursue its own agenda.

The government that in a few months will begin the move to Berlin—including to buildings once occupied by Hitler's ministers—will not be led by Mr Kohl, a Christian conservative whose war memories are firmly etched. Instead its chancellor is a left-of-centre lawyer who in 1978 represented the terrorist Horst Mahler, who omitted "so help me God" from his official oath and who, at 54, is too young to remember the Nazis.

In his government declaration—the equivalent of a US inauguration speech—Mr Schröder spoke of a "grown-up, self-confident" country that for the first time since the second world war had voted a government out of office; "a self-confidence of a grown-up nation that doesn't have to feel superior or inferior to anyone, that accepts its history and responsibility—but is forward looking".

It is a Social Democrat-led coalition government of a "new" political centre that has brought the environmentalist, pacifist Greens into federal office for the first time. It is looking for alternative answers to mass unemployment and to the country's 19 atomic power stations. And it is looking to bring "social justice" to a reunited Germany where the initial euphoria over the liberation of the east has given way to pessimism and demands for greater economic equality.

It is also a government that takes a more questioning stance towards the European Union, where it holds the presidency in the first six months of 1999. That does not mean a halt to economic and political integration—the opposite is the case—but ensuring that the EU functions as a community and international economic powerhouse, at an acceptable cost to the German taxpayer.

Does, then, the start of the Berlin republic signal a more assertive or energetic Germany? A glance at the country's corporate sector suggests the answer is 'Yes'. Years of industrial restructuring and reorienation towards the demands of global markets led to the merger in May of Daimler-Benz and Chrysler.

Then, last month, Deutsche Bank swooped to buy Bankers Trust, the eighth-largest US bank. Deutsche Bank has also signalled a break with the traditional cosy relationship between banks and industry by spinning off its DM40bn ($23.9bn) industrial holdings into separate companies, possibly as a prelude to eventual disposals. Meanwhile, the Viag power-based conglomerate is merging with Alusuisse-Lonza of Switzerland; the Hoechst pharmaceuticals group is teaming up with Rhône-Poulenc of France. The message is that German industry can act fast to remain world-beating.

Can the government be as bold? For all the hearalding of change, the omens are not good. The main task it has set itself is combating an unemployment total of 4m (about 10 per cent of the workforce). Its response is centred on building a consensus between labour, employers and the state of the sort that fashioned Germany's post-war economic recovery. Mr Schröder's "alliance for jobs" is aimed, deliberately, at rectifying the damage his advisers believe was inflicted even by Mr Kohl's modest achievements in reforming generous sick pay and employment protection laws.

But Mr Kohl tried an "alliance for jobs" unsuccessfully and it is arguable whether, even in Germany, a consensus approach is possible in 1999.

For business, the "alliance for jobs" has to focus on containing costs, lowering taxes and continuing wage moderation. The unions want a redistribution of working opportunities in Germany's highly capital-intensive economy through limits on overtime or reductions in maximum working hours.

> The result is a pragmatic approach to Europe from a new generation of political leaders

The government's priorities also differ in significant respects to those of business. The "socially just" tax reform plans of Oskar Lafontaine, finance minister, are calculated to help average households by cutting basic rate income tax and raising child allowances—with industry largely footing the bill through reduced tax breaks.

Professor Meinhard Miegel, director of the Bonn institute for economic and social research, argues that there remains strong social resistance to the creation of lower-paid, lower status jobs of the sort that have cut unemployment in the US. "The alliance for jobs is about distributing work—distribution, distribution, distribution," he says. "It is not about value creation. It is not an economic question. We are not going the way that would create more dynamic growth—because that would be socially unacceptable."

Where the new German government has been more determined, and even confrontational, is in European policy. Mr Schröder and Mr Lafontaine believe the introduction of the Euro will force the formation of economic and financial policies—as well as monetary policy—at European level. That means, above all, a European pact on job creation with binding and verifiable goals.

For some in Europe the talk in Bonn and Paris of tax harmonisation and greater use of majority voting—as opposed to the principle of unanimity—has been a harsh reminder of the pace at which the debate is moving. But Mr. Lafontaine and Mr Schröder find the UK's protests hard to understand. "In Germany it was difficult to give up the D-Mark," says Mr Lafontaine. "We have had our own experience in trying to convince people."

Mr Schröder argues that Germany is part of an increasingly integrated Europe, not through compulsion but by choice. "I belong to those for whom Europe is a perfectly natural thing," he says. "By that I mean a single Europe. That is something I want. I am a German, but also a European."

Germany's history still reinforces that European identity. But it is a different calculation to that of Mr Kohl, or Hans-Dietrich Genscher, foreign minister between 1974 and 1992, who co-authored Germany's final settlement with the victors of the 1939–45 war.

Mr Schröder's election has, to an extent, proved cathartic. Martin Walser, the novelist, has sparked controversy by suggesting Germans should no longer be preoccupied by the events of the 1930s and 1940s and by complaining of the media's "constant presentation of our shame".

Michael Naumann, the former publisher who is Mr Schröder's minister for cultural affairs, is opposing plans for a giant Holocaust memorial near the Brandenburg Gate in the centre of Berlin. The proposal for a field of stone slabs designed by Peter Eisenmann, the New York architect—which Mr Naumann criticises as being overwhelming—is likely to be replaced by a less brutal exhibition or depository of Holocaust evidence.

Germany's reflections on the past are far from extinguished, however. Mr Fischer talks about a "collective memory of our neighbours"—which could include potential new members of the EU—that obliges restraint in the extent to which Germany pursues national interests. Martin Mantzke, editor at the German foreign policy association, argues: "No reasonable German politician would ever talk about Germany first—but they would certainly not talk about Germany last." It requires a stress on international solidarity; German official support for this month's US and UK air strikes on Iraq was loyal, despite private misgivings about the moral and strategic objectives.

The result is a pragmatic approach to Europe from a new generation of political leaders. In contrast with Mr Kohl, the government does not see peace within an integrated Europe or nationalist wars as the only alternatives. As one European policy strategist in Bonn says: "We have to make the European Union worthwhile [for Germans]."

Mr Schröder recognises the associations created by the move to Berlin. "Sometimes 'Berlin' still sounds too authoritarian-Prussian, too centralist," he admitted in his government declaration. "Against that, we are setting our—completely unaggressive—vision of a Republic of the New Centre. This New Centre excludes nobody. It stands for solidarity and innovation, for enterprise and a sense of citizenship, for ecological responsibility and a political leadership that seizes chances. Symbolically, this New Centre is taking shape in Berlin—in the middle of Germany and the middle of Europe."

Thus, his pursuit of a distinct German agenda is hedged by a recognition of geography and politics, as well as history. In the centre of Europe it is surrounded by potential allies—or partners that could quickly form coalitions against Germany's interests. That requires a cautions stance by the new Berlin republic.

# Perspectives on the German Model

## GERMANY
## IS THE MODEL BROKEN?

*Germany's social-market system—which has delivered enviable stability and prosperity for decades—is in worse shape than it looks*

COUNTRIES around the world are seeking to reform their welfare states and deregulate their economies in the face of international competition. In most, success, where it has come, has been bought only at the cost of considerable social disruption. Last winter, France endured weeks of public-sector strikes and even riots in response to the government's plans to reduce public spending in line with the Maastricht criteria for economic and monetary union. In the 1980s, Britain faced even more turbulence (including a year-long miners' strike) as Margaret Thatcher's government pushed through deregulation and sharp public-spending cuts. Now, Germany is taking its biggest step yet down this road.

Helmut Kohl has proposed public spending cuts amounting to DM70 billion ($46 billion) next year alone, the scrapping of antiquated laws controlling the energy market and a modest liberalisation of the country's notoriously restrictive shopping hours. As thousands took to the streets in protest on May Day, the Chancellor must be hoping that the opposition will ebb away and that his country's much-admired consensus model of government—a system that encourages co-operation between parties, federal and local governments and trade unions and bosses—will enable Germany to reform itself smoothly, as it has done in the past.

Over the past five years, Germany has coped with the largest external shock any western country has faced for half a century: the incorporation, in a single blow, of 16m people with an average standard of living only one-fifth that of the rest of the country. Despite the gigantic bills of unification—in 1995 gross transfers to the former East Germany totalled DM200 billion—inflation was kept in check and GDP grew by an average of $1\frac{1}{2}$ a year in 1991–95. This was slightly above the European average and more than Japan's growth.

But, though the model coped with unification well, that event still hit the system hard. On many measures, the economy has been lagging behind for a decade and a half: business productivity, for example, has grown by less than half the industrial-economy average since 1979; exporters have lost market share for nine of the past ten years. Now, according to the six big economic institutes, growth this year will be a mere 0.75%. Manifestly, considerable change has been possible within the existing model. Indeed, it was possible without the basic components of the system changing much. But what has happened is that unification has brought to the surface faults in the German model which were always there, but would otherwise have taken longer to become evident.

### How it works

At the heart of Germany's distinctive "social-market economy" is a system called *Mitbestimmung* (or co-determination): by law, employees have half the seats on large companies' supervisory boards, the top governing bodies which hire and fire senior managers. This is part of a network of arrangements which both foster close ties between workers and managers and encourage a distinctive form of corporate governance: firms and banks own shares in each other, thus minimising the ownership-dispersing effects of stockmarkets and shareholders. The political counterparts to these economic arrangements are a highly decentralised federal system which gives extensive powers to 16 *Länder* (states) and a consensual form of politics in which decisions are taken—as far as possible—with the tacit support of the main parties, the Christian Democrats and Social Democrats.

Despite the shock of unification, the system survived virtually unscathed. The main parties' policies were closer after 1990 than they had been for many years. There was some tinkering with the arrangements that link workers and managers, but the workers' supervisory role remained untouched and most wage settlements were reached in the traditional manner—by agreement between established unions and bosses' organisations which applied not to individual firms but to whole industries. The federal arrangements underwent expansion, not reform: the new states were added to a largely unchanged federation.

To its supporters, the model does not merely allow change to occur; some argue that it helps reform to happen more smoothly, more predictably—and

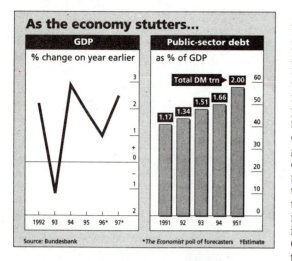

**As the economy stutters...**

GDP — % change on year earlier

Public-sector debt — as % of GDP

Total DM trn: 1.17 (1991), 1.34 (92), 1.51 (93), 1.66 (94), 2.00 (95†)

1992 93 94 95 96* 97*

Source: Bundesbank    *The Economist poll of forecasters   †Estimate

hence more effectively—than under adversarial systems. Because political parties eventually converge on one course of action, that course can be fixed more securely than in a confrontational country, such as Britain or America, where the possibility of policy reversal is greater. As a result, markets operate within a more stable framework.

So Mr. Kohl and his supporters are seeking to justify the government's new package by saying it is not an attack on the system, but a necessary measure to preserve it. "One cannot live beyond one's means", the chancellor told parliament. "If we do not act now, more jobs will disappear. Then welfare would be unfinanceable."

The reforms, as befits a consensual country, seek to spread the load evenly between the federal government, local governments and the social-security system. Some cuts threaten comfortable German ways and look a little like robbing the overfed of their third plum pudding; others affect the jobless and the sick. They include:

• A fall in unemployment benefits;

• A reduction of sick pay from 100% to 80% of basic wages;

• The limitation of state-subsidised cures at healthresorts—spas, beaches, moor and mountain retreats—to three weeks every four years instead of the present four weeks every three years;

• The postponment of a previously-agreed 10% raise in child benefit;

• A gradual rise in the retirement-age for women from 60 to 63 years starting next year, and for men from 63 to 65 from 2000;

• The removal from holiday pay of regular overtime earnings, hitherto included; and

• The removal of job-protection guarantees for firms with 10 or fewer employees.

When the government began this latest round of public-sector reform with a get-together of ministers, unions and bosses in January, Günter Rexrodt, the economy minister, said with pardonable pride that "there's bitter conflict over this sort of thing elsewhere, and here everyone gets together with the chancellor and we find the right direction." But the sheer size of the welfare reform suggests that, this time, something new is happening. Far from smoothing the needed changes, the German model may be being tested to destruction by them.

## Broken or chipped?

If implemented in full (admittedly a big if) these spending cuts would be equivalent to 2% of GDP next year. That is a huge sum, comparable to Margaret Thatcher's fiercest years. In contrast, the controversial "austerity" plan in France cuts public spending in real terms barely at all. Admittedly, welfare reform is not special to the German model: it is high on the agenda of other rich countries too. But because generous welfare payments help give everyone a stake in the system, and hence buttress consensus, it is hard to unravel the welfare state without affecting other parts of the consensual system too. Chancellor Kohl swears that he is determined to defend both—but the sheer scale of the welfare reform suggests that the cost of maintaining the wider system is rising to levels previously unheard of in Germany.

At least as important as the scale of the cuts is the manner of proposing

them. Mr. Rexrodt's self-congratulatory comments came after a first meeting of ministers, unions and bosses. But by the time Mr. Kohl got round to unveiling the proposed reforms to parliament, negotiations with the unions had been broken off. The government nevertheless decided to stick its neck out and proposed the whole programme to parliament. Hence the outcry from Germany's powerful unions and from the Social Democratic opposition. "Socially obscene . . . merciless," they cried. "A declaration of war on social justice," said Oskar Lafontaine, the Social Democratic leader. Even within the governing coalition, half a dozen supporters, both Christian Democrats and liberal Free Democrats, have balked at the plan. This is not the first time the government had gone out on a limb over an issue, but it is extremely rare for a step of this magnitude to be taken by the government alone.

So, paradoxically, in the name of preserving the model, the government has already dented two parts of it—the political-party consensus and the extensive welfare state. That alone might not be enough to make the whole system unravel. After all, there has been political conflict before, and the welfare state, which expanded hugely after the late 1960s, was not part of the original postwar model. The trouble is that the model has since developed in such a way that each part reinforces the others. Political consensus, for example, has been possible partly because, since the co-determination system helped defuse conflicts between managers and workers and the federal system lessened disputes involving regions and the centre, national parties were able to operate within a relatively narrow range of opinion. As a result, as one bit of the model goes awry, so could the rest.

**...labour pays the price**

Unemployment — %

Eastern Germany, Total, Western Germany

1991 92 93 94 95 96*

Trade union membership — m

1991 92 93 94 95

Labour costs — In manufacturing, $ per hour, 1994

0 5 10 15 20 25

Germany, Switzerland, Japan, United States, France, Italy, Britain, Poland

Sources: Bundesbank; DGB; Morgan Stanley; EIU    *March

## Workers v managers

It is one element of the rest—the contract between capital and labour—that is now coming most under strain. Take the labour side first. Despite having increased productivity in 1992–94, German workers are not so much more productive than their fellows in Poland or Japan that they can justify the world's highest labour costs.

Some of the biggest companies are expanding their production abroad and the small and medium-sized companies that are Germany's manufacturing backbone are following suit, lured especially across the border in central Europe, where wages are around a tenth of domestic levels. This might not matter if new investment were flowing in. But foreign firms are also reluctant to set up in high-wage Germany, while local ones are investing mainly in labour-saving technology. Western Germany has shed more than 1m workers in the past four years; last year, the country invested DM37 billion more in direct investment abroad than foreigners invested in the country.

Germany's unemployment level—at over 4m, it has reached its highest since the frightening 1930s, though remaining far smaller as a percentage of the workforce—is something that affects the model directly, in a way that even the financing crisis of the welfare system does not. This is because the link between managers and workers lies at the root of the whole system. Already, union power is eroding because unions speak for a shrinking share of the population: in 1995 membership of the German Trade Union Federation dropped by 3.9% to 9.4m. In addition, if the labour laws are making workers too expensive and inflexible, and if they are preventing people being priced back into work, then something has gone wrong at the heart of the model. In that sense, unemployment is a measure of the model's failure.

Now employers are demanding not just pay restraint but fundamental changes to the collective-bargaining system, under which wages and conditions are set by industry associations on behalf of employers and by unions on behalf of workers. Most managers still accept the principle that basic labour contracts should be negotiated collectively. But they want these general agreements to specify little more than basic wages and working hours. Everything else would be negotiated between individual firms and their workers, who are usually more pliant than the trade unions that represent them. They would decide, for example, how to distribute work across the week. Firms also want permission to pay less than the basic agreed wage in times of hardship, demanding, in effect, an escape clause from the basic contract that would be almost unheard-of in western Germany.

Some companies are not waiting for new contracts. Daimler-Benz, Germany's biggest industrial conglomerate, has insisted on introducing Saturday working at some of its factories, even though its labour contract rules this out; its workers, desperate to stop Daimler from moving their jobs abroad, have agreed. Following the government's decision to chop sick pay from 100% of a worker's wages to 80%, employers are eager to redraft their own labour contracts along similar lines.

Moreover, managers are busily undoing some of the distinctive features of German corporate governance. Traditionally, German finance directors worried first about pleasing their banks and only second about delivering profits to shareholders. But now, with firms competing globally for capital as well as for markets and production sites, finance directors must measure the performance of their firms' shares against those of competitors worldwide. Shareholders no longer cool their heels while the chairman entertains his bankers; now they walk straight into the chairman's office. The fad for "shareholder value" is bringing to Germany capitalist trappings that arouse resentment even in less egalitarian countries. Executives are starting to award themselves share options (the better to align their interests with those of shareholders); the stockmarket is booming; and companies are adopting new Anglo-American accounting standards that rip away the veils that once shrouded their profits.

In these circumstances, the new economic package represents a further and possibly decisive tilt in the balance of power between workers and managers. The government is proposing to let firms with ten employees or fewer sack workers easily (raising the threshold from five). Conceding business's long-standing argument that high taxes kill jobs, Mr. Kohl's fiscal package includes the abolition of a tax on capital and the reduction of one on profits, which finances mainly local governments. These cuts, admittedly, are to be financed by cutting tax breaks for depreciation (which could make investment even less attractive). But the government has made clear where its heart lies by proposing the abolition of a "wealth tax" on business.

## System failure or system reform?

Despite the changes that are starting to transform the nature of Germany's contract between unions and labour, it would be wrong to assume that every component of the German model is now doomed to radical transformation. For one thing, other parts of the system have changed comparatively little. Despite the emergence of new parties such as the Greens and the former communists in the eastern states, the two largest parties retain their traditional hold over electors' loyalty: the ruling Christian Democrats and the opposition Social Democrats continue to attract around 70% of all voters between them, roughly the same share as before unification. There is no sign of any sort of big political realignment.

For another, the government may well not command enough parliamentary support to ram its reform plans through over opposition from the SPD and from some of its own hesitating supporters. The coalition's majority in the lower house of parliament is only ten, while the SPD dominates the upper house (whose assent is required for some, though not all, of the reforms). It is a good bet that the government's proposed assault on the welfare state will be softened when it comes to a vote. In addition, one-third of the total spending cuts are supposed to come from a public-sector wage freeze—which the unions are unlikely to accept without a fight.

That said, it is clear that Germany's post-unification period is over and is giving way to change. Reform has begun and, at least in worker-manager relations, is likely to be deep. What remains in doubt is whether the changes will produce a new version of the model, better adapted to the next quarter-century, or whether the whole system will buckle under the strain of reform and end by producing in Germany a version of the Anglo-American model of capitalism, with its adversarial politics, and its red-in-tooth-and-claw economics. If the government and the companies have their way, the outcome is more likely to be a renewed, more flexible model. If the opponents of reform block real change, they risk the entire system unravelling.

# THE GERMAN WELFARE MODEL THAT STILL IS

### *Despite the Talk, Social Responsibility Remains This Country's Reigning Principle*

## Peter Ross Range and Robert Gerald Livingston

*Peter Range is a freelance writer who has covered Germany. Robert Livingston, a former U.S. diplomat in Germany, is chief development officer at the American Institute for Contemporary German Studies at Johns Hopkins University.*

**A**S AMERICA debates the fundamentals of its welfare state—Medicare, Aid to Families With Dependent Children, Social Security and health care—the example of Germany looms in the background.

Trashing the German economy, the world's third-largest, has become editorial blood sport. The New York Times op-ed page proclaims "The End of Germany's Economic Model"; Newsweek offers dire discourse on "the German disease"; and the Wall Street Journal calls Germany a "Failed Model." Washington Post columnist James K. Glassman, looking for a cudgel with which to fail the Clinton administration and this year's minimum wage hike, cavalierly dismissed the German model and all its works—national health care, guaranteed pensions, the uniquely successful vocational training system—as an outright "failure."

Is the German economic model, the so-called social market economy and its attendant welfare state, really dead?

Hardly. The political agenda of some commentators has edged out accurate reporting. True, Germany has been through a bad patch lately: double-digit unemployment, stagnant growth, lagging foreign investment, record bankruptcies. Germans are rightly worried about global competitiveness when wages and benefits make their manufacturing costs the highest in the world. And it's true that the German welfare state's generous benefits have outrun the economy's ability to pay for them and must be trimmed. Those is-

sues are being fought out in the parliament.

But reports of the imminent demise of the German system are not only premature—they are wrong. They ignore Germany's continuing high performance by most long-term indicators, its successful shouldering of the gigantic burden of absorbing East Germany, the solid and long-standing support it enjoys among Germans and the advantages it has brought not only to workers but to business.

Seen over time—the only reasonable way to judge comparative performance—Germany's economy is not in as bad shape as some argue. It certainly has not been seriously enough wounded to discredit the social market model that has guided Germany for the last 47 years.

Over the last decade, the German economy has performed as well as ours or better. Germany's real annual growth between 1986 and 1995 was 2.7 percent; that of the United States, 2.3 percent (over a 20-year period, the United States was marginally ahead). Germany's annual productivity gains over the past 10 years outpaced America's, 3.6 percent to 2.7. Still more striking was German superiority in the measure that truly counts in business—unit labor costs (the cost of labor per unit of output). Germany's grew by a mere 2 percent in the past decade, America's by 3 percent. Germany remains, by far, the world's leading exporter on a per capita basis—$4,950 in 1995. Germany's lead is unchallenged by America, with exports of only $2,240 per capita, or even by mighty Japan, with $3,530 per Japanese.

**S**till, Germany's recent mini-recession and swollen social costs have sparked a long-overdue national debate about reforming the system. Even though the latest indicators show

that the downturn is already over and predict 2.6 percent growth in 1997, the long-standing consensus among labor, management and government, a pillar of the social market economy, is being tested by a $33 billion "savings package"—cutbacks in the welfare system—proposed by Chancellor Helmut Kohl. Kohl wants to knock total government spending down from 50 percent of gross domestic product to 46 percent, where it was in 1989, just before German unification.

These austerity measures were largely prompted by the huge and unexpected cost of unification, not the failure of the social welfare system. Since 1990, the German government has transferred more than $500 billion to formerly communist eastern Germany—more money in constant dollars that the United States transferred to all of Europe during the three years of the Marshall Plan. The costs of unification compounded the need for reform.

But reform is hardly rejection. "Restructuring, not destruction," is the name of the game, Kohl has announced. In fact, the changes Kohl envisions are laughably marginal by the standards of Ronald Reagan or Margaret Thatcher.

Under the proposed reforms, for instance, some workers would receive only 80 percent of their salaries, instead of 100 percent as is the case now, for the first six weeks of sick leave. Government insurance-paid visits to German's bucolic spas—where one takes the waters, breathes deeply and applies sulfurated mud to ailing body parts—would be reduced from four weeks every three years to three weeks every four years. The retirement age would be raised, after the turn of the century, from 63 to 65 for men and from 60 to 65 for women. Workers in the smallest firms would lose job protection.

What Kohl is *not* doing is uprooting the social contract. Rather, he is seek-

From the *Washington Post*, August 11, 1996, p. C2. © 1996 by Peter Ross Range and Robert Gerald Livingston. Reprinted by permission.

ing changes within the accepted framework of the German *soziale Marktwirtschaft*—best translated as a "socially responsible market economy." This is Germany's version of capitalism with a human face, a free market economy with a heavy emphasis on social equity.

The real key to understanding the German model is the word *sozial*. Germans use it to express a sense of society's underlying interconnectedness and mutual obligations. It is rooted not simply in the altruistic belief that the strong should help the weak, but in the self-interested conviction that the strong won't thrive if too many of the weak fall by the wayside.

Indeed, society's responsibility for all its citizens is built into Germany's legal definition of itself. "The Federal Republic is a democratic and socially responsible federal state," says the constitution's very first line after its bill of rights. The welfare of the society as a whole is considered key to the success of the individual, not the other way around—communitarianism versus individualism on the American model.

This powerful ethic fosters consensus, relative equality of incomes and wealth, and social peace. Even Germany's most profit-minded industrialists believe this consensual approach is good for business. Jurgen Schrempp, the aggressive CEO of Daimler-Benz, Germany's largest conglomerate, made precisely this point in June to a New York audience of Wall Street fat cats. "The emphasis on social stability has paid off for us," he reported; " . . . the German system of a cooperative approach . . . based on consensus [has been] a guarantor of everybody's fast and steadily growing prosperity. . . . The German consensus system should under no circumstances be abandoned."

And it won't be. The recent experience of the powerful public employees' unions, representing 3.2 million workers, is a case in point. After throwing a few rhetorical tantrums over Kohl's proposed social welfare cuts, and calling out 350,000 demonstrators for a

Sunday walkabout in Bonn to show a little muscle (no striking, please; we're Germans), the unions and the government sat down and did what they have always done: compromised in the interest of the commonweal.

The unions agreed to a mere 1.3 percent wage increase over the next 20 months, which is the functional equivalent of nothing since it's less than the rate of inflation. The Kohl government, in turn, backed off its plans to trim health insurance benefits right away and increase working hours. Consensus prevailed. The model worked.

Those who use Germany's current belt-tightening as proof of the blanket failure of the socially responsible market economy are grinding an ideological ax: the belief that the American model is the only one that works. They underestimate how committed most Germans—including Kohl's conservatives—are to their model. Worse, they mislead readers who deserve an accurate portrayal of how other countries cope with painful economic transitions.

# GERMANS CUT LABOR COSTS WITH A HARSH EXPORT: JOBS

## By EDMUND L. ANDREWS

FRANKFURT, March 20—It would be hard to find a more vivid example of the revival of German industry than the renowned sports car manufacturer Porsche AG. Six years after the company came perilously close to bankruptcy, sales and profits are booming and its snappy new two-seater, the Boxster, is a hit.

But that is cold comfort for its workers. Having stretched its plants to their limit, Porsche has vowed not to build any more assembly plants and to farm out work to contractors.

Last September, in an unprecedented move for Porsche, it hired a Finnish company to start building some Boxsters. Though the move does not save Porsche much in costs, it frees the company from the expense of building a factory, hiring workers and laying them off if Boxster falters.

Porsche is one small example of the most striking economic feature in Germany: growth without jobs.

Europe is enjoying its best economic growth in years. But employers are not hiring many people. After years of layoffs and cost cutting, unemployment remains at record rates—11.6 percent in Germany and more than 10 percent across the European Union. Though there are signs that the problem has peaked nobody expects the rate to drop to single digits before late 1999, if then.

More and more, economists say, Europe's economies are growing without creating many jobs. Reasons vary from country to country but high labor costs—fringe benefits, plentiful vacations and holidays, rigid work rules—and high payroll taxes discourage companies from adding workers. The

main exceptions are Britain, Ireland and the Netherlands, which have more liberal work rules and lower taxes.

The labor costs are pushing companies to invest elsewhere. Last year German companies invested $25 billion abroad—ten times as much as foreign companies invested here, the biggest investment gap ever.

The political implications are potentially explosive. Unemployed workers have staged loud protests across France and Germany. Anger about joblessness in France was central to last summer's election victory by the Socialist Party, and it is a major threat to Chancellor Helmut Kohl in an election this September.

The upheaval is almost a mirror image of the American experience. In the United States, Rust Belt manufacturers shed hundreds of thousands of jobs in the 1980's. But in the 90's the unemployment rate has declined, partly because millions of jobs have been generated in the service economy. One price for those jobs has been workers' income, which declined in real terms throughout the 1980's and up to 1996.

In Europe, by contrast, wages and fringe benefits have remained high. The pain has come from a steady increase in unemployment.

The trends are particularly stark in Germany, Europe's biggest economy and most powerful exporter. Though exports are soaring, the domestic economy remains anemic. Retail sales actually declined a bit last year. After an acquisition binge, German banks are cutting jobs to improve profits. The dominant telephone company, forced into competition for the first time, is shedding 60,000 jobs.

## A Case Study:
## Hugo Boss Apparel

The divided world of renewed dynamism and fewer jobs is on display in Metzingen, a southern German city that is home to Hugo Boss AG. Originally known for its avant garde casual clothing, the company is branching into more conservative upscale apparel, including its first women's line. Boss brands and its stores are now familiar worldwide, and the company recently opened a high-profile store in Beverly Hills.

Sales climbed 14 percent last year, and the company surprised investors last month by announcing a 27 percent jump in profits. Part of Boss's success stems from shifting production outside Germany, mostly to Poland, Romania and Slovenia. Only about 20 percent of the clothing is produced in Germany now, down from about 40 percent five years ago.

"It used to be that if you wanted workers who cost $2.50 an hour, you had to travel 10,000 miles to Asia," remarked Joachim Vogt, the chief executive. "Now you just have to go 15 miles across the Oder River," to Poland.

Indeed, the main reason that Hugo Boss produces any clothing at all in Germany is to retain the technical expertise to supervise suppliers and insure quality. Company officials in Metzingen select the production equipment, develop procedures and even train many managers and workers from other countries.

The result is impressive. "A few years ago, our quality-control experts could look at the color of a jacket and tell what factory it came from," Mr.

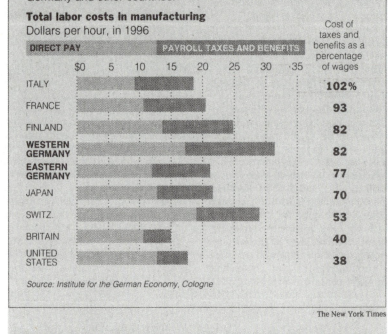

## Costly Compensation

Fringe benefits, generous vacation policies and steep payroll taxes add substantially to the cost of hiring permanent employees in Germany and other countries.

**Total labor costs in manufacturing**
Dollars per hour, in 1996

| | DIRECT PAY → PAYROLL TAXES AND BENEFITS | Cost of taxes and benefits as a percentage of wages |
|---|---|---|
| ITALY | | 102% |
| FRANCE | | 93 |
| FINLAND | | 82 |
| WESTERN GERMANY | | 82 |
| EASTERN GERMANY | | 77 |
| JAPAN | | 70 |
| SWITZ. | | 53 |
| BRITAIN | | 40 |
| UNITED STATES | | 38 |

*Source: Institute for the German Economy, Cologne*

The New York Times

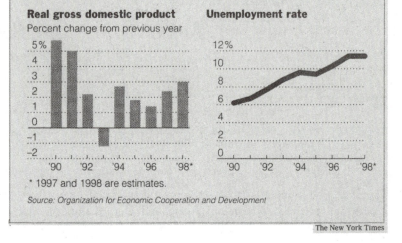

## Stunted Growth

Despite two years of increasing economic growth, experts say Germany's jobless rate will remain above 11 percent.

**Real gross domestic product**
Percent change from previous year

**Unemployment rate**

* 1997 and 1998 are estimates.

*Source: Organization for Economic Cooperation and Development*

The New York Times

Vogt said. "Today, not even the quality-control people can tell."

Thus the size of Boss's German work force has remained the same for several years and it has cut back on German suppliers.

## Where the Jobs Are:
## On the Managerial Level

The one silver lining is that within Hugo Boss, the decline in textile work-

ers has been offset by an increase in better-paid managers.

"Our core competence is to bring products to market and create brands on an international level," Mr. Vogt said. "Our industry doesn't need to produce in Europe. Europe's core competence comes from its highly educated and highly skilled people, and over the last 20 years there has been migration to jobs that are more brain-oriented."

Across Europe, corporate restructurings have put thousands of people out of work, but they have helped revitalize laggard companies.

For example Moulinex, a French company that makes coffee makers and other kitchen ware, lost hundreds of millions of dollars between 1993 and 1996. Under new management, the company closed two factories, announced plans to eliminate 2,600 jobs over three years and refocused on new products.

Today Moulinex has fewer workers but a slew of new appliances. Its annual sales stabilized at $1.3 billion last year, and the company earned its first profit in four years.

Porsche, on the other hand, got into trouble when recession hit the United States, then its largest market, and a plunge in the dollar pushed up sticker prices there. That would have been bad enough, but Porsche's production had slipped woefully behind the times. Cars took too long to design and build.

After a revolving door of executives, Wendelin Wiedeking was hired as chief executive in 1993 and quickly shocked workers by hiring Japanese to re-engineer the production system. The number of hours it took to assemble a Porsche was cut in half and many workers were laid off.

Today Porsche's German workforce has actually increased to 7,100 people, from its low of 6,350 in the mid-1990's. But when Porsche began running out of assembling capacity in late 1996, thanks largely [to] a surge in demand for the Boxster, Mr. Wiedeking had to make a choice between building a new plant and hiring more workers, or farming out the work.

It was not an easy decision. Though other German car companies had long since started building vehicles overseas, Porsche had always been a small, independent manufacturer with a rock-solid German identity.

Valmet of Finland, which has long run assembly lines for Saab and the Opel division of General Motors, offered to start assembling Porsches within nine months, using the same assembly lines used to make Saabs. It did not even need to hire new workers, because it was just reaching the end of a contract with Opel.

And if demand for Boxsters fell, Porsche could simply shut down production in Finland and let Valmet

worry about layoffs. In the end, Mr. Wiedeking decided the advantages were overwhelming, and 300 Finnish workers are now assembling about 5,000 Boxsters a year.

"This was not a decision taken against Germany," Mr. Wiedeking insisted. "This was a decision because we couldn't increase the production any faster."

But the decision did have to do with flexibility, and Prosche executives say they have made a firm decision not to build new plants for any future needs.

"It is our clear policy not to build any additional capacity," said Manfred Ayasse, a Porsche spokesman. "Porsche's view is that there is enough capacity around the world. We have almost no investment to make and we have almost no risk. If Boxster sales declined, we can stop production at Valmet within a year."

Economists here and abroad say the combination of high wages, high taxes and tight regulations have created a major barrier to hiring and investment.

The Institute for the German Economy, a business-backed research organization in Cologne, estimates that labor costs in most European countries remain far higher than in the United States. The Organization for Economic Cooperation and Development has calculated that the return on business investment in Europe has consistently been much lower than in the United States.

German business executives blame much of this on high labor costs and taxes. German workers pay about half their gross income in taxes and mandatory social security contributions, and employers have to match many of those payments.

The burden infuriates Arend Oetker, a fourth-generation business executive in Cologne who controls Schwartau, a producer of jams, snacks and other sweets. Mr. Oetker recently bought a controlling stake in a similar Swiss company called Hero and folded his non-German businesses into it because Swiss tax laws offer him savings compared with German laws.

"I am a German, and I want to keep employment here as much as possible," Mr. Oetker said. "But the more the labor costs rise, and the more that taxes rise, the more difficult it is to remain

in Germany. No one can be astonished that unemployment is going up."

In a report to the Government, Germany's top economic research institutes echoed that view. "Stronger growth alone will certainly not be sufficient to improve the labor market situation," the institutes said. The American example, the report continued, shows that greater flexibility in wage costs and regulation can help boost employment.

## A Bit of Change May Be Too Late

Some change is coming, slowly.

Last year at the huge Opel facility in Rüsselsheim, local union negotiators agreed to wage concessions in exchange for a commitment by Opel to cut jobs only through attrition and voluntary retirement incentives for the next five years.

But many German experts say the pace of change is far too slow.

A major tax-reform plan championed by Chancellor Kohl was blocked by opposition parties in Parliament. Labor unions, after grudgingly accepting negligible wage hikes in the past two years, are now demanding bigger increases.

The Government is trying to funnel more money toward job-creation programs and seed capital for new companies.

Gerhard Schröder, who will lead the opposition party in the fall, remains vague on what he would do if his party wins the elections. But he has talked about pumping more money into the economy to stimulate consumer demand.

Many union leaders continue to press for a shorter work-week, an idea the French Parliament is weighing, on the theory of dividing the current jobs among more people.

But economists say that such measures will not do the trick, and that both major political parties are too divided to force deeper changes.

"We all know what is to be done," said Klaus Friedrich, chief economist at Dresdner Bank. "But they can't get it done. Why? Because we don't have a Government in a position to do very much."

# Field Victory Colors French View of Themselves

**France:** Racially diverse team's World Cup success spurs discussion of virtues of a 'melting pot' nation.

By JOHN-THOR DAHLBURG
TIMES STAFF WRITER

PARIS—The French have renewed their very favorite love affair. With themselves.

Suddenly, "La Marseillaise" is cool again. Waving the tricolor flag no longer means a person sympathizes with the far-right, immigrant-hating National Front party of Jean-Marie Le Pen.

A stunning upset victory in the World Cup, the quadrennial international soccer tournament, has given the French immediate reason to feel good about themselves again. But it also has forced this ancient people—whose history texts once led with a controversial passage about "our ancestors," the blond and blue-eyed Gauls—to rethink who they are.

The new answer, in a phrase: *black, blanc, beur.* Black, white, French-born Arab.

"Of course I'm proud that France won," remarked one *beur*, Rachid Bourguiba, 20, whose mother and father come from Morocco. As he sat, smoking one evening with friends in a park near the Canal Saint-Martin in northeastern Paris, he added: "I was born here, and this is my country. This is where I'm going to live."

But citizens like Bourguiba who have black, brown or yellow faces are nearly invisible on French television. They are absent from the country's political and business elite. And they have been driven to the fringes of most cities over the decades.

Disenchantment with immigrants, especially the non-white, had grown so widespread that former Prime Minister Edouard Balladur, a figure of the establishment right, last month suggested a nationwide debate on whether there should be a "national preference" for some jobs.

Them came Les Bleus (the Blues)—the 22-member French soccer team, whose players could trace their ancestry not only to Normandy and Provence but also to Algeria, Argentina, sub-Saharan Africa, Armenia, Brittany, the Basque Country, Portugal, the Pacific isles and the West Indies.

The squad was a living reminder that the land of the Gauls has become, at the end of the 20th century, a "rainbow republic." Its shocking 3–0 victory over Brazil on July 12 was an unassailable argument that generations of immigrants have brought into France a rich flow of talent, physical strength and brains.

"The team of France is a symbol—that France is a mixed country but with a common ideal," said Fode Sylla, president of SOS Racisme, a grass-roots organization that battles racial prejudice. "They proved that far from being a handicap, that diversity could lead to victory, and that they are all defenders of the republic."

In fact, the hero of the semifinal win over Croatia was Lilian Thuram, 26, a black man from the "overseas department" of Guadeloupe in the Caribbean. He scored both French goals. In the final, France's first two points came on headers from Zinedine Zidane, 26, son of an immigrant construction worker from Algeria's Kabyle minority and native of the slums of Marseilles.

"Now the young *beurs* can say, 'We too can be part of France,'" said Monique Boisserie, 69, a widow from the upscale Paris suburb of Neuilly-sur-Seine.

Demographer Michele Tribalat gushed: "The French team has done more for in-tegration than years of pro-active government policies."

It is more than that: Its victories suddenly have gotten many French discussing the virtues of the U.S.-style "melting pot," rather than insisting as before that newcomers must "integrate" themselves into French society and embrace its culture and "republican" traditions.

Even Le Pen, who turned 70 during the World Cup and was caught flat-footed by the outburst of joyful patriotism, was forced to backtrack on his statement two years ago that immigrants should not be allowed to play on the national team.

Meanwhile, some of France's European neighbors have been looking on enviously. In Germany, it is much more difficult for a Turk or immigrant of another foreign ethnic stock to obtain citizenship than in France. Staunchly Teutonic, anchored by players with names like Matthaus, Klinsmann, Kohler and Koepke, the German World Cup squad was blown away by Croatia, 3–0. "White, old and tired," was how one German TV commentator summed up the losers.

Italy, another ethnically homogeneous European squad, was bested by France, 4–3. "If we want to save the Italian team, we should build our soccer fields near refugee camps," a commentator for La Repubblica, a Rome daily newspaper, concluded.

Victory brought more than 1 million of the French onto the Champs-Elysees, the biggest crowd since the Liberation in World War II. *Beurs* and *blacks* mingled with stylishly attired bourgeois from Passy and other chic capital neighborhoods. Longtime Parisians said they never had seen such a sea of blue-white-and-red French flags brandished by ordinary people. Crowds sang the stirring national anthem out of sheer pride and pleasure—another reported first.

Bourguiba, the Parisian of Moroccan lineage, was there, waving a tricolor with friends. "It was a joy for everybody—we're in France after all," he said.

These extraordinary, shared moments banished, at least for now, the moroseness and doubt that seemed to have become as much a part of contemporary French life as freshly baked croissants, high taxes and strikes by public-sector workers.

The shift has more to do with factors beyond football, of course: France's economy, the world's fourth biggest, is growing again; consumers are more confident than at any time in the recent past; and even naggingly high unemployment—the rate now stands at 11.9%, with almost 3 million people out of work—is projected to come down by the end of 1998.

A year-old left-of-center government, presided over by Socialist Prime Minister Lionel Jospin, has convinced most voters of its competence and probity. The country has become more certain of itself, less fearful of the trends threatening its way of life that often are summed up by the grab-bag term "globalization" and include American fast food, movies and dog-eat-dog capitalism.

France's soccer team "had a secret mission, which was to give a lesson of confidence, ambition and unity to the French," said Alain Peyrefitte of the Academie Francaise, a former right-wing minister.

After the easy-money, scandal-ridden years of the '80s and early '90s, Les Bleus also seemed to be the incarnation of some basic but long-neglected virtues: the ability to work hard and work together, the eschewing of big talk and glamour in favor of results.

"This is the France we would love to see: valiant, stubborn, enterprising, multiracial but accepting its crossbreeding as a fact of life," said the newsmagazine L'Evenement du Jeudi.

But does any of this mirror real life? "A victory in the [soccer] final . . . doesn't change social reality, but it can change the image that the French have of themselves," said Serge July, editor of the left-wing Paris newspaper Liberation.

Others are dubious. "In sports, it's really the person's ability alone that counts," said Mohammed Soufi, 25, a supermarket manager and Parisian of Algerian descent. "But in the business world, I have friends where, as soon as the boss gets a look at them, he's no longer interested."

Rene Oliviero, 48, an engineer who lives near Rouen, said, "The team won, but had they lost, it would have been the fault of A, B, or C, and origins would have become an issue."

Just as Jackie Robinson's breaking of the color bar in major league baseball 51 years ago hardly meant the end of racial discrimination in the U.S., achievements on soccer fields don't necessarily extend to all realms of society.

"There are no beurs and very few blacks in competitive examinations for high government jobs. There are no Zidanes or Thurams at the Ecole Polytechnique," an elite school, said Jean Levi, professor at the Institute of Political Sciences in Paris.

One recent Europe-wide opinion poll found the French classifying themselves as one of the most bigoted countries in Western Europe, second only to Belgians.

Catherine Pell, 37, is skeptical that French society now will change. "What we have lived through is a joyous, enthusiastic mob scene," the black Parisian said. "These are passing fancies, and then people forget them."

But Alain Beyer, sports editor of Le Parisien, the country's biggest mass-circulation tabloid, disagrees. He believes that a "new French Revolution" has just happened—and that it must not be limited to sports. "Soccer has played its part, but its part stops here," he wrote. "Now it's for others—politicians, bosses, labor leaders, artists and creators of all kind to take up the baton, to score the next point."

## INSTITUTIONAL REFORM

# Resisting reform to de Gaulle's old constitution

A conservative senate has forced Jospin to move with caution on overdue plans to change the balance of presidential power

## by Robert Graham

After 40 years, the constitution of the French Fifth Republic attracts much criticism for being outdated. Yet no one dares contemplate serious change.

The fear is that tampering with a presidential system designed to bring Charles de Gaulle to power will create more problems than it solves. The present government is aware of the constitution's shortcomings, but lacks sufficient influence on the conservative dominated senate without whose support no alteration can be made.

As a result, premier Lionel Jospin is moving cautiously, concentrating on aspects of reinforcing French democracy without questioning the fundamentals of the presidential system.

The present constitution, endorsed by referendum on September 28, 1958, was tailor-made for General de Gaulle's assumption of power after almost two decades of instability amid the crisis of French Algeria.

The president was given effective executive power and control of the armed forces, presiding for seven years over a parliament whose members were elected every five years and whose legislative functions were generally subordinate to the wishes of the Elysé presidential palace.

This authoritarian position was reinforced in 1962, when in the wake of an unsuccessful assassination attempt, General de Gaulle resorted to a referendum to allow the president to be elected by universal suffrage instead of a college of about 75,000 notables.

The ensuing referendum converted de Gaulle's France into a sort of "republican monarchy" even though the constitution clearly stated "the government determines the policy of the nation".

From President Georges Pompidou in 1973 through to the Mitterrand era, abortive efforts were made to reduce the seven-year mandate to five years or limit it to one term.

The aim was to address the problems created by cohabitation—of the president having to live with a government of a different political colour.

These always foundered on the conservative composition of the senate, elected for nine years by the so-called *grands elec-teurs*—persons holding elected public office and mostly made up of rural municipal councillors. The constitution gave blocking powers to the senate on constitutional change.

Nevertheless, France is now in its third "co-habitation" since 1986, due to the ambiguity of the constitution. Divisions of authority between the president and premier have evolved through precedent. But in the present case matters are more awkward.

Mr Jospin won an election after President Jacques Chirac miscalculated an early dissolution of parliament and the two will probably have to live together for a full parliament. Since President Chirac was elected on his RPR party ticket, this leaves him the unstated head of opposition.

Mr Jospin's tactic is to press for a reform of the senate to make the upper chamber reflect more closely the composition of the national assembly and cut the nine-year term to five. This in turn would simplify any altering of presidential office. But the conservative parties will not easily relinquish their long-standing privileged control of the upper chamber.

Out of frustration at this impasse, more attention is concentrated on ending the *cumuls des mandats,* the system of holding several elected offices. A high proportion of both houses of parliament hold down more than one elected office, whether mayorships, posts as regional or local councillors or as head of regional and departmental administrations. In the past, ministers have also been simultaneously deputies and local mayors.

Defenders of this system, of whom there are many in all parties, claim they are better able to represent their local voters because they are close to the heart of power.

The fact that they are not often present in their constituencies or even managing daily business at the "mairie" is mitigated by the ability to bend ministers' ears in Paris and ensure funding for local projects. Mr Jospin insists this is a distorted version of democracy and raises serious questions of conflict of interest.

He himself imposed strict rules on his own ministers on taking office. As a result, in the March regional elections Dominique Strauss-Kahn, the finance minister, backed away from plans to stand as head of the Ile-de-France region. However, the level of vested interest is so strong that the plan to prevent parliamentarians from holding other elected office could founder.

The difficulties of introducing institutional change were also highlighted in the wake of the March regional elections. Faced with a strong showing from the racist National Front and the prospect of right-wing regional leaders seeking the Front's support to form administrations, President Chirac announced an important review of all the country's electoral systems. The unstated purpose was to limit the influence of the National Front.

This appeared to boost Mr Jospin's own plans for a shake-up of the way the French elect their European MPs ahead of the 1999 European parliamentary elections. But four months later, in July, objections from within the ruling left-wing coalition, and from Mr Chirac's allies on the right, led Mr Jospin to shelve his scheme for creating seven new geographical units in continental France (plus one for overseas territories) to elect the 87 Euro-deputies.

The only electoral reform now likely to proceed is that for the regional elections. This could well involve adopting the first-past-the-post system for municipal elections. Regional elections use proportional representation which encourages a plethora of parties.

Mr Jospin also plans to write into the constitution the principle of parity between men and women. Although criticised by the right as a propagandist gesture towards the feminist lobby, the prime minister believes he is justified in highlighting the paucity of women in elected office.

# Right and Left in France: Two Recent Reports

## France's Right: An utter mess

**PARIS**

### The French right has little chance of defeating the reigning Socialists until it gets its own higgledy-piggledy house in order

**B**ATTERED in parliamentary elections last year, and again at regional polls this year, France's mainstream right is no nearer pulling itself together again. It remains divided on policy, buffeted by corruption scandals, and riven by rivalries. The only reason Jacques Chirac, the Gaullist president, is basking in his highest approval ratings since taking office three years ago is the economic upturn, and his friendliness with his popular Socialist prime minister, Lionel Jospin.

France's right is suffering from four main ills: contradictory views on Europe; opposing strategies toward the extreme-right National Front; an inability to agree on domestic policies, particularly over the economy; and too many chiefs (see table). As the right prepares for next summer's election to the European Parliament, each bit seems to be pulling in a different direction.

Philippe Séguin, once a noisy critic of the Maastricht treaty and now boss of the nominally pro-European Gaullist party, wants to create, and head, a single centre-right list of candidates for the European election. But Charles Pasqua, his party deputy and a fierce opponent of European integration, has been hinting that he may join forces with Philippe de Villiers, leader of a small, hard-right, Europhobic party, the Movement for France, to form a rival Eurosceptic list. Mr de Villiers got over 12% of the vote in the previous European Parliament election, four years ago.

François Bayrou, leader of Democratic Force, the main bit of the pro-European Union for French Democracy (UDF), which he also now heads, wants a single centre-right list too. After all, he asks, what is the point of the new Alliance, set up with great fanfare only in May by the three main parties of the moderate right—the Gaullists, UDF, and Alain Madelin's Liberal Democracy—if they cannot even get their act together for the first electoral show?

But many of Mr Bayrou's strongly Europhile colleagues are reluctant to go into battle behind such a Euro-minimalist general as Mr Séguin. They are even more nervous about joining ranks with the Liberal Democrats, their erstwhile partners in the UDF.

## Deconstructing the fissured French right

| The Alliance | | | The Right | Movement for France | National Front |
|---|---|---|---|---|---|
| Loose alliance of centre-right parties set up by Philippe Séguin and François Léotard in May 1998, which says it rejects any deal with the National Front. Provisional executive council, led by Mr Séguin, embraces leaders of the founding parties (below). | | | Founded and led since April 1998 by Charles Millon. Free-market and officially pro-European, but attracts many anti-Maastricht, anti-immigrant voters. Excluded from Alliance, suspected of sympathy for National Front. | Founded and led since 1994 by Philippe de Villiers. Far-right, nationalist, anti-Maastricht. Anti-Alliance. | Founded and led since 1972 by Jean-Marie Le Pen. Extreme-right, anti-immigrant, nationalist, protectionist and anti-Maastricht. |
| **Rally for the Republic (RPR)** | **Union for French Democracy (UDF)** | **Liberal Democracy (formerly Republican Party)** | | | |
| Founded in 1976 by Jacques Chirac. Led by Mr Séguin since 1997. Biggest opposition party. Divided over Europe. Traditionally Gaullist, nationalist and dirigiste, but now keener on free market. | Founded in 1978 by Valéry Giscard d'Estaing, France's then president. Loose federation of five centre-right, pro-European parties. François Bayrou replaced François Léotard as head on September 16th. | Formed in 1977. Renamed and led since June 1997 by Alain Madelin. Thatcherite, free-market, pro-European. Split from UDF in May 1998. | | | |
| **Democratic Force (formerly Centre of Social Democrats)** | **Radical Party** | **Popular Party for French Democracy** | **UDF "Direct Members"** | **Republican Independent and Liberal Group** | |
| Formed in 1976 by fusion of centre-right parties. Renamed and led since 1995 by Mr Bayrou. Centrist, pro-devolution, European federalist. Now the UDF's main part. | Led by Thierry Cornillet. | Led by Hervé de Charette, a former foreign minister. | Led by Pierre-André Wiltzer. | Led by Alain Lamassoure. Split from Liberal Democracy in 1998. | |

Reprinted with permission from *The Economist*, September 19, 1998, pp. 63-64. © 1998 by The Economist, Ltd. Distributed by The New York Times Special Features.

Not only did Mr Madelin and his pals abandon them in May to set up their own party, but they were also suspected of hanky-panky with Jean-Marie Le Pen's National Front. Though members of the Alliance have supposedly ruled out any truck with the Front, Mr Madelin last month welcomed back into his parliamentary group Jacques Blanc, one of the five regional-council presidents elected with Front support earlier this year. Seventeen Democratic Force deputies resigned from the party in protest.

Mr Madelin, himself once a member of an obscure far-right movement, says that his aim is to "reduce the influence" of the Front, which now attracts 15% of the national vote: in other words, presumably, to pinch its voters. How can he do this without also pinching some of its policies? For now, while resisting demands to dump Mr Blanc, he has agreed that his reviled colleague should not take part in any of the activities or structures of the Alliance. But this awkward compromise satisfies almost no one. What happens to Mr Blanc, for example, when the Alliance sets up its own parliamentary group, which it is about to do, composed of all members of its founding parties? Nobody knows the answer.

Outside the Alliance, matters are no less chaotic. Charles Millon, another regional-council president elected with Front support and a former UDF defence minister, has set up his own broad-church, right-wing movement, called simply the Right. Presenting itself as free-market, anti-racist and pro-European, it argues against deals with the Front. But the new party has been attracting a lot of hardline Eurosceptics, many from the far right, who want to create a single opposition party that includes the Front. Banned from both the UDF and the Alliance because of his suspected extreme-right sympathies, Mr Millon has been forced to sit by himself outside their parliamentary group.

In other words, the right is still a shambles—from which the Front looks likely to gain most. If the moderate right fails to agree on a single list for the European election, the right-wing vote will be split—and the Front could emerge as a dominant force. If the mainstream right offers a single, mildly pro-European list, Mr Le Pen might well grab a chunk of the Eurosceptic vote. As for Mr Chirac, he looks down in horror from the isolated splendour of the Elysée at his troops' squabbling, but can do little. He is supposed to be above party politics. But word is out that he is thinking of setting up his own Presidential Party. As if there were not enough confusion already.

# The French left begins to falter

**PARIS**

## After 18 months in office, the outlook is no longer quite so bright for Lionel Jospin's government. This is good news for President Jacques Chirac

A MARKED slowdown in the French economy. A more upbeat opposition, buoyed by a split in the far-right National Front. A newly pugnacious president back at the high levels of popularity reached at the start of his presidency. Divisions in the ruling left-wing coalition before the elections to the European Parliament in June. Will 1999 mark the end of the exceptional period of popularity enjoyed by Lionel Jospin, the prime minister, and his team since they came to power 18 months ago?

Mr Jospin continues to enjoy remarkably high levels of public support, with ratings mostly above 60%. But polls now suggest that Jacques Chirac would defeat him in a presidential poll. Why?

The darkest cloud for Mr Jospin hangs over the economy. After GDP grew by 3.1% last year, its strongest performance in the 1990s, economists predict an increase of a meagre 2-2.5% for 1999. Even the government now describes the 2.7% growth rate it used as the basis for this year's budget as a "target" rather than a "forecast". IN-SEE, an independent statistical body, predicts a mere 0.3% growth in the first quarter of this year. So unemployment, which had been falling—from a post-war record of 12.6% when Mr Jospin took over—is likely to remain stuck at its present level of over 11%.

The timing of the downturn is bad for Mr Jospin. He already has a delicate economic balancing act to carry out to keep his left-wing friends happy without losing the centrist voters who helped elect him. The government is pressing ahead with plans to create 350,000 public-sector jobs for the young; 150,000 have been found so far. He also hopes to create another 100,000 or so a year by reducing the working week from 39 to 35 hours. But early indications are that employers will not respond by creating many jobs. And the trade unions, faced with wage freezes and the imposition by employers of un-social work shifts to get round the shorter week, are beginning to wonder whether they have not been sold a pup.

Elected on an uncompromisingly left-wing platform, including a promise to end privatisation and a rejection of the euro-zone's growth and stability pact, which requires members to keep their budget deficits down, and which he once described as "that absurd concession to the Germans", Mr Jospin has since adopted a more pragmatic line. He now says—to the dismay of the Communists, Greens and other left-wing allies—that, though he sticks by his goals, he intends to be "flexible as to the means". "What counts is what works," he says, in a deliberate echo of Tony Blair, Britain's prime minister and a proponent of a "Third Way".

Indeed, Mr Jospin these days could sometimes be mistaken for a Blairite. Where he once virulently rejected the "excesses" of economic liberalism, he now talks of the need to balance social justice with economic efficiency. "Yes to the free-market economy; no to the free-market society," he proclaims. Like Mr Blair, he says he wants to shift individuals off welfare benefits into work, though he has not yet done much about it. In another blatant echo, he promises to get "tough on crime and tough on the causes of crime". Even privatisation is no longer taboo.

His record is certainly not that of a typical left-wing ideologue. He put his name to the austerity measures needed to squeeze the franc successfully into the euro. He has announced plans to cut public spending from 54% of GDP to around 51%, and to shave the budget deficit further, from 3% of GDP to around 1%, by 2002. He has sold more state assets in 18 months than the previous right-wing government did in its two years. He has promoted share options for company employees; agreed to the creation of private pension funds; launched the biggest crackdown on terrorism and organised crime in Corsica ever seen; extended game-shooting rights; and continued far-reaching reforms, launched by the right, in the armed forces (to end conscription) and in the health service, even threatening to punish overspending doctors.

Naturally, with a wary eye on his restless coalition friends, Mr Jospin denies that he has betrayed the left. His credo, he insists, is "democratic socialism", not social democracy, whatever the difference may be. Not only has he created jobs and cut the work-

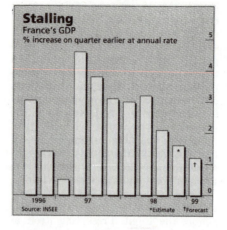

**Stalling**
France's GDP
% increase on quarter earlier at annual rate

1996    97    98    99
Source: INSEE    *Estimate    †Forecast

ing week, but he has given legal status to 80,000 illegal immigrants (though not as many as the Greens would have liked) and, separately, to homosexual couples.

Not enough, says the left. There are growing signs of rebellion within the government's own ranks. Late last year, the Greens decided to field their own strongly pro-European list of candidates for the June election, under the leadership of the iconoclastic Daniel Cohn-Bendit, a former leader of the 1968 student uprising. This is already causing Mr Jospin much heartache. The Communists are expected to follow suit with a Eurosceptic list of their own. This will leave the Socialists alone, and liable to be outwitted by the combined forces of a newly invigorated mainstream right.

Indeed, the moderate right now looks in better shape than it has since its shattering defeat in the snap 1997 general election. The former bitter rivalries and divisions have begun to fade. President Chirac is back in indisputable control of his Gaullist troops. Rumours that he will even set up a new movement after the European elections, to try to unite the mainstream right, are taken seriously. And the troubles of the National Front, which split last month into two rival factions, has raised centre-right hopes of scooping up at least some of its 15% of the vote.

Nor can Mr Jospin seek short-term comfort as he presses ahead with other potentially unpopular policies. These include the overhaul of public-sector pensions, the streamlining of the police forces and the reorganisation of the arms industry—not to mention proposed cuts, under German pressure, to European Union farm subsidies. Mr Chirac will move in for the attack wherever he finds a vulnerable flank.

All the same, Mr Jospin is head of a strong and popular government. He has managed to resolve the various social disputes that have beset his government—over lorry-drivers, Air France pilots, school pupils, and doctors—without too much political or financial cost. He has also succeeded in imposing himself as the sole plausible candidate of the left, in itself a feat never achieved by that arch-schemer, François Mitterrand. He could reach the Elysée yet.

# Perspectives on the French Model

## France vs. U.S.: Warring Views of Capitalism

### By ROGER COHEN

PARIS, Oct. 19—Anti-Americanism is an old theme here, almost a ritual, one that Prime Minister Lionel Jospin rehearsed recently when he declared that America could not impose its laws on the world and that "ultra-capitalism" was unacceptable.

What was surprising, though, was to find the new American Ambassador to Paris, Felix Rohatyn, agreeing with him. Not, of course, on the question of new French investments in Iran—the subject that gave Mr. Jospin the occasion for his gibes—but on the broader issue of American economic domination.

"We have no monopoly on ideas," Mr. Rohatyn said here the other day. "We do not believe that what works for us is automatically the best approach for anyone else." And as if to quash forever galloping French fears of an American "ultra-capitalist" system engulfing the globe, Mr. Rohatyn declared roundly: "There is no such thing as the American economic model."

These self-deprecatory remarks, made at the French Institute of International Relations, had a quite different ring from what was said just three months ago, at the Denver summit of major industrial powers. There, it was precisely America's unabashed vaunting of its economic successes and its exhortation to its European allies to follow its free-market recipes that led the French President, Jacques Chirac, to talk huffily about defending "our model."

The clash at Denver underscored the fact that the old sparring that strained but never undid an old alliance has gained a new edge, and a different scope, as France has set itself up as perhaps the nearest thing the United States has to a serious ideological rival in the last decade of the 20th century.

There used to be, of course, a shared enemy: the Soviet Union. Measured against that totalitarian power, the systems in America and France clearly had more in common than set them apart. France may identify the universal message of its Revolution with equality where Americans embrace liberty, but not even the French wanted to be equal on Soviet terms.

The situation has changed. Now that nobody wants to abolish capitalism, and its different forms lie at the heart of the global ideological debate, France and America offer two models whose different merits may be argued. The countries have been freed to explore their differences.

And differences there are: France has vastly better public medicine than America, safer cities, higher minimum wages, less crime and more job security, particularly in its huge state sector.

But it also has a 12.6 percent unemployment rate that is more than double the American, much higher taxes, a long-stagnant economy, crippling social security charges that discourage hiring, scant venture capital and a debilitating anxiety about change that has held back its investment in new technologies.

Which sort of society do you prefer? That is the essence of the debate that has raged here throughout this year and whose core question is: How much, if any, of French solidarity and social protection should be given up to achieve the faster growth and job-creation of the United States?

Unfortunately, the debate has tended to be argued in terms of caricature, increasing resentments between the countries that have then compounded real, if manageable, differences over their roles in Africa, Iran and elsewhere.

Here in France, the image of America generally presented is in some ways an echo of what the Soviets once drew: one of growing urban ghettos, overcrowded prisons, 19th-century wages and galloping capitalist cruelty. It is not uncommon to hear economists declare simply that the American system has failed.

In the United States, the French are almost uniformly presented as clinging stubbornly to archaic socialist ideals even as their unemployment rate climbs close to 13 percent and a wired world passes them by. It is not the merits of French public medicine that gain attention but the silliness of French strikers.

"The old Franco-American antagonism, the almost genetic rivalry, has been aggravated," said Jean Baudrillard, a sociologist. "The idea of a French exception, a French difference, is absurd, but a certain American triumphalism and our own relative decline has turned the idea into an obsession."

The new tone of Mr. Rohatyn, a former partner of the Lazard Frères investment firm in New York who took up his new post last month, was clearly intended to get beyond these obsessions and the accompanying caricatures.

If France was troubled by Medicare cuts, and if it does not want globalization to mean the relentless erosion of workers' rights, well, Mr. Rohatyn intimated, these were themes with which the Clinton Administration could sympathize.

### Anti-Americanism is used as camouflage.

He spoke of the need for fairness in the distribution of wealth, the need to promote "social values," the problems of big cities and crime, and the quest to insure "adequate retirement for our aging populations." In short, he seemed to make a limited defense of the very welfare state France is so determined to safeguard.

"The American in me is very pleased with our economic performance," said Mr. Rohatyn, who was born in Vienna. "The European in me understands your ambivalence about some of the choices that have been necessary to return to economic health."

The day after he spoke, Hubert Védrine, the French Foreign Minister, made remarks that were perhaps even more surprising. To a group of foreign correspondents, he declared, with disarming frankness: "We are a country that has trouble facing up to the reality of the world."

It was no good, Mr. Védrine said, to have excessive pretensions—to wallow in the old, rankling talk about the universality of French civilization and its values; the notion of occupying a position close to the center of the world; the harkening after past glory. "There is," he said, "something unhealthy in all that."

What was needed instead was a new realism, he said. And realism led France inexorably to the fact that there was only one superpower: the United States. To imagine otherwise was only to invite the terrible fits of melancholy that have periodically overcome France in the last year.

## An American envoy flatters French skeptics.

France, Mr. Védrine continued, was still very important, one of a group of perhaps seven countries—including Russia, China, Japan, Britain and Germany—with the power to have an influence throughout the world. It was firmly allied with the United States, but that did not mean it would always agree with America.

"France is not at the center of the world," he said, "but that is not a reason to despair. Let us try to have relations with the United States that are normal, calm, dispassionate and useful."

This new tone on both sides appears closer to the nuanced reality behind the caricatures. For it is not in fact so much America that is forcing France to reconsider its welfare state but the pressures

of a European integration of which France is a chief architect.

France has freed capital movements, sold off swathes of state industry, embraced budget austerity and made a strong franc a pillar of its policies because the opening of European borders and the push for a single European currency, the euro, have required such changes. But it is much easier to market these changes—and Mr. Jospin continues to push them—behind a veneer of anti-American statements than to dwell on what the euro means for France.

Similarly, the talk of the defense of "a French model of civilization" against the American masks the fact that the French private sector shows every sign of embracing a rugged American capitalism complete with storming corporate raiders.

In recent weeks, multibillion-dollar hostile takeover bids have been the talk of the bourse, as one giant supermarket chain tried to swallow two others and the rags-to-riches financier François Pinault bid $5 billion for the heart of the financial establishment, Worms & Cie. The fact that American pension funds are among the biggest investors in French companies suggests that the France-as-basket-case image is more than a little simplistic.

Moreover, French popular culture has embraced the American in a way not paralleled in Britain or Germany. The reversed baseball cap, basketball shoes, American movies and music—these are the frame of reference of a majority of French kids. The anti-Americanism glibly wheeled out by in-

tellectuals and politicians finds little echo among ordinary French people.

But this remains a people that wants to dream—"to aim for the ideal and understand the real," as the socialist Jean Jaurès once said. It is the legacy of the Revolution of 1789: the idea of a perfectible society, of equality and freedom reconciled, of what the historian François Furet called "a universal promise of earthly well-being."

In the same remarks that poured scorn on America's attempt to legislate for the world, Mr. Jospin outlined his own notions of "earthly well-being." He talked of his plans to institute a 35-hour work week in France in place of the current 39-hour week without a loss of salary. Thus, he suggested, more jobs would be created as the cake would be divided among more people.

Such ideas naturally make many Americans smile, laugh out loud or despair. They seem to confirm notions of the French basket-case.

But Mr. Jospin has proved a shrewd politician. He is as pragmatic as his Foreign Minister. He knows that without ideals and enemies, the French cannot function, and that a small dose of anti-Americanism is a useful camouflage for the changes that are inexorably bringing French society closer to the American.

Mr. Rohatyn—and the Clinton Administration—now seem equally aware of the need for camouflage: by questioning American economic failings, and implicitly flattering the French, they may actually encourage change faster than through confrontation.

---

JOSPIN'S CONTRADICTION: HE ACCEPTS THE AMERICAN MODEL BUT NOT ITS CONSEQUENCES.

# Is There a French Alternative?

## DANIEL SINGER

France used to be described, particularly in the nineteenth century, as the international laboratory in which political ideas were being tested. This function comes back to mind as the leftish government of Prime Minister Lionel Jospin is facing its first serious domestic trial of strength, presiding over a tense confrontation between employers and labor unions in a conference designed

*Daniel Singer is* The Nation's *Europe correspondent.*

to reduce the workweek from thirty-nine hours to thirty-five. The idea now being tested in France is whether it is possible—and how—to resist the repeated attempts to impose on Western Europe a new system of exploitation, based on the absolute reign of profit, the dismantling of the welfare state, the deregulation of the labor market and the growing gap between rich and poor, a system loosely called the American model. The U.P.S. strikers have shown spectacularly that the system can be tackled on its home ground. But one successful strike, however good for

labor's mood, does not alter the whole situation. The French experiment will show what problems must be solved and what pitfalls avoided in this common struggle over the shape of the world, of which these are still the early skirmishes.

The snag is that, judging from two recent lengthy articles on the cure in *The New York Times* by Roger Cohen on September 18 and 19, the reports making it back from the European front are highly biased. The bankers, businessmen and bosses who lent Cohen their insight (trade unionists were conspicuously absent) quite naturally share "the American conviction that lower taxes, deregulation, labor market flexibility and a dwindling social safety net are the route to success in the global economy." For them, Britain is, naturally, the best pupil of the model. Indeed, the vision of Europe I derived from these pieces is one of an Italy peopled by fraudulent pensioners and a France whose employers are taking flight across the Channel, relocating to escape unbearable tax burdens (how, with their allegedly huge labor costs, the businesses have managed to be major exporters and make profits is a detail the reader is not asked to ponder).

Now, there is no doubt that social services will have to be reformed throughout Western Europe, and not just in Italy. But the problem is whether they will be improved and modernized, or drastically cut and partly privatized. Similarly, the 50 cents of social contributions that a French employer has to add to each dollar of wages, and which so shocked a stooge from Normandy quoted by Cohen, is no novelty. For years these contributions were the financial foundation of the national health system and other benefits of the welfare state, which in France and the rest of Western Europe was presented as the solution to the problems of capitalism and one of the main reasons we need not think of radically altering society. It makes perfect sense that the moneybags would welcome a substitute social contract based on the principle "unto everyone that hath, shall be given." More relevant, however, is the reaction of the bulk of the European people. The question that Lionel Jospin has really put on the historical agenda is whether it is possible to have capitalism with a human face. (This was taken for granted throughout the so-called Golden Age, but now once more appears to be an illusion.)

For, whatever you may have read about him, Jospin is no revolutionary, and is best defined as a "normalized Socialist." He was one of the key participants in the transformation carried out by François Mitterrand after 1983, which converted French Socialists to consensus politics and the acceptance of capitalism as the "unsurpassable horizon," and had them join the cult of enterprise with the acceptance of globalized deregulation. But Jospin the Prime Minister is also the byproduct of the European resistance to the American model. It is not surprising that the test should be staged in Paris,

because it was in France that the biggest revolt so far against the allegedly inexorable model took place, in November and December 1995. Paralyzing Paris through a transport strike and shaking the country through huge demonstrations, the French adamantly refused the future they were being offered, despite the official argument that they had no choice. That French winter of discontent, while admittedly

*Can France develop a different logic within the E.U.'s free-trade framework? Unless pushed, this government may be likelier to yield.*

not offering an alternative, did change the political climate. It forced the conservative government to yield to the strikers and then prompted President Jacques Chirac to gamble its fate on a snap parliamentary election this past June. It pushed the Socialists to use more radical language on Europe, privatization and immigration and thus facilitated the coalition with the Communists and the Greens. And finally, it led to the victory in the June poll of the "plural left," headed by the Socialists. But Jospin's basic contradiction—his acceptance of the system and his refusal of its consequences—is weighing on this government, as can be seen from its performance during the first four months in office.

In a country with some 3.1 million jobless—12.5 percent of the labor force—the main task, everyone is aware, is to bring down unemployment. The social treatment of that issue was entrusted to 47-year-old Martine Aubry, known in the past mainly for being the daughter of Jacques Delors (former president of the European Commission) but who is fast making a name for herself as the government's second in command in charge of employment and solidarity. It is her duty to supervise fulfillment of the government's pledge to create 700,000 new jobs for people between the ages of 18 and 26. Half of those are to be set up in the private sector with state aid, and are yet to be defined. The 350,000 posts in the social-services sector have already been created and are being filled with junior supervisors and computer aides in

schools, assistants in libraries and post offices, and all sorts of posts in community services. The contradiction emerges when Minister Aubry claims that in the long run, all these jobs will cease to be subsidized. The new hires are given five-year contracts, during which the state will provide 80 percent of the French minimum wage (now about $1,100 a month); their employer pays the difference, or more. But what will happen when state aid ends? These jobs are shaped in response to social need, while the commercial ones rest on money-backed demand. The two logics clash. Aubry, like other advocates of the so-called third sector, is unable to explain how that sector is going to survive and expand without a radical transformation of the function and organization of work in society.

The gap between electoral promise and fulfillment is widening in another initiative designed to fight unemployment, the proposed rapid reduction of the workweek to thirty-five hours. During their campaign, the Socialists suggested that while employers and labor unions would be allowed to discuss specifics, the government would provide the legal framework, offering nationally binding rules and a fixed timetable. As the date of the government conference—October 10—approached, the employers began to raise objections. They did not mind reductions if those were flexible and calculated on an annual, not a weekly, basis; and if the process were negotiated case by case, without national rules or time limits. The hesitations of the government were revealed when Jospin, in a *Le Monde* interview, suddenly stated that the slogan "Thirty-five hours paid thirty-nine" was not his, as it was "anti-economic." But he also said in the same interview that he was in favor of the thirty-five-hour week "without loss of income." These verbal acrobatics strengthened the impression that the government might be ready to yield to employers unless labor reaction forced it to keep its pledge.

Signs of retreat can also be discerned on the privatization front. The Socialists proclaimed they would be "undogmatic" on the subject, which in this instance meant that they would not follow the fashion of denationalizing industries. Now one is entitled to doubts on the subject. True, the chairman of Air France, a big state company, did resign, allegedly on the ground that he was not allowed to sell at once a majority stake in it. But it is an open secret that Air France is not yet profitable enough to be sold, and the Communist transportation minister has now accepted the principle of the sale of a minority stake. More perturbing still is the volte-face on the French telecommunications giant France Télécom. In response to appeals by labor unions, which have the support of the majority of the employees, the Socialists promised to reverse the proposed privatization plan. After a pause in office, it reversed its reversal. Now, in the juiciest privatization deal so far, the government should get some $7.1 billion for 22.5 percent of the company's shares sold to the public and another 2.5 percent sold to the staff. (Later, about 7.5 percent will be swapped with Deutsche Telekom, its privatized German equivalent.) The government can argue that what really matters, in a case like that of Air France, is that the state will preserve a controlling interest. But the suspicion that this is the thin edge of the wedge is based on the fact that the French left no longer seems to conceive of the nationalized sector as a place where labor is organized differently or as an instrument for a different economic policy. How can a public sector thrive if it has no logic of its own?

Yet how can France develop such a logic within the free-trade framework of the European Union? Here, in fairness, it must be admitted that Jospin never concealed his acceptance of the Maastricht Treaty or his support of Europe's common currency, the euro. But this acceptance was qualified by serious reservations, two of them particularly significant. Jospin maintained that he was not bound by the deflationary "stability pact," added to Maastricht under German pressure, which extended a budget-deficit limit of 3 percent of G.D.P. on member nations till doomsday, with penalties for breaches, thus ruling out any Keynesian attempts at economic stimulus. He also argued that since Europe will now have a joint central bank, it must have some form of "government" to control its activity. Once in office, these splendid resolutions vanished. At his first European meeting in Amsterdam in June, Jospin lifted his veto on the stability pact in exchange for a mere face-saving device, the promise of a conference (to be held next month in Luxembourg) to see how the European

Union can fight unemployment and not exclusively inflation. As to the central bank, what started as a proposal to set up an instrument of control will produce at best a toothless organ of consultation due to German insistence on the bank's total independence. On its own, France could not move mountains, say the official pleaders. But a Socialist government could have come up with concrete, popular proposals by appealing, if necessary, to the people of Europe above the heads of their governments.

I, in turn, may be painting a distorted, because too bleak, picture. Actually, the "plural left" French government is doing well. With a slight economic recovery—including a pickup in exports—it has proved easier than expected to fulfill the Maastricht criteria. The budget deficit will hit the 3 percent target in 1998 and should be only fractionally higher this year. The government reached this objective in decent progressive fashion, raising the tax on big corporations, whose profits are so fat they cannot scream too loudly, and shifting the tax burden slightly from earned to unearned income. Nothing spectacular, but since not much was expected from this government, Jospin is, for the moment, fairly popular. To explain why I am, nevertheless, hinting that the various concessions mentioned above are signs of potential surrender, we shall now have to switch from the issue of unemployment to that of immigration.

Immigration is a hot potato the Socialists do not like to handle, on the unproven assumption that a liberal attitude on the matter is electorally a losing proposition. This is why, despite demands from various associations, Jospin for a long time refused to promise that if he won, he would abolish the anti-immigrant laws bearing the names of conservative former interior ministers. The latest, the Debré law, was clearly introduced this year by Chirac as part of his electoral strategy: Immigrant bashing was supposed to woo the voters from Jean-Marie Le Pen's National Front and put the Socialists in an awkward position. What nobody bargained for was that this obvious pandering to Le Pen at a time when his party had conquered a town hall in southern France would provoke one of those rare outbursts of moral indignation. Several hundred thousand people signed a petition stating that they would disobey the law, which incidentally required that the French act as informers and report to the government the departure of foreign

guests. When, spontaneously, without any party infrastructure, hundreds of thousands of protesters marched through Paris, Jospin was sufficiently impressed to promise, belatedly, that his government would "abrogate the Pasqua and Debré laws." It is this pledge that he now refuses to keep, although he has agreed to alter the laws by eliminating their worst features. The difference is both symbolic and significant. It makes one believe that, unless it is pushed strongly, this government is not ready to take risks; keen on consensus, it is likely to retreat, to yield, to seek compromise.

Two conclusions may be drawn on the prospects for this government. One is highly pessimistic: that it will go the way of all Socialist flesh—betray its promises and its principles, demobilize the movement and, by disappointing even limited hopes, pave the way for a backlash. There is also a more open-ended and perhaps more realistic conclusion: Nothing is yet frozen. If the labor unions show muscle, official policy on wages and working hours will take a different shape. Should the French people seize the political stage again, as they did in 1995, the Greens would remember that they did not enter government just to stop one nuclear reactor; Jean-Pierre Chevènement, the Interior Minister, would recall that he once was a Maastrichtmonger; and the Communists would be mindful that sitting in ministerial offices is not a virtue in itself. Above all, the Socialists would be reminded that the sinister Le Pen, rather than the clumsy Chirac, would benefit most from their failure.

Thus the future of this government is uncertain. But you can already draw from the French experience two lessons for the common struggle against the American model. One is that politics is not simply casting a ballot every few years, nor does it all happen at the top. The Teamsters and Télécom, the daily battles in factories and offices, in hospitals and shops or on campuses, the struggles at the grass roots, do shape the course of events. But the second lesson is that if we want those movements from below to unite and really matter, we must forge a common project, reinvent the vision of a different world. For it is increasingly plain that if we wish to live in an environment with a human face, it is imperative to look beyond the confines of our really existing societies.

France

# Jospin discovers America

PARIS

"MY VIEW of the United States has changed," Lionel Jospin, France's prime minister, confessed during his first official visit across the Atlantic this month. "Contrary to what we [in France] have claimed, and indeed believed, the jobs being created in the United States are not only, or even mainly, low-paid, dead-end jobs, but skilled ones in the service and high-tech industries." France, he admitted, could learn much about America's economic dynamism, the vitality of its research and innovation, its competitive spirit and capacity for renewal.

Was this really a Frenchman—and a supposedly *dirigiste* Socialist to boot—talking about a country hitherto regarded as the embodiment of cruel free-market excess? In the French press, and not just on the left, America is often portrayed as "ultra-capitalist" and arrogant, a place where the "law of the jungle" reigns. After the G7 group of rich countries met in Denver last year, President Jacques Chirac declared: "I do not want that model." Until now, Mr Jospin has echoed him.

For their part, many Americans caricature France as hidebound, strike-ridden, protectionist, clinging to old statist, socialist ideals, resistant to change, obsessed with its own fading glory, constantly bemoaning America's economic, military, and cultural "hegemony", and with an irritating, seemingly reflex, tendency to oppose the Americans on the world stage.

En route to America, Mr Jospin said he would "do away, once and for all, with the old stereotypes on both sides". And he took with him his government's two most ardent fans of America: Dominique Strauss-Kahn, his finance minister, and Claude Allègre, an eminent physicist, now minister for education and research. Both these fluent English-speakers, who have taught in the United States, have done much to make Mr Jospin friendlier to such notions as the entrepreneurial spirit and the global economy—once dirty terms in the French socialist lexicon. "Socialist thinking is in full evolution," said Mr Allègre, one of Mr Jospin's closest friends and advisers.

Throughout his trip, Mr Jospin, who has promised France a 35-hour week and 350,000 public-sector jobs for the young unemployed, was at pains to cast himself as a pragmatic reformist bent on "taking France into the modern era". He and President Bill Clinton apparently hit it off. Globalisation, among other topics, was said to have proved fascinating at lunch.

The French are not, however, about to adopt what they call the servile *suivisme* of other Europeans, especially Britain, for all things American. Though French business, youth, and the man-in-the-street are broadly keen on America, a strong anti-American current permeates many parts of the French political class, including the Communists, parts of the Socialist Party, the Gaullists and the far-right National Front. Many still suspect that Charles de Gaulle was right to say that "American imperialism" was the only real obstacle to "French greatness". Such people accused Mr Allègre of "capitulation" when he dared suggest that English should "no longer be considered a foreign language".

For sure, French complaints about American pushiness will still rumble. Americans will go on grumbling about France's haughty need to "go it alone". But the tone may be softening.

---

# Those revolutionary French shots

PARIS

FRANCE's parliament cocked a snook at the European Commission on June 19th when it adopted a law letting migrant birds and waterfowl be shot for up to seven-and-a-half months a year, giving the country by far the longest hunting season in Europe. But the commission is blasting back. The fiery French are already facing fines for a previous act of defiance over EU shooting laws.

Under the wild-birds directive, adopted by all EU countries in 1979, game birds may not be shot during migratory periods or during various stages of the breeding cycle. No dates are laid down. But in 1994 the European Court of Justice, the Union's rule-enforcer, said that all EU countries should "guarantee complete protection [of gamebirds] during the premating migration period". So shooting must stop as soon as birds begin to fly back home to nest.

Most EU countries allow people to shoot gamebirds from around early September until the end of January. But in France the season begins as early as mid-July and may run until the end of February, depending on the area and the species. After the commission told France last November to bring its laws into line with the rest of the Union's, 11 of France's 96 administrative departments decided to obey, by closing their season a month early—to the fury of *chasseurs*.

A group of senators from the mainstream right then popped up with a bill enabling parliament to fix each department's seasonal shooting dates and got plenty of support across the spectrum. Only 11 Socialists and three other left-wingers joined six Greens to vote against the bill. It was the turn of France's environment minister, Dominique Voynet, the leader of the Greens, who keenly support the EU directive, to be furious.

But France's 1.6m regular shooters (not counting another 3.5m occasionals), out-gunning their British and German counterparts by factors of two and five, are a powerful lobby. Most are blue-collar workers or small farmers; many vote left. Brussels, they say, has no right to deprive them of the hard-won spoils of the Revolution. And Lionel Jospin, the prime minister, does not want to be winged by them.

# Tocqueville in Italy

DAVID L. KIRP

*MAKING DEMOCRACY WORK: Civic Traditions in Modern Italy. By Robert Putnam. Princeton, 258 pp. $24.95.*

What makes a government responsive to the just wishes of its citizens? *Making Democracy Work* offers provocative and persuasive new ways to think about this ancient and pivotal political question. Political scientist Robert Putnam pays close attention to evidence—from historical accounts, personal narratives and survey data collected during a twenty-year experiment with local government—about how ordinary people's lives intersect with the power of the state. *Making Democracy Work* makes the past—a millennium's worth of the past—entirely relevant to today's headline stories. It takes up the classic chicken-and-egg puzzle of public life—does economic prosperity make *civitas* possible or is it the other way around?—and reaches conclusions that should prompt students of politics and economics alike to rethink their assumptions.

Seminal, epochal, path-breaking: All those overworked words apply to a book that, to make the point brazenly, is a *Democracy in America* for our times. But while Tocqueville drew his insights from a new nation famously experimenting with representative government, Putnam has voyaged to Italy, perhaps the most unlikely place among Western nations to look for instruction in matters democratic. For nearly half a century in that country, coalition governments dominated by the Christian Democrats came and went with breathtaking speed, even as the very same politicians stayed on.

*David L. Kirp is professor of public policy at the University of California, Irvine.*

And on—Amintore Fanfani, several times a prime minister and holder of innumerable Cabinet jobs into the 1980s, was a contemporary of Harry Truman. While the Christian Democrats were loved only by their families, they nonetheless regularly found their way back to Rome through the expedient of Communist-bashing. When the Socialists became a politically credible force, they too styled themselves as an alternative to the evils for which Communism stood. Always the Communists were in opposition.

In the aftershock of the end of the cold war, these arrangements started to collapse; keeping the Communists out of the government was no longer a rationale for ruling. Early in 1992, some brave Italian magistrates began poking around in the dustbins of national political life. While the investigations initially concentrated on petty misdeeds in Milan, the sweep of the corruption unearthed by Operation Clean Hands was stunning: Boatloads of politicians, Christian Democrats and Socialists alike, turned out to be on the payrolls of the biggest private and state companies, as well as the Mafia. This has proved too much to stomach, even in a country where, as Sicilian novelist Guiseppe Tomasi di Lampedusa observed, everything must change so that nothing will change. Now there is a new government led by a banker with no discrediting political ties, a new electoral law and a new emphasis on regional rather than national authority.

It is in Italy's twenty regional governments, not in the Roman corridors of power, that Putnam and his colleagues have been nosing about for more than two decades (forever in the world of social science research, usually impatient for quick results). In 1970, barely a century after the country was first unified,

the regions were granted new power to manage their affairs; and this taste of authority led, not surprisingly, to demands for more. Now these regions control as much as a third of the national budget, and their responsibilities include managing hospitals and health care, public safety, economic development, agriculture and housing.

Across Italy, the regional governments get more respect from the citizenry than do the overseers in Rome. Far more striking are the differences from one region to the next. In some places, public services are efficiently managed, with innovations ranging from family health clinics to environmental standards; officials are responsive and citizens are genuinely pleased. By contrast, other regional governments are cesspools, corrupt and exploitative, where personal connections rather than public priorities count for everything and the populace is grudging and resentful. What explains why the same form of government functions so well in some places, so badly in others? What makes democracy work?

None of the obvious explanations suffice. The formal administrative structures are almost identical from one region to another. Party politics or ideology isn't critical either, since Communists, Socialists and Christian Democrats can all handle or bungle the job. Social stability doesn't account for the performance of government, nor does the educational level of the populace. Most surprising, economic modernization isn't the key either. Some "have not" regions actually do a better job of managing their public business than their economically better-off counterparts.

What's crucial, it turns out, is the "civic-ness" of regional life—voter turnout (not homages to patronage), newspaper readership and membership in associations ranging from sports clubs to Lions Clubs, unions to choral societies—any kind of participation that "seems to depend less on *who* you are than on *where* you are." Where people perceive a public world framed by exploitation, corruption, individual powerfulness, citizenship is stunted. In such places, civic life only confirms the wisdom of cynicism—everyone is expected to violate the rules and to do otherwise is foolish. Once again, Tocqueville was right. "The most democratic country in the world now," he wrote in *Democracy in America,* "is that in which men have in our time carried to the highest perfection the art of pursuing in common the objects of common desires and have applied this new technique to the greatest number of purposes."

Writing a quarter of a century ago, in *The Moral Basis of a Backward Society,* political scientist Edward Banfield argued that "amoral familism"—"maximize the material, short-run advantage of the nuclear family; assume that all others will do likewise"—explained the failure of

civic life in some regions of Italy. Putnam puts the community and its "stocks of social capital" first. The supply of mutual trust, civic involvement and reciprocity naturally grows, as "virtuous circles" take on a life of their own. By contrast, someone trapped in a world of distrust and exploitation is unlikely to survive by promoting collaboration, for "the strategy of 'never cooperate' is a stable equilibrium."

The conclusion leads Putnam to search for the historic roots of the civic community, an inquiry that takes him all the way back to the twelfth century, when radically different political regimes first appeared in different regions of Italy. Autocratic rule, imposed in the South by Norman conquerers, became the regional norm, while unprecedented forms of self-government emerged in the very parts of the North where civic engagement and successful government presently prevail.

These successful communities, says Putnam, did not become civic because they were rich. On the contrary: The historical record strongly suggests that, over the past 150 years at least, they became rich because they were civic,

even as feudal, fragmented regions have slipped deeper into backwardness. The mutual aid societies and choral groups of our times can be traced back to the guilds, religious fraternities and tower societies in the medieval communes of Northern Italy, while in parts of the South, as a nineteenth-century writer observed, "One feels too much the 'I' and too little the 'we.' "

This is an account of Italy, but its implications are global—and sobering. There are no quick fixes, no mass inoculations of social capital that will turn Bosnia into Bologna, no ready way to imprint P.T.A.s or AIDS services organizations (or, more pertinently, their underlying values) in the Slovak Republic or the old East Germany. Nor, closer to home, is it an easy matter to nurture the practice of civic life that Tocqueville praised but that seems imperiled in the daily news accounts—the chronicles of our own amoral familism—whether about the highways of Miami or the hopelessly homeless on the streets of Anytown, U.S.A. In this respect, *Making Democracy Work* is one of the saddest stories a social scientist has ever told.

# FORMER COMMUNIST INSTALLED IN ITALY

## Names Eclectic Cabinet in Bid to Please Many Factions

**By ALESSANDRA STANLEY**

ROME, Oct. 21—A former Communist became Italy's Prime Minister today, the first ever to do so, and he quickly appointed an eclectic Cabinet that is not solidly to the left.

If Parliament approves the Cabinet of the new Premier, Massimo D'Alema, he will be the only former Communist to head a major Western European government.

But Mr. D'Alema, 49, chose a cabinet that has something for everyone: Communists, conservatives, and six women. That is twice the number who served under the departing Prime Minister, Romano Prodi, whose center-left government collapsed two weeks ago, when it lost a parliamentary election by one vote.

Among other compromises, Mr. D'Alema was forced to give such key ministries as Defense and Communications to supporters of Francesco Cossiga, a former Christian Democrat who now leads a small center-right party.

There are at least 17 parties in Parliament. Seven are represented in the new Government, eight if you include Mr. Prodi's Olive Tree coalition.

Mr. D'Alema's effort to forge across-the-board allegiances to secure a majority signals a classic Italian paradox: A Government whose stated goal is the introduction of a two-party system is itself a mirror of the patchwork quilt of small, constantly, mutating parties that is the source of Italy's chronic political instability.

Mr. D'Alema, who tried and failed to pass reforms in Parliament this year, has already pledged to make electoral reform a top priority. Many Italians wonder how he will manage.

"I find it hard to believe that so heterogeneous a coalition will be prepared to reform the electoral system," said Sergio Romano, a former diplomat and political expert. "Too many people behind this Government, like Cossiga, thrive on the very system of proportionality that the reform is supposed to change."

The irrepressible Mr. Cossiga, 70, is distrusted by left and right in Italy, but having survived the collapse of the old political system dominated by the Christian Democrats, of which he was a leader, he created the Union of Democrats for the Republic six months ago and is now a power broker.

Mr. Cossiga navigates from one political side to another. While he was President of Italy in 1991, Mr. D'Alema's party sought to have him impeached. Mr. Cossiga's new bond with Mr. D'Alema has infuriated his former allies in the opposition.

"We shall see how men who only yesterday insulted and attacked each other can stay clasped together in a grab for power," said Silvio Berlusconi, a media tycoon and former conservative Prime Minister.

Mostly, however, Italians are waiting to see how the Communists and Mr. Cossiga's forces will clash at Cabinet meetings.

Some Government priorities—like passing a 1999 budget that allows Italy to meet the requirements for joining a single European currency in January—seem widely shared and well within reach.

Mr. D'Alema reappointed the two top economic ministers, who are credited with helping Mr. Prodi trim Italy's bloated economy and qualify for membership in the euro last spring: Carlo Azeglio Ciampi will stay on as Treasury and Budget Minister, and Vincenzo Visco will continue as Finance Minister. Italy's respected Foreign Minister, Lamberto Dini, was also reappointed.

Mr. D'Alema has already said he will present to Parliament the same budget that caused Mr. Prodi's Government to collapse. Fausto Bertinotti, general secretary of the Marxist Communist Refounding Party, withdrew his support from Mr. Prodi over budget disputes.

But that move quickly split Communist Refounding. A more moderate faction led by Armando Cossutta, unwilling to be blamed for sabotaging the first center-left Government in 50 years, split off, forming yet another small leftist party, the Italian Communists' Party. A week ago, Mr. Cossutta vowed that he could never join forces with Mr. Cossiga. He relented, and his party was rewarded with the Ministries of Justice and Regional Affairs.

There are new faces, like Giovanna Melandri, 36, a member of Mr. D'Alema's Democratic Party of the Left, who was named Minister of Culture and Sports, and Enrico Letta, 32, a member of the Popular Party, who will take over European Affairs and is the youngest member of the Cabinet.

But Mr. D'Alema also brought back Giuliano Amato, 60, a former Prime Minister and one of the few Socialist leaders who escaped unscathed from the scandals that toppled former Prime Minister Bettino Craxi, who is now living in exile in Tunisia. Mr. Amato was awarded a newly revived post, Minister of Institutional reform, which includes drafting new electoral laws.

# The July 1998 Election: Two Reports

## *JAPANESE REBUKE GOVERNING PARTY IN NATIONAL VOTE*

### *Stage Set for Premier's Resignation—More Disarray Expected*

#### By NICHOLAS D. KRISTOF

TOKYO, Monday, July 13—Voters in parliamentary elections on Sunday gave Japan's governing party a brutal drubbing, setting the stage for the resignation of Prime Minister Ryutaro Hashimoto and creating new uncertainties about the country's political and economic course.

"The results are attributable to my lack of ability," a grim Mr. Hashimoto told Japanese television early this morning. "We could not live up to the people's expectations, and it is all my responsibility."

He strongly hinted that he would resign after meeting later today with officials of his Liberal Democratic Party.

But while the voters were apparently punishing the confusion and lack of decisiveness in the Government as it faces Japan's worst economic crisis in more than half a century, the results of the elections—for Parliament's upper house—may create more disarray than ever in the coming days.

No one knows who will lead the country—whose economy is second only to that of the United States in size—as it tries to extricate itself from recession, or what will happen to Japan's recently announced plans to deal with its mountain of bad loans held by banks.

It will now be harder than ever for the Liberal Democrats to govern Japan and push economic legislation through Parliament.

None of the main contenders for the Prime Minister's job is the kind of new and dynamic leader that many Japanese say they want, and that the United States and other countries fervently desire. There is some risk that the job will go from a man who exhibited little leadership to a rival who has shown none.

In an early verdict on the result, currency traders sent the yen plunging in trading against the dollar this morning. Japanese stocks also tumbled, adding to the nation's economic troubles.

The markets would have tumbled more if it were not for the possibility that the election shock may force the Liberal Democrats—who have changed policy in the past in reaction to electoral defeat—to become more aggressive in tackling the nation's economic problems.

There may now be more possibility of tax cuts and of another economic stimulus package, although it is not clear that there will be any push for the kind of market-oriented reorganization that many economists urge.

Since the elections on Sunday were for the upper house of Parliament, not the more important lower house, they do not directly affect Mr. Hashimoto's post as Prime Minister or his party's lock on power. But he billed the vote as a referendum on his leadership, and the party won only 44 of the 126 seats up for election this year.

That was still far more than the 27 seats won by the leading opposition group, the Democratic Party, but far less than the 61 seats that the Liberal Democrats held going into the election.

Other seats were won by the Communists, who did exceptionally well as winners of protest votes, and by independents and other groups in Japan's deeply fragmented opposition.

The upheaval comes at an odd time in the Japanese political world, when the country is neither exactly the one-party state it used to be nor a Western-style country where parties go in and out of power.

The Liberal Democrats ran the country for decades with only token opposition, but they were evicted from power in 1993 after a poor election performance and a series of defections by members of Parliament.

At that time, many thought that old-style Japanese politics were gone forever, but a year later the Liberal Democrats clawed their way back to power as part of a coalition.

Then Mr. Hashimoto took over as Prime Minister in January 1996 and led the Liberal Democrats in a long slog in which they managed to regain majority control of the lower house of Parliament, so that five years later the situation is much as it was before—but with much less sense of expectation that the political system can be a vehicle for far-reaching change anytime soon.

While Sunday's vote was an unambiguous rebuke to the Liberal Democrats, it is less clear whether it was a vote in favor of anything. By most accounts the voters were simply annoyed by the Liberal Democrats' lack of strong leadership at a time of national economic crisis.

"The biggest reason is the lack of economic recovery," Taku Yamasaki, a Liberal Democratic leader, told NHK Television. Mr. Yamasaki said the top party officials, including Mr. Hashimoto and himself, should resign, but he added that he worried about the impact of the move on the economy.

"What if something happens like the collapse of a financial institution while our financial restructuring scheme is still unfinished?" Mr. Yamasaki mused. "I'm very worried about the power vacuum created by this election result."

Prime Minister Hashimoto planned to go to Washington for a state visit later this month, but that will almost certainly be called off or postponed until a new leader is in place.

The Liberal Democrats will be under strong pressure to act within a week to choose a replacement, and probably to summon Parliament into session so a new person can formally take the Prime Minister's post.

The main contenders are Keizo Obuchi, the Foreign Minister and leader of the largest faction in the Liberal Democratic Party; Seiroku Kajiyama, a veteran politician who was the chief Cabinet spokesman for a time under Mr. Hashimoto; Kiichi Miyazawa, a former Prime Minister,

## The Japanese electorate punishes indecisiveness in an economic crisis.

and Yohei Kono, who was the Liberal Democratic leader until he resigned to make way for Mr. Hashimoto.

Whoever takes over, fundamental changes are not expected.

"The L.D.P. has a firm lock on power in the lower house, and that's not going to change," said John F. Neuffer, an analyst of Japanese politics at the Mitsui Marine Research Institute in Tokyo. "Hashimoto was being pulled around by his nose by party elders, and whoever is in there is going to continue party-established policies."

Mr. Neuffer said that while financial markets would be jittery, the humiliation might encourage the Liberal Democrats to become more aggressive in tackling bad debt problems, cutting taxes and approving a new economic stimulus package.

"In the long term I think this is good for the nation and the world, but in the short term I think everybody's going to be nervous," Mr. Neuffer said.

One important winner was the Democratic Party, which consolidated its role as the leading opposition force.

While the party is a poorly organized and newly formed coalition of various factions, it shows hints that it may eventually emerge as a Western-style opposition force, distinguishing itself from the governing party on issues and seen by voters as a credible alternative force.

The Democratic Party is led by Naoto Kan, who opinion polls suggest is by far Japan's most popular politician. Mr. Kan, who made his name as a Cabinet minister crusading against the bureaucracy, will now push to build his party's organization so it can wrest power from the Liberal

Democrats in the general elections that must be held by 2000.

"I take it very seriously that the newborn Democratic Party has been given a chance by the people," a jubilant Mr. Kan told reporters at his party headquarters. "People said no to what the Liberal Democratic Party has done. They realized that the Liberal Democratic Party cannot reform, is totally bound by special interests."

"People rejected the bureaucracy-led Government," Mr. Kan added, calling for early elections for the lower house.

Ichiro Ozawa, who once was the main opposition leader but now heads only a small opposition party, said, "I think lower-house elections are inevitable."

The Liberal Democrats may see things differently, since they would almost certainly lose ground in a general election.

With Sunday's election, Mr. Hashimoto becomes the latest in a series of politicians who entered the Prime Minister's residence strong and self-confident and then left ignominiously with his reputation in tatters.

When he took office, he was welcomed enthusiastically as a dynamic leader who was an expert on policy issues and was contrasted sharply with his predecessor, Tomiichi Murayama, a grandfatherly Socialist who was widely viewed as extremely nice and extremely lackadaisical.

Mr. Hashimoto initially did indeed exhibit leadership and decisiveness, but in retrospect he chose to exercise it in the wrong way: he pushed through an increase in the national sales tax from 3 percent to 5 percent. It was a bold and politically courageous attempt to put Japan's finances on a better footing, but it turned out to be economically catastrophic, tipping the nation into recession.

Moreover, Mr. Hashimoto proved much less firm in tackling the recession. He eventually pushed through a large stimulus package, but it took so long to put into place that the economy tumbled in the meantime and further endangered the country's weak banks.

# ELECTION AS REPROOF: JAPAN CHALLENGES THE SYSTEM

## By STEPHANIE STROM

TOKYO, July 25—The last two weeks have seen a stunning revolt in Japanese politics.

True, it was quashed. The election of Keizo Obuchi as president of the governing Liberal Democratic Party, a position that all but guarantees he will become Prime Minister next week, was pure Japanese politics as usual.

**News Analysis**

But the election itself—in which two party members openly challenged Mr. Obuchi—was a condemnation of the party and its longstanding system of choosing leaders, under which heads of its powerful factions meet privately to select one of them to run the country for the next few years.

In the tactics of its participants, in its openness and in the loud, angry voices of voters that accompanied it, the election was a wake-up call to the party that has governed Japan for 41 of the last 43 years with little challenge.

"We are seeing the start of a real end to the L.D.P. period," said Shinichi Yoshida, a columnist and senior political correspondent for Asahi Shimbun, one of Japan's largest papers.

Mr. Yoshida pointed out that the Liberal Democrats have not won a majority in an election since 1993, when an opposition coalition took power for 11 months. Since then, the party has governed either in coalition or by luring opposition members into its fold after an election to insure a majority.

"The voters have not given them a majority since 1993," he said. "With the voters, the L.D.P. is not popular."

Indeed, a poll taken last week by Yomiuri Shimbun, another large paper, showed support for the party slipping to an all-time low of 20.7 per cent, a drop of 8 percentage points in one month.

Everything about the election pointed to the party's unpopularity. An unexpected upset in the upper house elections two weeks ago forced the party president, Prime Minister Ryutaro Hashimoto, to resign. Plans to present a united front behind Mr. Obuchi fizzled when junior party members started clamoring for competition. Candidates were forced to discuss policy on television, and their neighbors found themselves being interviewed by reporters.

The party's loss of control was evident in the election's competitive nature, in the attention to public opinion about the race, in the voting across factional lines that determined the winner and in the edge-of-the-seat atmosphere that descended on Tokyo as party members cast their ballots Friday afternoon.

It all added up to what one analyst described as "the most open and democratic L.D.P. presidential election in history."

Only the outcome was predictable—and that may further weaken the party.

As Glen Fukushima, the American Chamber of Commerce president, put it: "There was enough concern expressed in the media and among certain L.D.P. members that the choice of Obuchi could lead to a potential backlash in the future, but despite that warning the party leaders went ahead and did their own thing. They probably think people will forget, but I wonder."

Two things could work in the Liberal Democrats' favor, however. The righteous indignation that voters are expressing now may evaporate if the economy takes a turn for the better.

Also, the opposition may have an attractive leader in Naoto Kan, head of the Democratic Party, but the party is still torn by dissension. Although

voters like Mr. Kan, it is doubtful whether he could put together a lasting coalition government.

---

## 'The start of a real end' to the Liberal Democratic Party's era?

---

Instability is the last thing that world leaders want to see in Japan, which must move quickly and without distraction to address the problems in its financial sector and to stimulate the economy. Should the party be forced into a coalition with the opposition, analysts fear a period in which very little would be accomplished.

"People have broken off from the party many times over the last two or three decades only to come back," a senior diplomat in Tokyo said. "It could happen again, I suppose, but there is certainly a lot of force in the party structure in the sense that its numbers put it in a position to offer a lot of rewards to its members." In fact, the 1993 voter revolt did not result in any lasting changes in party procedures or the Japanese system.

But Japanese voters are beginning to find their voices now, goaded by economic distress and changes in the electoral system five years ago that have given their votes more clout in the choice of district representatives.

One could not interview a legislator last week without hearing about how many of his constituents had faxed him in hopes of swaying his vote, and after the election last night, many were dreading their trips back to their districts. "I think a lot of people are going to be upset," said Taro Kono, a 35-year-old party member who had scheduled a series of meetings with constituents over the weekend in his district in

# New Party Chief Gets Low Ratings on Tokyo Streets

## By MARK LANDER

TOKYO, July 25—Japan's governing party may have elected Keizo Obuchi as its president and the country's future Prime Minister by a comfortable margin on Friday. But to walk the streets of this capital on a gloomy morning after Mr. Obuchi's election is to conclude that Japan's kingmakers live in a parallel universe.

"I'm not at all happy with the result," said Masakozu Nakamura, 21, a psychology student at Keio University in Tokyo, as his girlfriend nodded vigorously in agreement. "He doesn't look like a Prime Minister."

Tekuo Ichihara was equally dismissive. "Japan needs a leader who will make drastic changes," said Mr. Ichihara, 66, who is the president of Wako, an upscale department store in Tokyo's fashionable Ginza district. "Under his leadership, no drastic changes will happen."

From shoppers in the boutiques of Ginza to groundskeepers in the park near the Imperial Palace, people today were almost unanimously dissatisfied with Mr. Obuchi's election. They regard him as bland and overly cautious—the product of a system that favors consensus over conflict, evolution over revolution, and seems to produce Prime Ministers in varying shades of gray.

To be sure, the governing Liberal Democratic Party is especially unpopular in urban areas like Tokyo, where Japan's economic troubles have exacted the highest toll. But if today's opinion sample is any guide, Mr. Obuchi will face an uphill struggle persuading people that his party is not hopelessly out of touch.

"This was an intraparty battle," said Takako Kurihara, a 40-year-old executive at a retail company. "It doesn't reflect the will of the people."

But rather than vent their anger at the Liberal Democrats, people seem resigned to Mr. Obuchi's election as the inevitable consequence of the political process here. Several said they were doubtful that his opponents, Seiroku Kajiyama and Junichiro Koizumi, would have been any more successful in repairing Japan's debt-ridden banks or reviving its listless consumer confidence.

"It's like a garage sale, and it makes no difference whether Obuchi takes

## Many Japanese feel resigned to the new political leader: same as the old boss.

the job, , Kajiyama takes the job, or Koizumi takes the job" said Ms. Kurihara, borrowing a metaphor from Makiko Tanaka, an independent-minded Liberal Democratic legislator who was expressing her frustration with the election.

Mr. Obuchi conceded he was not the people's choice. In a victory speech on Friday that sounded almost like an apology, Mr. Obuchi said he recognized he was "inferior" to the other candidates in popularity, and he pledged to travel the country in an campaign to buff his image and win public support.

"I know well now that popularity among the people and popularity in the party should match each other," Mr. Obuchi said.

But with Japan in an economic quagmire, people may not be patient enough to listen. Some said they were already looking past Mr. Obuchi to the general election, which is set for September of next year. In that race, for control of the lower house of Parliament, the Liberal Democrats have only a slim majority, and a coalition of opposing parties could conceivably sweep them from power.

"This was predictable, but there will be a general election next year and Obuchi will be gone," said Mr. Ichihara matter-of-factly.

Of the potential alternatives to Mr. Obuchi, the leader of the Democratic Party of Japan, Naoto Kan, seemed the most attractive to people today. Mr. Kan had proposed a $43 billion tax cut and the disclosure of Japan's bad bank loans as a remedy for Japan's economic ills. But more than his message, people seem drawn to his fresh image—a vivid contrast to Mr. Obuchi's familiar persona.

"I don't care who takes over this week because I'm supporting the Democrats," said Satoko Ikeda, 21, who is studying textile manufacturing

at a technical college in Tokyo. "Maybe they can make a difference."

Ms. Ikeda is in her final year of studies, and with graduation looming, she said she was having trouble finding work. "In the present economic environment, it is hard to find a job, particularly for women," she said.

Not everybody dismisses Mr. Obuchi, but even those who were satisfied by his election offered only faint praise. "I don't think he's a bad man," said David Moriya, 47, who installs plate-glass windows in office buildings. "No matter who our Prime Minister is, we have to trust him."

And some people believe that one or the other of Mr. Obuchi's challengers could have made an effective leader. Mr. Nakamura, the psychology student, said he was disappointed that Jonichiro Koizumi, the Minister of Health and Welfare, did not win. Mr. Nakamura said he was impressed that Mr. Koizumi presented Japan's economic problems in a straightforward manner.

But after a week in which Mr. Obuchi and his challengers held several debates about the future of the country—culminating in a first-ever televised vote count for the party leadership—the overriding impression here is that people are exhausted by politics and deeply pessimistic that any leader can turn things around.

"I have watched so many Prime Ministers," said a 73-year-old man, as he stooped to pluck weeds from a gravel walkway near the Imperial Palace. "Hashimoto tried and he couldn't fix things. The guy before him tried and he couldn't fix things."

"I don't think anybody can fix the economy," said the man, who declined to give his name because, he said, he was a government worker.

His pessimism was shared by Kyoko Okano, 71, who was walking nearby. Mrs. Okano, who was wearing a traditional kimono and instructs young men and woman on the art of the Japanese tea ceremony, said she believed it was the duty of her generation to impart solid values to young Japanese.

And what did she make of the 61-year-old Mr. Obuchi? "He is like all the others, and they are not strong enough to teach things to young people."

Kanagawa prefecture. He said he had voted for Seiroku Kajiyama, one of Mr. Obuchi's challengers.

In particular city dwellers, who have never been big supporters of the Liberal Democrats, are angry. That was obvious in the upper house elections on July 12, when the party did not win a single seat in an urban area and thus lost its majority.

And since the recession has bitten harder in the conservative rural areas that are traditionally party strongholds, those voters are not feeling as friendly as they otherwise might.

"It doesn't matter whether they're from urban areas or the country, it's all Japan saying that Obuchi is the wrong choice," said Nobutero Ishihara, whose district is in central Tokyo and who supported Junichiro Koizumi, the crusading Health and Welfare Minister, in the party contest. "Unless the party un-derstands that, I don't think the L.D.P. has a future."

Mr. Ishihara left his faction before the election, even though the faction was supporting his candidate, because, he said, his constituents do not like factional politics.

Now, he and other younger legislators are wondering whether their party affiliation is going to become a liability. About 20 junior party members representing urban districts threatened to leave the party on Friday should Mr. Obuchi win, although his strong victory has made them think twice.

"I'm going back and forth, I don't know what I'll do," said Shinichiro Kurimoto, a supporter of Mr. Koizumi, who was wildly popular with the public but received the fewest votes on Friday. "As only one person, I can't make a difference, but if I had 12 friends, we could all make a difference."

The party's grip on power relies on a 13-seat majority in the lower house of the legislature, and were elections held any time soon, it would almost certainly lose its control. The lower house election is scheduled for September 1999, although the opposition, hoping to seize the moment, is pushing for an immediate dissolution of the legislature.

That is not likely, since most junior party members are terrified of an early election and would almost certainly stay in the party long enough to guarantee its ability to squelch a no-confidence vote.

But some members are even worrying about their prospects a year from now. "If the party cannot resurrect the economy, if there isn't a recovery," said Hakubun Shimomura, a junior legislator from Tokyo, "some people who are L.D.P. members now won't run as L.D.P. members in the next general election."

"The severe international repercussions of Japan's continued political procrastination have . . . generated intense pressures that will make it much more difficult for Japan's political leaders to remain at a standstill. . . . If [they] do not move Japan along a new path, others will surely emerge to lead the way."

# Japan's Search for a New Path

### T. J. PEMPEL

**W**hen you get to a fork in the road, take it!" Yogi Berra's advice would seem to be especially apt for a Japan suffering from an apparently relentless recession and political paralysis. But for the Japanese standing at the fork, the unanswered question is, "Which one?" Adherents of Anglo-American market approaches naturally see the choice as self-evident: the road that leads to stricter market rationality, reduced financial regulation, enhanced transparency, heightened sensitivity to the costs of capital and shareholder return, fewer cartels, and more vigorous corporate competition.

Having long trod a very different path and anxious to avoid the social disruption of further bankruptcies and unemployment, Japanese leaders have resisted moving along such an AngloAmerican road. Episodically, a few political and business groups have suggested alternative routes. Yet neither the Japanese government nor Japanese business has shifted with conviction in a new direction. Instead, most remain seemingly stumped by the question, "Which road?"

The magnitude of Japan's current problems undoubtedly complicates the decision making: the worst recession of the postwar era; stock market indices at their lowest point in 12 years; land prices 60 percent below those of a decade ago; the financial sector burdened by at least $1 trillion in bad loans; national economic growth essentially stagnant for eight years; bankruptcies and corporate failures at postwar highs for small and medium-sized firms (and increasingly toppling major financial corporations); seriously underfunded pension funds; industrial production roughly the same as it was in 1990; upward of 2 million manufacturing jobs lost in this decade; official

unemployment at the highest levels in four decades; annual debt service sucking up 18.6 percent of the government budget; and cumulative debt at over 100 percent of GNP. Action is certainly needed, but there is little consensus on how to address such a mountain of problems. Still, most outside observers remain perplexed: "What," they wonder, "is taking so long for action—of any sort?"

Until the summer of 1997, Japan's economic meltdown had been essentially national in scope. The sequence of rapid-fire financial crises in Thailand, South Korea, Malaysia, and Indonesia, however, suddenly wove Japan's problems into a region-wide epidemic while the summer 1998 financial crisis in Russia, Ukraine, and Brazil heightened the fear that Japan's continued inaction could trigger a global meltdown. Typical was the IMF's criticism in September 1998 that the main risk to the world economy was Japan's failure to "address its financial-sector problems while ensuring adequate domestic demand." Certainly, the expectations of the late 1980s that Japan would play a leading regional or global political role have diminished with the country's ebbing economic prowess.

The number of difficult choices complicates Japan's current situation, but present problems and the hesitancy in dealing with them are rooted in much deeper structural predicaments. Most analysis of Japan's economic troubles has concentrated on the magnitude of the problems and on possible ways to resolve them. Missing has been a serious examination of the inaction of Japan's leaders; surely it is not because of lack of intelligence, resources, or suggestions for action.

Japan's difficulties in committing to a new course of action are instead the result of the fundamental regime shift the country is undergoing. The interconnected structure of institutions, norms, alliances, and policies that shaped the Japanese political economy from the 1950s through the 1980s is no longer working as smoothly as it once did; indeed, it is rapidly coming unglued. Yet replacement institutions, norms, alliances, and policies have yet to gain sufficient acceptance to supersede

T. J. PEMPEL *is Boeing Professor of International Studies at the University of Washington. His latest book,* Regime Shift: Comparative Dynamics of the Japanese Political Economy, *was published in November by Cornell University Press.*

those of the past. Until this happens, Japan will find it increasingly difficult to move beyond the current crossroads, where its leaders now stand immobilized, and stride confidently in some pathbreaking new direction.

## THE ANCIEN RÉGIME

The main features of Japan's old regime are familiar. The conservative and pro-American Liberal Democratic Party (LDP), with its peculiar socioeconomic support base fusing both big and small business as well as organized agriculture, enjoyed an unparalleled 38 years of electoral and government dominance. The Liberal Democrats faced only a splintered collection of opposition parties, the largest of which was the committedly Marxian, anti-American, labor-based Japan Socialist Party (JSP, later the Social Democratic Party of Japan). Bureaucratic agencies enjoyed extensive regulatory powers over most spheres of public life, including the economic.

Most (though not all) sectors of the Japanese economy enjoyed insulation from foreign investment and import competition. A relatively small number of huge conglomerates (*keiretsu*) dominated the domestic economy. A web of formal and informal mechanisms linked scores of large corporations in different economic sectors to one another and to layers of subcontractors, distributors, and middlemen. Most larger companies relied on a core of (male) workers whose jobs were relatively secure and whose social welfare benefits and pay were closely tied to corporate profitability.

*Japan's political and bureaucratic world continues to resist restructuring the economy in deep, fundamental ways.*

Conservative politics and cartelized, protectionist economics reinforced one another. From the early 1970s onward, a number of Japanese companies in consumer electronics, automobiles, and machinery gained sufficient international strength to generate highly positive trade balances for Japan. At the same time, improvements in manufacturing productivity, GNP, and living standards were typically double those of the rich democracies of North America and Western Europe, while social welfare and defense expenditures remained vastly lower. Yet low social welfare spending did not prevent an overall economic equality that made Japan more like the Scandinavian social democracies than any other nominally conservative country.

The greatest virtue of the postwar Japanese system was its capacity to fuse corporate dynamism and rapid growth with social stability and high levels of equality. Japan more than matched the economic dynamism of Anglo-American capitalism yet spared most firms' workers the often high human costs of Anglo-American adjustment. At the same time, the Japanese system replicated much of the social cohesiveness of the continental European countries without their concomitantly burgeoning taxes and government budgets.

From the 1950s into the mid-1970s, the LDP and the economic ministries, most notably the Ministry of Finance and the Ministry of International Trade and Industry, cooperated to generate fiscal, monetary, and industrial policies that restructured the national economy and enhanced Japan's international competitiveness. Pork, protection, and privilege were hardly absent but they remained primarily subthemes unable to overwhelm the broader symphonic focus on rapid economic growth.

Ironically, the very longevity and adaptability of this Japanese system contributed heavily to the country's current problems and the procrastination in solving them. In the past, marginal tinkerings typically enabled leaders to cope with most problems without challenging the underlying regime. Consequently, by the late 1980s and early 1990s, many parts of the system had developed tenacious institutional roots that made them extremely effective in resisting any adjustments that threatened their entrenched powers.

Simply stated, Japan's crisis can be traced to two related developments. First, some Japanese companies adjusted successfully to Japan's growing profitability and to changing world market conditions but far more did not. Second, Japanese politics was slow to reflect the changes generated by Japan's overall economic success and international power position.

National economic success, however, masked both trends. In corporate terms, Japan increasingly became two disconnected economies. As companies such as Toyota, Honda, Canon, Matsushita, Hitachi, and Sony catapulted to international market leadership, far more firms in cartelized and protected sectors such as cement, power generation, food services, construction, banking, brokerage, and insurance, devoid of the rejuvenating rigors of international competition, continued to depend for their profitability on government regulation, domestic capital, and home markets. Increasingly, firms in these latter sectors came to rely on politicians who, in exchange for increased votes and campaign contributions, provided various forms of assistance, including exceptions to complex economic regulations. The consequent high costs, obviously, were borne by consumers and intermediate corporate or individual users. But rapid national growth and continued jumps in living standards muted most complaints.

Economic growth simultaneously induced dramatic demographic changes. The proportion of the population dependent on farming and small business shrank from 50 percent in 1946–1948 to below 6 percent today, and birth rates fell and life expectancy rose, leaving Japan with fewer young workers and more elderly retirees. Living standards also improved, and three-quarters of the population became urbanized. Combined, these trends reshaped Japanese society—making most Japanese middle class, middle-aged, urban, and salaried.

International conditions also changed considerably. During the height of the cold war, the strategic and foreign policy goals of the United States gave Japanese exporters access to the American market without requiring Japan to open its home market or expand its military role. Only in the late 1970s and early 1980s did United States concerns about jobs and competitiveness lead American officials to make serious demands for enhanced access to Japanese markets.

By the late 1980s and early 1990s, Japanese institutions found it increasingly difficult to deliver their earlier blend of dynamism and equality. Despite the myriad corporate, socioeconomic, and international changes occurring at home and in Japan's external environment, key Japanese political and economic institutions that had once been the crucibles of creative adjustment now inhibited flexibility, dynamism, and movement in new directions. These rigidities stymied the critical process that Joseph Schumpeter long ago identified as "creative destruction."

It was in the 1989 elections for the Diet's upper house that the complex tensions challenging the old regime first climaxed politically. Economically they burst into undeniability with the collapse of the economic bubble a year or so later.

## THE BUBBLE BURSTS . . .

The Japanese bubble lasted roughly from 1985 to 1990. At least two of its elements are important. First, the Japanese yen had accelerated greatly in value after the 1985 Plaza Accord (the agreement by the United States, Japan, West Germany, France, and Britain to pursue a collective lowering of the dollar's value). In response, the Ministry of Finance, fearing the possible negative effects on Japanese exports and worried about possible electoral retaliation against the LDP if the economy slowed, ordered the Bank of Japan to open the monetary floodgates while the ministry itself injected massive amounts of fresh spending into the economy through fiscal packages and the expanded investment of postal savings funds. Predictably, as the prime interest rate was lowered to a postwar low of 2.5 percent, asset markets in both stocks and land jetted upward.

Second, the rising yen and a liberalization of Japanese capital markets eroded prior linkages between major manufacturing firms and financial institutions. Many Japanese-owned firms developed production (and capital-raising) operations overseas while others began financing their activities through bonds and foreign capital markets. Cut off from their normal sources of income (highly competitive corporate borrowers) and yet flush with cheap capital, Japanese financial institutions began lending money to ever more dubious borrowers and providing less and less oversight. Smaller subsidiaries, fiscally marginal firms, land speculators, real estate companies, nonbank financial intermediaries, politicians, and members of organized crime families were among those who suddenly found bank loans thrust their way. Stock and real estate speculations became prime uses for the new easy money and the prices for both ratcheted steadily skyward.

In short, the late 1980s witnessed a massive increase in the value of assets such as stocks and land and the rising paper value of these assets then became collateral in a growing spiral of borrowing and speculation. Previously cautious firms engaged in more dubious financial speculations. Wider socioeconomic gaps opened between those who owned stocks or land and those who did not. Yet these and other underlying divergences in Japan's economy remained concealed behind the overweening triumphalism that surrounded the country's apparently unstoppable prosperity and its "new economic model." Unseen by most was the fragility of this new model. Instead, seduced by the visions of unstoppable profitability and a giddy citizenry, neither the banks, the bureaucrats, nor the LDP were anxious to apply the brakes. Like Icarus, the Japanese economy soared ever closer to the sun, lofted by a self-congratulatory euphoria.

When Bank of Japan Governor Mieno finally punctured the bubble with a sharp rise in the national discount rate in 1989–1990, asset prices collapsed dramatically, setting off what proved to be a decade of downward spiraling economics that culminated in today's recession. As stock and land prices plummeted, the collateral underlying the riskiest loans evaporated, leaving banks and financial institutions with trillions of yen in unrecoverable debt. As banks tried to call in loans, borrowers sold stock, land, and other assets, triggering further downward spirals. Public exposure of imprudent investments and corruption by brokerages led to their loss of both clients and profitability. By the mid-1990s, it was clear that Japan was in the midst of a structural financial crisis and a mounting liquidity shortage. For virtually the entire decade, political, financial, and bureaucratic officials who attempted to "solve" these problems did so wearing the institutional and policy blinders of the old regime. Not surprisingly, they usually found each effort stymied by new revelations about how much more the economic cancer had metastasized.

Political tensions rose in parallel to the economic downturn, reflecting the widening differences in economic interests. The LDP had long avoided serious internal divisions over economics by successfully accommodating a heterogeneous alliance that bridged the gap between Japan's most and least productive sectors. That alliance held together largely because the exceptional economic successes of the former allowed for politically brokered side payments to the latter. Thus, the high annual growth rates catalyzed by export successes in manufacturing provided government revenues to support not only high-tech research and development programs but also extensive subsidies for agriculture and the underwriting of expensive public utilities and transportation. Rising personal incomes meant greater total tax revenue for government coffers, effectively underpinning costly loans to small businesses and expensive public construction projects. As long as high growth continued and pressures for deregulation and decartelization were weak, the LDP's economically irrational alliance retained its political viability. Conservative politicians remained insulated from making harsh policy choices that systematically favored one group at the expense of the other.

## . . . WITHOUT THE POLITICAL HISS

By the late 1980s, the underlying policy tensions between Japan's internationally competitive and noncompetitive sectors had become politically inescapable. Largely in response to foreign pressures, but also in an effort to enhance its electoral appeal among urban residents, the LDP, in the middle and late 1980s, began to liberalize the market for agricultural goods, including beef, citrus fruits, and—albeit tentatively—rice. In late 1988, a government advisory committee also proposed revisions in laws that had long protected small shopkeepers from competitive superstores. In 1989, the government introduced a 3 percent consumption tax that made it tough for small shopkeepers and farmers to evade taxes. Meanwhile the nation's major business federation, Keidanren, cut off its previously automatic funding to the LDP, thereby expressing its own frustration with LDP economic policies. The cumulative result was an anti-LDP revolt by some of the party's core supporters; indeed the National Association of Agricultural Cooperatives seriously considered abandoning the LDP and forming a Farmers' Party. In the upper house election of 1989, voter preferences by farmers and small business owners shifted more than in any previous election. For the first time since its formation in 1955, the LDP no longer enjoyed control of both houses of parliament.

During this period the LDP was also rocked by a host of political scandals linked largely to the kinds of corporate bribery for regulatory exceptions previously noted. It became increasingly evident that the party could no longer guarantee the Japanese people a strong economy, nor could it ensure a successful electoral career for aspiring young conservatives. Party members divided over how best to adjust economically and institutionally. Beginning in 1993, the LDP went through a sequence of splits, with many younger, more urban, and reformist LDP members leaving, ultimately depriving the party of its majority in the lower House of Representatives as well.

Since the 1993 LDP split, Japan's party system has gone through a whirlwind of combinations and recombinations so that it now bears little resemblance to the party system of 1965 to 1985. Only the LDP and the Japan Communist Party (JCP) retain their earlier labels, and the LDP has a much narrower economic base than before. No longer is there a political party of organized labor, or any party hostile to continued United States security ties with Japan (except for the JCP, although it has agreed to "suspend" its prior opposition). Instead, a flurry of small new parties bid for various slices of urban, consumerist, pacifist, and other voter blocs.

But these party recombinations still have not led to any division reflective of the growing dualism in the economy or affording clear choices about Japan's future economic direction. There have been several false starts toward such a division, however. For example, the eight-party coalition government that replaced the LDP in 1993 made vague promises of internationalization and more economic openness and pro-urban policies, but it lacked a cohesive policy agenda. Prime Minister Hosokawa Morihiro did force through an important new electoral system, but, implicated in a financial scandal,

he resigned after only eight months in office, thus ending one possible mustering of energy to pursue a new economic direction.

Simultaneously, Ozawa Ichiro led a breakaway group that promised, among other things, a less protected and more open economy. This group eventually crystallized as the New Frontier Party (NFP). It gained allies within many government agencies. As an August 1996 survey of parliamentarians in the Japanese journal *Bungei Shunjû* showed, the NFP served as a temporary rallying point for parliamentary deregulators and internationalists while the LDP's members disproportionately favored continued regulation and protection. The NFP also proved to be short-lived, leaving antiprotectionist and deregulatory forces to go through another round of fragmentation and recoherence.

By 1996, the LDP had regained a majority in the lower house and controlled a noncoalition cabinet under Prime Minister Hashimoto Ryutaro. But by then the party had moved further away from its prior "catch-all" quality toward increased support for core protected constituents, despite efforts by some of its backbenchers to reduce such dependency and embrace new constituencies linked to more market-compatible economics. Tensions within the LDP were evident in the Hashimoto government's inability to generate any effective and consistent economic policy. Instead, it seesawed between fiscal stimulation based on public works, construction, and rural assistance, and fiscal tightness and a rise in the consumption tax. At one time it hinted that it would allow troubled financial institutions to fail but just as quickly it shifted to the virtually unlimited use of public funds to prevent such failures.

Electoral frustration with the Hashimoto government's lack of direction crystallized in the upper house elections of July 1998. Voter turnout jumped from 44.5 percent in the 1995 elections to 58.8 percent. The LDP won only 44 of 126 seats, none of which came from Japan's largest cities. The major victors were the Democratic Party of Japan (DPJ), the JCP, and independents.

After the election, the opposition mobilized around DPJ leader Kan Naoto, forcing a sequence of compromises to the LDP's proposed plans for financial reform, the essence of which involves restricting the use of public monies to bail out failing banks; a temporary nationalization of the insolvent Long-Term Credit Bank; no bailout for over-loaned agricultural co-ops; and hints of a reduction in the Ministry of Finance's regulatory powers. Tellingly, the opposition was joined in its efforts by many younger members of the LDP, such as Shiozaki Yasuhisa, Ishihara Nobuteru, and Nemoto Takumi, hinting at the LDP's internal divisions over future economic directions.

The ability of an upper house opposition to force compromises onto a reluctant LDP should be neither under- nor overestimated. Indeed, by late October 1998 the LDP had split the opposition by cutting deals with several of the opposition parties and passing a less transparent $500 billion bank bailout that isolated the formerly pivotal DPJ. To date, a new electoral system, party reorganization, and business and voter frustrations have not generated a political party with sufficient muscle and cohesion to provide a viable alternative to the LDP. Nor have the LDP and the bureaucratic elite been sufficiently threatened to abandon the long-standing roots of their own power. As a result, Japan's political and bureaucratic world continues to resist restructuring the economy in deep, fundamental ways.

## THE REALITIES OF ECONOMIC CHANGE

Despite the current political gridlock, economic changes have gained momentum. For example, the keiretsu are no longer as monolithic or as integrated as before. The main banks are losing their roles as the principal providers of capital to large firms, while keiretsu cross-holding of stocks has diminished. The debt-to-equity ratio of new borrowings for Japanese firms was nearly 90 percent in 1965; by 1995, this had fallen to 69.4. Bond issues, reliance on equity, foreign borrowing, and the like have correspondingly increased, especially for firms manufacturing internationally tradable goods. Meanwhile, as late as 1987, approximately 72 percent of the Tokyo Stock Exchange capitalization involved cross-holdings of shares by related companies. By 1996, this had fallen to 60 percent, and it was dropping at the rate of about 4 percent per year.

*Japan is in the midst of a struggle over how to move beyond the arrangements that served it so well for more than 30 years.*

Also sharply diminished has been Japan's previously single-minded orientation toward the manufacture and export of industrial goods. By the 1990s, large numbers of Japanese-owned manufacturing firms had moved their activities away from production in and export from Japan to embrace far more global production and investment strategies. Symbolically, by 1995, Japanese-owned firms were manufacturing more overseas than they exported from the home islands.

As a result, previously tight connections between large Japanese firms and their subcontractors and distributors have been loosened, reliance on part-time and contract workers has risen, and the job security of many long-term employees has decreased. In short, numerous pillars of Japan's old economic structures are eroding.

Nowhere is this erosion more important than in the increased penetration of the Japanese market by foreign firms. This has occurred in areas from food service and catalog sales to computers, telecommunications, and pharmaceuticals; most recently it has begun to include the once sacrosanct "commanding heights" of Japanese capitalism. Recent financial alliances involving Nippon Credit and Bankers Trust, Nikko Securities and Smith Barney, Merrill Lynch and Yamaiichi, GE Capital and Toho Mutual Life Insurance, Meiji Life and Dresdner Bank, and Nikko Securities and Travelers Group have typically involved Western partners with clear product and technological advantages over their Japanese counterparts. Not only have Western firms gained quick access to the previously restricted Japanese market, but their corporate practices are likely to exert substantial influences over their partners and the fields that they enter.

Western investors have also been gobbling up properties and property-related loans as quickly as Japanese banks can bundle them into attractive packages for sale. Western investors, such as Goldman Sachs, Morgan Stanley, GE Capital, and others have thereby been able to tap quickly into the Japanese real-estate market. The June 1, 1998, *Nikkei Weekly* estimated that in the 12 months prior to March 1998, some 30 property-related loan packages with a face value of $21.6 billion were bought by Western investors, at an average price of about 10 cents to the dollar.

Although Japan remains the industrialized country with the lowest per capita foreign direct investment, the centrality of these foreign firms with wildly different performance standards is beginning to force serious changes across a range of existing Japanese practices, including employment, stock options, performance-linked salaries, pricing, flexible commissions, higher rates of return, 24-hour ATMs, derivative products, and the cost of gasoline. Pressures will continue to mount for changes in many of Japan's long-standing but economically inefficient practices.

## THE CHALLENGE

Japan is in the midst of a struggle over how to move beyond the arrangements that served it so well for more than 30 years but are now proving incapable of delivering the previous mix of economic dynamism and social egalitarianism. The battle is being played out most acutely along the fault line between the strikingly different economic interests of its least dynamic and most protected sectors, most of which have strong allies in the political world, and those of its more internationally competitive sectors, which lack the political allies to match their obvious economic clout.

How this struggle will play out remains unclear. For the moment, changes are advancing far more speedily within Japan's economic sphere. The severe international repercussions of Japan's continued political procrastination have, however, generated intense pressures that will make it much more difficult for Japan's political leaders to remain at a standstill. If these politicians hope to avoid squandering the country's regional and international goodwill and retain or reestablish Japan's social cohesion, they will have to move quickly onto a path that embraces new institutions, new socioeconomic partnerships, and new public policies. They must do nothing less than oversee the creation of a new regime. Failure to do so will not make the problems disappear. The economic and international pressures for change have become sufficiently strong that the very ground beneath Japan's leadership is shifting. If its current leaders do not move Japan along a new path, others will surely emerge to lead the way.

# Unit 2

## Unit Selections

Political Ideas, Movements, Parties

18. **Europe: A Continental Drift—to the Left,** *The Economist*
19. **Europe's Right: Displaced, Defeated and Not Sure What to Do Next,** *The Economist*

Women and Politics

20. **Women in Power: From Tokenism to Critical Mass,** Jane S. Jaquette

The Institutional Framework of Representative Government

21. **What Democracy Is . . . and Is Not,** Philippe C. Schmitter and Terry Lynn Karl
22. **Devolution Can Be Salvation,** *The Economist*
23. **Parliament and Congress: Is the Grass Greener on the Other Side?** Gregory S. Mahler
24. **Campaign and Party Finance: What Americans Might Learn from Abroad,** Arthur B. Gunlicks

## Key Points to Consider

❖ How do you explain the apparent shifts toward the political center made by parties of the moderate Left and moderate Right in recent years? Discuss the recent trend toward governments of the moderate Left in Western Europe. How do Social Democrats present themselves as reformers of capitalism? What are the main sources of electoral support for the far-right political parties?

❖ Why are women so poorly represented in Parliament and other positions of political leadership? In what way is this beginning to change? How do institutional arrangements, such as electoral systems, sometimes help or hinder an improvement in this situation? Which parties and which countries tend to have a better record of female representation?

❖ Would you agree with the inventory of democratic essentials as discussed by Schmitter and Karl? What do you regard as most and least important in their inventory? What are some of the major arguments made in favor of the parliamentary system of government?

❖ What, if anything, do you think the United States could learn from the manner in which other democracies handle campaign and party finance?

DUSHKIN ONLINE **Links**  |  **www.dushkin.com/online/**

9. **Carnegie Endowment for International Peace**
   *http://www.ceip.org*
10. **Communications for a Sustainable Future**
    *gopher://csf.colorado.edu*
11. **DiploNet**
    *http://www.clark.net/pub/diplonet/DiploNet.html*
12. **Inter-American Dialogue**
    *http://www.iadialog.org*
13. **The North American Institute**
    *http://www.santafe.edu/~naminet/index.html*

These sites are annotated on pages 6 and 7.

Observers of contemporary Western societies frequently refer to the emergence of a new politics in these countries. They are not always very clear or in agreement about what is supposedly novel in the political process or why it is significant. Although no one would dispute that some major changes have taken place in these societies during the past third of a century, affecting both political attitudes and behavior, it is very difficult to establish clear and comparable patterns of transformation or to gauge their endurance and impact. Yet making sense of continuities and changes in political values and behavior must be one of the central tasks of a comparative study of government.

Since the early 1970s, political scientists have followed Ronald Inglehart and other careful observers who first noted a marked increase in what they called postmaterial values, especially among younger and more highly educated people in the skilled service and administrative occupations in Western Europe. Such voters showed less interest in the traditional material values of economic well-being and security, and instead stressed partici-patory and environmental concerns in politics as a way of improving democracy and the general "quality of life." Studies of post-materialism form a very important addition to our ongoing attempt to interpret and explain not only the so-called youth revolt but also some more lasting shifts in lifestyles and political priorities. It makes intuitive sense that such changes appear to be especially marked among those who grew up in the relative prosperity of Western Europe, after the austere period of reconstruction that followed World War II. In more recent years, however, there appears to have been a revival of material concerns among younger people, as economic prosperity and security seem to have become less certain. There are also some indications that political reform activities evoke less interest and commitment than they did earlier.

None of this should be mistaken for a return to the political patterns of the past. Instead, we may be witnessing the emergence of a still somewhat incongruent new mix of material and post-material orientations, along with "old" and "new" forms of political self-expression by the citizenry. Established political parties appear to be in somewhat of a quandary in redefining their positions, at a time when the traditional bonding of many voters to one or another party seems to have become weaker. Many observers speak about a widespread condition of political malaise in advanced industrial countries, suggesting that it shows up not only in opinion polls but also in a marked decline in voter participation and, on occasion, a propensity for voter revolt against the establishment parties and candidates. Without suggesting a simple cause-effect relationship, the British observer Martin Jacques has pointed to connections between electoral malaise or dealignment and the vague rhetoric offered by many political activists and opinion leaders. He believes that the end of the cold war and the collapse of communism in Europe have created a situation that demands a reformulation of political and ideological alternatives. In that sense, he finds some paradig-matic significance in the great political shakeup of the Italian party system.

At this point, at least, it seems unlikely that Italy will set an example for many other democracies. Most established parties seem to have developed an ability to adjust to change, even as the balance of power within each party system shifts over time and occasional newcomers are admitted to the club. Each country's party system remains uniquely shaped by its political history, but there does seem to be some very general patterns of development. One frequently observed trend is toward a narrowing of the ideological distance between the moderate Left and Right in many European countries. It now often makes more sense to speak of the Center-Left and Center-Right, respectively.

Despite such convergence, there are still some important ideological and practical differences between the two orientations. Thus the *Right* is usually far more ready to accept as "inevitable" the existence of social or economic inequalities, along with the hierarchies they produce. It normally favors lower taxes and the promotion of market forces—with some very important exceptions intended to protect the nation as a whole (national defense) as well as certain favorite groups and values within it. In general, the Right sees the state as an instrument that should provide security, order, and protection of an established way of life. The *Left*, by contrast, emphasizes that government has an important task in promoting opportunities, delivering services, and reducing social inequities. On issues such as higher and more progressive taxation, or their respective concern for high rates of unemployment and inflation, there continue to be considerable differences between moderates of the Left and Right.

Even as the ideological distance between Left and Right narrows but remains important, there are also signs of some political differentiation within each camp. On the Center-Right side of the party spectrum in European politics, economic *neoliberals* (who speak for business and industry) must be clearly distinguished from the *social conservatives* (who are more likely to advocate traditional values and authority). European liberalism has its roots in a tradition that favors civil liberties and tolerance but that also emphasizes the importance of individual achievement and laissez-faire economics. For such European neoliberals, the state has an important but very limited role to play in providing an institutional framework within which individuals and social groups pursue their interests. Traditional conservatives, by contrast, emphasize the importance of social stability and continuity, and point to the social danger of disruptive change. They often value the strong state as an instrument of order, but many of them also show a paternalist appreciation for welfare state programs that will help keep "the social net" from tearing apart.

In British politics, Margaret Thatcher promoted elements from each of these traditions in what could be called her own mix of "business conservatism." The result is the peculiar tension between "drys" and "wets" within her own Conservative Party, even after she ceased to be its leader. In France, on the other hand, the division between neoliberals and conservatives has run more clearly between the two major Center-Right parties, the very loosely united Giscardist UDF, and the seemingly more stable neo-Gaullist RPR, who have been coalition partners in several recent governments (until 1997). In Germany, the Free Democrats would most clearly represent the traditional liberal position, while some conservative elements can be found among the Christian Democrats.

There is something of a split identity also among the Christian Democrats, who until recently were one of the most successful political movements in Europe after World War II. Here idealists, who subscribe to the socially compassionate teachings of the Church, have found themselves losing influence to more efficiency-oriented technocrats or success-oriented political managers. The latter seem to reflect little of the original ideals of personalism, solidarity, and subsidiarity that originally distinguished the Christian Democrats from both neoliberals and conservatives in post-war Europe. It remains to be seen whether political setbacks for the Christian Democrats in Italy will lead to more than a facelift. Their new name of Popular Party seems unintentionally self-ironic and has done little, if anything, to stem their recent electoral losses. In Germany, however, the Christian Democrats managed to remain the chancellor party for very long periods before their major setback in the Bundestag election of 1998.

On the Left, democratic socialists and ecologists stress that the sorry political, economic, and environmental record of Communist-ruled states in no way diminishes the validity of their own commitment to social justice and environmental protection in modern industrial society. For them, capitalism will continue to produce its own social problems and dissatisfactions. No matter how efficient capitalism may be, they argue, it will continue to result in inequities that require politically directed redress. Many on the Left, however, show a pragmatic acceptance of the modified market economy as an arena within which to promote their reformist goals. Social Democrats in Scandinavia and Germany have long been known for taking such positions. In recent years their colleagues in Britain and, to a lesser degree, France have followed suit by abandoning some traditional symbols and goals, such as major programs of nationalization. The Socialists in Spain, who governed that new democracy after 1982, went furthest of all in adopting some very business-friendly policies before their loss of power in early 1996.

Some other Western European parties further to the left have also moved in the centrist direction in recent years. Two striking examples of this shift can be found among the Greens in Germany and in what used to be the Communist Party of Italy. The Greens are by no means an establishment party, but they have served as a pragmatic coalition partner with the Social Democrats in several state governments and have gained respect for their mixture of practical competence and idealism. Their so-called realist faction (*Realos*) appears to have outmaneuvered its more radical rivals in the party's so-called fundamentalist (or *Fundi*) wing. Despite some loss in voter support, which can be explained by a revival of the party's internal divisions over strategy and goals, the Greens were finally able to enter government at the national level in 1998. In Gerhard Schröder's government of Social Democrats and Greens, the leading "realo" Joschka Fischer is foreign minister and two other cabinet posts are held by fellow environmentalists. The Italian Communists have come even further toward a center-left position. Many years before they adopted the new name of Democratic Party of the Left (PDS), in 1991, they had abandoned the Leninist revolutionary tradition and adopted reformist politics similar to those of social democratic parties elsewhere in Western Europe. Not every Italian Communist went along, and a fundamentalist core broke away to set up a new far-left party of Refounded Communists. In 1998, however, the post-Communists fully joined the establishment they had once fought, when PDS leader Massimo D'Alema became Italy's new prime minister, heading an unusually broad coalition of several parties.

Both Center-Left and Center-Right moderates face a dual challenge from the populists on the Right, who often seek lower taxes and drastic cuts in the social budget as well as a curtailment of immigration, and the neo-fascists on the ultra-Right. These two orientations on the Right can often be distinguished, as in Italy where the populist Northern League and the neofascist-descended National Alliance represent positions that are polar opposites on such key issues as government devolution (favored by the former, opposed by the latter). Sometimes a charismatic leader can speak to both orientations, by appealing to their shared fears and resentments. That seems to be the case of Jsrg Haider, whose Freedom Party has managed at times to attract over one-quarter of the vote in Austria. The electoral revival of the right-wing parties can be linked in considerable part to the anxieties and tensions that affect some socially and economically insecure groups in the lower middle class and some sectors of the working class.

Ultra-Right nationalist politicians and their parties typically eschew a complex explanation of the structural and cyclical problems that beset the European economies. Instead, their simple answer blames external scapegoats, namely the many immigrants and refugees from Eastern Europe as well as developing world countries in northern Africa and elsewhere. The presence of the far-Right parties inevitably has an effect on both the balance of power and the political agendas that occupy the more centrist parties. Almost everywhere, for example, some of the established parties and politicians have been making symbolic concessions on the refugee issue, in order to prevent it from becoming monopolized by extremists.

*Women in politics* is the concern of the second section in this unit. There continues to be a strong pattern of underrepresentation of women in positions of political and economic leadership practically everywhere. Yet there are some notable differences from country to country, as well as from party to party. Generally speaking, the parties of the Left have been readier to place women in positions of authority, although there are some remarkable exceptions, as the Center-Right cases of Margaret Thatcher in Britain and Simone Weil in France illustrate.

On the whole, the system of proportional representation gives parties both a tool and an added incentive to place female candidates in positions where they will be elected. But here too, there can be exceptions, as in the case of France in 1986 when women did not benefit from the one-time use of proportional representation in the parliamentary elections. Clearly it is not enough to have a relatively simple means, such as proportional representation, for promoting women in politics: there must also be an organized will among decision makers to use the available tool for the purpose of such a clearly defined reform.

This is where a policy of affirmative action may become chosen as a strategy. The Scandinavian countries illustrate better than any other example how the breakthrough may occur. There is a markedly higher representation of women in the parliaments of Denmark, Finland, Iceland, Norway, and Sweden, where the political center of gravity is somewhat to the left and where proportional representation makes it possible to set up party lists that are more representative of the population as a whole. It is of some interest that Iceland has a special women's party with parliamentary representation, but it is far more important that women are found in leading positions within most of the parties of this and the other Scandinavian countries. It usually does not take long for the more centrist or moderately conservative parties to adopt the new concern of gender equality, and they may even move to the forefront. Thus women have recently held the leadership of three of the main parties in Norway (the Social Democrats, the Center Party, and the Conservatives), which together normally receive roughly two-thirds of the total popular vote. It is worth pointing out that in contrast to Margaret Thatcher, who included no women in her cabinet between 1979 and 1990, Norway's first female prime minister, Dr. Gro Harlem Brundtland, used that position to advance the number of women in ministerial positions (8 of 18 cabinet posts). The present Swedish government of Social Democrats has an equal number of women and men in the cabinet.

In another widely reported sign of change, the relatively conservative Republic of Ireland several years ago chose Mary Robinson as its first female president. It is a largely ceremonial post, but it had a symbolic potential that Mary Robinson, an outspoken advocate of liberal reform in her country, was willing to use on behalf of social change. In 1998, a second woman president was elected in Ireland. Perhaps most remarkable of all, the advancement of women into high political ranks has now also touched Switzerland, where women did not get the right to vote until 1971.

Altogether, there is undoubtedly a growing awareness of the pattern of gender discrimination in most Western countries. It seems likely that there will be a significant improvement in this situation over the course of the next decade if the pressure for reform is maintained. Such changes have already occurred in other areas, where there used to be significant political differences between men and women. At one time, for example, there used to be a considerably lower voter turnout among women, but this gender gap has been practically eliminated in recent decades. Similarly, the tendency for women to be somewhat more conservative in party and candidate preferences has given way to a more liberal disposition among younger women in foreign and social policy preferences than among their male counterparts. These are aggregate differences, of course, and it is important to remember that women, like men, do not represent a monolithic bloc in political attitudes and behavior but are divided by other interests and priorities. One generalization seems to hold, namely, that there is much less inclination among women to support parties or candidates that have a decidedly "radical" image. Thus the vote for extreme right-wing parties in contemporary Europe tends to be considerably higher among male voters.

In any case, there are some very important policy questions that affect women more directly than men. Any statistical study of women in the paid labor force of Europe could supply conclusive evidence to support three widely shared impressions: (1) There has been a considerable increase in the number and relative proportion of women who take on paid jobs; (2) These jobs are more often unskilled and/or part-time than in the case of men's employment; and (3) Women generally receive less pay and less social protection than men in similar positions. Such a study would also show that there are considerable differences among Western European countries in the relative position of their female workers, thereby offering support for the argument that political intervention in the form of appropriate legislation *can* do something to improve the employment status of women—not only by training them better for advancement in the labor market but also by changing the conditions of the workplace to eliminate some obvious or hidden disadvantages for women.

The relative socioeconomic status of women in other parts of the world is often far worse.

According to reports of the UN Development Program, there have been some rapid advances for women in the field of education and health opportunities, but the doors to economic opportunities are barely ajar. In the field of political leadership, the picture is more varied, as the UN report indicates, but women generally hold few positions of importance in national politics. To be sure, there have been some remarkable breakthroughs, for example, in South Africa, where women won 100 of the 400 seats in the first post-apartheid parliament in 1994.

*The institutional framework of representative government* is the subject of the third section of this unit. Here the authors examine and compare a number of institutional arrangements: (1) essential characteristics and elements of a pluralist democracy, (2) the trend toward devolution of power in several European countries, (3) two major forms of representative government, and (4) various rules governing campaign and party finance.

The topic of pluralist democracy is a complex one, but Phillipe Schmitter and Terry Lynn Karl manage to present a very comprehensive discussion of the subject in a short space. Gregory Mahler focuses on the legislative- executive relationship of parliamentary and congressional systems, drawing mainly upon the British, Canadian, and American examples. He avoids the trap of idealizing one or the other way of organizing the functions of representative government. Arthur Gunlicks approaches the issue of campaign and party finance from an interesting angle. He asks what Americans might learn from the manner in which this problem is resolved in several other democracies.

# EUROPE

## A continental drift—to the left

### Left-of-centre parties have swept to power across the European Union. But that does not mean they can agree on what they stand for

THIS whole election result has been a tremendous triumph," gushed Tony Blair, Britain's prime minister, after the victory of Gerhard Schröder's Social Democrats in Germany, "for him, and the fact that we have governments in France and Germany and Great Britain and elsewhere who share the same perspective." And, he might have added, in Italy and the Netherlands and Greece and Portugal and Sweden and Luxembourg and Denmark and Finland and Belgium and Austria. For Mr Schröder's election brings to 13 the tally of EU countries where the left either holds power or shares it as a chief party. That means all EU countries bar Ireland, whose main parties defy the poles of left and right, and Spain, where the right squeaked in after 13 years of so-

cialism. This tilt of Europe to the left is startling. Does it matter?

The left certainly believes so. For the first time since 1929, the heads of the big three EU governments—France, Germany and Britain—are of the left, and a left that is flush with the self-confidence of its electoral triumphs. The hope is not only that governments will share ideas, nor just that they might for once pull in the same direction in the EU. It is that, call it what you like—the third way (Blair), democratic socialism (Jospin), the new centre (Schröder)—this marks the rebirth of a modern, fashionable, pan-European centre-left.

Already, the election of leftish governments in Britain and France last year has breathed new life into the left-wing pan-European party net-

work. Not so long ago the meeting-houses for a political faith in despondency, gatherings such as those set up by members of the Party of European Socialists (PES), an umbrella group of socialist and social-democratic parties to which all 13 governing parties belong, have begun to have influence—on the continent at least, if not in more sceptical Britain. So in June Sweden's Social Democrats held a day's round-table, with like-minded Europeans, on jobs. The French Socialist Party holds another, on social matters, on October 3rd. A week later, the Italians will talk education in Bologna. Ministers often turn up. Next month there are six more to digest, not to mention other bilateral party think-ins.

On top of this, leftish ministers in every field get together about four

### A reddish glow
Centre-left governments in the European Union

Left and centre-left parties in bold

| Country | Main governing party | % cabinet posts | Head of government (party if not from leading party) | Coalition partners | Welfare cuts | Income-tax cuts | Privatisation |
|---|---|---|---|---|---|---|---|
| | | | | | Government policy on | | |
| Austria | **Social Democrats** | 53 | Viktor Klima | Christian Democrats | ✓ | ✓ | ✓ |
| Belgium | **Socialists\*** | 53 | Jean-Luc Dehaene (Christian Democrat) | Christian Democrats\* | ✓ | ✗ | ✓ |
| Britain | **Labour** | 100 | Tony Blair | None | ✓ | ✓ | ✓ |
| Denmark | **Social Democrats** | 80 | Poul Nyrup Rasmussen | **Radicals** | ✓ | ✗ | ✓ |
| Finland | **Social Democrats** | 39 | Paavo Lipponen | Conservatives, People's Party, **Greens, Left‡** | ✓ | ✗ | ✓ |
| France | **Socialists** | 72 | Lionel Jospin | **Greens, Communists** | ✗ | ✗ | ✓ |
| Germany | **Social Democrats** | ? | Gerhard Schröder | **Greens§** | ? | ✓ | ? |
| Greece | **Socialists** | 100 | Costas Simitis | None | ✓ | ✗ | ✓ |
| Italy | **Democrats of the Left‡** | 65 | Romano Prodi (Popular Party) | **Socialists, Greens,** Popular Party and other centrists (rely on **Communists** for majority) | ✓ | ✗ | ✓ |
| Luxembourg | **Social Democrats\*** | 50 | Jean-Claude Juncker (Christian Democrat) | Christian Democrats\* | ✓ | ✗ | ✗ |
| Netherlands | **Labour** | 46 | Wim Kok | Liberals, **D-66** | ✓ | ✓ | ✓ |
| Portugal | **Socialists** | 100† | Antonio Guterres | None | ✓ | ✗ | ✓ |
| Sweden | **Social Democrats** | ? | Goran Persson | **Left‡§, Greens§** | ✓ | ✗ | ✗ |

\*Equal partners †35% of government posts held by independents ‡Ex-communists §Likely times a year. A few years ago, tentatively, only finance ministers met; now they all do. Germany's Social Democratic victory will give these shindigs even more clout: Rudolf Scharping, who could become Germany's foreign minister, is the PES president. Indeed, the PES summits of party leaders have turned into something of a caucus ahead of meetings of the European Council of Ministers; Britain's new Labour, at first suspicious of continental socialists still daring to call themselves such, is taking such meetings more seriously.

In government, too, there is more shuttling back and forth. French and German officials have long spent time in and out of each other's ministries, regardless of the ruling party's hue. Mr Schröder may even take on as an adviser Brigitte Sauzay, a French woman who used to work for François Mitterrand and helped out in the recent German campaign. Still somewhat reluctant to take their mesmerised eyes off their American friends, even the British have been making an effort. Members of Mr Blair's Downing Street policy unit regularly visit and e-mail those in Lionel Jospin's *cabinet*. Even before the election, Mr Blair's young men in suits were bustling about, trying to pep up Mr Schröder's glitzy election campaign, and peddling his new centre.

All of which might help the left draft a common leftish manifesto, however vague, for next year's elections to the European Parliament. It might even spur on Europe's leftists to get to know one another, and work out how to extract concessions from each other in the EU.

It does not, however, add up to a shared, European, centre-left view. True, in government, the left has inched closer to the centre. Many governments have embraced privatisation, even trimmed income taxes on the rich, abandoning former articles of faith. Indeed, more state companies have been sold off under Mr Jospin than under his right-wing predecessor. Besides which, the euro has bound governments' hands: its rules require them to keep inflation low and spending within their means.

But there is plenty of room for division. The continentals still, on the whole, defiantly distrust the market, which translates into quite different policies from those of Mr Blair, particularly on issues such as jobs and workers' protection. While Mr Jospin is busy bringing in a 35-hour week and old-fashioned job-creation schemes, it is all Mr Blair can do just to swallow a 48-hour week. For all his Blairish electoral razzmatazz, Mr Schröder is unknown, while sidekicks, such as

Oskar Lafontaine, a good friend of Mr Jospin's, stand decidedly on the left: "Old Labour", whisper Mr Blair's people darkly.

Through French leftish eyes, there is precious little to separate Mr Blair from continental Christian democracy—belief in strong families, tough on crime—except his zeal for the market. His social conservatism sets him quite apart from, say, the Scandinavian social democrats and their insouciance about family breakdown. When Mr Blair and Bill Clinton went last week to a seminar in New York on the third way, which symbolically did not take place in Europe, Romano Prodi, Italy's prime minister, who counts Mr Blair as a pal, was the only other EU leader to turn up.

The most conspicuous absence was that of Mr Jospin, who was "busy". The word in Paris is that it would have been an embarrassment for him, who governs with Communists and Greens, to be seen hobnobbing with people who sound like transatlantic neo-liberals. "If the third way is between communism and ultra-liberalism, I'm in favour of it," Mr Jospin declared recently. "If it's between liberalism and social democracy, I'm against it."

# EUROPE'S RIGHT

## Displaced, defeated and not sure what to do next

**Does the right try to charge straight back into the trenches from which the left has driven it, or does it attempt to outflank the left—and, if so, how?**

IT IS a lonely conservative soul who peers around the horizon of Europe's politics these days. Across the European Union, voters have swung to the magnet of the new left, putting modern-looking socialists and social democrats into power in 11 of the Union's 15 countries, and leaving parties to the right of centre out of favour, out of power, and out of sorts. Today in the EU the right governs alone in only one country, Spain. In Belgium and Luxembourg it shares power with social democrats. (In Ireland, the 15th country, politics defies the categories of left and right.) Stunned by a series of defeats, Europe's centre-right is demoralised and divided, groping for ideas it might use to organise a return to power.

The right's malaise seems contagious. Since the mid-1990s, parties of the centre-right have tumbled from power all the way from Sweden to Portugal. In 1997, governments of the right fell both in France and in Britain, the latter after 18 years in power. The latest casualty is Germany's Helmut Kohl, the Christian Democrat booted out last September after a 16-year reign.

There is no shortage of competing explanations. Parties in power too long (Germany, Britain) looked tired, arrogant and in need of refreshing. The same was true in Spain, though the other way round: the left, grown tired and corrupt after nearly 14 years in office, was ejected in favour of the conservatives.

In many places, the right is fragmented and poorly led. In France, where even the mainstream right is a tangle of five parties (one of them itself made up of four factions), the moderate right has seen its support sapped by the far-right National Front, which bags over 15% of the vote. In Italy, voters can choose from an uninspiring trio of centre-right leaders: Silvio Berlusconi has been convicted three times on charges of bribery or fraud; Gianfranco Fini used to be a neo-fascist; and Francesco Cossiga has now half-changed sides, serving in the current leftish government.

There may also have been a shift in voters' ideas as the century draws to a close. Centre-right politicians mutter about the prevailing sense of insecurity brought about by economic globalisation. The left, they concede, has done better at presenting itself as a source of reassurance, a comforting pair of hands to protect ordinary people against the wicked forces of unfettered market economics. The new left stands for a kind of anti-post-cold-war-capitalist-triumphalism, which plays mercilessly on the caricature of an unfeeling right.

Most important, however, the left has changed. It is not only in Britain under Labour's Tony Blair that the left, in reconquering the centre, has stolen the right's clothes, and managed to look sharper and smarter in them. "In many ways Blair is to the right of us on the family and on economics," comments one puzzled and irritated Christian Democrat in Bonn. The left's new look is far-reaching. It covers both a vigorous military policy (it was Mr Blair's government that was busy bombing Iraq last month) and narrowed eyes about immigration (France's Socialist prime minister, Lionel Jospin, enraged his Green friends by denying papers to 63,000 illegal immigrants last year).

But the most basic change is in economics. The architect of Mr Blair's New Labour, Peter Mandelson (who resigned from the trade ministry last month over a financial indiscretion), sums it up by saying that there is nothing wrong with becoming "filthy rich". Not every leftish continental would go that far. But the basic principle—accepting the virtues of private enterprise and fiscal responsibility—is widely shared. France's Socialists have sold off more companies than their immediate right-wing predecessors did. Greece's Socialists are cutting state spending to try to squeeze the drachma into the euro. As Maurice Fraser of the London School of Economics, who used to write speeches for Douglas Hurd, a Conservative foreign minister, puts it, "The right has won the argument, but lost the electoral battle."

### Blurring with Blair

Across Europe these days, two words trip from the tongue of many a right-of-centre politician: Tony Blair. Spain's conservative prime minister, Jose Maria Aznar, confesses that Mr Blair is a widely admired man. Gabriele Albertini, an ex-businessman who is the centre-right mayor of Milan (he posed last year in a pair of Valentino swimming-trunks to promote the city's fashion industry), admits that he can see no difference between his policies and those of Mr Blair. Klaus Welle, secretary-general of the European People's Party, the umbrella party for the EU's Christian Democrats, explains with some dismay: "Blair says he wants something between socialism and capitalism. But that's exactly what traditional Christian Democracy is."

There is a sense of bedazzlement, tinged with indignation, on Europe's right about Mr Blair and his "Third Way". His pragmatic mix of markets and intervention seems to capture the popular mood and thus to look fashionably modern. By contrast, many politicians on Europe's right look—and feel—sad, tweedy and tired.

Robbed by the end of the cold war of its old claim to be the chief guardian of democratic liberty, and muscled out of the centre by the new left, the right is fumbling for a way to redefine itself. Broadly speaking, it is divided between those who believe that the way back to power lies in reconquering the centre ground, "middle Europe", on which the left has so rudely trespassed—in other words, doing what the left is doing but doing it better—and those who seek a radical alternative, a new right, which can draw a sharp line between itself and the left.

Those in favour of seizing back the centre often talk about the Spanish model. Under Mr Aznar, Spain's ruling People's Party, longing to distance itself from the legacy of Franco, has edged steadily leftwards, putting less emphasis on economic liberalism and more on the need for compassionate government. In Spain, as in Italy and Germany, even the term "the right" makes the People's Party wince, for fear that the label carries the historical whiff of fascism. Such has been its march towards the centre that the People's Party now feels quite at home among the Christian Democrats of the pan-European EPP, whose traditions, particularly in the Benelux countries, belong more to the centre than to the right.

In part, this centrist model draws on the "caring conservatism" preached by, among others, the Bush brothers, George and Jeb, governors of the American states of Texas and Florida. It blends small government with compassionate government; champions the little man against the big state; believes in "a hand-up, not a hand-out". In other words (whisper it), just like Mr Blair.

For those who look at things this way, the electoral battle will be fought on competence rather than ideology. Everybody wants to create individual prosperity while protecting the poor: but who can do it best? "It is no longer a question of the left versus the right," argues Hervé de Charette, leader of one of the parties that make up the centre-right Union of French Democracy (UDF), "but of one team in power, and one that prepares to replace it."

All the same, some on the right think they too need a grand new idea—or at least a brand-new packaging of their existing ideas—to distinguish their team from that of the governing left. Late last year, Mr Aznar got in touch with Wolfgang Schäuble, the new leader of Germany's Christian Democratic Union (CDU), and Jean-Claude Juncker, Luxembourg's Social Christian prime minister, to talk about an alternative to the "Third Way": some centre-right formula to grab the headlines and seduce the voters. What this could possibly be, apart from marketing the existing values of continental Christian Democracy, is, to say the least, hazy. Unless, argue some, you care to consider the ideas of the radical right. Of these, three stand out.

## Christian crusaders

From the lofty heights of the 30th floor of Milan's tallest tower block, one of Italy's few centre-right regional presidents, Roberto Formigoni, an ambitious politician with his eyes on a top job in Rome should the centre-right return to power, presides over the Lombardy region. If anywhere is natural recruiting ground for the centre-right it is here, the heartland of Italian industry and the cosmopolitan centre of the Italian north, which looks down its nose at the poorer, rural southerners.

But Mr Formigoni is not the sort of man who would easily gather the modern business vote in Frankfurt or London. A vast Catholic icon dominates an entire wall of his huge office. A man of the religious right, he wears his Catholicism on his sleeve as well as on his wall. Despite his efforts to introduce radical ideas—such as *buoni* (vouchers) to allocate nursery-school places through a market based on parental choice—Milan's voters know him best for his resolute stand against abortion and divorce.

Particularly in southern Europe, Christian values provide one rallying-point around which some politicians believe a new right could take shape. Certainly, some Christian Democrats in Central and Eastern Europe, notably in Catholic Poland (where abortion is illegal), are far bolder in standing up for explicitly Christian values. Last year Poland's Catholic right, part of the Solidarity-led governing coalition, pushed through a bill to remove sex-education from the school syllabus.

Many of Western Europe's Christian Democrats, however, are reluctant to sound preachy on such matters as the family. "We are quite simply amazed to hear Tony Blair talking about family values," says one in Germany. Although Christian Democracy has its roots in the (mostly) Catholic resistance to the anti-clerical movement of the 19th century, the Christian element is now for many of these parties' members only vaguely religious. In the easy-going Netherlands, for instance, there is little appetite for such talk; one leading Dutch Christian Democrat says breezily that his country's Christian democracy is actually "post-Christian". As for Spain's Mr Aznar, he would shrink from emphasising his Christian beliefs for fear of evoking the ghost of Franco.

A second project for the new right might be a return (in Britain) or a new move (almost anywhere else) to the liberal economics of Thatcherism. It is nonsense to talk of a blurring of left and right, goes this argument, when there is a clear line to be drawn between the tax-and-spend zealots of the left, however hard they try to dress themselves up as something else, and the fiscally responsible, light-government types on the right. Just wait, say the latter. The more the left demands such policies as "harmonised" taxes across the EU—meaning, in this view, higher taxes—the plainer it will become that social democrats such as Oskar Lafontaine, Germany's finance minister, have not really changed at all.

Europe does have economic liberals: they include Germany's Free Democrats; France's Alain Madelin, who broke away from the UDF last year to set up his new party, Liberal Democracy; and Antonio Martino, Italy's best-known Thatcherite. But they do not get much of the vote. Nor do the new recruits in Central and Eastern Europe, many of whom once had the free-market zeal of the newly converted, now look quite the disciples they once were. Vaclav Klaus, for instance, a former Czech prime minister and protégé of Margaret Thatcher, recently attacked the Czech central bank's tight monetary policy, and questioned the wisdom of more privatisation.

Even those working on new ideas for the British Tories do not advocate a return to Thatcherism pure and simple. "It would be a great mistake to think that the 1980s provided us with a timeless philosophy," says one. Some Tories argue that the libertarian ideas which the party borrowed in the 1980s were a means of rescuing Britain from the statist culture dominating it at the time, and reviving the individualism this had squashed, rather than of laying down a permanent conservative doctrine.

## Two sorts of nationalism

What does that leave for the new right? The third possibility is the one that has recently most captivated the centre-right's imagination. This is the nationalist option.

This option takes two possible forms, one respectable, the other potentially dangerous. The respectable version has lately been given new impetus by the onward march of European integration. The relinquishing of sovereignty required by the European project irks many people, by no means all normally supporters of the right. Under the euro, monetary authority has been surrendered in all but four of the EU countries. The looming prospect of "ever-closer" European unification gives new life to those who, rightly or wrongly, doubt the workability of a United States of Europe.

So far, the Christian Democratic parties of Europe have on the whole been loyal pro-integrationists. European voters, however, are deeply divided. Only a sliver over a half of the Germans, whose leaders have been the prime motor of integration, told pollsters last year that they were in favour of joining the single currency. For those who care to plough it, there is fertile ground here for a revival of nationalist feeling: suspicion that Brussels will trample over local cheese makers and beer-brewers, and harmonise Europe's cultures into a bland Euro-purée; fear of immigrants flooding in from Eastern Europe and pinching jobs in an expanded EU; and so on.

Euroscepticism was partly behind the nationalist appeal made by Britain's Tory leader, William Hague, this week. Britain is not alone. On January 1st Charles Pasqua, a leader of the Rally for the Republic (RPR) and a former French interior minister, declared that he would not take part in a combined pro-union centre-right list for the elections to the European Parliament in June, but would put forward his own list of anti-federalist candidates. This, he explained, was in order to defend the "personality of France".

Even some members of Germany's CDU, battered by their defeat last year, are eyeing with guarded envy the success of their sister party, the Bavarian-based Christian Social Union. The CSU is, by German standards, Eurosceptic; it also stands to the right of the CDU on matters such as law and order and immigration (Edmund Stoiber, its leader, talks of the dangers of "excessive immigration"). In Bavaria's state election last September, it scooped up a handy 53% of the vote. Mr Stoiber now barely conceals his ambition to stand as a "union" candidate for the two parties at the next general election. If the more centrist-minded and much bigger CDU agreed, this would be a clear shift to the nationalist right.

This is the basis of a defensible and democratic new nationalism for the centre-right to take a stand on. The other nationalist option is of a different, poisonous sort: it is the xenophobic brand of the far right.

## Vitriol in Vitrolles

As good a place as any to peer into the murky hole into which the wrong sort of nationalism can plunge is the southern French town of Vitrolles, a 1970s creation that has grown into a spillover suburb for those who want to flee from Marseilles. In 1985, the National Front, France's far-right party, was already gathering over a quarter of the vote in local elections here. In 1997, the town elected a National Front mayor, Catherine Mégret, with over half the votes.

Mrs Mégret is most famous as the wife of Bruno, the Front's wily number two, whose refusal to fall into line behind the party leader, Jean-Marie Le Pen, led last month to a bitter falling-out and a split in the party. In Vitrolles, one of the four big towns controlled by the Front, Mrs Mégret has been busy creating a showpiece of good Front leadership. She has closed down Le Sous-Marin, a bar that played "tribal" black-American music; re-baptised roads with such subversive names as Place Nelson Mandela, now Place de Provence; tripled the number of municipal policemen; and started to implement the policy of "national preference" hatched by her husband and designed to benefit white Frenchmen by paying a FFr5,000 ($880) bonus to the French or other EU parents of newborn babies—a policy that was subsequently ruled illegal by the courts.

None of this, perhaps, comes as a surprise from a party that advocates sending 3m immigrants back home. What took many aback, however, was that in France's regional elections last year some members of the centre-right took the hand of the National Front, thus offering it a degree of respectability, in order to cling on to power themselves. This was precisely the way to *dédiabolise* the far right that Mr Mégret had been pushing for. Five regional presidents were elected thanks to pacts with the Front. One resigned a week later; another was subsequently disqualified. All were expelled from their party, the UDF.

Now that the National Front has split—the Mégret camp meets on January 23rd and 24th to plan its future—some people argue that the temptation for the centre-right to seduce it will evaporate. Between them, the two bits of a divided Front will probably not manage to pull in the 15% of the French vote the united party got in the 1997 election. But the nationalist insecurities which propelled that slice of the electorate into the arms of the Front will not vanish. Mr Pasqua, no friend to immigrants when he was interior minister, will surely have had that in mind when he decided to go ahead with his separate, right-wing list for the coming Euro-elections.

In other European countries with far-right parties, such as Austria, Belgium and Germany, the centre-right has not given in to the same urge. Certainly in Germany, as in Spain, living memory of nationalist excess is enough to check any such temptation. But the popular anxiety that feeds such xenophobic movements is tempting ground for the centre. Only this month, Germany's CDU and CSU began to rail against the Social Democrat government's plans to liberalise Germany's citizenship laws and to allow millions of "foreigners" dual citizenship. Last week the two parties launched a petition in protest.

Shell-shocked by defeat, mesmerised by the "Third Way", Europe's right has not yet found out how to reinvent itself. But this does not mean it is condemned to perpetual opposition. It can find an issue, good or bad, from which it can eventually seize the commanding heights of politics and thus defeat the now triumphant left. Or it can hope that the left in power will in time become as arrogant as the right was before it, and offer the right a role as a fresh pair of safe hands all over again. "The only strategy for us right now", believes one glum German Christian Democrat, "is to wait."

# Women in Power: From Tokenism to Critical Mass

*by Jane S. Jaquette*

**N**ever before have so many women held so much power. The growing participation and representation of woman in politics is one of the most remarkable developments of the late twentieth century. For the first time, women in all countries and social classes are becoming politically active, achieving dramatic gains in the number and kind of offices they hold. Why is political power, off limits for so long, suddenly becoming accessible to women? And what are the implications of this trend for domestic and foreign policy?

Women have been gaining the right to vote and run for office since New Zealand became the first country to authorize women's suffrage in 1893. By 1920, the year the United States amended the Constitution to allow women to vote, 10 countries had already granted women the franchise. Yet many European countries did not allow women to vote until after World War II, including France, Greece, Italy, and Switzerland. In Latin America, Ecuador was the first to recognize women's political rights, in 1929; but women could not vote in Mexico until 1953. In Asia, women voted first in Mongolia, in 1923; then, with the U.S. occupation after 1945, women secured the right to vote in Japan and South Korea. The former European colonies in Africa and Asia enfranchised women when they gained independence, from the late 1940s into the 1970s.

Historically, women began to demand the right to vote by claiming their equality: If all men are created equal, why not women? The American and British suffrage movements inspired "women's emancipation" efforts among educated female (and sometimes male) elites worldwide, and most contemporary feminist movements trace their roots to these stirrings at the turn of the century. The nineteenth-century European movements had a strong influence on the thinking of Friedrich Engels, who made gender equality a central tenet of socialist doctrine. A similar movement among the Russian intelligentsia ensured that the equality of women in political and economic life would be an important goal of the Soviet state—and subsequently of its Central and Eastern European satellites.

> *Historically, a country's level of economic development has not been a reliable indicator of women's representation.*

But if the logic existed to support women's claims to political equality, the facts on the ground did not. As educated women mobilized to demand the right to vote, men in all countries largely resisted, with the result that

JANE S. JAQUETTE *is chair of the department of diplomacy and world affairs and B. H. Orr professor of liberal arts at Occidental College. Her latest book* Women and Democracy: Latin America and Central and Eastern Europe *was published by The Johns Hopkins University Press in 1998.*

most of the world's women gained this basic right of citizenship only in the last 50 years. Before women could vote, they organized to influence legislation, from the marriage and property rights acts of the mid-nineteenth century to the early twentieth century wave of Progressive legislation in the United States and Western Europe's generous maternal and protective labor laws.

However, the vote itself did not bring women into politics. On the contrary, some countries gave women the right to vote but not to run for office. In virtually every nation, women who tried to enter politics were subject to popular ridicule. Political parties routinely excluded women from decision-making positions, resisted nominating them as candidates, and denied their female candidates adequate campaign support.

Cultural factors partially explain the varying degrees of women's representation from region to region and country to country. Predictably, women in the Nordic and northern European countries, with long traditions of gender equality, have been the most successful in breaking through traditional resistance and increasing their representation. In contrast, those in Arab countries, with curbs against women in public life and contemporary pressures to abandon secular laws for religious rules, have consistently registered the lowest levels of female participation (and the lowest levels of democratization).

But "culture" does not fully explain why women in the United States and Great Britain, which rank high on various measures of gender equality, accounted for less than 7 percent of all parliamentarians as late as 1987. Nor have women been excluded from politics in all Islamic nations. The legislatures of Syria and Indonesia, while decidedly undemocratic,

are composed of 10 to 12 percent women. Former prime ministers Benazir Bhutto of Pakistan and Khaleda Zia of Bangladesh have wielded major power in Muslim societies.

Historically, a country's level of development has not been a reliable indicator of women's representation. Of the 32 most developed countries that reported electoral data in 1975, 19 had fewer than 10 percent female legislators and 11 had fewer than 5 percent. In France, Greece, and Japan—all developed, industrialized countries—female members accounted for 2 percent or less of their legislatures.

Although more women than ever are working for wages, even an increase in female participation in the work force does not necessarily translate into greater political clout for women. In recent years, for example, much of the growth in participation has been in low-wage labor. And although women's managerial participation has increased dramatically in many countries, from New Zealand to Peru, women are still rarely found at the highest levels of corporate management and ownership. Their underrepresentation in top management limits the number of private sector women invited to enter government as high-level appointees; women's lower salaries, in turn, restrict an important source of financial support for female candidates.

One can, however, discern significant worldwide increases in female representation beginning in 1975, the year in which the United Nations held its first international women's conference. From 1975 to 1995, the number of women legislators doubled in the developed West; the global average rose from 7.4 percent to nearly 11 percent.

Between 1987 and 1995 in particular, women's representation registered a dramatic increase in the developed countries, Africa, and Latin

## Percent of Women in National Legislatures, by region, 1975–97

|  | 1975 | 1987 | 1997* |
|---|---|---|---|
| Arab States | 3.5 | 2.8 | 3.3 |
| Asia | 8.4 | 9.7 | 13.4 |
| (Asia excluding China, Mongolia, N. Korea, Vietnam)† | (3.8) | (6.2) | (6.3) |
| Central and Eastern Europe and Former Soviet Union | 23.3 | 23.1 | 11.5 |
| Developed countries (excluding East Asia) | 5.1 | 9.6 | 14.7 |
| Latin America and the Caribbean | 6.0 | 6.9 | 10.5 |
| Nordic Countries | 16.1 | 28.8 | 36.4 |

* 1997 statistics for lower houses and single house systems. (Mongolia excluded.)
† women's representation under party control

Sources: *Democracy Still in the Making: A World Comparative Study* (Geneva: Inter-Parliamentary Union, 1997) and *The World's Women, 1970–1990: Trends and Statistics* (New York: United Nations, 1991).

## Women on Women

*"A man, who during the course of his life has never been elected anywhere, and who is named prime minister (it was the case with George Pompidou and Raymond Barre, who had never been elected to any position)—everyone found that absolutely normal. A woman who has been elected for 10 years at the National Assembly . . . at the regional level, who is the mayor of a city, it is as if she were coming out of nowhere."*
—**Edith Cresson, former prime minister of France**

*"I really do think that women are more cautious in adopting . . . decisions [to go to war]. . . . But I don't think that the woman will ever sacrifice the interests of the nation or the interest of the state due to . . . weakness."*
—**Kazimiera Prunskiene, former prime minister of Lithuania**

*"The traditional issues we were steered into—child care, health care, and education—have now become the sexy issues of the decade."*
—**Nancy K. Kopp, former speaker pro tem. of the Maryland House of Delegates**

*"Women cannot lead without men, but men have to this day considered themselves capable of leading without women. Women would always take men into consideration. That's the difference."*
—**Vigdis Finnbogadóttir, former president of Iceland**

*"Do I have an option?"*
—**Patricia Schroeder, former U.S. representative, when asked by the press if she was "running as a woman."**

Sources: Laura Liswood, *Women World Leaders* (London: HarperCollins, 1994); Linda Witt, Karen M. Paget, & Glenna Matthews, *Running as a Woman: Gender and Power in American Politics* (New York: Free Press, 1994).

America. Of the 32 women who have served as presidents or prime ministers during the twentieth century, 24 were in power in the 1990s. In the United States, women now make up 11.2 percent of Congress, about one-third the proportion in Nordic countries, but substantially higher than the 5 percent in 1987. And although only 23 women won seats in the Diet in Japan's 1996 elections, an unprecedented 153 women ran for office. In 1997, the Inter-Parliamentary Union reported only nine countries with no women in their legislatures. From 1987 to 1995, the number of countries without any women ministers dropped from 93 to 47, and 10 countries reported that women held more than 20 percent of all ministerial-level positions, although generally in "female" portfolios like health, education, and environment rather than the "power ministries" like finance and defense.

The only exception to the global acceleration in women's representation during the past decade is in the New Independent States of the former Soviet Union and the former members of the Eastern bloc. Here, representation has dropped from earlier highs under communist rule of 25 to 35 percent women (although they exercised little real power) to around 8 to 15 percent today, and numbers are lower in the largely Muslim states of Central Asia. Where women's representation is still under Communist Party control, as in China, North Korea, and Vietnam, women still account for about 20 percent of the national legislators.

## THE GLOBALIZATION OF THE WOMEN'S MOVEMENT

Why the surge in women officeholders in the last 10 years?

Three interconnected reasons seem to stand out: First, the rise of women's movements worldwide has heightened women's awareness of their political potential and developed new issues for which women are ready to mobilize. Second, a new willingness by political parties and states to ease the constraints on women's access to politics, from increasing their recruitment pools to modifying electoral systems and adopting quotas. And third, as social issues supplant security concerns in the post–Cold War political environment, opportunities have opened for new styles of leadership and have reordered political priorities.

The recent wave of female mobilization is a response to a series of political and economic crises—and opportunities—over the last two decades. On the political front, women's groups like the Madres de la Plaza de Mayo (Argentine mothers who demonstrated on behalf of their "disappeared" husbands and children) helped to inspire the defense of human rights in Latin America and beyond. Women were also recognized as valued participants in the opposition to authoritarian rule in the former Soviet bloc, where they took up the cause of human rights when their husbands and sons were arrested—dissident Andrei Sakharov's wife, Yelena Bonner, is just one example. In Africa and Asia, women are increasingly regarded as important opposition figures. In South Africa, for example, women were among prominent anti-apartheid leaders and have helped to lead the new government-sponsored effort to develop a women's charter for the post–apartheid period. In Iran, women have played an important role in defining electoral outcomes, despite the conventional wisdom that they are powerless.

On the economic front, the widespread adoption of market-oriented reforms, often accompanied by austerity programs, has had a severe impact on many women, who in turn have organized against price rises and the loss of health care and other public services. Women created communal kitchens in Chile and Peru to help feed their communities. Other small-scale, self-help programs like the Grameen Bank in Bangladesh and the Self-Employed Women's Association in India were developed to meet women's needs for credit. The war in Bosnia put an international spotlight on rape as a weapon of war and led to the demand that "women's rights" be considered "human rights" rather than some different or lesser category of concern.

These efforts were reinforced by international connections, many of which were created by the U.N. Decade for Women (1976–85). Three times during the decade (in 1975, 1980, and 1985) and again in 1995, the United Nations convened official delegations from member countries to report on the status of women and to commit governments to remedy women's lack of access to political, economic, and educational resources. Not only did these conferences encourage a flurry of local and national organizing, but they produced parallel meetings of nongovernmental organizations (NGOs), including the nearly 30,000 women who participated in the NGO conference in Beijing in 1995.

The Decade for Women originally meant that women's issues were geared to the U.N. agenda, which in the 1970s focused on the creation of a "new international economic order" and a more equitable sharing of resources between North and South. By the mid-1980s, however, attention had shifted from integrating women into world development efforts to enhancing roles for women in the promotion of market economics and democracy. The turn toward democracy made it easier for women to seek explicitly political goals, and the footdragging by the U.N. and its member countries on implementing their international pledges helped to stimulate women's interest in increasing their political power.

### Breaking The Political Class Ceiling

Since some of the public policies holding women back from greater political power—particularly women's access to education—

## The Old Girls Network

Historically, one of the greatest barriers to elected office for women has been inadequate financial support. Often lacking incumbent status or access to financial networks, they have had to build their own fund-raising networks from scratch.

One of the most successful such groups has been EMILY's List (EMILY stands for Early Money is Like Yeast), the first partisan organization set up to fund women candidates in the United States. Ironically for an organization that is now America's largest political action committee (PAC), its roots lie in a political defeat. In 1982, Harriet Woods won the Democratic primary for a Senate seat in Missouri but then received only token financial backing from her party. She called on Washington, D.C., philanthropist Ellen Malcolm for help. But the money proved to be too little and too late to counter her male opponent's negative advertising campaign. Stung by this defeat, Malcolm went on to found EMILY's List in 1985 to raise money for Democratic women candidates who support abortion rights (a.k.a., "pro-choice").

EMILY's List received a major boost in 1992, when the all-male Senate Judiciary Committee confirmed Clarence Thomas to the U.S. Supreme Court despite law professor Anita Hill's accusations of sexual harassment. A torrent of female outrage turned into a record flood of financial support for female candidates in that year's elections. EMILY's List grew from 3,000 to 23,000 members and raised $6 million. It also inspired several state-level imitators, including May's List in Washington State and the Minnesota $$ Million. And EMILY's List now has a number of Republican competitors, including WISH (Women in the Senate and House), which supports pro-choice female candidates, and the Women's Leadership Fund.

According to Rutgers University's Center for the American Woman and Politics, 11 national and 47 state or local PACS and donor networks now either give money predominantly to women or receive most of their contributions from women. Organizations to fund women candidates have been established in several other nations as well. In 1993, Britain's Labour Party launched EMILY's List U.K. In 1995, the Australian Labor Party decided to form its own version of EMILY's List to meet its target of a 35 percent female Parliament by 2002.

have been easing rapidly, attention has turned to other barriers. Chief among them have been the constraints on the pool of women available to run for office. Although women constitute a growing proportion of the rank and file in political parties, unions, and civil services, they still account for only a small proportion of the higher echelons that provide a springboard to higher political office.

Although women participate more actively in local government than they do at the national level, many more men make the jump from local to national leadership. One problem has been a lack of campaign funds. In the United States, women began to address that obstacle in the 1980s through innovative fund-raising strategies. In other countries, women have organized voting blocs to support female candidates. Yet there is only one women's political party, in Iceland, that has succeeded over time in electing women to office. By the mid-1990s, the European-based Inter-Parliamentary Union was holding meetings twice a year for female parliamentarians aimed at improving their electoral skills as well as their abilities to perform more effectively in office. In another innovative effort, a group called Women of Russia organized to stem the decline in women's representation under the new democratic electoral rules. Women of Russia surprised everyone by gathering over 100,000 signatures and winning 8 percent of the vote in the 1993 Duma elections, but in the 1995 elections they failed to maintain the minimum level of support necessary under Russian electoral rules. As a result of Women in Russia's initial success, however, other Russian parties are nominating more women.

Research has shown that different kinds of voting systems can dramatically affect women's chances of election. The widely accepted explanation for the relatively low numbers of female legislators in the United States and Britain is their "single-member district" electoral systems. When each district elects only one candidate, minority votes are lost. Significantly more women are elected in countries with electoral systems based on proportional representation (in which candidates are elected from party lists according to the percentage of total votes the party receives) or on at-large districts ("multi-member constituencies"). Several countries have experimented with different electoral systems, including mixed single-member and multi-member district systems, to improve the participation of underrepresented groups, particularly women.

The surest way to achieve an increased number of women in national legislatures is to adopt a quota system that requires a certain percentage of women to be nominated or elected. Although the issue of quotas is scarcely open to debate in the United States—where Lani Guinier's nomination for U.S. attorney general in 1993 was torpedoed by detractors' interpretations of essays she had written in support of "group" representation—many political parties (especially on the Left) and national legislatures around the world are experimenting with gender quotas. Quotas account for the

high levels of female representation in the Nordic countries and for the recent doubling (to 18 percent) of the number of women in the House of Commons in Britain when the Labour Party swept the election. A quota law in Argentina increased the women in its house of representatives from 4 percent in 1991 to over 16 percent in 1993 and 28 percent in 1995. In Brazil, when quotas were used in the 1997 congressional elections, the number of women legislators increased by nearly 40 percent since the last elections.

Quotas are used in Taiwan, by some of the political parties in Chile, and are under active discussion in Costa Rica, Ecuador, Paraguay, South Korea, and several other countries. The Indian constitution now mandates that one-third of the seats in local government bodies be "reserved" for women, and Pakistan is debating a similar measure. In Mexico, the Institutional Revolutionary Party (PRI) and its leftist opposition have adopted quotas, while the right-of-center party accepts the goal but maintains that it can promote women as effectively without them. Japan has adopted measures to ensure that more women are appointed to ministerial posts, and Bangladesh, among other countries, is experimenting with quotas for top civil service jobs.

It is obvious that quotas increase the number of women officeholders, but why are they being adopted now? Even where quotas are not seen to violate fundamental notions of democracy, as they appear to be in the United States, there are powerful arguments against them. Some insist that they will ghettoize women legislators and their issues. Others object that quotas lead to "proxy" representation, where women legislators run as "fronts" for their husbands or other male interests. In India, for example, there are many anecdotal cases of this phenomenon, and in Argentina there are complaints that many of the women nominated by the majority Peronist Party (which pushed through the quota law) have been chosen because of their unquestioning loyalty to President Carlos Saul Menem rather than because of their qualifications as candidates—as if only women could be considered party hacks.

Despite the controversy quotas raise, they have become popular not only because women have organized to push for them, but—importantly—because more men have become convinced that quotas serve useful political goals in a more democratic environment. A sea change in attitudes about women in public office is occurring at a time when the number of countries under some form of democratic governance is expanding rapidly, giving new salience to the question of whether national legislatures are truly representative of pluralistic societies. Adequate representation of all groups could strengthen the consolidation of democracies that are open and responsive—and thus make them more durable.

## WHAT DO WOMEN WANT?

The post–Cold War shift in national priorities from defense and security concerns to social and environmental issues also plays to women's strong suits. So do the negative impacts of economic globalization and structural adjustment policies, which have put the need for effective social safety nets high on domestic agendas. Many observers argue that the rejection of "unbridled capitalism" and the desire to retain social welfare policies explain the victories of the Labour Party in Britain, the socialists in France, and the electoral loss of the PRI in Mexico last July. Rightly or wrongly, many voters also associate market reforms with a rise in corruption. Despite accusations of corruption against leaders such as Pakistan's Bhutto and Tansu Ciller in Turkey, women's perceived "purity" and their status as outsiders, once considered political weaknesses, are now seen as strengths. In the last 10 years, it is not so much the case that women have come to politics; rather, politics has come to women.

If the trend continues, quotas will soon produce a quantum leap in women's political power. For the first time, women will form a "critical mass" of legislators in many countries, able to set new agendas and perhaps create new styles of leadership. How will women use their growing political influence?

One way to predict the direction of change is to look at how the political attitudes of women differ from those of men. Surveys show that one of the most persistent gender differences regards attitudes toward peace and war: Women are more pacifistic than men, less likely to favor defense spending, or to support aggressive policies abroad. Recent

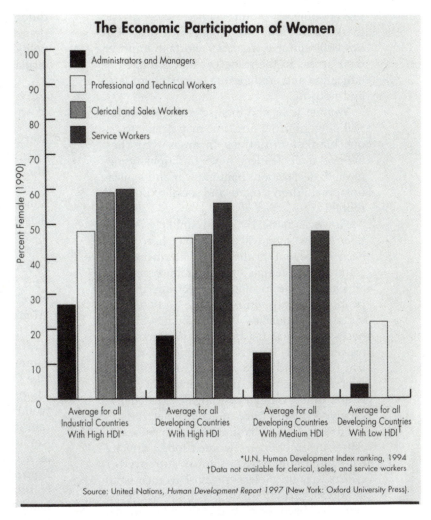

**The Economic Participation of Women**

- Administrators and Managers
- Professional and Technical Workers
- Clerical and Sales Workers
- Service Workers

Percent Female (1990)

Average for all Industrial Countries With High HDI*

Average for all Developing Countries With High HDI

Average for all Developing Countries With Medium HDI

Average for all Developing Countries With Low HDI†

*U.N. Human Development Index ranking, 1994
†Data not available for clerical, sales, and service workers

Source: United Nations, *Human Development Report 1997* (New York: Oxford University Press).

interviews of women heads of state show that most believe that they are more committed to peace than their male counterparts. Historically and today, women and women leaders are more interested in the so-called "soft" issues, including the environment and social welfare. On some measures, women are more conservative than men: They are less likely to vote for the parties on the Left, and rather than pursue their own self-interests, they more often mobilize for defensive reasons—namely to protect the interests of the family. As a result, these tendencies will probably place more focus on policies to support the family and to strengthen local communities.

But women are far from conservative in one important sense: Women are more likely than men to support state regulation of business to protect the consumer and the environment and to assure that the needs of society's weakest members are addressed. Because women are often more skeptical than men about the effectiveness of market reforms, the election of more women may signal a softening of some of reform's harsher aspects. The market's continued dominance in global politics will reinforce women s efforts to improve their access to the resources that count, from education and credit to the ownership of land and housing.

Women who find themselves experiencing real power for the first time may decide to try out blanket initiatives in areas that they believe male leaders have traditionally neglected: declarations banning war and legislation on children's rights and social or political morality.

However, radical change is unlikely. Predictions that women will act as a bloc have never been borne out in the past. Like their male counterparts, female officeholders come from all parts of the ideological spectrum and depend on the support of diverse and often divided constituencies. Women leaders are not necessarily pacificists or environmentally oriented. While former prime minister Gro Harlem Brundtland of Norway or Ireland's president Mary Robinson may support the "soft" issues, Indira Gandhi or Margaret Thatcher is capable of using force to achieve her ends.

Further, few of the initiatives on those social issues mobilizing women today directly confront male power. Global support for efforts to stem violence against women is an important exception. Antidiscrimination legislation has been developed at the international level through the U.N. Convention on the Elimination of All Forms of Discrimination Against Women—which has been ratified by 160 countries, but not the United States. The implementation of the instrument by signatories, however, lags far behind. And women leaders themselves disagree on many of the issues affecting women most, from reproductive rights and family law to genital mutilation.

Today, women are recruited aggressively into politics not to right past inequities or to recognize their equal citizenship—but to bring a different, explicitly female perspective to the political arena and to appeal to the women's vote. Whether the rationale for increasing female representation is equality or difference, women will have an unprecedented opportunity to put their stamp on politics and to increase the range of alternatives available to policymakers across the globe.

## WANT TO KNOW MORE?

Merilee Karl's compendium *Women and Empowerment: Participation and Decision-Making* (London: Zed Books, 1995) discusses women's participation in a range of institutional settings from an activist perspective. A rich and thoughtful treatment of women's political participation covering a variety of cases is *Women and Politics Worldwide,* Barbara Nelson & Najma Chowdhury, eds. (New Haven: Yale University Press, 1994). Laura Liswood interviews 15 female politicians in *Women World Leaders* (London: Pandora, 1994). For information on the impact of electoral systems, consult Wilma Rule & Joseph F. Zimmerman's *Electoral Systems in Comparative Perspective: Their Impact on Women and Minorities* (Westport, Connecticut: Greenwood Press, 1994). The story of women's ascent into U.S. politics is found in Linda Witt, Karen M. Paget, & Clenna Matthews' *Running as a Woman: Gender and Power in American Politics* (New York: The Free Press, 1994). Nancy Adler & Dafna Izraeli, on the other hand, present notable research on women in the private sector in *Competitive Frontiers: Women Managers in a Global Economy* (Cambridge: Blackwell, 1994).

A key source for data on women in power is the United Nations' *Human Development Report 1995* (New York: Oxford University Press, 1995), which is dedicated to gender comparisons. For some historical statistics, see *The World's Women, 1970–1990: Trends and Statistics* (New York: United Nations, 1991). Updates and special studies on women's political participation are available through the Inter-Parliamentary Union's Web page. Access this site and others on women in political and economic power through **www.foreign-policy.com.**

# WHAT DEMOCRACY IS . . . AND IS NOT

## Philippe C. Schmitter & Terry Lynn Karl

**Philippe C. Schmitter** *is professor of political science and director of the Center for European Studies at Stanford University.* **Terry Lynn Karl** *is associate professor of political science and director of the Center for Latin American Studies at the same institution. The original, longer version of this essay was written at the request of the United States Agency for International Development, which is not responsible for its content.*

For some time, the word democracy has been circulating as a debased currency in the political marketplace. Politicians with a wide range of convictions and practices strove to appropriate the label and attach it to their actions. Scholars, conversely, hesitated to use it—without adding qualifying adjectives—because of the ambiguity that surrounds it. The distinguished American political theorist Robert Dahl even tried to introduce a new term, "polyarchy," in its stead in the (vain) hope of gaining a greater measure of conceptual precision. But for better or worse, we are "stuck" with democracy as the catchword of contemporary political discourse. It is the word that resonates in people's minds and springs from their lips as they struggle for freedom and a better way of life; it is the word whose meaning we must discern if it is to be of any use in guiding political analysis and practice.

The wave of transitions away from autocratic rule that began with Portugal's "Revolution of the Carnations" in 1974 and seems to have crested with the collapse of communist regimes across Eastern Europe in 1989 has produced a welcome convergence toward [a] common definition of democracy.[1] Everywhere there has been a silent abandonment of dubious adjectives like "popular," "guided," "bourgeois," and "formal" to modify "democracy." At the same time, a remarkable consensus has emerged concerning the minimal conditions that polities must meet in order to merit the prestigious appellation of "democratic." Moreover, a number of international organizations now monitor how well these standards are met; indeed, some countries even consider them when formulating foreign policy.[2]

## WHAT DEMOCRACY IS

Let us begin by broadly defining democracy and the generic *concepts* that distinguish it as a unique system for organizing relations between rulers and the ruled. We will then briefly review *procedures,* the rules and arrangements that are needed if democracy is to endure. Finally, we will discuss two operative *principles* that make democracy work. They are not expressly included among the generic concepts or formal procedures, but the prospect for democracy is grim if their underlying conditioning effects are not present.

One of the major themes of this essay is that democracy does not consist of a single unique set of institutions. There are many types of democracy, and their diverse practices produce a similarly varied set of effects. The specific form democracy takes is contingent upon a country's socioeconomic conditions as well as its entrenched state structures and policy practices.

*Modern political democracy is a system of governance in which rulers are held accountable for their actions in the public realm by citizens, acting indirectly through the competition and cooperation of their elected representatives.* [3]

A *regime or system of governance* is an ensemble of patterns that determines the methods of access to the principal public offices; the characteristics of the actors admitted to or excluded from such access; the strategies that actors may use to gain access; and the rules that are followed in the making of publicly binding decisions. To work properly, the ensemble must be institutionalized—that is to say, the various patterns must be habitually known, practiced, and accepted by most, if not all, actors. Increasingly, the preferred mechanism of institutionalization is a written body of laws undergirded by a written constitution, though many enduring political norms can have an informal, prudential, or traditional basis.[4]

For the sake of economy and comparison, these forms, characteristics, and rules are usually bundled together and given a generic label. Democratic is one; others are autocratic, authoritarian, despotic, dictatorial, tyrannical, totalitarian, absolutist, traditional, monarchic, obligarchic, plutocratic, aristocratic, and sultanistic.[5] Each of these regime forms may in turn be broken down into subtypes.

Like all regimes, democracies depend upon the presence of *rulers,* persons who occupy specialized authority roles and can give legitimate commands to others. What distinguishes democratic rulers from nondemocratic ones are the norms that condition how the former come to power and the practices that hold them accountable for their actions.

The *public realm* encompasses the making of collective norms and choices that are binding on the society and backed by state coercion. Its content can vary a great deal across democracies, depending upon preexisting distinctions between the public and the private, state and society, legitimate coercion and voluntary exchange, and collective needs and individual preferences. The liberal conception of democracy advocates circumscribing the public realm as narrowly as possible, while the socialist or social-democratic approach would extend that realm through regulation, subsidization, and, in some cases, collective ownership of property. Neither is intrinsically more democratic than the other—just *differently* democratic. This implies that measures aimed at "developing the private sector" are no more democratic than those aimed at "developing the public sector." Both, if carried to extremes, could undermine the practice of democracy, the former by destroying the basis for satisfying collective needs and exercising legitimate authority; the latter by destroying the basis for satisfying individual preferences and controlling illegitimate government actions. Differences of opinion over the optimal mix of the two provide much of the substantive content of political conflict within established democracies.

> "*However central to democracy, elections occur intermittently and only allow citizens to choose between the highly aggregated alternatives offered by political parties . . .*"

*Citizens* are the most distinctive element in democracies. All regimes have rulers and a public realm, but only to the extent that they are democratic do they have citizens. Historically, severe restrictions on citizenship were imposed in most emerging or partial democracies according to criteria of age, gender, class, race, literacy, property ownership, tax-paying status, and so on. Only a small part of the total population was eligible to vote or run for office. Only restricted social categories were allowed to form, join, or support political associations. After protracted struggle—in some cases involving violent domestic upheaval or international war—most of these restrictions were lifted. Today, the criteria for inclusion are fairly standard. All native-born adults are eligible, although somewhat higher age limits may still be imposed upon candidates for certain offices. Unlike the early American and European democracies of the nineteenth century, none of the recent democracies in southern Europe, Latin America, Asia, or Eastern Europe has even attempted to impose formal restrictions on the franchise or eligibility to office. When it comes to informal restrictions on the effective exercise of citizenship rights, however, the story can be quite different. This explains the central importance (discussed below) of procedures.

*Competition* has not always been considered an essential defining condition of democracy. "Classic" democracies presumed decision making based on direct participation leading to consensus. The assembled citizenry was expected to agree on a common course of action after listening to the alternatives and weighing their respective merits and demerits. A tradition of hostility to "faction," and "particular interests" persists in democratic thought, but at least since *The Federalist Papers* it has become widely accepted that competition among factions is a necessary evil in democracies that operate on a more-than-local scale. Since, as James Madison argued, "the latent causes of faction are sown into the nature of man," and the possible remedies for "the mischief of faction" are worse than the disease, the best course is to recognize them and to attempt to control their effects.[6] Yet while democrats may agree on the inevitability of factions, they tend to disagree about the best forms and rules for governing factional competition. Indeed, differences over the preferred modes and boundaries of competition contribute most to distinguishing one subtype of democracy from another.

The most popular definition of democracy equates it with regular *elections,* fairly conducted and honestly counted. Some even consider the mere fact of elections—even ones from which specific parties or candidates are excluded, or in which substantial portions of the population cannot freely participate—as a sufficient condition for the existence of democracy. This fallacy has been called "electoralism" or "the faith that merely holding elections will channel political action into peaceful contests among elites and accord public legitimacy to the winners"—no matter how they are conducted or what else constrains those who win them.[7] However central to democracy, elections occur intermittently and only allow citizens to choose between the highly aggregated alternatives offered by political parties, which can, especially in the early stages of a democratic transition, proliferate in a bewildering variety. During the intervals between elections, citizens can seek to influence public policy through a wide variety of other intermediaries: interest associations, social movements, locality groupings, clientelistic arrangements, and so forth. *Modern democracy, in other words, offers a variety of competitive processes and channels for the expression of interests and values—associational as well as partisan, functional as well as territorial, collective as well as individual. All are integral to its practice.*

Another commonly accepted image of democracy identifies it with *majority rule.* Any governing body that makes decisions by combining the votes of more than half of those eligible and present is said to be democratic, whether that majority emerges within an electorate, a parliament, a committee, a city council, or a party caucus. For exceptional purposes (e.g., amending the constitution or expelling a member), "qualified majorities" of more than 50 percent may be required, but few would deny that democracy must involve some means of aggregating the equal preferences of individuals.

A problem arises, however, when *numbers* meet *intensities.* What happens when a properly assembled majority (especially a stable, self-perpetuating one) regularly makes decisions that harm some minority (especially a threatened cultural or ethnic group)? In these circumstances, successful democracies tend to qualify the central principle of majority rule in order to protect minority rights. Such qualifications can take the form of constitutional provisions that place certain matters beyond the reach of majorities (bills of rights); requirements for concurrent majorities in several different constituencies (confederalism); guarantees securing the autonomy of local or regional governments against the demands of the central authority (federalism); grand coalition governments that incorporate all parties (consociationalism); or the negotiation of social pacts between major social groups like business and labor (neocorporatism). The most common and effective way of protecting minorities, however, lies in the everyday operation of interest associations and social movements. These reflect (some would say, amplify) the different intensities of preference that exist in the population and bring them to bear on democratically elected decision makers. Another way of putting this intrinsic tension between numbers and intensities would be to say that "in modern democracies, votes may be counted, but influences alone are weighted."

*Cooperation* has always been a central feature of democracy. Actors must voluntarily make collective decisions binding on the polity as a whole. They must cooperate in order to compete. They must be capable of acting collectively through parties, associations, and movements in order to select candidates, articulate preferences, petition authorities, and influence policies.

But democracy's freedoms should also encourage citizens to deliberate among themselves, to discover their common needs, and to resolve their differences without relying on some supreme central authority. Classical democracy emphasized these qualities, and they are by no means extinct, despite repeated efforts by contemporary theorists to stress the analogy with behavior in the economic marketplace and to reduce all of democracy's operations to competitive interest maximization. Alexis de Tocqueville best described the importance of independent groups for democracy in his *Democracy in America*, a work which remains a major source of inspiration for all those who persist in viewing democracy as something more than a struggle for election and re-election among competing candidates.[8]

In contemporary political discourse, this phenomenon of cooperation and deliberation via autonomous group activity goes under the rubric of "civil society." The diverse units of social identity and interest, by remaining independent of the state (and perhaps even of parties), not only can restrain the arbitrary actions of rulers, but can also contribute to forming better citizens who are more aware of the preferences of others, more self-confident in their actions, and more civic-minded in their willingness to sacrifice for the common good. At its best, civil society provides an intermediate layer of governance between the individual and the state that is capable of resolving conflicts and controlling the behavior of members without public coercion. Rather than overloading decision makers with increased demands and making the system ungovernable,[9] a viable civil society can mitigate conflicts and improve the quality of citizenship—without relying exclusively on the privatism of the marketplace.

*Representatives*—whether directly or indirectly elected—do most of the real work in modern democracies. Most are professional politicians who orient their careers around the desire to fill key offices. It is doubtful that any democracy could survive without such people. The central question, therefore, is not whether or not there will be a political elite or even a professional political class, but how these representatives are chosen and then held accountable for their actions.

As noted above, there are many channels of representation in modern democracy. The electoral one, based on territorial constituencies, is the most visible and public. It culminates in a parliament or a presidency that is periodically accountable to the citizenry as a whole. Yet the sheer growth of government (in large part as a byproduct of popular demand) has increased the number, variety, and power of agencies charged with making public decisions and not subject to elections. Around these agencies there has developed a vast apparatus of specialized representation based largely on functional interests, not territorial constituencies. These interest associations, and not political parties, have become the primary expression of civil society in most stable democracies, supplemented by the more sporadic interventions of social movements.

The new and fragile democracies that have sprung up since 1974 must live in "compressed time." They will not resemble the European democracies of the nineteenth and early twentieth centuries, and they cannot expect to acquire the multiple channels of representation in gradual historical progression as did most of their predecessors. A bewildering array of parties, interests, and movements will all simultaneously seek political influence in them, creating challenges to the polity that did not exist in earlier processes of democratization.

## PROCEDURES THAT MAKE DEMOCRACY POSSIBLE

The defining components of democracy are necessarily abstract, and may give rise to a considerable variety of institutions and subtypes of democracy. For democracy to thrive, however, specific procedural norms must be followed and civic rights must be respected. Any polity that fails to impose such restrictions upon itself, that fails to follow the "rule of law" with regard to its own procedures, should not be considered democratic. These procedures alone do not define democracy, but their presence is indispensable to its persistence. In essence, they are necessary but not sufficient conditions for its existence.

Robert Dahl has offered the most generally accepted listing of what he terms the "procedural minimal" conditions that must be present for modern political democracy (or as he puts it, "polyarchy") to exist:

1. Control over government decisions about policy is constitutionally vested in elected officials.
2. Elected officials are chosen in frequent and fairly conducted elections in which coercion is comparatively uncommon.
3. Practically all adults have the right to vote in the election of officials.
4. Practically all adults have the right to run for elective offices in the government....
5. Citizens have a right to express themselves without the danger of severe punishment on political matters broadly defined....
6. Citizens have a right to seek out alternative sources of information. Moreover, alternative sources of information exist and are protected by law.
7. ... Citizens also have the right to form relatively independent associations or organizations, including independent political parties and interest groups.[10]

These seven conditions seem to capture the essence of procedural democracy for many theorists, but we propose to add two others. The first might be thought of as a further refinement of item (1), while the second might be called an implicit prior condition to all seven of the above.

8. Popularly elected officials must be able to exercise their constitutional powers without being subjected to overriding (albeit informal) opposition from unelected officials. Democracy is in jeopardy if military officers, entrenched civil servants, or state managers retain the capacity to act independently of elected civilians or even veto decisions made by the people's representatives. Without this additional caveat, the militarized polities of contemporary Central America, where civilian control over the military does not exist, might be classified by many scholars as democracies, just as they have been (with the exception of Sandinista Nicaragua) by U.S. policy makers. The caveat thus guards against what we earlier called "electoralism"—the tendency to focus on the holding of elections while ignoring other political realities.
9. The polity must be self-governing; it must be able to act independently of constraints imposed by some other overarching political system. Dahl and other contemporary democratic theorists probably took this condition for granted since they referred to formally sovereign nation-states. However, with the development of blocs, alliances, spheres of influence, and a variety of "neocolonial" arrangements, the question of autonomy has been a salient one. Is a system really democratic if its elected officals are unable to make binding decisions without the approval of actors outside their territorial domain? This is significant even if the outsiders are relatively free to alter or even end the encompassing arrangement (as in Puerto Rico), but it becomes especially critical if neither condition obtains (as in the Baltic states).

## PRINCIPLES THAT MAKE DEMOCRACY FEASIBLE

Lists of component processes and procedural norms help us to specify what democracy is, but they do not tell us much about how it actually functions. The simplest answer is "by the consent of the people"; the more complex one is "by the contingent consent of politicians acting under conditions of bounded uncertainty."

In a democracy, representatives must at least informally agree that those who win greater electoral support or influence over policy will not use their temporary superiority to bar the losers from taking office or exerting influence in the future, and that in exchange for this opportunity to keep competing for power and place, momentary losers will respect the winners' right to make binding decisions. Citizens are expected to obey the decisions ensuing from such a process of competition, provided its outcome remains contingent upon their collective preferences as expressed through fair and regular elections or open and repeated negotiations.

The challenge is not so much to find a set of goals that command widespread consensus as to find a set of rules that embody contingent consent. The precise shape of this "democratic bargain," to use Dahl's expression,[11] can vary a good deal from society to society. It depends on social cleavages and such subjective factors as mutual trust, the standard of fairness, and the willingness to compromise. It may even be compatible with a great deal of dissensus on substantive policy issues.

All democracies involve a degree of uncertainty about who will be elected and what policies they will pursue. Even in those polities where one party persists in winning elections or one policy is consistently implemented, the possibility of change through independent collective action still exists, as in Italy, Japan, and the Scandinavian social democracies. If it does not, the system is not democratic, as in Mexico, Senegal, or Indonesia.

But the uncertainty embedded in the core of all democracies is bounded. Not just any actor can get into the competition and raise any issue he or she pleases—there are previously established rules that must be respected. Not just any policy can be adopted—there are conditions that must be met. Democracy institutionalizes "normal," limited political uncertainty. These boundaries vary from country to country. Constitutional guarantees of property, privacy, expression, and other rights are a part of this, but the most effective boundaries are generated by competition among interest groups and cooperation within civil society. Whatever the rhetoric (and some polities appear to offer their citizens more dramatic alternatives than others), once the rules of contingent consent have been agreed upon, the actual variation is likely to stay within a predictable and generally accepted range.

This emphasis on operative guidelines contrasts with a highly persistent, but misleading theme in recent literature on democracy—namely, the emphasis upon "civic culture." The principles we have suggested here rest on rules of prudence, not on deeply ingrained habits of tolerance, moderation, mutual respect, fair play, readiness to compromise, or trust in public authorities. Waiting for such habits to sink deep and lasting roots implies a very slow process of regime consolidation—one that takes generations—and it would probably condemn most contemporary experiences *ex hypothesi* to failure. Our assertion is that contingent consent and bounded uncertainty can emerge from the interaction between antagonistic and mutually suspicious actors and that the far more benevolent and ingrained norms of a civic culture are better thought of as a *product* and not a producer of democracy.

## HOW DEMOCRACIES DIFFER

Several concepts have been deliberately excluded from our generic definition of democracy, despite the fact that they have been frequently associated with it in both ev-eryday practice and scholarly work. They are, nevertheless, especially important when it comes to distinguishing subtypes of democracy. Since no single set of actual institutions, practices, or values embodies democracy, polities moving away from authoritarian rule can mix different components to produce different democracies. It is important to recognize that these do not define points along a single continuum of improving performance, but a matrix of potential combinations that are *differently* democratic.

1. *Consensus:* All citizens may not agree on the substantive goals of political action or on the role of the state (although if they did, it would certainly make governing democracies much easier).

2. *Participation:* All citizens may not take an active and equal part in politics, although it must be legally possible for them to do so.

3. *Access:* Rulers may not weigh equally the preferences of all who come before them, although citizenship implies that individuals and groups should have an equal opportunity to express their preferences if they choose to do so.

4. *Responsiveness:* Rulers may not always follow the course of action preferred by the citizenry. But when they deviate from such a policy, say on grounds of "reason of state" or "overriding national interest," they must ultimately be held accountable for their actions through regular and fair processes.

5. *Majority rule:* Positions may not be allocated or rules may not be decided solely on the basis of assembling the most votes, although deviations from this principle usually must be explicitly defended and previously approved.

6. *Parliamentary sovereignty:* The legislature may not be the only body that can make rules or even the one with final authority in deciding which laws are binding, although where executive, judicial, or other public bodies make that ultimate choice, they too must be accountable for their actions.

7. *Party government:* Rulers may not be nominated, promoted, and disciplined in their activities by well-organized and programmatically coherent political parties, although where they are not, it may prove more difficult to form an effective government.

8. *Pluralism:* The political process may not be based on a multiplicity of overlapping, voluntaristic, and autonomous private groups. However, where there are monopolies of representation, hierarchies of association, and obligatory memberships, it is likely that the interests involved will be more closely linked to the state and the separation between the public and private spheres of action will be much less distinct.

9. *Federalism:* The territorial division of authority may not involve multiple levels and local autonomies, least of all ones enshrined in a constitutional docu-

ment, although some dispersal of power across territorial and/or functional units is characteristic of all democracies.

10. *Presidentialism:* The chief executive officer may not be a single person and he or she may not be directly elected by the citizenry as a whole, although some concentration of authority is present in all democracies, even if it is exercised collectively and only held indirectly accountable to the electorate.

11. *Checks and Balances:* It is not necessary that the different branches of government be systematically pitted against one another, although governments by assembly, by executive concentrations, by judicial command, or even by dictatorial fiat (as in time of war) must be ultimately accountable to the citizenry as a whole.

While each of the above has been named as an essential component of democracy, they should instead be seen either as indicators of this or that type of democracy, or else as useful standards for evaluating the performance of particular regimes. To include them as part of the generic definition of democracy itself would be to mistake the American polity for the universal model of democratic governance. Indeed, the parliamentary, consociational, unitary, corporatist, and concentrated arrangements of continental Europe may have some unique virtues for guiding polities through the uncertain transition from autocratic to democratic rule.[12]

## WHAT DEMOCRACY IS NOT

We have attempted to convey the general meaning of modern democracy without identifying it with some particular set of rules and institutions or restricting it to some specific culture or level of development. We have also argued that it cannot be reduced to the regular holding of elections or equated with a particular notion of the role of the state, but we have not said much more about what democracy is not or about what democracy may not be capable of producing.

There is an understandable temptation to load too many expectations on this concept and to imagine that by attaining democracy, a society will have resolved all of its political, social, economic, administrative, and cultural problems. Unfortunately, "all good things do not necessarily go together."

First, democracies are not necessarily more efficient economically than other forms of government. Their rates of aggregate growth, savings, and investment may be no better than those of nondemocracies. This is especially likely during the transition, when propertied groups and administrative elites may respond to real or imagined threats to the "rights" they enjoyed under authoritarian rule by initiating capital flight, disinvestment, or sabotage. In time, depending upon the type of democracy, benevolent long-term effects upon income distribution, aggregate demand, education, productivity, and creativity may eventually combine to improve economic and social performance, but it is certainly too much to expect that these improvements will occur immediately—much less that they will be defining characteristics of democratization.

Second, democracies are not necessarily more efficient administratively. Their capacity to make decisions may even be slower than that of the regimes they replace, if only because more actors must be consulted. The costs of getting things done may be higher, if only because "payoffs" have to be made to a wider and more resourceful set of clients (although one should never underestimate the degree of corruption to be found within autocracies). Popular satisfaction with the new democratic government's performance may not even seem greater, if only because necessary compromises often please no one completely, and because the losers are free to complain.

Third, democracies are not likely to appear more orderly, consensual, stable, or governable than the autocracies they replace. This is partly a byproduct of democratic freedom of expression, but it is also a reflection of the likelihood of continuing disagreement over new rules and institutions. These products of imposition or compromise are often initially quite ambiguous in nature and uncertain in effect until actors have learned how to use them. What is more, they come in the aftermath of serious struggles motivated by high ideals. Groups and individuals with recently acquired autonomy will test certain rules, protest against the actions of certain institutions, and insist on renegotiating their part of the bargain. Thus the presence of antisystem parties should be neither surprising nor seen as a failure of democratic consolidation. What counts is whether such parties are willing, however reluctantly, to play by the general rules of bounded uncertainty and contingent consent.

Governability is a challenge for all regimes, not just democratic ones. Given the political exhaustion and loss of legitimacy that have befallen autocracies from sultanistic Paraguay to totalitarian Albania, it may seem that only democracies can now be expected to govern effectively and legitimately. Experience has shown, however, that democracies too can lose the ability to govern. Mass publics can become disenchanted with their performance. Even more threatening is the temptation for leaders to fiddle with procedures and ultimately undermine the principles of contingent consent and bounded uncertainty. Perhaps the most critical moment comes once the politicians begin to settle into the more predictable roles and relations of a consolidated democracy. Many will find their expectations frustrated; some will discover that the new rules of competition put them at a disadvantage; a few may even feel that their vital interests are threatened by popular majorities.

Finally, democracies will have more open societies and polities than the autocracies they replace, but not necessarily more open economies. Many of today's most successful and well-established democracies have historically resorted to protectionism and closed borders, and have relied extensively upon public institutions to promote economic development. While the long-term compatibility between democracy and capitalism does not seem to be in doubt, despite their continuous tension, it is not clear whether the promotion of such liberal economic goals as the right of individuals to own property and retain profits, the clearing function of markets, the private settlement of disputes, the freedom to produce without government regulation, or the privatization of state-owned enterprises necessarily furthers the consolidation of democracy. After all, democracies do need to levy taxes and regulate certain transactions, especially where private monopolies and oligopolies exist. Citizens or their representatives may decide that it is desirable to protect the rights of collectivities from encroachment by individuals, especially propertied ones, and they may choose to set aside certain forms of property for public or cooperative ownership. In short, notions of economic liberty that are currently put forward in neoliberal economic models are not synonymous with political freedom—and may even impede it.

Democratization will not necessarily bring in its wake economic growth, social peace, administrative efficiency, political harmony, free markets, or "the end of ideology." Least of all will it bring about "the end of history." No doubt some of these qualities could make the consolidation of democracy easier, but they are neither prerequisites for it nor immediate products of it. Instead, what we should be hoping for is the emergence of political institutions that can peacefully compete to form governments and influence public policy, that can channel social and economic conflicts through regular procedures, and that have sufficient linkages to civil society to represent their constituencies and commit them to collective courses of action. Some types of democracies, especially in developing countries, have been unable to fulfill this promise, perhaps due to the circumstances of their transition from authoritarian rule.[13] The democratic wager is that such a regime, once established, will not only persist by reproducing itself within its initial confining conditions, but will eventually expand beyond them.[14] Unlike authoritarian regimes, democracies have the capacity to modify their rules and institutions consensually in response to changing circumstances. They may not immediately produce all the goods mentioned above, but they stand a better chance of eventually doing so than do autocracies.

## Notes

1. For a comparative analysis of the recent regime changes in southern Europe and Latin America, see Guillermo O'Donnell, Philippe C. Schmitter, and Laurence Whitehead, eds., *Transitions from Authoritarian Rule*, 4 vols. (Baltimore: Johns Hopkins University Press, 1986). For another compilation that adopts a more structural approach see Larry Diamond, Juan Linz, and Seymour Martin Lipset, eds., *Democracy in Developing Countries*, vols. 2, 3, and 4 (Boulder, Colo.: Lynne Rienner, 1989).

2. Numerous attempts have been made to codify and quantify the existence of democracy across political systems. The best known is probably Freedom House's *Freedom in the World: Political Rights and Civil Liberties*, published since 1973 by Greenwood Press and since 1988 by University Press of America. Also see Charles Humana, *World Human Rights Guide* (New York: Facts on File, 1986).

3. The definition most commonly used by American social scientists is that of Joseph Schumpeter: "that institutional arrangement for arriving at political decisions in which individuals acquire the power to decide by means of a competitive struggle for the people's vote." *Capitalism, Socialism, and Democracy* (London: George Allen and Unwin, 1943), 269. We accept certain aspects of the classical procedural approach to modern democracy, but differ primarily in our emphasis on the accountability of rulers to citizens and the relevance of mechanisms of competition other than elections.

4. Not only do some countries practice a stable form of democracy without a formal constitution (e.g., Great Britain and Israel), but even more countries have constitutions and legal codes that offer no guarantee of reliable practice. On paper, Stalin's 1936 constitution for the USSR was a virtual model of democratic rights and entitlements.

5. For the most valiant attempt to make some sense out of this thicket of distinctions, see Juan Linz, "Totalitarian and Authoritarian Regimes" in *Handbook of Political Science*, eds. Fred I. Greenstein and Nelson W. Polsby (Reading Mass.: Addison Wesley, 1975), 175–411.

6. "Publius" (Alexander Hamilton, John Jay, and James Madison), *The Federalist Papers* (New York: Anchor Books, 1961). The quote is from Number 10.

7. See Terry Karl, "Imposing Consent? Electoralism versus Democratization in El Salvador," in *Elections and Democratization in Latin America, 1980–1985*, eds. Paul Drake and Eduardo Silva (San Diego: Center for Iberian and Latin American Studies, Center for US/Mexican Studies, University of California, San Diego, 1986), 9–36.

8. Alexis de Tocqueville, *Democracy in America*, 2 vols. (New York: Vintage Books, 1945).

9. This fear of overloaded government and the imminent collapse of democracy is well reflected in the work of Samuel P. Huntington during the 1970s. See especially Michel Crozier, Samuel P. Huntington, and Joji Watanuki, *The Crisis of Democracy* (New York: New York University Press, 1975). For Huntington's (revised) thoughts about the prospects for democracy, see his "Will More Countries Become Democratic?," *Political Science Quarterly* 99 (Summer 1984): 193–218.

10. Robert Dahl, *Dilemmas of Pluralist Democracy* (New Haven: Yale University Press, 1982), 11.

11. Robert Dahl, *After the Revolution: Authority in a Good Society* (New Haven: Yale University Press, 1970).

12. See Juan Linz, "The Perils of Presidentialism," *Journal of Democracy* 1 (Winter 1990): 51–69, and the ensuing discussion by Donald Horowitz, Seymour Martin Lipset, and Juan Linz in *Journal of Democracy* 1 (Fall 1990): 73–91.

13. Terry Lynn Karl, "Dilemmas of Democratization in Latin America" *Comparative Politics* 23 (October 1990): 1–23.

14. Otto Kirchheimer, "Confining Conditions and Revolutionary Breakthroughs," *American Political Science Review* 59 (1965): 964–974.

## EUROPE

# Devolution can be salvation

**Decentralisation has spread across Europe. On the whole, it has kept countries together rather than broken them up.**

The decision by three-quarters of Scotland's voters on September 11th to opt for their own parliament could—Scottish Nationalists hope—lead to Scotland's snapping clean away from the United Kingdom. Scotland might, indeed, be as viably independent as Denmark, Finland or Ireland, countries of comparable size and wealth.

But experience elsewhere in Europe suggests that devolution has proved widely popular without generally leading to secession; indeed, it can help to hold a country together. When strong regional or national identities, silent or suppressed for many years, are suddenly given a voice, the paradoxical result has often been greater harmony and a greater desire to stick together rather than anguish, chaos and disintegration. The end of the cold war and the inexorable rise of the European Union have both weakened the grip of Europe's main nation-states but without threatening to break them up, except when involuntary unions fragmented after communists lost control.

Take the seven most populous countries on Europe's continent: Russia, Germany, Turkey (yes, it is European as well as Asian), France, Italy, Ukraine and Spain.

Russia is, perhaps, *sui generis*, because of its immense size and ethnic diversity, the exceptional brutality of its history, and the suffocating uniformity forced on its various peoples by communists and tsars. After the 14 non-Russian republics of the old Soviet Union went their ways, Russia was left with more than a score of autonomous ethnically named regions and republics. Chechnya apart, ramshackle Russia has been a big success: by offering all these peoples a measure of genuine self-rule, the country has held itself together. Ukraine too, by giving Crimea

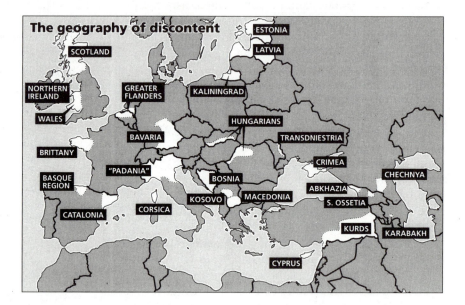

The geography of discontent

and its ethnic-Russian majority plenty of autonomy, has managed to hold on to its Black Sea peninsula without bloodshed. Devolution is working in both these Slav places.

Germany has—with its post-1945 determination never to let power again sit in the palm of one hand—given much power to its 16 *Länder* (states), including the five eastern ones added after the Berlin Wall came down in 1989. Indeed, their power to block reform, through their representation in the federal republic's second chamber, the Bundesrat, may nowadays be too much. But, on the whole, Germany's federal devolution has worked too. And worried Britons should remember that former kingdoms such as Bavaria and—a recent addition from the east—Saxony, both now *Länder*, have as great a sense of historic identity as Scotland, and (even compared with

Scotland's coming dispensation) much more constitutional power. Yet none of them threatens to secede.

France, famously centralised since Louis XIV's reign (1643–1715), has also usefully loosened its Parisian bonds since the 1980s by creating 22 new mainland regions with budgets of their own. France has dealt sensibly with its nastiest would-be separatist danger: Napoleon's native isle of Corsica, some fifth of whose people are nationalists of one kind or another, has been pacified with a mixture of subsidy and devolution. And Lionel Jospin, France's prime minister, now says that non-French languages in France, such as Breton, should be given greater due.

Spain, since General Franco died in 1975, has boldly devolved, giving more power to 17 new regions, and extra power still to Basques and Catalans.

For sure, Basque separatists, who take about 12% of the vote in the Basque region, connive at a lingering terror campaign that has taken some 800 lives in 30 years. But there is no doubt that Spanish decentralisation has, with minimal post-Franco coercion, kept the country together.

Italy, too, is contemplating some degree of devolution as the cold-war glue of old parties and their loyalties to a Roman centre has gone. The separatist Northern League has made electoral inroads in Italy's north, but may now have peaked. Once again, devolution from Rome is likely to hold things better together.

Devolution is occurring in some new ways, too. Regional co-operation across old national borders (some of them evaporating as the EU integrates) may in time engender a new set of economics-driven loyalties that weaken the pull of the old nation-states but without necessarily breaking them up. The Catalans, for instance, seem set to stay in Spain, but hope to use their vaunted status as a European region to play Madrid off against Brussels. Tolerant Irishmen likewise hope that closer links within the EU between their island's north and south may soften the edges of competing nationalisms. Maybe, in time, they will.

Devolution is trickier when disaffected components of larger units—eg, Bosnia, as it broke away from old Yugoslavia—consist of populations whose ethnic make-up is mixed and whose loyalties are therefore divided. In such places, the least hopeless course may be to ensure as wide a measure of democracy as possible at the lowest local level (for instance, in last weekend's Bosnian town elections, whose results are not yet clear). But "ethnic cleansing" and partition are still brutally effective in places where people with divided loyalties cannot co-exist side by side.

It is easier, of course, if people who do not love each other in one country already inhabit separate bits of it. Hence, in 1993, Czechs and Slovaks could amicably agree to divorce. Greeks and Turks in Cyprus are unlikely ever to integrate. But Russians are coming to terms with living among newly dominant Balts. And, with the lure of European Union membership, Hungarians and Romanians are treating their minorities much better; the Slovak government, alas, is not so gentle.

The chief illustration of a country whose short-sighted and prickly nationalism nourishes a belief that devolution is but a slippery slope to separation is Turkey. If only it would learn from Spain. The Turks' refusal to grant any serious autonomy to their large Kurdish minority has helped prolong a guerrilla war that has cost at least six times as many lives, over a much shorter period, as have been lost in the Basque and Irish conflicts put together. If the Kurds had autonomy, their urge to break off completely from Turkey would be scarcely stronger than that of the Basques or Scots wanting to abandon Spain or Britain. If there is a turn-of-the-century message in Europe, it may be "devolve or die".

# Parliament and Congress:

## Is the Grass Greener on the other side?

*Gregory S. Mahler*

**Gregory Mahler is chair of the Political Science Department at the University of Mississippi.**

Aristotle long ago observed that man is a "political animal." He could have added that man, by his very nature, notes the political status of his neighbours and, very often, perceives their lot as being superior to his own. The old saying "the grass is greener on the other side of the fence" can be applied to politics and political structures as well as to other, more material, dimensions of the contemporary world.

Legislators are not immune from the very human tendency to see how others of their lot exist in their respective settings, and, sometimes, to look longingly at these other settings. When legislators do look around to see the conditions under which their peers operate in other countries, they occasionally decide they prefer the alternative legislative settings to their own.

Features which legislators admire or envy in the settings of their colleagues include such things as: the characteristics of political parties (their numbers, or degrees of party discipline), legislative committee systems, staff and services available to help legislators in their tasks, office facilities, libraries, and salaries. This essay will develop the "grass is greener" theme in relation to a dimension of the legislative world which is regularly a topic of conversation when legislators from a number of different jurisdictions meet: the ability or inability of legislatures to check and control the executive.

## The Decline of Parliament

The theme of the "decline of parliament" has a long and well-studied history.[1] It generally refers to the gradual flow of true legislative power away from the legislative body in the direction of the executive. The executive does the real law-making—by actually drafting most legislation—and the legislature takes a more "passive" role by simply approving executive proposals.

Legislators are very concerned about their duties and powers and over the years have jealously guarded them when they have appeared to be threatened. In Canada (and indeed most parliamentary democracies in the world today), the majority of challenges to legislative power which develop no longer come from the ceremonial executive (the Crown), but from the political executive, the government of the day.

It can be argued that the ability to direct and influence public policy, is a "zero sum game" (i.e. there is only room for a limited amount of power and influence to be exercised in the political world and a growth in the relative power of the political executive must be at the expense of the power of the legislature). It follows, then, that if the legislature is concerned about maintaining its powers, concerned about protecting its powers from being diminished, it must be concerned about every attempt by the political executive to expand its powers.

Others contend that real "legislative power" cannot, and probably never did reside in the legislature. There was no "Golden Age" of Parliament. The true legislative role of parliament today is not (and in the past was not) to create legislation, but to scrutinize and ratify legislation introduced by the Government of the day. Although an occasional exception to this pattern of behavior may exist (with private members' bills, for example), the general rule is clear: the legislature today does not actively initiate legislation as its primary *raison d'être*.

Although parliamentarians may not be major initiators of legislation, studies have indicated a wide range of other functions.[2] Certainly one major role of the legislature is the "oversight" role, criticizing and checking the powers of the executive. The ultimate extension of this power is

From *Canadian Parliamentary Review,* Winter 1985/86, pp. 19–21. Reprinted by permission of the Committees and Parliamentary Associations Branch of the House of Commons in Ottawa, Ontario.

the ability of the legislature to terminate the term of office of the executive through a "no confidence" vote. Another role of the legislature involves communication and representation of constituency concerns. Yet another function involves the debating function, articulating the concerns of the public of the day.

Professor James Mallory has indicated the need to "be realistic about the role of Parliament in the Westminster system."[3] He cites Bernard Crick's classic work, *The Reform of Parliament*: ". . . the phrase 'Parliamentary control," and talk about the 'decline of parliamentary control," should not mislead anyone into asking for a situation in which governments can have their legislation changed or defeated, or their life terminated. . . . Control means influence, not direct power; advice, not command; criticism, not obstruction; scrutiny, not initiation; and publicity, not secrecy."[4]

The fact that parliament may not be paramount in the creation and processing of legislation is no reason to condemn all aspects of parliamentary institutions. Nor should parliamentarians be convinced that legislative life is perfect in the presidential-congressional system. In fact, some American legislators look to their parliamentary brethren and sigh with envy at the attractiveness of certain aspects of parliamentary institutions.

## Desirability of a Congressional Model for Canada?

Many Canadian parliamentarians and students of parliament look upon presidential-congressional institutions of the United States as possessing the answers to most of their problems. The grass is sometimes seen as being greener on the other side of the border. The concepts of fixed legislative terms, less party discipline, and a greater general emphasis on the role and importance of individual legislators (which implies more office space and staff for individual legislators, among other things) are seen as standards to which Canadian legislators should aspire.

A perceived strength of the American congressional system is that legislators do not automatically "rubber stamp" approve executive proposals. They consider the president's suggestions, but feel free to make substitutions or modifications to the proposal, or even to reject it completely. Party discipline is relatively weak; there are regularly Republican legislators opposing a Republican president (and Democratic legislators supporting him), and vice versa. Against the need for discipline congressmen argue that their first duty is to either (a) their constituency, or (b) what is "right", rather than simply to party leaders telling them how to behave in the legislature. For example, in 1976 Jimmy Carter was elected President with large majorities of Democrats in both houses of Congress. One of Carter's major concerns was energy policy. He introduced legislative proposals (that is, he had congressional supporters introduce legislation, since the American president cannot introduce legislation on his own) dealing with energy policy, calling his proposals "the moral equivalent of

war." In his speeches and public appearances he did everything he could to muster support for "his" legislation. Two years later when "his" legislation finally emerged from the legislative process, it could hardly be recognized as the proposals submitted in such emotional terms two years earlier.

The experience of President Carter was certainly not unique. Any number of examples of such incidents of legislative-executive non-cooperation can be cited in recent American political history, ranging from President Wilson's unsuccessful efforts to get the United States to join the League of Nations, through Ronald Reagan's contemporary battles with Congress over the size of the federal budget. The Carter experience was somewhat unusual by virtue of the fact that the same political party controlled both the executive and legislative branches of government, and cooperation still was not forthcoming. There have been many more examples of non-cooperation when one party has controlled the White House and another party has controlled one or both houses of Congress.

This lack of party discipline ostensibly enables the individual legislators to be concerned about the special concerns of their constituencies. This, they say, is more important than simply having to follow the orders of the party whip in the legislature. It is not any more unusual to find a Republican legislator from a farm state voting against a specific agricultural proposal of President Reagan on the grounds that the legislation in question is not good for his/her constituency, than to find Democratic legislators from the southwestern states who voted against President Carter's water policy proposals on the grounds that the proposals were not good for their constituencies.

Congressional legislators know that they have fixed terms in office—the President is simply not able to bring about early elections—and they know that as long as they can keep their constituencies happy there is no need to be terribly concerned about opposing the President, even if he is the leader of their party. It may be nice to have the President on your side, but if you have a strong base of support "back home" you can survive without his help.

Are there any benefits to the public interest in the absence of party discipline? The major argument is that the legislature will independently consider the executive's proposals, rather than simply accepting the executive's ideas passively. This, it is claimed, allows for a multiplicity of interests, concerns, and perspectives to be represented in the legislature, and ostensibly results in "better" legislation.

In summary, American legislative institutions promote the role of the individual legislator. The fixed term gives legislators the security necessary for the performance of the functions they feel are important. The (relative) lack of party discipline enables legislators to act on the issues about which they are concerned. In terms of the various legislative functions mentioned above, congressmen appear to spend a great deal of their time in what has been termed the legislative aspect of the job: drafting legislation, debating, proposing amendments, and voting (on a more or less independent basis).

While many parliamentarians are impressed by the ability of individual American legislators to act on their own volition it is ironic that many congressional legislators look longingly at the legislative power relationships of their parliamentary brethren. The grass, apparently, is greener on the *other* side of the border, too.

## Desirability of a Parliamentary Model

The "decline of congressional power" is as popular a topic of conversation in Washington as "the decline of parliamentary power" in Ottawa or London. Over the last several decades American legislators have sensed that a great deal of legislative power has slipped from their collective grasp.[5] Many have decried this tendency and tried to stop, or reverse this flow of power away from the legislative branch and toward the executive.

One of the major themes in the writings of these congressional activists is an admiration for the parliamentary model's (perceived) power over the executive. Many American legislators see the president's veto power, combined with his fixed term in office, as a real flaw in the "balance of powers" of the system, leading to an inexorable increase in executive power at the expense of the legislature. They look at a number of parliamentary structures which they see as promoting democratic political behavior and increased executive responsibility to the legislature, including the ability to force the resignation of the executive through a non-confidence vote. The regular "question period" format which insures some degree of public executive accountability is also perceived as being very attractive.

Critics of the congressional system do not confine their criticism only to the growth of executive power. There are many who feel there is too much freedom in the congressional arena. To paraphrase the words of Bernard Crick cited earlier, advising has sometimes turned into issuing commands; and criticism has sometimes turned into obstruction. This is not to suggest that congressional legislators would support giving up their ability to initiate legislation, to amend executive proposals, or to vote in a manner which they (individually) deem proper. This does suggest, however, that even congressional legislators see that independence is a two-sided coin: one side involves individual legislative autonomy and input into the legislative process; the other side involves the incompatibility of complete independence with a British style of "Responsible Government".

In 1948 Hubert Humphrey, then mayor of Minneapolis, delivered an address at the nomination convention of the Democratic Party. In his comments he appealed for a "more responsible" two party system in the United States, a system with sufficient party discipline to have *meaningful* party labels, and to allow party platforms to become public policy.[6] Little progress has been made over the last

thirty-seven years in this regard. In the abstract the concept of a *meaningful* two party system may be attractive; American legislators have not been as attracted to the necessary corollary of the concept: decreased legislative independence and increased party discipline.

While American Senators and Representatives are very jealous of executive encroachments upon their powers, there is some recognition that on occasion—usually depending upon individual legislators' views about the desirability of specific pieces of legislation—executive leadership, and perhaps party discipline, can serve a valuable function. Congressional legislators are, at times which correspond to their policy preferences, envious of parliamentary governments' abilities to carry their programs into law because MPs elected under their party labels will act consistent with party whips' directions. They would be loath to give up their perceived high degrees of legislative freedom but many of them realize the cost of this freedom in this era of pressing social problems and complex legislation. Parliamentary style government is simply not possible without party discipline.

A Democratic Congressman supporting President Carter's energy policy proposals might have longed for an effective three-line whip to help to pass the energy policies in question. An opponent of those policy proposals would have argued, to the contrary, that the frustration of the president's proposals was a good illustration of the wisdom of the legislature tempering the error-ridden policy proposals of the president. Similarly, many conservative Republican supporters of President Reagan have condemned the ability of the Democratic House of Representatives to frustrate his economic policies. Opponents of those policies have argued, again, that the House of Representatives is doing an important job of representing public opinion and is exercising a valuable and important check on the misguided policies of the executive.

## Some Concluding Observations

The parliamentary model has its strengths as well as its weaknesses. The individual legislator in a parliamentary system does not have as active a role in the actual legislative process as does his American counterparts, but it is not at all hard to imagine instances in which the emphasis on individual autonomy in the congressional system can be counterproductive because it delays much-needed legislative programs.

The problem, ultimately, is one of balance. Is it possible to have a responsible party system in the context of parliamentary democracy which can deliver on its promises to the public, and also to have a high degree of individual legislative autonomy in the legislative arena?

It is hard to imagine how those two concepts could coexist. The congressional and parliamentary models of legislative behavior have placed their respective emphases on two different priorities. The parliamentary model, with its responsible party system and its corresponding party discipline in the legislature, emphasizes efficient policy delivery, and the ability of an elected government to deliver on its promises. The congressional model, with its lack of party discipline and its emphasis on individual legislative autonomy, placed more emphasis on what can be called "consensual politics": it may take much more time for executive proposals to find their way into law, but (the argument goes) there is greater likelihood that what does, ultimately, emerge as law will be acceptable to a greater number of people than if government proposals were "automatically" approved by a pre-existing majority in the legislature acting "under the whip".

We cannot say that one type of legislature is "more effective" than the other. Each maximizes effectiveness in different aspects of the legislative function. Legislators in the congressional system, because of their greater legislative autonomy and weaker party discipline, are more effective at actually legislating than they are at exercising ultimate control over the executive. Legislators in the parliamentary system, although they may play more of a "ratifying" role in regard to legislation, do get legislation passed promptly; they also have an ultimate power over the life of the government of the day.

The appropriateness of both models must also be evaluated in light of the different history, political culture and objectives of the societies in which they operate. Perhaps the grass is just as green on both sides of the fence.

## Notes

1. There is substantial literature devoted to the general topic of "the decline of legislatures." Among the many sources which could be referred to in this area would be included the work of Gerhard Loewenberg. *Modern Parliaments: Change or Decline?* Chicago: Atherton. 1971; Gerhard Loewenberg and Samuel Patterson, *Comparing Legislatures,* Boston: Little, Brown, 1979; or Samuel Patterson and John Wahlke, eds., *Comparative Legislative Behavior: Frontiers of Research,* New York: John Wiley, 1972.
2. A very common topic in studies of legislative behavior has to do with the various functions legislatures may be said to perform for the societies of which they are a part. For a discussion of the many functions attributed to legislatures in political science literature, see Gregory Mahler, *Comparative Politics: An Institutional and Cross-National Approach* (Cambridge, Ma.: Schenkman, 1983, pp. 56–61.
3. J. R. Mallory, "Can Parliament Control the Regulatory Process?" *Canadian Parliamentary Review* Vol. 6 (no. 3, 1983) p. 6.
4. Bernard Crick, *The Reform of Parliament,* London, 1968, p. 80.
5. One very well written discussion of the decline of American congressional power in relation to the power of the president can be found in Ronald Moe, ed., *Congress and the President,* Pacific Palisades, Calif.: Goodyear Publishing Co., 1971.
6. Subsequently a special report was published by the Committee on Political Parties of the American Political Science Association dealing with this problem. See "Toward a More Responsible Two-Party System," *American Political Science Review* Vol. 44 (no. 3, 1950), special supplement.

# Campaign and Party Finance:
# What Americans Might Learn from Abroad

## Arthur B. Gunlicks
*University of Richmond*

When the Clinton Administration took office in January 1993 with a Democratic-controlled Congress, many Americans were hoping that the long-standing "gridlock" between the Congress and President would finally be broken on a wide variety of issues, not the least of which was a reform of campaign finance laws and practices. Ross Perot had raised the issue during the presidential campaign, and Democratic-passed reform legislation which had been vetoed by President Bush now seemed to have a good chance of being revived, perhaps modified, passed, and signed by the new President.

It was not to be. Democratic House leaders gave President Clinton's campaign reform proposals of May 7, 1993, a lukewarm reaction, and Senator Robert Dole threatened to use the filibuster to block congressional action. Reform is a risky business for both parties, and what looks good from the perspective of political scientists or even the White House may not be very appealing to politicians in the trenches who worry that would-be challengers might actually have a fighting chance. In any case, the Democrats in the Senate and House could not agree on a compromise bill, and by the time they finally did in the fall of 1994 their efforts were defeated by the inability to end a Republican filibuster in the Senate.

After the Republican takeover of both the Senate and House following the 1994 midterm elections, any serious hope for political finance reform was dead. First, because the Republican "Contract with America" set entirely different priorities, and, second, because "gridlock" had returned and there was little hope that the Republican-dominated Congress and the Democratic President could agree on reform measures. Certainly any proposals calling for federal subsidies or tax expenditures would have no chance in a Republican Congress determined to reduce drastically federal expenditures and the federal deficit. Still, Ross Perot continued to talk about political finance reform, and House Speaker Newt Gingrich and President Clinton agreed informally in early summer 1995 to work together to promote campaign finance reform. In fact, not much has happened since then, although the issue refuses to go away.

It is easy and very tempting to argue that we should look at what other Western democracies do and adopt some of their practices. One of the difficulties we face, however, lies in the uniqueness of our political system, which raises questions about the relevance of foreign experiences. First, we have to focus on the party system. Our politics are candidate-oriented. In most democracies, they are more party-oriented. Many of us may regret this fact and even devote some energy and effort toward strengthening American parties, but the probability of a major change seems slight. The party orientation found elsewhere has an effect on political financing. Indeed, the concept of "political finance" is likely to mean candidate and campaign financing in the United States and party financing in other democracies. Therefore, it is not surprising that the administration backed away from the idea of funneling public funds to the parties.

Second, our institutions are different. Virtually all countries that we might look to for comparison are parliamentary democracies. France may have a semi-presidential system, but its parliamentary features still distinguish it from the United States. Most democracies are unitary states. Canada, Australia, Germany, Switzerland and Austria are federal states, but they differ in significant respects from the United States in their division of powers as well as in population and/or size of territory. They are also parliamentary democracies.

Third, we have a political culture which is not very conducive to government assistance to political parties. Anti-party and anti-government sentiments in the United States have deep roots, and reform proposals that might cost taxpayers money and bring about more government involvement must overcome serious obstacles. It may be that public financing is not very popular in other countries, either, but the fact remains that it is widespread abroad and not here.

It is clear that the kind of massive public funding of parties found, for example, in Germany, Austria, and Sweden has little prospect of being implemented in the United States. The generously funded party foundations which perform a number of useful tasks in Germany and Austria also are unlikely ever to gain majority support

Original version of this revised article first appeared in *Party Line,* Spring/Summer 1993, pp. 7–8. © 1993 by Arthur B. Gunlicks. Reprinted by permission.

in Congress. Public funding on this scale would be unacceptable for very practical budgetary reasons, let alone the different American party system and political culture.

What, then, are some foreign practices that might be deserving of some careful consideration in spite of the odds against their passage? It should be possible to convince the public—and then Congress—that television and radio stations must provide a certain amount of free media time, a common practice in almost every other democracy. The Clinton Administration's proposal to provide congressional candidates vouchers to pay for television, printing and postage if they agree to adhere to spending limits is a step in the right direction, but it differs significantly from other democracies where free time is provided to the parties rather than individual candidates. Free billboard and poster space for political advertisements might also be offered by local governments, as is common in Europe. There can be no question, however, that the focus on individual candidates in this country makes free television time and billboard space more complicated to administer. It would probably be very difficult to convince Americans to ban altogether the purchase of media time by individual candidates, as is done in Canada, Britain and the European Continent.

In order to reduce the influence of the widely disliked PACs, which are not found abroad, one can make a strong case for limiting the amounts they may give individual candidates. Thus it is not surprising that the Clinton Administration has moved at least modestly in this direction. But placing limits on PACs raises the question of where the necessary campaign money is to come from besides wealthy candidates, their supporters, and other private interests. Some European countries, e.g., Germany, provide generous tax deductions for donations to political parties. The very modest deductions that were available in the United States were eliminated in the 1986 tax reforms. Surely small donations of up to at least $250 should be encouraged through tax deductions and/or public matching funds for candidates who have demonstrated that they enjoy minimal political support. Contributions to political parties should be promoted, and parties should be encouraged to assume more responsibility for financing the campaigns of their candidates. Perhaps "soft money" *to the parties* could be better regulated rather than banned, as appears to be a goal of the Clinton proposals.

We do, of course, have a $3 federal tax check-off to pay for *presidential* campaigns and national political conventions, but only a small percentage (15–18 percent) of taxpayers actually check the appropriate boxes even though it costs them nothing. A few states also have tax check-offs for helping to finance certain candidates or parties, while another handful of states have tax add-ons, where the taxpayer actually increases his or her tax liability by giving up a small portion of the refund due.

As a result, only about one percent of state taxpayers participate in tax add-on schemes. In other words, the amount of public political financing that exists in the United States, except for presidential races, is minimal.

To level the playing field even more, Congress could again try to impose limits on individual spending by candidates in the hope that the Supreme Court might reconsider its decision in *Buckley v. Valeo*. The British and Canadians have limited expenditures by individual candidates without, at last check, weakening freedom of speech in any notable way. The British also require candidate approval of what we call "independent expenditures," which has hardly led to a serious undermining of free speech.

Some reformers have argued that tightening the regulation of parties and candidates, such as improved disclosure and reporting procedures, would "clean up" problems of political finance. Aside from the suspicion that such proposals reflect the "puritan" streak in American political culture, it is difficult to see how these measures would deal effectively with the funding problems we face.

If large amounts of money are being spent by individual candidates, PACs and special interests in general, and there is understandable public dissatisfaction with this state of affairs, it seems apparent that alternate sources of financing must be found. Placing ceilings on expenditures is probably not a very effective solution. Tightening regulations will not produce more private donations. The dilemmas—and there are several—are that alternatives seem to be very expensive, and there is the problem of increasing dependency on the state. This dependency may lead to a separation of the party from the grassroots, as appears to be happening in Germany and several other countries, especially Italy, which voted *recently* in a referendum to end public subsidies for the parties.

American parties are a very long way from becoming dependent on the state for their finances. Indeed, by international comparison we rank low on the dependency scale, especially if one excludes the presidential campaigns. Were we to adopt free media time, free billboard space, tax deductions for small donations to parties and candidates, or modest public subsidies for legislative candidates, all of which are practices common in numerous other democracies, we would not solve all of our current problems. But it seems difficult to believe that the conditions of political financing in the United States would not benefit from the adoption of some of these measures.

---

Arthur B. Gunlicks is the editor of *Comparative Party and Campaign Finance in Europe and North America,* published by Westview Press.

## Unit Selections

The European Union
25. **The Untied States of Europe,** Tyler Marshall
26. **What Is Europe? The Changing Idea of a Continent,** Richard Rose
27. **The Institutional Framework of the EU,** *The Economist*
28. **Europe's Censure Motion,** Quentin Peel and Peter Norman

The Introduction of the Euro
29. **Europe's New Currency: Gambling on the Euro,** The Economist

Post-Communist Central and Eastern Europe
30. **Eastern Europe a Decade Later: The Postcommunist Divide,** Jacques Rupnik

Russia and the Other Post-Soviet Republics
31. **What Now for Russia?** John-Thor Dahlburg
32. **Russia's Summer of Discontent,** Michael McFaul
33. **Can Russia Change?** David Remnick

## Key Points to Consider

❖ What are the major obstacles to the emergence of a more unified Europe? What differentiates the optimists and the skeptics as they assess the outlook for greater integration? What are the major institutional characteristics of the European Union, and why is there a widespread call for reform? How will the introduction of the euro change relations within the EU?

❖ What is the evidence that the economic problems of Western Europe are not just cyclical but also structural in origin? What has been the impact of economic stagnation on the social services provided by the welfare state?

❖ What are the main problems facing the newly elected governments in Eastern and Central Europe? How well are they doing in coping with the transition to political pluralism and a market economy?

❖ Was Gorbachev mistaken in believing that the Soviet Union could be reformed without being dissolved? How have the recent parliamentary and presidential elections set back the cause of political and economic reform in Russia? What explains the electoral support received by the Communists and the nationalists?

 **Links**      ## www.dushkin.com/online/

14. **Europa: European Union**
    *http://europa.eu.int*

15. **NATO Integrated Data Service**
    *http://www.nato.int/structur/nids/nids.htm*

16. **Research and Reference (Library of Congress)**
    *http://lcweb.loc.gov/rr/*

17. **Russian and East European Network Information Center, University of Texas at Austin**
    *http://reenic.utexas.edu/reenic.html*

These sites are annotated on pages 6 and 7.

Most of the articles in this unit are in some way linked to one or the other of two major developments that have fundamentally altered the political map of Europe in recent years. The first of these major changes is the long-term movement toward supranational integration of many Western European states within the institutional framework of the European Community, or EC, which officially became the European Union, or EU, on November 1, 1993. Here the development has primarily been one by which sovereign states piecemeal give up some of their traditional independence, especially in matters dealing with economic and (so far, to a lesser degree) monetary policy. Some important decisions that used to be taken by national governments in Paris, Rome, Bonn, Dublin, or Copenhagen have become the province of EU policymakers in Brussels.

It is an important indication of the EU's continuing attractiveness that other countries seek to join the club. Austria and two of the Scandinavian countries (Sweden and Finland) became the newest EU members in 1995, after the entry had been approved in national referendums in each country.

The second major challenge to the established European state system is of a more disruptive nature. It consists of the disintegration brought about by the sudden collapse of Communist rule in Central and Eastern Europe at the end of the 1980s. Here states, nations, and nationalities have broken away from an imposed system of central control, and now assert their independence from the previous ruling group and its ideology. In their attempts to construct a new order for themselves, the post-Communist countries are encountering enormous difficulties. Their transition from one-party rule to pluralist democracy and from centrally planned state socialism to a market-based economy has turned out to be much rougher than had been anticipated. There is already considerable evidence that many people have a nostalgia for the basic material security and "orderliness" provided by the communist welfare states of the past. Communist-descended parties have responded by abandoning much of their Leninist baggage and engaging in the competitive bidding for votes with promises of social fairness and security. In Poland and elsewhere, such parties have recently gained political leverage. By contrast with the recent past, however, they must now operate in a pluralist political setting and have adopted different strategies and goals than in the past.

A closer look at the countries of Western Europe reveals that they have their own internal problems, even if in a far less acute form than their counterparts to the East. Their relative prosperity rests on a base built up during the prolonged postwar economic boom of the 1950s and 1960s. By political choice, a considerable portion of their affluence was channeled toward the public sector and was used to develop relatively generous systems of social services and social insurance. Between the early 1970s and the mid-1980s, however, Western industrial societies were beset by economic disruptions that brought an end to the long period of rapidly growing prosperity. The last half of the 1980s marked some improvement in the economic situation throughout most of Western Europe, partly as a result of some favorably timed positive trade balances with the United States. In the early 1990s, however, economic recession gripped these countries once again. It is becoming clear that there are more fundamental reasons why they no longer can take increasing affluence for granted in a more competitive global economy. Almost every one of them is today beset by economic problems that appear to be structural in origin, rather than just cyclical and therefore passing.

The economic shock that first interrupted the prolonged postwar boom had come in the wake of sharp rises in the cost of energy, linked to successive hikes in the price of oil imposed by the Organization of Petroleum Exporting Countries (OPEC) after 1973. In the 1980s, OPEC lost its organizational bite, as its members began to compete against each other by raising production and lowering prices rather than abiding by the opposite practices in the manner of a well-functioning cartel agreement. The exploitation of new oil and gas fields in the North Sea and elsewhere also helped alleviate the energy situation, at least for the present. The resulting improvement for the consumers of oil and gas helped the Western European economies recover, but as a whole they did not rebound to their earlier high growth rates.

Because of their heavy dependence on international trade, Western European economies are especially vulnerable to the kind of global recessionary tendencies we have encountered in recent years. Another important challenge to these affluent countries is found as they face stiff competition from the new industrial countries (NICs) of East and South Asia. The emerging Asian factor probably contributed to the increased tempo of the European drive for economic integration in the late 1980s.

A related issue is how the increase in international trade within and outside the European Union will affect the established "social market economies" of continental Europe. The economic gains derived from international competition could have a positive consequence by providing a better base for consolidating and invigorating the social welfare systems. However, a different scenario seems to be starting, which will result in a drastic pruning and reduction in social services, carried out in the name of efficiency and international competitiveness. Several writers allude to the social problems that have resulted in Europe's growing "underclass." It also seems evident that the corporatist and welfare state arrangements, which appear to serve these countries so well for so long, now face other demographic and economic challenges as well. The debate about the best policy response to such problems will probably continue to agitate West Europeans for years to come.

In the mid-1980s, there was widespread talk of a malaise or "Europessimism" that had beset these countries. Thereafter, the mood appeared to become more upbeat, and for a while some observers even detected a swing toward what they labeled "Euro-phoria." By now there seems once again to be a more sober or even pessimistic spirit abroad in Western Europe.

The demise of the Soviet bloc removed one major external challenge but replaced it with a set of others. The countries of Western Europe were simply unprepared for the chaotic conditions left behind by the former Communist regimes to the East. They are now affected by the fierce comp-etition for scarce capital, as the countries in Eastern Europe seek to attract investments that will build a new and modern economic infrastructure. At the same time, the daily poverty and disorder of life in Eastern Europe have encouraged a migration to the relatively affluent societies of the West.

Those who attempt the big move to the "Golden West" resemble in many ways the immigrants who have been attracted to the United States in the past and present. But many West Europeans are unwilling to accept what they regard as a flood of unwanted strangers, who are widely portrayed as outsiders whose presence will further drain the generous welfare systems and threaten their economic security. One serious political consequence has been the emergence of anti-immigrant populism on the far Right. In response, the governments in several countries have changed their laws on citizenship, asylum, and immigration.

There can be no doubt that the issues of immigration and cultural tensions in Eastern Europe will occupy a central place on the political agenda in the coming years. Some of the established parties have already made symbolic and substantive accommodations to appease protesting voters, for fear of otherwise losing them to extremist ultra-Right movements. But it is important to remember that there are also groups that resist such compromises and oppose the xenophobic elements in their own societies. Some enlightened political leaders promote the reasonable perspective that migrants could be an important asset. This argument may concede that the foreign influx also involves some social cost in the short run, but it emphasizes that the newcomers can be a very important human resource. Quite apart from any such economic considerations, of course, the migrants and asylum-seekers have become an important test of liberal democratic tolerance on the continent.

Prudent observers had long warned about a premature celebration of "Europe 1992," which referred to the abolition on restrictions in the flow of goods, capital, services, and labor after January 1, 1993, under the EC's Single Europe Act (SEA), adopted and ratified a few years earlier. They suggested that the slogan served to cover up some remaining problems and some newly emerging obstacles to the full integration of the European Community. The skeptics seemed at least partly vindicated by the setbacks that have followed the new and supposedly decisive "leap" forward that was taken in the summit meeting of EC leaders at the Dutch town of Maastricht in December of 1991. The Maastricht Treaty went beyond the SEA in delineating additional steps toward supranational integration during the last half of the 1990s. It envisaged a common European monetary system and a federal European Reserve Bank as well as common policies on immigration, environmental protection, external security, and foreign affairs.

In 3 of the then 12 member countries—Denmark, Ireland, and France—ratification of the Maastricht Treaty was tied to the outcome of national refer-endums. In the first of these expressions of the popular will, Danish voters in June 1992 decided by a very slim majority of less than 2 percent to reject the treaty. A huge Irish majority in favor of the treaty was followed by a very slim French approval as well. The negative Danish vote seemed to have had the effect of legitimating and releasing many pent-up reservations and second thoughts in other member countries, not least Germany. But in May 1993 Danish voters approved a modified version of agreement, pruned down with special "opt-out" provisions that meet Denmark's particular reservations. Some weeks later British prime minister John Major was able to hammer together a fragile parliamentary majority for the treaty in the House of Commons. Here too, however, the agreement was a customized version of the treaty designed to meet Britain's reservations. The last formal hurdle to the Maastricht Treaty was passed in Germany, where the Constitutional Court turned down a legal challenge based on an alleged violation of national sovereignty. But the ratification process has revealed widespread political resistance that continues to hamper the course toward a federal union.

As several of the articles in this section point out, European Union has effectively reached a cross-roads, even with the adoption of a common currency, the euro, by 11 of the 15 member nations. The European nation-state has turned out to have more holding power than some federalists had expected. The absence of a quick and coherent West European response to the violent ethnic conflict in Bosnia and other parts of former Yugoslavia has added a further reason for doubt concerning the EU's imminent progression toward an elementary form of political federation. For these and other reasons, the present seems to be a time for new thought and debate about the EU's further goals and its route for reaching them.

While much academic and political ink has been spilled on the problems of a transition from a market economy to state socialism, we have little theory or practice to guide Central and East European countries that are trying to move in the opposite direction. The question of what would be the best strategy for restructuring the economies of the former Communist countries is far more than an interesting theoretical issue. Some academics believe that a quick transition to a market economy is a preferable course, even though such an approach would be very disruptive and painful in the short run. They argue that such a "shock therapy" approach will release human energies and bring economic growth more quickly and efficiently. At the same time, these supporters of a "tough love" approach warn that compassionate halfway measures could end up worsening the economic plight of these countries.

Other strategists have come out in favor of a more gradual approach to economic reconstruction in these countries. They warn that the neoclassical economists, who would introduce a full-scale market economy by fiat, not only ignore the market system's cultural and historical preconditions but underestimate the turmoil that is likely to accompany the big transition. These gradualists therefore recommend pragmatic strategies of incremental change, accompanied by a rhetoric of lower expectations, as a more prudent course of action.

After a few years we may have some better insights into the merits of each argument. A pluralist society, however, rarely permits itself to become a social laboratory for controlled experiments of this kind. Instead, it seems likely that political factors will promote a "mix" of the two approaches as the most acceptable and practical policy outcome.

A similar debate about the best strategy for economic reconstruction has been carried out in the former Soviet Union during the past few years. In some ways, it could be argued that Mikhail Gorbachev, the last Soviet head of government (1985 to 1991), failed to opt clearly for one or the other approach to economic reform. He seems not only to have been ambivalent about the means but about the ends of his perestroika, or restructuring, of the centrally planned economy. In the eyes of some born-again Soviet marketeers, he remained far too socialist, while Communist hard-liners never forgave him for dismantling a system in which they had enjoyed at least a modicum of security and privilege.

More than anything else, however, the Achilles' heel of the now defunct Soviet Union turned out to be its multiethnic character. Gorbachev was not alone in underestimating the potential centrifugal tendencies of a country that was based on an ideological and political redefinition of the Russian Empire. Many of the non-Russian minorities were ethnic majorities within their own territory, and this made it possible for them to want greater autonomy or even national independence, unlike the scattered ethnic groups of the United States.

Gorbachev appears to have regarded his own policies of glasnost, or openness, and democratization as essential accompaniments of perestroika in his modernization program. He seems to have understood (or become convinced) that a highly developed industrial economy needs a freer flow of information along with a more decentralized system of decision making, if its component parts

are to be efficient, flexible, and capable of self-correction. In that sense, a market economy has some integral feedback traits that make it incompatible with the traditional Soviet model of a centrally directed, authoritarian command economy.

But glasnost and democratization were clearly incompatible with a repressive political system of one-party rule as well. They served Gorbachev as instruments to weaken the grip of the Communist hard-liners and at the same time to rally behind him some reform groups, including many intellectuals and journalists. Within a remarkably short time after he came to power in 1985, a vigorous new press emerged in the Soviet Union headed by journalists who were eager to ferret out misdeeds and report on political reality as they observed it. A similar development took place in the history profession, where scholars used the new spirit of openness to report in grim detail about past Communist atrocities that had previously been covered up or dismissed as bourgeois lies. There was an inevitable irony to the new truthfulness. Even as it served to discredit much of the past along with any reactionary attempts to restore "the good old days," it also brought into question the foundations of the Soviet system and the leading role of the Communist Party. Yet Gorbachev had clearly sought to modernize and reform the system, not to bring it down.

Most important of all, democratization gave those ethnic minorities in the Soviet Union, which had a territorial identity, an opportunity to demand autonomy or independence. The first national assertions came from the Baltic peoples in Estonia, Latvia, and Lithuania, which had been forced back under Russian rule in 1940, after some two decades of national independence. Very soon other nationalities, including the Georgians and Armenians, expressed similar demands through the political channels that had been opened to them. The death knell for the Soviet Union sounded in 1991, when the Ukrainians, who constituted the second largest national group in the Soviet Union after the Russians, made similar demands for independence.

In a very real sense, then, Gorbachev's political reforms ended up as a mortal threat not only to the continued leadership role by the Communist Party but also to the continued existence of the Soviet Union itself. Gorbachev seems to have understood neither of these ultimately fatal consequences of his reform attempts until quite late in the day. This explains why he could set in motion forces that would ultimately destroy what he had hoped to make more attractive and productive. In August 1991, Communist hard-liners attempted a coup against the reformer and his reforms, but they acted far too late and were too poorly organized to succeed. The coup was defeated by a popular resistance, led by Russian president Boris Yeltsin, who had broken with Communism earlier and, as it seemed, far more decisively. In fact, the would-be coup d'état became instead a coup de grace for the Soviet Communists and the Soviet Union as well.

Somewhat reluctantly, Gorbachev declared the party illegal soon after he returned to office.

After his formal restoration to power following the abortive coup, Gorbachev had become politically dependent on Yeltsin and was increasingly seen as a transitional figure. His days as Soviet president were numbered when the Soviet Union ceased to exist a week before the end of 1991. It was formally replaced by the Commonwealth of Independent States (CIS), a very loose union that lacked both a sufficient institutional framework and political will to keep it together. Almost from the outset, the CIS seemed destined to be a loosely structured transitional device. It could serve a practical purpose for the former Soviet republics, while they negotiated what to do with the economic, military, and other institutional leftovers of the old system and tried to shape new and useful links to each other. Understandably, some political leaders would like to find a way to restore a stronger union among these new states.

There is an undeniable gloom or hangover atmosphere in many of the accounts of post-Communist and post-Soviet Europe. It seems clear that much will become worse before it will become better in the economic and social life of these countries. The political consequences could be very important, for social frustrations can now be freely articulated and represented in the political process. Here the transition from one-party rule to pluralist democratic forms resembles the economic passage to a market economy in being neither easy nor automatic. A turn to some form of authoritarian nationalist populism cannot be ruled out in several countries, including Russia. Former Communists with leadership skills are likely to play a major role in the process in countries like Poland and Ukraine. They sometimes cooperate with ultra-Right nationalists, with whom they share the passion for a much stronger societal control by the state.

Specialists on the former Soviet Union disagree considerably in their assessments of the current situation or what brought it about. One of the hotly debated issues concerns President Yeltsin's decision in September 1993 to use a preemptive strike to break a deadlock between his government and a majority in the Russian parliament. When a majority of the legislators, who had been elected over 2 years earlier, blocked some of his major economic reforms, Yeltsin simply dissolved parliament and called new elections for December 1993.

The electoral result was a political boomerang for Yeltsin. It resulted in a major setback for the forces that backed rapid and thoroughgoing market reforms. The new parliament, based on a two-ballot system of elections, was highly fragmented, but

Nationalists and former Communists occupied pivotal positions in the Duma. Henceforth, President Yeltsin played a more subdued role than previously, and the new government pursued far more cautious reform policies than previously. The military invasion of Chechnya, a breakaway Caucasian republic located within the Russian federation, did not give Yeltsin a quick and easy victory that might have reversed his slide into political unpopularity among Russians. Nor could it stem the surge of authoritarian and nationalist political expression, which also thrived as a reflex to crime and social disorder. But neither the ultra-Right nor the former Communists, who both resist far-reaching market reforms, seem eager to return to the tradition of a centrally planned economy. In that limited sense, at least, the long Soviet chapter of Russian history appears to have been closed, even though the experience will continue to disturb the pattern of the country's development. That does not rule out a "Bonapartist" solution, in the form of a coup, or the danger that a Russian form of fascism could come to power, as Russian-watchers continue to warn.

New parliamentary elections in December 1995 provided a further setback for the democratic and economic reformers in Russia. However, it was far less their rivals' strength than their own disunity and rivalry both before and after the election that weakened their parliamentary position. Together, the reformers received close to a quarter of the vote. That was slightly more than the Communists, led by Gennady Zyuganov, received and it was twice as much as the far-right nationalists in Vladimir Zhirinovsky's Liberal Democratic Party. Under Russian electoral law, however, the Communists received 35 percent of the seats in the new Duma. Observers of Russian politics differed in their assessments of this, but all agreed that it left the cause of political and economic reform in some disarray.

During the spring of 1996, Russian political leaders had their eyes fixed on the presidential elections of June, in which the incumbent Boris Yeltsin faced the toughest political challenge of his career. As expected, he did not win a clear majority in the first vote, but he defeated Zyuganov with relative ease in a run-off election. David Remnick gives an informed and balanced account of the presidential election and some later developments in Russia, where ill health has added seriously to Yeltsin's governing problems. His successive replacements of prime ministers has not improved the situation. By early 1999, Russia faced a financial disaster as international investors and banks drew back from taking further risks in the shaky post-Soviet economy. The outlook could hardly have been worse.

# The Untied States of Europe

■ Cultural differences, myths and rivalries are stymieing the quest for a continental union. Diversity—Latin verve! British pragmatism!—once was seen as strength. But now it is proving divisive.

## TYLER MARSHALL

Times Staff Writer

*Heaven is where the police are British, the chefs French, the mechanics German, the lovers Italian and it's all organized by the Swiss.*

*Hell is where the police are German, the chefs British, the mechanics French, the lovers Swiss and it's all organized by the Italians.*
    **—An oft-told European joke**

MAASTRICHT, Netherlands—For decades, those struggling to build a united Europe saw the Continent's rich cultural diversity as an asset in fulfilling their dream.

They noted how a Latin flair for the grand gesture helped generate such unifying symbols as the single lavender-colored passport now issued by all 15 European Union countries. And how British pragmatism helped streamline and decentralize the Union's formidable bureaucracy.

"Europe's strength is in its diversity" argued Richard Hill, a British-born specialist on cross-cultural dynamics who lives in Brussels.

Others are no longer so sure.

Efforts are moving ahead to strengthen the Union, and member states are beginning to hitch their economic fate to a common currency and mull revolutionary political steps such as adopting a single foreign and security policy. But the enormous differences in culture, values and outlook that have separated the nations of Europe for centuries now loom as a large impediment to deeper unity.

Although governments of several EU members devote resources to smoothing relations among linguistic or cultural groups within their countries, the issue of bridging these far greater divisions across the Union is largely ignored.

While in the United States diversity is a gut issue that triggers constant, often heated, public discourse and action, in Europe the architects of integration have hardly addressed the subject.

### Stereotypes Thrive

Amid this inaction, raw national stereotypes continue to thrive, cropping up in jokes, offhand comments and easy banter.

As for the once conventional wisdom that Western Europe's economic and political convergence over the decades would gradually erode many of the differences, it simply hasn't happened.

"There was the belief that the Common Market, the European Union and [the goal of] unification would lead to a common culture, but it apparently doesn't work that way," said Niels G. Noorderhaven, director of the Institute for Research on Intercultural Cooperation, which is based in this picture-book Dutch town where the treaty on European political and economic unity was signed more than four years ago.

Today, Noorderhaven is only one of many who believe the experiment of forming a united Europe will probably fall well short of a "United States of Europe"—in part because of deep and fundamental divisions.

He and others go so far as to argue that there is evidence to suggest the opposite is happening—that cultural differences in Europe may be hardening.

"When you start talking about pulling down political boundaries or becoming part of a greater whole, people have a desire to want to preserve what is unique about themselves," noted Ralf Dahrendorf, the respected German-born social scientist who is now a British lord and head of Oxford University's St. Antony's College. "It's not surprising."

It's also unsettling, because history has proved that convictions of such uniqueness among people in Europe can, with only a little tension, quickly lead to friction and tragedy—as the recent Balkan conflict has underscored.

Some experts argue that either the notion of European diversity or the goal of integration must give.

### Divided by History

Dutch academic Geert Hostede, who studied European cultural differences for U.S. computer giant International Business Machines Corp. in the 1970s and later emerged as one of the leading experts in the field, has argued that Europeans remain inevitably divided by their history.

"Countries have remained separate precisely because there existed fundamental differences in thinking and feeling between them," he said in a 1993 farewell lecture at the University of Limburg here. "Why do you think the Belgians revolted against the Dutch in 1830? The border between Belgium and the Netherlands revives the border between the Roman Empire and the barbaric Germanic tribes . . . in about 4 AD."

Hofstede said he found no other instance in the world in which two neighboring countries had so much in common yet still showed such differences in what he termed "their mental programming."

"The inheritance of the Roman Empire survives in the minds of the populations of the Latin countries," he said. "The Germanic countries never knew the same centralization of power, nor a universal system of laws, implying greater equality and tolerance for uncertainty."

### Schooling Differs

Relationships between the individual and authority diverge at an early age among Europeans, according to Noorderhaven, with elementary school teachers in northern countries such as the Netherlands and Scandinavia having far less "distance" between themselves and their pupils than their counterparts in Mediterranean countries.

Dutch children, for example, are schooled to keep low profiles and taught that being first at something isn't necessarily a virtue. The message prepares

From the *Los Angeles Times*, May 20, 1996, pp. A1, A8. © 1996 by the Los Angeles Times. Reprinted by permission.

them for life in one of the globe's most egalitarian societies.

At home and in school, children in Mediterranean countries such as Greece and Italy tend to be nurtured as special, unique (and, implicitly, superior) individuals.

In Britain, it's acceptable to finish first—but only if one can do it without seeming to work harder in the process.

For those nurturing the ideal of a united Europe, such diverse values carry important implications. "These cultural differences go very deep, and they aren't just about culture," Dahrendorf said. "Attitudes to the economy and to the state are fundamentally different in different countries."

He described the tough anti-inflation criteria for monetary union written into the Maastricht Treaty as "German culture put into an international treaty," but he questioned how nations such as Italy or Britain, which have no such allergy to inflation, can settle into such a system. "In Britain, there is a feeling that a bit of inflation may not be such a bad thing."

In business, cross-border mergers in Europe historically have a high failure rate, usually because of "culture blindness."

Richard Branson, the British-based entrepreneur, in 1995 gave up a four-year attempt to face down recalcitrant German trade unions and closed his Virgin Megastore music, book and video outlet in Frankfurt, in part because German employees refused to wear T-shirts with the Virgin logo. Since trade union power in Britain was crushed in the early 1980s by then-Prime Minister Margaret Thatcher, such confrontations are a rarity in Britain.

At the political level, countries such as Britain and Denmark, with long traditions of relatively non-intrusive government but respect for law, have tended to resist proposals for new regulations from the EU's executive, the European Commission, in Brussels. Yet they have the best record of implementing those regulations once they are agreed upon.

On the other hand, Belgium—where bureaucracy is oppressive and evading laws and regulations is a national sport—ranks among the quickest to propose new EU rules yet has the worst record in the Union for implementing adopted legislation.

The relative importance of rules and regulations in European countries is sometimes easy to spot. Contrast the picture of the German woman unwilling to cross an empty road until the red light turns green with the Italian taxi driver in Naples who looks on red lights as little more than a suggestion to slow, views stop signs with disdain and considers a

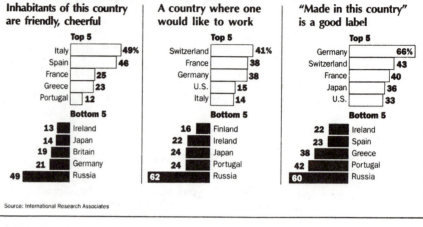

# What Europeans Think of Others

The study was based on face-to-face interviews with 1,000 people in each country. Each person was shown a list of countries and for each item was asked to choose three countries for which that item was most applicable and three countries for which the item was least applicable. The numbers below show the percentage of people who named each country.

**Inhabitants of this country are friendly, cheerful**

Top 5
| | |
|---|---|
| Italy | 49% |
| Spain | 46 |
| France | 25 |
| Greece | 23 |
| Portugal | 12 |

Bottom 5
| | |
|---|---|
| 13 | Ireland |
| 14 | Japan |
| 19 | Britain |
| 21 | Germany |
| 49 | Russia |

**A country where one would like to work**

Top 5
| | |
|---|---|
| Switzerland | 41% |
| France | 38 |
| Germany | 38 |
| U.S. | 15 |
| Italy | 14 |

Bottom 5
| | |
|---|---|
| 16 | Finland |
| 22 | Ireland |
| 24 | Japan |
| 24 | Portugal |
| 62 | Russia |

**"Made in this country" is a good label**

Top 5
| | |
|---|---|
| Germany | 66% |
| Switzerland | 43 |
| France | 40 |
| Japan | 36 |
| U.S. | 33 |

Bottom 5
| | |
|---|---|
| 22 | Ireland |
| 23 | Spain |
| 38 | Greece |
| 42 | Portugal |
| 60 | Russia |

Source: International Research Associates

Los Angeles Times

right turn from the left lane as a logical, routine maneuver.

Just why the unprecedented mobility of Europeans over the past 40 years—plus close economic and political cooperation—has not been a greater cultural leveler is unclear.

## Few Lessons on Unity

But the absence of any moves toward common educational standards or school curricula are cited as one key reason. That children of all ages in EU member states are taught little about the Union, its origins or goals may be another factor, social scientists suggest. That only 3% of EU citizens reside outside their native countries also helps answer why even the crudest national stereotypes remain powerful:

• An American recalled being trapped on a Paris-Brussels express train, already hours late and going nowhere fast, and watching three Britons in the same car come to a slow boil over their plight and eventually spill out their prejudices. "The French and the Belgians don't know how to run anything," one said. "What they need is some good German control."

• At a seminar of former world leaders in Colorado Springs, Colo., last fall, Thatcher, the former British prime minister, commented that she remained apprehensive about reunified Germany despite the country's four decades of model democracy. "Her natural character is to dominate," she said of Germany. "There's something in this that I still fear."

• And polls conducted by the French Tourism Ministry about travelers' complaints seemed to tell more about visitors than about France: Germans said they found the French undisciplined, Belgians said they were nice but wrapped up in themselves, the Swiss said they weren't clean enough, and the British described them as quarrelsome and chauvinistic.

Many argue that, with Europe's cultural differences so deeply ingrained, the best that advocates of greater unity can hope for is broader understanding of what they face.

## Taboo Subject

But social scientists such as Noorderhaven note that within the EU's formidable bureaucracy of 20,000, not one official studies the impact of the Continent's cultural diversity. "It's more or less a taboo within the European Commission that these differences might have an impact," he said. "Perhaps they see it as a threat to the idea of unification. But if you try to deny them, then the trouble really begins."

He cites a highly successful student exchange program that underwrites foreign studies for 150,000 high school and university students as the best EU weapon to foster awareness of diversity.

"It's a chance to study material with a European dimension," he said. "People also really get exposed to life in another culture, and, through that experience, they become aware of their own values and prejudices. This is the best-spent money in the European Union."

# WHAT IS EUROPE?

## The changing idea of a continent

**Richard Rose**

Europe is often referred to as a timeless ideal, a civilisation as well as a continent. Yet there is no agreement about what the idea of Europe symbolises. It can be invoked as a symbol of war or of peace; of freedom or oppression; of economic dynamism or backwardness; of great achievements in music and art or as a passive audience for American television sitcoms.

GEOGRAPHY appears to offer certainty. Europe is one continent among a number. It definitely excludes North America, Africa, Latin America and Asia. Egypt is an older civilization than Greece, and the Greeks regarded Persia, not Rome, as their rival. Even though England is geographically only 20 miles from France, many English people feel closer to America, Canada or Australia than to their continental neighbours.

The significance of European geography has been fundamentally transformed by modern technology. Today, jet planes fly between major European cities in less time than it takes their passengers to travel to and from the airport. Telecommunications enable Europeans to communicate with each other at the touch of a few keys, and the spread of English as the common international language makes this especially easy for Britons. Barriers to communication today are not physical; they reflect political cultures and political institutions.

Locating Europe on a map is a test of political values. Where we look depends upon what we are looking for. A philosopher might locate the heart of Europe in Athens, the home of ancient Greek philosophers. But Athens today is the capital of a small, rela-

tively poor European state. To describe Europe as representative of Christian civilisation ignores the religious schisms and wars that have torn Christianity throughout its history. To define contemporary Europe as a set of advanced industrial societies implies that any country that becomes industrialised, such as Japan or Korea, thereby becomes 'European'.

### DIVERSITY AND COMPLEXITY

Any attempt to reduce contemporary Europe to a single idea is bound to fail, for Europeans differ about almost everything imaginable. Between countries there are striking differences in language, religion and eco-

> **'Locating Europe on a map is a test of political values. Where we look depends upon what we are looking for.'**

nomic prosperity. The two great wars of this century have been European civil wars, fought between the major countries of Europe, and affecting smaller countries too. Even when countries share a commitment to democratic institutions, there are differences in the conduct of free elections between Britain, with its first-past-the-post electoral system, and the great majority of European countries, which elect their parliaments by proportional representation.

There are also differences within every European country. Income, class, regional and urban/rural differences are found in every European society. Religious commitment or indifference divides societies too. In the Netherlands differences between Protestants, Catholics and secular groups have been so strong that the state recognises separate educational and cultural institutions for each religious group. In a few European countries, such as Switzerland and Belgium, there are also major divisions of language.

### WHEN IS EUROPE?

To say what Europe is we must specify which time period and which history we are talking about, the history of Nazi Germany

From *Politics Review*, January 1997, pp. 26-30. © 1997 by Philip Allan Publishers, Ltd. Reprinted by permission.

or the history of a democratic, consensus-oriented and rich Federal Republic.

The modern European state was created in the seventeenth and eighteenth centuries as a 'hard' state, legal in form but authoritarian in practice. The monarch's power was subject to some restraint by other élites, but ordinary subjects had no rights. Bureaucrats enforcing laws and collecting taxes were servants of the crown and acted on its authority. In eighteenth century Prussia, the King claimed to be an enlightened despot, who promoted the collective good rather than the interests of 'mere' individuals. From the end of the Napoleonic wars in 1815 to the outbreak of World War I in 1914, the modern state spread throughout Europe. Nationalism became a potent political force, too.

In 1900, Europe was *a set of undemocratic, multinational empires* (Figure 1). Countries in which the vote of a majority of the adult male population could choose a government were few, and in none had men and women the right to vote on equal terms. Many states were what the Germans call a *Rechtsstaat* (rule of law state)—but the law granted far more power and rights to the state than to individuals. Authoritarian regimes were the norm.

Pre-1914 European states were multinational. They were not formed to represent people with a common language and identity; they were the property that a monarch had acquired by inheritance, politically convenient marriages and/or conquest. The Austro-Hungarian Empire ruled over peoples speaking more than a dozen different languages and territories since scattered among ten different states. The Ottoman Empire ruled an extraordinarily cosmopolitan collection of peoples of Europe and the Middle East from Constantinople (now Istanbul). The British Empire was a global empire. France, Germany, Italy and Czarist Russia sought to expand outside Europe too. World War I brought about the collapse and disappearance of the multinational Austrian Hapsburg, German, Ottoman and Russian empires.

## SELF-DETERMINATION UNDER STRAIN

The 1919 Versailles peace conference established the idea of Europe as *a set of nation-states, democratic or undemocratic,* and many new states appeared on the map of Europe (Figure 2). However, the principle of national self-determination was difficult to apply, because several nationalities often lived in the same city or region, for example, Czechs and Germans in Prague, Austrians and Italians in Northern Italy, Germans and Poles in what had been Prussia and became western Poland, and Hungarians and Romanians in Transylvania.

In the interwar period the attempt to spread democracy throughout Europe failed. Most important states were undemocratic and Europe invented novel forms of totalitarian rule, coercing people far more thoroughly than earlier regimes. The Czarist empire was succeeded by the Communist Soviet Union, a state governed by Marxist-Leninist ideology without regard for 'bourgeois' ideas of democracy or civil rights. In Italy, Benito Mussolini created a fascist regime. In 1933 Adolf Hitler took power in Germany in the name of the Nazi Party. In the 1930s, no democratically elected government in Europe except Sweden offered its economically depressed population the hope of a new deal, similar to that of President Franklin D. Roosevelt in the United States.

## POSTWAR DIVISION

In World War II, Allied victory brought two new super-powers to the centre of Europe, the United States and the Soviet Union. Soon they became opponents, as Soviet troops and political commissars imposed Communist regimes across almost half the continent, creating what Sir Winston Churchill described as an Iron Curtain dividing the continent.

In Western Europe there was fear of a Communist takeover too. The United States, previously outside the European balance of power, became the economic and military leader of the West. Economic aid was given through the Marshall Plan, launched in 1947. The North Atlantic Treaty Organisation (NATO) was created in 1949 as a military alliance under American leadership with strong support from the Labour government of Clement Attlee. A few democratic countries remained neutral, including Switzerland, Sweden, Finland, Ireland and Austria. For the four decades of the Cold War, the Soviet bloc was opposed by a league of North Atlantic democracies.

The Organisation for Economic Cooperation and Development (OECD) was founded in 1961 to link advanced industrial nations. Its membership is not confined to one continent. OECD member states span four continents, including the United States and Canada; Australia and New Zealand—and Japan. If number of countries is the criterion, then OECD is primarily an association of European states, but if economic wealth is the measure, then no continent can claim dominance. Europe has the greatest population and the largest gross domestic product (GDP) in total; Japan has the highest GDP per capita; and the United States has the greatest military force.

Meanwhile, from East Germany and Czechoslovakia to the Baltics and the Balkans, Soviet-style regimes ruled, denying their subjects free elections and freedom of speech, travel and religion. A command economy was introduced, in which state ownership and bureaucratic controls replaced private property and choice in the market place. The Iron Curtain distorted historical links, especially in Germany, where

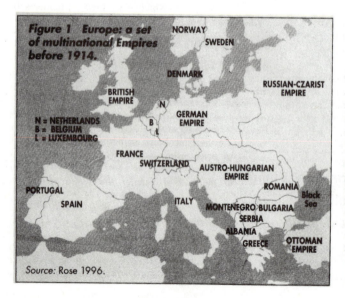

Figure 1 Europe: a set of multinational Empires before 1914.

N = NETHERLANDS
B = BELGIUM
L = LUXEMBOURG

Source: Rose 1996.

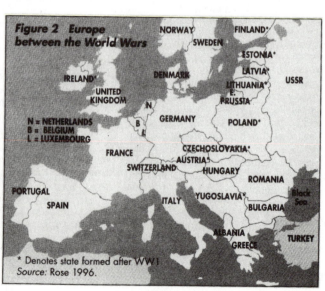

Figure 2 Europe between the World Wars

N = NETHERLANDS
B = BELGIUM
L = LUXEMBOURG

* Denotes state formed after WW1
Source: Rose 1996.

even its historic capital, Berlin, was divided between two states, the Federal Republic and the German Democratic Republic. Prague, geographically to the west of Vienna, was placed politically in Eastern Europe.

## EUROPE TODAY

The opening of the Berlin Wall on 9 November 1989 and the subsequent collapse of Soviet power ushered in a new era in Europe. Central Europe is once again a meaningful region, embracing Germany, Austria, the Czech Republic, Slovakia, Hungary, Poland and a few other parts of the old Austro-Hungarian Empire. East Europeans are now free to travel, trade and study with Westerners. But their idea of a West European city may be Berlin or Vienna rather than London or Brussels.

The defining characteristic of Europe today is *democracy on a continental scale*. West European countries do not want as neighbours authoritarian regimes, whether Communist, fascist or nationalist. Nor do the majority of peoples in post-Communist countries. In 1990, free competitive elections were held across Central and Eastern Europe, and new governments were formed. Second elections have now been held too, often leading to a peaceful change of control of government. In countries such as Poland, Hungary and Bulgaria, shortcomings of governments have enabled ex-Communist parties to win the largest share of votes and office, giving opportunistically minded ex-Communists the incentive to respect democratic rules of competition.

Democratic Europe now extends far more widely than at any time in the past.

However, European countries have arrived at the use of free elections to choose a parliament, and hold government accountable, by very different routes. But countries have followed four different routes (Table 1). The textbook path to democracy is through evolution. However, uninterrupted progress toward democracy, as in Britain, has occurred in only a third of contemporary European states. The Republic of Ireland is unique in gradually evolving democratic institutions under the tutelage of the Westminster Parliament, which introduced free elections before the Irish war of independence gave Ireland its own Parliament in 1921.

The majority of European states have followed a trial and error course, introducing their current democratic system in a political vacuum, after the collapse of authoritarian regimes under internal or external pressures. In 1945 the defeat and occupation of Germany and Austria led these countries to adopt democratic constitutions under the eyes of occupying armies. The domestic collapse of an authoritarian regime is an alternative cause of the abrupt introduction of democracy. In Spain, the death of a dictator,

| Primary pressure | |
|---|---|
| **Internal** | **External** |
| **Evolution** | **Tutelage** |
| Belgium | Ireland |
| Britain | |
| Denmark | |
| Finland | |
| Luxembourg | |
| Netherlands | |
| Norway | |
| Sweden | |
| Switzerland | |
| **Domestic trial and error** | **Defeat and occupation** |
| France | Austria |
| Greece | Germany |
| Portugal | Italy |
| Spain | |
| | **Liberation** |
| | Bulgaria |
| | Czech Republic |
| | Hungary |
| | Poland |
| | Romania |
| | Slovakia |

(left margin labels: Gradual / Tempo / Abrupt)

Source: R. Rose (1996) *What is Europe?*, HarperCollins.

**Table 1 Alternative paths to democracy**

General Franco, was the trigger; in Portugal a revolt against an ageing authoritarian regime; and in Greece the surrender of power by colonels. France has been exceptional in replacing one democratic regime, the Fourth Republic, with another, the presidentialist Fifth Republic under General de Gaulle, as a consequence of a military coup in 1958. In Central and Eastern Europe, the withdrawal of Soviet influence was critical. When Moscow showed it would no longer use its force to suppress opponents of Communist regimes, countries were free to become democratic if they wished.

## CHALLENGES FOR DEMOCRACY

The introduction of democracy does not mean that all a country's problems are resolved, or that there is an end to politics, that is, debate about who should govern or what the government ought to do. Nor does democracy promise an end to problems of managing the economy, as is shown by countries under governments as different as those of Sweden and Britain. Economic problems are particularly acute in post-Communist countries, where the problem is not that of managing a market economy but the

unprecedented challenge of creating a market economy in place of a highly centralised command economy.

Post-Communist countries differ in the extent to which they have progressed toward consolidating democracy and introducing the institutions of a market economy, whether on the Swedish, German, British or American model. Yet all have made significant progress compared to their position a decade ago. This is true not only in the Czech Republic, now a member of OECD, but also of Romania, where today's regime, whatever its shortcomings, is a lesser evil than the brutally repressive Ceausescu regime. Surveys of public opinion in post-Communist countries endorse the Churchill hypothesis that democracy is the worst form of government known—except for all the others that have ever been tried. People who have known the Communist alternative and, in the older generation, nationalist and fascist alternatives too, tend to prefer the present system.

Two Communist states—Yugoslavia and the Soviet Union—disintegrated; the dividing line between democracy and its alternatives lies within their former territories. Slovenia has peacefully advanced toward becoming a democracy with an expanding economy, but Croatia and Serbia have been at war and Bosnia displays some of the worst features of past European history. In the Soviet Union many successor republics still hold elections by Soviet standards, where the ruler claims 99% rather than half the vote. In the Russian Federation there are big debates about the future direction of the polity and the economy. Moreover, President Boris Yeltsin's claim to being an economic reformer, or even a democrat, is increasingly challenged by his former allies, and figures such as Vladimir Zhirinovsky represent the anti-democratic face of Eastern Europe.

## THE BOUNDARIES OF EUROPE

The states of the European Union (EU) are the core countries of Europe today. The origins of the Union lie in the desire of France and Germany to integrate their economies to prevent the recurrence of war. The subsequent creation of a single European market

> **'The deepening significance of political and economic ties within the European Union means that member countries now give relations with America less attention than before.'**

has been achieved by political bargaining. The European Union today is not a state; but its treaty obligations bind members together in ways that both supporters and opponents agree increasingly set limits on the freedom of action of national governments. It lacks an army but it can make laws and enforce them through the courts, raise revenue and spend money, too.

The boundaries of Europe are broader than the current boundaries of the European Union. Norway and Switzerland are certainly part of Europe, even though referendums there have rejected membership in the EU. Many post-Communist countries now also belong in Europe (Figure 3). Membership in the European Union is one way of strengthening their commitment to democracy and market economies. One post-Communist country, the former German Democratic Republic, immediately became part of the EU upon its integration in the Federal Republic of Germany. Six countries of Central and Eastern Europe—the Czech Republic, Slovakia, Hungary, Poland, Bulgaria and Romania—have already applied for membership. Three former republics of the Soviet Union, Estonia, Latvia and Lithuania plus Slovenia, have already signed association agreements.

The military boundaries of Europe are altering. NATO was created to defend against the threat of Soviet takeover of Western Europe. The Soviet Union is no more; today there are new and less predictable threats of ethnic conflicts spilling over national boundaries, such as have occurred in the successor states of Yugoslavia. There is common interest in avoiding a small country's gaining atomic weapons to use for political blackmail, and avoiding another Chernobyl. Thus, the boundaries of the Organisation on Security and Cooperation in Europe are very broad, including civil and military nuclear powers across the former Soviet Union.

Boundaries exclude some countries. The deepening significance of political and economic ties within the European Union means that member countries now give relations with America less attention than before. The *Deutsche Mark,* not the US dollar, is the primary currency of Europe, and border wars in the former Yugoslavia rather than trouble on other continents the main military worry. Americans, too, are looking toward other continents; big states such as California,

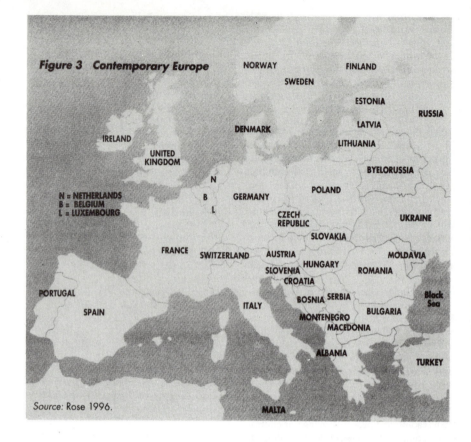

**Figure 3  Contemporary Europe**

N = NETHERLANDS
B = BELGIUM
L = LUXEMBOURG

Source: Rose 1996.

> 'There are only two kinds of countries in Europe today; those that are small and know it, and those that are small and do not.'

Texas and Florida are closer to Latin America or Asia than to Europe, and the changing ethnic composition of the United States is rapidly reducing the population that identifies its heritage with Europe. Congress is unlikely to make a long-term, open-ended guarantee to defend European countries against the threat of 'local' wars in Central or Eastern Europe.

## WHAT ROLE FOR BRITAIN IN EUROPE?

Historically, Britain has always seen its role as apart from Europe, rather than as a part of Europe. It relied on the open sea to forge an empire that reached around the world. The Commonwealth is the chief reminder of former Imperial ties—but its members differ about almost everything imaginable, politically, economically and militarily. A generation ago, an American government official noted: 'Britain has lost an Empire, but has not yet found a role.' It is not the only former imperial power uncertain about its place in the new Europe: Germany, France and Russia, too, are facing new challenges as a result of the collapse of the Soviet bloc.

In contemporary Europe, *interdependence* is a political fact of life: what happens in other countries affects national government elsewhere. The legal doctrine of 'sovereignty' of Parliament did not enable the British government of John Major to defend

the foreign exchange value of the pound in 1992, nor did it save two post-war Labour governments from having to devalue the pound. The decisions of Downing Street or the House of Commons in an international crisis are less important than decisions taken in Washington or on the Continent. Small countries have long known that they must respond when others make decisions. In the words of a Belgian political leader: 'There are only two kinds of countries in Europe today; those that are small and know it, and those that are small and do not.'

Britain is a power in Europe, but not a great power that can dominate all others. While it is similar to France and Italy in population, it is almost a third less than Germany. The GDP of Britain is today no larger than Italy's, and half that of the enlarged Federal Republic of Germany. Slow rates of economic growth have resulted in the average Briton having an income with a purchasing power less than that in ten other European countries. Nor has the British welfare state made people outstandingly healthy. A British woman will not live as long as a woman in eleven other European countries. Britain's relative decline in Europe has occurred even though great progress in British living standards has been made in the postwar era. Britain is now 'around' average on many criteria of well-being because other European countries have been progressing faster.

The political controversies about Europe today reflect the importance of the subject and the difficulties of securing agreement. Britain is not the only country to disagree about whether the Maastricht agreement aimed at strengthening the European Union is a good thing. In every member state that held a referendum on the Maastricht Treaty, voters split into two relatively equal groups. A majority rejected it in the first Danish referendum; after cosmetic changes, a majority endorsed it the second time around.

One thing is certain: in contemporary Europe, success is no longer defined as victory on a battlefield. European leaders have learned the hard way that viewing politics as a zero-sum battleground creates more losers than winners. Today, for the first time in European history, more than two dozen governments have abandoned the idea of preparing to win a war against their neighbours, and instead are concentrating on maintaining peace and prosperity through democratic institutions of national governance.

## REFERENCES AND FURTHER READING

Hayward, J. and Page, E. C. (eds) (1995) *Governing the New Europe,* Polity.

Koole, R. and Mair, P. (annual) *Political Data Yearbook,* December issue of the *European Journal of Political Research.*

Mackie, T. T. and Rose, R. (1991) *The International Almanac of Electoral History,* 3rd edn. Macmillan.

Rose, R. and Haerpfer, C. (1995) 'Democracy and enlarging the European Union eastwards', *Journal of Common Market Studies,* Vol. 33, No. 3.

Rose, R. (1996) *What Is Europe? A Dynamic Introduction,* HarperCollins.

Therborn, G. (1995) *European Modernity and Beyond,* Sage.

Urwin, D. W. (1989) *Western Europe since 1945,* 4th edn. Longman.

## QUESTION

• Does the process of European integration necessarily undermine the power of sovereign nation-states?

---

**Richard Rose is Director of the Centre for the Study of Public Policy at the University of Strathclyde, Glasgow. He has been a visiting Professor at the European University Institute, Florence, and the Central European University, Prague.**

# The Institutional Framework of the EU

## European Parliament
# Looking for legitimacy

STRASBOURG

**If the European Union is to expand eastwards, the club's members must reform their institutions. In the first of a series of occasional articles, we look at the European Parliament**

NEXT week Jose-Maria Gil-Robles, a courtly hidalgo whose father was an influential right-wing politician just before the Spanish civil war, will almost certainly be elected the European Parliament's new president. The choice was fixed in advance by the two biggest groups in the parliament, the Socialists and the European People's Party (EPP). Mr Gil-Robles is capable enough, but unlikely to set the Rhine on fire. Nor will he be recognised on any European street. His rigged election symbolises the institution's main problem. To quote from a standard textbook, "The European Parliament is remote and unfamiliar to a majority of the European electorate."

This is not because the parliament is particularly feeble. In every treaty change over the past 20 years, it has won extra powers. It shares almost equal control over the budget with the Council of Ministers, made up of governments. In many areas it has "co-decision" powers that enable it to amend or even reject draft laws. It would like the EU's 15 countries (now enmeshed in their inter-governmental conference to reform club rules) to extend co-decision to all laws passed in the council by qualified majority vote, on the ground that if there is no national veto only the parliament can offer democratic input. The hordes of lobbyists prowling the parliament's corridors in Strasbourg testify to its growing influence.

Even so, it remains a body that few of the Union's 370m citizens recognise, let alone love. One reason is that its job is misunderstood. Most voters expect an elected parliament to produce a government and to function in an adversarial way. The European Parliament does neither; in the words of the leader of the European People's Party, Wilfried Martens, it is a forum, not a parliament. It is supposed to exert democratic control over the club's bureaucracy, the European Commission. But national governments still choose all the commissioners, though Euro-MPs now vote on the appointment of the commission's president (almost rejecting Jacques Santer in 1994). And the parliament is far from adversarial: it needs consensus among its political groups to create absolute majorities to amend laws. It tends to work in cahoots with the commission. Its real enemy is the Council of Ministers.

There is more to the parliament's woes, however, than misunderstanding. It is hamstrung by having to function in three places: Strasbourg for monthly sessions, Brussels for committees and "mini-plenaries", and Luxembourg for its 3,800-strong secretariat. What the outgoing president, Klaus Hänsch, calls "this nonsense" costs some 100m ecus ($124m) a year in extra rent for lavish buildings and travel. More seriously, it reduces the parliament's influence, partly because reporters find the slog down to Strasbourg tiresome. Many Euro-MPs sympathise,

but say they can do nothing: government leaders agreed in Edinburgh in 1992 that it would remain in Strasbourg, and the French are taking the parliament to court for holding only 11 (not 12) sessions there each year.

Critics say that a determined parliament could decide where it is to meet, whatever the governments say. They also argue that Euro-MPs are themselves far too prone to extravagance, feathering their own nests and even indulging in fraud. They are also far too tolerant of the parliamentary farce of having to operate in 11 languages (Finnish, for instance), though conceivably enlargement will one day limit the babble of tongues.

### Where's that whip?

Perhaps Mr Gil-Robles's biggest obstacle—one of the parliament's biggest failings—is indiscipline among the political groups. They often splinter along national lines. Britain's Tories, nominally part of the EPP, are just one culprit. The Socialists, led by Pauline Green, a formidable British ex-policewoman, are little better. Although the groups have coalesced a bit over the years, so that there are now only four that really count, they will never be able to exert real control over their members until they correspond to, and fight elections as, genuine Europe-wide parties. Such a change could take decades.

But the problem of elections to the parliament may be even trickier. In most countries they are fought on purely national, not European, issues. Turnout is low—57% in the last round of polls—and falling, though still higher than in congressional elections in America. Several countries, such as Italy, France and Spain, use a list system that means there is no link between a Euro-MP and his constituency. Not surprisingly, these countries produce the worst members and the highest rates of absenteeism. British adherence to first-past-the-post voting distorts the parliament's make-up: the Socialists are the biggest group in Europe only because Labour scooped up 62 of Britain's 87 seats in 1994.

Even some Europhiles concede that direct elections to the parliament, started in 1979, may have come too early. Nominated Euro-MPs did at least keep a link between national parliaments and the European one. Numbers of Euro-MPs have shot up too, to 626 today, and are set to rise even higher after enlargement. Long-standing Euro-MPs such as Piet Dankert, a Dutch socialist who once served as president, think the parliament would do better if it were chopped to 500 members or fewer.

The case for reinvolving national parliaments is growing, too. In 1990 the European and national parliaments held a joint "assize" to discuss the forthcoming Maastricht treaty. It did not get anywhere. Had it done so, the treaty might have been less contentious.

Elizabeth Guigou, a French Socialist Euro-MP, wants to boost a body (known by its French acronym, COSAC) that brings together committees of the European and national parliaments. The French have also proposed the creation of a second chamber made up of members of national parliaments. But a third legislative chamber, alongside the parliament and the council, would be cumbersome and expensive. The real need is for national parliaments to exert greater control over the decisions of their ministers in the council.

Few can now argue that the parliament does not matter, even though it has yet to come of age. Yet genuine legitimacy still eludes it, and it is a bore—which is perhaps worse than being an irrelevance.

## European Commission

# The big squeeze

BRUSSELS

## The second article in our series on the European Union's institutions assesses whether the European Commission has lost influence

WHEN Eurosceptics denounce "Brussels", they usually have in mind its permanent bureaucracy, the European Commission. The commission, which has a full-time staff of around 16,000 people, presided over by 20 commissioners, is the EU's executive branch. It has the exclusive right to propose EU legislation. It monitors the implementation of laws after adoption by the Council of Ministers, which represents national governments. It executes the EU budget. And as guardian of the treaties, it enforces the rules, if need be taking members to court.

It is, in short, a powerful body. Yet its influence has waxed and waned. Today the commission is at a low ebb. Many people blame this on its president since January 1995, Jacques Santer, a cheery but unprepossessing former prime minister of Luxembourg. Mr Santer got the job, which he did not ask for, largely because it was the turn of the Benelux countries; the Germans blocked the Dutch prime minister, Ruud Lubbers; and the British vetoed the Belgian, Jean-Luc Dehaene. In comparison with his predecessor, the high-profile Jacques Delors, Mr Santer seemed rather like John Major coming after Margaret Thatcher.

Yet it is not wholly fair to blame Mr Santer for the commission's decline, which actually began under Mr Delors. The commission reached a peak of power around 1990, when it was pushing through the 1992 single-market programme. Mr Delors forecast a time when 80% of social and economic legislation in Europe would come from Brussels. Such hubris provoked a reaction; members, led by Britain and France, decided to cut him down to size. The 1992 Maastricht treaty was, in many ways, a failure for the commission, made worse by subsequent ratification difficulties. It endorsed a single currency, but members have a firm grip over progress towards the euro. And although it brought both foreign policy and home affairs into the EU's purview, it did so in two new "pillars" that deliberately curtailed the commission's role.

Mr Santer was, in any event, chosen for the job by governments that wanted him to refrain from grand initiatives. In his words, the commission was "to do less, but better". He has largely kept his promise: in 1996, for example, the commission made only 12 new legislative proposals, and it withdrew nearly 50 that had not been adopted by the council. As one senior official says, it is now only in subordinate legislation, especially on food safety and farming, that anyone could reasonably accuse the commission of being over-active.

The Santer commission can boast other advantages over its predecessor. It is more collegial; decisions are usually taken by consensus, whereas the Delors commission was disfigured by intrigues and, occasionally, by huge rows. The chefs de cabinet, the officials who run each commissioner's office and meet every Monday to prepare decisions to be taken at Wednesday's full commission meetings, are more co-operative. Jim Cloos, Mr Santer's chef, is less of a bully than was Pascal Lamy, who did the job for Mr Delors. And there are some unsung improvements. One is financial management, where Erkki Liikanen, the Finnish budget commissioner, is changing the institution's entire culture in favour of value-for-money and greater efficiency. A recent commission meeting to discuss the 1998 budget proved, for the first time, to be more austere about future spending plans than were the officials who had prepared it.

## So what's the snag?

Yet the commission still has glaring weaknesses. It is squeezed between an assertive Council of Ministers and an ambitious European Parliament. The six-monthly summit of heads of government is increasingly seizing the EU initiative. And, through a proliferation of management committees, governments are exerting more power over executing EU policies.

The parliament is also second-guessing the commission's management. It is about to adopt a critical report on the commission's handling of Britain's outbreak of mad-cow disease, which some Euro-MPs want to use as an excuse to sack the commission (something they have never done before). The commission claims to be "serene", but officials do not disguise their irritation over the parliament's report.

The commission has plenty of internal problems too. There are, for a start, too many commissioners. Mr Santer managed the task of allocating portfolios among the 20 with some skill, but several have been left with too little to do. External affairs, in particular, is a mess. It is now divided among no fewer than four commissioners, and it is also split among four directorates-general—units of the commission—which overlap and frequently clash.

The quality of the commissioners is, at best, uneven. Among the present lot there are stars with heavyweight portfolios such as competition (Belgium's Karel Van Miert), and external trade (Britain's Sir Leon Brittan). There are some odder successes: for example, Mr Liikanen and Emma Bonino, the Italian consumer-affairs and fisheries commissioner who is about to be given responsibility for food safety. There are also some notable failures: Ritt Bjerregaard, the Danish environment commissioner, and Martin Bangemann, the German industry commissioner, to name but two.

Inevitably, the commission is awkward to run. Its 16,000 officials make it relatively small: on a par, say, with a local council in Britain. But pulling together 15 different nationalities and administrative cultures is tough. Mr Liikanen, who is responsible for administration as well as the budget, observes sardonically that the commission mixes the traditions of "French hierarchy, German *Mitbestimmung* [worker consultation] and Italian trade unions". The allocation of top jobs, especially the 25 directors-general, often degenerates into a nightmare of lobbying, inserting senior officials and filling unspoken nationality quotas in which ability to do the job is forgotten.

And what, in the end, is it all for? Humbler officials (there are some) observe that the commission must, above all, serve the EU's members. So when the mood turns against Brussels, the commission should take notice. But experience also teaches another lesson: that without the initiative of the commission, little gets done in the EU. The two more inter-governmental pillars of Maastricht, which have largely been failures, testify to this.

Here is the big task for Mr Santer's commission, whose mandate lasts till 1999: to retain its low profile and limited agenda but to do enough to keep the European project going. The next two years will be hard: the arrival of a single currency, the revision of Maastricht, new budgetary and farm policies and the process of taking in new members—to say nothing of coping with testy ones like Britain. The risk is that Mr Santer's commission, after the big squeeze, will not have enough juice left to prevent the whole European idea from drying up.

## Europe's Council of Ministers
# Doing the splits

BRUSSELS

**The council, which represents national governments and adopts most EU laws, is the Union's pivot. But, in our third look at Europe's institutions, we spot weaknesses as well as strengths**

THE symbolism is almost too apt. For two years the European Commission building, the four-pronged Berlaymont, has been shrouded in white plastic while asbestos is removed. Meanwhile across the street glowers a grim pink fortress: the Justus Lipsius Building, new home of the Council of Ministers. Power is indeed seeping from one to the other. Under the classic EU design, the commission proposes, the parliament opines and the council disposes. But nowadays, especially in foreign policy and home affairs, commission and parliament barely get a peep; the council runs the whole show.

Yet this is too simple. The European Parliament, for instance, has grown more powerful as well. Even so, the EU clearly has a more "inter-governmental" flavour than it did—that is, national governments have managed to wrench back more of a say, in keeping with the public mood in most of the Union's 15 countries. Not only Euro-sceptical Britons, but also Danes, Swedes, Frenchmen and others want less bossiness from Brussels. Such feelings inevitably strengthen the council, the most inter-governmental of the EU's institutions.

They have also made the council somewhat schizophrenic. It is more than a collection of national ministers. Through regular ministerial meetings, a six-monthly presidency that rotates among all the members, a 2,300-strong secretariat and 15 national permanent missions in Brussels, the council has acquired its own European identity. It is, after all, the central body of a nascent confederation. The tension between national and supranational interest reaches right down to the humblest council working-group.

A big failure of the council is that it is far too secretive—perhaps the only law-making body in the democratic world that takes decisions behind closed doors. It is also sprawlingly big. Theoretically a single unit, it now meets in some 23 gatherings of national ministers, from foreign affairs and finance to education and environment. And it has suffered from enlargement. There is a huge difference between six five-minute speeches from ministers in 1970 and 15 from ministers today. If the Union grows to 25, entire council meetings could be taken up with a simple *tour de table*.

Such unwieldiness combines with only brief forays to Brussels by ministers to hand vast dollops of power to their officials, especially to the Committee of Permanent Representatives, better known by its French acronym, Coreper. Every day, 1,000 delegates attend some 20 council working-group meetings. About 90% of council decisions are taken before ministers ever get entwined. And ministers often prove bad even at agreeing on the 10% that are too controversial for officials to resolve, especially when they need unanimous approval.

If a specialist council cannot agree, the foreign ministers are meant to step in. But they increasingly discuss only foreign affairs; internal disputes are often referred up to the twice-yearly summits of heads of government. The growing dominance of the European Council, as this very top body is called, is one of the biggest EU changes since its inception. When it began in the early 1970s, the idea was that heads of government should meet informally for a fireside chat. Now each presidency works towards a climax of decisions at summits normally held in June and December. And the conclusions from each summit tend to map out the agenda for the whole EU.

Plenty of problems affect this system. Heads of government are not close enough to most issues to debate them properly, so they often rubber-stamp agreements reached by officials. Pushing so much up to summit meetings encourages a "package" approach that often wraps up unrelated issues in gargantuan and indigestible compromises. Knowing this, ministers at lower level are often reluctant to concede anything at all until summit meetings. The practice has also eroded the initiative of the commission, the traditional driver of the European project, without always providing an adequate alternative.

Describing weaknesses in the council is one thing; suggesting cures is harder. One favourite notion is to increase majority voting. Yet the council is naturally wedded to consensus; even when the treaties provide for voting, it seldom happens. Some officials maintain even so that it is the existence of majority voting, not its use, that makes agreement easier. Majority voting may be extended in the revision of the Maastricht treaty supposed to be agreed on at the Amsterdam summit in June, but hostility from Britain and others will stop it going at all far.

A second idea is to change the presidency system. The six-monthly rotation confuses the EU's interlocutors; gives chairmen of councils and working-groups short time-horizons; and puts undue pressure on small coun-

tries such as Luxembourg. Yet some cures would be worse. The council secretary-general, currently Germany's Jürgen Trumpf, could take the chair, as happens in NATO—though that would put huge power into unelected hands. The presidency could last longer, perhaps for a year—though it would then take 15 years to come round, making it hard for countries to gain experience. Or the presidency could rotate only among big countries—producing squeals from the smalls, who have often run the most adept presidencies.

Tensions among governments in the council seem bound to grow. Arguments loom over reducing the extra voting weight given to small countries, for a start. The newest members, Austria, Sweden and Finland, may have helped to foster the notion of a north-south split. But the biggest divide is neither big-small nor north-south. It is between founding members, which usually want further integration, and more recent recruits, which tend not to.

The favoured solution for this is "flexibility", enabling an inner group to go faster without waiting for the laggards. But flexibility could end up dividing the council more than uniting it. One ambassador from the original six observes, a little disdainfully, that "we have been building something for 40 years which is popular and works; newcomers must not drop it." Nor, it might be said, should the founders.

European Court of Justice

# Biased referee?

LUXEMBOURG

**Critics say the European Court of Justice wants to speed ever closer political union in Europe. Yet, as we argue in our fourth article on EU institutions, the court's real failing is that it refuses to explain itself**

ATTACKS on the Court of Justice long predate the birth of Euroscepticism. In the 1960s, one French politician accused it of "morbid megalomania". In 1975, another, Valéry Giscard d'Estaing, denounced what he called the court's "illegal acts". A Danish lawyer once said the court was running wild. Both France and Germany have had difficulty accepting the supremacy of European law. Indeed, some judges on the German Constitutional Court in Karlsruhe believe that,

in case of conflict, Germany's own constitution should prevail.

But by far the most vociferous recent critics have been the British, who think of the court as an unguarded back door through which national sovereignty is being carted away. In 1995, a celebrated analysis by Sir Patrick Neill, a former head of All Souls College, Oxford, concluded that the court was uncontrollable, skewed and dangerous. In the conference to revise the Maastricht treaty, Britain—confusing

legislative with judicial functions—proposed that a majority of members should be able to overturn court judgments. Eurosceptics in all parties want to "repatriate" the court's powers, to stop it overruling national courts and governments. Some of the diatribes aimed at the court in Luxembourg confuse it with the European Court of Human Rights in Strasbourg, which has nothing to do with the EU. It remains to be seen whether the new Labour government will be friendlier to the

Reprinted with permission from *The Economist*, May 17, 1997, pp. 59-60. © 1997 by The Economist, Ltd. Distributed by The New York Times Special Features.

court than the former Conservative one.

One reason to think it might is that Britain has one of the best records before the Luxembourg court (unlike the Strasbourg one). In the years 1973–96, the British government was taken to court for breaches of the treaty 39 times—far fewer than governments from other big states (see table on next page). Britain is also taken seriously in Luxembourg: it files more briefs in court proceedings than any other country, and the judges pay attention to its arguments.

Even more striking, what the court decides usually chimes with British interests. Most cases that come to the court are about enforcing single-market rules. A famous example was the 1979 *Cassis de Dijon* ruling which said that a product—in this case, a French liqueur—approved for sale in one country must be accepted by others. This paved the way for mutual recognition of standards to become a cornerstone of the single market.

To the charge that the court acts to promote federalism by stealth, David Edward, the British judge, retorts that its agenda is set by EU treaties, which talk of an ever closer union and make clear that EU law is directly enforceable through national courts. The supremacy of EU law over national law is also implicit in the treaties. Nor could the court's powers be repatriated, by Britain or anyone else, without a country leaving the Union altogether. Mr Edward dismisses the whole notion as "cloud-cuckoo land".

There are, even so, legitimate questions about the court. One that Britain, ironically, has fretted over is its lack of sanctions. Some countries—notably Italy and Belgium, joined more recently by Germany—have become habitual offenders. Until now, the court has been able to do little about this. The European Commission has just put into effect a provision of the Maastricht treaty, proposed by Britain, under which recalcitrant countries may

be fined. Its first targets were Germany and Italy. But the fines are still too small.

The court's overload is also worrying. It can take 18 months to deliver a "preliminary ruling"—the procedure under which national courts refer questions of European law to Luxembourg. Federico Mancini, Italy's judge at the court, jokes ruefully that the court upheld the 48-hour-maximum working week, but the judges do not apply it to themselves. The 15 judges often sit in chambers of three or five to speed things up. Referring all cases to an "advocate-general", who gives an opinion that helps to clarify them, also helps a bit.

In 1989 a new court of first instance, also 15-strong, was set up to relieve the pressure on the main court. Other measures may soon be needed. One possibility would be special tribunals to hear EU staff disputes, for instance, or anti-dumping suits. Mr Edward argues that the Union will one day have to reconsider its whole judicial architecture. The need for reform will become more urgent when the Union takes in new members, especially if the court is given a role in the EU's inter-governmental "third pillar" of justice and home affairs, from which it is largely excluded at present.

Perhaps the biggest questions surround how judges are appointed. At present each member nominates two judges, one to the main court and the other to the court of first instance. The five big members also nominate an advocate-general apiece; four more advocates-general rotate among the smalls. All appointments are for six-year renewable terms. The judges choose a president every three years.

Critics say this system is neither open nor democratic. Some appointees have little experience as judges; the court has a sprinkling of legal academics and even the odd politician. The public at large has no idea who these bigwigs are; nor, because all court judgments are published collectively

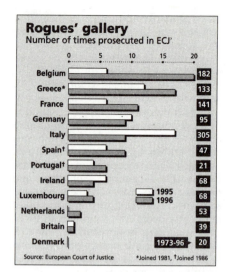

**Rogues' gallery**
Number of times prosecuted in ECJ'

| | 1995 | 1996 |
|---|---|---|
| Belgium | | 182 |
| Greece* | | 133 |
| France | | 141 |
| Germany | | 95 |
| Italy | | 305 |
| Spain† | | 47 |
| Portugal† | | 21 |
| Ireland | | 68 |
| Luxembourg | | 68 |
| Netherlands | | 53 |
| Britain | | 39 |
| Denmark | 1973-96 | 20 |

Source: European Court of Justice    *Joined 1981, †Joined 1986

with no record of dissenting votes, what any of them thinks. It is a far cry from America's Supreme Court, with its televised confirmation hearings and detailed examination of the opinions of individual justices.

Most judges recoil, unsurprisingly, from the American example. The continental European tradition is different from the Anglo-Saxon one: continental courts issue collective judgments and their judges remain largely anonymous. Judges fear that American-style confirmation hearings could politicise the court and turn the choice of new judges into a media circus.

Yet Europe's final court of appeal could do with a dose of Americanism. The European Parliament (or, if that seems federalist, national parliaments) could help vet new judges without turning confirmation into a circus. And publication of individual judges' opinions—especially dissenting ones—could improve future judgments. American experience shows that dissenting opinions often, a few years later, win the day. It could happen. As Mr Mancini observes, in its early days the Supreme Court in Washington also did not publish individual opinions.

# Coreper, Europe's managing board

**V**ISIT the seat of the Council of Ministers of the European Union in Brussels, and the chances are you will find no council of ministers there. The council is more of a process than an institution. Groups of ministers from national governments meet for a day or two, agree upon policy, adopt legislation, make a few declarations,

and disperse. Foreign ministers meet at least once a month, as do finance ministers and agriculture ministers. Most others meet less often. Steering the whole mass of intergovernmental business has been the job of the foreign ministers. The detailed work is done by the "permanent representatives" of member states and their deputies.

These high-ranking civil servants meet in a two-tier committee known for short as "Coreper". Most of them are career diplomats with long years of EU experience.

As proxies and problem-solvers for their national governments, the members of Coreper do not merely sift and prepare agendas for ministers. They and the working parties below them resolve nine-tenths of the issues before ministers even meet, leaving only the most politically sensitive points to be decided.

The secrecy, permanence and ubiquity of Coreper have led to its members being tagged, by those who know of them at all, as the "men who really run Europe". Alan Clark, a former British minister, recorded in his diaries the sour but flattering view that "it makes [not] the slightest difference to the conclusions of a meeting what Ministers say at it. Everything is decided, horse-traded off by officials at Coreper. . . . The ministers arrive on the scene at the last minute, hot, tired, ill or drunk (sometimes all of these together), read out their piece and depart."

From inside Coreper, naturally enough, the view is rather different. As good civil servants, the permanent representatives would never admit to "running" Europe. ("If ministers want to let Coreper decide, that is a ministerial decision.") At most they would admit to holding a vital part of its structure together. But even this role may soon be endangered. Some members of Coreper think the system they serve is beginning to fracture around them.

That prospect looms because the old masters of European policy across national governments—the foreign ministers—have been losing their clout. They are ceasing to achieve at the political level what Coreper does at the working level—take the broad view, strike the necessary balance, recognise the European interest. Finance ministers are wresting the big decisions away from them. Heads of government are intervening in European affairs more often and more directly. Minis-

ters have less incentive to speak from a single script, which Coreper can edit.

Opinions differ as to the cause of the foreign ministers' decline. One member of Coreper says (off the record, as always) that the current crop is simply not up to the calibre of its predecessors: "Name me a great man among them." Another suggests the foreign ministers may have made a conscious decision to "give up their role—I can find no other words" because they have found the work involved both too detailed and too boring and because they prefer to spend more of their time on world affairs.

The kindest view is that the decline of the foreign ministers' role follows inevitably from their past successes. The EU has permeated national affairs so completely that it has come to seem scarcely "foreign" at all. All ministries have grown confident and experienced enough to set European agendas for themselves. Business has become so voluminous that no one group of ministers can offer much in the way of overall leadership merely by meeting once a month.

The foreign ministers and Coreper have lost battles before. Agriculture ministers have led a life of their own since the 1960s, when they secured a Special Agricultural Committee, separate from Coreper, through which "technical" issues could be prepared.

But the new challenge to foreign ministers' dominance, coming from finance and economic ministers, is a much bigger one, which could prove fatal. The finance ministers' functional role in EU affairs has grown hugely with the approach of European monetary union. It has emboldened them to demand a last word on everything touched by finance—in effect, almost everything. They have begun strug-

gling openly with the foreign ministers for control of "Agenda 2000", a draft package of reforms that are mainly financial in character. If the foreign ministers lose this battle, says one member of Coreper, "they will become just another specialist council themselves."

It is too late already for Coreper to recoup one big loss: it has been offered no role at all in the work of "Euro-11", the new club for finance ministers of countries within the nascent monetary union. The finance ministers have said that they want to keep their proceedings low-key. "Apparently we will be 'informed' of developments there," fumes one Coreper ambassador. "But financial and economic policy touches on everything. On employment. How can we co-ordinate? We cannot. It is incredible. Incredible. And the only ones who get any satisfaction out of it are the narrow-minded ministers."

From a strictly procedural point of view, notes another ambassador, it need not matter much to Coreper if another set of ministers, or the heads of EU governments meeting with increased frequency, takes over the steering role in Europe. The job could even be done by a new, permanent body of "vice-prime ministers for Europe", of which there is scattered talk. Even now Coreper answers to governments, not to foreign ministries alone. But there must be some dedicated political body leading EU business at an intergovernmental level. Otherwise arguments and contradictions between ministerial interests and national interests would become all-consuming. Coreper, says this ambassador, "would become like the dinosaurs. The small predators would prevail". The dinosaur waits to see if he is right.

# Europe's censure motion

**Quentin Peel** and **Peter Norman** explain why the European parliament's vote yesterday matters, even though it did not bring the Commission down

It was "one of the most important votes that has ever taken place in the European parliament", says José Maria GilRobles, its Spanish president. At stake was the future of Jacques Santer, president of the European Commission, at least two of his commissioners, and possibly all of them.

The parliament had been asked to pass a motion of censure on the commissioners after accusations of financial mismanagement: 42 per cent of parliamentarians who voted chose to condemn the executive and seek its resignation.

All the same, that left Mr Santer trying not to look smug. After all, he survived the motion.

For days, he and his 19 fellow commissioners had been subjected to varying degrees of vilification for their lack of accountability, mismanagement, dilatoriness, and inability to root out fraud and corruption. Two commissioners were named and urged to step down for alleged maladministration in their departments.

But when it came to the vote, the critics (from both left and right) were unable to summon a majority, and the motion was lost by 232 votes to 293.

"What prime minister in Europe can claim to have such a majority?" Mr Santer demanded, as he rode up to face the press. "It was a double victory. They failed to get an absolute majority, and they failed to get a two-thirds majority, both of which they needed. It was a vote for confidence."

Perhaps. But that was not how members of the parliament saw it and the truth is that a week of extraordinary wrangling has left the Commission with a bloody nose, and the parliament feeling more powerful. Meanwhile, Europe's citizens probably feel more disenchanted than before with the workings of the European Union.

"No ordinary person can tell the difference between the Commission, the parliament, and the 15 member states in the Council of Ministers," according to one French diplomat. "So allegations of fraud and mismanagement affect us all."

In the long term, the dispute may be more positive than that suggests. Pat Cox, the Irish independent who leads the Liberal group in the parliament, called the vote a victory for democratic accountability because, he said, the Commission had been forced to defend itself in public and to concede a raft of reforms in its administration and appointments.

"Here is a parliament almost playing it by ear, and discovering all sorts of powers," said Peter Ludlow, director of the Centre for European Policy Studies in Brussels. "Life will never be the same again. No treaty will be needed in the future to remind the Commission that it is responsible to the parliament."

The escalation of the dispute to the point of yesterday's vote of censure partly reflected Mr Santer's inept mishandling of the parliament since it refused to sign off the 1996 budget last month—in itself a strong criticism of the executive's financial management. He challenged parliament to pass a motion of censure, in order to prove that he still had cross-party support. As a result, he unleashed the whole bruising debate, and the direct attack on Manuel Marin, his Spanish vice-president, and Edith Cresson, the French commissioner responsible for education and training.

But the tussle is also symptomatic of a longer-term power shift between parliament and Commission, which is likely to continue running in parliament's favour.

Mr Gil-Robles pointed out yesterday that the MEPs' greater militancy was a logical consequence of the powers granted to parliament by the 1992 Maastricht treaty. It had simply taken time to adjust to that new strength.

Under the present treaty, the Commission is a single college, and individual commissioners cannot be held responsible for their own programmes. They are appointed by the 15 member states in the Council of Ministers, and none has ever been dislodged, in spite of notorious cases of ineffectiveness and incompetence. The parliamentarians are determined to change that, as a step towards making Brussels more accountable. "The individual responsibility of commissioners has been put on the agenda," said Willy de Clercq, himself a former trade commissioner. "We will not take it off again."

That determination, even if it takes time to realise through treaty changes, will put pressure on member states to select more competent commissioners, and ensure the Commission is efficiently run.

That in turn will force further changes. Taking the long view, it is possible to argue that the Commission's power peaked relatively early in the history of the EU. It has been in decline since 1966, when the then six member states won a right of veto over matters of "vital national interest", undermining the Commission's role as the principal initiator of policy.

Under Jacques Delores, Mr Santer's charismatic and powerful predecessor, the commission still initiated a great deal of legislation. Under Mr Santer, its task has been rather one of managing the programmes. Yet, according to Mr Ludlow, the Commission's personnel has not been changed to suit the new more modest purpose. "In a private firm, you wouldn't turn the planning department into an accountancy unit," he says.

In addition, the commission has been ill-served by both member states and the parliament, which have heaped responsibilities on it without proving extra resources. The Commission has been guilty of accepting them, and of taking on too many tiny programmes.

"We had far too high a number of small projects," says Erkki Liikanen, the Finnish commissioner responsible for the budget. "We should create a minimum size of project, and never accept one where the cost of control and management are higher than the expense of the project itself."

All that is practical good sense. But the parliament has exposed a fundamental lack of accountability in the Commission itself.

And because of the vote, that is no longer just the commission's problem. In the wake of yesterday's censure motion—and the broader powers being given to the European parliament by treaty—the responsibility for sorting out the mess will in future be shared more widely. If there are more scandals over mismanagement, it will be far more difficult for the member states and the parliament to escape their share of blame.

From *Financial Times*, January 15, 1999, p. 10. © 1999 by Financial Times Syndication. Reprinted by permission.

# EUROPE'S NEW CURRENCY

## Gambling on the euro

**Europe's monetary union is neither bound to succeed nor doomed to fail. Leadership, circumstances and luck will combine to decide its fate**

THE architects of the euro, looking back this weekend on what they have achieved, are entitled to feel pleased with themselves. As recently as ten years ago, the idea of merging the European Union's national monetary systems seemed fantastic. A plan for doing it was drawn up nonetheless. Then, with the ink on this blueprint hardly dry, the forerunner of the single currency (the exchange-rate mechanism of the European Monetary System) collapsed, casting new doubt on the whole enterprise. No matter. The prime movers, Helmut Kohl in Germany and François Mitterrand in France, carried on regardless. On January 4th their remarkable vision becomes a reality: the currencies of the 11 participating members of Europe's Economic and Monetary Union will be "irrevocably" fused.

To have come this far is in itself an amazing political feat. Nobody can claim that EMU was forced upon Europe's governments by force of events, still less by popular demand.

**Solid foundations?** `1`

| Euro countries | % in favour of EMU end '97 | % in favour of EMU mid '98 | Tested by referendum? (if Yes, % in favour) | % feeling well-informed about EMU* |
|---|---|---|---|---|
| Germany | 40 | 51 | No | 32 |
| France | 58 | 68 | Yes (52) | 33 |
| Italy | 78 | 83 | No | 17 |
| Spain | 61 | 72 | No | 22 |
| Netherlands | 57 | 73 | No | 43 |
| Belgium | 57 | 68 | No | 31 |
| Austria | 44 | 56 | No | 42 |
| Portugal | 45 | 52 | No | 11 |
| Finland | 33 | 53 | No | 34 |
| Ireland | 67 | 68 | Yes (69) | 17 |
| Luxembourg | 62 | 79 | No | 43 |
| Euro-11 | 60 | 66 | | 25 |
| **Non-participating countries** | | | | |
| Britain | 29 | 34 | No | 13 |
| Sweden | 34 | 39 | No | 16 |
| Denmark | 40 | 51 | Yes† | 42 |
| Greece | 59 | 67 | No | 12 |

Sources: Eurobarometer; Keesings
*Mid '98 †In a first referendum the Danes voted against the treaty. In a later one they voted in favour of the treaty with an opt-out from EMU

Events have, if anything, conspired to wreck the plan. Europe's voters, perhaps reflecting the weight of official pro-euro propaganda, are by and large in favour, and opinion has moved further in this direction of late (see table 1). However, the balance in Germany, which could prove decisive, is still quite narrow. And it is disturbing that so few voters anywhere consider themselves "well-informed" about the project.

This is an initiative of extraordinary ambition, given that it is to be carried through despite quite shallow support in popular opinion. EMU is an elite project. Europe's governments are saying: Our people may not be convinced of the euro's benefits just yet, but once it is in place and they come to understand it, they will change their minds. Europe's leaders had better be right. Otherwise, when the system comes under strain, its political foundations may prove too weak to sustain it.

Even before construction of the euro is complete, governments can point to one notable success. The past year has seen extraordinary turmoil in global financial markets. Rich-country stockmarkets and currencies have not been spared. Yet Europe has been, comparatively speaking, a safe haven. Intra-European movements in exchange rates have been tiny. This is something that the euro-11 governments had committed themselves to, but their success could not have been taken for granted a year ago. The fact is, at a time of unprecedented financial turbulence, the foreign-exchange markets regarded the promise to stabilise intra-European exchange rates as credible. Currencies have held steady and interest rates have converged: it augurs well for the transition to the new system.

The next few years are, after all, transitional. National currencies will continue to circulate until the end of 2001, albeit at permanently fixed parities. In the meantime, the European System of Central Banks undertakes to defend those parities. In principle this means that if, say, Italians decide to switch all their lire into D-marks, the supply of D-marks, will be expanded without limit to accommodate them. Even now there must be some small doubt as to whether, if push comes to shove, this will happen. But if the markets continue to regard the parities as credible—as they did throughout the exceptionally severe test of the past year—then Germany's offer to finance the early retirement of Italy's currency is unlikely to be called upon.

That danger aside, and for the moment considering EMU only in its economic aspect, two principal risks remain. The first, which will be most acute during the project's early years, is that economic policy in the euro area as a whole will be ill-judged, leading to a recession that discredits the whole venture. The other, which will remain a threat into the medium term, is that the system will prove too inflexible to cope with local (in the jargon, "asymmetric") economic shocks. Consider each in turn.

## Independent to a fault

In designing EMU, the architects laid great emphasis both on the independence of the European Central Bank (ECB) and on the simplicity and severity of its anti-inflation objective.

**Good timing?** [2]
Forecasts of growth and inflation, %

| Euro countries | GDP 1998 | GDP 1999 | Inflation* 1998 | Inflation* 1999 |
|---|---|---|---|---|
| Germany | 2.7 | 2.2 | 1.0 | 1.2 |
| France | 3.1 | 2.4 | 0.5 | 0.9 |
| Italy | 1.5 | 2.1 | 2.3 | 1.8 |
| Spain | 3.8 | 3.4 | 2.0 | 2.0 |
| Netherlands | 3.8 | 2.7 | 2.1 | 2.1 |
| Belgium | 2.9 | 2.3 | 1.0 | 1.2 |
| Austria | 3.1 | 2.4 | 1.0 | 1.0 |
| Portugal | 4.0 | 3.3 | 2.7 | 2.3 |
| Finland | 5.0 | 3.2 | 1.1 | 1.3 |
| Ireland | 9.1 | 6.7 | 2.7 | 2.4 |
| Luxembourg | 4.7 | 3.4 | 1.1 | 1.3 |
| Euro-11 | 2.9 | 2.5 | 1.3 | 1.4 |
| **Non-participating countries** | | | | |
| Britain | 2.7 | 0.8 | 2.0 | 2.8 |
| Sweden | 2.8 | 2.2 | 0.8 | 1.0 |
| Denmark | 2.4 | 2.0 | 1.9 | 2.5 |
| Greece | 3.0 | 3.2 | 4.8 | 3.0 |

Source: OECD    * Private-consumption deflators

In statutory terms, at least, the ECB may well be the most independent, and most single-minded, central bank in the world. America's Federal Reserve, for instance, is required by law to take output and employment into account alongside inflation, for which no numerical target is set. In addition, the Fed is accountable to Congress, which periodically questions its top officials and sometimes tries to influence their views. The restraint that Congress and the White House show in this regard is a matter of custom, reflecting the standing which the Fed has won for itself in financial markets over many years, and not a matter of law.

The position of the ECB is quite different. The Maastricht treaty allows for no clear accountability to any other arm of national or European government. In fact the treaty explicitly forbids the ECB and its decision-making bodies to "seek or take instructions from Community institutions or bodies, from any government of a member state or from any other body". It also stipulates that the proceedings of the ECB council's meetings will remain confidential. If he chose, Wim Duisenberg, the first chief of the ECB, could nonetheless announce the outcome of its deliberations, together with a commentary and forecasts justifying it. Mr Duisenberg says he is not against this sort of openness. Time will tell. The point is, everything is left for the ECB to decide: this is independence with a vengeance.

As to aims, the treaty further stipulates that the ECB's goal is "price stability", leaving the bank to decide what that means. In many other countries with "independent" central banks—in

Britain, for instance—the government sets a target for inflation and reserves the right to change it as circumstances, in its judgment, dictate. EMU has no such escape-clause. Moreover, the bank is forbidden to balance the goal of price stability against other aims. The treaty directs the ECB to "support the general economic policies of the Community" but, crucially, it is to do this "without prejudice to the objective of price stability".

The ECB has now defined "price stability" to mean inflation of less than 2% a year. In modern times, no major economy has hit such a target consistently over a run of years. America's inflation rate has averaged 3.3% over the past ten years; Germany's, despite the mighty Bundesbank, has averaged 2.8%. In short, a radically undemocratic institution has been charged to achieve, without compromise, an exceptionally demanding goal of virtually zero inflation.

Strong evidence suggests that central-bank independence is indeed a good idea: any given level of inflation can be achieved more cheaply, in terms of forgone output and employment, if firms and workers believe that monetary policy is free from undue political pressure. The danger is that EMU's architects have gone too far. The European Union, with its weak parliament, is acknowledged in any case to have a "democratic deficit" at its centre; the powers of the new central bank will make that deficit all the greater. In economic terms, the danger is simply that the ECB will take its instructions literally—and will try to screw inflation down to nothing regardless of wider economic repercussions.

As it happens, the circumstances seem likely to prove favourable. Forecasters at the OECD expect that output in the euro zone will grow by 2½% in the coming year, with inflation remaining at about its present 1½% (see table 2). This assumes that short-term interest rates in the euro area will average 3% in 1999, their current level, a full percentage point lower than the average for 1998. All that would presumably suit the ECB pretty well. But more awkward eventualities cannot be ruled out.

One is that governments, after years of post-Maastricht squeezing and fudging of budget deficits, will ease fiscal policy too much (despite the rule forbidding it, of which more in a moment). That could put upward pressure on inflation and lead the ECB, with little headroom beneath its inflation target, to assert itself at once and raise interest rates (or delay cutting them). An early conflict of this kind between loose fiscal policy and tight monetary policy would be an extremely discouraging start.

Another even more awkward possibility for monetary policy in EMU's first year or two is that the OECD's forecasts for output may prove too optimistic. This is not implausible. The health of the world economy is far from robust. With Wall Street overvalued on every historical measure, the danger of sharp falls in global equity prices in 1999 needs to be taken seriously. That in turn might prompt a worse slowdown in demand than is allowed for in the OECD's central-case forecasts. The question would then be whether the ECB would cut interest rates soon enough and far enough to avoid recession in Europe.

If the bank waited for inflation to fall before acting, that would be too late. Yet the bank might be reluctant to act more promptly, responding to forecasts of lower inflation rather than to out-turns, as it should, for fear of undermining its credibility with the markets.

Mr Duisenberg will prefer to err on the side of caution (that is, on the side of lower inflation and higher short-term unemployment) in any case; he will want to be judged by the euro zone's inflation record, maintaining that unemployment is none of his concern. Adding to his desire to establish a tough reputation at the outset will be his memory of the fiasco surrounding his appointment. France wanted to appoint its own candidate to the job; the other countries resisted. The absurd compromise that was settled upon allowed France to say that Mr Duisenberg will step down early in favour of its man, while Mr Duisenberg says that no such promise was made. When Mr Duisenberg comes to be tested, the price of that squabble may well be higher interest rates and fewer jobs.

## A shocking possibility

In principle, however, a recession that threatens the euro-11 as a group is not the most difficult scenario for the ECB. Once its reputation is established and any teething troubles overcome, a system-wide problem of that kind can be dealt with perfectly well by the system-wide response of a change in interest rates. Indeed, a single central bank is arguably better equipped to deal with such a case than would be 11 separate national banks, acting in an unco-ordinated way. That is why, beyond the transitional period, the larger challenge for the new system will be to deal with fluctuations that are not system-wide.

# Ins and outs

PERHAPS the biggest omission in the Maastricht treaty was the failure to clarify the status of the "outs"—the countries that decline to take part. (Britain, Denmark and Sweden have chosen to stay out; Greece would love to join but is nowhere near satisfying the Maastricht criteria for membership.) This was not an oversight but a deliberate gap, much in accord with the way Europe's architects have tended to proceed.

The EU'S members are pledged to move towards "ever closer union". Implicitly, the idea is that they will approach this goal (as yet undefined) at about the same speed—so the four countries not taking part in EMU at the outset are expected to join as soon as they can. To have designed a durable relationship between the ins and outs might have encouraged further delay.

It often happens in European politics that if you do not want a contingency to arise, you ignore it, hoping it goes away. Sometimes it does—and this time-honoured approach may also work in the case of EMU's outs. If monetary union is a success, the qualifying outsiders will warm to the idea. But the collapse of the ERM in 1992–93 showed that the head-in-the-sand method is not infallible. If EMU works badly, outsiders such as Britain are likely to become even more reluctant.

There is also the question of EU enlargement. Prospective new members in Eastern Europe may not be ready, or may not choose, to join EMU at the beginning. Indeed, they would be wise to be cautious. Their economies are still struggling with the legacy of socialism. For many years yet they are likely to remain structurally different from their western neighbours, leaving them more exposed to the danger of asymmetric economic shocks. This only adds to the case for lasting arrangements allowing EU countries to opt out of EMU indefinitely.

The main economic problem posed by a permanent division of the EU into EMU and non-EMU countries is that the outs will be seen by the others as cheats. It is easy to imagine circumstances in which the euro will strengthen against other European currencies, putting euro countries at a competitive disadvantage in trade. If this happens (as well it might) at a time of slowing growth in the euro zone and briskly expanding output elsewhere in the EU, the euro-zone governments will be obliged to object.

In due course, therefore, some form of "monetary co-operation" will probably be required of the outs, if only as a mark of good faith. One possibility would be a revived ERM, albeit a looser arrangement than the one that collapsed. (For instance, governments might promise to limit variations in their real, as opposed to nominal, exchange rates: this would preserve a measure of monetary discretion while ensuring that governments did not use it to pursue a policy of competitive devaluation.) Failing some such accord, the discussion may move to other ways of correcting the "unfair" advantage of the noneuro countries' depreciated currencies—and that is a discussion that could endanger the EU itself.

A permanent union of ins and outs would also raise a host of day-to-day political difficulties. The outs' great fear—and what eventually may force them into EMU—is that the centre of decision-making for the EU as a whole will move to the committee of euro-zone finance ministers. This seems certain to happen if EMU runs into trouble, and the euro-zone countries adopt remedies such as collective fiscal policy and/or increased harmonisation of taxes and economic regulations. Even if all goes well, though, a diminution of the outs' political sway seems likely. The ins will surely want to punish the outs, with or without a show of regret. How better to encourage the laggards to change their minds?

The euro zone is not what economists call an "optimum currency area"—that is, it is not a region whose constituent parts are affected in broadly the same way by typical economic disturbances, or among whose constituent parts labour moves freely. If it were, then no economic purpose would be served by retaining sub-European currencies. Admittedly, few if any national economies meet that ideal standard: regions within the United States often suffer asymmetric shocks because of local concentrations of particular industries, and although American labour migrates comparatively smoothly from one state to another, these shifts are by no means costless.

The point, though, is that the euro zone is very much further from being an optimum currency area than is the United States. Disparities in relative prices (after allowing for exchange-rate fluctuations) are greater among the euro-11 than among American states; and the mobility of labour within Europe is, according to one study, only one-third of the mobility of labour within America.

Advocates of monetary union argue that the euro will itself narrow the gap, by encouraging closer economic integration. This is quite true. However, even with the euro, the barriers of culture and language are likely to remain stronger in Europe. One perverse consequence of the euro may be that, precisely because it encourages closer integration, it will also promote greater local specialisation—increasing the chance of asymmetric shocks from that source. In sum, for many years to come, persistent national divergences in growth and unemployment are likely to recur from time to time.

Europe's governments all acknowledge that one way to reduce the costs of these divergences is to improve the supply-side flexibility of their economies. The price of European over-regulation is a both a higher unemployment rate over time, and a greater susceptibility to a further upward ratcheting of this average or equilibrium rate of unemployment with each serious recession. The trouble is, governments have so far proved better at paying lip-service to the need for deregulation than they have at dealing with the problem. The recent shift to the left in European politics makes this remedy all the less likely to be adopted.

That leaves macroeconomic policy. When a country with its own currency suffers a recession, it is free to cut interest rates. This stimulates demand

| No headroom | | 3 |
| --- | --- | --- |
| Budget deficit/(surplus) as % of GDP | | |
| Euro countries | 1998 | 1999 |
| Germany | 2.4 | 2.1 |
| France | 2.9 | 2.4 |
| Italy | 2.6 | 2.2 |
| Spain | 1.9 | 1.8 |
| Netherlands | 1.2 | 1.3 |
| Belgium | 1.5 | 1.3 |
| Austria | 2.2 | 2.2 |
| Portugal | 2.3 | 2.0 |
| Finland | (0.8) | (1.9) |
| Ireland | (2.5) | (2.8) |
| Luxembourg | (1.4) | (1.0) |
| Non-participating countries | | |
| Britain | 0.4 | 0.7 |
| Sweden | (1.2) | (0.3) |
| Denmark | (1.0) | (2.2) |
| Greece | 2.7 | 2.5 |
| Source: OECD | | |

twice over: first by lowering the cost of credit, and second by causing the currency to depreciate (which spurs exports). Countries in the euro zone will not have this option. Emigration cannot help much (as it would in the case of Michigan, say). And since Europe has only a tiny central budget, net assistance from faster-growing countries (in the form of bigger inflows of public spending and smaller outflows of taxes) will also play a far smaller part than the equivalent fiscal transactions in the United States.

All that remains is national fiscal policy. The recession-struck economy is still free to borrow on its own behalf, thus stimulating demand and speeding its recovery. Or it would be, except for EMU's "Stability and Growth Pact". This is a rule that governments agreed to at Germany's insistence, requiring budget deficits to be held to 3% of GDP or less. Violators will be fined, subject to a vote of governments, unless output has fallen by 2% or more in the year in question.

Despite this purported flexibility, the regime (like the rules defining the ECB's aims and freedoms) is exceptionally severe. Falls in output of 2% or more are extremely unusual; far smaller downturns would cause unemployment to rise quickly and be universally regarded as "recessions". And the restriction is too tight in another way: governments that tried to anticipate a downturn by relaxing fiscal policy early, thereby breaching the 3% limit before output fell by 2%, would also face fines.

The German doubts that led to the adoption of this procedure were exaggerated, albeit not entirely groundless.

The concern was that chronic overborrowers would become even more fiscally irresponsible once they had adopted the euro, because they would no longer face the financial-market sanction of higher interest rates and (in the end) a depreciating currency. Moreover, this overborrowing would henceforth be at least partly at the expense of Germany and the other euro countries, because they would bear some of the cost of default, if it came to that.

The fear is exaggerated because the Maastricht treaty rightly insists that the central bank cannot bail out national governments. Provided that promise is believed, and so long as the no-bail-out rule applies to other finance ministries as well as to the ECB, the markets would attach a risk premium (in the form of a higher interest rate) to borrowing by heavily indebted governments. That is as it should be—and no further discipline should be necessary. As it is, the stability pact calls that promise into doubt, by making budgets a collective responsibility. Worse, in the meantime it rules out counter-cyclical fiscal policy of the sort that will often be necessary, and for which there is no longer any plausible national substitute.

The crucial question regarding the stability pact, therefore, is the same as for the ECB: given that the design is so bad, how might it work in practice? Today, budget deficits in many euro economies (including the three biggest) stand at more than 2% of GDP (see table 3). If demand in Europe grows more slowly in 1999 than the forecasters expect, those deficits may rise. (In some cases they will tend to rise regardless, as assorted post-Maastricht fudges are unwound.) Governments may soon be faced with the stability-pact requirement to raise taxes and/or cut public spending—even as their economies slide toward recession. Again, therefore, the hope must be that the rules will be bent, or scrapped. If this does not happen, and one or more countries encounter a downturn that the ECB cannot remedy by means of system-wide monetary policy, there are only two alternatives.

One is that the countries concerned endure a deeper and longer recession than they are used to, or is necessary. This plainly runs the risk of calling forth mounting protests against EMU itself. The other is that the fiscal powers available to the centre—the money gathered and spent by Brussels—must be greatly enlarged. This would allow automatic fiscal stabilisers to work within Europe as they do within the

United States of America. Many in Europe would regard this second alternative as desirable in any case, which (if the stability pact survives) makes it the more probable outcome. In any event, this seems likely to be the issue on which Europe's political future turns.

## Ever closer union

Judged strictly as an economic venture, EMU will be a success if, over the coming years, the participating countries benefit from closer integration (measured by growing trade and investment in the euro area), satisfactory growth, declining unemployment and low inflation. If the single-currency project had been better designed, the chances of achieving this would have been good. Closer economic integration seems assured in any case. A plan that created a properly directed, properly accountable central bank and provided for adequate freedom in na-

tional fiscal policy would have done as much as macroeconomic policy can do to take care of the rest. To be sure, that would still have left governments to carry a heavy burden of supply-side reform—without which Europe cannot expect to cut its unemployment to the levels seen in America. Still, the outlook would have been promising.

As it is, the chances of success are no better than fair. The central bank will have to rise above its flawed design—winning the popular regard it will one day need both by explaining what it is up to, and by balancing the short-term demands of low inflation, on the one hand, and growth in output and employment, on the other, more intelligently than its statutes require. And governments will have to find a way to make fiscal policy respond far more flexibly to economic circumstances than the Maastricht rules allow.

Ideally this will be done by changing the rules—perhaps to require that budgets are balanced over the course

of the economic cycle, but leaving them free to run further into deficit at times of slowing demand than the 3% of GDP allowed by the stability pact. Needless to say, in this case too, efforts to liberalise Europe's markets for goods, services and labour far more determined than governments have made so far will also be required.

If EMU can overcome the flaws of its design and prove an economic success after all, Europe's governments (and, preferably, their citizens as well) will be able to weigh the coming political choices on their merits. If it fails in economic terms, those political choices may be severely constrained—and, as a result, far more divisive. Closer political integration built on the solid foundation of an EMU that worked would be one thing. The same course adopted in distress to save EMU from failure, or even outright collapse, would be an entirely different, and much more dangerous, enterprise.

# Eastern Europe a Decade Later

# THE POSTCOMMUNIST DIVIDE

## Jacques Rupnik

*Jacques Rupnik is senior fellow and professor at the Foundation Nationale des Sciences Politiques in Paris. He is the author of* Balkans: Paysage après la bataille *(1996) and* Le Déchirement des nations *(1995) and the editor of two forthcoming volumes, 1968:* Le Printemps tchécoslovaque *and* International Perspectives on the Balkans.

Ten years after the collapse of the Soviet empire, one thing is clear: The word "postcommunism" has lost its relevance. The fact that Hungary and Albania, or the Czech Republic and Belarus, or Poland and Kazakhstan shared a communist past explains very little about the paths that they have taken since. Indeed, it is striking how vastly different the outcomes of the democratic transitions have been in Central and Eastern Europe. Nonetheless, certain patterns do emerge. A new tripartite political geography of formerly communist Europe is emerging: a new Central Europe (the so-called Visegrád group, the Baltic countries, and Slovenia) as a clear "success story"; the Balkans, where the democratic transition has often been derailed by the priorities of nation-state building or undermined by the legacies of communism and economic backwardness; and Russia, in search of a postimperial identity and teetering on the brink of economic disaster. (The fate of democratization in Ukraine, Belarus, and Moldova will to a large extent depend on what happens in Russia.)

Shortly after the collapse of the communist system, Ralf Dahrendorf identified three interrelated areas of change with different "timetables": political democracy and the rule of law (six months), the conversion to a market economy (six years), and the emergence of a civil society (six decades). Almost a decade later, it appears that so far the new political elites in Central Europe have suc-

cessfully met the challenge posed by the disjunctive time spans of these three processes of change. They have established parliamentary democracy as the only game in town, creating a constitutional framework and political institutions that are seen as legitimate by all political actors; moreover, the formation of a relatively stable party system, allowing for smooth alternation in power, by now has taken place everywhere in Central Europe. A market economy has been established, with more than half of GNP produced in the private sector and over three quarters of trade now conducted with the OECD countries. A civil society is developing, with both its economic dimension (emerging new strata of entrepreneurs) and its networks of nongovernmental organizations (NGOs).

This picture contrasts not only with the former Soviet Union (the Baltic states excepted) but also with the Balkans. The most extreme case of a "derailed" transition, of course, is former Yugoslavia, because of the war and the breakup of the Federation into several successor states whose legitimacy and viability are still being questioned. The legitimacy of the territorial framework clearly remains the first prerequisite for a democratic transition.

To be sure, the situation in the Balkans should not be seen solely through the prism of the Yugoslav war and ethnonationalist conflict. There have been encouraging developments over the last year or two in both Bulgaria and Romania. In the former, the winter of discontent (1996–97), culminating in the ransacking of Parliament, forced the incompetent and corrupt ex-communist government to step down and call for an early election, opening the way for much delayed economic reforms. In Romania, a belated alternation in power ("We have lost seven years," said President Constantinescu when

taking over from Iliescu) saw the ex-communists replaced by a right-wing coalition, although after two years in power it has produced little or no reform. If the contrast between the Central European and Balkan models can be summed up as that between democratic consolidation and the rise of "illiberal democracies," then Romania and Bulgaria (as well as Slovakia) are in an intermediate position.

There is, of course, no single factor that accounts for this process of differentiation. One can only point to a combination of factors, explanations, or hypotheses that can help make sense of the uneven progress of the democratic transition in the region.

*1) The legacies of communism.* More important than the manner of the changeover in 1989–91 (gradual or sudden, negotiated from above or imposed from below) in influencing the longer-term prospects for democratic success are the nature of the old communist regime and the depth of its imprint on society. The harshest totalitarian domination in the postwar period tended to be in the Balkans (Albania, Romania, Bulgaria), whereas a greater degree of reform and accommodation was characteristic of the post-1956 regimes in Poland and Hungary. Of course, the contrasting cases of relatively liberal Yugoslavia (since the 1960s) and of "normalized" Czechoslovakia after 1968 show the limits of such a generalization.

Nonetheless, it is instructive to examine the nature of the pre-1989 crises of communism in the two regions. In Central Europe, communism experienced three major crises (the 1956 Hungarian revolution, the Prague Spring in 1968, and the rise of Poland's Solidarity movement in 1980–81) that posed primarily the issue of democracy and civil society, and only in a second phase (under

From the *Journal of Democracy*, January 1999, pp. 57-62. © 1999 by the National Endowment for Democracy and the Johns Hopkins University Press. Reprinted by permission.

growing external constraint) that of national independence. By contrast, the three major crises of communism in the Balkans (Tito's 1948 break with Stalin, Hoxha's 1961 switch of allegiance from Moscow to Peking, and Ceausescu's 1968 bid for foreign policy independence) all stressed the autonomy of the national communist apparatus vis-à-vis Moscow, while reinforcing the totalitarian features of the regime. The origins of the rebirth of civil society in Central Europe go back to the region's three major crises, as well as to the dissident movements of the 1970s and 1980s. The origins of "nationalism as the final stage of communism" (Adam Michnik's phrase) in the Balkans owe a great deal to the legacies of Tito, Hoxha, and Ceausescu. Similarly, the emergence of alternative political elites during and in the immediate aftermath of 1989 in Central Europe owes a great deal to the existence of organized democratic opposition movements. These were largely lacking in Southeastern Europe, where the first free elections were all won by the ex-communist parties.

*2) Market and civil society.* "No bourgeoisie, no democracy." Barrington Moore's famous phrase provides a second clue for a comparative assessment of the democratic transitions in Central and Eastern Europe. There were, of course, differences due to the uneven level of economic development dating back to the precommunist period or the degree of economic reform pursued in the decaying phase of communism (here Hungary and Poland were the frontrunners, while Romania and Bulgaria lagged behind). The most striking contrast, however, is between those who after 1989 embarked on radical market reforms and those who chose gradualism or simply the postponement of market reforms and privatization.

The results are fairly clear, not only in terms of the relative size of the private sector, but also in foreign trade, growth rates, and the level of foreign investment (nearly half of direct investment in Central and Eastern Europe went to Hungary alone). There are one million registered private entrepreneurs in the Czech Republic and over 800,000 in Hungary. The emergence of new middle classes is also related to the progress of the "information revolution" and the formidable expansion of the service sector, areas where "human capital" is rewarded. (Before 1989, less than a third of Czechs believed that education was related to success; today almost two-thirds do.) The development of these middle strata, along with the conversion (through the privatization process) of part of the old *nomenklatura* into the new bourgeoisie, provides the backbone of the new market.

As for civil society, a term that emerged within the dissident movement in the late 1970s, it was originally understood as a self-organizing alternative society (a "parallel polis," as Václav Benda put it in 1978) in opposition to totalitarian rule. After the collapse of the latter, the concept acquired two new meanings relevant to the democratic transition. The first, prevalent in Central Europe among "liberals on the right," tended to identify it with the above described economic revolution. This is civil society as *Bürgergesellschaft,* secured by the market economy.

The second definition of civil society, prevalent among "liberals on the left," divorced the term almost completely from the market economy and identified it with the so-called third sector, i.e., NGOs. According to this view, civil society is distinct from both state and market. The NGO is doubly pure, corrupted neither by power (i.e., politics) nor by money (i.e., the market). Civil society understood in terms of the first definition is more developed in Central Europe, while the NGO sector has been relatively more important to the transition in Southeastern Europe, where it can help compensate for the weakness of both the middle class and of political opposition to semi-authoritarian rule (Romania under Iliescu, ex-Yugoslavia). In the recent elections in Slovakia, which after 1993 seemed to be drifting away from the Central European model, the "third sector" demonstrated how effective it can be in mobilizing society and helping the opposition to overcome the "democratic deficit."

*3) The rule of law and the "Habsburg factor."* The recent debate about "illiberal democracies" has usefully reemphasized the crucial importance of the rule of law for democratic consolidation, a relationship that is underscored by the experience of the past decade. Although all generalizations are also exaggerations, one can say that the rule of law, constitutionalism, and the existence of an independent judiciary are undoubtedly more developed in Central Europe than in the Balkans. Explanations for this fact can be sought in specific political circumstances and in the degree of receptivity of the new elites to Western models of the separation of powers.

There is another factor, however, that warrants mention in this connection: the legacy of the Austrian as opposed to the Ottoman empire. It may be going too far to call the Habsburg empire liberal, but neither was it an autocracy like Czarist Russia. It was a *Rechtsstaat,* that is, a state run by the rule of law. Indeed Austrian turn-of-the-century literature (from Musil and Roth to Broch and Kafka) is dominated by the question of the law, the tension between legitimacy and legality. That Habsburg legacy of the rule of law has influenced several of its Central European successor states, as reflected in their legal scholarship, public administration, and political culture more generally. It was already being rediscovered in the last phase of communism, as the rulers began to accept some limitations on their powers and the opposition began to challenge their rule in the name of accepted domestic and international legal commitments. The 1990s have confirmed the trend. The weakness of the rule of law in the former Habsburg domains of Slovakia and Croatia qualifies but does not invalidate the general argument.

*4) Nation-state building and "homogeneity."* The return of democracy in 1989 was inseparable from the return of the nation: Popular sovereignty and national sovereignty became indistinguishable. In this respect, 1989 followed in the footsteps of 1848 and 1918, reaffirming the idea that the nation-state is the natural and most favorable framework for democracy. The demise of federalism inherited from communism in the Soviet Union, Yugoslavia, and Czechoslovakia seemed to validate this conviction. But a preoccupation with building the nation-state can also work against democracy and the rule of law, as we have seen in the former Yugoslavia. This classic dilemma was described by the Hungarian thinker István Bibo at the end of World War II in his essay on *The Misery of the Small Nations of Eastern Europe:* "Fascism exists in germ everywhere where, following a cataclysm or an illusion, the cause of the nation separates from that of freedom." The fear that freedom and democracy will "threaten the cause of the nation" was a major impediment to democracy during the interwar period and has no doubt been an important factor in the sidetracking of the democratic transition after 1989 in the Balkans.

One reason why Central Europe has been less troubled by the national question than Southeastern Europe is that today its populations are more homogeneous (and where they are not, as in Slovakia, is precisely where the transition has been least successful). Poland, where minorities once comprised a third of the population, today is a homogeneous state; this dream of Poland's old nationalist right was realized with the help of Hitler and Stalin. Similarly, the Czech Republic today is without Jews, Germans, and now even Slovaks. Alone at last! Slovenia, the only Yugoslav successor state where the democratic transition fits the Central European pattern, also does not have a significant minority population. In short, in Central Europe "ethnic cleansing" was completed half a century ago, whereas in the Balkans the process of "homogeneous" nation-state building is still under way. This, as Ernest Gellner once put it, is purely a description, not a prescription. It would be absurd to suggest that ethnic "homogeneity" is a prerequisite for democracy. Yet the contrasting situation in this respect of Central Europe and the Balkans accounts at least in part for the different fates of their democratic transitions.

*5) Culture.* This is one of the oldest arguments about the development of democracy, going back to Max Weber's classic thesis about the Protestant ethic and the spirit of capitalism. In looking at the balance sheet of the democratic transition in Central and Eastern Europe, is there a case for pushing the Weberian thesis one notch further and suggesting a correlation between Western Christianity and democratic success (Central Europe), or between Orthodox Christianity and difficulty in achieving democratic and market-oriented change? The argument revolves around the issue of whether the subordination of the Church to the State and the close identification between religion and ethnicity in Orthodox Christianity poses a significant obstacle to the emergence of a democratic public space and a civil society.

This whole subject has become politically loaded since the publication of Samuel Huntington's thesis about the "clash of civilizations," which has many ardent disciples in the Balkans and has been widely used and abused in analyzing not only the war in Bosnia but the goals of Western policy. Fortunately, democratic difficulties in Catholic Slovakia and Croatia (as well as encouraging developments in Orthodox Romania and Bulgaria) tend to disprove Huntington's thesis. My response to this controversy is both to reject cultural determinism (especially when reduced to its religious dimension) as misleading or politically dangerous, but also to avoid the kind of political correctness that would make Max Weber's classic sociological question taboo.

*6) The international environment.* The international environment, at least so far, has been exceptionally favorable to the democratic transition in Central Europe: Russia is weak and its sphere of influence shrinking; Germany is powerful but democratic and integrated in both the EU and NATO; and there are no significant regional conflicts. This favorable combination of factors, unprecedented in Central European history, contrasts with the instability in the Balkans—not merely the wars in the former Yugoslavia, but the collapse of the Albanian state at the very moment that the Kosovo issue is intensifying, and the latent Greek-Turkish rivalry.

This divergence is reinforced by the prospects of "Euro-Atlantic" integration, the Central European code word for the double enlargement of NATO and the EU. Both institutions insist on democracy as a condition for membership (and, as the case of Slovakia showed, they mean it). On the whole, it can be argued that both these institutions embodying democratic Western values have been preoccupied primarily with the integration of Central Europe. No Balkan country is high on the list of candidates for either NATO or the EU. It remains to be seen what impact the noninclusion of Romania and Bulgaria will have on the democratic process in those countries. Thus far the differentiation in the enlargement process between the "ins" and the "outs" has largely been a consequence of the relative success of their democratic transitions. In the future, however, the enlargement process itself could help to undermine the democratic transition precisely where it is most fragile.

# WHAT NOW FOR

# RUSSIA?

By JOHN-THOR DAHLBURG

TIMES STAFF WRITER

MOSCOW—It's impossible to understand this country with cold reason, cautioned 19th century poet Fyodor Tyutchev: "In Russia, you can only believe."

Grigory A. Tsvetkov, a computer programmer, is one 20th century Russian whose faith has run out.

The 45-year-old Muscovite's salary has been whittled by economic crisis to the equivalent of less than $20 a month. It was August when he last was paid. He wants to emigrate with his wife and children, ages 13 and 15.

"We were ready to wait and struggle for five, 10 years, but seven years have passed, and our leading democrats we trusted and loved turned out to be thieves and liars, our president turned into a senile old man who doesn't care, simply doesn't care, about his people," said the bearded and bespectacled Tsvetkov, who has been importing and selling used cars from Germany and France to support his family. "To put it briefly, we want to have a normal life now—and not in a generation or two."

Where once in post-Soviet Russia there was wildly optimistic talk about becoming a "normal, civilized country" in a decade or less, there is deep, pervasive gloom. Many, if not most, people wonder whether things will ever improve.

This autumn, a survey of 1,500 Russians found existence of late has become so much worse that fully half of those polled "don't know how they are going to live further."

"Where did we go wrong?" the director of a regional hospital asked as she flew recently on a Tupolev jetliner to St. Petersburg for a refresher course in medicine.

Also unpaid for months, the physician, in her late 60s, slipped the pat of butter from the airline meal into her pocket as she described how her hospital had no more funds to purchase pharmaceuticals or meet staff salaries.

"Perhaps we didn't have the right people at the top," she said.

Political paralysis in Russian ended with the September appointment as prime minister of Yevgeny M. Primakov, former foreign minister, head of the espionage service and Soviet-era Communist Party apparatchik. But distressing, seemingly insoluble economic problems, and dashed expectations, remain.

"In 1991, the regime of which everybody had been sick and tired collapsed, but people had savings, enthusiasm and hopes," Alexander I. Lebed, a former Soviet army general who hopes to use his position as governor of the Krasnoyarsk region as a springboard to the presidency, said recently in Moscow. "Today they have nothing of this. No savings. Their hopes are almost dead. The credit of trust is almost used up."

In contrast with the euphoria that crested with the end of the Soviet Union in December 1991, many thoughtful Russians believe that their homeland has entered a long and dreary phase of economic hard times and of inglorious political leadership.

For the United States, the fate of this former superpower is of great concern if only because it possesses about 10,240 nuclear warheads. In Washington, where a State Department official has likened Russia to a car that is spinning wildly after hitting a patch of ice, the debate is over whether Russia has been "lost"— and if so, who lost it.

Two competing scenarios—the return to some sort of socialism or the rise of a nationalist strongman—are said by some observers to be possible, but not as likely as a long, gray period of muddling through. Disappointed with a decade's worth of leaders who first promised a reformed Soviet system, then Western-level politics and economic bounty, many Russians are no longer ready to believe in anyone offering a miracle.

A crimson banner hanging near the White House, seat of the Russian government, sums up prevailing suspicions succinctly and rudely: "All bosses are bastards."

"Our people do not trust anyone anymore—they do not trust the government, they do not trust their neighbors, they do not trust the rest of the world," said Dmitri Y. Furman, a Russian historian. "But what is most important, they have lost faith in themselves. A nation that has never had a chance to determine its own fate does not trust its own judgment.

"But least of all," Furman added, "they trust the so-called elite, the highest echelons of power, which for decades attracted like a magnet the most despicable, unworthy, dishonest and immoral members of society—the ones who were capable of surviving in the Communist Party machine and rising to the very top."

## A Disastrous Plunge in Living Standards

For a people who endured decades of socialist shortages and bread lines, the free market promised to be a veritable horn of plenty. Perhaps it will prove to be yet. But the short-run results for many, if not most, Russians are little short of catastrophic.

According to Graham Allison of Harvard University, a former assistant secretary of Defense, ordinary citizens here have suffered, on average, a 75% plunge in living standards under President Boris N. Yeltsin's rule. That is almost twice the decline in Americans' income during the Great Depression.

Veniamim S. Sokolov, public accountant of the Audit Chamber, a government watchdog agency that tracks state expenditures, recently estimated that Russia was $200 billion in debt, while $300 billion had been pillaged and covertly transferred overseas.

It sounds like a one-liner from "The Tonight Show," but Russia's economy is performing so poorly that the Federal Security Service, the spy agency that is heir to the KGB, has said it will have to let some employees go.

"We pinned all our hopes on the free market, which we believed would cure the country and rectify all wrongs," said Pavel G. Bunich, an economist and lawmaker in the lower house of parliament who is also a member of the Russian Academy of Sciences. "Instead, we ended up with utter anarchy and disorder. We have a situation when everything is allowed, when thieves of all sorts have ripped the country off and gotten away with it, for there were no laws."

So the moroseness of the moment is understandable. But deeper and more subtle processes also have been at work in Russian society in the 1990s, which make the current question—whither Russia?—more difficult to answer.

Civil liberties, such as the freedom to speak one's mind, that the Soviet Communists tried to eradicate as bourgeois perversions have taken root speedily and firmly in Russian soil. So has the concept of private property—one former high-ranking Soviet official in the current government holds a controlling interest in half a dozen business ventures.

And a land that deliberately kept itself isolated—Russians in the 1960s could not understand Beach Boys songs played over the Voice of America radio because dictionaries here did not include the word "surfing," which Russians assumed was an obscene synonym for fornicating—has proved eager to rejoin the rest of the world. In the heart of Siberia, halfway around the globe from Hollywood, a newspaper on sale this autumn was carrying jokes about the movie "Titanic."

"I would not wholly subscribe to the point of view that one of the pillars of Western civilization, namely the principle of democracy, has not worked in Russia," political analyst Andrei A. Piontkovsky, usually a blistering critic of present-day Russia, told a foreign journalist. "For if that were so, we would not be able to have this interview, and I'd have to think many times before telling you what I really thought."

There are competing diagnoses of the changes experienced by Russia in recent years. One argument says that this continent-sized nation skirted by Roman law, the Renaissance, the Reformation and the Englightenment—in short, by the formative experiences of the West—does not have it in its collective gene pool to be democratically governed and prosperous.

"One has to bear a great deal of faith and love in one's heart in order to keep any hope at all for the future of the most powerful of the Slav tribes," T. N. Granovsky, a prominent Russian scholar,

sadly wrote to a friend abroad. That was in 1854. Events in the next few years will show whether, once again, the pessimists are right about Russia.

Underlying the new government's obvious priorities—shoring up the ruble, paying back wages, ensuring people have food and heat during the winter—is an urgent psychological task: winning back people's trust. It may be mission impossible; one poll this autumn found that Yeltsin's approval rating was a mere 1%.

With disconcerting regularity, Russian television has been showing the populace its sick and sometimes befuddled leader. Recently, after a bizarre public exchange between Primakov and Yeltsin's spokesman, it was uncertain whether Yeltsin was being kept informed about even the most crucial matters of state.

Late last month, aides to the 67-year-old Yeltsin said he was suffering from a debilitating disorder that will force him to play less of a role in government. He may not be able to serve out his full term, which runs until 2000. On the other hand, nothing compels him to leave office immediately.

"We have a czar again, who can sit in the Kremlin and drink," a 60-year-old tourist from the Urals, Yeltsin's home region, lamented during a visit to the Stalingrad battle memorial in Volgograd.

## Stranded in 'a Land of Permanent Promises'

There are already many hopeful successors—the retired Gen. Lebed, Moscow Mayor Yuri M. Luzhkov, Russian Communist leader Gennady A. Zyuganov, liberal economist Grigory A. Yavlinsky. Their challenge will be to build a nationwide base of support and straunch the hemorrhage of popular confidence in Russia's leaders.

Can it be done? Perhaps not. In 1992, a team of young Russian liberals lifted socialist-era economy controls, and Russians saw prices soar by more than 2,000%. Another, supposedly reformist plan to give each citizen an equal share in the businesses and industry built under the Soviets resulted in wealth and political power rapidly falling into the hands of a few nouveaux riches known as the oligarchs.

Last August, under Primakov's predecessor, political neophyte Sergei V. Kiriyenko, Russia in effect devalued its currency, defaulted on government treasury bills and delayed the repayment of private debts to foreigners. The ruble tumbled, big banks shut their doors, and Russia's leaders discredited themselves again.

"Yet another time, the government has told its people, 'You can't rely on us,'" said Vladimir A. Poleshchuk, deputy governor of the Kemerovo region, an area of Siberia as large as Maine.

Like many of his fellows elsewhere in the country, Poleshchuk is now working to insulate his region economically and politically from the whims of the capital.

Russia, with one dominant ethnic group, language and culture, seems in no serious danger of spinning apart, as did the Soviet Union. However, the logic of events should continue to drain power and influence from inside Moscow's Ring Road to the country's 89 oblasts, republics and other constituent areas.

"Now it is clear—the transition will take decades, with retreats, defeats and crisis," Anatoly B. Chubais, the former head of Russia's privatization program that turned into a fire sale of state assets to insiders, told a Moscow newspaper recently. His biggest mistake, Chubais said, was to believe that the Russian economy could be reinvented in a few years.

In this season of uncertainty, Alexi II, patriarch of the Russian Orthodox Church, has been urging his flock to have courage and be patient. The Orthodox prelate even went to a Moscow picture gallery in September to pray to the virgin of Vladimir, the icon said to have saved the Russian capital from invading Mongol horsemen six centuries ago.

"We believe that the Lord will spare our motherland misfortunes, suffering and civil strife," Alexi said.

Tsvetkov, the computer programmer who wants to emigrate, now believes that it will take a generation, maybe two, for things in Russia to stabilize.

"We want to live in a normal country," he said, "where if you have a job, you know that you can buy the things you want, you can pay rent and have an apartment or house, you can go to the hospital and expect to be treated rather than humiliated, cheated and murdered, where you can put your money in a bank or a mutual fund and not wake up in a cold sweat every night worrying about it, where you can trust your government leaders, where you can at least understand what they say on television and not be ashamed of them.

"I am sick and tired of this sort of living in a land of permanent promises, that looks like a huge dirty railway station where all the trains are late or going the wrong way," Tsvetkov said. "Now I know my train will never arrive. I am stranded at the wrong station."

**Sergei L. Loido of The Times'
Moscow Bureau contributed
to this report.**

> "*For the first time in several years, politicians across the spectrum—liberals, communists, and nationalists alike—have begun to speak about the specter of Russian fascism should the current economic and political crises continue. Others, including even President Yeltsin, have warned of coup plots aimed at toppling Russia's fragile democracy. What went wrong, so quickly?*"

# Russia's Summer of Discontent

### MICHAEL McFAUL

Nineteen ninety-eight was supposed to be the year that Russia turned the corner. The 1996 presidential election had marked the end of a transitional period for Russia's political system and had seen Boris Yeltsin receive a renewed mandate to pursue his reform agenda. Equally important, all major political actors participated in the election and accepted the results as legitimate. The street protests, mass social action, and violent conflict that had constituted Russian politics in the country's first years of independence had given way to the electoral process. Gubernatorial elections in the fall of 1996 and spring of 1997 reconfirmed the primacy of elections in determining who rules Russia. Because elections rather than revolution were the focus of attention for most politicians, 1997 was politically the quietest year in Russia since independence in 1991.

This relative calm provided the perfect context for finally tackling Russia's economic woes. When Yeltsin introduced his reform plan in January 1992 to transform Russia's command economic system into a market economy, he warned citizens of tough times ahead, but promised that the transitional economic downturn would last just 10 or 11 months. Six years later, only a handful of people had realized any benefit from this "reform"; Russia recorded negative growth rates from 1992 to 1997, while the

MICHAEL McFAUL, *an assistant professor of political science and a Hoover fellow at Stanford University, is also a senior associate at the Carnegie Endowment for International Peace. His books include* Russia's 1996 Presidential Election: The End of Polarized Politics (*Stanford, Calif.: Hoover Institution Press, 1997*) *and* Privatization, Conversion, and Enterprise Reform in Russia (*Boulder, Colo.: Westview, 1995*).

majority of citizens reported in opinion polls that they were worse off in 1997 than they had been in 1991.

But 1998 was going to be different. At the end of 1997, Russian government officials as well as several Western financial institutions predicted positive growth rates, increased foreign investment, and a continuing bullish stock market for 1998. Yeltsin had reorganized his government in the spring of 1997 to empower a group of young reformers. He made an even bolder reconfiguration in the spring of 1998 when he dismissed Prime Minister Viktor Chernomyrdin and appointed a more reformist government headed by a young banker, Sergei Kiriyenko. Labeled a reformer's "dream team" by many Russian and Western commentators, the new government came into office with the expressed desire to reform Russia's robber baron capitalism. As First Deputy Prime Minister Boris Nemtsov reflected, "A transition is now taking place from unlimited semibandit capitalism, where the rules are dictated by those who are trying to take control of state property, to a situation where the rules are dictated by the state."

The plans for radical economic reform were never realized. Instead, throughout the summer and fall of 1998, Russia has been mired in its most serious financial crisis since independence. The financial crisis, in turn, has threatened to undermine the political stability achieved in the previous two years. For the first time in several years, politicians across the spectrum—liberals, communists, and nationalists alike—have begun to speak about the specter of Russian fascism should the current economic and political crisis continue. Others, including even President Yeltsin, have warned of coup plots aimed at toppling Russia's fragile democracy. What went wrong, so quickly?

## INTO THE PRECIPICE

The immediate causes of Russia's financial crisis in 1998 were straightforward. Early in the year, falling international oil prices greatly reduced revenues anticipated for the Russian budget. More important, however, were the unrealistic projections underlying the 1998 budget. Projected tax revenues were more than double the actual amount. Moreover, 40 percent of taxes paid to the federal government in 1997 were paid in kind, not in cash, a practice that continued in 1998. In addition, the Asian financial crisis created a further international strain on Russia's economy as projected inflows of foreign capital into the country's emerging market also decreased.

Given these revenue shortages, the Russian government was compelled to borrow heavily through the international bond market and by issuing short-term domestic treasury bills known as GKOS (state short-term bonds). Over the course of the summer, holders (both foreign and domestic investors) of GKOS became increasingly nervous about the government's ability to honor its debts. Reflecting this lack of confidence, interest rates for GKOS soared, climbing to over 120 percent in the second week of July. Even at this rate, buyers for the government debt were still scarce. At the same time, the stock market continued to fall throughout the year and had lost 50 percent of its January value by July, giving Russia the distinction of having, along with Indonesia, the worse performing stock market in the world.

This situation was not sustainable over the long run, since the amount the government owed to holders of GKOS would soon exceed the foreign reserves held by the Russian central bank. Western analysts predicted that by August the government would be bankrupt and would face the difficult choice of devaluing the ruble or defaulting on outstanding debts.

Before the central bank depleted its reserves, however, the International Monetary Fund intervened. In cooperation with the World Bank and the Japanese government, the IMF offered Russia new loans amounting to $17.1 billion. In negotiations over this bailout package, IMF officials attempted to secure commitments from the Russian government to undertake several reform policies. This package of reforms was to include over 20 new draft laws that would streamline and rationalize the tax code, decrease the profit tax, raise individual income taxes, create a national sales tax and land tax, raise taxes on imported goods as well as on alcohol sales and precious metals exports, and cut government expenditures even further to bring the deficit under 2.8 percent of GDP in 1999.

The bailout package failed. The first transfer of IMF funds under the new agreement—totaling nearly $5 billion—disappeared almost immediately as investors converted their rubles into dollars to get their money out of Russia. This put extreme pressure on the value of the ruble. In a desperate response, the Kiriyenko government surprised the world in August by pursuing a policy of both default and devaluation. On August 17, the government announced a compulsory conversion of short-term GKOS into longer-term debt instruments. The Russian debt market immediately collapsed as investors became convinced that the government would never pay back the borrowed money. On this same day, the government also imposed a 90-day moratorium on payments of all hard currency loans owed to Western commercial banks. Simultaneously, it announced a new trading price for the ruble 30 percent lower than the day before. In a single day, the two major economic achievements of the Yeltsin era—control of inflation and a stable, transferable currency—were eliminated.

These emergency measures did little to halt the economic crisis. The stock market all but disappeared, the ruble continued to fall, and banks began to close. Responding desperately to a desperate situation, Yeltsin fired Kiriyenko and his government the next week and nominated Viktor Chernomyrdin as his candidate for prime minister. After Chernomyrdin was rejected twice by the Russian parliament, Yeltsin nominated Foreign Minister Yevgeni Primakov as a compromise candidate, and he was quickly approved. In the meantime, the economy continued to collapse. The ruble plummeted, banks refused to allow withdrawals, prices soared, and stores emptied as people started to stockpile goods such as cigarettes, sugar, and flour.

## THE CRISIS BEHIND THE CRISIS

No matter who emerges from the current crisis to rule the country, there are no immediate solutions to the economic problems. Russia's latest crisis was not caused by failed macroeconomic policy undertaken by the Kiriyenko government or the IMF. Rather, the roots are microeconomic: ill-defined property rights and a lack of institutions capable of clarifying and enforcing these rights. Failure to appreciate the importance of this problem will lead to further misdirected "reforms" and continued economic depression in Russia.

In 1992, the Russian government launched an ambitious and comprehensive program to privatize most of the economy. Two years later, the Russian government (as well as the United States Agency for International Development and its Western contractors who assisted the privatization effort) trumpeted the success of its program by noting that more than 100,000 enterprises had been privatized.

While speedy, this privatization program did not produce effective owners. At two-thirds of all large enterprises, insiders—the directors in cooperation with the trade union officials loyal to them—gained a controlling share. At the time of privatization, the vast majority of these enterprises subtracted rather than added value to the economy. Amazingly, with the exception of a handful of energy exporters and a few other companies, most have continued to operate as net subtractors of value since privatization. Directors are not accountable to outside shareholders interested in profit maximization, so they can avoid restructuring, downsizing, product improvement, and efficiency enhancements. Through complex arbitrage schemes, the withholding of wages, and the use of parasitic "offshore" companies, these directors can amass individual wealth while their companies continue to operate in the red. More recently, several of Russia's financial-industrial groups have begun to acquire control of the potentially profitable enterprises still operating at a loss, but these new outside owners have yet to pursue restructuring (let alone new investment) vigorously.

Under market conditions, these companies would be forced into bankruptcy, their assets would be reorganized and auctioned, and either owners interested in profit making would assume control or the enterprises would be shut down. In Russia, however, bankruptcies rarely occur. Instead, the state has continued to subsidize ailing companies, initially through direct transfers and now by allowing these companies not to pay taxes. In the wake of the latest financial crisis, many predict that the new Russian government will resort to printing money and issuing credits again, further delaying the reorganization of these enterprises into value-producing assets.

Given these conditions at the micro level, anti-crisis plans for raising revenues will not have an immediate positive effect. No matter what the tax code, most companies do not have the means to pay since they are bankrupt. There are some exceptions and the government must insist that profit generators like Gazprom, the energy monopoly, and oil companies pay their taxes. But this is only a short-term solution. After all, Gazprom responds to government requests for tax payments with its own unpaid invoices for gas supplied to government enterprises. At some point the government must break this vicious circle by enforcing bankruptcy procedures as the first step toward restructuring enterprises, clarifying property rights, and ultimately finding owners for these enterprises who are interested in profit maximization. And these new owners, it must be remembered, will invest only under the right conditions—conditions that include lower interest rates, a rational tax code, and state protection (rather than mafia protection) of their property.

The financial meltdown during the summer of 1998 will further delay fundamental reform at the firm level. Because the government defaulted on its loans, there will be little foreign capital flowing into the country in the immediate future. Strapped for cash, the government will be forced to print money, which will fuel inflation. Faced with the prospect of hyperinflation again, the new government will be tempted to introduce wage and price controls; some provincial governors already have begun to do so. Price controls will spawn a black market and the reintroduction of the dollar as the currency of choice. In the very near future, the Russian economy may come to resemble the Soviet economy in the year leading up to the collapse of the Soviet Union. The road to recovery from this bleak situation will be long and difficult, especially because the very concept of "market reform" has now been discredited.

## THE POLITICAL CONSEQUENCES

Soon after the announcement of the ruble's devaluation, Russia's economic crisis became a political crisis. Even before the devaluation, social tensions and workers' strikes had escalated throughout the summer, culminating in hundreds of unpaid miners camping outside the White House (the building that houses the government), demanding their back wages and Yeltsin's resignation. Given this highly charged political environment, not only liberal supporters of the government but

*Russian citizens have begun to lose faith in the democratic process because it has produced few tangible benefits to the average person.*

even communist and nationalist opponents of Yeltsin made dire predictions about the disastrous political consequences of a devaluation. Analysts speculated that a sudden rise in prices resulting from devaluation would trigger mass social unrest. Trade union officials and Communist Party leaders feared that they might lose the support of their constituencies, who would turn to more radical political groups in times of crisis. Yeltsin also appeared to be worried about these extremists when he issued a warning in early July to potential non-democratic challengers that his regime retained enough military force to defeat any coup attempt.

To date, Russia's patient citizens have not rebelled in response to devaluation. And in contrast to Weimar Germany, Russia does not have a nationally organized fascist party ready to take advantage of the situation. The Russian National Union, Russia's closest equivalent to Hitler's Nazi Party, still does not enjoy a mass following. The one nationalist group that has organized throughout the country, Vladimir Zhirinovsky's Liberal Democratic Party of Russia, has shunned radical solutions and has cooperated with Yeltsin (for a price) in finding a solution to the political crisis. On the left, some radical communist organizations have advocated revolutionary tactics, but the leadership of the Russian Communist Party has remained committed to following the democratic process. Most important, all major political actors adhered to the democratic rules of the game in appointing a prime minister, demonstrating the resilience of Russia's new democratic institutions.

As with any revolutionary situation, this social calm could evaporate quickly. If one trigger-happy soldier fires into a peaceful demonstration, calls for a violent overthrow of the regime will escalate. Likewise, if Yeltsin and his team violate the constitution by attempting to delay elections or rule by decree, their enemies also will no longer feel compelled to respect the democratic rules of the game.

## DEMOCRACY'S FRAGILITY

These scenarios of coups, state collapse, and revolution seem more compelling when one remembers how weak and fragile the current Russian political system has become. The administrative apparatus of the Russian state lacks the capacity to execute even the most basic of state policies. The Soviet state, like the Soviet economy, collapsed in the fall of 1991. After this collapse, Russian reformers rightly devoted energy and resources to transforming the economy from a command system to a market, but they failed to undertake a commensurate reform program to create a market-friendly, democratic, and effective state. Consequently, the Russian state cannot collect taxes, and fails to provide basic public goods such as security, welfare, and education. This is not a government that has the capacity to withstand even spontaneous and disorganized social challenges.

Russia's democratic institutions are also fragile and unconsolidated. As affirmed through successful parliamentary, presidential, and gubernatorial elections over the last several years, Russia is an electoral democracy. But the system still lacks many of the qualities of a liberal democracy. The constitution gives too many powers to the president, the judiciary does not act as a third and independent branch of government, political parties are weak, mass-based interest groups are marginal, the rule of law has only begun to take hold, and the media are becoming less independent. More generally, Russian citizens have begun to lose faith in the democratic process because it has produced few tangible benefits to the average person.

In addition to a weak state and fragile democratic institutions, Russia also has a president who lacks popular support and legitimacy. Yeltsin's approval rating has fallen back into single digits and even many of his longtime allies have begun to call for his resignation. Yeltsin is not the kind of leader who has the authority to carry out radical economic reforms. Nor could his regime mobilize a popular defense if challenged by a coup or other nondemocratic acts.

As pressures mount for Yeltsin's removal, many predict that Russia's next presidential election will be held sooner rather than later, and well before the end of Yeltsin's term in the summer of 2000. Opinion polls suggest that anyone affiliated with Yeltsin or the current government has little chance of winning the next election. Even in 1996, Yeltsin won not because voters approved of his record in office (his approval rating peaked on the day of the election at 29 percent), but because they feared a return to communism. Yeltsin was the lesser of two evils. However, in the next presidential election the anticommunist card will not work, since no one now believes in the threat of Soviet-style communist restoration. Given the economic and political uncertainties that erupted after his dismissal, former Prime Minister Viktor Chernomyrdin might be able to run as the candidate of stability. However, even with the generous backing of Gazprom and financial industrialists Boris Berezovsky and Vladimir Gusinsky, Chernomyrdin is still a long-shot candidate, since he presided as the head of government during years of economic stagnation.

A communist victory in a presidential election is also unlikely. Communist Party leader Gennadi Zyuganov has worked hard since his electoral defeat in 1996 to transform his party into a nationalist movement in an attempt to attract new supporters. To date, the strategy has not succeeded. If he runs again, Zyuganov will enjoy solid enough support from his party loyalists to ensure that he will make it into the runoff—which he is almost equally assured of losing. If given the choice between Zyuganov and any other leading presidential contender, the majority of voters in opinion polls say they would support the noncommunist on the ballot.

The absence of viable candidates from either the current government or the communist opposition opens the door for new challengers. Today, two dominate the pack: Moscow

*American foreign policymakers must make renewed efforts to promote liberal democracy and a liberal market economy in Russia.*

Mayor Yuri Luzhkov and Krasnoyarsk Governor Aleksandr Lebed. Luzhkov's program of state-led capitalism laced with ethnic nationalism offers a potentially attractive alternative to the more liberal economic reforms pursued by Yeltsin's government. Although his critics charge that Luzhkov is corrupt, authoritarian, and chauvinistic toward minorities, the city he governs has produced positive growth rates. His supporters hope that he can do for Russia what he has done for Moscow.

At a time of growing popular dissatisfaction, Lebed is the consummate protest candidate. A former general with a reputation for getting things done, Lebed appeals to those who long for law and order. His views regarding market reform and democracy are still ill-defined. But if Russia continues to record negative growth rates the next two years, Russian voters may be ready to reject markets and democracy altogether in favor of a new "third" way.

## THE UNITED STATES AND RUSSIA

Russia's latest crisis will deliver another blow to United States–Russian relations. Over the last several years, the Start II arms reduction treaty, NATO expansion, trade with Iran and Iraq, and Russia's new draconian law sanctioning only certain religions have dominated relations between the two countries. To historians of Soviet-American relations, this agenda should sound familiar: arms control, European security, regional conflicts, and human rights were the main components of most summit talks between the two superpowers during the cold war. This old agenda suggests that the promise of a new post-communist strategic partnership between the United States and Russia has yet to emerge. Some now argue that, given the balance of power in the international system, the United States and Russia are simply destined to be adversaries. This camp believes that Russia's latest economic crisis will propel to power Russian leaders hostile to the West, compelling the Western world to contain the Russian threat to markets and democracy once again.

This is a premature conclusion. The Soviet communist system—not Russia as a country or Russians as a people—threatened America's national interests during the cold war. As long as Russia continues on the path of democratization and marketization, Russian-American relations hold the promise of moving beyond these old issues of division and confrontation. It was the collapse of communism, not skilled diplomacy, that brought the greatest progress on all these issues earlier this decade. Consequently, United States strategic interests in the post–cold war era are tied intimately to the fate of Russia's new political and economic system.

The heightened domestic turmoil Russia has suffered during the last several months suggests that American foreign policy-makers must make renewed efforts to promote liberal democracy and a liberal market economy in Russia. If democracy and capitalism collapse there, then the issues of contention between Russia and the United States will multiply and new threats to American security will emerge.

President Bill Clinton's administration demonstrated leadership in responding aggressively to Russia's latest financial crisis by urging the IMF to negotiate a new set of loans to Russia, but the rescue mission failed. Until Russia forms a government and outlines a genuine anticrisis program, it is premature for the IMF, the Group of Seven, or the United States to provide additional funds to the Russian state (although assistance to nongovernmental actors and institutions can and should continue). Once the new Russian government devises a plan to end the crisis, however, it will need Western help to succeed.

In addition to assistance for achieving macroeconomic stabilization provided through the IMF, the United States should focus on facilitating the development of important market institutions such as laws governing property rights, financial disclosure, bankruptcy, pension funds, taxes, and securities markets to promote enterprise restructuring. Especially as American funds for assistance to Russia continue to decrease, a focus on institutions rather than individual projects or technical assistance for specific economic actors should remain a top priority.

The West must rethink basic assumptions about political reform in Russia. Russian reformers wrongly believed that economic reform had to precede political reform. American assistance programs also adopted this logic and channeled the lion's share of American aid to Russia into economic reform while only a fraction went to promoting democratic institutions. The record of reform in the postcommunist world, however, has demonstrated that the fastest democratizers also have conducted the most successful economic reforms.

Programs that provide expertise on the development of the basic institutions that constitute a liberal democracy—that is,

programs that promote parties, federalism, the rule of law, independent media, and civil society—should be expanded, not curtailed. The United States also can do more to foster basic democratic values in Russia by providing civics textbooks, funding public policy programs, developing higher education courses on democracy, and continuing student exchanges. While the market creates incentives for Russians to learn how to become entrepreneurs, Russians today have few incentives to learn how to be good democrats.

Finally, at the highest levels, American officials must send clear signals to Russian elites about the negative consequences of circumventing the democratic process. For instance, Clinton should urge Yeltsin to establish a precedent for the peaceful transfer of political power through the electoral process. Because such a transfer would be a first in Russian history, no single event is more important for the consolidation of Russia's democracy than the upcoming presidential election. The Clinton administration also must send an unequivocal message to the Russian government that the West will not condone any extraconstitutional seizures of power, be they radical plots to overthrow the current regime or plans by the Yeltsin group to institute martial law.

Many Americans have grown weary of Russia; achievements have been few and headaches many. Now is not the time to give up on it. Only seven years since the Soviet collapse, Russia's revolution has by no means ended. The country's current leaders remain committed to developing a market economy and a democratic polity, and to joining rather than threatening the community of democratic states; it is in the vital national interest of the United States to ensure that this trajectory remains in place. Continued engagement with Russia's reformers, sustained promotion of Russian liberal market and democratic institutions, and gradual integration of Russia into the world capitalist system and the international community of democratic states: these are the policies that will prevent Russia's transition from turning belligerent. Containment, isolation, and neglect of institutional development in Russia are policies that will help transform Russia's revolution into a security threat, both to democratic states in the West and to democratizing states closer to Russia.

# Can Russia Change?

*David Remnick*

*DAVID REMNICK is a Staff Writer at The New Yorker and was the Moscow Correspondent for The Washington Post from 1988 to 1991.*

## THE DISAPPOINTMENT OF THE PRESENT

THERE WAS celebration in the State Department when Boris Yeltsin won re-election last July, but polls show that in Moscow and other Russian cities and towns there was no joy, only relief, a sense of having dodged a return to the past and the Communist Party. Political celebration, after all, usually welcomes a beginning, and the Yeltsin regime, everyone understood, was no beginning at all. Yeltsin had accomplished a great deal both as an outsider and as a president, but now, in his senescence, he represented the exhaustion of promise.

To prevail, Yeltsin had been willing to do anything, countenance anything, promise anything. Without regard for his collapsed budget, he doled out subsidies and election-year favors worth billions of dollars; he gave power to men he did not trust, like the maverick general Aleksandr Lebed; he was willing to hide from, and lie to, the press in the last weeks of the campaign, the better to obscure his serious illness.

Power in Russia is now adrift, unpredictable, and corrupt. Just three months after appointing Lebed head of the security council, Yeltsin fired him for repeated insubordination, instantly securing the general's position as martyr, peacemaker, and pretender to the presidency. On the night of his dismissal, Lebed giddily traipsed off to see a production of Aleksei Tolstoy's *Ivan the Terrible*. "I want to learn how to rule," he said.

In the new Russia, freedom has led to disappointment. If the triumph of 1991 seemed the triumph of liberal democrats unabashedly celebrating a market economy, human rights, and Western values, Yeltsin's victory in 1996 was distinguished by the rise of a new class of oligarchs. After the election, the bankers, media barons, and industrialists who had financed and in large measure run the campaign got the rewards they wanted: positions in the Kremlin, broadcasting and commercial licenses, and access to the national resource pile. Before 1991, these oligarchs had been involved mainly in fledgling small businesses—some legitimate, some not—and then, under the chaotic conditions of the post-Soviet world, they made their fortunes. Anatoly Chubais, who led Yeltsin's privatization and presidential campaigns, suddenly forgot his vow never to re-join the government and became chief of staff in the new administration, a position Yeltsin's bad health made all the mightier. Perhaps personifying the Kremlin's shamelessness, Chubais led the push to appoint one of the leading oligarchs, Boris Berezovsky, as deputy minister of security. The few Muscovites with enough patience left to care about Kremlin politics wondered what qualifications Berezovsky, who had made his fortune in the automobile business, brought to his new job.

The new oligarchs, both within and outside the Kremlin, see themselves as undeniably lucky, but worthy as well. They righteously insist that their fortunes will spawn a middle class, property rights, and democratic values. No matter that the Kremlin lets them acquire an industrial giant like the Norilsk nickel works for a thief's price; they claim to be building a new Russia, and rationalize the rest. Mikhail Smolensky, who runs Moscow's powerful Stolichnii Bank from his offices in the restored mansion of a nineteenth-century merchant, told me, "Look, unfortunately, the only lawyer in this country is the Kalashnikov. People mostly solve their problems in this way. In this country there is no respect for the law, no culture of law, no judicial system—it's just being created." In the meantime, bribery greases the wheels of commerce. Government officials, who issue licenses and permissions of all sorts, "practically have a price list hanging on the office wall," Smolensky said.

The new oligarchs are humiliating to Russians, not because they are wealthy but because so little of their wealth finds its way back into the Russian economy. According to Interpol and the Russian Interior Ministry, rich Russians have sent more than $300 billion to foreign banks, and much of that capital leaves the country illegally and untaxed. Yeltsin's Kremlin capitalism has so far failed to create a nation of shopkeepers—the British middle-class model. It has, however, spawned hundreds of thousands of *chelnoki*, or shuttle traders, young people who travel to and from countries like China, Turkey, and the United Arab Emirates carrying all manner of goods for sale. This sort of trade is probably only a crude, transitional form of capitalism, but it is also uncontrolled, untaxed, and mafia-ridden.

Under Yeltsin, power at the Kremlin has become almost as remote from the people it is supposed to serve as it was under the last communist general secretaries. In its arrogance, in its refusals to answer questions from the press, Yeltsin's Kremlin seems to believe that its duty to observe democratic practices ended with the elections. The Russian people, understandably, believe the government has much to answer for. The poverty rate is soaring. Life expectancy for men is plunging. The murder rate is twice as high as it is in the United States and many times higher than in European capitals to the west. According to Russian government statistics, by late 1995, 8,000 criminal gangs were operating in the county—proportionately as many as in Italy. The fastest-growing service industry in Russia is personal security. Hundreds of thousands of men and women now work for private businesses as armed security guards. The police are too few, and usually too corrupt, to do the job.

Though far better than in Soviet times, the press is still not free. State television, which is largely owned by the new oligarchs, is extremely cautious, even sycophantic, when it comes to Yeltsin. After acting like cheerleaders during the election campaign, some newspapers and magazines have once again become aggressive and critical, even probing impolitely into the state of Yeltsin's health. An investigation by *Itogi*, a Moscow magazine, forced Yeltsin to go public with his heart ailments, which in turn led him to agree to quintuple-bypass surgery last November. But there is still no institution—not the press, not parliament, certainly not the weak judiciary—with the authority to keep the Kremlin honest.

One of the most troubling deficiencies in modern Russia is the absence of moral authority. The country lacks the kind of ethical compass it lost when Andrei Sakharov died in 1989. Human rights groups like Memorial, in the forefront of the democratic reform movement under Mikhail Gorbachev, are now marginal. If Sakharov had a leading protégé, it was Sergei Kovalyov, a biologist who spent many years in prison under Brezhnev and later helped lead the human rights movement. One of Yeltsin's most promising gestures was his appointment of Kovalyov as commissioner of human rights, and one of the most depressing events of his reign was Kovalyov's resignation when he recognized that he could not convince the government to end the war in Chechnya. Kovalyov is hardly a presence in public life these days—he appears more often in *The New York Review of Books* than in *Izvestia*—and no one seems to have replaced him. Even the most liberal journalists seem uninterested in Kovalyov or any-

one of his ilk. After years of talking about ideas and ideals, they are cynical, intent only on discussing economic interests; the worst sin is to seem naive, woolly, bookish—or hopeful.

"The quality of democracy depends heavily on the quality of the democrats," Kovalyov told me after the elections. "We have to wait for a critical mass of people with democratic principles to accumulate. It's like a nuclear explosion: the critical mass has to accrue. Without this, everything will be like it is now, always in fits and starts. Our era of romantic democracy is long over. We have finally fallen to earth."

## THE DAMAGE OF RUSSIAN HISTORY

WHEN AND HOW will that critical mass accumulate? Russia should not be mistaken for a democratic state. Rather, it is a nascent state with some features of democracy and, alas, many features of oligarchy and authoritarianism. When and how will a more complete transformation of its political culture occur? Is Russia capable of building a stable democratic state, or is it forever doomed to follow a historical pattern in which long stretches of absolutism are briefly interrupted by fleeting periods of reform?

First, it pays to review the legacy—the damage—of history. Russia seems at times to have been organized to maximize the isolation of the people and, in modern times, to prevent the possibility of democratic capitalism. For example, the Russian Orthodox Church, for centuries the dominant institution in Russian life, was by nature deeply suspicious of, even hostile to, the outside world. After the fall of Constantinople in 1453, the church distanced itself from transnational creeds like Protestantism, Catholicism, Judaism, and Buddhism. Xenophobia pervaded both church and state. During the Soviet regime that xenophobia only intensified. Under the banner of communist internationalism, the Bolsheviks successfully kept the world at bay until the glasnost policy was instituted in the late 1980s.

Russian absolutism has proved unique in its endurance and intensity. In many regards the authority of the tsars exceeded that of nearly all other European monarchs. As Richard Pipes points out in the June 1996 *Commentary*,

> throughout Europe, even in countries living under absolutist regimes, it was considered a truism that kings ruled but did not own: a popular formula taken from the Roman philosopher Seneca that "unto kings belongs the power of all things and unto individual men, property." Violations of the principle were perceived as a hallmark of tyranny. This whole complex of ideas was foreign to Russia. The Muscovite crown treated the entire realm as its property and all secular landowners as the tsar's tenants-in-chief, who held

their estate at his mercy on the condition of faithful service.

Tsarist absolutism was far more severe than the English variety because of its greater control of property. With the rise of the Bolshevik regime, property became, in the theoretical jargon of the period, the property of all, but in practice it remained the property of the sovereign—the Communist Party and its general secretary. And the communists were even less inclined to develop a culture of legality—of property rights, human rights, and independent courts—than the last of the Romanovs had been.

Likewise, under both the tsars and general secretaries, the government had only, in Gorbachev's rueful phrase, "the legitimacy of the bayonet." Violence and the threat of violence characterized nearly all of Russian political history. The two great breakthroughs—the fall of Nicholas II in February 1917 and the fall of Gorbachev as Communist Party leader in August 1991—came only after it was clear that both figures would refuse, or were incapable of, the slaughter necessary to prolong their regimes. Many Russian intellectuals today, including gulag survivors like the writer Lev Razgon, believe that the communist regime's policy of forced exile, imprisonment, and execution exacted a demographic, even genetic, toll on the Russian people's inherent capacity to create a democratic critical mass. "When one begins to tally up the millions of men and women, the best and the brightest of their day, who were killed or forced out of the country, then one begins to calculate how much moral and intellectual capacity we lost," Razgon told me. "Think of how many voices of understanding we lost, think of how many independent-minded people we lost, and how those voices were kept from the ears of Soviet citizens. Yes, I am furious beyond words at Yeltsin for the war in Chechnya and for other mistakes. But we have to look at our capacities, the injuries this people has absorbed over time."

Finally, Russia will have to alter its intellectual approach to political life. Even though Gennady Zyuganov failed to carry the elections last year with his nationalist-Bolshevik ideology, he proved that maximalist ideas still resonate among a certain segment of the population. In 1957 Isaiah Berlin, writing in the October issue *of Foreign Affairs*, accurately described the traditional Russian yearning for all-embracing ideologies rooted in the anti-intellectual and eschatological style of the Russian Orthodox Church. As Berlin pointed out, the Russian revolutionaries of the nineteenth and twentieth centuries were obsessed not with liberal ideas, much less political and intellectual pluralism, but were instead given to a systemic cast of mind—and in the most extreme ways. They first absorbed German historicism in its Hegelian form, in which history obeyed scientific laws leading it in a de-

terminate direction, and then the utopian prophecies of Saint-Simon and Fourier:

Unlike the West, where such systems often languished and declined amid cynical indifference, in the Russian Empire they became fighting faiths, thriving on the opposition to them of contrary ideologies—mystical monarchism, Slavophile nostalgia, clericalism, and the like; and under absolutism, where ideas and daydreams are liable to become substitutes for action, ballooned out into fantastic shapes, dominating the lives of their devotees to a degree scarcely known elsewhere. To turn history or logic or one of the natural sciences—biology or sociology—into a theodicy; to seek, and affect to find, within them solutions to agonizing moral or religious doubts and perplexities; to transform them into secular theologies—all that is nothing new in human history; But the Russians indulged in this process on a heroic and desperate scale, and in the course of it brought forth what today is called the attitude of total commitment, at least of its modern form.

By the end of the process, Russian intellectuals—not least Lenin himself—derided the weakness, the unsystematic approach, of Western liberalism. For Lenin, Marxism provided a scientific explanation for human behavior. All he needed was the technological means of altering that behavior.

But while the Russian and Soviet leadership have been xenophobic, absolutist, violent, and extremist, there have always been signs of what the scholar Nicolai Petro, in his 1995 book *The Rebirth of Russian Democracy,* calls an "alternative political culture." If Russians today were to attempt to create a modern state purely from foreign models and experience, if there was nothing in Russian history to learn from, rely on, or take pride in, one could hardly expect much. But that is not the case. Perhaps Russia cannot rely, as the Founding Fathers did, on a legacy like English constitutionalism, but the soil of Russian history is still far from barren.

Even the briefest survey of alternative currents in Russian history must take note of the resistance to absolutism under Peter I and Catherine the Great or, in the nineteenth century, the Decembrist revolt against Nicholas I. While Nicholas was able to crush the Decembrists, their demands for greater civil and political authority did not fade; in fact, their demands became the banner of rebellion that persisted, in various forms and movements, until the February revolution of 1917. Alexander II's decree abolishing serfdom was followed by the establishment of local governing boards, or *zemstvos,* and out of that form of limited grassroots politics came more pressure on the tsar. In May 1905, after a long series of strikes, the Third Zemstvo Congress appealed to the tsar for a transition to constitutional government, and the tsar soon issued an edict accepting constitutional monarchy. The constitution published in 1906 guaranteed the inviolability of person, residence, and property, the right of assembly, freedom of religion, and freedom of the press—so long as the press was not criticizing the tsar.

Under Soviet rule, the Communist Party was far quicker to suppress signs of an alternative political culture than Nicholas II had been, but expressions of resistance and creativity endured. Under Krushchev, in the thaw years, a few artists and journalists began to reveal the alternative intellectual and artistic currents flowing under the thick ice of official culture, and beginning in the late 1960s one began to see the varied currents of political dissent: Sakharov and the Western-oriented human rights movement; "reform" socialists like Roy Medvedev; religious dissidents like Aleksandr Men and Gleb Yakunin, both Russian Orthodox priests; and traditionalist neo-Slavophile dissidents like Solzhenitsyn and the authors of *From Under the Rubble.*

Yeltsin's government has not been especially successful in articulating the nature of the new Russian state. But, however formless, the new state has made a series of symbolic overtures. By adopting the prerevolutionary tricolor and double-headed eagle as national emblems, the government has deliberately reached back to revive a sense of possibility from the past. Similarly, the mayor of Moscow, Yuri Luzhkov, has had restored and rebuilt dozens of churches and monuments destroyed during the Soviet period, including the enormous Cathedral of Christ the Savior on the banks of the Moscow River. There is also a revived interest in Ivan Ilyin, Nikolai Berdyayev, and other émigré philosophers who tried to describe Russian political and spiritual values. Academics are struggling to write new textbooks. Religious leaders are coping with the revival of the Russian Orthodox Church among a people with little religious education and only a sentimental attachment to their faith. These outcroppings are not mere kitsch or intellectual fashions but an attempt to reconnect Russians to their own history and the notion of national development that was shattered with the Bolshevik coup of 1917.

## THE PROMISE OF RUSSIAN LIFE

ALTHOUGH DAILY life in Russia suffers from a painful economic, political, and social transition, the prospect over the coming years and decades is more promising than ever before. As former Deputy Prime Minister Yegor Gaidar has said, "Russia today is not a bad subject for long-term prognostication, and a very inappropriate subject for short-term analysis." There seems no reason why Russia cannot break with its absolutist past in much the way that Germany and Japan did after World War II.

Since the late 1980s, Russia has come a long way in this direction. The decades of confrontation with the West are over. Russia has withdrawn its talons, and except for the need to vent some nationalist rhetoric once in a great while, it offers little threat to the world. For all the handwringing by Henry Kissinger and other Russophobes, there is no imminent threat of renewed imperialism, even within the borders of the old Soviet Union. The danger of conflict between Russia and Ukraine over the Crimea or between Russia and Kazakstan over northern Kazakstan has greatly diminished in the last few years. After centuries of isolation, Russia seems ready to live not merely with the world but in it. The peril it poses is less a deliberate military threat than chaos and random events like the theft of "loose nukes." Russians are free to travel. They are free to consume as much foreign journalism, intellectual history, and popular culture as they desire. The authorities encourage foreign influence and business: more than 200,000 foreign citizens reside in Moscow, many times the number before 1990. Communication with the outside world is limited only by Russia's dismal international telephone system, and scholars and businesspeople have finessed that limitation with personal computers and electronic mail, which are rapidly becoming more widely available.

In the short term, most Russians cannot hope for much, especially from their politicians. If after his surgery Yeltsin's health does not improve dramatically, there will likely be an atmosphere of permanent crisis in Moscow. "I lived through the last days of Brezhnev, Andropov, and Chernenko, and I know how illness in power leads to danger," Mikhail Gorbachev told me shortly after the recent elections. "We survived back then thanks only to the inertia of the Soviet system. But Russia needs dynamic people in office and now, well . . ." Gorbachev has never been charitable to Yeltsin (nor Yeltsin, Gorbachev), but he was right.

The most important figures in the government will be Yeltsin's chief of staff, Chubais, the prime minister, Viktor Chernomyrdin, and Yeltsin's daughter, Tatyana Dyachenko. Such a government is likely to uphold a more or less friendly relationship with Washington and the West and to preside over a semicapitalist, semioligarchic economy. But unless the government begins to fight corruption, create a legal order, and strengthen the court system, the state will continue to be compared with the Latin American countries and the South Korea of the 1970s.

If Yeltsin dies sooner rather than later, his circle will either follow the letter of the constitution and hold presidential elections after three months, or it will find an excuse to avoid them. The latter choice would go a long way toward negating the limited progress made since 1991. Russia has yet to prove it can undergo a peaceful and orderly transfer of power—one of the most crucial tests in the development of a democracy. If the government does go forward with elections, the likely combatants would include Chernomyrdin, Luzhkov, Lebed, and Zyuganov.

Lebed's popularity is the highest of the four, but what kind of man he is and what sort of president he would be is unknown. He is considered flexible and educable by many Western visitors, but his is a flexibility born mainly of ignorance. Lebed is a military man, but unlike Colin Powell or Dwight Eisenhower—to say nothing of his hero, Charles de Gaulle—he has hardly any experience beyond the military. Lebed must be given credit for signing a peace treaty with the Chechens during his short tenure as security minister. He is also, by most accounts, a decent and honest man, which sets him apart from most who have set foot in the Kremlin. But he has displayed a willful, even outrageous, disregard for the president he was ostensibly serving. Aleksandr Lebed's first priority, so far, appears to be Aleksandr Lebed. It is discouraging that the most visible political alliance he formed after leaving the Kremlin was with Aleksandr Korzhakov, Yeltsin's crony and bodyguard before he was bounced from the government during the campaign. Korzhakov, for his part, has landed easily on his feet; he has decided to run for parliament from Lebed's home district, Tula, and should any old rivals threaten him, he has promised to release "incriminating evidence" against Yeltsin and his aides.

Lebed's potential rivals are more fixed in their views and political behavior, but they are not a promising lot. Zyuganov still has supporters, especially in the oldest and poorest sectors of the population, but he has little or no chance to win if he repeats the tactics and rhetoric of 1996. The communists would do well to jettison any traces of the past and adopt, as some are proposing, a new name for the party and younger faces to run it. A party of social democrats is inevitable in Russia, but not under Zyuganov.

Chernomyrdin represents a longed-for predictability abroad, but to Russians he represents the worst of Yeltsin's government: corruption, privilege, and an almost delusional disregard for the public. Chernomyrdin is also singularly inarticulate. The only way he could win the presidency would be to exploit the resources of the Kremlin and gain the support of the media to an even greater degree than Yeltsin did in 1996. As mayor, Luzhkov is extremely popular in Moscow—a kind of Russian Richard Daley—but he would have to cope with the traditional Russian tendency to be suspicious of political figures from the capital.

At this writing, the Kremlin depends on the heart tissue of one man and the conflicting economic and political interests of his would-be inheritors.

But not all depends on Yeltsin, or on Moscow. Russia is a far less centralized country than the Soviet Union was, for while Moscovite political life is rife with intrigue and gives off the whiff of authoritarian arrogance, it is also relatively weak. In Soviet times,

regional party leaders looked to Moscow as if to Mecca. Now one decree after another is issued, but local authorities adopt what they like and ignore the rest. Development and progress are wildly different in the country's 89 regions, and much depends on the local political map. Beyond Moscow, in the most encouraging region, centered around Nizhny Novgorod, young, progressive politicians like Mayor Boris Nemtsov have made good on their promises to create "capitalism in one country." One of the biggest problems with the Soviet economy was its heavy militarization; Nizhny Novgorod, the third-largest city in the country, was one of the most militarized. Yet not only has the city managed, by privatizating, breaking up monopolies, and issuing bonds, to create thriving service and manufacturing sectors, it has also converted 90 percent of its collective farms to private ownership. Meanwhile, 500 miles down the Volga River, the communist-run city government of Ulyanovsk, Lenin's hometown, has refused to participate in radical reform. Ulyanovsk's economy is a shambles. Unfortunately, too many Russian cities have followed the path of Ulyanovsk rather than Nizhny Novgorod.

Not all regions, however, can thrive simply by adopting the market reforms of Nizhny Novgorod. The coal-mining regions of western Siberia will continue to suffer for the same reasons the miners of many other countries have suffered: the mines are nearly exhausted and no alternative industry has developed. Most farming regions have resisted the difficult transformation to private enterprise, largely because of the vast amounts of capital needed for modern equipment and the inevitable reductions in the work force privatization entails. Agricultural areas like the Kuban or Gorbachev's home region of Stavropol have only suffered since 1991.

The mafia and tough moral questions also play a local role in deciding how or whether reform occurs. The mobster Vladimir "The Poodle" Podiatev controls the city of Khabarovsk to the extent that he has his own political party and television station. Chechnya will continue to gnaw at the attention, if not the conscience, of Moscow. Grozny, Chechnya's capital city, is in ruins, and the local authorities consider themselves victors; the rule of Islam, not the rule of Moscow, now prevails.

When describing Russia's situation and the country's prospects, analysts tend to grope for analogies with other countries and eras. The rise of oligarchy summons up Argentina, the power vacuum evokes Weimar Germany, the dominance of the mafia hints at postwar Italy, and the presidential constitution recalls de Gaulle's France of 1958. But while Russia's problems alarm the world on occasion, none of these analogies takes into account the country's possibilities.

Since 1991 Russia has broken dramatically with its absolutist past. The almost uniformly rosy predictions for China and the almost uniformly gloomy ones for Russia are hard to justify. Political reform is not the only advantage Russia has. Unlike China, where rural poverty and illiteracy still predominate, Russia is an increasingly urban nation with a literacy rate of 99 percent. Nearly 80 percent of the Russian economy is in private hands. Inflation, a feature of all formerly communist countries, dropped from a runaway 2,500 percent in 1992 to 130 percent in 1995. Russia's natural resources are unparalleled. In their perceptive 1996 book, *The Coming Russian Boom*, Richard Layard of the London School of Economics and John Parker, a former Moscow correspondent for *The Economist*, arm themselves with an array of impressive statistics allowing them to predict that by the year 2020 Russia "may well have outstripped countries like Poland, Hungary, Brazil and Mexico with China far behind."

Not least in Russia's list of advantages is that its citizens show every indication of refusing a return to the maximalism of communism or the xenophobia of hard-line nationalism. The idea of Russia's separate path of development is increasingly a losing proposition for communists and nationalists alike. The highly vulgarized versions of a national idea—Zyuganov's "National Bolshevism" or the various anti-Semitic, anti-Western platforms of figures like the extremist newspaper editor Aleksandr Prokhanov—have repelled most Russian voters, no matter how disappointed they are with Yeltsin. Anti-Semitism, for example, has no great political attraction, as many feared it would; even Lebed, who has his moments of nationalist resentment, has felt it necessary to apologize after making bigoted comments. He will not win

as an extremist. Rather, he appeals to popular disgust with the corruption, violence, and general lack of integrity of the Yeltsin government.

Perhaps it is a legacy of the Cold War that so many American observers demand so much so soon from Russia. Russia is no longer an enemy or anything resembling one, yet Americans demand to know why, for example, there are no developed political parties in Russia, somehow failing to remember that it took the United States—with all its historical advantages, including its enlightened founders—more than 60 years of independence to develop its two party system, or that in France nearly all the parties have been vehicles for such less than flawless characters as François Mitterrand and Jacques Chirac. The drama of 1991 so accelerated Western notions of Russian history that our expectations became outlandish. Now that many of those expectations have been disappointed, deferred, and even betrayed, it seems we have gone back to expecting only the worst from Russia.

The most famous of all nineteenth-century visitors to Russia, the Marquis de Custine, ended his trip and his narrative by writing, "One needs to have lived in that solitude without tranquillity, that prison without leisure that is called Russia, to appreciate all the freedom enjoyed in other European countries, no matter what form of government they have chosen . . . It is always good to know that there exists a society in which no happiness is possible, because, by reason of his nature, man cannot be happy unless he is free." But that has changed. A new era has begun. Russia has entered the world, and everything, even freedom, even happiness, is possible.

# Unit 4

## Unit Selections

*Politics of Development* 34. **Let's Abolish the Third World,** *Newsweek*
35. **The 'Third World' Is Dead, but Spirits Linger,**
   Barbara Crossette
*Latin America* 36. **Latin Economies Soar, Stumble with Reforms,**
   Chris Kraul and Sebastian Rotella
37. **Mexico: Sweeping Changes of Last Decade Translate
   into a Tale of 2 Economies,** James F. Smith
*Africa* 38. **After Mandela's Miracle in South Africa,** Michael Bratton
39. **Nigeria's Long Road Back to Democracy,** *The Economist*
*China* 40. **Jiang Zemin Takes Command,** Joseph Fewsmith
41. **In March toward Capitalism, China Has Avoided
   Russia's Path,** Henry Chu
*India* 42. **What a Difference a Year Can Make,** Mark Nicholson
*Newly Industrialized* 43. **Asian Values Revisited: What Would Confucius Say
*Countries* Now?** *The Economist*
44. **Asia and the "Magic" of the Marketplace,**
   Jeffrey A. Winters

## Key Points to Consider

❖ Why is the term Third World of little analytical value? What have these developing countries in common, and how are they diverse?

❖ How do explanations of Third World poverty and slow development differ in assigning responsibility for these conditions to external (foreign) and internal (domestic) factors?

❖ What is dependency theory, and why has it had so much appeal especially in Latin America? How do you explain the current wave of market-oriented reforms, and who are "winners" and "losers" in the process?

❖ Why do economic development and representative government run into such difficulties in most of Latin America and much of Africa? What are some of the major political, economic, and social problems that South Africa still has to face in overcoming the legacy of apartheid?

❖ How do you explain China's relative success in turning toward market reforms for the economy, as compared to the Soviet Union?

❖ How has India managed to maintain itself as a parliamentary democracy, given the many cleavages that divide this multiethnic society?

❖ What can the newly industrialized countries of Asia teach us about the possibility of economic modernization and democratic reform?

 **Links** **www.dushkin.com/online/**

18. **Africa News Online**
   *http://www.africanews.org*
19. **ArabNet**
   *http://www.arab.net*
20. **ASEAN Web**
   *http://www.asean.or.id*
21. **Human Rights Web**
   *http://www.hrweb.org*
22. **Inside China Today**
   *http://www.insidechina.com*
23. **InterAction**
   *http://www.interaction.org/advocacy/index.html*
24. **The North-South Institute**
   *http://www.nsi-ins.ca/info.html*

25. **Organization for Economic
   Cooperation and Development/
   FDI Statistics**
   *http://www.oecd.org/daf/cmis/fdi/statist.htm*
26. **Penn Library: Resources by Subject**
   *http://www.library.upenn.edu/resources/
   websitest.html*
27. **SunSITE Singapore**
   *http://sunsite.nus.sg/asiasvc.html*
28. **U.S. Agency for International
   Development**
   *http://www.info.usaid.gov*
29. **World Bank**
   *http://www.worldbank.org*

These sites are annotated on pages 6 and 7.

Until recently, the Third World was a widely used umbrella term for a disparate group of states that are now more frequently called the developing countries. Their most important shared characteristic may well be what these countries have *not* become—namely, relatively modern industrial societies. Otherwise they differ vastly from each other. The Third World designation has been used so loosely that it can now be dismissed as a category that produces more confusion than political insight. It seems high time to let go of the vague and slippery concept, as Charles Lane suggests in the first essay of this unit. However, as Barbara Crosette next explains, the "spirit" or "vision" of a third world still retains some of its evocative power.

Originally the term referred to countries—many of them recently freed former colonies—that had chosen to remain nonaligned in the cold war confrontation between the First World (or Western bloc) and the Second World (or Communist bloc). Thus, it was common to speak of "three worlds."

This derivative category makes very little sense today. It sometimes still carries the residual connotation of non-Western as well as non- Communist. Increasingly, however, the term has become used to cover all largely nonindustrial countries that are predominantly nonmodern in their economic and social infrastructures. In that sense, the remaining Communist-ruled countries would belong to the Third World category, with China and a few of its Asian neighbors as prime examples. In the same sense, Cuba is one of many Third World countries in Latin America, although it differs significantly from the others in (still) being Communist-ruled.

Most of these developing nations also share the problems of poverty and, though now less frequently, rapid population growth. However, their comparative economic situation and potential for development can vary enormously. Adding to the terminological inflation and confusion, the developing countries have often been referred to collectively as the "South" and contrasted with the largely industrialized "North." Most of them in fact are located in the southern latitudes of the planet—in Latin America, Africa, Asia, and the Middle East. But Greenland would also qualify for Third World status along with much of Russia and Siberia, while Australia or New Zealand clearly would not. South Africa would be a case of "uneven" or "combined" development, as would some Latin American countries where we find significant enclaves of advanced modernity located within a larger context of premodern social and economic conditions.

Thus, it is very important to remember that the developing countries vary tremendously in their sociocultural and political characteristics. Some of them have representative systems of government, and a few of these even have an impressive record of political stability, such as India. Many others are governed by authoritarian, often military-based regimes that often advocate an ideologically adorned strategy of rapid economic development. Closer

examination will reveal that the avowed determination of leaders to improve their societies is frequently less significant than their determination to maintain and expand their own power and privilege.

In recent years, market-oriented development has gained in favor in many countries that previously subscribed to some version of heavy state regulation or socialist planning of the economy. The renewed interest in markets resembles a strategic policy shift that has also occurred in former Communist-ruled nations or the more advanced industrialized countries. It usually represents a pragmatic acceptance of a "mixed economy" rather than a doctrinaire espousal of laissez-faire capitalism.

In studying the attempts by developing countries to create institutions and policies that will promote their socioeconomic development, it is important not to leave out the international context. In the recent past, the political and intellectual leaders of these countries have often drawn upon some version of what is called *dependency theory* to explain their plight, often combining it with demands for special treatment or compensation from the industrial world. In some of its forms, dependency theory is itself an outgrowth of the Marxist or Leninist theory of imperialism, according to which advanced capitalist countries have established exploitative relationships with the weaker economic systems of the less developed world. The focus of such theories has often been on alleged external reasons for a country's failure to generate self-sustained growth. They differ strikingly from explanations that give greater emphasis to a country's internal obstacles to development (whether sociocultural, political, environmental, or a combination of these).

The debate has had some tangible consequences in recent years. It now appears that dependency theory, at least in its simplest and most direct form, has lost intellectual and political support. There is much to be said for middle-range theory that pays attention to the contextual or situational aspects of each case of development. On the whole, multivariable explanations seem preferable to monocausal ones. Strategies of development that may work in one setting may come to naught in a different environment.

Sometimes called the Group of 77, but eventually consisting of some 120 countries, the developing states used to link themselves together in the United Nations to promote whatever interests they may have had in common. They focused on promoting changes designed to improve their relative commercial position vis-à-vis the affluent industrial- ized nations of the North. Their common front, however, turned out to be more rhetorical than real.

Outside the United Nations, some of these same countries have tried to increase and control the price of industrially important primary exports through the building of cartel agreements among themselves. The result has sometimes been detrimental to other developing nations. The most successful of these cartels, the Organization of Petroleum Exporting Countries (OPEC), was established in

1973 and held sway for almost a decade. Its cohesion eventually eroded, resulting in drastic reductions in oil prices. While this latter development was welcomed in the oil-importing industrial world as well as in many developing countries, it left some oil-producing nations, such as Mexico in economic disarray for a while. Moreover, the need to find outlets for the huge amounts of petrodollars, which had been deposited by some oil producers in Western banks during the period of cartel-induced high prices, led some financial institutions to make huge and often ill-considered loans to many developing nations. The frantic and often unsuccessful efforts to repay on schedule created new economic, social, and political dislocations, which hit particularly hard in Latin America during the 1980s.

The problems of poverty, hunger, and malnutrition in much of the developing world are socially and politically explosive. In their fear of revolution and their opposition to meaningful reform, the privileged classes have often resorted to brutal repression as a means of preserving a status quo favorable to themselves. In Latin America, this led to a political-ization of many lay persons and clergy of the Roman Catholic Church, who demanded social reform in the name of what was called *liberation theology*. For them, this variant of dependency theory filled a very practical ideological function by providing a relatively simple analytical and moral explanation of a complex reality. It also gave some strategic guidance for political activists who were determined to change this state of affairs. Their views on the inevitability of class struggle, and the need to take an active part in it, often clashed with the Vatican's more conservative outlook.

The collapse of Communist rule in Europe has had a profound impact on the ideological explanation of the developing world's poverty and on the resulting strategies to overcome it. The Soviet model of modernization appears to offer very little of practical value. The fact that the Communists who remain in power in China have been willing to experiment widely with market reforms, including the private profit motive, has added to the general discredit of the centrally planned economy. Perhaps even more important is the positive demonstration effect of some countries in Africa and Latin America that have pursued more market-oriented strategies of development. On the whole, they appear to have performed much better than some of their more statist neighbors with their highly regulated and protected economies.

**Latin America** illustrates the difficulty of establishing stable pluralist democracies in many parts of the developing world. Some authors have argued that its dominant political tradition is basically authoritarian and corporatist rather than competitively pluralist. They see the region's long tradition of centralized oligarchic governments, whether of the Left or Right, as the result of an authoritarian "unitary" bias in the political culture.

Today, however, one after the other dictatorship in the region has been replaced by an elected government. The demonstration effect of democratic governments in Spain and Portugal may also have been important for the Latin American countries. Finally, the negative social, economic, and political experience with authoritarian rulers may well be one of the strongest cards held by their democratic successors. But unless they also meet the pragmatic test ("Does it work?"), by providing evidence of social and economic progress, the new democracies in Latin America could also be in trouble shortly.

In much of Latin America there has been a turn toward a greater emphasis on market economics, replacing the traditional commitment to strategies that favored statist interventions. The two articles in this section both deal with some dilemmas that have accompanied this transformation. A basic problem is that the benefits of economic growth have not "trickled down" very much. Indeed, there are many real victims of the economic dislocation brought on by free market reforms.

In Mexico, in early 1997, the government announced that it had paid back a huge relief loan provided by the United States, and overall economic prospects for the struggling country appeared to have improved considerably.

The Mexican elections of July 1997 could become a political milestone in the country's recent history. They resulted in the defeat of the Institutional Revo-lutionary Party (PRI), something that would have been unthinkable until recently. In the lower house of Congress, two opposition parties denied the PRI its habitual controlling majority. They began to trans-form what had been regarded as a rubber stamp chamber into a political check on the president.

**South Africa** faces the monumental task of making democracy work in a multiracial society where the ruling white minority had never shared political or economic power with black Africans or Asian immigrants. A new transitional constitution was adopted in late 1993, followed by the first multiracial national elections in April 1994. Former president de Klerk seems destined to go into history as an important reformer, but his political work could not possibly please a broad cross section of South African society. His reforms were judged to have gone much too far and too fast by members of the privileged white minority, and they clearly did not go nearly far enough or come quickly enough for many more people who demanded measures that went far beyond formal racial equality.

Nelson Mandela, who succeeded de Klerk in the presidency, has faced an even more difficult historical task. He has some strong political cards, in addition to his undisputed leadership qualities. He clearly represents the aspirations of a long-repressed majority, but he has managed to retain the respect of a large number of the white minority. It will be important that he continues to bridge the racial cleavages that otherwise threaten to ravage South African society. In the interim constitution, the reformers had sought political accommodation through an institutional form of power sharing. A new constitution, adopted in 1996, lays the foundation for creating simple majority-based governments that are bound to be dominated for now by the African National Congress (ANC), Mandela's political party. The new charter contains many guarantees of individual and group rights, but political prudence will recommend some form of meaningful interracial coalition-building in South Africa's policy-making process.

The continued task of finding workable forms of power sharing will be only one of Mandela's many problems. In order for the democratic changes to have much meaning for the long-suppressed majority, it will be necessary to find policies that reduce the social and economic chasm separating the races. The politics of redistribution will be no simple or short-term task, and one may expect many conflicts in the future. Nevertheless, for the first time since the beginning of colonization, South Africa now offers some hope for a major improvement in interracial relations, and some sober optimists believe that a firm foundation has been laid that should ensure political stability in the post-Mandela era. In December 1997 Mandela stepped down from the leadership of the ANC as a first step in his eventual retirement from politics. His place was taken by Thabo Mbeki, the country's deputy president, who is scheduled to become president in 1999. It seems that the new leaders have done their best to provide for political continuity instead of a divisive power struggle after Mandela's departure. Mbeki (and everyone else) lacks Mandela's great moral authority, but he is widely described as "businesslike" and competent.

Another focus of attention in 1999 will be Nigeria. It covers a large area and has more than 100 million inhabitants, making it the most populous country in Africa. The former British colony is now returning to electoral politics after 15 years of oppressive military rule that brought economic havoc to the potentially rich nation. The path toward democratic governance in this culturally diverse country will be long and difficult. It bears close watching by students of comparative politics.

**China** is the homeland of over a billion people, or more than one-fifth of the world's population. Here the reform Communists, who took power after Mao Zedong's death in 1976, began much earlier than their Soviet counterparts to steer the country toward a relatively decontrolled market economy. They also introduced some political relaxation, by ending Mao's recurrent ideological campaigns to mobilize the masses. In their place came a domestic tranquillity such as China had not known for over half a century. But the regime encountered a basic dilemma: it wished to maintain tight controls over politics and society while freeing the economy. When a new openness began to emerge in Chinese society, comparable in some ways to the pluralism encouraged more actively by Gorbachev's glasnost

policy of openness in the Soviet Union, it ran into determined opposition among hard-line Communist leaders. The aging reform leader Deng Xiaoping presided over a bloody crackdown on student demonstrations in Beijing's Tiananmen Square in May 1989. The regime has refused to let up on its tight political controls of society, but it continues to loosen the economic controls in the areas or zones designated for such reforms. In recent years, China has experienced a remarkable economic surge with growth rates that appear unmatched elsewhere in the world. A still unanswered question is whether the emerging market-oriented society can long coexist with a tightly controlled political system. In February 1997 Beijing announced the death of Deng Xiaoping, whose long illness had prevented his appearance in public for a couple of years. Specialists in China differed in their analyses of the likely consequences of Deng's death, but they saw little likelihood of a major power struggle or de-stabilizing policy changes in the short run. Jiang Zemin, chosen by Deng as his successor in 1989, had been the country's president since 1993. As government and party leader, he appeared likely to continue the relatively pragmatic course adopted by Den. It needs to be added that the regime has revived a hard line in dealing with real, imagined, or potential political dissidence, which includes some forms of religious expression. Moreover, there are signs of social tension, as China's mixed economy leaves both "winners" and "losers" in its wake. With the country's undeniable problems and short-comings, however, China's leaders have steered clear of the chaotic condition of post-Soviet Russia. They seem determined to continue with their tight political controls, even as their economy becomes freer and more market-oriented. Some observers believe that the basic economic and political norms will eventually begin to converge, but that remains to be seen.

**India** is often referred to as a subcontinent. With some 900 million people, this country ranks second only to China in population and ahead of the continents of Latin America and Africa combined. India is deeply divided by ethnic, religious, and regional differences. In recent years, Hindu extremists have become politicized and now constitute a threat to the Muslim minority as well as to the secular foundation of the state. For the vast majority of the huge population, a life of material deprivation seems inescapable. However, some policy critics point to the possibility of relief if the country's struggling economy were freed from a long tradition of heavy-handed state interference. There have been some promising steps in that direction. The potential for political crisis never-theless looms over the country. In 1992 the national elections were marred by the assassination of Rajiv Gandhi, the former prime minister and leader of the Congress Party. Prime Minister P.V. Narasimha Rao, the political veteran who took charge of a tenuous minority government after the election, soon followed in the steps of other reform governments in the developing world by adopting more market-oriented policies. Several members of Rao's cabinet were linked to political corruption, and his Congress Party was badly defeated in the general election of May 1996. It subsequently went into parliamentary opposition, trying to heal its deep internal divisions. After a short interval, a new coalition government took over. It included 14 political parties and, at least in that sense, seemed to reflect the country's diversity. It pledged to continue the market-oriented reforms, but it was hampered in promoting new policies by deadlock among its many different partners. After 10 months in office, it was replaced by a new government, headed by Inder Kumer Gurjal. New elections in the spring of 1998 produced a result that seemed to promise more instability for the world's largest democracy. The Bharatiya Janata Party, dominated by Hindu nationalists, won the most seats, but it was only able to govern in alliance with several smaller parties. Such a coalition provided a weak parliamentary majority, but it appeared to be viable, because the BJP leader, Atal Behari Vajpayee, was able to tame the rhetoric of his own party's more militant Hindu-nationalist members. The Congress party still hopes to revive and eventually return to power.

Some observers believe that the "real action" in India now comes from a more dynamic economy, which has been energized by the relaxation of the country's long tradition of heavy state regulation and protectionism. They emphasize as a considerable achievement that India has so far managed to weather the financial storm, which has wreacked havoc throughout much of South Asia. Other India-watchers think the country's market reforms have caused social and economic dislocations that could spark new political turmoil and ethnic strife. As always, this huge country bears careful watching.

The **Newly Industrialized Countries** (NICs) have received much attention as former Third World nations that are breaking out of the cycle of chronic poverty and low productivity. It is not fully clear what lessons we can draw from the impressive records of the four or five "tigers" or "dragons" — Singapore, Hong Kong, South Korea, Taiwan, and possibly Thailand or Malaysia. Some observers have suggested that their combination of authoritarian politics and market economics provided a successful mix of discipline and incentives that made the economic take-off possible. Others point to the presence of special cultural factors in these countries (such as strong family units and values that emphasize hard work, postponement of gratification, and respect for education) that supposedly encourage rational forms of economic behavior. It would also be possible to cite some geopolitical and historical advantages that helped the NICs accumulate investment capital at a critical phase. The subject is of great importance and it seems bound to become one of the main topics in the field of study we call the politics of development.

These countries are of special interest not only as possible role models for rapid and sustained economic development, but also as reminders of what can go wrong: Hit by a tidal wave of financial turmoil in 1997 and 1998, several of the South Asian countries were shown to have extremely fragile economic infrastructures that seemed to be linked to the prevalence of cozy networks or "cronyism" in their interplay of government, banks, and business ventures. These countries had become used to being admired for their economic prowess, and this may have helped them ignore some early warnings about the financial dislocations to come. At this point it is still uncertain how and when the present havoc will end. Some countries, like Thailand, Malaysia, and Indonesia, appear to be far more heavily hit than others, but the spillover effects are likely to be felt in other nations as well. The turmoil has raised some serious questions about the role of mobile global capital in destabilizing the once booming economies of South Asia.

There is also disagreement over whether some of these countries can serve as examples of how authoritarian political and social traditions can be reformed in tandem with the development of a more affluent consumer society. The authors of one article give a perspective on the newly industrialized countries by carefully reviewing the debate concerning the relative contributions made to their remarkable economic development by market forces, state intervention, and cultural and social factors.

# LET'S ABOLISH THE THIRD WORLD

*It never made much sense, and it doesn't exist in practice.*
*So why not get rid of it in theory?*

Sometimes language lags history. Take the Third World. Did we ever have another name for the poor, unstable nations of the south? In fact, the Third World is a 1950s coinage, invented in Paris by French intellectuals looking for a way to lump together the newly independent former European colonies in Asia and Africa. They defined *le tiers monde* by what it wasn't: neither the First World (the West) nor the Second (the Soviet bloc). But now the cold war is over, and we are learning a new political lexicon, free of old standbys like "Soviet Union" that no longer refer to anything. It's a good time to get rid of the Third World, too.

The Third World should have been abolished long ago. From the very beginning, the concept swept vast differences of culture, religion and ethnicity under the rug. How much did El Salvador and Senegal really have in common? And what did either share with Bangladesh? One of the bloodiest wars since Vietnam took place between two Third World brothers, Iran and Iraq. Many former colonies remained closer to erstwhile European metropoles than to their fellow "new nations."

Nevertheless, the Third World grew. Intellectuals and politicians added a socioeconomic connotation to its original geopolitical meaning. It came to include all those exploited countries that could meet the unhappy standard set by Prime Minster Lee Kuan Yew of Singapore in 1969: "poor, strife-ridden, chaotic." (That was how Latin America got into the club.) There's a tendency now to repackage the Third World as the "South" in a global North-South, rich-poor division. To be sure, in this sense the Third World does refer to something real: vast social problems—disease, hunger, bad housing—matched by a chronic inability to solve them. And relative deprivation does give poor nations some common interests: freer access to Western markets, for example.

But there are moral hazards in defining people by what they cannot do or what they do not have. If being Third World meant being poor, and if being poor meant being a perennial victim of the First and Second Worlds, why take responsibility for your own fate? From Cuba to Burma, Third Worldism became the refuge of scoundrels, the "progressive" finery in which despots draped their repression and economic mismanagement. Remember "African socialism" in Julius Nyerere's Tanzania? It left the country's economy a shambles. A good many Western intellectuals hailed it as a "homegrown" Third World ideology.

Paternalism is one characteristic Western response to a "victimized" Third World. Racism is another. To nativists such as France's Jean-Marie Le Pen or Patrick Buchanan, "Third World" is a code phrase for what they see as the inherent inferiority of tropical societies made up of dark-skinned people. Either way, the phrase Third World, so suggestive of some alien planet, abets stereotyping. "The Third World is a form of bloodless universality that robs individuals and societies of their particularity," wrote the late Trinidad-born novelist Shiva Naipaul. "To blandly subsume, say, Ethiopia, India, and Brazil under the one banner of Third Worldhood is as absurd and as denigrating as the old assertion that all Chinese look alike."

Today, two new forces are finishing off the tattered Third World idea. The first is the West's victory in the cold war. There are no longer two competing "worlds" with which to contrast a "third." Leaders can't play one superpower off the other, or advertise their misguided policies as alternative to "equally inappropriate" communism and capitalism. The second is rapid growth in many once poor countries. The World Bank says developing countries will grow twice as fast in the '90s as the industrialized G-7. So much for the alleged immutability of "Third World" poverty—and for the notion that development must await a massive transfer of resources from north to south. No one would call the Singapore of Lee Kuan Yew poor, strife-ridden or chaotic: per capita GNP is more than $10,000, and its 1990 growth rate was 8 percent. South Korea, Taiwan and Hong Kong also have robust economies, and Thailand and Malaysia are moving up fast.

American steelmakers have recently lodged "dumping" complaints against half a dozen Asian and Latin American countries. Cheap wages explains much of these foreign steelmakers' success, but the U.S. industry's cry is still a backhanded compliment. "A nation without a manufacturing base is a nation heading toward Third World status," wrote presidential candidate Paul Tsongas. But Tsongas was using obsolete imagery to make his point: soon, bustling basic industries may be the *hallmark* of a "Third World" nation.

**Patina of modernity:** Nor can the Third World idea withstand revelations about what life was really like in the former "Second World." It was assumed that, whatever the U.S.S.R.'s political deformities, that country was at least modern enough to give the West a run for its money in science and technology. In fact, below a patina of modernity lay gross industrial inefficiency, environmental decay and ethnic strife. Nowadays, it's more common to hear conditions in the former Soviet Union itself described as "Third World," and Russia seeks aid from South Korea. Elsewhere in Europe, Yugoslavia's inter-ethnic war is as bad as anything in Asia or Africa. The United States itself is pocked with "Third World" enclaves: groups with Bangladeshi life expectancies and Latin American infant-mortality rates.

A concept invoked to explain so many things probably can't explain very much at all. The ills that have come to be associated with the Third World are not confined to the southern half of this planet. Nor are democracy and prosperity the exclusive prerogatives of the North. Unfair as international relations may be, over time, economic development and political stability come to countries that work, save and organize to achieve them. Decline and political disorder come to those who neglect education, public health—and freedom. The rules apply regardless of race, ethnicity, religion or climate. There's only one world.

CHARLES LANE

# The 'Third World' Is Dead, but Spirits Linger

*Indonesia saw a movement born, and now hosts its wake.*

**Barbara Crossette**

Not more than 60 miles down the highway from the Indonesian hill town of Bogor, where President Clinton will take part this week in an economic summit of Asian-Pacific nations, is a genteel city that once symbolized everything the third world believed in and hoped for when it was young. The city is Bandung. There, another generation of world leaders—Nehru, Nasser, Nkrumah, Sukarno, Zhou Enlai—met at another summit, the 1955 Afro-Asian Conference, a gathering full of postcolonial promise, with dreams of self-sufficiency, solidarity among newly independent nations and commitment to an anti-superpower international policy that became known as nonalignment.

"Sisters and brothers!" President Sukarno of Indonesia told the delegates. "How terrifically dynamic is our time!"

The fraternal third world these founders envisioned is dead. The agenda for Bogor, where the heirs of the Bandung generation plan to talk mostly about economic liberalization, competition for foreign investment and free trade, is its obituary. The hollowness of the dream of Afro-Asian commonality is never so starkly evident as when Pacific Rim countries get together, a number of them boasting higher living standards than some European nations. Nehru's India is barely on the horizon of this world; Nkrumah's Africa isn't even in the picture.

The "third world," a phrase first used by French journalists in the 1950's, was meant to describe those who were not part of the industrial world or the Communist bloc. The distinction has no more relevance now than the idea that developing nations automatically have much in common with each other. People speak of the "tigers" who form a class of their own, or a "fourth world" of the poorest countries. A "fifth world" might be found among proliferating populations of rootless refugees. And so on.

"We no longer have a coherent image of the third world," says Jean-Bernard Mérimée, France's chief delegate to the United Nations and a former Ambassador to India. "It is now composed of totally different elements. What do nations like Burkina Faso and Singapore have in common? Nothing, except a sort of lingering perception that they belong to something that had the tradition of opposing the West and the developed world." All that is left, the envoy said, are "remnants of the Bandung attitude" and memories of the fight against colonialism that once bonded emerging nations.

Bandung's oratory lives on, however, resurfacing regularly in the frustration of poor countries looking for easy explanations for development shortcomings. The new "imperialists" now tend to be lending organizations like the World Bank and International Monetary Fund, which have tried to impose stringent fiscal regimes. The "neocolonial" tag has also been attached to donor nations asking questions about rights abuses, child labor, religious or sex discrimination and population policy. At the recent United Nations population conference in Cairo, some of the hottest buttons and bumper stickers proclaimed angrily, "No to Contraceptive Imperialism."

The days of Bandung were heady days of shared underdevelopment, before yawning material gaps between the richest and poorest of these nations began to widen. In Asia, Pakistani business leaders say ruefully that a few decades ago their nation was roughly on a par with South Korea and both had military governments. Both are now democracies, at least on paper, but South Koreans live a decade longer, earn 10 times as much and send 10 times as many children to college with less than half Pakistan's population. In Egypt, intellectuals recall how their country once exported skilled labor to other Arabic-speaking nations that now import a more educated work force, even for menial jobs, from Southeast Asia. In decades of building organizations—the Non-aligned Movement, the Group of 77—third world never devised effective mechanisms to help one another.

Ideologies, economic policies, cultural differences and the creation of superpower clienteles all played a part in widening fissures among developing countries. Different growth rates were not always predictable. Singapore's lack of natural resources did not prevent it from growing into an economic powerhouse. A sea of oil has not turned Nigeria into Texas or Mexico. Authoritarian policies contributed to the boom in some

nations. Repression and corruption drained the life of others, or drove the dispossessed into violence.

## Dirt Poor, With Tanks

What happened to the shared dreams of the third world is documented in the United Nations' Human Development Index. Looking at daily lives rather than macroeconomic figures, the index has for the last five years ranked more than 100 developing nations in education, access to basic services and conditions of women, among other topics. "What emerges is an arresting picture of unprecedented human progress and unspeakable human misery, of humanity's advances on several fronts mixed with humanity's retreat on several others, of a breath-taking globalization of prosperity side by side with a depressing globalization of poverty," the 1994 report says.

This year, the index focuses on big military spenders. "Many nations have sacrificed human security in the search for more sophisticated arms," it says. "For example, India ordered 20 advanced MIG-29 fighters that could have provided basic education to all the 15 million girls now out of school. Nigeria bought 80 battle tanks from the United Kingdom at a cost that would have immunized all two million unimmunized children in that country while also providing family-planning services to nearly 17 million couples."

While the third world had divided itself into unequal streams of

development well before the end of the cold war, developing nations hoped there would be peace dividends for them after the collapse of communism. They have been disappointed. Not only have sources of aid from the former Soviet bloc withered, as Cuba has discovered most painfully, but also the European nations reborn as democracies—now labeled "economies in transition"—have moved in to claim a lot of attention and scarce development funds.

What to do? Development experts say doing nothing about the Global South—the new term—will lead only to more ethnic wars, migrations from overpopulated regions and rapid depletion of natural resources. On the other hand, those "remnants of the Bandung attitude" that the French envoy identified do not want the industrialized world to get an opportunity to intervene in national policies as a condition of granting more aid.

"You get a certain feeling that on many issues—social policies, environmental policies, human rights—the developing countries get a feeling of interference," said Austria's United Nations delegate, Ernst Sucharipa. "We would not say this is true, though I can see why some countries would feel that way. We have to have an open discussion on issues of global consequence." The need for universal sisterhood and brotherhood is now no longer confined to the world of Bandung.

# Latin Economies Soar, Stumble With Reforms

**Development:** Free markets yield benefits, but poverty and inequality persist—and in some cases worsen.

By CHRIS KRAUL
and SEBASTIAN ROTELLA
TIMES STAFF WRITERS

RIO DE JANEIRO—Latin America has been a laboratory for free-market reform over the last decade. And in many ways the experiment has worked, generating robust growth and billions of dollars in foreign investment while wiping out the hyperinflation that smothered the poor.

But don't talk to Sidney Setubal of Rio de Janeiro about the sweet winds of change or the blessings bestowed on his country by Ford or Wal-Mart or Motorola.

The former clerk was among nearly 3,000 workers fired in November by Telerj, Rio's telephone company, after the government sold the notoriously inefficient utility to private owners, who slashed costs.

Setubal, 48, sat recently among morose former co-workers in a union hall, filling out forms and waiting to talk to a lawyer. The father of two had the dark, slender look of a beach-loving Rio native. His 22 years at a desk job had ensconced him in the lower middle class.

Suddenly out on the street and lacking a college degree, Setubal sees little hope of landing work soon. Unemployment rates have climbed to 7.5% and Brazil is bracing for a deep recession in 1999.

"It's hard to find a job when you've worked a long time in the same company," Setubal said wearily. "You don't know how to work elsewhere."

The Brazilian's plight reflects the growing paradox—and brewing political tempest—underlying Latin America's all-out conversion to free markets in the 1990s.

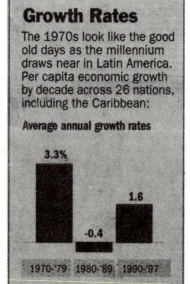

### Growth Rates

The 1970s look like the good old days as the millennium draws near in Latin America. Per capita economic growth by decade across 26 nations, including the Caribbean:

**Average annual growth rates**

3.3%    -0.4    1.6

1970-'79   1980-'89   1990-'97

Source: Inter-American Development Bank

Los Angeles Times

Productivity and consumerism have soared, and a statistical patina of growth blankets much of the region.

But job creation is actually slower than a decade ago, and unemployment across the region is unchanged at 10%.

A bigger proportion of working-age people—57% today versus 52% in the 1980s—is trapped in the "informal economy" as street vendors and the like, neither paying taxes nor receiving pensions, medical insurance and other forms of security, according to a number of recent studies.

## Reducing Poverty Remains Elusive Goal

The new economics is not replacing the inefficient jobs that have been slashed all across the region by the hundreds of thousands.

It's the "dirty little secret" of today's Latin America, as one economist puts it: While the wealthy enjoy the fruits of modernization, poverty and inequality persist and even worsen.

There is an increasing consensus among experts across the ideological spectrum that the ultimate goal of the reforms, the reduction of the region's grinding poverty, remains little or no closer than a decade ago.

Jobs in the region have increased an average of just 2.8% a year in this decade, down from 3.3% in the 1980s—and far short of the 5% to 6% needed to absorb the millions who reach working age each year.

"The whole process has not been sufficiently equitable. You've got a significant number of losers and a large number of people who have yet to see benefits," said Richard Feinberg, a UC San Diego political economist and former advisor on Latin America in the Bush administration.

To be sure, some of the disappointments are facts of life elsewhere, including the United States, where the gap between rich and poor also widened this decade.

However, the scale here is vast. Disillusionment is acute in Latin America because inequality was already the worst in the world, said Nancy Birdsall

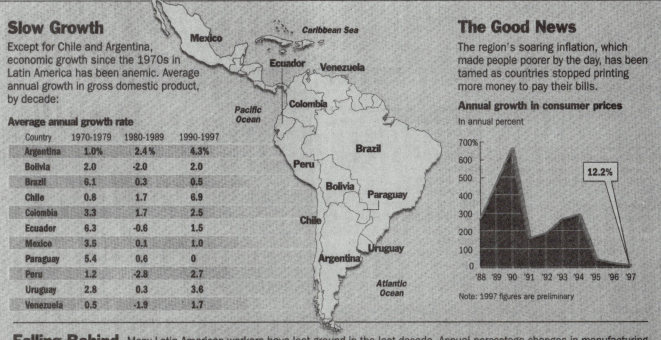

## Slow Growth

Except for Chile and Argentina, economic growth since the 1970s in Latin America has been anemic. Average annual growth in gross domestic product, by decade:

### Average annual growth rate

| Country | 1970-1979 | 1980-1989 | 1990-1997 |
|---|---|---|---|
| Argentina | 1.0% | 2.4% | 4.3% |
| Bolivia | 2.0 | -2.0 | 2.0 |
| Brazil | 6.1 | 0.3 | 0.5 |
| Chile | 0.8 | 1.7 | 6.9 |
| Colombia | 3.3 | 1.7 | 2.5 |
| Ecuador | 6.3 | -0.6 | 1.5 |
| Mexico | 3.5 | 0.1 | 1.0 |
| Paraguay | 5.4 | 0.6 | 0 |
| Peru | 1.2 | -2.8 | 2.7 |
| Uruguay | 2.8 | 0.3 | 3.6 |
| Venezuela | 0.5 | -1.9 | 1.7 |

## The Good News

The region's soaring inflation, which made people poorer by the day, has been tamed as countries stopped printing more money to pay their bills.

**Annual growth in consumer prices**
In annual percent

12.2%

Note: 1997 figures are preliminary

## Falling Behind

Many Latin American workers have lost ground in the last decade. Annual percentage changes in manufacturing wages, adjusted for inflation:

**Manufacturing wages** In annual percent

Source: Inter-American Development Bank

Argentina

Brazil

Chile

Mexico

VICTOR KOTOWITZ and LORENA IÑIGUEZ / Los Angeles Times

---

of the Carnegie Endowment for International Peace, a Washington economics policy research group. And so it remains.

"It looks as though when times are bad the poor are worse off, and when times are good it's not clear that the poor are better off," Birdsall said.

It has been a long journey even if, for many, the distance traveled is short.

Until the 1980s, Brazil and other Latin American nations dedicated half a century to keeping imports out and building local industries. They relied on heavy government investment in basic industry to stimulate growth.

The region became a bastion of massively inefficient cronyism and inflated, make-work payrolls. Success hinged less on marketing and technological prowess than on cultivating contacts with power brokers.

The debt crisis of the early 1980s exposed the inadequacies of the old policy, showing that governments were borrow-

ing enormous amounts in foreign loans to maintain unaffordable, socialist systems. The countries were being left behind in a rapidly globalizing, high-technology-based world.

Chile became the free-market pioneer. In the late 1970s and early 1980s, then-dictator Augusto Pinochet unleashed the so-called Chicago boys, technocrats molded by the conservative economics department at the University of Chicago.

## Source of Chile's Success Debated

Chile now has Latin America's most privatized and deregulated economy and has done a uniquely good job of reducing poverty, from 45% to 23% of the population from 1987 to 1996. Unemployment shrank by more than half, to 7%.

Yet an ideologically charged debate rages over who gets the credit: Pinochet's

purist free-marketeers, whose innovations included privatized pensions, or subsequent democratic governments, which presided over greater growth.

"The previous governments had an almost religious conviction that the market solves everything," said Richardo Ffrench Davis, a former top official of the government elected in 1990.

"What we did was introduce pragmatism. We invested more in production, in quality of education, in physical infrastructure, in equity."

By the early 1990s, Chile's neighbors had started down the free-market road. Mexico, Argentina, Peru, Colombia, Brazil and others gradually lowered trade barriers, invited foreign companies to invest and began selling off bloated, inefficient state-run industries.

But as progress has faltered or, in the case of Mexico, been reversed, the disappointments have accumulated, and a debate over market reforms has been building for years.

Many Latin Americans had already concluded what people elsewhere in the world have deduced in the last 18 months: that "free markets" can devastate developing nations.

## The Global Economy Domino Effect

The economic flu that began in Thailand in 1997 and spread across Asia, Russia and Brazil sent capital pouring out of all emerging markets. It still threatens to send Brazil over the brink, menaces economies across the hemisphere and led to a $41-billion international bailout in November. Regional economic growth is nearing the vanishing point, projected to slow to 1.5% this year.

This just a few years after nervous money fled Mexico and left that nation an economic shambles that will not be fully repaired until early in the new millennium.

"Hot money can break a country in 24 hours," lamented Gov. Tasso Jereissati of Ceara state in northeast Brazil. "Everyone can be happy today and then we wake up broke because of something that happened overnight in South Africa or Hong Kong. In this kind of world, it's hard for an emerging country to really emerge."

At the same time, most conservatives and leftists alike agree that landmark structural achievements of the 1990s should not be touched: monetary stability, open markets, leaner governments.

Indeed, purists say the changes did not go far enough. They blame the entrenched woes of working people on halfhearted modernization, pernicious corruption and a failure to accompany free markets with strong democratic institutions.

However, a chorus of critics wants to "reform the reforms" to make the economies more responsive to have-nots.

The region's heavy reliance on the market has caused nations to neglect the state's vital role in educating and training its people, said Jose Antonio Ocampo, director of the U.N.'s Economic Commission for Latin America and the Caribbean.

"The second wave of reforms is not more economic liberalization," he said in an interview. "There are these fictions that the problem is insufficient liberalization. Where? This has become incredibly simplistic. . . . We must seek more pragmatic solutions."

## A Huge Market for U.S. Exports

New solutions might well be necessary to mute a backlash that is already gaining strength as more citizens equate free-market democracy with lawlessness and lost jobs.

Venezuelans in December elected as president populist Hugo Chavez, an ex-paratrooper who once attempted a coup and denounces "savage capitalism." Center-left political movements have gained ground in Argentina, Chile and Mexico partly because they criticize "*el modelo*"—the dominant economic model.

The United States, of course, has a big stake in the health of the region's democracies and economies, particularly the working and middle classes—all potential consumers or, conversely, illegal emigres. U.S. exports to Latin America are expected to more than double to $240 billion by 2010, exceeding the projected combined exports to Europe and Japan.

That speaks to the particularly Latin American irony of all this: A sizable minority, tens of millions of people, are thriving. Brazil has been called "Bel-India" because the elite live as if they were in Belgium and the masses as if they were in India. That clash of images increasingly fits Latin America.

Thus, companies such as Compaq Computer Corp. and J.C. Penney Co. are scrambling to sell computers and bedsheets to Brazil's new middle class. More lasting investment—in factories, power plants and the like—continues to pour into the region on the bet that these economies will keep growing.

Brazil last year received $23 billion in direct foreign investment, up from $1 billion in 1990 and second only to China. In energy projects alone, about $170 billion will be invested in the region over the next decade.

## New Opportunities for Entrepreneurs

The lifestyle of Pilar Caicedo, a Colombian consultant who conducts sales and customer service training, proves that home-grown entrepreneurs are also part of the new economic pie.

Caicedo, 53, is a sophisticated, fashionable mother of four. She socializes with a former president, drives a sleek Mazda sedan and travels the globe for business and pleasure.

The opening of the hemisphere's economies has boosted her company, which is based in the hills above Cali and has representatives across the continent. Customers include Dow Chemical Co. and IBM Corp.

Neighboring countries used to obstruct foreign entrepreneurs, Caicedo said. But now taxes on foreign firms have been slashed, and she has expanded operations in Peru, Ecuador and Venezuela.

"This has helped us withstand the economic difficulties in Colombia," Caicedo said on a recent afternoon in her suburban villa.

But Caicedo's gilded world of professionals has little to do with the world where most Latin Americans live.

## A Region Lacking in Educational Resources

The time-honored way to narrow such a gap, of course, is education. Yet educational opportunities are shrinking compared to other parts of the world—a seemingly damning comment on how the region has used its resources.

The region's workers now have two fewer years of education than their Asian counterparts, whose schooling they equaled in the 1960s, according to an Inter-American Development Bank study. And technical training has failed to supply skilled workers or get the unemployed back to work.

As these nonworkers fall into the informal economy, streets have filled with tattered armies of itinerant peddlers from Mexico City to Caracas to La Paz. Not only are more workers shut out of health and pension coverage, but countries lose the productivity inherent in organized work.

Even the comparatively bright health statistics should be better than they are. Though some Latin American nations have dramatically improved life expectancy and infant mortality rates, those figures still trail countries with similar income patterns, according to the Inter-American Development Bank.

That such gloomy numbers co-exist with the cheerful macroeconomic evidence, analysts say, reflects the differing, irregular and incomplete stages of reform that these economies have reached. As such, reform advocates say, it's too early to pass judgment.

Brazil, for example—by far the dominant economy in Latin America—only five years ago tackled the kind of massive transformation others started in the 1980s. A generation or more might be needed for market-based reforms to reach full flower, said Amaury Bier, Brazil's finance undersecretary.

The Brazilian government, which once owned or controlled the nation's industries, is remaking itself as a creator of "human capital adequate to technological development" and of "macroeconomic conditions for future growth," Bier said in an interview.

As the region ponders the options, the free-market switch—despite the shortfalls—is widely perceived as better than the alternatives.

In fact, because the hyperinflation of earlier years acted as a tax on the poor, its elimination was a godsend to them—arguably the most important reform to date.

In Brazil in 1993, inflation went up 1% to 2% *every day,* robbing the poor of spending power while the wealthy shielded themselves or profited from the fallout.

President Fernando Henrique Cardoso's strategy of inflation-busting and a minimum-wage hike benefited the poor more than any other group and reduced their ranks in 1994, though the current downturn could partly reverse that progress.

## The Crucial Decline in Birthrates

The latest thinking among many intellectuals and politicians would replace traditional free-market policies with an approach closer to the British Labor Party's "third way" between capitalism and socialism.

"The [economic] opening has had no good effect on the poor," Ciro Gomes, former finance minister and a future contender for [the] presidency, said in an interview. "In trying to shock our companies into being more efficient, we've drowned them instead."

Sounding like American tycoon and politician Ross Perot, Gomes complains that the lowering of trade barriers against foreign auto manufacturers caused more than 1,000 Brazilian auto parts companies to go broke. He wants the state to grant low-cost credit to help small and mid-size businesses compete. He also adds his voice to those around the world demanding limits on the free flow of capital.

But in the long term, such policy options might pale in importance compared to another change spreading across the regions: a decline in the birthrate.

For many reasons, notably urbanization and the growth of women in the work force, birthrates are falling throughout Latin America. Population growth in

the 1990s has slowed to 1.7% a year from 2% in the 1980s.

Until now, Latin America's soaring birthrates defied efforts to create enough jobs for those flooding the ranks of would-be workers. And large families worsened the burden on wage earners, completing the poverty circle.

"If you are working and gaining income and on top of that have fewer kids to take care of, the easier it is to educate the kids you have, which raises their income levels," says Ricardo Hausmann, chief economist at the Inter-American Development Bank.

Lower birthrates allow more of the region's resources to be dedicated to such critical needs as education, land redistribution, pension reform, revisions of labor law and better tax collection.

## Brazil's Landscape of Inequality

Northeast Brazil offers a panorama of the challenges.

It is an alternately lush and desolate landscape of almost feudal injustice, the poorest and most unequal region in a nation with the world's most unequal income distribution. In Ceara state, rural and urban desperation has been aggravated by a serious drought and the loss in Fortaleza, the capital, of industries shuttered by the new competitive climate.

"We can't wait for the process of economic opening to take care of itself," Gov. Jereissati said. "The state has to be more active to stimulate jobs."

Land reform is a priority. By turning sharecroppers into owners, land redistribution makes them more productive and provides land as collateral, giving them the use of credit.

During the last four years, Brazil's agrarian reform program has provided land to about 270,000 needy farm families. However, an estimated 2 million more landless peasants pose one of the society's most difficult challenges.

The World Bank hopes to resettle 175,000 families in 13 Brazilian states over the next six years, based on a pilot program in the northeast that is resettling 15,000 families.

Francisco Dominguez de Souza and his fellow farmers, resilient men clad in linen shirts, work pants and sandals, are mulattoes and mestizos—like most of the almost 200 million Latin Americans

trapped in poverty. Until February, they were the poorest of the poor.

As a tenant farmer, Dominguez was forced to move his family every year at the whim of landowners known as "colonels," rural bosses who control political machines, county-size estates and regiments of private gunslingers. The landowners told him what crops he could grow, when and where. And he had to give them half of his harvest.

"I was kind of a slave," Dominguez said.

Then a loan helped their 13-family collective buy an 800-acre farm from an absentee owner near the town of Acarau in Ceara. Land ownership means the difference between decent daily meals and going to bed hungry, between misery and dignity.

"There's enough to eat," said Dominguez, 54, a weather-beaten father of five interviewed in his small but sturdy new house. "And also there is liberty: the fact that I can pound this table and say it's mine."

Now he is his own master. He hopes for a bumper crop of coconuts next year and aspires to earn $2,500, which is five times the subsistence income he earned annually as a renter.

Such efforts might one day be part of a recipe that will move the majority of Latin Americans closer to prosperity. Yet until the region's economies are deeply transformed, any such recipe will inevitably yield a bitter taste.

Consider the new $210-million electric power project in Cali, Colombia, being built by InterGen, a joint venture of San Francisco-based Bechtel Corp. and Shell Oil Co. It was made possible when Colombia agreed to let foreigners invest in the national power grid.

When the plant fires up this month, it will add 25% to Cali's power capacity, improve reliability and reduce pollution. However, it will employ only half as many workers while generating five times the energy.

The same kind of wholesale job loss continues all across the region. Paper manufacturer Smurfit Carton de Colombia laid off 10% of its work force to compete with Finnish, Chilean and Brazilian challengers.

"We know changes are necessary," union leader James Molina said at the paper plant. "But we need to put a human face on the changes."

# MEXICO

## Sweeping Changes of Last Decade Translate Into a Tale of 2 Economies

**By JAMES F. SMITH,**
TIMES STAFF WRITER

ECATEPEC, Mexico

Ask Isidra Sanchez what Mexico's decade of reform has done for her and the 26-year-old maid and mother replies without hesitation: "I now have to work. Before, my husband's pay was enough for us to live on."

But ask the same question of Gustavo de Leon, a proud young engineer at a gleaming new Shell petrochemical plant in the gulf Coast city of Tampico, and he is just as clear: "There are many new opportunities for young people in high-tech jobs, and that lets us support Mexico's growth."

Seen through a macroeconomic lens, the Mexican landscape looks more competitive, more productive, leaner and healthier than a decade ago. But through an average family's eyes, the reforms of the last 10 years too often have meant less food on the table.

Consider: The average non-farm, non-government worker in Mexico last year earned one-third *less* than he did in 1982.

The first grudging economic reforms in Mexico took place in the early 1980s, but the headlong plunge into the global market economy really began with Carlos Salinas de Gortari's inauguration as president in December 1988. So it's ex-

actly a decade since the reforms began in earnest.

The reformist Salinas left as part of his disgraced legacy the worst recession in postwar Mexico. Yet the same Salinas is credited with crafting the North American Free Trade Agreement, or NAFTA, as well as other sweeping changes that redefined modern Mexico and made it the world's 10th-largest trading nation.

So when people write report cards on the past wrenching decade for Mexico and its 95 million people, the grades are far lower when they come from the vast numbers of working poor than from the sizable minority of Mexicans who have cashed in on the changes.

Still, the shift toward an open economy is unlikely to be reversed in a world that is less and less tolerant of countries that try to buck the free market. And very few people would dispute that change was necessary in a country drowning in bureaucracy and strangled by protectionism.

In addition to opening up trade through NAFTA, Mexico has privatized banks, the telephone monopoly **Telmex** and other state-controlled enterprises; invited foreign investment and foreign companies into the economy; and legalized the sale of communal land. On

Jan. 1, even subsidies for the sacred tortilla were abandoned.

Mexico's transformation coincided with similar changes all over Latin America. Yet Mexico stands apart because of its tangled but overpowering relationship with the U.S. In particular, NAFTA, which took effect Jan, 1, 1994, transformed the country into a low-wage production platform for U.S., European and Asian manufacturers building things for the U.S. market.

Last summer, for example, the number of workers employed in the NAFTA-driven export assembly industry passed the 1 million mark—often 50-cent-an-hour jobs, but nevertheless a vast pool of opportunity that has prompted at least some Mexicans to stay home rather than sneak across the Rio Grande. In October, Mexico overtook Japan as the second-largest U.S. trading partner after Canada.

At the same time, the opening of the economy exposed protected domestic businesses to fierce competition, and many failed to measure up. And privatization became a mantra. In 1982, there were 2,255 state-owned firms in Mexico. By January 1997 the number was down to 185, and many remaining state-controlled enterprises went through fierce efficiency programs that also stripped out thousands of jobs.

Rather than judge the reforms good or bad, political scientist Jorge Castaneda casts two opposing scenarios:

The positive view is that "Mexico is poised for takeoff, and that after the crash of 1995 and '96 ... we are now on the verge of a Chile-like situation with 10 years ahead of 6% to 7% annual growth."

The converse view is that "Mexico is not really poised for growth, that the problems we saw this year—falling federal revenues, higher inflation because of devaluation, more difficult access to capital—all are leading to a new cycle of lethargic growth of 2% to 3%."

Castaneda leans to the pessimistic view, reasoning that good results cannot come from reforms "designed by elite groups in the United States and Mexico." The reforms ignore the reality that "the majority of people do not have a satisfactory standard of living," he said. "This development challenge is not being addressed."

## Paychecks as Bottom Line

Yet other statistics point to useful improvements—at least for those with moderate cash incomes. A decade ago people waited years for a phone line. The telephone company, Telmex, was privatized in 1991 and has invested billions, doubling the number of phone lines and reducing the waiting list to a matter of days.

Savings was a chronic Achilles' heel for Mexico. But compulsory private retirement funds were introduced in 1996, and more than 13 million workers have signed up for new types of funds over the last year. They had saved $4.1 billion by August 1998, already a huge new source of domestic capital for investment and growth.

Yet the bottom-line evidence of economic well-being—paychecks badly eroded by the peso's decline—helps explain Mexicans' skepticism toward economic reform. Just when things seem to be settling down, a new crisis erupts. Ground that was gained is suddenly lost. Inevitably, the least well-off suffer most.

Isidra Sanchez and her cousin Teresa live in Ecatepec, a smog-filled, rough town on the northern edge of Mexico City. They, like many residents here, came several years ago from a village in the mountains of adjacent Puebla state, trading the uncertainties of subsistence farming for a couple of rooms in a two-story boarding house shared by eight families.

"It got much worse in 1995, when all the prices went up and there was no work," Isidra said, recalling the 52% inflation that year. She and Teresa both went to work as domestics, and earn about $30 a week—the same as their husbands, who work in a nearby factory making shelves for stores. Teresa, who has two young children, must travel two hours each way to work. "Now we both have to work, and we barely make it," she said.

Their tiny apartments are immaculate, with precious space set aside for a shrine to the Virgin of Guadalupe and the living rooms ingeniously adapted to include bunk-bed space for four. The walls are crammed with tidy sections of toiletries, books and an ancient color TV.

## Opportunities Available to Few

There are prospects for improvement. Both husbands contribute to a government-backed housing program that could land the two families modest homes of their own in years to come.

The original reason for the families' move—better schooling for each couple's two children—remains the principal motive, and they feel the quality is indeed much better. Isidra's son Felipe, 10, wants to be a doctor.

For engineer Gustavo de Leon in Altamira, the reforms have opened up a new world. Parts of Mexico's petroleum industry are slowly being opened to competition. That encouraged **Shell** to open a huge new polyester plant, creating well-paying jobs for local talent like De Leon. He noted proudly that while 25 U.S. experts had helped get the state-of-the-art plant up and running last year, the factory will soon be run entirely by Mexican technicians, many in their 20s and 30s and most of whom studied at the state technical university.

But the percentage of ordinary Mexicans who have such opportunities remains small.

Independent economist Rogelio Ramirez de la O broadly characterized the reforms in Latin America as "very positive, and probably most positive for Mexico."

Yet the reforms have fallen short, he said, because the government has lacked the resolve to push them further and deeper, and change fundamentally the way Mexico operates.

President Ernesto "Zedillo couldn't capitalize on the confidence that arose with the original opening of the economy. Part of that opening was accidental, chaotic, forced by the 1995 crisis," Ramirez said, referring to reforms such as the floating exchange rate adopted after

Mexico ran out of foreign reserves trying in vain to defend a fixed value for the peso.

"But the government didn't exploit the crisis to get to the bottom of problems," Ramirez said. "This has meant that the reforms haven't reached the ordinary people, and salaries haven't risen. So Zedillo is making an annual apology that the new order isn't delivering the goods for the average person. I think we have become a lot more polarized between the haves and the have-nots."

Still languishing, for example, are proposed reforms to the labor laws to create more flexibility in hiring and firing and to offer better job training. Better, fairer tax collection remains elusive—a critical problem as slumping oil prices rob the government of revenue. Some financial reforms remain stuck in Congress. And everyone agrees the judicial system needs restructuring to end a culture of impunity—including tougher measures against corruption and white-collar crime.

But what Mexico has done well, Ramirez and others agree, is build its manufacturing export capacity.

Whereas growth under Salinas was fed by consumption and fattened by an artificially strong peso, growth under Zedillo has been more disciplined and built on industrial output—up an average 9.2% per year since 1996. The number of exporting firms has risen from 22,000 in 1994 to 34,000 in 1998.

In the process, fixed investment has poured into Mexico at more than $10 billion a year to create new export-driven factories, while the proportion of volatile liquid capital—so-called hot money—invested on the stock market has declined.

"So in Latin America, Mexico is the exporter par excellence," Ramirez said. Productivity has risen steadily and modern manufacturing quality systems are the norm. But the productivity still hasn't translated into higher real wages for workers.

Thirty years ago, the economist noted, Mexican craftsmen producing relatively complex goods in a closed economy could command a premium wage. Now Mexicans are more often laborers on an assembly line. That means that in real terms, today's workers are often less well-off than their fathers were.

"The abrupt entry of Mexico into the global economy, while correct, put the Mexican laborer at the bottom rung in world terms," Ramirez said. "It will take a long time for the worker to recover."

## Benefits Don't Filter Down

U.S. Ambassador Jeffrey Davidow, who previously served as assistant secretary of state for Inter-America Affairs, acknowledged that "the openings in the economy have generally not yet percolated down to the 50% of Mexico that is poor. . . . The challenge for the next 10 years is how do the benefits become more evenly distributed?" But Davidow added: "If Mexico had not changed, would the poor be any better off? My guess is not."

Commerce Secretary Herminio Blanco said: "Now development opportunities are spreading across the entire country. Before, only the big cities developed. Now growth is occurring from the northern border to the Yucatan Peninsula."

The reforms did feed one bad Mexican habit. The many privatizations that came with the apertura, or process of opening the economy, meant in at least some spectacular cases a bonanza for corruption.

The privatization of the banks in the early 1990s earned the government about $20 billion. But many unqualified non-bankers allegedly won the frenzied bidding by fraud and corruption and eventually needed to be bailed out. That rescue, still underway, is likely to cost taxpayers at least $60 billion—and has undermined the credibility of privatization.

While wages for workers have lagged, there's little doubt that productivity and competitiveness have improved dramatically, boosting profits for companies instead of pay for workers. For many, that has bred resentment. For political scientist Castaneda's optimist scenario, it means Mexico and its people should be better positioned for real gains in the years ahead.

In 1970, according to figures from the national statistical service, Mexico's labor productivity in manufacturing stood at 70 on an index measuring output per hours worked. It has since soared to 132.3, a far faster growth rate than that achieved by the United States.

From President Zedillo to laboring families in towns like Ecatepec, there is broad agreement that the next phase of Mexico's development must bring more equitable distribution of wealth to a broader spectrum of Mexicans than occurred in the first decade of reform.

If not, the risk of a backlash against the market will grow. Already, even the right-wing National Action Party has raised the idea of putting restrictions on stock market investments.

Jesus Silva-Herzog, a finance minister from 1982 to 1986 and more recently ambassador to the United States, reflected on the reform model in a recent address to politicians—and found it wanting.

"There has to be a review and adjustment of the economic model," said Silva-Herzog, a possible presidential candidate for the ruling PRI in 2000. "Arithmetically, without citing ideologies, the income per person has fallen, and simply and plainly, the number of unemployed has risen. And this has occurred not in the space of three or five years, but over 15 years. So something is going wrong."

"South Africa has entered a more rough-and-tumble era of open multiparty competition... To generate the deep reserves of trust and civic responsibility necessary for a brighter future, black and white South Africans will have to recognize afresh that their futures are inexorably connected."

# After Mandela's Miracle in South Africa

## MICHAEL BRATTON

A miracle is a hard act to follow. Well-wishers celebrated South Africa's peaceful passage from a racial oligarchy to one of the world's most liberal democracies not least because it seemed so splendidly far-fetched. Who would have thought that hard-line political opponents could span the bitter chasms of color and class to create a compromise solution? Their constitutional pact seemed to give each side what it most wanted: the black majority gained control of the state, and the white minority received guarantees of a place in the economic sun.

Four years after the country's founding elections of April 1994, fissures are beginning to appear in South Africa's historic truce. Black and white South Africans have different understandings of the terms of the transition agreement, especially whether the political miracle marked the beginning or the end of a broad process of change. At the same time, because the pact was struck between elites, political leaders have not been able to guarantee that all their followers will embrace the new order.

In their attempt to resolve deep-seated differences, South Africans will soon lose the guidance of one of the twentieth century's true political visionaries. In 1999,

Nelson Rolihlahla Mandela will step down as president, thus depriving the country of its main unifying symbol. Already the era of "reconciliation"—the policy of forgiveness and partnership that has been Mandela's hallmark—is being superseded. With the second national election coming in 1999, his African National Congress (ANC) has embarked on a strategy of "transformation" that emphasizes African expectations for economic advancement and downplays minority concerns. Unable to avoid the reality that transformation must embody the redistribution of wealth, leaders of all political parties are lapsing into a defensive racial discourse.

## AN ACCELERATED TRANSITION

South Africa's transition to democracy was meant to be gradual. Because they could not agree on immediate majority rule, the principal protagonists—represented by the ANC, the National Party, and the Inkatha Freedom Party—agreed on a temporary power-sharing arrangement. Conducted under an interim 1993 constitution, the founding elections inaugurated a Government of National Unity in which the largest parties obtained cabinet seats in proportion to their share of the vote. This consensual dispensation was to last until the 1999 elections, which were to pass the reins of power to the winners and consign other parties to the role of loyal opposition. Only then would South Africa's transition to a competitive, multiparty democracy be complete.

In practice this timetable has been shortened. An expansive new constitution was signed into law on International Human Rights Day 1996 and entered into force

*MICHAEL BRATTON is a professor of political science and African studies at Michigan State University. He is the coauthor with Nicolas van de Walle of* Democratic Experiments in Africa *(New York: Cambridge University Press, 1997) and coeditor with Goran Hyden of* Governance and Politics in Africa *(Boulder, Colo.: Lynne Rienner Publishers, 1992). He is currently a visiting Fulbright scholar at the Universities of Natal and Durban in South Africa.*

in February 1997. Applauding the text as a monumental achievement, South Africa's Constitutional Court nonetheless insisted on adding provisions to strengthen the bill of rights, provincial autonomy, and public oversight. Significantly, Chief Gatsha Buthelezi and his Zulu-based Inkatha Freedom Party chose to remain entirely outside the process of constitutional negotiations, contending that promises of international mediation of disputes with the ANC had not been honored. And the National Party, still led at the time by former President F. W. de Klerk, withdrew from the national unity government on June 30, 1996, claiming that the new constitution discarded power-sharing and that his party could better serve the country in opposition. Thus, for all practical purposes, the "season for power-sharing," as South African scholar Vincent Maphai put it, has already run much of its course, and South Africa has entered a more rough-and-tumble era of open multiparty competition.

To this accelerated transition must be added Mandela's phased withdrawal from the political scene. The "old man" has taken the presidency in an increasingly ceremonial direction, delegating all but the most knotty executive decisions to others in the ANC hierarchy. Deputy President Thabo Mbeki has taken charge of policy-making, notably on the economy. Yet the expected accession of Mbeki to the national presidency in 1999 signals more a change of governing style than a new policy direction. Lacking Mandela's gift for fusing moral authority with a common touch, Mbeki will be a more aloof, professional chief executive. The political succession has been skillfully managed and will likely occur without the debilitating power struggles that often arise when great leaders bow out. While South Africans do not know Mbeki well, and while they will surely never love him as they do Mandela, they are growing accustomed to having him in charge.

## ECONOMIC IMPERATIVES

Any South African leader is bound to be preoccupied with the economy, which must generate enough employment to ease chronic black impoverishment. As the government's own targets reflect, economic growth must reach 6 percent per year to keep up with population growth and at the same time lift the poor. Although the South African economy has expanded steadily for five years, growth rates (just 2 percent in 1997, the same rate forecast by the government for 1998) have not been able to make a dent in unemployment, which is rising alarmingly in the nonagricultural sector; at least 30 percent of adults do not have formal jobs. The situation could worsen because of external uncertainties like the price of gold, which has plunged to its lowest level in almost two decades and led to the closure of unprofitable mines. On the positive side, inflation is steadily declining to an expected 5 percent for 1998, the rand has retained its value

against many major currencies, and foreign direct investment has begun to trickle in.

After four years in power, much of the credit—and blame—for the performance of the economy can be placed at the feet of the ANC government. In the 1994 election campaign, the party promised to make job creation and social service delivery top priorities under its Reconstruction and Development Program. This ambitious public-spending scheme was supplemented in June 1996 by a more orthodox package of monetary controls and investment incentives known as GEAR, which stands for Growth, Employment, and Redistribution. This homegrown macroeconomic strategy is so market friendly that foreign donors report that they do not even raise economic policy conditions when negotiating grants to the government. Such is the newfound zeal of ANC ministers for neoliberal policies that one easily forgets that, as an exile movement, the party was bent on nationalizing mines, industry, and banking. Not only has the ANC government adjusted to global economic realities by repudiating these commitments, but it now speaks the language of privatization in relation to broadcasting, the airlines, and telecommunications.

This turnabout in economic thinking has been painful and politically controversial, especially for the Confederation of South African Trade Unions (COSATU) and the South African Communist Party. These partners in the ANC's triple alliance have neither abandoned faith in interventionist economics nor ceased to defend organized labor's globally uncompetitive wages; at COSATU's 1997 national conference, hundreds of delegates jeered GEAR. Nevertheless, Thabo Mbeki has vowed that he will stick to his economic policy even if it costs him his friends.

In the face of extreme social inequalities, any democratically elected government will face powerful demands for redistribution. And policies of economic reapportionment will inevitably engender conflict between would-be winners (who will always want more) and prospective losers (who will resist making sacrifices). For example, black businesspeople have taken control of 9 percent of the capital assets on the Johannesburg Stock Exchange, but official efforts at black empowerment are criticized as elitist. A 1998 initiative to enact an Employment Equity Bill that includes ambitious affirmative action requirements has ignited protests and preemptive countermeasures from the private sector. And, even though the government has steadily shifted spending priorities away from defense and toward poverty relief, it still faces popular impatience. Since 1994, the government has provided electricity to 1.2 million households and furnished water supply for 1.7 million people; yet it remains dogged by complaints that fewer than one-third of the 1 million houses that it promised to build have actually been constructed.

## POLITICS POLARIZED

Although the country's leaders would prefer to keep attention focused on the positive possibilities of economic growth, pressures for social justice are making for polarized politics. Three current events illustrate this trend: the fiftieth National Conference of the ANC, the twilight of the Truth and Reconciliation Commission, and the dawning 1999 election campaign.

When 3,000 ANC delegates gathered in Mafikeng for the party's fiftieth congress in December 1997, Mandela gave a vituperative valedictory speech. Before cataloguing the ANC's achievements, he lashed out at "a counter-revolutionary network [based among those] who have not accepted the reality of majority rule." Accused of subverting the government's program were apartheid holdovers in the bureaucracy, the main white opposition parties, foreign-funded nongovernmental organizations, and "the bulk of the mass media." Although the text of the speech was reportedly prepared by Mbeki's office and is thought to reflect his views, it was presented by Mandela, perhaps because his vast authority made a strident message more palatable, and because a reversal of roles enabled Mbeki, whose supremacy is still being established, to rise above the fray.

International press coverage of the speech was adverse, seeing in the president's sweeping attack an unhealthy defensiveness and a failure to distinguish between critics and enemies. Black domestic audiences reacted much more favorably to a public rebuke of those white South Africans who insist on the preservation of what are widely perceived as ill-gotten gains. Indeed, Mandela probably enhanced his status with core constituents who felt that he had gone too far to accommodate white interests.

Certainly the speech helped the ANC reunify a fragmented party. In the elections for the party's deputy presidency, the hierarchy headed off the insurgent candidacy of former First Lady Winnie Mandela who, despite a popularity born of campaigning among the marginal poor, had become an embarrassment because of her penchant for corrupt and high-handed tactics. The party instead stage-managed the ascent of Jacob Zuma, Mbeki's hand-picked associate, to the number two position and in the process laid claim to political support in KwaZulu-Natal, Zuma's homeland. To their credit, the delegates (who were overwhelmingly African) helped the ANC reaffirm its well-established nonracial credentials by electing seven non-Africans to the party's ten top executive positions.

## TRUTH AND ITS CONSEQUENCES

This reaffirmation comes at a time when platitudes about South Africa's "rainbow nation" have worn thin and doubts have surfaced about South Africa's respected Truth and Reconciliation Commission. Set up in July 1995 under the supervision of Nobel Peace Prize winner Archbishop Desmond Tutu, the TRC was a bold attempt to confront the country's brutal past without the cost and

divisiveness of Nuremberg-style trials. It was charged with three tasks: to uncover the truth about human rights abuses; to offer amnesty to those who confess a politically motivated involvement; and to make reparations to victims. Armed with the stick of subpoena power and the carrot of amnesty, it is easily the broadest, most powerful commission of its kind ever created.

Since 1995, several thousand victims have testified before the TRC's public hearings, providing, at last, a chance for those who suffered to be heard. At the same time, a stream of low-level apartheid functionaries has come forward to admit, often in chilling detail, how they served as the covert hit men of a deranged regime. Moreover, in December 1997, under the glare of international media coverage, the commission delved into the alleged involvement of Winnie Mandela in several murders in the late 1980s, revealing damaging new information. The TRC has accumulated a repository of apartheid's inner secrets, making denial difficult and a recurrence that much more remote.

However, as the commission prepares its final report for release this June, it faces dwindling confidence from across the political spectrum. The truth about the chain of command in the torture and killing of anti-apartheid activists will remain obscured until senior figures such as former Prime Minister P. W. Botha and Chief Buthelezi drop their boycotts of the TRC proceedings and agree to testify in person. The families of victims express growing anger at a process that opens old wounds but offers little succor afterward. From the right-wing side of the fence, the Freedom Front's Constand Viljoen and his followers suspect that the TRC is a plot to scapegoat Afrikaners as a people. They are especially troubled by the revelation that, without public hearings, the commissioners granted a blanket amnesty to 37 top ANC leaders for acts committed during the liberation war.

The Truth and Reconciliation Commission is discovering that truth does not automatically lead to reconciliation. Even more than for Mandela, Archbishop Tutu's career has been built on peaceful accommodation: but as Tina Rosenberg remarked in the November 18, 1996, *New Yorker*, it is far from clear that his "gospel of reconciliation [will] triumph over the human impulse to seek vengeance." The graffito scrawled on a Pretoria underpass—"Tutu has made them confess; now we will kill them!"—surely represents an extreme view, but it nonetheless captures the missing element: justice. For many South Africans, the righting of wrongs will require more than criminal justice for official perpetrators; as the scholar Mahmood Mamdani recently argued, it must also include a meaningful measure of social justice that involves broad sacrifices from apartheid's multiple beneficiaries. A vice-chancellor of a former black university put it succinctly: "Lasting reconciliation will be achieved only when there is health care and education for every South African child."

The most ambitious goal of the TRC, targeted through extensive radio and television coverage of its public hearings, is to change how white South Africans think. In this it has so far failed. Few whites are willing to admit complicity in apartheid. Shocked, threatened, and ultimately fatigued, many are shutting out the TRC's findings. Tutu summed up the mood of the country by saying in late December last year that whites begrudge being asked to carry a burden of guilt and blacks resent the failure of whites to acknowledge how lucky they are: "And so we sit in our little corners feeling angrier and angrier . . . But I still think we have a great deal going for us . . . if [only] we could have the courage maybe to be a little more honest."

## TALKING AND NOT HEARING

The opening volleys of the campaign for South Africa's second national elections (expected to be held between April and July 1999) have only confirmed that contending parties talk past each other. At the opening of parliament in Cape Town in February 1998, opposition leaders came out swinging against Mandela's ANC conference speech. Tony Leon, the head of the Democratic Party, introduced a party document entitled "The Death of the Rainbow Nation" that sought to paint affirmative action as reverse discrimination. In the Western Cape, the National Party is trying to woo "coloured" (mixed race) voters by splitting them from Africans and promising promotions within the party. In response, black parties are closing ranks.

To play the race card would seem to be a losing strategy for small white parties whose only chance of gaining access to government lies in attracting black voters. More realistic is the United Democratic Movement (UDM), formed in March 1997 by Bantu Holomisa and Roelf Meyer, after they broke with the ANC and the National Party respectively to form a multiracial alliance. In February 1998, Meyer announced that he would defer leadership to Holomisa, but it remains to be seen whether the party can rise above the latter's reputation for opportunism. The UDM's best opening would seem to lie in a policy platform that challenges the ANC's progressive positions on abortion, criminal rights, and the death penalty, and that taps into the strong currents of social conservatism among Africans. Opinion polls from late 1997, however, suggest that the UDM attracts no more than 4 to 7 percent of the national vote.

If these figures hold, the results of the 1999 elections will be similar to those of 1994. Because the euphoria of a founding election cannot be replicated, voter turnout will drop, but the ANC will still likely receive about six out of ten votes nationally. As in neighboring Zimbabwe, there may be a heightening of racial rhetoric and a rash of redistribution promises as elections approach. But such polarization can be read as a product of, rather than a threat to, the gradual consolidation of democracy. No political party—including Inkatha and Freedom Front on the right, or the Pan Africanist Congress on the left—is questioning the legitimacy of elections, seeing them instead as the main game in town.

## FROM POLITICAL TO CRIMINAL VIOLENCE

Political violence is in decline. Most encouraging is the apparent determination of national ANC and Inkatha leaders to broker a rapprochement that will reduce deadly interparty clashes during the next election. The idea of an ANC-Inkatha merger has been floated, only to be denied by Buthelezi, who is nonetheless capable of changing his mind at the last minute. Moreover, the prospect of right-wing extremists taking up arms to secure an Afrikaner *volkstaat* (people's state) now seems increasingly quixotic. None of these observations rules out the possibility of local feuds in rural KwaZulu-Natal or disruptive skirmishes by remnants of the old regime's more shadowy supporters.

The larger threat to social stability comes from criminal violence. The murder rate in South Africa—65 people per day in the first nine months of 1997—is among the highest in the world. The carnage is concentrated in Johannesburg, Cape Town, and Durban—and further concentrated in black residential areas of the latter two cities—while the rest of the country remains reasonably safe. In early 1998, President Mandela claimed that the ANC's tenure had been accompanied by a decrease in major crimes. The facts, however, are mixed. Some serious crimes (murder, aggravated theft, and robbery of businesses) seem to have fallen slightly in 1997, while others (assault, residential burglary, and rape especially) continue to climb. But the police admit that crime statistics are unreliable, due in part to ignorance about conditions in the former black homelands, and are reluctant to say the tide has turned.

Conventional wisdom connects crime with joblessness. The abolition of influx controls and the growth of informal squatter settlements, coupled with the shortage of jobs, lend credence to an economic interpretation. It does not explain, however, the connection between crime and violence. Here it is necessary to remember that South Africa's seemingly smooth transition was actually very

> Popular demands for a better life are especially intense in South Africa, whose transition was in large part a revolution of rising expectations.

turbulent. Both the state security forces and a generation of guerrilla fighters adopted tactics of intimidation and vigilantism. A gap in authority opened between an ever more repressive state and the increasingly ungovernable townships—into which large numbers of weapons have continued to flow.

By early 1998 the country's security crisis was epitomized by a rash of high-profile problems: gang violence, farm murders, and a spate of armed bank heists. Crime is becoming increasingly organized and internationalized, with Russians, Colombians, and Nigerians believed to be involved in smuggling drugs and guns into South Africa and diamonds and luxury cars out. The national police commissioner has warned that endemic crime is "the biggest threat to democracy in South Africa." The business press emphasizes the negative economic repercussions in the form of high insurance premiums, emigration of skills, and a downturn in tourism. And public opinion surveys confirm that fear of crime is pervasive among South Africans.

## THE FRAYED STATE

The perceived ubiquity of crime raises tough questions about state capacity in the new South Africa. Is the state defaulting in its most basic duty to provide law and order?

The performance of the South African Police Service certainly leaves much to be desired. The force makes arrests for just 16 percent of crimes reported, many suspects escape custody before they are brought to trial, and when trials are held witnesses often refuse to testify because the authorities cannot protect them. Similarly, the justice system shows signs of disintegration; for example, delays in bringing cases to trial have lengthened as senior prosecutors have resigned and their junior replacements have refused to work overtime without pay. For cases that do make it to court, the rate of successful prosecutions is in decline.

The root of these problems lies in the apartheid era, which saw black South Africans reject the authority of a state they regarded as politically illegitimate. The restoration of public confidence in the police and courts (not to mention the army and the prison service) will take time, a process that has not been helped by the ANC's slow start in grappling with issues of law and order.

The new government was at first torn between a liberal impulse to protect individual rights and a growing popular outcry for action against violent criminals. Over the last year it has taken a few decisive steps: to tighten bail laws, to introduce minimum sentences for serious crimes, and to establish the country's first detective academy. In an effort to shore up confidence, the government also appointed a no-nonsense businessman to revamp the mission, management, staffing, and training of the police force.

Citizens also expect the state to improve material welfare. Popular demands for a better life are especially intense in South Africa, whose transition was in large part a revolution of rising expectations. Indeed, South Africans view democracy instrumentally, associating it with jobs, incomes, and housing rather than with its intrinsic guarantees of civil and political freedoms. The ANC government is thus under strong pressure to deliver basic goods and services, preferably before the next election. In attempting to do so, it encounters other state weaknesses. Some central government ministries are paralyzed as inexperienced new recruits and intransigent old-order functionaries struggle to implement an expanded range of tasks. Among local authorities (overloaded with responsibilities for water, sanitation, electricity, roads, and refuse services), the problems are manifestly financial, though they go much deeper. In March 1997, the minister for local government said that about one out of three local authorities lacked the discretionary funds to deliver basic services at an acceptable level, with one out of eight possessing insufficient cash reserves to cover monthly obligations.

A large part of the fiscal crisis of local government originates in the rent and service-charge boycotts launched by the mass democratic movement against township boards appointed by the apartheid government. These mass actions bred a culture of nonpayment that has proved difficult to eradicate. Boycotts have even spread to upscale white suburbs as rate-payers dodge local taxes or escape into private fee-paying services. Because the ANC government's *masakhane* (let's work together) campaign to encourage payments induced little voluntary compliance, new approaches are being tried, from community self-mobilization to abrupt service cutoffs. Still, it is unclear whether municipalities that once served only an affluent minority can command enough resources to address all needs even if everyone pays. Clearly the state alone cannot solve the problem of distributing basic services: what is required is a collaborative governance scheme that yokes state and civil society in a common project.

## AFTER THE MIRACLE

The approaching retirement of the 79-year-old Nelson Mandela comes as the transitional era of reconciliation and power-sharing in South Africa is winding down. The constitutional order will most likely remain democratic: major political players will operate according to agreed-on rules of the game by observing the bill of rights, the electoral laws, and the judgments of the courts. The economic strategy will become increasingly mixed as the ANC government strains to balance its commitment to generating employment through private investment with the rising insistence of its key constituencies for material and social justice. And political discourse will be sharply polarized, even if the distribution of power is not: the ANC will consolidate its hold on the central government while small parties, consigned to permanent opposition, will snap at the ANC's heels with charges of eroding privilege or betraying the poor.

Seasoned observers of African politics see in the ANC's dominance the portents of a de facto one-party state, with all the threats to accountable democracy that such a scenario entails. They worry that the ANC may win two-thirds of the seats in the 1999 parliamentary elections, thus enabling the government, should its present commitments change, to amend the constitution at will. These concerns are valid to the extent that evidence is already available that some ANC officials cut legal corners and practice or condone corruption. In a weakness typical of other African leaders, both Mandela and Mbeki have yet to come out against graft among party loyalists. But concerns about the threat of political monopoly overlook countervailing powers, unusually strong by African standards, embedded in South Africa's state (especially the constitutional court and numerous public watchdog agencies) and its civil society (which features a plural press and nongovernmental organizations). These elements can quickly call into question the legitimacy of a corrupt government.

Which brings us to the central issue. The threat to the South African miracle emanates not so much from a state that governs too much, but from one that governs too little. The most serious flaw in the new South Africa is not imminent authoritarianism but the relentless erosion of political authority. It is most evident in a frayed government that cannot effectively control crime or redistribute services quickly and broadly enough, highlighting the need to reconstruct both police services and local government from the ground up. State incapacity would appear to be at least as serious a constraint to overcoming poverty as persistently low rates of economic growth.

While popular discourse casts these challenges in terms of "delivery," this puts altogether too much onus on the state. The bureaucratic apparatus in South Africa is weak in good part because its inherited structures are historically disconnected from its mass clientele. The ANC is well placed to help mediate a new social contract between state and citizen that restores state legitimacy. To accomplish this, the country needs a new generation of visionary leaders who can help South Africans see that crime and poverty are not only linked problems, but also shared ones. To generate the deep reserves of trust and civic responsibility necessary for a brighter future, black and white South Africans will have to recognize afresh that their futures are inexorably connected.

# Nigeria's long road back to democracy

LAGOS

## At last Nigeria seems on a credible course to end 15 years of military rule. But it's a long and difficult route

CAMELS and donkeys carried the ballot boxes to far-flung polling stations in northern Nigeria. In the southern swamps boats were used. Last weekend, millions of Nigerians queued up to vote in the first of a series of elections that should result in Nigeria's first elected civilian government in 15 years. It may have been the country's biggest ever electoral turn-out. Streets, normally bustling, were deserted as people formed long lines in front of the 110,000 polling stations to vote for new local councils and an end to military rule.

These polls are to be followed by state elections in January, and elections for a new parliament and president in February. On May 29th, if all goes well, the new president will take office, and civilians will rule, from the lowest level to the top.

A rare thing in Nigeria, this election has been applauded on almost all sides. General Abdulsalami Abubakar, the head of state who called it, said it showed Nigeria was ready for a return to democracy. The Commonwealth called it well-conducted. Even normally sceptical human-rights activists called it "credible".

Since independence from Britain in 1960, Nigeria has known only one reasonably successful election, in 1979, when Shehu Shagari, a little-known northern politician, defeated the veteran southerner Obafemi Awolowo. The next election, in 1983, was rigged to return a by-then unpopular Mr Shagari to power. Later that year he was overthrown by the army, which has ruled ever since. The last presidential election, in 1993, appeared to have been won by a southern business tycoon, Moshood Abiola, but before all the results were out, the soldiers annulled the polls.

This time, the elections appear to have been properly, if hastily, organised, with nine parties contesting this initial round of voting. Knowing that politicians had bought up millions of voter cards, the government ordered that voters must queue up to register; and, once registered, must stay in polling stations until registration was complete and voting started. This, and transparent ballot boxes, at least limited multiple voting and fraud.

Still more important, the usually sceptical public appears to believe the general when he says he wants Nigeria under accountable elected rule and the army back in barracks. Just whose elected rule is far from clear. The winner this week has been the Peoples' Democratic Party (PDP), whose most eminent member is General Olusegun Obasanjo, a former military ruler and now a presidential hopeful. Recently formed by a group of politicians hostile to military rule, the party has eschewed regionalism, building support across the country. It won 60% of all councils, compared with 25% for the All Peoples' Party and 15% for the Alliance for Democracy, strong only among the Yorubas of the south-west (which includes, not least, Lagos). The PDP hardly won a single council there. For the fiercely self-regarding Yorubas, General Obasanjo, one of their number, has committed what is for them the ultimate sin—he rejects Yoruba nationalism.

Victory in these local elections will probably mean victory for the PDP later at state, legislative and presidential levels, as new members flood in seeking to back the winner. And then? To learn what the PDP stands for is not easy. Like its rivals, it made no commitment to ideology or policies on important issues such as devolving power, changing the distribution of oil revenues, ending the much-criticised dual-exchange rate or speedier privatisation. Its stated aims were slogans: "Power to the People" and "Justice Unity Progress". Its officials say that the party, formed only in August, is still in the process of formulating policies.

In practice, its formulations may matter less than the realities that its candidate—or any other winner of the presidency—will inherit. Huge problems await the next government: social unrest in the oil-producing areas of the Niger Delta, grinding poverty in the north, everywhere a collapse of long-neglected infrastructure, particularly in telecommunications and electricity. Tackling these at the best of times would be hard; with oil at $10 a barrel, the new government will have to sweat to persuade Nigerians that democracy makes you better off than military rule.

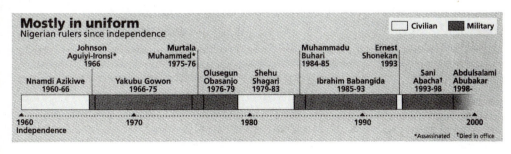

**Mostly in uniform**
Nigerian rulers since independence

Civilian   Military

| Nnamdi Azikiwe 1960-66 | Johnson Aguiyi-Ironsi* 1966 | Yakubu Gowon 1966-75 | Murtala Muhammed* 1975-76 | Olusegun Obasanjo 1976-79 | Shehu Shagari 1979-83 | Muhammadu Buhari 1984-85 | Ibrahim Babangida 1985-93 | Ernest Shonekan 1993 | Sani Abacha† 1993-98 | Abdulsalami Abubakar 1998- |

1960 Independence     1970     1980     1990     2000

*Assassinated  †Died in office

Even after Deng Xiaoping's death last year, few predicted that Chinese President Jiang Zemin would be able to escape from the longtime leader's shadow. But in reviewing developments at the top of Chinese politics, Joseph Fewsmith concludes that "more than outside observers had anticipated, Jiang has demonstrated political strength and flexibility, and perhaps even vision."

# Jiang Zemin Takes Command

## JOSEPH FEWSMITH

As Bill Clinton prepared for his historic trip to China this June—the first by an American president in nearly a decade—critics of the president and his China policy raised the rhetorical ante to a new level. Fueled by accusations that illegal campaign contributions had influenced administration policy on satellite launches, and outraged that the president would be received on Tiananmen Square (where other government leaders have routinely been received), they accused the administration of compromising United States national security and of "kowtowing" to China on human rights. Over 150 members of Congress signed a letter urging the president to postpone his trip, and the House of Representatives overwhelmingly passed a resolution that called on him not to go to Tiananmen Square. Meanwhile, some 75 China-related bills, most imposing sanctions, were under discussion in various congressional committees.

Behind the rhetoric of the president's critics and supporters raged an ongoing debate over the question, "Whither China?" Since the Chinese government's crackdown on demonstrators in and around Tiananmen Square in June 1989, a fundamental division has opened between those who believe that China can be persuaded, over time, to adopt more moderate policies at home and abroad and those who believe that China is emerging as a latter-day fascist state that threatens the economic and security interests of Asia, the United States, and indeed the world. Few have articulated this difference in perception as

JOSEPH FEWSMITH *is an associate professor of international relations and director of the East Asian interdisciplinary studies program at Boston University. He is the author, most recently, of* Dilemmas of Reform in China: Economic Debate and Political Conflict *(Armonk, N.Y.: M. E. Sharpe, 1994).*

sharply as Representative Chris Smith (R-NJ), who wrote in the February 28, 1997, issue of the conservative *Weekly Standard* that the "fundamental basis of the disagreement" on how to deal with Beijing is that some "think the men who rule China are more like businessmen, and others think they are more like Nazis."

Lurking behind this breathtaking reductionism is another argument about the prospects for China's democratization. The terms of this argument have largely been defined in relation to dissidents who have left China since Tiananmen. Early on, the Clinton administration's China policy appeared premised on the belief that such people might become the future leaders of China and that the administration should therefore position itself on the "right side of history." It was also widely believed that an early democratic transition was possible and that, without such a transition, China would become a dangerous adversary. It is just such Manichaean reasoning that lies behind comments such as Representative Smith's.

Framing the debate over China in this manner has done a disservice, both to any realistic understanding of what is happening inside China (which has seemed entirely peripheral to the concerns of many) and to the task of forming a consistent policy toward the country. The China of 1998 is not the China of 1989. Although tolerance of political dissent remains extremely limited, there have been important changes that should not be ignored. The economy is far more market oriented and open to the outside world, the political leadership has changed considerably and the intellectual and political atmosphere is far different from that of just a few years ago.

Although China continues to present a mixed picture of good and bad to the outside world, the overall trend is clearly in the right direction. Critics have focused too narrowly on the absence of a democratic transition and not enough on the possibilities for sustainable democratic governance. If China is to have a democratic government in the future, it needs a reasonably efficient bureaucracy, a system of law, an economy that is more independent of the government, and—most of all—a political culture in which all issues are not seen in zero-sum terms. The changes under way in China are supportive of such trends.

## IN DENG'S END, A BEGINNING

To understand the present political dynamic in China, one must go back to the death of Deng Xiaoping in February 1997. The passing of the "paramount" leader had long been anticipated, and it occurred with such orchestrated smoothness that its impact has been obscured.

Jiang Zemin, elevated by Deng in 1989 to be general secretary of the Communist Party, had been in his position for nearly eight years and had increasingly assumed the substance as well as the appearance of power. Nevertheless, Deng's passing, combined with the scheduled convening of the fifteenth party congress in the fall, gave Jiang his first opportunity to step out from under the shadow of Deng. Stability and continuity seemed to be the order of the day, but in his eulogy at Deng's funeral Jiang hinted that he had something more than mere continuity in mind. Jiang quoted Deng as saying when he returned to power in the late 1970s that there are two possible attitudes: "One is to act as a bureaucrat, the other is to work."

It seemed a risky quote for Jiang to cite, given his reputation for caution. In retrospect, it appears that Jiang was using Deng to make a personal declaration, namely that he was determined to "work" too. Everything since then has confirmed that Jiang, aware that he is likely to serve only a single five-year term as president in the post-Deng era, is conscious of his place in history and wants to leave his mark.

Jiang's intimation of important changes to come was perhaps as much a reflection of the dilemmas facing the party as it was of personal ambition. As Deng had entered his final decline, the party had fought vigorously over his legacy. How would the program of reform and opening up that Deng had pioneered be continued or amended? This was not an easy question. By the late 1990s, it was possible for party conservatives to argue—and they did so vigorously—that reform and opening up were threatening the party's control and even China's sovereignty.

For years, these conservatives had argued that President Mikhail Gorbachev's reforms had destroyed the Soviet Union. Deng's reforms, they believed, were leading China in the same direction, albeit more slowly. The decline of state-owned enterprises, the rapid growth of the private economy, the massive importation of foreign capital and management, the enervation of the party, and the reemergence of "bourgeois liberalism" (ideas that disagree with more orthodox readings of Marxism-Leninism) were repeatedly cited as threats to Chinese socialism. Although raised mainly by older conservatives ("leftists"

in Chinese political jargon), such concerns do have a substantial social foundation. Managers of state-owned enterprises prefer their cozy relationships with the government bureaucracy, while workers in state-owned enterprises fear losing their jobs. Local leaders want to protect their local economy, and bureaucrats charged with maintaining social order can hardly welcome socially wrenching changes.

Conservatives gave voice to these concerns in a series of "10,000-character manifestos"—anonymously written critiques of reform—that were circulated in party circles between the spring of 1995 and the spring of 1997. These manifestos posed a serious dilemma for the party leadership. Unanswered, they would exert an influence on party policy; rebutting them risked opening up dangerous rifts in the party.

Arrayed against vested interests and the concerns of party conservatives, however, were stark economic facts and ultimately a persuasive political logic. China's state-owned enterprises had become a serious drag on the economy and increasingly posed a threat to the banking system as loans went unpaid. Moreover, the growth of township and village enterprises, the engine that had driven so much of China's economic development in recent years, had slowed, leading to concerns about their viability as a form of collective ownership as well as about where the roughly 14 million workers entering the workforce annually were supposed to find jobs. Apparently the answer is to be found in China's private sector, which has been growing rapidly. But both the idea of reforming state-owned enterprises and the financial sector and the recognition of the expanding role of the private sector present substantial challenges to Chinese ideas about socialism.

In short, China had reached a crossroads, and it was not long before Jiang was forced to choose. In March 1997, the draft of Jiang's report to the fifteenth party congress was circulated among officials for comment, and it met with a barrage of criticism from the left. Jiang either had to water down his proposals extensively or break with the left, something he had refrained from doing in the years since his arrival in Beijing. Indeed, Jiang had drawn much support from the left wing of the party in his early years. As late as 1996, Jiang had reached out to the left with the famous (or infamous) statement in a party resolution that building "spiritual civilization would not be sacrificed to material civilization."

In late May 1997, with Deng dead and the need to launch an identifiable "Jiang Zemin era," Jiang went to the Central Party School to give the most important political speech of his career. In a thinly veiled jab at the left, Jiang declared that "there is no way out if we study Marxism in isolation and separate and set it against vivid development in real life." In the unpublicized portion of the speech, Jiang went further, explicitly criticizing the left and laying out his rationale for reform of the ownership structure. Deng had raised the slogan "guard against the right, but guard primarily against the left" in his 1992 trip to southern China in support of the reform effort, but it had been largely dropped from the official media following the fourteenth party congress later that year. Now Jiang was reviving it and identifying himself with Deng's reforms. For a leader often criticized as bland, cautious, and technocratic, Jiang was beginning to reveal a boldness previously visible only in his deft maneuvers against political enemies.

## REORGANIZING THE PARTY...

Although Jiang had previewed some of his major themes in his May speech to the Central Party School, it was not until the fifteenth party congress convened in Beijing in September that the full scope of Jiang's program and his personnel arrangements for carrying it out were unveiled. One of the most interesting aspects of Jiang's report to the congress was that even as he touted Deng's reputation and legacy, he hinted that he himself would push that legacy forward. Jiang cited Deng's 1978 battle with party Chairman Hua Guofeng's "two whatevers" ("whatever decisions Chairman Mao made, we resolutely support; whatever instructions Chairman Mao made, we will steadfastly abide by") as a period of "emancipating the mind"; he said Deng's 1992 trip to the south was a second such period. Intimating that he would continue this process, Jiang called for an "emancipation of the mind in the new period." Conservative Prime Minister Li Peng, of all people, made this implication clear when he told a group of delegates that the present was a third period of "emancipating the mind." This theme would be picked up and expanded in the months that followed during the limited political opening that has become known as the "Beijing Spring."

The central theme of Jiang's report, however, was his argument that China is in the "primary stage of socialism," which was originally expounded at the thirteenth party congress in 1987 but quietly dropped after 1989. Jiang used this thesis to endorse the joint-stock system as a way to reform state-owned enterprises. "The joint-stock system," Jiang declared, "can be used both under capitalism and socialism." At the same time, Jiang declared that large and medium-sized state-owned enterprises would be reorganized into "standard corporations" with "clear ownership" that would be genuinely independent of government control. Jiang also called for the development of diverse forms of ownership, a formulation that would permit the continued rapid development of the private economy. Together these reforms will allow a massive restructuring of the Chinese economy in the years ahead.

The other news that caught the Western media's attention was Qiao Shi's dismissal from the leadership of the Central Committee. Qiao, the number three person in the Politburo Standing Committee and the chairman of the National People's Congress, had made a reputation by repeatedly calling for greater attention to law, seemingly challenging Jiang Zemin's authority in doing so. Many interpreted Qiao's removal as a retreat from the liberal themes he had been touting. Qiao did indeed present a political problem for Jiang, and Jiang responded by lining up support for Qiao's ouster. Although Jiang apparently surprised Qiao by calling for all those over 70 years

*Jiang is conscious of his place in history and wants to leave his mark.*

of age to step down (only to have party elder Bo Yibo say that the rule should not apply to Jiang himself), the real work had been done behind the scenes. Qiao supporters Wan Li and Yang Shangkun reportedly sat mute through the meeting, realizing that they had been outmaneuvered.

Lost in much of the Western press coverage of Qiao's ouster was that dropping Qiao from the Central Committee facilitated Jiang's move to the "right." Qiao would have taken advantage of any movement to relax political control and emphasize the rule of law in order to increase the role of the National People's Congress at Jiang's expense. Removing Qiao gave Jiang the freedom to adopt much of Qiao's program, which he proceeded to do with a vengeance.

In his report to the party congress, Jiang devoted considerable space to political and legal reform, saying, "Without democracy there can be no socialism and no socialist modernization." Although Jiang stopped well short of endorsing anything resembling Western-style democracy, his repeated use of the word "democracy" has prompted hopes of greater opening up. More important for many listeners was his use of the term "rule of law" instead of the standard formula "rule by law." This formulation seemed to presage a new era in institution building and an acceptance of limitations on the arbitrary use of power.

Personnel arrangements made at the congress support the fresh image Jiang has been cultivating, and the removal of many older party personnel is likely to enhance Jiang's ability to control the party. Overall, 60 percent of the 193 people selected as full members of the Central Committee are new. The Central Committee is younger, better educated, and more professionally capable than any of its predecessors. Military representation on the committee has declined from five years ago, and, more important, no military representatives now sit on the powerful Politburo Standing Committee. This, combined with Jiang's call to reduce the military by 500,000 people—including 100,000 officers—indicates a clear effort to make China's military smaller, better equipped, more professional, and less political.

## ... AND REORGANIZING THE GOVERNMENT

The sweeping changes in China's political leadership continued this spring when the National People's Congress convened. Delegates to the NPC meet every five years to select a new government leadership, including the prime minister, the head of the NPC, and the president and vice president. Li Peng, who had served two terms as prime minister, was chosen to head the NPC, replacing Qiao Shi. Li's selection reflected a delicate political arrangement. As the first top leader (prime minister or general secretary) to face a constitutional limit on his time in office—not to mention one of China's most controversial figures because of his role in Tiananmen—the leadership had to find a face-saving way to ease Li out without stirring up divisive calls for a reevaluation of Tiananmen. Making Li the NPC chairman solved the problem and also opened up the post of prime minister for the vastly popular Zhu Rongji while removing Jiang's nemesis, Qiao Shi.

These personnel decisions had been made internally at the party congress the previous fall and were duly confirmed by the NPC. More interesting was the plan for government reorganization announced at the session. Pointing to the costs of bloated government, to the demands posed by the reform of state-owned enterprises, and to the challenges presented by the Asian financial crisis, the NPC adopted a sweeping plan to reduce the 40 departments of the government, known as the State Council, to 29.

The reorganization plan simultaneously centralized economic management in the hands of the State Economic and Trade Commission (SETC) and emphasized the indirect management of the economy by eliminating the major economic ministries and reorganizing them as bureaus under SETC management. The SETC will act as a superministry, the command center of a leaner, meaner economic bureaucracy

Accompanying this sweeping reorganization was the promise to cut the central bureaucracy by 50 percent by the end of 1998, to be followed by similar cuts in the provincial and county-level bureaucracies over the next two years. Bureaucratic organs were told to decide on the "three fixes"—what their functions were, how many people were needed to carry out those functions, and which personnel were to be dismissed—by the end of April. Although that target was not met, Zhu has staked so much of his reputation on his promised cuts that he will almost certainly achieve them, or come close to doing so. If he does come reasonably close, it would be a remarkable administrative revolution in China, which has seen repeated efforts over the years to reduce the government bureaucracy only to have it quickly swell again to its original size and beyond.

Although Zhu's plan for government reform addresses real problems—the cost of administration, the paternalistic relations between the bureaucracy and state-owned enterprises, and the gross inefficiency of bloated government—he clearly had a populist goal in mind as well. The reorganization of state-owned enterprises announced at the fifteenth party congress requires heavy personal sacrifices, since thousands of people will be laid off. Zhu's government reform plan responded to the pain of the populace by, in effect, saying that reforms will hurt the government too.

Zhu is clearly the most popular politician in China today. His declaration at his post-NPC news conference that "No matter whether there is a minefield ahead of me or whether there is a deep ravine in front of me, I will bravely forge ahead, will not turn my back, and will do my best until my last breath" seized the public imagination. When asked if the recent political demonstrations that brought down the Suharto government in Indonesia could spread to China in a new expression of "people power," Chinese repeatedly responded, "Not with Zhu Rongji as prime minister." Zhu has won himself and

China a honeymoon period. He will surely need it, for the road ahead will not be easy.

## A STILL CHILLY BEIJING SPRING

The past year has seen a limited opening for political expression. This opening can perhaps be traced to the letter Beijing University Professor Shang Dewen sent to the Central Committee in August 1997, the first of three such letters to date. Shang argued that economic reform could not go further without an opening of the political system. Far more sensitive than Shang's letter, which received greater coverage abroad than domestically was a letter former General Secretary Zhao Ziyang wrote to Jiang Zemin before the opening of the fifteenth party congress, calling for a reappraisal of Tiananmen. Zhao's letter, which was authentic, was tightly held at the time, and delegates to the party conclave were unaware of its existence. Jiang displayed his displeasure by ordering Zhao's confinement to his house, although he later relaxed this order. Zhao nevertheless repeated his call for a reappraisal of Tiananmen in June, just as President Clinton arrived in the country.

Following the party congress last fall, Jiang visited the United States. By all accounts the leadership was pleased with the results of this trip, and the message was soon sent out, to a sometimes skeptical audience, that building relations with the United States was in China's interest. One indication of this new atmosphere was the broadcast of a television movie depicting the role of the "Flying Tigers" and Sino-American cooperation in the Second World War. Many Chinese learned for the first time how General Claire Lee Chennault and his ragtag group of fighter pilots had prevented the Japanese from bombing cities such as Kunming. Another sign was the improvement in the treatment authoritative Chinese media accorded the United States.

China's intellectuals, as Shang Dewen's inaugural letter suggests, were quick to sense the changing mood. In October, a month after the party congress, Fang Jue, a reform-minded official in the southeastern province of Fujian, distributed a statement calling for political reform. In December, Hu Jiwei, the crusading former editor-in-chief of *People's Daily,* published a series of articles in a major Hong Kong daily calling for political reform. In January the economics journal *Reform* carried an article advocating political reform by Li Shenzhi, the highly respected former head of the Institute of American Studies at the Chinese Academy of Social Sciences who had been removed in the wake of Tiananmen. In March, the previously obscure journal *Methods* ran a special issue on political reform. And in May a rapidly edited book called *Beijing University's Tradition and Modern China* took advantage of the approaching centennial anniversary of the university to emphasize the liberal tradition in China. A preface by Li Shenzhi noted that although liberalism is not native to China, it has struck roots and become a part of China's tradition since its introduction through Beijing University.

In contrast to only a couple of years ago—when *The China that Can Say No* topped the best-seller list and spawned a host of imitators—books that depict the United States in a more favorable light have begun to appear on the market. One notable work is *China Will Not Be "Mr. No,"* by senior intellectual Shen Jiru, which joined the long-standing debate about the causes of the collapse of the Soviet Union. Shen argued that it had been the steadfast refusal of Soviet leaders to cooperate with other countries and open their country up (which earned Soviet Foreign Minister Andrei Gromyko the nickname "Mr. No") that had brought about its demise. In opposition to conservatives' argument that it was reform that led to collapse, Shen and others held that it was the *lack* of reform that brought about the failure of socialism in the Soviet Union and Eastern Europe.

The most controversial book of the spring was *Crossed Swords.* Written by Ma Licheng and Ling Zhijun, two journalists at *People's Daily,* the book traces the history of the emergence of the Dengist reforms—particularly the opening up of intellectual freedom—against the opposition of Mao's successor, Hua Guofeng. *Crossed Swords* goes on to link this early period of relaxation to the heated debates surrounding Deng Xiaoping's trip to the south in 1992, a trip that reenergized reform in the aftermath of Tiananmen. Finally and most controversially the book details the sharp political debates of 1995–1997. These debates pitted those who wanted to further advance reform against leftist ideologues who continue to oppose the marketization, and especially the privatization, of the Chinese economy as well as China's continued integration into the world economy and the progressive abandonment of Marxism. Ignoring certain historical realities, particularly that much of Deng's animus in his 1992 trip was directed against Jiang Zemin, who was then seen as lukewarm at best toward reform, the book portrays Jiang as inheriting and pushing forward the "emancipation of the mind" begun in 1978. Picking up on Jiang's report to the fifteenth party congress and Li Peng's remarks at the same time, the book calls the current opening China's "third emancipation of the mind."

*Crossed Swords* was even more controversial than any of the other works published during the spring because it was included in a series on China's problems that is under the general editorship of Liu Ji. Liu is a vice president of the Chinese Academy of Social Sciences (CASS) and a close personal friend of Jiang Zemin's. This does not mean that *Crossed Swords* reflects, or reflects fully, Jiang's thinking. In an effort to maintain a balance among different constituencies in the party, Jiang has surrounded himself with a variety of advisers, some conservative, some liberal and some cautious, some bold. It is clear that Jiang's advisers do not all agree with each other, and that personal animosities among them run deep.

Jiang brought Liu Ji to Beijing in 1993, in part to provide balance to his group of advisers and in part to cultivate a coterie of young intellectuals who could provide him with policy advice. This was inevitably conflictual because Liu Ji was given the post of vice president of CASS, where the very conservative Wang Renzhi (whom Deng had criticized in his 1992 southern trip and had forced to step down as head of the powerful Propaganda Department) held sway as vice president and party secretary (the CASS president at the time, Hu Sheng, was old and largely inactive).

In 1996 Liu sponsored the publication of *Heart-to-Heart Talks with the General Secretary,* which was aimed at providing policy advice to Jiang, giving Jiang a new and more reformist image, and shaking up the political atmosphere by taking exception to the nationalistic themes then dominating political discourse in Beijing. Predictably the book angered leftists, who responded with disparaging remarks about it and about Liu personally.

The atmosphere following the publication of *Crossed Swords* was even more heated. Ding Guan'gen, the conservative head of the Propaganda Department who is widely disliked by intellectuals, quickly condemned the book. Leftists, who were angered by *Crossed Swords'* wholesale criticism of them, organized a meeting in April to offer their own critique of the book; the decision to invite Communist ideologues from Russia provoked liberals to mock the gathering as one of the "Communist International."

Jiang was under great pressure to criticize *Crossed Swords,* which is apparently why party elder Wan Li, the person directly responsible for the inauguration of the rural reforms two decades ago, met with the authors on two occasions and expressed strong support for the book. As Wan pointed out, if you don't "cross swords," you can never make progress. Wan emphasized his point, albeit indirectly in a rare press interview carried in the May 18, 1998, *Farmers' Daily.* In discussing development of the rural reforms, Wan repeatedly criticized "leftism," never once coupling it with opposition to rightism. Wan's sympathies were abundantly clear. Jiang, under pressure from both sides, has refrained from making any comment on the book.

With this clash of criticism and countercriticism swirling around him, Jiang nevertheless decided to go to Beijing University on May 4 to participate in the university's centennial ceremonies. Jiang made this decision on his own and against the counsel of some of his advisers; they feared the trip would be too controversial and perhaps even stir up a new student movement. Beijing University has been the fount of liberal thinking in modern China and, more specifically, was the leading force in the 1989 Tiananmen demonstrations. Wang Dan, the former student leader released to the United States this April, was a Beijing University student.

Critics have argued that Jiang's visit paid too much attention to patriotism and the university's role in the development of the Chinese Communist Party (the cofounders of the party Li Dazhao and Chen Duxiu, were both Beijing University fac-

> *In seeking a better relationship with the United States . . . Jiang is linking the forces of change within Chinese society to the demands of globalization.*

ulty). Nevertheless, what seems important was Jiang's personal gesture in reaching out to intellectuals. According to professors at the school, the president's visit was highly successful. Jiang spent an entire morning addressing faculty in French, English, Russian, and Japanese (which he said he would speak better if he had not been forced to learn it under the Japanese occupation) and exchanging couplets of Tang poetry with students.

Jiang's visit to Beijing University appears to have been part of a strategy to assuage the anger left by Tiananmen without formally revising the party's judgment on the event. Like the removal of the Yang brothers from the military in 1992, the ouster of the widely disliked Beijing party secretary Chen Xitong in 1995, the various campaigns against corruption, Jiang's ambiguous comments at Harvard University last spring that "sometimes mistakes are made," and the easing out of Li Peng as prime minister, Jiang's visit to the university was an important gesture that tried to put Tiananmen behind him and reach out to the intellectual community at the same time. Perhaps Jiang will eventually reverse the verdict on Tiananmen, but until that time he will at least have tried to distance himself from the event and set a different course.

## WEIGHING THE RISKS AHEAD

Sometimes history moves faster than at other times. Such has been the case since Deng's death. Although there seemed little doubt that Jiang would continue as general secretary, it was unclear how he would handle challenges from the left (the various "10,000-character manifestos") and right (Qiao Shi), or what tone he would set for the post-Deng era. More than outside observers had anticipated, Jiang has demonstrated political strength and flexibility and perhaps even vision. In a matter of months, Jiang made clear not only that he would continue Deng's line of reform and opening up but that he would carry it further by endorsing a new period of "emancipating the mind." He then managed to oust Qiao Shi while

stealing his program of legal reform. He also paved the way for Prime Minister Zhu Rongji to carry out sweeping reforms of state-owned enterprises and the state bureaucracy. Finally Jiang has allowed a more tolerant political atmosphere to emerge, however tentatively.

It could be argued that Jiang is merely responding to the pressures in China, both social and economic, that demand continued change, but the deftness of Jiang's maneuvers suggests that he is taking the initiative. Despite the declaration of the fifteenth party congress that it would "hold high" the banner of "Deng Xiaoping Theory," it is clear that a new, distinctive Jiang Zemin era is beginning to take shape.

The risks for China and the world are high. Nothing in politics is more difficult than engineering a controlled opening. Next year the challenges of layoffs, enterprise reform, bureaucratic restructuring, and the Asian financial crisis will converge at the same time that China faces the tenth anniversaries of the death of Hu Yaobang and Tiananmen, as well as the fiftieth anniversary of the People's Republic and the eightieth anniversary of the May Fourth Movement (the patriotic protest against the Treaty of Versailles that prompted both an intellectual renaissance and the founding of the Chinese Communist Party). It will be an uneasy time, but Jiang is evidently willing to forge ahead despite the risks—a welcome change from the cautious, uncertain attitude that has prevailed in recent years. Moreover, Jiang has made it clear that he views China's relationship with the United States as critical to the reforms he is undertaking.

In seeking a better relationship with the United States—against his domestic critics—Jiang is linking the forces of change within Chinese society to the demands of globalization. Jiang's efforts may fail. But in trying to bring about better governance and a more efficient economic system, Jiang may, whether intentionally or not, be preparing the way for sustainable democratic governance in the long run.

# In March Toward Capitalism, China Has Avoided Russia's Path

**Asia:** Unlike its onetime idol, Beijing has used a gradual approach to developing a market-oriented economy.

By HENRY CHU

TIMES STAFF WRITER

BEIJING—If the Soviet Union always seemed like the terrifying embodiment of Big Brother to the West, then for years it was something of a big brother to China toward the south.

Inspired by the same Marxist-Leninist ideals that first took root in Russia, Beijing alternately held up Moscow as its role model and, in times of disillusionment, its nemesis.

But since the Soviet Union's collapse, China has come to regard Russia as one thing only: its worst nightmare—a country with a political system in disarray; a society in sometimes violent flux; and, now, an economy in free fall.

In attempting to remake itself from a Communist behemoth into a capitalist beacon, China has studiously tried to avoid the path of its onetime idol, preferring a more gradual approach to change. Over the last 20 years, the result has been shaky but mostly upward progress: steady economic growth, an emerging middle class, a new breed of entrepreneurs.

As world leaders and economists reassess the wisdom of free markets amid today's global turmoil, the China model—from the perspective of Russia's collapse and the pain in lesser Asian countries that wholeheartedly embraced capitalism—looks wise enough.

Yet even as Beijing silently congratulates itself on the wisdom of its go-slow approach, analysts say that historical conditions here have been nearly as big a contributor to China's improvement as current policy.

And as in Russia, major domestic reforms—especially China's latest efforts to shed its money-losing state enterprises and streamline its bloated bureaucracy—have brought about a whole new set of problems, making the final outcome of one of the most ambitious economic transitions in history far from certain.

"It is too soon to say whether China's reforms will succeed," Nicholas Lardy, an economist with the Brookings Institution in Washington, wrote recently.

Like Russia, China has struggled to redesign a planned economy into a market-oriented one. But even though both were Communist in name, the two countries launched their modernization drives at very different stages in their development.

"The Communist revolution in the former Soviet Union was over 70 years old; the Communist revolution in China was 30," said Harry Harding, a Sinologist at George Washington University. "The former Soviet Union was more industrial-

ized; China was still an agricultural, rural society."

China embarked on its transformation when Deng Xiaoping, the nation's late "paramount leader," officially ended Beijing's isolation in 1978 with a series of measures designed to open up and liberalize the world's most populous country.

The enormous rural communes set up by Mao Tse-tung were dismantled. Peasant farmers were permitted to sell food on the private market. Two years later, the doors to foreign investment were thrown open in specially designated zones along the southern coast.

### Setting the Stage

Radical Maoism was dead, discredited after the 1966–76 Cultural Revolution, one of China's darkest periods, during which hundreds of thousands of citizens were killed.

Ironically, however, many scholars now argue that some of Mao's wrongheaded policies actually fostered the political climate and infrastructure necessary for the success of China's long march toward capitalism—or, in Deng's wordplay, "socialism with Chinese characteristics." Fanaticism was replaced by pragmatism and a thirst for a new national direction.

"The Cultural Revolution deinstitutionalized the political system and de-legitimized the Communist Party in ways that made reform both necessary and more possible," Harding said.

Under Mao, much of China's economic decision-making and planning had already devolved to local authorities. After Deng's reforms began, local officials used their knowledge and the fledgling industrial development across China to push for rapid industrialization of the countryside through a combination of tax breaks and enterprising schemes.

Labor was cheap—and plentiful. Three of every four Chinese toiled in the fields and could be redirected into industrial jobs and big, capital-intensive projects. In the Soviet Union, by contrast, industrialization was largely complete when the Soviet empire collapsed, leaving 75% of workers scrambling for hard-to-find jobs in new sectors of the economy.

Chinese cities such as Shenzhen, the first of the special economic zones, mushroomed with activity.

Shiny new skyscrapers now rise from a robust manufacturing base. Millions of Barbie dolls roll off assembly lines into the eager hands of children worldwide. The population of Shenzhen, a onetime fishing village with 30,000 inhabitants across from the Hong Kong border, skyrocketed a hundredfold to 3 million.

Traders work the Shenzhen stock market. This year, foreign investment through July totaled an impressive $1.6 billion.

Much of the investment in Shenzhen and throughout the rest of China comes from a natural resource that Russia does not have: the ethnic Chinese around the world who still feel strong ties with "the motherland" and who have become one of China's primary engines for growth.

Whereas the Soviet Union splintered along nationalist and ethnic lines after its breakup, overseas Chinese, about 55 million in all, have remained remarkably unified through their common cultural heritage across boundaries of state and time.

"Hong Kong, Taiwan, Singapore and the Chinese diaspora in South [and] East Asia and North America are filled with ethnic Chinese entrepreneurs who have proved to be valuable sources of knowledge and investment and who have served as important bridges to the world economy," Andrew G. Walder, sociologist and specialist in China market reforms at Stanford University, observed in the China Quarterly magazine.

Amazingly, between 75% and 80% of all foreign investment in China (including money from Hong Kong) comes out of the pockets of ethnic Chinese across the globe, whose ranks boasted three dozen billionaires in East Asia in 1994.

Although the regional financial crisis has pinched some of the capital flow from the outside, economists say that money keeps pouring in at a fast clip.

In addition to abundant foreign investment, a comparatively low foreign debt—thanks to Mao's insistence on national self-sufficiency—has been crucial to China's revival as one of the world's major economies.

In stark contrast to Russia, China has not had to resort to crushing bailout packages by the International Monetary Fund to shore up its economy. While the government is struggling to keep expenditures in check as central tax revenue dwindles, Beijing does not need to devote huge resources to servicing short-term foreign debt; 80% of its debt is long-term, according to Hu Biliang, a senior economist with a French securities firm here.

Moscow, meanwhile, has buckled under the weight of $31.2 billion in IMF cash since 1992. And those loans have invariably come with political strings attached, reflecting one of the widest and most important divergences between China and Russia on the way to the free market: their different political systems.

For Russia, economic reform has gone hand in hand with political restructuring. At about the same time that Moscow relinquished its stranglehold on the economy, the Russian people also flung off the totalitarian Communist regime in one violent shudder.

Since then, prescriptions for a free market have been intertwined with efforts to build a free society. Economic shock treatment and the massive unloading of nationalized industries in Russia are bound up with ending the political monopoly of the Communist Party and building a raucous, but functional democracy.

Beijing, on the other hand, represents the last great bastion of Communist control, a one-party dictatorship that oversees one-fifth of humanity. Its authoritarian rule has greatly loosened over the last two decades—some detect the signs of a civil society emerging—but the one-party Communist regime remains China's government.

As such, China's leaders can still rule by fiat, pushing through relatively unpopular measures when necessary, although the regime is careful not to push too hard lest it provoke a popular uprising such as the 1989 Tiananmen Square demonstrations. Even the ensuing massacre that year put only a temporary crimp in the economy, which flagged until Deng launched a "southern tour" of China in 1992 to jump-start greater economic liberalization.

Now many Chinese appear content to ignore the government so long as it allows some personal freedom, such as easier internal movement within China, and the liberty to pursue a higher living standard.

Beijing knows its legitimacy increasingly rests on its handling of the economy, and it has tried to help its citizens discover the truth of Deng's famous maxim: "To get rich is glorious." China's leaders are hoping that an economic overhaul is enough, without knitting it together with a political one, as happened in the former Soviet bloc.

"Where in Eastern Europe [economic] shock therapy and mass privatization are designed in part to dismantle communism and strip former Communists of power and privilege," Walder wrote, "in China gradual reform is intended to allow the party to survive as an instrument of economic development."

As a multi-party state, Russia is now full of vested interests jockeying for position. Politicians, elected by popular vote, must cater to them to stay in power.

The result has been a crony capitalism and democracy stage-managed by a handful of "oligarchs" behind the scenes, who have gobbled up the wealth and used it to wrest favors from Moscow.

So far, China has stayed largely immune to such stresses. But it has spawned a crony capitalism of its own that threatens the stability that the government is obsessed with maintaining.

Among those who have enriched themselves the most from Beijing's market reforms are not the *laobaixing*, or common people, but the families of high officials, who have used their connections to gain control of some of the most lucrative businesses in China.

Indeed, such corruption was one of the main grievances that drove the *laobaixing* to Tiananmen Square in 1989, marching for an end to Communist Party privilege and nepotism.

## Fighting Corruption

The issue still ranks as China's No. 1 public beef. Frustrated locals and foreigners alike complain that preferential treatment for party "princelings" or through money passed under the table kills competition and undermines their ability to do honest business.

The Asian financial crisis has put enormous pressure on the government as exports have slowed and the economy tightens. Production surpluses in industries such as steel sit untouched in huge stockpiles. Devastating flooding across China has made government promises of an 8% economic growth rate this year ring hollow.

Unemployment, officially at 3.5% but probably higher, is rising as local authorities eagerly shed their small and medium-sized state-owned enterprises at a speed the government was evidently not prepared for. In some cases, the enterprises were sold for pennies on the dollar to friends and relatives of local officials, though not on the scale of the "false" privatization in Russia that concentrated assets in just a few hands, analysts say.

"There are as yet no media moguls like [Boris] Berezovsky or energy czars like [Viktor] Chernomyrdin, but localities are seething with resentment against those who appropriated local collective enterprises over the past five to 10 years," said Douglas Paal, president of the Asia Pacific Policy Center in Washington and former National Security Council senior staffer under Presidents Reagan and Bush.

Last month, in a sign of growing alarm, the Communist regime issued an official editorial calling for a halt to "blind selling of state-owned firms."

"Leaders in some localities have simplified these serious and complicated reforms, and have taken them to mean merely selling such enterprises," the New China News Agency said. Local authorities should "carefully study" the proper guidelines regulating such sales, it added.

With joblessness on the rise, Beijing has backed off from ambitious plans to make residents buy their own homes and to slash China's bureaucracy in half, a potential loss of 4 million jobs.

Worker protests have already broken out, from Sichuan province in central China to Heilongjiang in the northeast, but are not reported in the official media.

These days, no one is willing to write off China as a potential economic success story, but pessimism hangs in the air among economists and some citizens here over the current state of China's gradual, multi-pronged reform program. It seems clear, however, that the Russian strategy is not an alternative.

"There probably are no panaceas in this world," said Harding. "Neither the Russian model nor the Chinese model is perfect. Or, as the cynic once said, 'The grass is brown on both sides of the fence.' "

# What a difference a year can make

Indians have escaped the worst of east Asia's economic storms during a period when the political mood at home and abroad has shifted. **Mark Nicholson** reports from New Delhi

By default and design in equal part, India's economic, political and strategic place in the world suddenly looks vastly different this year from last. Who, for example, would have forecast that India's likely growth rate this year of 5 per cent of GDP would make the country one of Asia's best economic performers? The relatively closed nature of India's previously straggling economy has helped it, so far, survive mostly unscathed the financial hurricanes which have ripped through other economies.

No one, likewise, correctly forecast that the Bharatiya Janata party, installed six months ago as the head of a fractious coalition government, would so suddenly and dramatically alter India's global strategic relations, as it did by detonating five nuclear test blasts in May and claiming status as a "nuclear weapons power".

The Hindu nationalist-led government, settling somewhat into the seat of power after a discomfiting and disappointing start, currently takes great heart from both altered relationships. "Suddenly," says Yashwant Sinha, finance minister, "there has been a feeling that India has not become part of the east Asian meltdown, and India is being perceived as a stable pole of economic development and progress in an environment which appears very difficult."

In its global relations, too, officials speak confidently of a "resurgent" India. "There is a new element, a new reality," says Brajesh Mishra, principal secretary to the prime minister and an architect of India's evolving post-nuclear foreign policy. "This is the nuclear status. Whether it is formally recognised or not doesn't matter. But it's having an impact on people."

There are, however, less partisan ways of viewing India's changed status. Though India can claim some credit for having weathered the Asian financial storm this is largely because its economy is still much less than fully open and has as much to do with India's lack of liberalisation and globalisation since reforms began seven years ago.

Moreover, disconcerting cracks have become apparent in the financial system.

As both the World Bank and International Monetary Fund have recently pointed out, there remains a long and politically tough list of reforms ahead before India can ever aspire to the rates of growth enjoyed across the rest of east Asia before the crisis—and to which many currently suffering Asian economies can hope to rebound. India's economy remains among the world's most highly regulated, state dominated and protected; export performance after seven years of reform remains dismal—India's share of world trade declined last year—and full convertibility on the capital account is a distant notion, under current circumstances more distant than ever.

Strategically, too, there are troubling questions. While Indian officials boast of a new foreign policy assertiveness and knock on the doors of the established nuclear club, others—including Japan, China and many western governments—worry that India's nuclear tests, and Pakistan's matching blasts, have destabilised south Asia, torn a hole in the global nuclear non-proliferation regime, and generally raised questions about the intended direction of Indian foreign policy.

On a recent visit to Delhi, Richard N. Haass, director of foreign policy studies at the Brookings Institution, argued that the Indian and Pakistani blasts had made south Asia considerably more dangerous and unstable—not a view widely aired in New Delhi. "The presence of nuclear weapons in the arsenals of India and Pakistan increases the danger that nuclear weapons would be used in any conflict," he said. And he noted that the south Asian standoff was vastly different from the Cold War.

chiefly because India and Pakistan sustain a low-level conflict over the border of Jammu and Kashmir, the Himalayan territory they dispute and over which they have already fought two wars.

At the UN General Assembly meeting last month, Atal Behari Vajpayee gave his clearest indication yet that India would eventually accede to the Comprehensive Test Ban Treaty, given successful negotiations—now into their sixth round—with the US. These talks with the US are, under close secrecy, apparently making some progress—though Delhi appears more optimistic about the pace of their success than Washington.

Whatever the immediate prospect for such talks, some believe they contain the kernel of a fundamental and possibly positive realignment of Indian foreign policy towards the more pragmatic from several decades of moral-based dealings with the outside world. The US-India talks, says C. Raja Mohan, a security and defence analyst, are perhaps the first true strategic dialogue with Washington since Indian independence and perhaps herald a maturing of bilateral Indo-US relations following several prickly decades.

Some analysts have also taken heart from the apparent warmth with which Mr Vajpayee and Nawaz Sharif, his Pakistani counterpart, undertook to resume a bilateral dialogue, one to include both security matters and the thorny issue of Kashmir. Such moves offered hope that the crisis inspired by India's nuclear blasts might, in fact, prove a foreign policy opportunity, though it remains very early days to be confident that Indo-Pakistani relations are indeed on a more even track.

On the home front, too, there are reasons for cheer. One is simply the likely longevity of the BJP-led coalition. Having manufactured an awkward and vulnerable parliamentary coalition of some 18 parties in March after India's indeterminate 12th post-independence election, the BJP weathered several months' threat to its survival under assault from its own allies.

The political squalls which have come to characterise India's increasingly fractured and federalising polity are, however, likely to continue. And while the opposition Congress party under Sonia Gandhi, who sprang from self-imposed reclusion to rescue party fortunes during the April elections, currently seems content to sit in opposition and concentrate on rebuilding, successes in a series of critical state elections in November could revive calls within the party for it to move against the BJP.

Also cheering has been the fact that the Hindu nationalist BJP has, by and large, refrained from promoting any of its more contentious and divisively religious-based policies. Restrained somewhat by its secular allies, there have been no significant moves from the leadership to revive debate over the disputed building of a Hindu temple at Ayodhya, where Hindu zealots sacked a mosque in 1992, nor over other perceived Hundu nationalist items on the party's agenda.

Even the party's economic nationalist policies of "swadeshi" (broadly, India for the Indians) have been muted. As Mr Sinha points out, no "negative list" of foreign investment has been drawn up and, in fact, foreign investment approvals have proceeded apace. The party has even drawn criticism from hard-line "swadeshi" affiliates for being too "pro-multinational".

Indeed, the nuclear adventure apart, it has been the economy which has chiefly exercised the government. After three successive years of growth averaging more than 7 per cent, the BJP inherited an economy which had slowed to around 5 per cent, seen exports slump to negative growth, and witnessed, in some key manufacturing sectors, something approaching outright recession.

The BJP's recipe was to increase protection for ailing domestic industry, "calibrate" further integration with the local economy and focus instead on deregulating domestically and offering a fiscal stimulus to the economy, largely through more spending on infrastructure and agriculture.

In addition, the government promised a sea change in public sector reform, saying it would in most cases reduce government holdings in public enterprises to 26 per cent, identifying Air India as an early candidate for sale, while promising to push through a host of share offerings and strategic sales of state assets. For the first time since India embarked on reforms, its government now speaks out loud about "privatisation" rather than just "disinvestment".

Should Mr Sinha and his reformist finance secretary, Vijay Kelkar, succeed in giving this programme momentum, it could stand as the BJP's most significant contribution to India's continuingly cautious reform programme.

Whether Mr Sinhja's policies can boost growth this year to his target of 6.5 per cent—a figure doubted by most private economists—is one thing. Whether India can start comparing itself proudly with the currently wounded economies to its east is, however, quite another.

Though the World Bank and IMF have, in their recent reviews of the Indian economy, grown more muted on the need for faster global opening of the economy, both have highlighted the crippling effects of India's stubbornly high fiscal deficits and the need for concerted and politically tough action to contain them.

Added together, the combined deficits of centre and states now sits at over 9 per cent of GDP, a level which western economists say will be tough even to sustain without serious efforts to reform the public sector, increase India's slim tax base, restructure government spending and attack subsidies. Failure to do so, said the IMF, threatened "heavy costs" to future growth.

The measure of India's current economic performance, therefore, is perhaps not relative to this or next year's rates of growth in Thailand or South Korea but to the sustained 7, 8 or 9 per cent rates needed to make inroads into India's still deep and widespread poverty. There remain serious questions about the current quality of India's growth, over the problems facing its creaking infrastructure, and its prospects for boosting export growth.

In a recent article in the Economic Times, Omkar Goswami, a leading economic commentator, warned against the "danger and absurdity" of Indian officials' "congratulatory talk" about the country having weathered the current economic storms. For India to reach the current levels of income per head even now enjoyed by a slumping Indonesia, he noted, would take 15 years of 7 per cent growth. It would take India 37 years of 7 per cent growth to reach the income level of a depressed Thailand, and 46 years to achieve Malaysia's current GDP per capita.

Mr Goswami reckoned India might enjoy at best six months of being Asia's "stable economic pole", as Mr Sinha puts it. He recommended six months of reform at "blistering pace" to take advantage. There are so far few signs of that.

# ASIAN VALUES REVISITED

# What would Confucius say now?

**SINGAPORE**

**Asian values did not explain the tigers' astonishing economic successes, and they do not explain their astonishing economic failures**

MAYBE the cycles of intellectual fashion are speeding up. Just 20 years ago, Chinese communists and many western historians alike blamed the set of moral teachings and social mores known as Confucianism for China's backwardness. Despite its ancient civilisation and technological breakthroughs, it had been humbled in the 19th century by western barbarians, partly, it was argued, because of the Confucians' contempt for trade. Then, in the early 1990s, some Asians argued that those same intellectual and social traditions, now subsumed into a broader concept—Asian values, they were called—helped explain East Asia's remarkable economic success, and prepared the region for global dominance in what was to be the "Pacific century". The aftershocks from the region's economic earthquake of the past year now rumble through this debate. Those Asians—and some westerners—who argued that there was something inherently superior about Asia's social structures have been proven wrong. Indeed, the very values they touted have contributed to the collapse.

Or perhaps not. To believe that Asian values caused either miracle or crash is to accept two dubious premises: that there is a common core of distinctively Asian principles, and that this core has been accurately defined

by the most outspoken and articulate Asian participants in this debate, most of them from South-East Asia, notably Malaysia and Singapore.

According to Kishore Mahbubani, a Singaporean diplomat and writer, Asian values include "attachment to the family as an institution, deference to societal interests, thrift, conservatism in social mores, respect for authority". This list is not exhaustive. Indeed, Asians are also said to prize consensus over confrontation, and to emphasise the importance of education. Put together, these values are held to justify regimes which, to the West, look illiberal. Invoking Asian values, authoritarian governments are said only to be providing their people with what they want. While they delivered unprecedented economic success, the claim was taken seriously.

Asians moved off the back foot, and on to the offensive. Westerners, they argued, had confused ideas rooted in their own traditions—about individual freedom and liberal democracy—with universal truths. Asians, however, stick to eternal verities forgotten by western countries in their headlong pursuit of individualism, and their descent into a morass of broken families, drug-taking, promiscuity, mud-slinging and violence. In 1996, after the first Asia-Europe summit, Malaysia's prime minister made the bold assertion

"Asian values are universal values. European values are European values."

So it appears both that there is something different about Asian values, and that they, unlike western ones, are somehow "universal". The picture is further muddied by occasional suggestions that these values change with time, but are appropriate for Asia's present stage of economic development, just as "Victorian values" suited 19th-century Britain. But Asians, broadly defined, make up more than 60% of the world's population. Any attempt to distil essential, but non-universal, beliefs across such a huge swathe of humanity is ambitious to say the least. And in practice, the debate has concentrated on East Asia, largely ignoring South Asia, except in negative comparisons sometimes drawn between India's rumbustious democracy and its relatively poor economic performance on the one hand, and the tough but successful systems to the east on the other.

Even in East Asia, talking of a single set of values involves blending many of the world's intellectual traditions—Confucianism, Buddhism and Islam, to name but three. However, it was not in doubt that the region had produced many authoritarian regimes and, until last year, some fantastic rates of economic growth. First, Tai-

# The sage, 2,549 years on

FOR most of the 25 centuries since Confucius was alive, scholars have been debating what he was on about. As with any influential thinker, people tend to pick and choose which elements of his ideas most appeal. In recent years, he has been cited favourably by those on both sides of the debate about Asian values.

The only (nearly) direct source of Confucius's thoughts is "The Analects", a collection of his *obiter dicta* compiled by disciples after his death. It is more of a scrap-book than a thesis. Its classical Chinese is terse and elliptical. Some of it is hard to interpret. Indeed, some passages are understood in diametrically opposed ways by different scholars.

Confucius lived at a time when the old feudal order had disintegrated into warring satrapies. His advice to the rulers he sought to influence reflected a conservative hankering for the old rituals, the old certainties and the old stability. Modern exponents of Asian values like to stress his emphasis on "filial piety", scholarship and meritocracy.

But others point out that "the rectification of names" (a son should behave like a son, a subject like a subject) was a two-way street: fathers and rulers also had obligations. In this sense, argues Simon Leys in a recent book*, "Confucius was certainly not a Confucianist... More essential notions were conveniently ignored [by him]—such as the precepts of social justice, political dissent, and the moral duty for intellectuals to criticise the ruler." Confucius believed in a loyal opposition. Asked how to serve a prince, he replied: "Tell him the truth even if it offends him."

---

* "The Analects of Confucius, Translation and Notes" by Simon Leys. W.W. Norton, New York, 1997.

Lee Kuan Yew, Singapore's senior minister, is accepted even in China as a great Confucianist: he spoke at a big conference in China in 1994 to celebrate the 2,545th anniversary of the great man's birth. But others use the sage's words to argue a different line from Mr Lee's. Malaysia's Anwar Ibrahim, for example, cites Confucius to denounce the idea that "the state must always precede the individual". Another scholar argues that Mr Lee's policies owe less to Confucianism than to the rival Chinese tradition of "legalism". A Confucian state, he says, would not need to pass a law, as Singapore has done, requiring children to look after elderly parents.

The legalists were famous for laying the intellectual basis for the rule, through strict laws, of China's first emperor, Qinshi Huangdi—he of the terracotta warriors, the Great Wall, the burning of books and the burial alive of Confucianists. Nowadays, legalism, mercifully, takes milder forms.

---

wan, South Korea, Hong Kong (all of which industrialised before they democratised) and Singapore; and then China, Indonesia, Malaysia and Vietnam.

But now some of the sins laid at the doors of the region's economic systems look suspiciously like Asian values gone wrong. The attachment to the family becomes nepotism. The importance of personal relationships rather than formal legality becomes cronyism. Consensus becomes wheel-greasing and corrupt politics. Conservatism and respect for authority become rigidity and an inability to innovate. Much-vaunted educational achievements become rote-learning and a refusal to question those in authority.

Goenawan Mohamad, an Indonesian writer, tells a story of his country during President Suharto's last months in office. A young journalist came across some traffic policemen engaged in the odd pursuit of drying out banknotes at the roadside. On inquiry, it emerged the money came from bribes routinely paid by bus and lorry drivers. To shorten procedures, they stuffed the cash in cigarette packs and threw them from their cab windows. The banknotes were wet because first they would spit on them.

It is a tale of petty, futile yet rebellious compliance that could be told of many corrupt and arbitrary regimes in the world. Yet it casts doubt on the proposition that Asians have a greater respect for authority—however exercised—than do westerners, as does other evidence. In the past 12 years, the region has seen a series of mass protests: in the Philippines in 1986, South Korea in 1987, Myanmar in 1988, China in 1989, Taiwan in 1990, Thailand in 1992, Indonesia in 1998. Some of these popular protests were manipulated by factions among the elite, but that was possible only because of the large pool of disaffection to draw on. Their success or failure depended, ultimately, not on the inherent support enjoyed by the government, but on the willingness (as in China), or otherwise (as in the Philippines) of the army to shoot civilians.

Nor is such protest just a phenomenon of a "westernised" middle class. In 1990, even the people of Myanmar, among the world's poorest, voted decisively against the military junta and for the party of the western-educated, "liberal" Aung San Suu Kyi. In 1993, the benighted, long-suffering people of Cambodia also voted against the established powers-that-be and, despite threats of intimidation and threats of violence, may do so again in the general election to be held there on July 26th.

Nor do Asia's intellectuals and politicians come close to unanimity about the notion of Asian values propagated by the concept's leading promoters, Lee Kuan Yew, Singapore's senior minister, and Mahathir Mohamad, the prime minister of Malaysia. Among the many Asians who have argued that "human rights" and "freedom" are universally held aspirations are Miss Suu Kyi, Kim Dae Jung, the veteran campaigner for democracy elected in December as president of South Korea, and Wei Jingsheng, a well-known dissident expelled from China. In apparent defiance of his boss, Malaysia's deputy prime minister, Anwar Ibrahim, claims that "no Asian tradition can be cited to support the proposition that in Asia the individual must melt into a faceless community."

The argument about Asian values is usually presented as an intellectual joust between Asia and the West. But it is probably more important as a political debate going on in Asia itself both among leaders (like Mr Anwar and Dr Mahathir) and between governments and their opponents. It is notable that so much of it is conducted in—or with—Singapore. Singapore is the youngest, richest, smallest (Brunei aside) and most westernised country in South-East Asia. No other is so dependent on international trade and investment from multinational companies, giving it, you might have thought, an incentive to pipe down a bit.

Mr Mahbubani explains Singapore's assertiveness as in part shrugging off a colonial chip—"an effort to define [Asians'] own personal and national identities in a way that enhances their sense of self-esteem where their immediate ancestors had subconsciously accepted that they were lesser beings in a western universe." But that explains only national values, not Asian ones. Tommy Koh, another Singaporean diplomat and Asian-values theorist, says he once asked one of his Japanese colleagues why they were so quiet in this debate. "We're more Asian than you," was the reply. It meant, apparently, that the Japanese were less confrontational. Another interpretation is that they are surer of their identity and place in the world.

A multi-media exhibition currently running in Singapore is part of a recent effort to foster an understanding of the island's history. The visitors sit on a mobile "people carrier" which transports them through a series of tableaux designed as a "journey through time", from the arrival of Britain's Sir Stamford Raffles in 1819 to the glorious, three-dimensional (special glasses are provided) but "challenging" future. There are gory pictures of past communal riots, and an explanation of how vulnerable Singapore felt after its expulsion from federation with Malaysia in 1965. Singapore itself is an accident of history in a dangerous part of the world. Complacent young Singaporeans, the display suggests, could do with some of their elders' edginess, as well as a commitment to a "shared pledge" beginning "Nation before community and society above self".

## The internal stresses

In spreading that message across the region, other factors may have come into play, such as the desire to seek a shared view of the world with countries which in the past have been hostile. Singapore, a small and mostly Chinese island surrounded by largely Muslim Malaysia and Indonesia, hopes that its neighbours, seeking an alter-

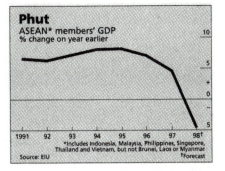

**Phut**
ASEAN* members' GDP
% change on year earlier

1991  92  93  94  95  96  97  98†

*Includes Indonesia, Malaysia, Philippines, Singapore, Thailand and Vietnam, but not Brunei, Laos or Myanmar
Source: EIU          †Forecast

native to wholesale westernisation, will not veer towards more extreme forms of Islam; Mr Anwar in Malaysia, and B.J. Habibie, Indonesia's new president, evoke some alarm—not so much because both seem to have rather "liberal" views, but because in both their backgrounds is a link with Islamic groups. The recent orchestrated rape and murder of ethnic Chinese in Indonesia's riots is a grim enough reminder of the lingering dangers of ethnic and religious antipathies as economic hardships worsen.

Asia has rarely been without intraregional tension, and much less in any sense united. Indeed Asia itself is a western concept: the Chinese word for it, *Yazhou*, is a coinage translating a foreign notion. Even South-East Asia is a remarkably diverse and potentially fractious region. The assertion of Asian values partly represents a desire to increase regional cohesion, both to ease tensions between the countries of the region, and to put on weight internationally. Whereas, say, the European Union is a collection of largely Christian, democratic countries, the regional club, the Association of South-East Asian Nations, includes communist states (Vietnam and Laos), a military dictatorship (Myanmar), an "Islamic monarchy" (Brunei) and parliamentary democracies of varying sorts. ASEAN has countries with Buddhist, Muslim and Christian majorities. Hinduism from India and Confucianism from China have left deep imprints. So have periods of Dutch, British, Spanish, French, German, Portuguese, American and Japanese rule.

There is nothing wrong in seeking some common ground in such diverse terrain, especially given the instability and mutual hostility that until recently marked intraregional relations. But, to quote Mr Anwar again, "It is altogether shameful, if ingenious, to cite Asian values as an excuse for autocratic practices and denial of basic rights and liberties." That, neverthe-

less, is what many Asians believe has happened.

## Don't interfere

The debate may seem to be over. It is not. Both Mr Mahbubani and Mr Koh have this year produced books* collecting their essays. But the discussion is now taking rather different forms. One will be felt at the meetings that begin this week in Manila, among ASEAN's foreign ministers and later with their foreign partners in the security talking-shop, the ASEAN Regional Forum. Since its foundation in 1967, ASEAN's most fundamental policy has been "non-interference" in its neighbours' affairs. This, "the ASEAN way", applied Asian values—even before the term was coined—of consensus and non-confrontation to diplomacy. But in the past two years it has been under threat.

The admission of Myanmar to ASEAN a year ago has created trouble in the group's relations with Europe and America. Without an effective mechanism for telling Myanmar its behaviour is unacceptable, ASEAN is powerless to resolve the dispute. Similarly, the contagious effect of the region's financial turmoil has shown how vulnerable members are to their neighbours' policy mistakes. But, without "interfering", it is hard to exert influence. Thailand and the Philippines have argued for a new policy of "flexible engagement" among members. This is unlikely to overcome the objections of Indonesia and Malaysia, let alone ASEAN's newer recruits, like Vietnam and Myanmar, which would resent any attempt by such a convivial club wanting to change its rules so soon after they have joined.

Nor has economic collapse led to a sudden rush to embrace liberal democracy, although it has entrenched democratic change in some countries. Only in South Korea, with the once-imprisoned Mr Kim now president, is a former inmate running the asylum. Thailand has adopted a constitution that should lead to a more representative, less corrupt, form of democracy, and the economic mess encouraged Fidel Ramos in the Philippines not to try to amend the constitution last year and run for a second term as president. Mr Habibie is introducing liberal reforms in Indonesia. Some of the in-

---

* "Can Asians Think?" by Kishore Mahbubani. Times Books International, Singapore.
"The Quest for World Order" by Tommy Koh. Federal Publications, Singapore.

tellectuals advising him have long taken issue with what they call "the Singapore school" of Asian values, as have some of those close to Mr Anwar. But the country's political future remains beholden to the army.

And in Singapore and Malaysia, the proponents of Asian values are unrepentant. Dr Mahathir continues to rail against decadent western liberals. This week he accused the opposition leader, Lim Kit Siang, of simply mouthing any criticism he found in the foreign press. Two newspaper editors have resigned because, many believe, their loyalty to the prime minister is less than wholehearted. In Singapore, there is not much opposition left. Two leading government critics, Chee Soon Juan and Tang Liang Hong, who have lost lawsuits brought by the government, are in Australia. A third, J.B. Jeyaretnam, recently saw the court of appeal increase fivefold the damages awarded

to the prime minister by a lower court in another defamation suit. If the judgment is enforced, he will be bankrupted and lose his seat in Parliament.

Elsewhere—especially in the worst afflicted economies, Thailand, and Indonesia—there remains a big risk of an anti-western backlash, as people lose their jobs, see foreigners buy up local companies, and generally force tough policies on weakened national governments. The next time the Asian-values debate flares up, it may be in a new guise, concentrating not so much on individual freedom and human rights, and whether or not they are universal, but on the global financial system and its dominance by the West. Now is not the time for westerners to crow about their superior ways. Such triumphalism has, in fact, been rather muted. Yet noting how some western commentators have reacted to the disaster, Mr Mahbubani's book argues that "the desire to bury Asian values revealed the real pain" inflicted during the debate.

Yet that pain was felt not just by smug westerners whose ingrained sense of superiority was challenged. It was shared by Asians who believed their values were being misrepresented, and their traditions selectively culled to justify policies. In Asia, as everywhere, there is disagreement about which traditions are worth preserving and nurturing. South-East Asia, for example, with its history of maritime trade, has in some ways an admirable record of tolerance and openness to foreign influence. The urge to avoid wholesale westernisation is understandable. But it need not mimic former colonial prejudices about the ineffable otherness of the East. Dr Mahathir was right: Asian values are universal values. But he should have added, vice versa.

"It is evident that the reemergence of global finance on a scale last seen at the end of the nineteenth century, in combination with late-twentieth-century technology and communications, is a volatile mix that wrenches governments and populations alike ... The political question is whether people want their fates to be determined so thoroughly, randomly, suddenly, and irrationally by the controllers of mobile capital."

# Asia and the "Magic" of the Marketplace

JEFFREY A. WINTERS

To make sense of the crisis that began in Asia in 1997, it is crucial to consider where the ravages of economic destabilization hit hardest and where they were felt much less severely. Why were such varied countries as Indonesia, South Korea, Thailand, and Malaysia badly damaged, while such equally varied cases as Singapore, Vietnam, the Philippines, Taiwan, and China punched and bruised but not knocked to the ground?

The answer lies in systemic changes in international capitalism: specifically the control of capital flows to developing countries, and the growing prominence of highly mobile and volatile forms of capital and transactions. It is clear that the vulnerability of a country varies with the nature of its linkages and exposure to external capital flows, which can change course more rapidly than ever before and on a scale that can easily overwhelm all but a few economies. Like a huge electrical grid, as the current in the system grows more unstable and potentially dangerous, it matters first the degree to which

JEFFREY A. WINTERS, *a* Current History *contributing editor, is an associate professor in the department of politics at Northwestern University. He is the author of* Power in Motion: Capital Mobility and the Indonesian State *(Ithaca, N.Y: Cornell University Press, 1996).*

one is plugged in and second, whether surge protectors are in place to dampen the effects of massive fluctuations.

No country in Asia has been untouched by the destabilizing economic impact of the crisis. All have seen exports hurt, stock market capitalizations reduced, rates of foreign investment slowed, and currency values eroded. But where the crisis began, which countries were pulled in quickly and deeply, and where the devastation has been greatest has depended on how exposed a country was to the external financial system.

The key considerations were the convertibility of currency; the existence, size, and international exposure of capital markets; the degree of private foreign borrowing by local corporations; the share of this borrowing that was short-term; and the ease with which currency traders could raise local credit to launch an attack on a national currency. These factors were more important than the economic fundamentals of the countries in question, their degree of crony capitalism, or even whether governments were resolute and skilled in adopting policies to dampen the crisis once it began to spread throughout the region—although policy responses have certainly had an impact over the medium term after the crisis moved through different phases.

There are three aspects of the crisis that are especially surprising. The first is that a region everyone believed was so strong could stumble and crumble so rapidly. The second is that so many countries could get swept simultaneously into a crisis. And the third is that the crisis has remained so deep and durable, despite domestic and international efforts to restore stability and confidence, including some $120 billion in rescue packages sponsored by the International Monetary Fund (IMF). Indeed, what began in Thailand, Malaysia, and Indonesia soon spread to South Korea, shook Hong Kong, and threatened China and Japan. These crises caused ripple effects that disrupted the capital markets of Europe and North America, with graphs of the daily fluctuations on the New York Stock Exchange resembling the brain waves of a patient caught in a nightmare.

## UNDERSTANDING THE CONTEXT

"In nearly every economic crisis, the root cause is political, not economic," concluded Singapore's senior minister, Lee Kuan Yew, in an address to leading American businesspeople at the Fortune 500 Forum in Boston last year. Lee did not mean political in the same sense as Malaysian Prime Minister Mahathir Mohamad, who blamed the crisis on an international conspiracy of Jews who, he implied, were upset to see Muslims prosper economically (a view that is not only odious but odd, since the crisis began in Thailand). Lee meant that the behaviors of economic actors are a response to prior government decisions and policies. Governments oversee and enforce the context in which economic activity unfolds; their policies create the opportunities and set the rules. They can also produce the kind of time bomb that exploded in Southeast Asia at the beginning of July 1997. This is because the interaction between government and economy does not stop with the context created by governments. Economic actors react according to their own interests, and in the 1990s they do so in an increasingly connected transnational environment.

Thus, the Asian crisis is not just the result of government policies, but specifically how they interact in an international environment dominated by private controllers of capital who are willing and able to relocate massive resources away from perceived danger in a very short time frame—and are not necessarily willing to bring them back as quickly as they withdrew them. Significantly, once this process starts, it does not matter if the danger is real or perceived. This suggests important lessons regarding transparency and information.

When the stakes are high, information is crucial. Investors operate well with *risk*, by which probabilities of different outcomes can be calculated. They do not operate well with *uncertainty*, which means the absence of quality information on which to base investment decisions. Transparency transforms uncertainty into risk. In the world of Asian business, transparency means bringing into public view much more information about who is doing what; who owns what; who is borrowing, from where, how much, for what; and how well everyone is doing (including the government itself), as well as who is being bailed out, protected, and subsidized, and at whose expense.

These questions strike at the heart of power relations across Asia. Failing to answer them satisfactorily over extended periods, which was the norm during the cold war, is no longer a viable option. Indeed, as hidden information about the economies of Southeast Asia seeped out in July 1997, it triggered an escape psychology among private capital controllers that by November had erased some $400 billion of value from the region's capital markets (measured from the beginning of 1997). All the economies in the region saw their growth slow in 1998, and several went into recessions and contractions that are projected to continue into 1999. Along the way billions of dollars in production and hundreds of millions of jobs are being lost. According to estimates in October 1998, since the crisis began, $1 trillion in loans had gone bad, $2 trillion in equity capitalization for Asian stock markets had been vaporized, and $3 trillion in GDP growth had been lost.

It is also important to note that even if analysts or policymakers can successfully diagnose the superficial and deep causes of crises, it is not obvious what policies will create stability. Even the Mexico crisis of 1994 and 1995 provides few clear parallels and lessons for dealing with the disaster that has spread like wildfire across Asia. It appears that many policymakers in the region, together with powerful international institutions like the IMF, took actions that were tailored more to standard balance of payments difficulties than to the kind of crisis that hit Asia. As they groped for a policy combination that worked, their actions sometimes helped deepen and prolong the crisis.

Finally, any analysis of the crisis and the responses to it (including one that strongly emphasizes external factors, as I do here) must be linked analytically to the struggles over power within the governments of the region. For instance, one consequence of the close arrangement in Southeast Asia between the state and its clients in business and politics is that there is a built-in tendency for economic reformers in government, who are marginalized from power in normal times, to seize moments of crisis as a window of opportunity to ram through as many fundamental changes in the domestic political economy as possible. Some of these policies may help address the immediate crisis, but just as often they extend it. Far from being a rational, methodical, planned, phased, or integrated set of policies to stabilize the economy and set it on a more prosperous course, the actions of frustrated reformers are sometimes driven by a desire simply to make as many sweeping changes as possible before the window closes and power swings back to those who traditionally enjoy it during the interim between crises.

This is of interest for three reasons. First, it helps explain why seemingly useful and even crisis-averting policies are delayed so long, as well as why reforms tend to be introduced in wrenching packages that only make sense as acts of desperation. Second, it suggests a twisted relationship between economic crises and the power of economic reformers in clientelist Asian states: crises sharply increase the influence of reformers, but once solved, often result in an equally sharp decrease in reformers' influence. And third, it provides an important reminder that despite nationalist public statements and

# SURGE PROTECTORS IN PLACE?

INDONESIA, MALAYSIA, SOUTH KOREA, AND THAILAND were decidedly more exposed to the crisis than Taiwan, where smaller-scale firms attracted very little foreign debt, the turnover in foreign exchange markets was only $150 million to $200 million daily (with banks limited in lending local currency for foreign exchange dealings), and where currency markets with a low volume of trade prevented hedge fund speculators from gaining a toehold for attack. Foreign investment in stocks could be withdrawn from the island, though in most instances only under a variety of restrictions.

The Philippines was also less exposed because it had the good luck of only recently having reappeared on the radar screen of international financial interests. Unlike their counterparts in neighboring countries, Filipino companies had neither the credit rating not the lure of a vibrant economy to attract billions in foreign bank credits that could be deployed at home in various speculative assets.

Singapore also escaped because gross national savings routinely exceeded investment, thus allowing corporate investment capital to be drawn overwhelmingly from local rather than external funds or retained earnings. Large foreign reserves enabled Singapore to beat back most attacks on its currency, and the country has enjoyed one of the smallest currency depreciations in the region.

One of the least exposed countries in the region was Vietnam. It was shielded because it had a nonconvertible currency, capital markets still only in the early planning stage in 1997, and foreign debt that consisted mostly of medium- and long-term bilateral and multilateral loans extended to the government and state-owned firms. Private firms were few in number, small-scale, and had not enjoyed much success in attracting private foreign credit. The banking sector was dominated by state banks, and borrowing from foreign private banks was limited and highly controlled.

*J.A.W.*

posturing, economic ministers often use the conditions imposed by international agencies like the IMF for maximum advantage in their intragovernmental and domestic struggles. This was especially true in Indonesia, where ministers responsible for the economy insisted on including many policy changes and reforms as conditions for the IMF bailout that the fund had not demanded but for which it was later criticized. Thus, those who would cast the conflict as pitting foreign versus domestic forces miss one of the most important political dimensions of the crisis.

## PHASE ONE: THE ONSET

The first public indication of problems in Southeast Asia came on July 2,1997, when Thailand announced that its currency, the baht, would be floated. To the casual observer this was a curious development, but hardly worth more attention than the thousands of other facts filling the newspapers that day. But to individuals controlling huge pools of investment

resources in Southeast Asia, this was a flashing red light signaling danger for the whole region. Within weeks, the Indonesian government also floated its currency the rupiah—yet another stunning announcement for investors, both local and global, whose entire game plan for Southeast Asia was founded on stable exchange rates pegged to the United States dollar. It was in this moment that the liberalization of investment flows into and out of developing countries made its impact felt with a vengeance. It was also the moment when the latent vulnerabilities linked to high external exposure, especially to private and short-term bank debt, became explosive.

The already thin economic analysis by most capital controllers prior to these announcements was soon replaced by a pure psychology of escape. All controllers of liquid capital, including domestic actors, began behaving like spooked wildebeests on the Serengeti. Frustrated policymakers, economists, and even managers and analysts at major institutional investing firms tried desperately to break the grip of the escape syndrome by pointing out that, despite some obvious and even deep problems with the political economies of Southeast Asia, the region's economic fundamentals simply did not warrant such a mass exodus. But when the managers and analysts were done talking to reporters, most of them went back to their terminals and phones and rejoined those selling shares and local currency because they knew that words of assurance would not be enough to stop the stampede.

In the weeks and months that followed, several countries in Southeast Asia endured devaluations in their currencies averaging over 50 percent and declines in local stock markets that were even higher. Millions of workers and managers were fired from companies that either went bankrupt or had to scale back operations because economic growth rates were suddenly much lower, imported components were much more expensive, or major government projects were postponed or canceled. At the epicenter of the crisis were the region's ailing banking and property sectors, which only grew more unstable as the crisis deepened.

If it is true that there were serious underlying problems in the political economies of Southeast Asia, then why did the crisis not occur six, twelve, or even eighteen months earlier? All the problems confronting the region's economies—weak banks, wasteful and nonproductive investment, overbuilding in the property sector, excessive borrowing by private sector firms, and speculation in local stock markets with borrowed funds—had been chronic for years. Part of the answer is that it took time for these trends to mature and converge in the right (or wrong) mix. But part of the answer also concerns information (or the lack of it), a psychology among investors that inflates an economic bubble, and a triggering moment that causes the bubble to burst.

That moment came when currency traders, suspecting that Thailand's economic situation was much worse than investors thought, were proved correct. The day was July 2, when policymakers in the Thai government, who had spent a staggering $23 billion buying baht in a vain attempt to maintain the dollar peg, gave up their defensive effort because they realized that they would run out of foreign exchange reserves long before there would be any good economic news to report about the country's property and banking sector. Only an immediate, genuine, and reliable upturn in the health of the economy could have stopped the pressure from the currency traders (by causing them to lose large amounts of money for betting the news would be bad). And given the realities in the Thai economy, there would be no such upturn.

It would be incorrect to draw the simple conclusion that the big problem was the peg to the dollar. It was a smart thing to do and worked rather well as long as the dollar was weak. Pegged currencies gave Thai and other regional exporters a competitive edge, especially against producers based in Japan. This, in turn, generated high growth, which attracted capital and helped strengthen the belief—some would say hype—that the economies of Southeast Asia would sustain high growth rates indefinitely. Those who pointed to serious and growing problems in the region's economies were shouted down by others who responded that the countries would grow their way out of the bottlenecks they faced, be they national debt, balance of payments problems, insolvent banks, or oversupplies in office space and expensive residential property.[1] Between 1990 and 1995, when the dollar was weak and exports were still booming, Thailand ran current account deficits of 7.7 percent of GDP, a level that normally signals serious problems to investors, rating agencies like Moody's Investors Service and Standard and Poor's, and such watchdog institutions as the World Bank and IMF. But no one seemed to care and no alarm bells were rung.

*Most of the portfolio capital supplied to developing countries ends up in the hands of just 100 extremely important [fund managers.]*

When the dollar appreciated in value, the peg went from being a blessing to a curse as Thailand's exports became relatively more expensive. At the same time, there was a global slowdown in key Southeast Asian exports, especially electronics. China's massive devaluation in 1994 played a central role in the slowdown, since Chinese exports undercut exports of similar products from Southeast Asia. By the first quarter of 1997 it was clear that private Thai companies, encouraged by the stable exchange rate, were running up their short-term debts even more aggressively by borrowing tens of billions of dollars from foreign commercial banks.

Currency traders were the first to notice the sharp rise in Thailand's current account deficit. And since most currency traders are based at commercial banks, they were also the first to notice the surge in Thai businesses' and financial institutions' borrowing of large amounts of dollars with relatively short maturities. The final blow came in the spring of 1997 when, against the advice of local and foreign economists who were already worried that Thailand was sitting on a bubble, five new banking licenses were issued to individuals with

strong government connections. It was at this point that currency traders became convinced that Thailand was in trouble, and began to bet with their resources that they were right.

## PHASE TWO: THE CHAIN REACTION

This story helps explain how Thailand got into trouble, and even how that trouble quickly pulled the country into a crisis. But why should a crisis in Thailand have triggered a chain reaction that not only pulled in other major countries in the region, but spread to distant and diverse areas of the globe? To understand this, the analysis must shift to an entirely different set of actors and forces.

The chain reaction was set in motion by currency traders and managers of large pools of portfolio capital who operate under intense competitive pressures. These pressures cause them to behave in a manner that is objectively irrational and destructive for the whole system (especially for the countries involved), but subjectively both rational and necessary for any hope of individual investor survival. Since an increasing proportion of private capital flowing to developing countries in the early 1990s was in the form of commercial loans and portfolio investments, meaning stocks, bonds, and other securities, countries across Southeast Asia moved rapidly to open up capital markets; selling shares is an important alternative to raising capital from commercial banks. But where does this capital originate and how does it reach the market?

The majority of capital invested in Southeast Asia's capital markets is owned and managed by local actors. But a substantial portion comes from many millions of private citizens from around the world. This money is gathered together in a variety of institutional forms, such as pension funds and mutual funds, which have management teams that decide where to invest the capital and how much to allocate.

It is through these large institutional investors that, collectively, tens of billions of dollars in portfolio capital get invested in the capital markets of developing countries. But there is still another stage in the system before the money reaches capital markets in areas such as Southeast Asia. Often even the largest institutional investors lack the staff and expertise to invest intelligently in emerging markets. To solve this problem, specialized mutual funds have arisen that are designed to invest in emerging markets. At the head of these funds are emerging market fund managers (EMFMS). It is the EMFMS who make the micro-level decisions about which countries and companies in emerging markets will receive the investments as purchases of shares in capital markets around the world. This structure for channeling investment capital produces what political economist Mary Ann Haley calls a precarious "funnel" effect. Hundreds of millions of independent investors and savers entrust

---

[1] Even MIT economist Paul Krugman's mild observation that as GDPs in Asia grew ever larger, annual growth rates on a much larger base would have to slow down, was dismissed as overly pessimistic.

their money to a much smaller number of institutional investors, who then entrust a portion of their capital to an even smaller number of EMFMS. The disturbing result is that most of the portfolio capital supplied to developing countries ends up in the hands of just 100 extremely important EMFMS.

Of course, EMFMS are paid handsomely for serving this specialized role as the eyes, ears, and decision makers for millions of people and their money. Justified or not, these individual investors (plus a range of institutional investors) expect that EMFMS will act prudently and responsibly with the capital under their control.[2] Yet even when they are behaving at their analytical best, there are still two major problems for EMFMS: the intense pressure they are under in a highly competitive environment to outperform all the other EMFMS, and the poor quality of information about the world's emerging markets.

It is the combination of these three elements—the funnel effect, intense competitive pressures, and bad information—along with currency traders and high short-term bank debt, that produced the explosive volatility and the chain reaction that has rocked Asia. Having severe problems in one's political economy is a necessary precondition for being vulnerable to the forces of this chain reaction. But it is not sufficient. China and Vietnam shared many of the same political economic pathologies of their Asian neighbors, and should have been swept into the crisis and felt its full disruptive force. But because neither country had a convertible currency and Vietnam lacked a capital market, the behavior of currency traders and EMFMS had a delayed and muted effect. Elsewhere, however, currency traders lost confidence, started betting local currencies would go down in value, and unloaded them en masse, thus commencing a self-fulfilling downward spiral that is exceedingly difficult for government officials with limited reserves and a convertible currency to counter. Meanwhile, EMFMS started selling shares across the region, and then beyond it. Entire banking and corporate sectors that had borrowed heavily in yen- and dollar-denominated currencies sank into immediate insolvency.

With profit-seeking and risk-averse private investors now in charge of most capital flows, displacing bureaucratically and politically motivated actors controlling official flows, the psychology, motivations, and volatility of these investors take on great significance. One of the least understood aspects of investments channeled through capital markets—or, indeed, bank deposits—is that the decision to invest, to keep the capital where it is, or to withdraw it is only partly based on the direct information the individual investor has about the quality, safety, and stability of the investment, whether it is in a coun-

try's capital market, a bank, or in an individual company. It is also based on what the investor believes other investors will do.

And so there is a paradox: even if there is no good reason to panic, the more individual controllers of money and capital act to protect themselves in times of uncertainty, the more genuine reason there is to panic. And the logic of the syndrome applies equally to foreign and domestic capital controllers. The chain reaction starts because once a major triggering event like the float of the Thai baht occurs, EMFMS realize that the positive (buy/bullish) psychology regarding other similar emerging markets—which is a very delicate bubble because it is rarely based on solid data and information—can burst and cause tremendous financial losses. A trigger like that seen in Thailand also causes EMFMS to ask tougher questions, look much more closely at the data on the economies in which they are invested, and demand better answers and immediate policy actions to prevent a loss of confidence. If the answers and policies are late or never come, the chain reaction continues and deepens as it widens. Once a crisis starts, it also has the effect of exposing weaknesses in an economy that had previously been well hidden, such as high debt levels, poor sales or export performance, problem loans in the banking sector, or dangerous interlocking relationships between capital markets, banks, and the property sector. As this happens, what begins narrowly as a financial crisis enters a vicious cycle that quickly turns it into a full-scale economic crisis.

## PHASE THREE: THE VICIOUS CYCLE

Although strictly speaking it was not the poor condition of the Southeast Asian economies that caused the crisis, the political economies of the region were not completely healthy on the eve of the crisis. For years Asia's corporate and political leaders had borrowed more money than they could invest productively. Believing growth rates would remain strong indefinitely, they built hundreds of office towers, thousands of luxury condominiums (whereas the real shortage was in low-cost housing), and scores of resorts, and also used borrowed funds to speculate in the capital markets. According to one estimate, Asian (excluding Japanese) companies had borrowed at least $700 billion from the rest of the world just since 1992. Japanese banks lent Asians $263 billion, European banks lent them $155 billion, and American banks lent $55 billion. Conservative estimates were that by mid-1997, Indonesia, Malaysia, Thailand, Singapore, and the Philippines had accumulated bad bank loans that totaled $73 billion, or 13 percent of these countries' combined GDPS. That makes Southeast Asia's banking mess larger in relative terms than the savings and loan crisis in the United States in the 1980s and the bursting of the Japanese bubble in the 1990s.

A highly damaging downward spiral was triggered by initial pressures on the region's currencies and capital markets. In Indonesia, when the economic ministers raised interest rates to try to pull rupiah liquidity out of the market and defend the currency, they unwittingly deepened the crisis by increasing investors' alarm about how serious circumstances were; this

---

[2]There are indications that many EMFMs in fact did not act prudently and responsibly. "Before [the crisis], people could just close their eyes and blindly buy Asia as a whole," said Nitin Parekh, regional strategist at Credit Suisse First Boston (HK) Ltd. "Now you can't do that; you have to pick carefully what you buy and why you're buying it." According to one of the world's leading specialists on financial markets, "When the market rises, there may be a rush of 'noise traders' wanting to get in on the action. Noise traders care little about underlying values [of companies' stock] and are simply betting that the rising trend will continue. Their buying can drive prices up, providing them with the capital gains they hoped for. This, in turn, spurs more buying, and so on." See Meir Kohn, *Financial Institutions and Markets* (New York: McGraw-Hill, 1994), p. 727.

tempted them to shift their money out of the potentially volatile Jakarta Stock Exchange and into the banking system, especially the large state banks. In Malaysia, Prime Minister Mahathir played to domestic nationalist and religious sentiment by lashing out at currency speculators and others who he felt had turned against the Malaysian economy for no good reason. Mahathir's statements, along with other signs that his government would not produce any serious policy responses to the spreading crisis, caused the pressure on Malaysia to increase. In Thailand, the crisis provoked infighting among coalition partners in the government, leading to the resignation of Prime Minister Chavalit Yongchaiyudh and the formation of a new government. The Chavalit government's initial response had been fragmented and contradictory causing investor confidence in the country and the economy to drop to unprecedented levels.

> *It is not technology but the policies of states that confer power to those controlling and moving investment resources around the globe.*

## INSTITUTIONAL FAILURES

The blame for the crisis spreads in several directions. The IMF and the World Bank are supposed to be watchdogs that alert governments and capital controllers to serious trouble on the horizon. But these institutions did not perform their jobs. The IMF failed to anticipate the Mexican peso fiasco. After that record bailout, a new "early warning system" to provide more extensive and timely information to policymakers and market actors was created. But the IMF provided no warnings in the weeks and months before July 2, 1997. In May the IMF had issued its annual *World Economic Outlook,* but it contained no clear signals indicating that Thailand or the other countries of Southeast Asia were in serious trouble. In response to these criticisms, the IMF claimed that it had known there were problems and that it had the internal documents to prove it. But as one observer asked pointedly, "Is secrecy the hallmark of an early warning system?"

Rating agencies like Standard and Poor's and Moody's have special access to corporate ledgers and boardrooms, yet businesses and banks that they had rated highly were crumbling under the weight of the region's financial crisis. Executives from these rating firms defended themselves by saying that as early as two years before the crisis they had already sent clear signals of problems, but that these concerns did not appear in their credit ratings. Why? Because, according to a top manager at Moody's, such signals are not supposed to appear in the ratings. "An institution run by a bunch of bureaucrats who couldn't run a corner candy store is not necessarily a bad credit risk," the manager pointed out. What matters is the willingness of governments to intervene and bail out management teams that the man from Moody's admits may in fact be "dumbos." A high credit rating does not mean that a company or bank is well managed. It means that despite "bad management, lax regulations, corrupt lending practices, and all other maladies,"

creditors will be paid because governments can be expected to provide public funds as backing. It happens that these rating agencies provide another measure, called financial ratings, and it is these that reflect what the agency thinks of a company's or bank's actual management and operation. But investors do not appear to consult these ratings.

The United States has also been criticized for the actions it took, or failed to take, that contributed to the crisis. One example was the almost reflexive response against the idea of setting up a regional monetary authority dominated by the Japanese. Especially when comparing the far more engaged United States response to the Mexican crisis, it is important to realize that the mostly counterproductive role of the United States government was more by neglect and distraction than by design. Because Mexico shares a long, porous border with the United States, and because immigration from Mexico is a sensitive political issue in Washington, the crisis that broke out late in 1994 received immediate and generous attention. The massive exposure of United States investors and bankers in Mexico also played an important role in the response from the Clinton administration. There were no parallel economic and political concerns regarding Asia. The crisis that began in Thailand and appeared to be spreading did not set off alarm bells in Washington.

Policymakers in the United States clearly misread the dimensions of the crisis, and certainly were very late in appreciating the negative impact it could have on the United States stock market and economy. By the time the Clinton administration began to engage the crisis more directly, it had a difficult time selling a deeper commitment to and intervention in Asia to the people and to Congress.

## THE LARGER IMPLICATIONS

It is evident that the reemergence of global finance on a scale last seen at the end of the nineteenth century, in combination with late-twentieth-century technology and communications, is a volatile mix that wrenches governments and populations alike. United States Federal Reserve chairman Alan Greenspan noted in early 1998 that "these virulent episodes" seen in the Mexican and Asian crises may be "a defining characteristic of the new high-tech financial system." Greenspan admitted that no one fully understands the workings of that system. "At one point, the economic system appears stable," he said, while "the next it behaves as though a dam has reached a breaking point, and water—confidence—evacuates its reservoir." Hinting at a crack in the dam known as neoclassical economic theory, Greenspan concluded: "We have observed that global financial markets, as currently organized, do not always achieve an appropriate equilibrium."

The political question is whether people want their fates to be determined so thoroughly, randomly suddenly, and irrationally by the controllers of mobile capital. Although it will be a difficult struggle, with capital controllers putting up a fight, decisions can be taken to severely limit the power and influence of hot money and those who wield it. Many people around the globe feel immobilized by abstractions like "globalization." Yet it is not technology but the policies of states that confer power to those controlling and moving investment resources around the globe. In September 1998, Malaysia's Mahathir decided to pull the plug, impose capital controls, and try a strong dose of Keynesian stimulation in an effort to regain some semblance of control over the domestic economy. Where this bold move will take Malaysia is unclear, but supporters and opponents of free markets are watching closely.

On the question of political participation, arguments about the wonders of authoritarianism for rapid economic development have been floating around government, business, and academic circles for several decades. It is striking, however, that Thailand and South Korea handled their crises better than Indonesia, and that both managed peaceful changes in government leadership at the peak of economic disruption—and did so without violence and bloodshed. In Indonesia, the country faced a political impasse for months as President Suharto clung to power despite his age, poor health, and role in making the country vulnerable to the crisis in the first place. Suharto was finally deposed at the cost of more than 1,000 Indonesian lives. The relatively more participatory political systems in Thailand and South Korea allowed discredited leaders to be eased out and new leaders to take the reins and push through painful reforms with a legitimacy that was utterly lacking in the half-hearted efforts of Suharto's New Order regime and the B. J. Habibie government that followed.

It is not yet clear how this crisis will affect Asian countries or international capitalism. For the present, controllers of mobile capital are in charge. Either through the direct signals of their capital investments and withdrawals or through the spins and policy reforms pushed by organizations like the IMF or individuals like Alan Greenspan, the capital controllers are able to punish and reward countries they dislike or favor. Of course, along the way jobs and goods get created. But over time, and with successive crises, especially in finance, it becomes apparent that the motives of these investors have little to do with jobs and production. These are by-products of the profit-making drive, not its central concern or goal. Neoclassical economists consider this to be the genius of market systems. You do not have to want to create employment or develop a society: it happens as if by magic.

But it does not happen automatically or magically. Nor does it happen without a good dose of coercion, conflict, and now the constant threat of tremendous economic upheaval. Private investors are choosy. Some 80 percent of total private capital flowing to developing countries goes to just a dozen countries. This means that until major changes are made in how capital is controlled, countries will face intense pressures to be responsive to the demands of capital controllers. This is going to yield reforms in the short and medium term that could undermine much of what has long defined business-government relations across many parts of Asia. But even as these crises produce reforms favoring mobile capital, they could also strengthen the resolve of governments and their citizens over the medium and long term to gain more control over how capital is controlled.

# Unit 5

## Unit Selections

*The Democratic Trend*    45. **Is the Third Wave Over?** Larry Diamond
*The Turn toward Markets*  46. **Serial Utopias,** Christian Tyler
                          47. **Capitalism and Democracy,** Gabriel A. Almond
*Ethnic and Cultural Conflict*  48. **Cultural Explanations: The Man in the Baghdad Cafe,** *The Economist*
                          49. **A Debate on Cultural Conflicts,** Samuel Huntington; Josef Joffe; Chandra Muzaffar
                          50. **Jihad vs. McWorld,** Benjamin R. Barber

## Key Points to Consider

❖ What is meant by the first, second, and third waves of democratization? Discuss the reversals that followed the first two.

❖ Where are most of the countries affected by the third wave located? What factors appear to have contributed to their democratization? What are the signs that the third wave may be over?

❖ What are some main problems and dilemmas of old and new democracies, according to Gabriel Diamond?

❖ In what ways can market capitalism and liberal democracy be said to be mutually supportive? How can they undermine each other? What is the implication of the argument that in economics, one model or "size" is unlikely to "fit all"?

❖ Why is it so difficult to resolve political conflicts that arise from the political assertion of an exclusive religious or ethnic identity?

❖ What does Benjamin Barber mean when he warns that democracy is threatened by globalism and tribalism?

## DUSHKIN ONLINE Links
## www.dushkin.com/online/

30. **Commission on Global Governance**
    *http://www.cgg.ch*
31. **IISDnet**
    *http://iisd1.iisd.ca*
32. **ISN International Relations and Security Network**
    *http://www.isn.ethz.ch*
33. **United Nations Environment Program**
    *http://www.unep.ch*
34. **Virtual Seminar in Global Political Economy/Global Cities & Social Movements**
    *http://csf.colorado.edu/gpe/gpe95b/resources.html*

These sites are annotated on pages 6 and 7.

The articles in this unit deal with three major political trends or patterns of development that can be observed in much of the contemporary world. It is important at the outset to stress that, with the possible exception of Benjamin Barber, none of the authors predict some form of global convergence in which all political systems would become alike in major respects. On closer examination, even Barber turns out to argue that a strong tendency toward global homogenization is offset by a concurrent tendency toward intensified group differentiation and fragmentation.

Thus the trends or patterns discussed here are neither unidirectional nor universal. They are situationally defined, and therefore come in a great variety. They may well turn out to be temporary and partly reversible. Moreover, they do not always reinforce one another, but show considerable mutual tension. Indeed, their different forms of development are the very stuff of comparative politics, which seeks an informed understanding of the political dimension of social life by making careful comparisons across time and space.

After such cautionary preliminaries, we can proceed to identify three recent developments that singly and together have had a very important role in changing the political world in which we live. One is *the democratic revolution,* which has been sweeping much of the world. This refers to a widespread trend toward some form of *popular government* that often, but not always, takes the form of a search for representative, pluralist democracy in countries that were previously ruled by some form of authoritarian oligarchy or dictatorship.

Another trend, sometimes labeled *the capitalist revolution,* is the even more widespread shift toward some form of *market economy.* It includes a greater reliance on private enterprise and the profit motive, and involves a concurrent move away from heavy regulation, central planning, and state ownership. But this need not mean laissez-faire capitalism. The "social market economy," found in much of Western Europe, allows a considerable role for the state in providing services, redistributing income, and setting overall societal goals. In some of the Asian Communist-ruled countries, above all China, we have become used to seeing self-proclaimed revolutionary socialists introduce a considerable degree of capitalist practices into their formerly planned economies. Some wags have suggested that it is time to speak of "market-Leninists."

The third major trend could be called the *revival of ethnic or cultural politics.* This refers to a growing emphasis on some form of an *exclusive group identity* as the primary basis for political expression. In modern times, it has been common for a group to identify itself by its special ethnic, religious, linguistic, or other cultural traits and to make this identity the basis for a claim to rule by and for itself. The principle of national self-determination received the blessing of Woodrow Wilson, and it continues to have appeal, even though some critics

warn against the potential dangers that may stem from a fractious politics of ethnocracy. They detect a collectivist or antipluralist potential in this form of political expression, and point out that it can contribute to intolerance and conflicts among groups as well as between the group and the individual.

The article in the first section covers democratization as the first of these trends, that is, the startling growth in the number of representative governments in recent years. Even if this development is often fragile and likely to be reversed in some countries, we need to remember how remarkable it has been in the first place. Using very different criteria and data, skeptics on both right and left for a long time doubted whether representative government was sufficiently stable, efficient, accountable, attractive, or, ultimately, legitimate to survive and spread in the modern world. It would be instructive to review their more recent discussion of the 1970s and early 1980s to learn from their insights and oversights.

Samuel Huntington's widely discussed thesis concerning a recent wave of democratization is usefully summarized and carried further by Larry Diamond. Huntington is one of the best-known observers of democratization, who in the past emphasized the existence of cultural, social, economic, and political obstacles to representative governments in most of the world. Even before the collapse of the Communist regimes in Europe, however, he had begun to identify a broad pattern of democratization that started already in the mid-1970s, when three dictatorships in southern Europe came to an end (in Greece, Portugal, and Spain). In the following decade, democratization spread to most of Latin America. Central and Eastern Europe then followed, and the trend has also reached some states in East and South Asia as well as in some parts of Africa, above all South Africa and now Nigeria.

In a widely adopted phrase, Huntington identified this trend as the "third wave" of democratization in modern history. The "first wave" had been both slow and long in its reach. It began in the 1820s and lasted about one century, until the 1920s, a period during which first the United States and subsequently 28 other countries established governments based on a wide and eventually universal suffrage. In 1922, however, Mussolini's capture of power in Italy began a period of reversal, which lasted until the mid-1940s. During these two decades, the number of democracies fell from 29 to 12, as many became victims of dictatorial takeovers or subsequent military conquests.

A "second wave" of democratization started with the Allied victory in World War II and continued during the early postwar years of decolonization. This wave lasted until about 1962 and resulted in the conversion of about 2 dozen previous authoritarian systems into democracies or quasi democracies, sometimes of very short duration. There followed a second reverse wave, lasting from

1962 to 1974. During this period, the number of democracies fell from 36 to 30 and the number of nondemocracies increased from 75 to 95 as various former colonies or fresh democracies fell under authoritarian rule. In the mid-1970s, then, the important "third wave" of democratization got its start.

At the beginning of the 1990s, Huntington counted about 60 democracies in the world, which roughly amounts to a doubling of their number in less than two decades. Today there are even more. It is an impressive change, but Huntington also pointed out that the process is likely to be reversed once again in a number of the new and unstable democracies. Both Huntington and Diamond's findings lend support to the conclusion that democracy's advance has been at best a "two steps forward, one step back" kind of process.

The expectations associated with the coming of democracy are in some countries so high that disappointments are bound to follow. Already, the earlier "third wave" democratic advances in countries like Sudan, Nigeria, Algeria, and Peru have been followed by authoritarian reversals. Haiti (like Nigeria) has gone through its own double wave. The prospects for democracy on that poverty-stricken Caribbean island do not seem bright, but there have been some positive news to report. In 1994 Jean-Bertrand Aristide returned to the presidential office for which he had been elected in 1991 and overthrown by a military coup in the same year. He stepped down at the end of his regular term in 1996, and Haiti came to experience its first democratic succession in office. There are ominous signs of authoritarian revivals elsewhere in the world.

What are the general conditions that inhibit or encourage the spread and stabilization of democracy? Huntington and other scholars have identified some specific historical factors that appear to have contributed to the third wave. One important factor is the loss of legitimacy by both right- and left-wing authoritarian regimes, as they have become discredited by failures. Another factor is the expansion in some developing world countries of an urban middle class, with a strong interest in representative government and constitutional rule. In Latin America, especially, the influence of a more liberal Catholic Church has been important. There have also been various forms of external influence by the United States and the European Community, as they have tried to promote a human rights agenda. A different but crucial instance of external influence took the form of Mikhail Gorbachev's shift toward nonintervention by the Soviet Union in the late 1980s, when he abandoned the Brezhnev Doctrine's commitment to defend established Communist rulers in Eastern Europe and elsewhere against counterrevolution. Finally, there is the "snowballing" or demonstration effect of a successful early transition to democracy in countries such as Spain or Poland, which served as models for other countries in similar circumstances. This has also been very important in Latin America.

Huntington's rule of thumb is that a democratic form of government can be considered to have become stable when a country has had at least two successive peaceful turnovers of power. Such a development may take a generation or longer to complete, even under fortunate circumstances. Many of the new democracies have little historical experience with a democratic way of life. Where there has been such an experience, it may have been spotty and not very positive. There may be important cultural or socioeconomic obstacles to democratization, according to Huntington. Like most other observers, he sees extreme poverty as a principal obstacle to successful democratization.

Both old and new democracies face dangers, as Larry Diamond points out. He analyzes the special problems that tend to dog the new democracies, including the difficulty of living up to initial expectations. Popular dissatisfaction normally focuses on a particular government in the established political systems, but where a representative form of government is a new development there is a special danger that the democratic system itself may become the target of criticism rather than the governing group that can be replaced.

Germany provides a valuable case study for testing some of these interpretations of democracy. After World War I, antidemocratic critics identified its Weimar Republic with international disaster, socioeconomic ruin, and political weakness and instability. After World War II, by contrast, the Federal Republic became increasingly credited with stability and prosperity. At first accepted passively, the fledgling West German democratic system soon generated an increasing measure of pragmatic support from its citizenry, based on its widely perceived effectiveness. In time, the new republic also appeared to gain a deeper, more effective support from much of the population. A major question is how national reunification, with its accompanying wrenching changes and inevitable disappointments, will influence German attitudes toward representative government. In the new eastern states, in particular, reunification was linked to unrealistic expectations of almost immediate socioeconomic alignment with the prosperous West. How have East Germans reacted, as the new polity failed to deliver promptly and bountifully? Comparatively speaking, Germany is fortunate in having a stable set of institutions, a well-developed democratic culture in the "old" or western states of the Federal Republic, and a solid economic structure.

The second section of this unit covers the trend toward capitalism or, better, market economics. Here Gabriel Almond explores the connections between capitalism and democracy in an article that draws upon both theory and empirical studies. His systematic discussion shows that there are ways in which capitalism and democracy support each other, and ways in which they tend to undermine each other. Is it possible to have the best of both? Almond answers at length that there is a nonutopian manner in which capitalism and democracy can be reconciled, namely in democratic welfare capitalism.

Almond's discussion can be linked to a theme emphasized by some contemporary political economists. They point out that the economic competition between capitalism and socialism, in its Communist form of state ownership and centralized planning, has become a largely closed chapter in history. The central question now is which form of capitalism or market economy will be more successful. A similar argument has been made by the French theorist, Michel Albert, who also distinguishes between the British-American and the continental "Rhineland" models of capitalism. The former is more individualistic, antigovernmental, and characterized by such traits as high employee turnovers and short-term profit-maximizing. It differs considerably from what the Germans themselves like to call their "social market economy." The latter is more team-oriented, emphasizes cooperation between management and labor, and leaves a considerable role for government in the setting of economic strategy, the training of an educated labor force, and the provision of social welfare services.

These different conceptions of capitalism can be linked to different histories. Both Britain and the United States experienced a head start in their industrial revolutions and felt no need for deliberate government efforts to encourage growth. By contrast, Germany and Japan both played the role of latecomers, who looked to government protection in their attempts to catch up. To be sure, governments were also swayed by military considerations to promote German and Japanese industrialization. But the emergence of a kind of social capitalism in other continental countries of Europe suggests that cultural rather than military factors played a major role in this development. A crucial question is whether the relative prosperity and social security associated with this kind of mixed economy can be maintained in a time of technological breakthroughs and global competition. One possible answer will come from the policies and strategies adopted by the new "Red-Green" government in Germany. Because it seems unlikely that one economic model or size will fit all, as Christian Tyler emphasizes, we should continue to expect differently mixed economies.

The third section deals with the revival of the ethnic and cultural dimension in politics. Until recently, relatively few observers foresaw that this element would play such a divisive role in the contemporary world. There were forewarnings, such as the ethnonationalist stirrings in the late 1960s and early 1970s in peripheral areas of such countries as Britain, Canada, and Spain. It also lay behind many of the conflicts in the newly independent countries of the developing world. But most Western observers seem to have been poorly prepared for the task of anticipating or understanding the resurgence of politicized religious, ethnic, or other cultural forces. Many non-Westerners were taken by surprise as well. Mikhail Gorbachev, for example, grossly underestimated the centrifugal force of the nationality question in his own country.

The politicization of religion in many parts of the world falls into this development of a "politics of identity." In recent years, religious groups in parts of Latin America, Asia, the Middle East, sub-Saharan Africa, Asia, and southern Europe have variously set out on the political road in the name of their faith. As Max Weber warned in a classic lecture shortly before his death, it can be dangerous to seek "the salvation of souls" along the path of politics. The coexistence of people of divergent faiths is possible only because religious conviction need not fully determine or direct a person's or a group's politics. Where absolute and fervent convictions take over, they make it difficult to compromise pragmatically and live harmoniously with people who believe differently. Pluralist democracy requires an element of tolerance, which for many takes the form of a casual "live and let live" attitude.

There is an important debate among political scientists concerning the sources and scope of politics based on ethnic, religious, and cultural differences. Samuel Huntington argues forcefully that our most important future conflicts will be based on clashes of civilizations. In his view, they will be far more difficult to resolve than those rooted in socio-economic or ideological differences. His critics, including Josef Joffe, argue that Huntington distorts the differences *among* civilizations and trivializes the differences *within* civilizations as sources of political conflict. Chandra Muzaffar, a Malaysian commentator, goes further by contending that Huntington's thesis provides a rationalization for a Western policy goal of dominating the developing world. Others have pointed out that ethnic conflicts are in fact often the result of political choices made by elites. This can be a hopeful thesis, because it contains the conclusion that such conflicts are avoidable if other political choices were made.

In the final article, Benjamin Barber brings a broad perspective to the discussion of identity politics in the contemporary world. He sees two major tendencies that threaten democracy. One is the force of globalism, brought about by modern technology, communications, and commerce. Its logical end station is what he calls a "McWorld," in which human diversity, individuality, and meaningful identity are erased. The second tendency works in the opposite direction. It is the force of tribalism, which drives human beings to exacerbate their group differences and engage in holy wars or "jihads" against each other. Barber argues that globalism is at best indifferent to democracy, while militant tribalism is deeply antithetical. He argues in favor of seeking a confederal solution, based on democratic civil societies, which could provide human beings with a nonmilitant, parochial communitarianism as well as a framework that suits the global market economy fairly well.

# IS THE THIRD WAVE OVER?

## Larry Diamond

*Larry Diamond is coeditor of the* Journal of Democracy, *codirector of the National Endowment for Democracy's International Forum for Democratic Studies, and a senior research fellow at the Hoover Institution. Various portions of this essay will appear in his forthcoming book* Developing Democracy: Toward Consolidation, *to be published by Johns Hopkins University Press.*

Since the overthrow of Portugal's dictatorial regime in April 1974, the number of democracies in the world has multiplied dramatically. Before the start of this global trend toward democracy, there were roughly 40 countries that could be classified as more or less democratic. The number increased moderately through the late 1970s and early 1980s as a number of states experienced transitions from authoritarian (predominantly military) to democratic rule. in the mid-1980s, however, the pace of global democratic expansion accelerated markedly, and today there are between 76 and 117 democracies, depending on how one counts. *How* one counts is crucial, however, to thinking about *whether* democracy will continue to expand in the world, or even hold steady at its current level. In fact, it raises the fundamental question of what we mean by democracy.

In a seminal formulation, Samuel Huntington has dubbed this post–1974 period the "third wave" of global democratic expansion. He defines a "wave of democratization" simply as "a group of transitions from nondemocratic to democratic regimes that occur within a specified period of time and that significantly outnumber transitions in the opposite direction during that period."[1] He identifies two previous waves of democratization: a long, slow wave from 1828 to 1926 and a second wave from 1943 to 1964. Significantly, each of these ended with what he calls a "reverse wave" of democratic breakdowns (the first lasting from 1922 to 1942, the second from 1961 to 1975), in which some of the newly established (or reestablished) democracies failed. Overall, each reverse wave reduced the number of democracies in the world significantly but still left more democracies in place than had existed prior to the start of the preceding democratic wave. Reverse waves do great harm to political freedom, human rights, and peace. Thus, as I will argue, preventing a reverse wave should be paramount among the policy goals of democratic actors and institutions around the world.

## Conceptualizing Democracy

Essential to tracking the progress of democracy and understanding both its causes and its consequences is a high degree of conceptual clarity about the term "democracy." Unfortunately, what prevails instead in the burgeoning empirical and theoretical literature on democracy is conceptual confusion and disarray so serious that David Collier and Steven Levitsky have identified more than 550 "subtypes" of democracy.[2] Some of these nominal subtypes merely identify specific institutional features or types of full democracy, but many denote "diminished" forms of democracy that overlap with one another in a variety of ways. Fortunately, most conceptions of democracy today (in contrast with the 1960s and 1970s, for example) do converge in defining democracy as a system of political authority, separate from any social and economic features. Where conceptions still diverge fundamentally (but not always very explicitly) is in the range and extent of political attributes encompassed by democracy.

Minimalist definitions descend from Joseph Schumpeter, who defined democracy as a system "for arriving at political decisions in which individuals acquire the power to decide by means of a competitive struggle for the people's vote."[3] Huntington, among others, explicitly embraces Schumpeter's emphasis on electoral competition as the essence of democracy.[4] Over time, however, Schumpeter's appealingly concise definition has required periodic elaboration (or what Collier and Levitsky call "precising") to avoid inclusion of cases that do not fit the implicit meaning. The most influential elaboration has been Robert Dahl's concept of "polyarchy," which requires not only extensive political competition and participation but also substantial levels of freedom (of speech, press, and the like) and pluralism that enable people to form and express their political preferences in a meaningful way.[5]

Contemporary minimalist conceptions of democracy—what I term here *electoral democracy*, as opposed to *liberal democracy*,—commonly acknowledge the need for minimal levels of civil freedom in order for competition and participation to be meaningful. Typically, however, they do not devote much attention to the basic freedoms involved, nor do they attempt to incorporate them into actual measures of democracy. Such Schumpeterian conceptions—particularly common among Western policy makers who track and celebrate the expansion of democracy—risk exemplifying what Terry Karl has called the "fallacy of electoralism." That mistake consists of privileging electoral contestation over other dimensions of democracy and ignoring the degree to which multiparty elections, even if genuinely competitive, may effectively deny significant sections of the population the opportunity to contest for power or advance and defend their interests, or may leave significant arenas of decision-making power beyond the reach or control of elected officials.[6] As Philippe Schmitter and Terry Karl emphasize, "However central to democracy, elections occur intermittently and only allow citizens to choose between the highly aggregated alternatives offered by political parties."[7]

As Collier and Levitsky note, minimalist definitions of democracy have been refined in recent years to exclude regimes with substantial "reserved domains" of military (or bureaucratic, or oligarchic) power that are not accountable to elected officials.[8] On such grounds, Guatemala in particular has often been classified as a "pseudo" or quasi democracy. But such refined definitions of democracy can still fail to acknowledge political repression

that marginalizes significant segments of the population—typically the poor or ethnic and regional minorities. While conceptual "precising" has been constructive, it has left behind a welter of what Collier and Levitsky term "expanded procedural" conceptions that occupy various intermediate locations on the continuum between electoral and liberal democracy.

This conceptual disorder is not surprising given that scholars are trying to impose categories on a phenomenon—political freedom—that in fact varies only by degree. Whereas the presence or absence of competitive elections is relatively clear-cut, individual and group rights of expression, organization, and assembly can vary considerably even across countries that meet the criteria for electoral democracy.

How large and overtly repressed or marginalized must a minority be for the political system to be disqualified as a polyarchy, or, in my terms, a liberal democracy?[9] Is Turkey disqualified by the indiscriminate violence it has used to suppress a ruthless Kurdish insurgency, and its historical constraints (recently relaxed) on the peaceful expression of Kurdish political and cultural identity? Is India disqualified by the human rights violations its security forces have committed in secessionist Kashmir; or Sri Lanka by the brutal excesses on both sides in the secessionist war of Tamil guerrillas; or Russia by its savage war against Chechen secessionists; or Colombia by its internal war against drug traffickers and left-wing guerrillas, and its exceptionally high rates of political assassination and other human rights abuses? Do these polities not have a right to defend themselves against violent insurgency and secessionist terror? Or does democracy fall short—despite the presence in all five countries of highly competitive elections that in recent years have produced party alternation in power? As indicated below, this problem affects a growing group of

countries that are commonly considered "democracies" today.

By a minimalist, electoral definition, all five of the above-mentioned countries qualify as democracies. But by a stricter conception of liberal democracy, all fall short. All suffer sufficiently serious abridgments of political rights and civil liberties that they failed to attain a rating of "free" in the most recent "Comparative Survey of Freedom," the annual global survey of political rights and civil liberties conducted by Freedom House. This gap between electoral democracy and liberal democracy, which has become one of the most striking features of the "third wave," has serious consequences for theory, policy, and comparative analysis.

## Liberal Democracy and Pseudodemocracy

How does *liberal* democracy extend beyond the minimalist (or formal) and intermediate conceptions of democracy described above? In addition to regular, free, and fair electoral competition and universal suffrage, it requires the absence of "reserved domains" of power for the military or other social and political forces that are not either directly or indirectly accountable to the electorate. Second, in addition to the "vertical" accountability of rulers to the ruled (which is secured most reliably through regular, free, and fair elections), it requires "horizontal" accountability of officeholders to one another; this constrains executive power and so helps protect constitutionalism, the rule of law, and the deliberative process.[10] Third, it encompasses extensive provisions for political and civic pluralism, as well as for individual and group freedoms. Specifically, liberal democracy has the following features:

1) Real power lies—in fact as well as in constitutional theory—with elected officials and their appointees, rather than with unaccountable internal actors (e.g., the military) or foreign powers.

2) Executive power is constrained constitutionally and held accountable by other government institutions (such as an independent judiciary, parliament, ombudsman, and auditor general).

3) Not only are electoral outcomes uncertain, with a significant opposition vote and the presumption of party alternation in government over time, but no group that adheres to constitutional principles is denied the right to form a party and contest elections (even if electoral thresholds and other rules prevent smaller parties from winning representation in parliament).

4) Cultural, ethnic, religious, and other minority groups, as well as traditionally disadvantaged or unempowered majorities, are not prohibited (legally or in practice) from expressing their interests in the political process, and from using their language and culture.

5) Beyond parties and intermittent elections, citizens have multiple, ongoing channels and means for the expression and representation of their interests and values, including a diverse array of autonomous associations, movements, and groups that they are free to form and join.

6) In addition to associational freedom and pluralism, there exist alternative sources of information, including independent media, to which citizens have (politically) unfettered access.

7) Individuals have substantial freedom of belief, opinion, discussion, speech, publication, assembly, demonstration, and petition.

8) Citizens are politically equal under the law (even though they are invariably unequal in their political resources), and the above-mentioned individual and group liberties are effectively protected by an independent, impartial judiciary whose decisions are enforced and respected by other centers of power.

9) The rule of law protects citizens from unjustified detention, exile, terror, torture, and undue interference in their personal lives

not only by the state but also by organized antistate forces.

These elements of liberal democracy constitute most of the criteria used by Freedom House in its annual survey of freedom around the world. Two dimensions of freedom—political rights (of contestation, opposition, and participation) and civil liberties—are measured on a seven-point scale, with a rating of 1 indicating the most free and 7 the least free. Countries whose two scores average 2.5 or below are considered "free"; those scoring 3 to 5.5, "partly free"; and those scoring 5.5 and above, "not free," with the determination for countries with the borderline score of 5.5 made on the basis of a more discriminating raw-point score.[11]

The "free" rating in the Freedom House survey is the best available empirical indicator of "liberal democracy." Of course, as with any multipoint scale, there is inevitably an element of arbitrariness in the thresholds used for each category. Yet there is a significant difference even between average scores of 2.5 and 3. In the 1995—96 survey, all nine countries with a score of 2.5—the highest score a country could attain and still be rated "free"—received a rating of 2 on political rights and 3 on civil liberties. The difference between a 2 and a 3 on political rights is substantial, with the latter typically indicating significantly more military influence in politics, electoral and political violence, or electoral irregularities, and thus political contestation that is appreciably less free, fair, inclusive, and meaningful. For example, El Salvador and Honduras each scored 3 on political rights and 3 on civil liberties, as did Venezuela, where military autonomy and impunity and political intimidation have eroded the quality of democracy in recent years. The difference between a 2 and a 3 on civil liberties is also significant, with the higher-scoring countries having at least one area—such as freedom of speech or the press, personal security from terror and arbitrary ar-

rest, or associational freedom and autonomy—where liberty is significantly constrained.

The intermediate conceptions of democracy, which fall somewhere in between "electoral" and "liberal" democracy, explicitly incorporate basic civil freedoms of expression and association, yet still allow for considerable restriction of citizenship rights. The crucial distinction turns on whether political and civil freedoms are seen as relevant mainly to the extent that they ensure meaningful electoral competition and participation, or are instead viewed as necessary to ensure a wider range of democratic functions.

To appreciate the dynamics of regime change and the evolution of democracy, we must also allow for a third class of regimes that are less than even minimally democratic but still distinct from purely authoritarian regimes. Such regimes—which I call here *pseudodemocracies*—have legal opposition parties and perhaps many other constitutional features of electoral democracy, but fail to meet one of its crucial requirements: a sufficiently fair arena of contestation to allow the ruling party to be turned out of power.

There is wide variation among pseudodemocracies as I use the term here. They include "semidemocracies," which approach electoral democracies in their pluralism, competitiveness, and civil liberties, as well as "hegemonic party systems," such as Mexico before 1988, in which an institutionalized ruling party makes extensive use of coercion, patronage, media control, and other tools to reduce opposition parties to decidedly "second-class" status.[12] But they also encompass multiparty electoral systems in which the undemocratic dominance of the ruling party may be weak and contested (as in Kenya), or in the process of decomposing into a more competitive system (as in Mexico today), or highly personalistic and poorly institutionalized (as in Kazakhstan).

What distinguishes pseudodemocracies from the residual category of "authoritarian" regimes is that they tolerate the existence of independent opposition parties. This distinction is important theoretically. If we view democracy in *developmental* terms, as emerging in fragments or parts, by no fixed sequence or timetable, then the presence of legal opposition parties that may compete for power and win some seats in parliament, and of the greater space for civil society that tends to exist in such systems, provides important foundations for future democratic development.[13] In Mexico, Jordan, Morocco, and a number of states in subSaharan Africa where former one-party dictators engineered their reelection under pseudodemocratic conditions, these democratic fragments are pressing out the boundaries of what is politically possible, and may eventually generate breakthroughs to electoral democracy.

## Empirical Trends During the Third Wave

By any measure, democracy has expanded dramatically since the beginning of the third wave. Using a minimalist or formal conception of democracy that emphasizes electoral competition, both the number and the proportion of the world's democracies have risen sharply. In 1974 there were only 39 democracies in the world, 28 of which had populations over one million (or so close to one million that they would exceed that mark by 1995). Only about 23 percent of countries with populations over one million and about 27 percent of all countries were formally democratic. The difference between these proportions illustrates an interesting relationship between country size and regime type that has held continuously throughout the third wave: very small countries (those with populations under one million) are significantly more likely than larger countries to be democracies (especially liberal democracies). In fact, two-thirds of states with populations under one million are

| Year | Number of Democracies | Number of Countries | Democracies as a % of All Countries |
|------|------|------|------|
| 1974 | 39 | 142 | 27.5% |
| 1990 | 76 | 165 | 46.1% |
| 1991 | 91 | 183 | 49.7% |
| 1992 | 99 | 186 | 53.2% |
| 1993 | 108 | 190 | 56.8% |
| 1994 | 114 | 191 | 59.7% |
| 1995 | 117 | 191 | 61.3% |

Table 1—Number of Formal Democracies, 1974, 1990–95

*Sources:* Data from Freedom House, *Freedom in the World: The Annual Survey of Political Rights and Civil Liberties, 1990–91, 1991–92, 1992–93, 1993–94, 1994–95* (New York: Freedom House, 1991 and years following); and *Freedom Review* 27 (January–February 1996).

*Note:* Figures for 1990–95 are for the end of the calendar year. Figures for 1974 reflect my estimate of the number of democracies in the world in April 1974, at the inception of the third wave.

liberal democracies today, compared with only about one-third of states with populations over one million.

By the beginning of 1996, the number of countries meeting at least the requirements for electoral democracy had increased to 117. Moreover, even though the number of independent states has steadily grown throughout the third wave (by more than a third), the proportion of countries that are at least formally democratic has more than doubled, to over 60 percent. More striking still is how much of this increase has occurred in the 1990s, with the collapse of Soviet and East European communism and the diffusion of the third wave to sub-Saharan Africa. As Table I shows, the number and percentage of democracies in the world have increased *every year* since 1990. This can only be described as an unprecedented democratic breakthrough. As recently as 1990, when he was writing *The Third Wave*, Huntington found only 45 percent of the world's states (with populations over one million) to be democratic, a proportion virtually identical to that in 1922 at the peak of the first wave.[14] Even if we similarly restrict our view to countries with populations over one million, the proportion of formal democracies in the world now stands at 57 percent.

What has been the trend with respect to *liberal* democracy? As one

would expect, both the number of countries and the proportion of countries in the world rated "free" by Freedom House have also increased significantly, albeit not as dramatically. From the survey's inception in 1972 until 1980, the number of free states increased by only ten (and the proportion of free states in the world rose only slightly, from 29 to 32 percent). Moreover, change was not in one direction. During the first six years of the third wave, five states suffered breakdowns or erosions of democracy that cost them their free ratings. In fact, although the overall global trend of regime change during the third wave has been toward democracy and freedom, 22 countries suffered breakdowns of democracy between 1974 and 1991, and further deterioration has occurred since then.

During the third wave, freedom took its biggest jump in the latter half of the 1980s and the early 1990s. As Table 2 shows, between 1985 and 1991 (a crucial year, which witnessed the demise of Soviet communism), the number of free states jumped from 56 to 76 and the proportion of free states in the world increased from a third to over 40 percent. Moreover, the proportion of blatantly authoritarian ("not free") states declined to a historic low of 23 percent in 1991, falling further to just over 20 percent in 1992. By contrast, in 1972 almost half the independent states in the world were rated "not free."

The 1991–92 period seems to have been the high-water mark for freedom in the world. Since 1991, the proportion of free states has declined slightly, and since 1992, the proportion of "not free" states has jumped sharply. Despite the steady growth in the number of electoral democracies, the number of free states has stagnated in the first half of this decade, with gains in freedom offset by losses. In 1993, 43 countries registered a decline in their freedom score, while 18 posted a gain. In 1994, eight countries improved their freedom category (e.g., from partly free to free) and four declined in category; overall, however, freedom scores increased in 22 countries while declining in 23.15. In 1995, the trend was slightly more positive, with four category upgrades and three downgrades and a total of 29 increases in freedom scores and 11 decreases. Yet the total number of free states did not change at all.

Juxtaposing the two divergent trends of the 1990s—continued growth of electoral democracy, but stagnation of liberal democracy—demonstrates the increasing shallowness of democratization in the latter part of the third wave. During the 1990s, the gap between electoral and liberal democracy has steadily grown. As a proportion of all the world's democracies, free states (liberal democracies) have declined

from 85 percent in 1990 to 65 percent today (Table 3). During this period, the quality of democracy (as measured by the extent of political rights and civil liberties) has eroded in many of the most important and influential new third-wave democracies—including Russia, Turkey, Brazil, and Pakistan—while an expected transition to democracy in Africa's most populous country, Nigeria, imploded. At the same time, political freedom has deteriorated in several of the longest-surviving democracies in the developing world, including India, Sri Lanka, Colombia, and Venezuela. In fact, with a few notable exceptions (including South Korea, Poland, and South Africa), the overall trend of the past decade among regionally influential countries that are electoral democracies today has been toward a decline in freedom. This is particularly disturbing given that, as Huntington has argued in *The Third Wave*, the "demonstration effects" that are so important in the wavelike diffusion or recession of democracy emanate disproportionately from the more powerful countries within a region and internationally.

The undertow in the third wave has been particularly striking in Latin America. Of the 22 countries below the Rio Grande with populations over one million, 10 have experienced significant declines in freedom since 1987, while 6 have seen increases. While five countries made transitions to formal democ-

racy (Chile, Nicaragua, Haiti, Panama, and Paraguay), only Chile became a free state, and six countries lost their free status. Even in some free states (such as Argentina, Ecuador, and Jamaica), Freedom House has observed a downward trend in recent years. Although it is commonly assumed that Latin America today is overwhelmingly democratic, only 8 of the 22 principal countries in the region were rated free at the end of 1995, compared with 13 in 1987. While blatantly authoritarian rule has receded in the hemisphere, so has liberal democracy, as the region has experienced a "convergence" toward "more mixed kinds of semi-democratic regimes."[16]

Some consider it remarkable that Latin American democracies have survived at all considering the enormous stresses they have experienced over the past decade: dramatic economic downturns and increases in poverty (only recently reversed in some countries), the mushrooming drug trade, and the violence and corruption that have flourished in its wake. Since the redemocratization of Latin America began in the early 1980s, the response to severe adversity and political crisis—including scandals that have forced presidential resignations in several countries—has primarily been adherence to constitutional process and electoral alternation in office (although the military did nearly overthrow democracy in Venezuela in 1992, and has rattled its sabers loudly elsewhere). In the practice of "voting the bums out" rather than mobilizing against democracy itself, Latin American publics have given many observers cause to discern a normalization and maturation of democratic politics not seen in previous eras. Indeed, a number of democratic governments (in Southern and Eastern Europe as well as in Latin America) have been able to make considerable progress in economic reform during the third wave, and in one sizeable sample of such reform experiences, "the party that initiated cuts in working-class income

### Table 2—Freedom Status of Independent States, 1972–95

| Year | Free | Partly Free | Not Free | Total |
|------|------|-------------|----------|-------|
| 1972 | 42 (29.0%) | 36 (24.8%) | 67 (46.2%) | 145 (100%) |
| 1980 | 52 (31.9%) | 52 (31.9%) | 59 (36.2%) | 163 (100%) |
| 1985 | 56 (33.5%) | 56 (33.5%) | 55 (32.9%) | 167 (100%) |
| 1991 | 76 (41.5%) | 65 (35.5%) | 42 (22.9%) | 183 (100%) |
| 1992 | 75 (40.3%) | 73 (39.2%) | 38 (20.4%) | 186 (100%) |
| 1993 | 72 (37.9%) | 63 (33.2%) | 55 (28.9%) | 190 (100%) |
| 1994 | 76 (39.8%) | 61 (31.9%) | 54 (28.3%) | 191 (100%) |
| 1995 | 76 (39.8%) | 62 (32.5%) | 53 (27.7%) | 191 (100%) |

*Sources:* For 1972, 1980, and 1985: Raymond D. Gastil, ed., *Freedom in the World: Political Rights and Civil Liberties, 1988–89* (New York: Freedom House, 1989). For 1991–95: See Table 1.
*Note:* Ratings refer to the status of the countries at the end of the calendar year. See text for an explanation of the basis of the ratings.

| Table 3—Formal and Liberal Democracies, 1990–95 |||||
| Year | Number of Formal Democracies | Number of Free States (Liberal Democracies) | Free States as a % of Formal Democracies | Total |
| --- | --- | --- | --- | --- |
| 1990 | 76 (46.1%) | 65 (39.4%) | 85.5% | 165 |
| 1991 | 91 (49.7%) | 76 (41.5%) | 83.5% | 183 |
| 1992 | 99 (53.2%) | 75 (40.3%) | 75.8% | 186 |
| 1993 | 108 (56.8%) | 72 (37.9%) | 66.7% | 190 |
| 1994 | 114 (59.7%) | 76 (39.8%) | 66.7% | 191 |
| 1995 | 117 (61.3%) | 76 (39.8%) | 65.0% | 191 |

*Sources:* See Table 1.

there, all that is required is the presence of opposition parties that can contest for office, even if they are manipulated, hounded, and robbed of victory at election time.

## A Period of Stasis

With the number of liberal democracies now stagnating, with the quality of many third-wave and Third World democracies sharply deteriorating, and with the world's most powerful and influential authoritarian states—China, Indonesia, Iran, and Saudi Arabia—showing little or no prospect of democratization in the near term, the question arises: Is the third wave over?

The evidence in the affirmative appears to be mounting. If we look beyond the form of democracy—a form that is increasingly expected by world culture and organizations—we see erosion and stagnation offsetting liberalization and consolidation. *Liberal* democracy has stopped expanding in the world, and so has political freedom more generally. If we take the liberal content of democracy seriously, it seems that the third wave of democratic expansion has come to a halt, and probably to an end. We may or may not see in the coming years the emergence of a few new electoral democracies, but a further sizeable increase seems unlikely, given that democratization has already occurred in the countries where conditions are most favorable. Movement to electoral democracy also seems likely to be offset by movement away from it, as some fledgling electoral democracies in Africa and elsewhere are either blatantly overthrown (as in Gambia and Niger), squelched just before birth (as in Nigeria) or strangled by deterioration in the fairness of contestation and the toleration of opposition (as in Peru, Cambodia, and some of the former communist states). In these circumstances, more and more countries may seek to satisfy the expectation of "democracy" with its most hollow form, pseudo-democracy.

has been defeated in less than half the cases."[17]

This persistence of constitutional procedures gives grounds for hope about the future of democracy in Latin America, as do recent reforms that have decentralized power and opened up the electoral process in Venezuela and Colombia, instituted an independent electoral commission in Panama, and improved judicial functioning in several countries. But these positive steps have been outweighed by conditions that render electoral democracy in the region increasingly hollow, illiberal, delegative, and afflicted. These trends, evident in the resurgence of authoritarian practices under elected civilian presidents in countries such as Peru and Venezuela, and in a general erosion of the rule of law under pressure from the drug trade, reflect the growing gap between electoral and liberal democracy in the region.

As mentioned above, the trends of increasing (or persisting) disorder, human rights violations, legislative and judicial inefficacy, corruption, and military impunity and prerogatives have been evident in other third-wave democracies around the world—not only major countries like Turkey and Pakistan but smaller ones such as Zambia and most of the electoral regimes of the former Soviet Union. Indeed, in the former Soviet Union, Africa, parts of Asia, and the Middle East, elections themselves are increasingly hollow and uncompetitive, a thin disguise for the authoritarian hegemony of despots and ruling parties: "As recogni-

tion grows of the right freely to elect one's governmental representatives, more governments [feel] compelled to hold elections in order to gain [international] legitimacy."[18] In 1995 these contests degenerated into "an electoral charade" in Kazakhstan, Turkmenistan, Tajikistan, Armenia, and Azerbaijan (not to mention Iraq, Iran, Egypt, and Algeria) because of intimidation, rigging, and constriction (or, in extreme cases, utter obliteration) of the right of opposition forces to organize and contest. Since the most recent wave of democratization began its sweep through Africa in early 1991, at least ten civilian regimes have held multiparty elections so flawed that they do not meet the minimal criteria for electoral democracy.[19] All of these regimes are "pseudodemocracies."

Perhaps the most stunning feature of the third wave is how few regimes are left in the world (only slightly over 20 percent) that do not exhibit some degree of multiparty competition, whether that level corresponds with liberal democracy, electoral democracy, or pseudo-democracy. This broad diffusion signals the ideological hegemony of "democracy" in the post–Cold War world, but also the superficial nature of that hegemony. In Latin America and the Caribbean, the United States and the international community demand electoral democracy in exchange for recognition and economic rewards, but are not too insistent about human rights and the rule of law. For Africa, a lower standard is set by the major Western powers:

Does this mean that we are on the edge of a third "reverse wave" of democracy? This more frightening prospect is not yet apparent; indeed, a reverse wave may well be avoidable. It is theoretically possible for a wave of democratic expansion to be followed for some time not by a reverse wave but rather by equilibrium, in which the overall number of democracies in the world neither increases nor decreases significantly. It is precisely such a period of stasis that we seem to have entered.

Many of the new democracies of the third wave are in serious trouble today, and it could be argued that the erosion of democratic substance is a precursor to the actual suspension or overthrow of democracy, whether by executive or military coup. The *autogolpe* of President Alberto Fujimori of Peru was preceded by years of steady deterioration in political rights and civil liberties. Historically, the path to military coups and other forms of democratic breakdown has been paved with the accumulation of unsolvable problems, the gross corruption and malfunctioning of democratic institutions, the gradual aggrandizement of executive power, and the broad popular disaffection with politics and politicians that is evident today in many third-wave democracies (and a few of longer standing).

Yet three things are different today:

1) Military establishments are extremely reluctant to seize power overtly, for several reasons: the lack of popular support for a coup (due in part to the discredit many militaries suffered during their previous periods of brutal and inept rule); their sharply diminished confidence in their ability to tackle formidable economic and social problems; the "disastrous effects on the coherence, efficiency, and discipline of the army" that they have perceived during previous periods of military rule;[20] and, not least, the instant and powerful sanctions that the established democracies have shown an increasing resolve to impose against

such democratic overthrows. In addition, many third-wave democracies have made great progress toward establishing the conditions of "objective civilian control" that prevail in the industrialized democracies: high levels of military professionalism, constrained military roles, subordination of the military to civilian decision makers, autonomy for the military in its limited area of professional competence, and thus "the minimization of military intervention in politics and of political intervention in the military."[21]

2) Even where, as in Turkey, the Philippines, Brazil, Pakistan, and Bangladesh, progress toward democratic consolidation has been partial and slow, and the quality of democracy has deteriorated in some respects, publics have shown no appetite for a return to authoritarian rule of any kind; culturally, democracy remains a valued goal.

3) Finally, no antidemocratic ideology with global appeal has emerged to challenge the continued global ideological hegemony of democracy as a principle and a formal structure of government.

Together, these factors have so far prevented a new wave of democratic breakdowns. Instead of expiring altogether, democracy has gradually been "hollowed out" in many countries, leaving a shell of multiparty electoralism—often with genuine competition and uncertainty over outcomes—adequate for the attainment of international legitimacy and economic rewards. Rather than mobilize against the constitutional system, political leaders and groups that have no use for democracy, or are (to use Juan Linz's term) "semi-loyal" to the system, are more likely to choose and condone oblique and partial assaults on democracy, such as the repression of particularly troublesome oppositions and minorities. Instead of seizing power through a coup, the military may gradually reclaim more operational autonomy and control over matters of internal security and counterinsurgency, as they have done in Gua-

temala, Nicaragua, Colombia, Pakistan, Turkey, and probably India and Sri Lanka. Instead of terminating multiparty electoral competition and declaring a one-party (or no-party) dictatorship, as they did during the first and second reverse waves, frustrated chief executives (like Alberto Fujimori in Peru) may temporarily suspend the constitution, dismiss and reorganize the legislature, and reshape to their advantage a constitutional system that will subsequently retain the formal structure or appearance of democracy. Or they may engage in a cat-and-mouse game with international donors, liberalizing politically in response to pressure while repressing as much as they can get away with in order to hang on to power—as the former one-party regimes of Daniel arap Moi in Kenya, Omar Bongo in Gabon, and Paul Biya in Cameroon have done in Africa.

Is this, then, the way the third wave of democratization ends: death by a thousand subtractions?

## The Imperative of Consolidation

If the historical pattern is to be defied and a third reverse wave avoided, the overriding imperative in the coming years is to consolidate those democracies that have come into being during the third wave. In essence, consolidation is the process of achieving broad and deep legitimation, such that all significant political actors, at both the elite and mass levels, believe that the democratic regime is better for their society than any other realistic alternative they can imagine. As Juan Linz and Alfred Stepan, among others, have stressed, this legitimation must be more than a commitment to democracy in the abstract; it must also involve a shared normative and behavioral commitment to the specific rules and practices of the country's constitutional system.[22] It is this unquestioning embrace of democratic procedures that produces a crucial element of consolidation: a reduction in the uncertainty of democracy, regarding not so much the outcomes as the rules and methods of political competition. As consolidation advances, "there is a widening of the range of political actors who come to assume democratic conduct [and democratic loyalty] on the part of their adversaries," a transition from "instrumental" to "principled" commitments to the democratic framework, a growth in trust and cooperation among political competitors, and a socialization of the general population (through both deliberate efforts and the practice of democracy in politics and civil society).[23] Although many contemporary theorists are strangely determined to avoid the term, I believe that these elements of the consolidation process encompass a shift in *political culture.*

Democratic consolidation is fostered by a number of institutional, policy, and behavioral changes. Many of these changes improve governance directly by strengthening state capacity, liberalizing and rationalizing economic structures, securing social and political order while maintaining basic freedoms, improving horizontal accountability and the rule of law, and controlling corruption. Others improve the representative functions of democratic governance by strengthening political parties and their linkages to social groups, reducing fragmentation in the party system, strengthening the autonomous capacity and public accountability of legislatures and local governments, and invigorating civil society. Most new democracies need these types of institutional reform and strengthening. Some also require a steady program of reforms to reduce military involvement in nonmilitary issues and subject the military and intelligence establishments to oversight and control by elected civilian leaders. And some require legal and institutional innovations to foster accommodation and mutual security among different ethnic and national groups.

Underlying all of these specific challenges, however, is an intimate connection between the deepening of democracy and its consolidation. Some new democracies have become consolidated during the third wave, but none of the "nonliberal" electoral democracies that have emerged during the third wave has yet achieved consolidation. And those electoral democracies that predate the third wave and that have declined from liberal to nonliberal status during it (India, Sri Lanka, Venezuela, Colombia, Fiji) have become less stable and consolidated.

The less respectful of political rights, civil liberties, and constitutional constraints on state power are the behaviors of key state, incumbent-party, and other political actors, the weaker will be the procedural consensus underpinning democracy. Consolidation is then obstructed, by definition. Furthermore, the more shallow, exclusive, unaccountable, and abusive of individual and group rights is the electoral regime, the more difficult it will be for that regime to become deeply legitimated at the mans level (or to retain such legitimacy), and thus the lower will be the perceived costs for the elected president or the military to overthrow the system or to reduce it to pseudodemocracy. Consolidation is then obstructed or destroyed causally, by the effects of institutional shallowness and decay. If they are to become consolidated, therefore, electoral democracies must become deeper and more liberal. This will require greater executive (and military) accountability to both the law and the scrutiny of other branches of the government, as well as the public; the reduction of barriers to political participation and mobilization by marginalized groups; and more effective protection for the political and civil rights of all citizens. Deepening will also be facilitated by the institutionalization of a political-party system that stimulates mass participation, incorporates marginalized groups, and forges vibrant linkages with civil society organizations

and party branches and officials at the local level.

## Holding Democratic Ground

None of this should be seen as ruling out the possibility of democratic progress in the world's autocratic and pseudodemocratic states. Indeed, a developmental perspective should sensitize us to the real scope for partial gains and sudden breakthroughs that no theory of the "preconditions for democracy" could anticipate. However, if we think strategically about democracy's future, the key question must be, to borrow Huntington's analogy to a military campaign, how the democratic idea can hold the vast new territory it has conquered.[24]

The overriding imperative for the long-term global advance of democracy is to prevent its near-term recession into a new reverse wave. That encompasses three challenges. First, the new liberal democracies of the third wave must become consolidated (only a few of them have so far). Since consolidation is partly a process of habituation, time is on their side, but only if they can avoid major crises, sink institutional roots, and provide some degree of effective governance. Second, the merely electoral democracies must be deepened and liberalized politically so that their institutions will become more broadly and intrinsically valued by their populations.

Finally, the established, industrialized democracies must show their own continued capacity for democratic vitality, reform, and good governance. The ideological hegemony of democracy in the world has flourished on two foundations: the clear moral and practical superiority of the political systems of the established democracies; and their increasing use of pressure and conditional assistance to promote democratic development around the world. If the world's wealthy, established democracies have the wisdom and energy to preserve those two foundations, more democracies will become "established" in the coming decade, even if the overall expansion of (electoral) democracy draws to a halt. As the universe of stable liberal democracies expands, new points of democratic diffusion, pressure, and assistance will emerge, and cultural arguments that liberal democracy is a Western, ethnocentric concept will become increasingly perverse and untenable.

At some point in the first two decades of the twenty-first century—as economic development transforms the societies of East Asia in particular—the world will then be poised for a "fourth wave" of democratization, and quite possibly a boon to international peace and security far more profound and enduring than we have seen with the end of the Cold War.

## Notes

1. Samuel P. Huntington, *The Third Wave: Democratization in the Late Twentieth Century* (Nonnan: University of Oklahoma Press, 1991), 15.
2. David Collier and Steven Levitsky, "Democracy 'With Adjectives': Conceptual Innovation in Comparative Research" (unpubl. ms., Department of Political Science, University of California at Berkeley, 8 April 1996).
3. Joseph Schumpeter, *Capitalism, Socialism and Democracy*, 2nd ed. (New York: Harper, 1947), 269.
4. Huntington, *The Third Wave*, 5–13.
5. Robert A. Dahl, *Polyarchy: Participation and Opposition* (New Haven: Yale University Press, 1971), 3.
6. See Terry Lynn Karl, "Imposing Consent? Electoralism versus Democratization in El Salvador," in Paul Drake and Eduardo Silva, eds., *Elections and Democratization in Latin America, 1980–1985* (San Diego: Center for Iberian and Latin American Studies and Center for U.S.-Mexican Studies, University of California at San Diego, 1986), 9–36; "Dilemmas of Democratization in Latin America," *Comparative Politics* 23 (October 1990): 14–15; and "The Hybrid Regimes of Central America," *Journal of Democracy* 6 (July 1995): 72–86.
7. Philippe C. Schmitter and Terry Lynn Karl, "What Democracy Is... and Is Not," *Journal of Democracy* 2 (Summer 1991): 78.
8. An important discussion of reserved domains appears in J. Samuel Valenzuela, "Democratic Consolidation in Post–Transitional Settings: Notion, Process and Facilitating Conditions," in Scott Mainwaring, Guillermo O'Donnell, and J. Samuel Valenzuela, eds., *Issues in Democratic Consolidation: The New South American Democracies in Comparative Perspective* (Notre Dame, Ind.: University of Notre Dame Press, 1992), 64–66.
9. I use the term "liberal" to refer not to an economic regime featuring a limited state and an open economy but to a political regime in which individual and group liberties are particularly strong and well protected. There is obviously some affinity between economic and political liberty in these senses, but there are tensions and complexities as well that are beyond the scope of this discussion. Moreover, the term "liberal" should be construed here very broadly, even in the political sense. It requires sufficient civil liberties and pluralism to allow for free and meaningful competition of interests and the rule of law between elections as well as during them. But this still leaves substantial scope for variation in the balance a society places on individual rights versus responsibilities—or, to put it another way, in the emphasis on the individual versus the community.
10. Richard L. Sklar, "Developmental Democracy," *Comparative Studies in Society and History* 29 (October 1987): 686–714, and "Towards a Theory of Developmental Democracy," in Adrian Leftwich, ed., *Democracy and Development: Theory and Practice* (Cambridge, England: Polity Press, 1996), 26–27; and Guillermo O'Donnell, "Delegative Democracy," *Journal of Democracy* 5 (January 1994): 60–62. Sklar terms the lateral form "constitutional democracy" and emphasizes its mutually reinforcing relationship to vertical accountability.
11. Raw-point scores are determined by assigning from 0 to 4 points to each country on each of 8 checklist items for political rights and each of 13 checklist items for civil liberties. For a full explanation of the survey methodology, see Freedom House, *Freedom in the World: The Annual Survey of Political Rights and Civil Liberties, 1994–1995* (New York: Freedom House, 1995), 672–77, or *Freedom Review* 27 (January–February 1996): 11–15.
12. Giovanni Sartori, *Parties and Party Systems: A Framework for Analysis* (Cambridge: Cambridge University Press, 1976), 230–38.
13. Both my use of the term "developmental" and my emphasis on the continuous and open-ended nature of change in the character, degree, and depth of democratic institutions owe much to the work of Richard L. Sklar ("Developmental Democracy" and "Towards a Theory of Developmental Democracy"). Readers will nevertheless note important differences in our perspectives.
14. Huntington, *The Third Wave*, 25–26.
15. Freedom House, *Freedom in the World 1994–1995*, 5–7.
16. Jonathan Hartlyn, "Democracies in Contemporary South America: Convergences and Diversities," in Joseph Tulchin, ed., *Argentina: The Challenges of Modernization* (forthcoming). Quotations are from page 14 of a draft manuscript written in November 1995.
17. Barbara Gpeddes, "Challenging the Conventional Wisdom," in Larry Diamond and Marc F. Plattner, eds., *Economic Reform and Democracy* (Baltimore: Johns Hopkins University Press, 1995), 67.
18. Human Rights Watch, *Human Rights Watch World Report 1996* (New York: Human Rights Watch, 1995), xxv.
19. These ten are Senegal, Côte d'Ivoire, Burkina Faso, Ghana, Togo, Cameroon, Gabon, Zimbabwe, Kenya, and Ethiopia.
20. Samuel P. Huntington, "Armed Forces and Democracy: Reforming Civil-Military Relations," *Journal of Democracy* 6 (October 1995): 13.
21. Ibid., 9–10.
22. Juan J. Linz and Alfred Stepan, *Problems of Democratic Transition and Consolidation: Southern Europe, South America, and Post–Communist Europe* (Baltimore: Johns Hopkins University Press, forthcoming), ch. 2, and "Toward Consolidated Democracies," *Journal of Democracy* 7 (April 1996): 14–33; and Richard Gunther, Hans-Jürgen Puhle, and P. Nikiforos Diamandouros, "Introduction," in Gunther, Diamandouros, and Puhle, eds., *The Politics of Democratic Consolidation: Southern Europe in Comparative Perspective* (Baltimore: Johns Hopkins University Press, 1995), 7–10.
23. Laurence Whitehead, "The Consolidation of Fragile Democracies: A Discussion with Illustrations," in Robert A. Pastor, ed., *Democracy in the Americas: Stopping the Pendulum* (New York: Holmes and Meier, 1989), 79.
24. Samuel P. Huntington, "Democracy for the Lang Haul," *Journal of Democracy* 7 (April 1996): 5.

# Serial Utopia

Economic models, like their fashion equivalents, come and go.
But will one size ever fit all, asks **Christian Tyler**

Like any fashion model, today's ideal economy is supposed to be slim to the point of anorexic. In a post-collective, minimal-welfare age, the model must carry no fat. She must be long in the leg but light on her feet, not top-heavy nor too comfortable, but flexible, wiry—and competitive.

She should have the racing lines of, let us say, Irma Pantaeva, the six-foot supermodel from Siberia who wears an (American) dress size six. Pantaeva left her home on the shores of Lake Baikal in Russia after the collapse of communism—and found her way to New York where her doll-like Eskimo looks have landed her a part in a Woody Allen film.

Miss Pantaeva knew where she was going. Many economic theorists, especially American ones, regard the US as the ultimate model for an era famously described by Francis Fukuyama as "the end of history."

Others disagree, even violently. Too slim a line, they protest, is bad for the public health.

Starve your social structure too much, rely too much on material palliatives (sport, sex, shopping) for assuaging people's insecurity and spiritual hunger, and you are in danger of falling right off the catwalk. If not the US, who is the millennial supermodel?

The tiger-cub economies of Asia—especially Thailand, Malaysia, and Indonesia—are out of the contest for the moment. They have been put back in their cages, tails between their legs, punished by the markets for practising a fat-cat capitalism in which the banking system was allowed to become the plaything of the rich and powerful.

We must look elsewhere in a world ever more locked together by trade and technology.

Utopias have always been with us. But they are not always places we would choose to live in. For even the most zealous economic libertarian prizes his quality of life, his slippers warming by a thermally inefficient hearth.

Sir Thomas More, Chancellor under Henry VIII, was mockingly ambivalent about his *Utopia,* according to Peter Ackroyd's new biography. More appeared to praise its Platonic *dirigisme.* Yet he called his narrator Hythlodaeus, which means "babbler" in Greek, the island's capital Amaurotum ("gloomy") and its principal river Anydrus ("waterless").

The poet Coleridge could find no subscribers for his "Pantisocracy", an egalitarian commune in the New World. And no doubt Samuel Butler would have run a mile rather than live in his *Erewhon* ("Nowhere").

And how many will sign up for the latest Utopian project: a 1,400-metre, 2.7m-tonne, 30-storey ship called "Freedom" designed to carry 65,000 rich residents in tax-exempt bliss round the globe in "the world's first ideal community"?

Many "ideal communities" have been held up for admiration this century. Even the Siberian supermodel's homeland, now in the grip of gangster capitalism, had its moment of glory.

According to the historian Eric Hobsbawin, Soviet central planning was an influential precedent for political leaders in the west anxious to forge a social contract—

> **Germany lacks the will to break up a labour hierarchy which goes back to the Middle Ages**

full employment and a welfare state—that would prevent a recurrence of economic slump, political extremism and war.

From the rubble of wartime Germany a powerful new model emerged, even as Britain began to understand the reality of its own post-imperial decline. Envious eyes were cast on this virtuous example of a high-wage, high-output economy where everyone, from baker's boy to finance director, had to serve his apprenticeship; where wage negotiations took account of the size of the national cake and rarely ended in strikes; where workers had seats on big company boards.

What was "concerted action" to Germany was "corporatism" to Thatcher's Britain. Today, Germany, having paid the bill to absorb its bankrupt eastern half after the fall of the Berlin wall, is considered too fat to prosper in the lean regime demanded by global competition. Even its most loyal supporters suspect it lacks the will to break up a labour hierarchy which goes back (as it did in the UK) to the guilds of the Middle Ages.

Among other social market economies, Austria has its adherents, but none attracts such devotion as the glamorous Swedish model. Exotically high taxes supported generous public services, and each year better-off white-collar workers conceded a "solidarity" wage transfer to their poorer comrades. Sweden was glamorous, but lacked stamina. In 1990, under a coalition government, the model repented of its public expenditure excesses.

In the 25 years of post second world war prosperity which Hobsbawm has described as a golden age, France attracted supporters for its modernising *élan.* Railways, airports and nuclear power plants were built, homes were computer-linked, and cultural monuments were erected by a ruling elite which moved effortlessly between civil service, government and industry. They wrote books, talked philosophy—and never cut short their lunch.

Italy had its 15 mInutes of fame. In spite of a corrupt and chaotic political system, a ludicrous bureaucracy and massive national debt, it managed to pull ahead, briefly, of the UK.

The *sorpasso* of 1987 may have been statistical sleight-of-hand, but it left thrifty north Europeans musing about the strengths of a family-based, moonlighting economy.

There was even a small vogue—among trade union visionaries—for the Yugoslav model. After breaking with Stalin in 1948, Tito became the west's Good Communist, challenged for the title only by the "maverick", as he was so often described, Nicolae Ceausescu of Romania.

Tito liberalised the economy, devolved power to the regions, eased up a bit on political dissent, and gave his vizier Edvard Kardelj the unenviable job of reconciling "self-management"—workers chose their bosses and paid themselves wages—with the leading and guiding role of the party.

By the 1970s, of course, the world was being dazzled by the rising sun of Japan. Craftily borrowing western production ideas without at the same time compromising their

From *Financial Times*, March 21/22, 1998, pp. 14. © 1998 by Financial Times Syndication. Reprinted by permission.

culture, the Japanese had the audacity to make them work better than the west could.

At first, competitors laughed at the company songs, the lifetime employment, the pitifully few holidays, the stay-at-work strikes. Soon they were trembling for their jobs.

By fair means or foul (including strange excuses for low import penetration—that Japanese snow was "the wrong kind" for American skis, for instance) Japan inundated the world with its exports of cars and electronics.

Then suddenly, in 1990, following a stock market blowout, Japan hit the buffers. Today, kids wear baseball caps, and cars are imported; and there has been a surge in youth crime, along with a credit crunch, bankruptcies and rising unemployment.

The Asian tigers were on Japan's heels. South Korea, now also in crisis, was the industrial powerhouse but western pundits were more fascinated by the island states. Hong Kong, hitherto derided for making cheap plastic toys, began building textile factories in Switzerland. Taiwan gave the west an ideologically useful stick with which to beat communist China, then itself beginning to open.

As for Singapore, the streets were cleared of litter and riff-raff, miscreants were given a sound thrashing, and opposition politics became the riskiest choice of career. It was, the writer William Gibson observed, that rare place where residents went to a neighbouring Moslem country for their hanky-panky. Yet law-and-order capitalism appeared to work. Perhaps there was something in these "Asian values" after all.

The current blizzard in Asia has confirmed Fukuyama in his belief that economies will converge round a western (if not specifically US) model.

"Of all the alternatives, only a kind of paternalist Asian one looked remotely plausible," he said this week, speaking from George Mason University, Virginia. "Now that has been shown not to be viable."

What about China's version of a market economy? "I would be extremely surprised if the Communist party stays in power," he declared. Others are beginning to wonder if this conventional wisdom is correct, as they observe Beijing's increasingly pragmatic management of its economic revolution.

If another "third way" is emerging, the fashion show is not over yet. Indeed, the world could see a proliferation of capitalisms, says Professor John Gray, of the London School of Economics. In a new polemic, *False Dawn,* Gray warns that US efforts to impose a free-market, free-trade diet on the rest of the world will be rejected.

A defector from the radical right, Gray thinks the US has neither the power, nor the will, to enforce what he calls just another form of social engineering. Americans may tolerate the consequences—ghettoes, gross income inequalities and a huge prison population; but exported to other cultures, this brand of capitalism is doomed to self-destruction.

So who now takes the crown?

"If you are talking about efficiency," says Nicholas Crafts, professor of economic history at the LSE, "then I still think the US has got it more nearly right than most. But the model is deeply unattractive to many people, including me. My judgment is that Americans care too little about redistribution."

Asked to pick the supermodel for the millennium, Fukuyama nominated Canada, as a free-market country, socially liberal, with its own cultural accessories.

Gray nominated the Netherlands for its combination of reformed welfare state, freed-up labour market and social tolerance. Sweden still has her fans, as do Austria and Denmark.

In any beauty contest, jurors cannot conceal their local bias. But it is not just for that reason that Blair's "cool Britannia", which lost the crown early this century, is getting votes these days from its native judges. Britain, they say, could be the model for Europe. At the least, it is looking like a plausible model for itself.

And this is the conclusion pundits seem to like best. Countries may pinch one another's clothes, but they should not dress up in gear that doesn't suit the body they were born into. "There is no One Size Fits All," says Roderick Nye of the Social Market Foundation, a London think-tank.

Geoff Mulgan, another tankie now working at Tony Blair's policy unit, puts it well: "The fashion for using other countries is waning, and that's a healthy thing. It's bound to end in mistaken borrowings, and it's bound to end in tears."

# Capitalism and Democracy*

## Gabriel A. Almond

Gabriel A. Almond, professor of political science emeritus at Stanford University, is a former president of the American Political Science Association.

Joseph Schumpeter, a great economist and social scientist of the last generation, whose career was almost equally divided between Central European and American universities, and who lived close to the crises of the 1930s and '40s, published a book in 1942 under the title, *Capitalism, Socialism, and Democracy.* The book has had great influence, and can be read today with profit. It was written in the aftergloom of the great depression, during the early triumphs of Fascism and Nazism in 1940 and 1941, when the future of capitalism, socialism, and democracy all were in doubt. Schumpeter projected a future of declining capitalism, and rising socialism. He thought that democracy under socialism might be no more impaired and problematic than it was under capitalism.

He wrote a concluding chapter in the second edition which appeared in

1946, and which took into account the political-economic situation at the end of the war, with the Soviet Union then astride a devastated Europe. In this last chapter he argues that we should not identify the future of socialism with that of the Soviet Union, that what we had observed and were observing in the first three decades of Soviet existence was not a necessary expression of socialism. There was a lot of Czarist Russia in the mix. If Schumpeter were writing today, I don't believe he would argue that socialism has a brighter future than capitalism. The relationship between the two has turned out to be a good deal more complex and intertwined than Schumpeter anticipated. But I am sure that he would still urge us to separate the future of socialism from that of Soviet and Eastern European Communism.

Unlike Schumpeter I do not include Socialism in my title, since its future as a distinct ideology and program of action is unclear at best. Western Marxism and the moderate socialist movements seem to have settled for social democratic solutions, for adaptations of both capitalism and democracy producing acceptable mixes of market competition, political pluralism, participation, and welfare. I deal with these modifications of capitalism, as a consequence of the im-

pact of democracy on capitalism in the last half century.

At the time that Adam Smith wrote *The Wealth of Nations,* the world of government, politics and the state that he knew—pre-Reform Act England, the French government of Louis XV and XVI—was riddled with special privileges, monopolies, interferences with trade. With my tongue only half way in my check I believe the discipline of economics may have been traumatized by this condition of political life at its birth. Typically, economists speak of the state and government instrumentally, as a kind of secondary service mechanism.

---

*The relation between capitalism and democracy dominates the political theory of the last two centuries.*

---

I do not believe that politics can be treated in this purely instrumental and reductive way without losing our analytic grip on the social and historical process. The economy and the pol-

*Lecture presented at Seminar on the Market, sponsored by The Ford Foundation and the Research Institute on International Change of Columbia University, Moscow, October 29–November 2.

From *PS: Political Science and Politics,* September 1991, pp. 467–474. © 1991 by The American Political Science Association. Reprinted by permission.

ity are the main problem solving mechanisms of human society. They each have their distinctive means, and they each have their "goods" or ends. They necessarily interact with each other, and transform each other in the process. Democracy in particular generates goals and programs. You cannot give people the suffrage, and let them form organizations, run for office, and the like, without their developing all kinds of ideas as to how to improve things. And sometimes some of these ideas are adopted, implemented and are productive, and improve our lives, although many economists are reluctant to concede this much to the state.

My lecture deals with this interaction of politics and economics in the Western World in the course of the last couple of centuries, in the era during which capitalism and democracy emerged as the dominant problem solving institutions of modern civilization. I am going to discuss some of the theoretical and empirical literature dealing with the themes of the positive and negative interaction between capitalism and democracy. There are those who say that capitalism supports democracy, and those who say that capitalism subverts democracy. And there are those who say that democracy subverts capitalism, and those who say that it supports it.

The relation between capitalism and democracy dominates the political theory of the last two centuries. All the logically possible points of view are represented in a rich literature. It is this ambivalence and dialectic, this tension between the two major problem solving sectors of modern society—the political and the economic—that is the topic of my lecture.

## Capitalism Supports Democracy

Let me begin with the argument that capitalism is positively linked with democracy, shares its values and culture, and facilitates its development. This case has been made in historical, logical, and statistical terms.

Albert Hirschman in his *Rival Views of Market Society* (1986) examines the values, manners and morals of capitalism, and their effects on the larger society and culture as these have been described by the philosophers of the 17th, 18th, and 19th centuries. He shows how the interpretation of the impact of capitalism has changed from the enlightenment view of Montesquieu, Condorcet, Adam Smith and others, who stressed the *douceur* of commerce, its "gentling," civilizing effect on behavior and interpersonal relations, to that of the 19th and 20th century conservative and radical writers who described the culture of capitalism as crassly materialistic, destructively competitive, corrosive of morality, and hence self-destructive. This sharp almost 180-degree shift in point of view among political theorists is partly explained by the transformation from the commerce and small-scale industry of early capitalism, to the smoke blackened industrial districts, the demonic and exploitive entrepreneurs, and exploited laboring classes of the second half of the nineteenth century. Unfortunately for our purposes, Hirschman doesn't deal explicitly with the capitalism–democracy connection, but rather with culture and with manners. His argument, however, implies an early positive connection and a later negative one.

Joseph Schumpeter in *Capitalism, Socialism, and Democracy* (1942) states flatly, "History clearly confirms . . . [that] . . . modern democracy rose along with capitalism, and in causal connection with it . . . modern democracy is a product of the capitalist process." He has a whole chapter entitled "The Civilization of Capitalism," democracy being a part of that civilization. Schumpeter also makes the point that democracy was historically supportive of capitalism. He states, " . . . the bourgeoisie reshaped, and from its own point of view rationalized, the social and political structure that preceded its ascendancy . . ." (that is to say, feudalism). "The democratic method was the political tool of that reconstruction." According to Schum-

peter capitalism and democracy were mutually causal historically, mutually supportive parts of a rising modern civilization, although as we shall show below, he also recognized their antagonisms.

Barrington Moore's historical investigation (1966) with its long title, *The Social Origins of Dictatorship and Democracy; Lord and Peasant in the Making of the Modern World,* argues that there have been three historical routes to industrial modernization. The first of these followed by Britain, France, and the United States, involved the subordination and transformation of the agricultural sector by the rising commercial bourgeoisie, producing the democratic capitalism of the 19th and 20th centuries. The second route followed by Germany and Japan, where the landed aristocracy was able to contain and dominate the rising commercial classes, produced an authoritarian and fascist version of industrial modernization, a system of capitalism encased in a feudal authoritarian framework, dominated by a military aristocracy, and an authoritarian monarchy. The third route, followed in Russia where the commercial bourgeoisie was too weak to give content and direction to the modernizing process, took the form of a revolutionary process drawing on the frustration and resources of the peasantry, and created a mobilized authoritarian Communist regime along with a state-controlled industrialized economy. Successful capitalism dominating and transforming the rural agricultural sector, according to Barrington Moore, is the creator and sustainer of the emerging democracies of the nineteenth century.

Robert A. Dahl, the leading American democratic theorist, in the new edition of his book (1990) *After the Revolution? Authority in a Good Society,* has included a new chapter entitled "Democracy and Markets." In the opening paragraph of that chapter, he says:

> It is an historical fact that modern democratic institutions . . . have existed only in countries with pre-

dominantly privately owned, market-oriented economies, or capitalism if you prefer that name. It is also a fact that all "socialist" countries with predominantly state-owned centrally directed economic orders—command economies—have not enjoyed democratic governments, but have in fact been ruled by authoritarian dictatorships. It is also an historical fact that some "capitalist" countries have also been, and are, ruled by authoritarian dictatorships.

To put it more formally, it looks to be the case that market-oriented economies are necessary (in the logical sense) to democratic institutions, though they are certainly not sufficient. And it looks to be the case that state-owned centrally directed economic orders are strictly associated with authoritarian regimes, though authoritarianism definitely does not require them. We have something very much like an historical experiment, so it would appear, that leaves these conclusions in no great doubt. (Dahl 1990)

Peter Berger in his book *The Capitalist Revolution* (1986) presents four propositions on the relation between capitalism and democracy:

Capitalism is a necessary but not sufficient condition of democracy under modern conditions.

If a capitalist economy is subjected to increasing degrees of state control, a point (not precisely specifiable at this time) will be reached at which democratic governance becomes impossible.

If a socialist economy is opened up to increasing degrees of market forces, a point (not precisely specifiable at this time) will be reached at which democratic governance becomes a possibility.

If capitalist development is successful in generating economic growth from which a sizable proportion of the population benefits, pressures toward democracy are likely to appear.

This positive relationship between capitalism and democracy has also been sustained by statistical studies. The "Social Mobilization" theorists of the 1950s and 1960s which included

## There is a logic in the relation between level of economic development and democratic institutions.

Daniel Lerner (1958), Karl Deutsch (1961), S. M. Lipset (1959) among others, demonstrated a strong statistical association between GNP per capita and democratic political institutions. This is more than simple statistical association. There is a logic in the relation between level of economic development and democratic institutions. Level of economic development has been shown to be associated with education and literacy, exposure to mass media, and democratic psychological propensities such as subjective efficacy, participatory aspirations and skills. In a major investigation of the social psychology of industrialization and modernization, a research team led by the sociologist Alex Inkeles (1974) interviewed several thousand workers in the modern industrial and the traditional economic sectors of six countries of differing culture. Inkeles found empathetic, efficacious, participatory and activist propensities much more frequently among the modern industrial workers, and to a much lesser extent in the traditional sector in each one of these countries regardless of cultural differences.

The historical, the logical, and the statistical evidence for this positive relation between capitalism and democracy is quite persuasive.

## Capitalism Subverts Democracy

But the opposite case is also made, that capitalism subverts or undermines democracy. Already in John Staurt Mill (1848) we encounter a view of existing systems of private property

as unjust, and of the free market as destructively competitive—aesthetically and morally repugnant. The case he was making was a normative rather than a political one. He wanted a less competitive society, ultimately socialist, which would still respect individuality. He advocated limitations on the inheritance of property and the improvement of the property system so that everyone shared in its benefits, the limitation of population growth, and the improvement of the quality of the labor force through the provision of high quality education for all by the state. On the eve of the emergence of the modern democratic capitalist order John Staurt Mill wanted to control the excesses of both the market economy and the majoritarian polity, by the education of consumers and producers, citizens and politicians, in the interest of producing morally improved free market and democratic orders. But in contrast to Marx, he did not thoroughly discount the possibilities of improving the capitalist and democratic order.

Marx argued that as long as capitalism and private property existed there could be no genuine democracy, that democracy under capitalism was bourgeois democracy, which is to say not democracy at all. While it would be in the interest of the working classes to enter a coalition with the bourgeoisie in supporting this form of democracy in order to eliminate feudalism, this would be a tactical maneuver. Capitalist democracy could only result in the increasing exploitation of the working classes. Only the elimination of capitalism and private property could result in the emancipation of the working classes and the attainment of true democracy. Once socialism was attained the basic political problems of humanity would have been solved through the elimination of classes. Under socialism there would be no distinctive democratic organization, no need for institutions to resolve conflicts, since there would be no conflicts. There is not much democratic or political theory to be found in Marx's writings. The basic reality is the mode of economic production and the consequent class structure from which other institutions follow.

For the followers of Marx up to the present day there continues to be a negative tension between capitalism, however reformed, and democracy. But the integral Marxist and Leninist rejection of the possibility of an autonomous, bourgeois democratic state has been left behind for most Western Marxists. In the thinking of Poulantzas, Offe, Bobbio, Habermas and others, the bourgeois democratic state is now viewed as a class struggle state, rather than an unambiguously bourgeois state. The working class has access to it; it can struggle for its interests, and can attain partial benefits from it. The state is now viewed as autonomous, or as relatively autonomous, and it can be reformed in a progressive direction by working class and other popular movements. The bourgeois democratic state can be moved in the direction of a socialist state by political action short of violence and institutional destruction.

Schumpeter (1942) appreciated the tension between capitalism and democracy. While he saw a causal connection between competition in the economic and the political order, he points out "...that there are some deviations from the principle of democracy which link up with the presence of organized capitalist interests.... [T]he statement is true both from the standpoint of the classical and from the standpoint of our own theory of democracy. From the first standpoint, the result reads that the means at the disposal of private interests are often used in order to thwart the will of the people. From the second standpoint, the result reads that those private means are often used in order to interfere with the working of the mechanism of competitive leadership." He refers to some countries and situations in which "...political life all but resolved itself into a struggle of pressure groups and in many cases practices that failed to conform to the spirit of the democratic method." But he rejects the notion that there cannot be political democracy in a capitalist society. For Schumpeter full democracy in the sense of the informed participation of all adults in the selection of political leaders and consequently the making of public policy, was an impossibility because of the number and complexity of the issues confronting modern electorates. The democracy which was realistically possible was one in which people could choose among competing leaders, and consequently exercise some direction over political decisions. This kind of democracy was possible in a capitalist society, though some of its propensities impaired its performance. Writing in the early years of World War II, when the future of democracy and of capitalism were uncertain, he leaves unresolved the questions of "... Whether or not democracy is one of those products of capitalism which are to die out with it ..." or "... how well or ill capitalist society qualifies for the task of working the democratic method it evolved."

Non-Marxist political theorists have contributed to this questioning of the reconcilability of capitalism and democracy. Robert A. Dahl, who makes the point that capitalism historically has been a necessary precondition of democracy, views contemporary democracy in the United States as seriously compromised, impaired by the inequality in resources among the citizens. But Dahl stresses the variety in distributive patterns, and in politico-economic relations among contemporary democracies. "The category of capitalist democracies" he writes, "includes an extraordinary variety ... from nineteenth century, laissez faire, early industrial systems to twentieth century, highly regulated, social welfare, late or postindustrial systems. Even late twentieth century 'welfare state' orders vary all the way from the Scandinavian systems, which are redistributive, heavily taxed, comprehensive in their social security, and neocorporatist in their collective bargaining arrangements to the faintly redistributive, moderately taxed, limited social security, weak collective bargaining systems of the United States and Japan" (1989).

In *Democracy and Its Critics* (1989) Dahl argues that the normative growth of democracy to what he calls its "third transformation" (the first being the direct city-state democracy of classic times, and the second, the indirect, representative inegalitarian democracy of the contemporary world) will require democratization of the economic order. In other words, modern corporate capitalism needs to be transformed. Since government control and/or ownership of the economy would be destructive of the pluralism which is an essential requirement of democracy, his preferred solution to the problem of the mega-corporation is employee control of corporate industry. An economy so organized, according to Dahl, would improve the distribution of political resources without at the same time destroying the pluralism which democratic competition requires. To those who question the realism of Dahl's solution to the problem of inequality, he replies that history is full of surprises.

---

*... one of the dominant traditions of economics from Adam Smith until the present day stresses the importance for productivity and welfare of an economy that is relatively free of intervention by the state.*

---

Charles E. Lindblom in his book, *Politics and Markets* (1977), concludes his comparative analysis of the political economy of modern capitalism and socialism, with an essentially pessimistic conclusion about contemporary market-oriented democracy. He says

We therefore come back to the corporation. It is possible that the rise of the corporation has offset or more than offset the decline of class as an instrument of indoctrination.... That it creates a new core of wealth and power for a newly constructed upper class, as well as an overpowering loud voice, is also reasonably clear. The executive of the large corporation is, on many counts, the contemporary counterpart to the landed gentry of an earlier era, his voice amplified by the technology of mass communication. . . . [T]he major institutional barrier to fuller democracy may therefore be the autonomy of the private corporation.

Lindblom concludes, "The large private corporation fits oddly into democratic theory and vision. Indeed it does not fit.

There is then a widely shared agreement, from the Marxists and neo-Marxists, to Schumpeter, Dahl, Lindblom, and other liberal political theorists, that modern capitalism with the dominance of the large corporation, produces a defective or an impaired form of democracy.

## Democracy Subverts Capitalism

If we change our perspective now and look at the way democracy is said to affect capitalism, one of the dominant traditions of economics from Adam Smith until the present day stresses the importance for productivity and welfare of an economy that is relatively free of intervention by the state. In this doctrine of minimal government there is still a place for a framework of rules and services essential to the productive and efficient performance of the economy. In part the government has to protect the market from itself. Left to their own devices, according to Smith, businessmen were prone to corner the market in order to exact the highest possible price. And according to Smith businessmen were prone to bribe public officials in order to gain special privileges, and legal monopolies. For Smith good capitalism was competitive capitalism, and good government provided just those goods and services which the market needed to flourish, could not itself provide, or

would not provide. A good government according to Adam Smith was a minimal government, providing for the national defense, and domestic order. Particularly important for the economy were the rules pertaining to commercial life such as the regulation of weights and measures, setting and enforcing building standards, providing for the protection of persons and property, and the like.

For Milton Friedman (1961, 1981), the leading contemporary advocate of the free market and free government, and of the interdependence of the two, the principal threat to the survival of capitalism and democracy is the assumption of the responsibility for welfare on the part of the modern democratic state. He lays down a set of functions appropriate to government in the positive interplay between economy and polity, and then enumerates many of the ways in which the modern welfare, regulatory state has deviated from these criteria.

A good Friedmanesque, democratic government would be one " . . .which maintained law and order, defended property rights, served as a means whereby we could modify property rights and other rules of the economic game, adjudicated disputes about the interpretation of the rules, enforced contracts, promoted competition, provided a monetary framework, engaged in activities to counter technical monopolies and to overcome neighborhood effects widely regarded as sufficiently important to justify government intervention, and which supplemented private charity and the private family in protecting the irresponsible, whether madman or child . . . ." Against this list of proper activities for a free government, Friedman pinpointed more than a dozen activities of contemporary democratic governments which might better be performed through the private sector, or not at all. These included setting and maintaining price supports, tariffs, import and export quotas and controls, rents, interest rates, wage rates, and the like, regulating industries and banking, radio and television, licensing professions and occupations, pro-

viding social security and medical care programs, providing public housing, national parks, guaranteeing mortgages, and much else.

Friedman concludes that this steady encroachment on the private sector has been slowly but surely converting our free government and market system into a collective monster, compromising both freedom and productivity in the outcome. The tax and expenditure revolts and regulatory rebellions of the 1980s have temporarily stemmed this trend, but the threat continues. "It is the internal threat coming from men of good intentions and good will who wish to reform us. Impatient with the slowness of persuasion and example to achieve the great social changes they envision, they are anxious to use the power of the state to achieve their ends, and confident of their own ability to do so." The threat to political and economic freedom, according to Milton Friedman and others who argue the same position, arises out of democratic politics. It may only be defeated by political action.

In the last decades a school, or rather several schools, of economists and political scientists have turned the theoretical models of economics to use in analyzing political processes. Variously called public choice theorists, rational choice theorists, or positive political theorists, and employing such models as market exchange and bargaining, rational self interest, game theory, and the like, these theorists have produced a substantial literature throwing new and often controversial light on democratic political phenomena such as elections, decisions of political party leaders, interest group behavior, legislative and committee decisions, bureaucratic, and judicial behavior, lobbying activity, and substantive public policy areas such as constitutional arrangements, health and environment policy, regulatory policy, national security and foreign policy, and the like. Hardly a field of politics and public policy has been left untouched by this inventive and productive group of scholars.

The institutions and names with which this movement is associated in the United States include Virginia State University, the University of Virginia, the George Mason University, the University of Rochester, the University of Chicago, the California Institute of Technology, the Carnegie Mellon University, among others. And the most prominent names are those of the leaders of the two principal schools: James Buchanan, the Nobel Laureate leader of the Virginia "Public Choice" school, and William Riker, the leader of the Rochester "Positive Theory" school. Other prominent scholars associated with this work are Gary Becker of the University of Chicago, Kenneth Shepsle and Morris Fiorina of Harvard, John Ferejohn of Stanford, Charles Plott of the California Institute of Technology, and many others.

One writer summarizing the ideological bent of much of this work, but by no means all of it (William Mitchell of the University of Washington), describes it as fiscally conservative, sharing a conviction that the " . . .private economy is far more robust, efficient, and perhaps, equitable than other economies, and much more successful than political processes in efficiently allocating resources. . . ." Much of what has been produced " . . .by James Buchanan and the leaders of this school can best be described as contributions to a theory of the failure of political processes." These failures of political performance are said to be inherent properties of the democratic political process. "Inequity, inefficiency, and coercion are the most general results of democratic policy formation." In a democracy the demand for publicly provided services seems to be insatiable. It ultimately turns into a special interest, "rent seeking" society. Their remedies take the form of proposed constitutional limits on spending power and checks and balances to limit legislative majorities.

One of the most visible products of this pessimistic economic analysis of democratic politics is the book by Mancur Olson, *The Rise and Decline*

*of Nations* (1982). He makes a strong argument for the negative democracy–capitalism connection. His thesis is that the behavior of individuals and firms in stable societies inevitably leads to the formation of dense networks of collusive, cartelistic, and lobbying organizations that make economies less efficient and dynamic and polities less governable. "The longer a society goes without an upheaval, the more powerful such organizations become and the more they slow down economic expansion. Societies in which these narrow interest groups have been destroyed, by war or revolution, for example, enjoy the greatest gains in growth." His prize cases are Britain on the one hand and Germany and Japan on the other.

> The logic of the argument implies that countries that have had democratic freedom of organization without upheaval or invasion the longest will suffer the most from growth-repressing organizations and combinations. This helps explain why Great Britain, the major nation with the longest immunity from dictatorship, invasion, and revolution, has had in this century a lower rate of growth than other large, developed democracies. Britain has precisely the powerful network of special interest organization that the argument developed here would lead us to expect in a country with its record of military security and democratic stability. The number and power of its trade unions need no description. The venerability and power of its professional associations is also striking. . . . In short, with age British society has acquired so many strong organizations and collusions that it suffers from an institutional sclerosis that slows its adaptation to changing circumstances and technologies. (Olson 1982)

By contrast, post-World War II Germany and Japan started organizationally from scratch. The organizations that led them to defeat were all dissolved, and under the occupation inclusive organizations like the general trade union movement and general organizations of the industrial and commercial community were first formed.

These inclusive organizations had more regard for the general national interest and exercised some discipline on the narrower interest organizations. And both countries in the post-war decades experienced "miracles" of economic growth under democratic conditions.

The Olson theory of the subversion of capitalism through the propensities of democratic societies to foster special interest groups has not gone without challenge. There can be little question that there is logic in his argument. But empirical research testing this pressure group hypothesis thus far has produced mixed findings. Olson has hopes that a public educated to the harmful consequences of special interests to economic growth, full employment, coherent government, equal opportunity, and social mobility will resist special interest behavior, and enact legislation imposing antitrust, and anti-monopoly controls to mitigate and contain these threats. It is somewhat of an irony that the solution to this special interest disease of democracy, according to Olson, is a democratic state with sufficient regulatory authority to control the growth of special interest organizations.

## Democracy Fosters Capitalism

My fourth theme, democracy as fostering and sustaining capitalism, is not as straightforward as the first three. Historically there can be little doubt that as the suffrage was extended in the last century, and as mass political parties developed, democratic development impinged significantly on capitalist institutions and practices. Since successful capitalism requires risk-taking entrepreneurs with access to investment capital, the democratic propensity for redistributive and regulative policy tends to reduce the incentives and the resources available for risk-taking and creativity. Thus it can be argued that propensities inevitably resulting from democratic politics, as Friedman, Olson and many others argue, tend to reduce productivity, and hence welfare.

But precisely the opposite argument can be made on the basis of the historical experience of literally all of the advanced capitalist democracies in existence. All of them without exception are now welfare states with some form and degree of social insurance, health and welfare nets, and regulatory frameworks designed to mitigate the harmful impacts and shortfalls of capitalism. Indeed, the welfare state is accepted all across the political spectrum. Controversy takes place around the edges. One might make the argument that had capitalism not been modified in this welfare direction, it is doubtful that it would have survived.

This history of the interplay between democracy and capitalism is clearly laid out in a major study involving European and American scholars, entitled *The Development of Welfare States in Western Europe and America* (Flora and Heidenheimer 1981). The book lays out the relationship between the development and spread of capitalist industry, democratization in the sense of an expanding suffrage and the emergence of trade unions and left-wing political parties, and the gradual introduction of the institutions and practices of the welfare state. The early adoption of the institutions of the welfare state in Bismarck Germany, Sweden, and Great Britain were all associated with the rise of trade unions and socialist parties in those countries. The decisions made by the upper and middle class leaders and political movements to introduce welfare measures such as accident, old age, and unemployment insurance, were strategic decisions. They were increasingly confronted by trade union movements with the capacity of bringing industrial production to a halt, and by political parties with growing parliamentary representation favoring fundamental modifications in, or the abolition of capitalism. As the calculations of the upper and middle class leaders led them to conclude that the costs of suppression exceeded the costs of concession, the various parts

of the welfare state began to be put in place—accident, sickness, unemployment insurance, old age insurance, and the like. The problem of maintaining the loyalty of the working classes through two world wars resulted in additional concessions to working class demands: the filling out of the social security system, free public education to higher levels, family allowances, housing benefits, and the like.

Social conditions, historical factors, political processes and decisions produced different versions of the welfare state. In the United States, manhood suffrage came quite early, the later bargaining process emphasized free land and free education to the secondary level, an equality of opportunity version of the welfare state. The Disraeli bargain in Britain resulted in relatively early manhood suffrage and the full attainment of parliamentary government, while the Lloyd George bargain on the eve of World War I brought the beginnings of a welfare system to Britain. The Bismarck bargain in Germany produced an early welfare state, a postponement of electoral equality and parliamentary government. While there were all of these differences in historical encounters with democratization and "welfarization," the important outcome was that little more than a century after the process began all of the advanced capitalist democracies had similar versions of the welfare state, smaller in scale in the case of the United States and Japan, more substantial in Britain and the continental European countries.

We can consequently make out a strong case for the argument that democracy has been supportive of capitalism in this strategic sense. Without this welfare adaptation it is doubtful that capitalism would have survived, or rather, its survival, "unwelfarized," would have required a substantial repressive apparatus. The choice then would seem to have been between democratic welfare capitalism, and repressive undemocratic capitalism. I am inclined to believe that capitalism as such thrives more with the demo-

cratic welfare adaptation than with the repressive one. It is in that sense that we can argue that there is a clear positive impact of democracy on capitalism.

We have to recognize, in conclusion, that democracy and capitalism are both positively and negatively related, that they both support and subvert each other. My colleague, Moses Abramovitz, described this dialectic more surely than most in his presidential address to the American Economic Association in 1980, on the eve of the "Reagan Revolution." Noting the decline in productivity in the American economy during the latter 1960s and '70s, and recognizing that this decline might in part be attributable to the "tax, transfer, and regulatory" tendencies of the welfare state, he observes,

> The rationale supporting the development of our mixed economy sees it as a pragmatic compromise between the competing virtues and defects of decentralized market capitalism and encompassing socialism. Its goal is to obtain a measure of distributive justice, security, and social guidance of economic life without losing too much of the allocative efficiency and dynamism of private enterprise and market organization. And it is a pragmatic compromise in another sense. It seeks to retain for most people that measure of personal protection from the state which private property and a private job market confer, while obtaining for the disadvantaged minority of people through the state that measure of support without which their lack of property or personal endowment would amount to a denial of individual freedom and capacity to function as full members of the community. (Abramovitz 1981)

Democratic welfare capitalism produces that reconciliation of opposing and complementary elements which makes possible the survival, even enhancement of both of these sets of institutions. It is not a static accommodation, but rather one which fluctuates over time, with capitalism being compromised by the tax-transfer-regulatory action of the state at one point, and then correcting in the direction of the reduction of the intervention of the state at another point, and with a learning process over time that may reduce the amplitude of the curves.

The case for this resolution of the capitalism-democracy quandary is made quite movingly by Jacob Viner who is quoted in the concluding paragraph of Abramovitz's paper, " . . . If . . . I nevertheless conclude that I believe that the welfare state, like old Siwash, is really worth fighting for and even dying for as compared to any rival system, it is because, despite its imperfection in theory and practice, in the aggregate it provides more promise of preserving and enlarging human freedoms, temporal prosperity, the extinction of mass misery, and the dignity of man and his moral improvement than any other social system which has previously prevailed, which prevails elsewhere today or which outside Utopia, the mind of man has been able to provide a blueprint for" (Abramovitz 1981).

## References

Abramovitz, Moses. 1981. "Welfare Quandaries and Productivity Concerns." *American Economic Review,* March.

Berger, Peter. 1986. *The Capitalist Revolution.* New York: Basic Books.

Dahl, Robert A. 1989. *Democracy and Its Critics.* New Haven: Yale University Press.

_____. 1990. *After the Revolution: Authority in a Good Society.* New Haven: Yale University Press.

Deutsch, Karl. 1961. "Social Mobilization and Political Development." *American Political Science Review,* 55 (Sept.).

Flora, Peter, and Arnold Heidenheimer. 1981. *The Development of Welfare States in Western Europe and America.* New Brunswick, NJ: Transaction Press.

Friedman, Milton. 1981. *Capitalism and Freedom.* Chicago: University of Chicago Press.

Hirschman, Albert. 1986. *Rival Views of Market Society.* New York: Viking.

Inkeles, Alex, and David Smith. 1974. *Becoming Modern: Individual Change in Six Developing Countries.* Cambridge, MA: Harvard University Press.

Lerner, Daniel. 1958. *The Passing of Traditional Society.* New York: Free Press.

Lindblom, Charles E. 1977. *Politics and Markets.* New York: Basic Books.

Lipset, Seymour M. 1959. "Some Social Requisites of Democracy." *American Political Science Review,* 53 (September).

Mill, John Stuart. 1848, 1965. *Principles of Political Economy,* 2 vols. Toronto: University of Toronto Press.

Mitchell, William. 1988. "Virginia, Rochester, and Bloomington: Twenty-Five Years of Public Choice and Political Science." *Public Choice,* 56: 101–119.

Moore, Barrington. 1966. *The Social Origins of Dictatorship and Democracy.* New York: Beacon Press.

Olson, Mancur. 1982. *The Rise and Decline of Nations.* New Haven: Yale University Press.

Schumpeter, Joseph. 1946. *Capitalism, Socialism, and Democracy.* New York: Harper.

# CULTURAL EXPLANATIONS

## The man in the Baghdad café

### Which "civilisation" you belong to matters less than you might think

GOERING, it was said, growled that every time he heard the word culture he reached for his revolver. His hand would ache today. Since the end of the cold war, "culture" has been everywhere—not the opera-house or gallery kind, but the sort that claims to be the basic driving force behind human behaviour. All over the world, scholars and politicians seek to explain economics, politics and diplomacy in terms of "culture-areas" rather than, say, policies or ideas, economic interests, personalities or plain cock-ups.

Perhaps the best-known example is the notion that "Asian values" explain the success of the tiger economies of South-East Asia. Other accounts have it that international conflict is—or will be—caused by a clash of civilisations; or that different sorts of business organisation can be explained by how much people in different countries trust one [an]other. These four pages review the varying types of cultural explanation. They conclude that culture is so imprecise and changeable a phenomenon that it explains less than most people realise.

To see how complex the issue is, begin by considering the telling image with which Bernard Lewis opens his history of the Middle East. A man sits at a table in a coffee house in some Middle Eastern city, "drinking a cup of coffee or tea, perhaps smoking a cigarette, reading a newspaper, playing a board game, and listening with half an ear to whatever is coming out of the radio or the television installed in the

corner." Undoubtedly Arab, almost certainly Muslim, the man would clearly identify himself as a member of these cultural groups. He would also, if asked, be likely to say that "western culture" was alien, even hostile to them.

Look closer, though, and the cultural contrasts blur. This coffee-house man probably wears western-style clothes—sneakers, jeans, a T-shirt. The chair and table at which he sits, the coffee he drinks, the tobacco he smokes, the newspaper he reads, all are western imports. The radio and television are western inventions. If our relaxing friend is a member of his nation's army, he probably operates western or Soviet weapons and trains according to western standards; if he belongs to the government, both his bureaucratic surroundings and the constitutional trappings of his regime may owe their origins to western influence.

The upshot, for Mr Lewis, is clear enough. "In modern times," he writes, "the dominating factor in the consciousness of most Middle Easterners has been the impact of Europe, later of the West more generally, and the transformation—some would say dislocation—which it has brought." Mr Lewis has put his finger on the most important and least studied aspect of cultural identity: how it changes. It would be wise to keep that in mind during the upsurge of debate about culture that is likely to follow the publication of Samuel Huntington's new

book, "The Clash of Civilisations and the Remaking of World Order".

### The clash of civilisations

A professor of international politics at Harvard and the chairman of Harvard's Institute for Strategic Planning, Mr Huntington published in 1993, in *Foreign Affairs,* an essay which that quarterly's editors said generated more discussion than any since George Kennan's article (under the by-line "x") which argued in July 1947 for the need to contain the Soviet threat. Henry Kissinger, a former secretary of state, called Mr Huntington's book-length version of the article "one of the most important books . . . since the end of the cold war."

The article, "The Clash of Civilisation?", belied the question-mark in its title by predicting wars of culture. "It is my hypothesis", Mr Huntington wrote, "that the fundamental source of conflict in this new world will not be primarily ideological or primarily economic. The great division among humankind and the dominating source of conflict will be cultural."

After the cold war, ideology seemed less important as an organising principle of foreign policy. Culture seemed a plausible candidate to fill the gap. So future wars, Mr Huntington claimed, would occur "between nations and groups of different civilisations"—western, Confucian, Japanese, Islamic, Hindu, Orthodox and Latin American, perhaps African and Buddhist. Their disputes would "dominate global politics" and the battle-lines of the future would follow the fault-lines between these cultures.

No mincing words there, and equally few in his new book:

Culture and cultural identities... are shaping the patterns of cohesion, disintegration and conflict in the post-cold war world... Global politics is being reconfigured along cultural lines.

Mr Huntington is only one of an increasing number of writers placing stress on the importance of cultural values and institutions in the confusion left in the wake of the cold war. He looked at the influence of culture on international conflict. Three other schools of thought find cultural influences at work in different ways.

• **Culture and the economy.** Perhaps the oldest school holds that cultural values and norms equip people—and, by extension, countries—either poorly or well for economic success. The archetypal modern pronouncement of this view was Max Weber's investigation of the Protestant work ethic. This, he claimed, was the reason why the Protestant parts of Germany and Switzerland were more successful economically than the Catholic areas. In the recent upsurge of interest in issues cultural, a handful of writers have returned to the theme.

It is "values and attitudes—culture", claims Lawrence Harrison, that are "mainly responsible for such phenomena as Latin America's persistent instability and inequity, Taiwan's and Korea's economic 'miracles', and the achievements of the Japanese." Thomas Sowell offers other examples in "Race and Culture: A World View". "A disdain for commerce and industry", he argues, "has... been common for centuries among the Hispanic elite, both in Spain and in Latin America." Academics, though, have played a relatively small part in this debate: the best-known exponent of the thesis that "Asian values"—a kind of Confucian work ethic—aid economic development has been Singapore's former prime minister, Lee Kuan Yew.

• **Culture as social blueprint.** A second group of analysts has looked at the connections between cultural factors and political systems. Robert Putnam, another Harvard professor, traced Italy's social and political institutions to its "civic culture", or lack thereof. He claimed that, even today, the parts of Italy where democratic institutions are most fully developed are similar to the

areas which first began to generate these institutions in the 14th century. His conclusion is that democracy is not something that can be put on like a coat; it is part of a country's social fabric and takes decades, even centuries, to develop.

Francis Fukuyama, of George Mason University, takes a slightly different approach. In a recent book which is not about the end of history, he focuses on one particular social trait, "trust". "A nation's well-being, as well as its ability to compete, is conditioned by a single, pervasive cultural characteristic: the level of trust inherent in the society," he says. Mr Fukuyama argues that "low-trust" societies such as China, France and Italy—where close relations between people do not extend much beyond the family—are poor at generating large, complex social institutions like multinational corporations; so they are at a competitive disadvantage compared with "high-trust" nations such as Germany, Japan and the United States.

• **Culture and decision-making.** The final group of scholars has looked at the way in which cultural assumptions act like blinkers. Politicians from different countries see the same issue in different ways because of their differing cultural backgrounds. Their electorates or nations do, too. As a result, they claim, culture acts as an international barrier. As Ole Elgstrom puts it: "When a Japanese prime minister says that he will 'do his best' to implement a certain policy," Americans applaud a victory but "what the prime minister really meant was 'no'." There are dozens of examples of misperception in international relations, ranging from Japanese-American trade disputes to the misreading of Saddam Hussein's intentions in the weeks before he attacked Kuwait.

## What are they talking about?

All of this is intriguing, and much of it is provocative. It has certainly provoked a host of arguments. For example, is Mr Huntington right to lump together all European countries into one culture, though they speak different languages, while separating Spain and Mexico, which speak the same one? Is the Catholic Philippines western or Asian? Or: if it is true (as Mr Fukuyama claims) that the ability to produce multinational firms is vital to economic success, why has "low-trust" China, which has few such companies, grown so fast? And why has yet-more successful "low-trust" South Korea been able to create big firms?

This is nit-picking, of course. But such questions of detail matter because behind them lurks the first of two fundamental doubts that plague all these cultural explanations: how do you define what a culture is?

In their attempts to define what cultures are (and hence what they are talking about), most "culture" writers rely partly on self definition: cultures are what people think of themselves as part of. In Mr Huntington's words, civilisation "is the broadest level of identification with which [a person] intensely identifies."

The trouble is that relatively few people identify "intensely" with broad cultural groups. They tend to identify with something narrower: nations or ethnic groups. Europe is a case in point. A poll done last year for the European Commission found that half the people of Britain, Portugal and Greece thought of themselves in purely national terms; so did a third of the Germans, Spaniards and Dutch. And this was in a part of the world where there is an institution—the EU itself—explicitly devoted to the encouragement of "Europeanness".

The same poll found that in every EU country, 70% or more thought of themselves either purely in national terms, or primarily as part of a nation and only secondly as Europeans. Clearly, national loyalty can coexist with wider cultural identification. But, even then, the narrower loyalty can blunt the wider one because national characteristics often are—or at least are often thought to be—peculiar or unique. Seymour Martin Lipset, a sociologist who recently published a book about national characteristics in the United States, called it "American Exceptionalism". David Willetts, a British Conservative member of Parliament, recently claimed that the policies espoused by the opposition Labour Party would go against the grain of "English exceptionalism". And these are the two components of western culture supposedly most like one another.

In Islamic countries, the balance between cultural and national identification may be tilted towards the culture. But even here the sense of, say, Egyptian or Iraqi or Palestinian nationhood remains strong. (Consider the competing national feelings unleashed during the Iran-Iraq war.) In other cultures, national loyalty seems preeminent: in Mr Huntington's classification, Thailand, Tibet and Mongolia all count as "Buddhist". It is hard to imagine that a Thai, a Tibetan and a Mongolian really have that much in common.

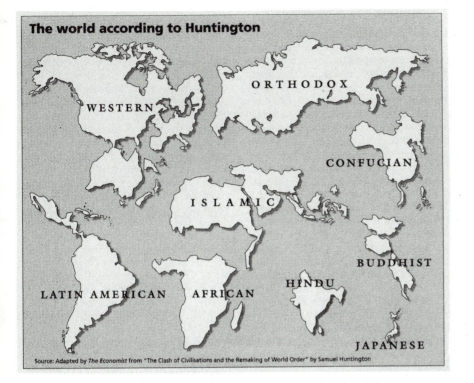

**The world according to Huntington**

WESTERN · ORTHODOX · CONFUCIAN · ISLAMIC · BUDDHIST · LATIN AMERICAN · AFRICAN · HINDU · JAPANESE

Source: Adapted by *The Economist* from "The Clash of Civilisations and the Remaking of World Order" by Samuel Huntington

So the test of subjective identification is hard to apply. That apart, the writers define a culture in the usual terms: language, religion, history, customs and institutions and so on. Such multiple definitions ring true. As Bernard Lewis's man in the Levantine café suggests, cultures are not singular things: they are bundles of characteristics.

The trouble is that such characteristics are highly ambiguous. Some push one way, some another.

## Culture as muddle

Islamic values, for instance, are routinely assumed to be the antithesis of modernising western ones. In Islam, tradition is good; departure from tradition is presumed to be bad until proven otherwise. Yet, at the same time, Islam is also a monotheistic religion which encourages rationalism and science. Some historians have plausibly argued that it was the Islamic universities of medieval Spain that kept science and rationalism alive during Europe's Dark Ages, and that Islam was a vital medieval link between the ancient world of Greece and Rome and the Renaissance. The scientific-rationalist aspect of Islam could well come to the fore again.

If you doubt it, consider the case of China and the "Confucian tradition" (a sort of proxy for Asian values). China has been at various times the world's most prosperous country and also one of its poorest. It has had periods of great scientific innovation and times of technological backwardness and isolation. Accounts of the Confucian tradition have tracked this path. Nowadays, what seems important about the tradition is its encouragement of hard work, savings and investment for the future, plus its emphasis on co-operation towards a single end. All these features have been adduced to explain why the tradition has helped Asian growth.

To Max Weber, however, the same tradition seemed entirely different. He argued that the Confucian insistence on obedience to parental authority discouraged competition and innovation and hence inhibited economic success. And China is not the only country to have been systematically misdiagnosed in this way. In countries as varied as Japan, India, Ghana and South Korea, notions of cultural determination of economic performance have been proved routinely wrong (in 1945, India and Ghana were expected to do best of the four—partly because of their supposed cultural inheritance).

If you take an extreme position, you could argue from this that cultures are so complicated that they can never be used to explain behaviour accurately.

Even if you do not go that far, the lesson must be that the same culture embraces such conflicting features that it can produce wholly different effects at different times.

That is hard enough for the schools of culture to get to grips with. But there is worse to come. For cultures never operate in isolation. When affecting how people behave, they are always part of a wider mix. That mix includes government policies, personal leadership, technological or economic change and so on. For any one effect, there are always multiple causes. Which raises the second fundamental doubt about cultural explanations: how do you know whether it is culture—and not something else—that has caused some effect? You cannot. The problem of causation seems insoluble. The best you can do is work out whether, within the mix, culture is becoming more or less important.

## Culture as passenger

Of the many alternative explanations for events, three stand out: the influence of ideas, of government and what might be called the "knowledge era" (shorthand for globalisation, the growth of service-based industries and so forth). Of these, the influence of ideas as a giant organising principle is clearly not what it was when the cold war divided the world between communists and capitalists. We are all capitalists now. To that extent, it is fair to say that the ideological part of the mix has become somewhat less important—though not, as a few people have suggested, insignificant.

As for the government, it is a central thesis of the cultural writers that its influence is falling while that of culture is rising: cultures are in some ways replacing states. To quote Mr Huntington again "peoples and countries with similar cultures are coming together. Peoples and countries with different cultures are coming apart."

In several respects, that is counter-intuitive. Governments still control what is usually the single most powerful force in any country, the army. And, in all but the poorest places, governments tax and spend a large chunk of GDP—indeed, a larger chunk, in most places, than 50 years ago.

Hardly surprising, then, that governments influence cultures as much as the other way around. To take a couple of examples. Why does South Korea (a low-trust culture, remember) have so many internationally competitive large firms? The answer is that the government decided that it should.

Or another case: since 1945 German politicians of every stripe have been insisting that they want to "save Germany from itself"—an attempt to assert political control over cultural identity.

South Korea and Germany are examples of governments acting positively to create something new. But governments can act upon cultures negatively: ie, they can destroy a culture when they collapse. Robert Kaplan, of an American magazine *Atlantic Monthly,* begins his book, "The Ends of the Earth", in Sierra Leone: "I had assumed that the random crime and social chaos of West Africa were the result of an already-fragile cultural base." Yet by the time he reaches Cambodia at the end of what he calls "a journey at the dawn of the 21st century" he is forced to reconsider that assumption:

Here I was . . . in a land where the written script was one thousand two hundred years old, and every surrounding country was in some stage of impressive economic growth. Yet Cambodia was eerily similar to Sierra Leone: with random crime, mosquito-borne disease, a government army that was more like a mob and a countryside that was ungovernable.

His conclusion is that "The effect of culture was more a mystery to me near the end of my planetary journey than at its beginning." He might have gone further: the collapse of governments causes cultural turbulence just as much as cultural turbulence causes the collapse of governments.

## Culture as processed data

Then there is the "knowledge era". Here is a powerful and growing phenomenon. The culture writers do not claim anything different. Like the Industrial Revolution before it, the knowledge era—in which the creation, storage and use of knowledge becomes the basic economic activity—is generating huge change. Emphasising as it does rapid, even chaotic, transformation, it is anti-traditional and anti-authoritarian.

Yet the cultural exponents still claim that, even in the knowledge era, culture remains a primary engine of change. They do so for two quite different reasons. Some claim that the new era has the makings of a world culture. There is a universal language, English. There are the beginnings of an international professional class that cuts across cultural and national boundaries: increasingly, bankers, computer programmers, executives, even military officers are said to have as much in common with their opposite numbers in other countries as with their next-door neighbors. As Mr Fukuyama wrote in his more famous book: the "unfolding of modern natural science . . . guarantees an increasing homogenisation of all human societies." Others doubt that technology and the rest of it are producing a genuinely new world order. To them, all this is just modern western culture.

Either way, the notion that modernity is set on a collision course with culture lies near the heart of several of the culture writers' books. Summing them up is the title of Benjamin Barber's "Jihad versus McWorld". In other words, he argues that the main conflicts now and in future will be between tribal, local "cultural" values (Jihad) and a McWorld of technology and democracy.

It would be pointless to deny that globalisation is causing large changes in every society. It is also clear that such influences act on different cultures differently, enforcing a kind of natural selection between those cultures which rise to the challenge and those which do not.

But it is more doubtful that these powerful forces are primarily cultural or even western. Of course, they have a cultural component: the artefacts of American culture are usually the first things to come along in the wake of a new road, or new television networks. But the disruptive force itself is primarily economic and has been adopted as enthusiastically in Japan, Singapore and China as in America. The world market is not a cultural concept.

Moreover, to suggest that trade, globalisation and the rest of it tend to cause conflict, and then leave the argument there, is not enough. When you boil the argument down, much of its seems to be saying that the more countries trade with each other, the more likely they are to go to war. That seems implausible. Trade—indeed, any sort of link—is just as likely to reduce the potential for violent conflict as to increase it. The same goes for the spread of democracy, another feature which is supposed to encourage civilisations to clash with each other. This might well cause ructions within countries. It might well provoke complaints from dictators about "outside interference". But serious international conflict is a different matter. And if democracy really did spread round the world, it might tend to reduce violence; wealthy democracies, at any rate, are usually reluctant to go to war (though poor or angrily nationalist ones may, as history has shown, be much less reluctant).

In short, the "knowledge era" is spreading economic ideas. And these ideas have three cultural effects, not one. They make cultures rub against each other, causing international friction. They also tie different cultures closer together, which offsets the first effect. And they may well increase tensions within a culture-area as some groups accommodate themselves to the new world while others turn their back on it. And all this can be true at the same time because cultures are so varied and ambiguous that they are capable of virtually any transformation.

The conclusion must be that while culture will continue to exercise an important influence on both countries and individuals, it has not suddenly become more important than, say, governments or impersonal economic forces. Nor does it play the all-embracing defining role that ideology played during the cold war. Much of its influence is secondary, ie, it comes about partly as a reaction to the "knowledge era". And within the overall mix of what influences people's behaviour, culture's role may well be declining, rather than rising, squeezed between the greedy expansion of the government on one side, and globalisation on the other.

**The books mentioned in this article are:**

Benjamin Barber. Jihad versus McWorld (Random House; 1995; 400 pages; $12.95).

Francis Fukuyama. The End of History and the Last Man (Free Press; 1992; 419 pages; $24.95. Hamish Hamilton; £20.) and Trust: The Social Virtues and the Creation of Prosperity (Free Press; 1995; 480 pages; $25. Hamish Hamilton; £25).

Lawrence E. Harrison. Who Prospers? How Cultural Values Shape Economic and Political Success (Basic Books; 1992; 288 pages; $14).

Samuel Huntington. The Clash of Civilisations? *Foreign Affairs* Vol. 72 (Summer 1993) and The Clash of Civilisations and the Remaking of World Order (Simon & Schuster; 1996; 367 pages; $26).

Robert Kaplan. The Ends of the Earth (Random House; 1996; 475 pages; $27.50. Papermac; £10).

Bernard Lewis. The Middle East (Wiedenfeld & Nicolson; 1995; 433 pages; £20. Simon & Schuster; $29.50).

Seymour Martin Lipset. American Exceptionalism (Norton; 1996; 352 pages; $27.50 and £19.95).

Robert Putnam. Making Democracy Work: Civic Traditions in Modern Italy (Princeton; 1993; 288 pages; $24.95 and £18.95).

Thomas Sowell. Race and Culture: A World View (Basic Books; 1994; 331 pages; $14).

# A Debate on Cultural Conflicts

## The Coming Clash of Civilizations —Or, the West Against the Rest

### Samuel P. Huntington

*Samuel P. Huntington is professor of government and director of the Olin Institute for Strategic Studies at Harvard. This article is adapted from the lead essay in the summer issue of* Foreign Affairs.

World politics is entering a new phase in which the fundamental source of conflict will be neither ideological or economic. The great divisions among mankind and the dominating source of conflict will be cultural. The principal conflicts of global politics will occur between nations and groups of different civilizations. The clash of civilizations will dominate global politics.

During the cold war, the world was divided into the first, second and third worlds. Those divisions are no longer relevant. It is far more meaningful to group countries not in terms of their political or economic systems or their level of economic development but in terms of their culture and civilization.

A civilization is the highest cultural grouping of people and the broadest level of cultural identity people have short of that which distinguishes humans from other species.

Civilizations obviously blend and overlap and may include sub-civilizations. Western civilization has two major variants, European and North American, and Islam has its Arab, Turkic and Malay subdivisions. But while the lines between them are seldom sharp, civilizations are real. They rise and fall; they divide and merge. And as any student of history knows, civilizations disappear.

---

## Global conflict will be cultural.

---

Westerners tend to think of nation-states as the principal actors in global affairs. They have been that for only a few centuries. The broader reaches of history have been the history of civilizations. It is to this pattern that the world returns.

Civilization identity will be increasingly important and the world will be shaped in large measure by the interactions among seven or eight major civilizations. These include the Western, Confucian, Japanese, Islamic, Hindu, Slavic-Orthodox, Latin American and possibly African civilizations. The most important and bloody conflicts will occur along the borders separating these cultures. The fault lines between civilizations will be the battle lines of the future.

Why? First, differences among civilizations are basic, involving history, language, culture, tradition and, most importantly, religion. Different civilizations have different views on the relations between God and man, the citizen and the state, parents and children, liberty and authority, equality and hierarchy. These differences are the product of centuries. They will not soon disappear.

Second, the world is becoming smaller. The interactions between peoples of different civilizations are increasing. These interactions intensify civilization consciousness: awareness of differences between civilizations and commonalities within civilizations. For example, Americans react far more negatively to Japanese investment than to larger investments from Canada and European countries.

Third, economic and social changes are separating people from long standing local identities. In much of the world, religion has moved in to fill this gap, often in the form of movements labeled fundamentalist. Such movements are found in Western Christianity, Judaism, Buddhism, Hinduism and Islam. The "unsecularization of the world," George Weigel has remarked, "is one of the dominant social facts of life in the late 20th century."

Fourth, the growth of civilization consciousness is enhanced by the fact that at the moment that the West is at the peak of its power a return-to-the-roots phenomenon is occurring among non-Western civilizations— the "Asianization" in Japan, the end of the Nehru legacy and the "Hinduization" of India, the failure of Western ideas of socialism and nationalism and, hence, the "re-Islamization" of the Middle East, and now a debate over Westernization versus Russianization in Boris Yeltsin's country.

More importantly, the efforts of the West to promote its values of democracy and liberalism as universal values, to maintain its military predominance and to advance its economic interests engender countering responses from other civilizations.

The central axis of world politics is likely to be the conflict between "the West and the rest" and the responses of non-Western civilizations to Western power and values. The most prominent example of anti-Western cooperation is the connection between Confucian and Islamic states that are challenging Western values and power.

Fifth, cultural characteristics and differences are less mutable and hence less easily compromised and resolved than political and economic ones. In the former Soviet Union, Communists can become democrats, the rich can become poor and the poor rich, but Russians cannot become Estonians. A person can be half-French and half-Arab and even a citizen of two countries. It is more difficult to be half Catholic and half Muslim.

Finally, economic regionalism is increasing. Successful economic regionalism will reinforce civilization consciousness. On the other hand, economic regionalism may succeed only when it is rooted in common civilization. The European Community rests on the shared foundation of European culture and Western Christianity. Japan, in contrast, faces difficulties in creating a comparable economic entity in East Asia because it is a society and civilization unique to itself.

As the ideological division of Europe has disappeared, the cultural division of Europe between Western Christianity and Orthodox Christianity and Islam has re-emerged. Conflict along the fault line between Western and Islamic civilizations has been going on for 1,300 years. This centuries-old military interaction is unlikely to decline. Historically, the other great antagonistic interaction of Arab Islamic civilization has been with the pagan, animist and now, increasingly, Christian black peoples to the south. On the northern border of Islam, conflict has increasingly erupted between Orthodox and Muslim peoples, including the carnage of Bosnia and Sarajevo, the simmering violence between Serbs and Albanians, the tenuous relations between Bulgarians and their Turkish minority, the violence between Ossetians and Ingush, the unremitting slaughter of each other by Armenians and Azeris and the tense relations between Russians and Muslims in Central Asia.

The historic clash between Muslims and Hindus in the Subcontinent manifests itself not only in the rivalry between Pakistan and India but also in intensifying religious strife in India between increasingly militant Hindu groups and the substantial Muslim minority.

Groups or states belonging to one civilization that become involved in war with people from a different civilization naturally try to rally support from other members of their own civilization. Decreasingly able to mobilize support and form coalitions on the basis of ideology, governments and groups will increasingly attempt to mobilize support by appealing to common religion and civilization identity. As the conflicts in the Persian Gulf, the Caucasus and Bosnia continued, the positions of nations and the cleavages between them increasingly were along civilizational lines. Populist politicians, religious leaders and the media have found it a potent means of arousing mass support and of pressuring hesitant governments. In the coming years, the local conflicts most likely to escalate into major wars will be those, as in Bosnia and the Caucasus, along the fault lines between civilizations. The next world war, if there is one, will be a war between civilizations.

If these hypotheses are plausible, it is necessary to consider their implications for Western policy. These

---

## Only Japan is non-Western and modern.

---

implications should be divided between short-term advantage and long-term accommodation. In the short term, it is clearly in the interest of the West to promote greater cooperation and unity in its own civilization, particularly between its European and North American components; to incorporate into the West those societies in Eastern Europe and Latin America whose cultures are close to those of the West; to maintain close relations with Russia and Japan; to support in other civilizations groups sympathetic to Western values and interests; and to strengthen international institutions that reflect and legitimate Western interests and values. The West must also limit the expansion of the military strength of potentially hostile civilizations, principally Confucian and Islamic civilizations, and exploit differences and conflicts among Confucian and Islamic states. This will require a moderation in the reduction of Western military capabilities, and, in particular, the maintenance of American military superiority in East and Southwest Asia.

In the longer term, other measures would be called for. Western civilization is modern. Non-Western civilizations have attempted to become modern without becoming Western. To date, only Japan has fully succeeded in this quest. Non-Western civilizations will continue to attempt to acquire the wealth, technology, skills, machines and weapons that are part of being modern. They will attempt to reconcile this modernity with their traditional culture and values. Their economic and military strength relative to the West will increase.

Hence, the West will increasingly have to accommodate to those non-Western modern civilizations, whose power approaches that of the West but whose values and interests differ significantly from those of the West. This will require the West to develop a much more profound understanding of the basic religious and philosophical assumptions underlying other civilizations and the ways in which people in those civilizations see their interests. It will require an effort to identify elements of commonality among Western and other civilizations. For the relevant future, there will be no universal civilization but instead a world of different civilizations, each of which will have to learn to co-exist with others.

---

## Global debate on a controversial thesis

# A Clash Between Civilizations —or Within Them?

### SüddeutscheZeitung

■ *A recent essay by Harvard professor Samuel P. Huntington in "Foreign Affairs" magazine—"The Clash of Civilizations?"—has attracted a good deal of attention not only in the U.S. but abroad, as well. Huntington is attempting to establish a new model for examining the post-cold-war world, a central theme around which events will turn, as the ideological clash of the cold war governed the past 40 years. He finds it in cultures. "Faith and family, blood and belief," he has written, "are what people identify with and what they will fight and die for." But in the following article, Josef Joffe, foreign-affairs specialist at the independent "Süddeutsche Zeitung" of Munich, argues that "kulturkampf"—cultural warfare—is not a primary threat to world security. And in a more radical view, Malaysian political scientist Chandra Muzaffar writes for the Third World Network Features agency of Penang, Malaysia, that Western dominance—economic and otherwise—continues to be the overriding factor in world politics.*

A ghost is walking in the West: cultural warfare, total and international. Scarcely had we banished the 40-year-long cold war to history's shelves, scarcely had we begun to deal with the seductive phrase "the end of history," when violence broke out on all sides. But this time it was not nations that were behind the savagery but peoples and ethnic groups, religions and races—from the Serbs and Bosnians in the Balkans to the Tiv and Jukun in Nigeria. Working from such observations, one of the best brains in America, Harvard professor Samuel Huntington, produced a prophecy, perhaps even a philosophy of history. His essay "The Clash of Civilizations?" has caused a furor. For centuries, it was the nations that made history; then, in the 20th century, it was the totalitarian ideologies. Today, at the threshold of the 21st century, "the clash of civilizations will dominate global politics." No longer will "Which side are you on?" be the fateful question but "What are you?" Identity will no longer be defined by passport or party membership card but by faith and history, language and customs—culture, in short. Huntington argues that "conflicts between cultures" will push the old disputes between nations and ideologies off center stage. Or put more apocalyptically: "The next world war, if there is one, will be a war between civilizations."

Between which? Huntington has made a list of more than half a dozen civilizations, including the West (the U.S. plus Europe), the Slavic-Orthodox, the Islamic, the Confucian (China), the Japanese, and the Hindu. At first glance, he seems to be right. Are not Catholic Croats fighting Orthodox Serbs—and both of them opposing Muslim Bosnians? And recently, the ruthless struggle between the Hindus and Muslims of India has

Reprinted with permission from *World Press Review*, February 1994, pp. 24-26. Originally from SüddeutscheZeitung.

233

re-erupted. Even such a darling of the West as King Hussein of Jordan announced during the Persian Gulf war: "This is a war against all Arabs and all Muslims and not against Iraq alone." The long trade conflict pitting Japan against the United States (and against Europe) has been called a "war"—and not only by the chauvinists. Russian Orthodox nationalists see themselves in a two-front struggle: against the Islamic Turkic peoples in the south and the soulless modernists of the West. And even worse: The future could mean "the West against the rest."

But this first look is deceptive; after a closer look, the apocalypse dissolves, to be replaced by a more complex tableau. This second look shows us a world that is neither new nor simple. First of all, conflicts between civilizations are as old as history itself. Look at the struggle of the Jews against the Turks in the 19th century, or the revolt of the Greeks against the Turks in the 19th century. The Occident and Orient have been in conflict, off and on, for the last 1,300 years. Second, the disputes with China, Japan, or North Korea are not really nourished by conflicts among civilizations. They are the results of palpable national interests at work. Third, if we look only at the conflicts between cultures, we will miss the more important truth: Within each camp, divisions and rivalries are far more significant than unifying forces.

The idea of cultural war seems to work best when we examine Islam. The demonization of the West is a part of the standard rhetoric of Islamic fundamentalists. The Arab-Islamic world is one of the major sources of terrorism, and most armed conflicts since World War II have involved Western states against Muslim countries. But if we look more closely, the Islamic monolith fractures into many pieces that cannot be reassembled. There is the history of internecine conflicts, coups, and rebellions: a 15-year-long civil war of each against all in Lebanon (not simply Muslims against Maronite Christians), the Palestine Liberation Organization against Jordan, and Syria against the PLO. Then consider the wars among states in the Arab world: Egypt versus Yemen, Syria against Jordan, Egypt versus Libya, and finally Iraq versus Kuwait. Then the wars of ideologies and finally, the religiously tinted struggles for dominance within the faith—between Sunnis and Shiites, Iraq and Iran.

But more important: What does the term "Islam" really mean? What does a Malay Muslim have in common with a Bosnian? Or an Indonesian with a Saudi? And what are we to understand by "fundamentalism"? The Saudi variety is passive and inward-looking, while the expansive Iranian variety arouses fear. It is true that, from Gaza to Giza, fundamentalists are shedding innocent blood. But most of the Arab world sided with the West during the Gulf war. And, beyond this, only 10 percent of the trade of the Middle East takes place within the region; most of it flows westward. Economic interdependence, a good index of a common civilization, is virtually nonexistent in the Islamic world.

The real issue is not a cultural war but actually another twofold problem. Several Islamic nations are importing too many weapons, and some are exporting too many people. The first demands containment and denial, calling for continued military strength and readiness in the West. And what of the "human exports"? They are not just a product of the Islamic world but of the entire poor and overpopulated world—no matter what culture they are part of. Along with the spread of nuclear weapons and missiles, this is the major challenge of the coming century, because massive migrations of people will inevitably bring cultural, territorial, and political struggles in their wake. No one has an answer to this. But a narrow vision produced by the "West-against-the-rest" notion is surely the worst way to look for answers.

—*Josef Joffe*

# The West's Hidden Agenda

Third World Network
**FEATURES**

Like Francis Fukuyama's essay "The End of History?" published in 1989, Samuel Huntington's "The Clash of Civilizations?" has received a lot of publicity in the mainstream Western media. The reason is not difficult to fathom. Both articles serve U.S. and Western foreign-policy goals. Huntington's thesis is simple enough: "The clash of civilizations will dominate global politics. The fault lines between civilizations will be the battle lines of the future."

The truth, however, is that cultural, religious, or other civilizational differences are only some of the many factors responsible for conflict. Territory and resources, wealth and property, power and status, and individual personalities and group interests are others. Indeed, religion, culture, and other elements are symbols of what Huntington would regard as "civilization identity" are sometimes manipulated to camouflage the naked pursuit of wealth or power—the real source of many conflicts.

But the problem is even more serious. By overplaying the "clash of civilizations" dimension, Huntington has ignored the creative constructive interaction and engagement between civilizations. This is a much more constant feature of civilization than conflict per se. Islam, for instance, through centuries of exchange with the West, laid the foundation for the growth of mathematics, science, medicine, agriculture, industry, and ar-

Reprinted with permission from *World Press Review*, February 1994, pp. 25-26. Originally from *Third World Network Features*.

chitecture in medieval Europe. Today, some of the leading ideas and institutions that have gained currency within the Muslim world, whether in politics or in economics, are imports from the West.

# "U.S and Western dominance is at the root of global conflict."

That different civilizations are not inherently prone to conflict is borne out by another salient feature that Huntington fails to highlight. Civilizations embody many similar values and ideals. At the philosophical level at least, Buddhism, Christianity, Hinduism, Islam, Judaism, Sikhism, and Taoism, among other world religions, share certain common perspectives on the relationship between the human being and his environment, the integrity of the community, the importance of the family, the significance of moral leadership, and indeed, the meaning and purpose of life. Civilizations, however different in certain respects, are quite capable of forging common interests and aspirations. For example, the Association of Southeast Asian Nations encompasses at least four "civilization identities," to use Huntington's term—Buddhist (Thailand), Confucian (Singapore), Christian (the Philippines), and Muslim (Brunei, Indonesia, and Malaysia). Yet it has been able to evolve an identity of its own through 25 years of trials.

It is U.S. and Western dominance, not the clash of civilizations, that is at the root of global conflict. By magnifying the so-called clash of civilizations, Huntington tries to divert attention from Western dominance and control even as he strives to preserve, protect, and perpetuate that dominance. He sees a compelling reason for embarking on this mission. Western dominance is under threat from a "Confucian-Islamic connection that has emerged to challenge Western interests, values, and power," he writes. This is the most mischievous—and most dangerous—implication of his "clash of civilizations."

By evoking this fear of a Confucian-Islamic connection, he hopes to persuade the Western public, buffeted by unemployment and recession, to acquiesce to huge military budgets in the post-cold-war era. He argues that China and some Islamic nations are acquiring weapons on a massive scale. Generally, it is the Islamic states that are buying weapons from China, which in turn "is rapidly increasing its military spending." Huntington observes that "a Confucian-Islamic military connection has thus come into being, designed to promote acquisition by its members of the weapons and weapons technologies needed to counter the military power of the West." This is why the West, and the U.S. in particular, should not, in Huntington's view, be "reducing its own military capabilities."

There are serious flaws in this argument. One, it is not true that the U.S. has reduced its military capability; in fact, it has enhanced its range of sophisticated weaponry. Two, though China is an important producer and exporter of arms, it is the only major power whose military expenditures consistently declined throughout the 1980s. Three, most Muslim countries buy their weapons not from China but from the U.S. Four, China has failed to endorse the Muslim position on many global issues. Therefore, the Confucian-Islamic connection is a myth propagated to justify increased U.S. military spending.

It is conceivable that Huntington has chosen to target the Confucian and Islamic civilizations for reasons that are not explicitly stated in his article. Like many other Western academics, commentators, and policy analysts, Huntington, it appears, is also concerned about the economic ascendancy of so-called Confucian communities such as China, Hong Kong, Taiwan, Singapore, and overseas Chinese communities in other Asian countries. He is of the view that "if cultural commonality is a prerequisite for economic integration, the principal East Asian economic bloc of the future is likely to be centered on China." The dynamism and future potential of these "Confucian" economies have already set alarm bells ringing in various Western capitals. Huntington's warning to the West about the threat that China poses should be seen in that context—as yet another attempt to curb the rise of yet another non-Western economic competitor.

As far as the "Islamic threat" is concerned, it is something that Huntington and his kind have no difficulty selling in the West. Antagonism toward Islam and Muslims is deeply embedded in the psyche of mainstream Western society. The rise of Islamic movements has provoked a new, powerful wave of negative emotions against the religion and its practitioners. Most Western academics and journalists, in concert with Western policy makers, grant no legitimacy to the Muslim resistance to Western domination and control. When Huntington says, "Islam has bloody borders," the implication is that Islam and Muslims are responsible for the spilling of blood. Yet anyone who has an elementary knowledge of many current conflicts will readily admit that, more often than not, it is the Muslims who have been bullied, bludgeoned, and butchered.

The truth, however, means very little to Huntington. The title of his article "The Clash of Civilizations?" is quoted from [British educator] Bernard Lewis's "The Roots of Muslim Rage," an essay that depicts the Islamic resurgence as an irrational threat to Western heritage. Both Huntington and Lewis are "Islam baiters" whose role is to camouflage the suffering of and the injustice done to the victims of U.S. and Western domination by concocting theories about the conflict of cultures and the clash of civilizations. Huntington's "The Clash of Civilizations?" will not conceal the real nature of the conflict: The victims—or at least some of them—know the truth.
—*Chandra Muzaffar*

# Jihad vs. McWorld

*The two axial principles of our age—tribalism and globalism—clash at every point except one: they may both be threatening to democracy*

## Benjamin R. Barber

*Benjamin R. Barber is the Whitman Professor of Political Science at Rutgers University. Barber's most recent books are* Strong Democracy *(1984),* The Conquest of Politics *(1988), and* An Aristocracy of Everyone.

Just beyond the horizon of current events lie two possible political figures—both bleak, neither democratic. The first is a retribalization of large swaths of humankind by war and bloodshed: a threatened Lebanonization of national states in which culture is pitted against culture, people against people, tribe against tribe—a Jihad in the name of a hundred narrowly conceived faiths against every kind of interdependence, every kind of artificial social cooperation and civic mutuality. The second is being borne in on us by the onrush of economic and ecological forces that demand integration and uniformity and that mesmerize the world with fast music, fast computers, and fast food—with MTV, Macintosh, and McDonald's, pressing nations into one commercially homogenous global network: one McWorld tied together by technology, ecology, communications, and commerce. The planet is falling precipitately apart and coming reluctantly together at the very same moment.

These two tendencies are sometimes visible in the same countries at the same instant: thus Yugoslavia, clamoring just recently to join the New Europe, is exploding into fragments; India is trying to live up to its reputation as the world's largest integral democracy while powerful new fundamentalist parties like the Hindu nationalist Bharatiya Janta Party, along with nationalist assassins, are im-

periling its hard-won unity. States are breaking up or joining up: the Soviet Union has disappeared almost overnight, its parts forming new unions with one another or with like-minded nationalities in neighboring states. The old interwar national state based on territory and political sovereignty looks to be a mere transitional development.

The tendencies of what I am here calling the forces of Jihad and the forces of McWorld operate with equal strength in opposite directions, the one driven by parochial hatreds, the other by unversalizing markets, the one re-creating ancient subnational and ethnic borders from within, the other making national borders porous from without. They have one thing in common: neither offers much hope to citizens looking for practical ways to govern themselves democratically. If the global future is to pit Jihad's centrifugal whirlwind against McWorld's centripetal black hole, the outcome is unlikely to be democratic—or so I will argue.

## McWORLD, OR THE GLOBALIZATION OF POLITICS

Four imperatives make up the dynamic of McWorld: a market imperative, a resource imperative, an information-technology imperative, and an ecological imperative. By shrinking the world and diminishing the salience of national borders, these imperatives have in combination achieved a considerable victory over factiousness and particularism, and not least of all over their most virulent traditional form—nationalism. It is the realists who are now Europeans, the uto-

pians who dream nostalgically of a resurgent England or Germany, perhaps even a resurgent Wales or Saxony. Yesterday's wishful cry for one world has yielded to the reality of McWorld.

*The market imperative.* Marxist and Leninist theories of imperialism assumed that the quest for ever-expanding markets would in time compel nation-based capitalist economies to push against national boundaries in search of an international economic imperium. Whatever else has happened to the scientist predictions of Marxism, in this domain they have proved farsighted. All national economies are now vulnerable to the inroads of larger, transnational markets within which trade is free, currencies are convertible, access to banking is open, and contracts are enforceable under law. In Europe, Asia, Africa, the South Pacific, and the Americas such markets are eroding national sovereignty and giving rise to entities—international banks, trade associations, transnational lobbies like OPEC and Greenpeace, world news services like CNN and the BBC, and multinational corporations that increasingly lack a meaningful national identity—that neither reflect nor respect nationhood as an organizing or regulative principle.

The market imperative has also reinforced the quest for international peace and stability, requisites of an efficient international economy. Markets are enemies of parochialism, isolation, fractiousness, war. Market psychology attenuates the psychology of ideological and religious cleavages and assumes a concord among producers and consumers—categories that ill fit narrowly conceived national or religious cultures. Shopping has little toler-

 From *The Atlantic Monthly,* March 1992, pp. 53–55, 58–63. © 1992 by Benjamin R. Barber. Reprinted by permission.

ance for blue laws, whether dictated by pub-closing British paternalism, Sabbath-observing Jewish Orthodox fundamentalism, or no-Sunday-liquor-sales Massachusetts puritanism. In the context of common markets, international law ceases to be a vision of justice and becomes a workaday framework for getting things done—enforcing contracts, ensuring that governments abide by deals, regulating trade and currency relations, and so forth.

Common markets demand a common language, as well as a common currency, and they produce common behaviors of the kind bred by cosmopolitan city life everywhere. Commercial pilots, computer programmers, international bankers, media specialists, oil riggers, entertainment celebrities, ecology experts, demographers, accountants, professors, athletes—these compose a new breed of men and women for whom religion, culture, and nationality can seem only marginal elements in a working identity. Although sociologists of everyday life will no doubt continue to distinguish a Japanese from an American mode, shopping has a common signature throughout the world. Cynics might even say that some of the recent revolutions in Eastern Europe have had as their true goal not liberty and the right to vote but well-paying jobs and the right to shop (although the vote is proving easier to acquire than consumer goods). The market imperative is, then, plenty powerful; but, notwithstanding some of the claims made for "democratic capitalism," it is not identical with the democratic imperative.

*The resource imperative.* Democrats once dreamed of societies whose political autonomy rested firmly on economic independence. The Athenians idealized what they called autarky, and tried for a while to create a way of life simple and austere enough to make the polis genuinely self-sufficient. To be free meant to be independent of any other community or polis. Not even the Athenians were able to achieve autarky, however: human nature, it turns out, is dependency. By the time of Pericles, Athenian politics was inextricably bound up with a flowering empire held together by naval power and commerce—an empire that, even as it appeared to enhance Athenian might, ate away at Athenian independence and autarky. Master and slave, it turned out, were bound together by mutual insufficiency.

The dream of autarky briefly engrossed nineteenth-century America as well, for the underpopulated, endlessly bountiful land, the cornucopia of natural resources, and the natural barriers of a continent walled in by two great seas led many to believe that America could be a world unto itself. Given this past, it has been harder for Americans than for most to accept the inevitability of interdependence. But the rapid depletion of resources even in a country like ours, where they once seemed inexhaustible, and the maldistribution of arable soil and mineral resources on the planet, leave even the wealthiest societies ever more resource-dependent and many other nations in permanently desperate straits.

Every nation, it turns out, needs something another nation has; some nations have almost nothing they need.

*The information-technology imperative.* Enlightenment science and the technologies derived from it are inherently universalizing. They entail a quest for descriptive principles of general application, a search for universal solutions to particular problems, and an unswerving embrace of objectivity and impartiality.

Scientific progress embodies and depends on open communication, a common discourse rooted in rationality, collaboration, and an easy and regular flow and exchange of information. Such ideals can be hypocritical covers for power-mongering by elites, and they may be shown to be wanting in many other ways, but they are entailed by the very idea of science and they make science and globalization practical allies.

Business, banking, and commerce all depend on information flow and are facilitated by new communication technologies. The hardware of these technologies tends to be systemic and integrated—computer, television, cable, satellite, laser, fiber-optic, and microchip technologies combining to create a vast interactive communications and information network that can potentially give every person on earth access to every other person, and make every datum, every byte, available to every set of eyes. If the automobile was, as George Ball once said (when he gave his blessing to a Fiat factory in the Soviet Union during the Cold War), "an ideology on four wheels," then electronic telecommunication and information systems are an ideology at 186,000 miles per second—which makes for a very small planet in a very big hurry. Individual cultures speak particular languages; commerce and science increasingly speak English; the whole world speaks logarithms and binary mathematics.

Moreover, the pursuit of science and technology asks for, even compels, open societies. Satellite footprints do not respect national borders; telephone wires penetrate the most closed societies. With photocopying and then fax machines having infiltrated Soviet universities and *samizdat* literary circles in the eighties, and computer modems having multiplied like rabbits in communism's bureaucratic warrens thereafter, *glasnost* could not be far behind. In their social requisites, secrecy and science are enemies.

The new technology's software is perhaps even more globalizing than its hardware. The information arm of international commerce's sprawling body reaches out and touches distinct nations and parochial cultures, and gives them a common face chiseled in Hollywood, on Madison Avenue, and in Silicon Valley. Throughout the 1980s one of the most-watched television programs in South Africa was *The Cosby Show.* The demise of apartheid was already in production. Exhibitors at the 1991 Cannes film festival expressed growing anxiety over the "homogenization" and "Americanization" of the global film industry when, for the third year running, American films dominated the awards ceremonies. America has dominated the world's popular culture for much longer, and much more decisively. In November of 1991 Switzerland's once insular culture boasted best-seller lists featuring *Terminator 2* as the No. 1 movie, *Scarlett* as the No. 1 book, and Prince's *Diamonds and Pearls* as the No. 1 record album. No wonder the Japanese are buying Hollywood film studios even faster than Americans are buying Japanese television sets. This kind of software supremacy may in the long term be far more important than hardware superiority, because culture has become more potent than armaments. What is the power of the Pentagon compared with Disneyland? Can the Sixth Fleet keep up with CNN? McDonald's in Moscow and Coke in China will do more to create a global culture than military colonization ever could. It is less the goods than the brand names that do the work, for they convey life-style images that alter perception and challenge behavior. They make up the seductive software of McWorld's common (at times much too common) soul.

Yet in all this high-tech commercial world there is nothing that looks particularly democratic. It lends itself to surveillance as well as liberty, to new forms of manipulation and covert control as well as new kinds of participation, to skewed, unjust market outcomes as well as greater productivity. The consumer society and the open society are not quite synonymous. Capitalism and democracy have a relationship, but it is something less than a marriage. An efficient free market after all requires that consumers be free to vote their dollars on competing goods, not that citizens be free to vote their values and beliefs on competing political candidates and programs. The free market flourished in junta-run Chile, in military-governed Taiwan and Korea, and, earlier, in a variety of autocratic European empires as well as their colonial possessions.

The *ecological imperative.* The impact of globalization on ecology is a chiché even to world leaders who ignore it. We know well enough that the German forests can be destroyed by Swiss and Italians driving gas-guzzlers fueled by leaded gas. We also know that the planet can be asphyxiated by greenhouse gases because Brazilian farmers want to be part of the twentieth century and are burning down tropical rain forests to clear a little land to plough, and because Indonesians make a living out of converting their lush jungle into toothpicks for fastidious Japanese diners, upsetting the delicate oxygen balance and in effect puncturing our global lungs. Yet this ecological consciousness has meant not only greater awareness but also greater inequality, as modernized nations try to slam the door behind them, saying to developing nations, "The world cannot afford your modernization; ours has wrung it dry!"

Each of the four imperatives just cited is transnational, transideological, and transcultural. Each applies impartially to Catholics, Jews, Muslims, Hindus, and Buddhists; to democrats and totalitarians; to capitalists and socialists. The Enlightenment dream of a universal rational society has to a remarkable degree been realized—but in a form that is commercialized, homogenized, depoliticized, bureaucratized, and, of course, radically incomplete, for the movement toward McWorld is in competition with forces of global breakdown, national dissolution, and centrifugal corruption. These forces, working in the opposite direction, are the essence of what I call Jihad.

## JIHAD, OR THE LEBANON-IZATION OF THE WORLD

OPEC, the World Bank, the United Nations, the International Red Cross, the multinational corporation... there are scores of institutions that reflect globalization. But they often appear as ineffective reactors to the world's real actors: national states and, to an ever greater degree, subnational factions in permanent rebellion against uniformity and integration—even the kind represented by universal law and justice. The headlines feature these players regularly: they are cultures, not countries; parts, not wholes; sects, not religions; rebellious factions and dissenting minorities at war not just with globalism but with the traditional nation-state. Kurds, Basques, Puerto Ricans, Ossetians, East Timoreans, Quebecois, the Catholics of Northern Ireland, Abkhasians, Kurile Islander Japanese, the Zulus of Inkatha, Catalonians, Tamils, and, of course, Palestinians—people without countries, inhabiting nations not their own, seeking smaller worlds within borders that will seal them off from modernity.

A powerful irony is at work here. Nationalism was once a force of integration and unification, a movement aimed at bringing together disparate clans, tribes, and cultural fragments under new, assimilationist flags. But as Ortega y Gasset noted more than sixty years ago, having won its victories, nationalism changed its strategy. In the 1920s, and again today, it is more often a reactionary and divisive force, pulverizing the very nations it once helped cement together. The force that creates nations is "inclusive," Ortega wrote in *The Revolt of the Masses.* "In periods of consolidation, nationalism has a positive value, and is a lofty standard. But in Europe everything is more than consolidated, and nationalism is nothing but a mania...."

This mania has left the post-Cold War world smothering with hot wars; the international scene is little more unified than it was at the end of the Great War, in Ortega's own time. There were more than thirty wars in progress last year, most of them ethnic, racial, tribal, or religious in character, and the list of unsafe regions doesn't seem to be getting any shorter. Some new world order! The aim of many of these small-scale wars is to redraw boundaries, to implode states and resecure parochial identities: to escape McWorld's dully insistent im-

peratives. The mood is that of Jihad: war not as an instrument of policy but as an emblem of identity, an expression of community, an end in itself. Even where there is no shooting war, there is fractiousness, secession, and the quest for ever smaller communities. Add to the list of dangerous countries those at risk: In Switzerland and Spain, Jurassian and Basque separatists still argue the virtues of ancient identities, sometimes in the language of bombs. Hyperdisintegration in the former Soviet Union may well continue unabated—not just a Ukraine independent from the Soviet Union but a Bessarabian Ukraine independent from the Ukrainian republic; not just Russia severed from the defunct union but Tatarstan severed from Russia. Yugoslavia makes even the disunited, ex-Soviet, nonsocialist republics that were once the Soviet Union look integrated, its sectarian fatherlands springing up within factional motherlands like weeds within weeds within weeds. Kurdish independence would threaten the territorial integrity of four Middle Eastern nations. Well before the current cataclysm Soviet Georgia made a claim for autonomy from the Soviet Union, only to be faced with its Ossetians (164,000 in a republic of 5.5 million) demanding their own self-determination within Georgia. The Abkhasian minority in Georgia has followed suit. Even the good will established by Canada's once promising Meech Lake protocols is in danger, with Francophone Quebec again threatening the dissolution of the federation. In South Africa the emergence from apartheid was hardly achieved when friction between Inkatha's Zulus and the African National Congress's tribally identified members threatened to replace Europeans' racism with an indigenous tribal war. After thirty years of attempted integration using the colonial language (English) as a unifier, Nigeria is now playing with the idea of linguistic multiculturalism—which could mean the cultural breakup of the nation into hundreds of tribal fragments. Even Saddam Hussein has benefited from the threat of internal Jihad, having used renewed tribal and religious warfare to turn last season's mortal enemies into reluctant allies of an Iraqi nationhood that he nearly destroyed.

The passing of communism has torn away the thin veneer of internationalism (workers of the world unite!) to reveal ethnic prejudices that are not only ugly and deep-seated but increasingly murderous.

Europe's old scourge, anti-Semitism, is back with a vengeance, but it is only one of many antagonisms. It appears all too easy to throw the historical gears into reverse and pass from a Communist dictatorship back into a tribal state.

Among the tribes, religion is also a battlefield. ("Jihad" is a rich world whose generic meaning is "struggle"—usually the struggle of the soul to avert evil. Strictly applied to religious war, it is used only in reference to battles where the faith is under assault, or battles against a government that denies the practice of Islam. My use here is rhetorical, but does follow both journalistic practice and history.) Remember the Thirty Years War? Whatever forms of Enlightenment universalism might once have come to grace such historically related forms of monotheism as Judaism, Christianity, and Islam, in many of their modern incarnations they are parochial rather than cosmopolitan, angry rather than loving, proselytizing rather than ecumenical, zealous rather than rationalist, sectarian rather than deistic, ethnocentric rather than universalizing. As a result, like the new forms of hypernationalism, the new expressions of religious fundamentalism are fractious and pulverizing, never integrating. This is religion as the Crusaders knew it: a battle to the death for souls that if not saved will be forever lost.

The atmospherics of Jihad have resulted in a breakdown of civility in the name of identity, of comity in the name of community. International relations have sometimes taken on the aspect of gang war—cultural turf battles featuring tribal factions that were supposed to be sublimated as integral parts of large national, economic, postcolonial, and constitutional entities.

## THE DARKENING FUTURE OF DEMOCRACY

These rather melodramatic tableaux vivants do not tell the whole story, however. For all their defects, Jihad and McWorld have their attractions. Yet, to repeat and insist, the attractions are unrelated to democracy. Neither McWorld nor Jihad is remotely democratic in impulse. Neither needs democracy; neither promotes democracy.

McWorld does manage to look pretty seductive in a world obsessed with Jihad. It delivers peace, prosperity, and relative unity—if at the cost of independence, community, and identity (which is generally based on difference).

The primary political values required by the global market are order and tranquility, and freedom—as in the phrases "free trade," "free press," and "free love." Human rights are needed to a degree, but not citizenship or participation—and no more social justice and equality than are necessary to promote efficient economic production and consumption. Multinational corporations sometimes seem to prefer doing business with local oligarchs, inasmuch as they can take confidence from dealing with the boss on all crucial matters. Despots who slaughter their own populations are no problem, so long as they leave markets in place and refrain from making war on their neighbors (Saddam Hussein's fatal mistake). In trading partners, predictability is of more value than justice.

The Eastern European revolutions that seemed to arise out of concern for global democratic values quickly deteriorated into a stampede in the general direction of free markets and their ubiquitous, television-promoted shopping malls. East Germany's Neues Forum, that courageous gathering of intellectuals, students, and workers which overturned the Stalinist regime in Berlin in 1989, lasted only six months in Germany's mini-version of McWorld. Then it gave way to money and markets and monopolies from the West. By the time of the first all-German elections, it could scarcely manage to secure three percent of the vote. Elsewhere there is growing evidence that *glasnost* will go and *perestroika*—defined as privatization and an opening of markets to Western bidders—will stay. So understandably anxious are the new rulers of Eastern Europe and whatever entities are forged from the residues of the Soviet Union to gain access to credit and markets and technology—McWorld's flourishing new currencies—that they have shown themselves willing to trade away democratic prospects in pursuit of them: not just old totalitarian ideologies and command-economy production models but some possible indigenous experiments with a third way between capitalism and socialism, such as economic cooperatives and employee stock-ownership plans, both of which have their ardent supporters in the East.

Jihad delivers a different set of virtues: a vibrant local identity, a sense of community, solidarity among kinsmen, neighbors, and countrymen, narrowly conceived. But it also guarantees parochialism and is grounded in exclusion.

Solidarity is secured through war against outsiders. And solidarity often means obedience to a hierarchy in governance, fanaticism in beliefs, and the obliteration of individual selves in the name of the group. Deference to leaders and intolerance toward outsiders (and toward "enemies within") are hallmarks of tribalism—hardly the attitudes required for the cultivation of new democratic women and men capable of governing themselves. Where new democratic experiments have been conducted in retribalizing societies, in both Europe and the Third World, the result has often been anarchy, repression, persecution, and the coming of new, noncommunist forms of very old kinds of despotism. During the past year, Havel's velvet revolution in Czechoslovakia was imperiled by partisans of "Czechland" and of Slovakia as independent entities. India seemed little less rent by Sikh, Hindu, Muslim, and Tamil infighting than it was immediately after the British pulled out, more than forty years ago.

To the extent that either McWorld or Jihad has a *natural* politics, it has turned out to be more of an antipolitics. For McWorld, it is the antipolitics of globalism: bureaucratic, technocratic, and meritocratic, focused (as Marx predicted it would be) on the administration of things—with people, however, among the chief things to be administered. In its politico-economic imperatives McWorld has been guided by laissez-faire market principles that privilege efficiency, productivity, and beneficence at the expense of civic liberty and self-government.

For Jihad, the antipolitics of tribalization has been explicitly antidemocratic: one-party dictatorship, government by military junta, theocratic fundamentalism—often associated with a version of the *Führerprinzip* that empowers an individual to rule on behalf of a people. Even the government of India, struggling for decades to model democracy for a people who will soon number a billion, longs for great leaders; and for every Mahatma Gandhi, Indira Gandhi, or Rajiv Gandhi taken from them by zealous assassins, the Indians appear to seek a replacement who will deliver them from the lengthy travail of their freedom.

## THE CONFEDERAL OPTION

How can democracy be secured and spread in a world whose primary tendencies are at best indifferent to it

239

(McWorld) and at worst deeply antithetical to it (Jihad)? My guess is that globalization will eventually vanquish retribalization. The ethos of material "civilization" has not yet encountered an obstacle it has been unable to thrust aside. Ortega may have grasped in the 1920s a clue to our own future in the coming millennium.

> Everyone sees the need of a new principle of life. But as always happens in similar crises—some people attempt to save the situation by an artificial intensification of the very principle which has led to decay. This is the meaning of the "nationalist" outburst of recent years . . . things have always gone that way. The last flare, the longest; the last sigh, the deepest. On the very eve of their disappearance there is an intensification of frontiers—military and economic.

Jihad may be a last deep sigh before the eternal yawn of McWorld. On the other hand, Ortega was not exactly prescient; his prophecy of peace and internationalism came just before blitzkrieg, world war, and the Holocaust tore the old order to bits. Yet democracy is how we remonstrate with reality, the rebuke our aspirations offer to history. And if retribalization is inhospitable to democracy, there is nonetheless a form of democratic government that can accommodate parochialism and communitarianism, one that can even save them from their defects and make them more tolerant and participatory: decentralized participatory democracy. And if McWorld is indifferent to democracy, there is nonetheless a form of democratic government that suits global markets passably well—representative government in its federal or, better still, confederal variation.

With its concern for accountability, the protection of minorities, and the universal rule of law, a confederalized representative system would serve the political needs of McWorld as well as oligarchic bureaucratism or meritocratic elitism is currently doing. As we are already beginning to see, many nations may survive in the long term only as confederations that afford local regions smaller than "nations" extensive jurisdiction. Recommended reading for democrats of the twenty-first century is not the U.S. Constitution or the French Declaration of Rights of Man and Citizen but the Articles of Confederation, that suddenly pertinent document that

stitched together the thirteen American colonies into what then seemed a too loose confederation of independent states but now appears a new form of political realism, as veterans of Yeltsin's new Russia and the new Europe created at Maastricht will attest.

By the same token, the participatory and direct form of democracy that engages citizens in civic activity and civic judgment and goes well beyond just voting and accountability—the system I have called "strong democracy"—suits the political needs of decentralized communities as well as theocratic and nationalist party dictatorships have done. Local neighborhoods need not be democratic, but they can be. Real democracy has flourished in diminutive settings: the spirit of liberty, Tocqueville said, is local. Participatory democracy, if not naturally apposite to tribalism, has an undeniable attractiveness under conditions of parochialism.

Democracy in any of these variations will, however, continue to be obstructed by the undemocratic and antidemocratic trends toward uniformitarian globalism and intolerant retribalization which I have portrayed here. For democracy to persist in our brave new McWorld, we will have to commit acts of conscious political will—a possibility, but hardly a probability, under these conditions. Political will requires much more than the quick fix of the transfer of institutions. Like technology transfer, institution transfer rests on foolish assumptions about a uniform world of the kind that once fired the imagination of colonial administrators. Spread English justice to the colonies by exporting wigs. Let an East Indian trading company act as the vanguard to Britain's free parliamentary institutions. Today's well-intentioned quick-fixers in the National Endowment for Democracy and the Kennedy School of Government, in the unions and foundations and universities zealously nurturing contacts in Eastern Europe and the Third World, are hoping to democratize by long distance. Post Bulgaria a parliament by first-class mail. Fed Ex the Bill of Rights to Sri Lanka. Cable Cambodia some common law.

Yet Eastern Europe has already demonstrated that importing free political parties, parliaments, and presses cannot establish a democratic civil society; imposing a free market may even have the opposite effect. Democracy grows from

the bottom up and cannot be imposed from the top down. Civil society has to be built from the inside out. The institutional superstructure comes last. Poland may become democratic, but then again it may heed the Pope, and prefer to found its politics on its Catholicism, with uncertain consequences for democracy. Bulgaria may become democratic, but it may prefer tribal war. The former Soviet Union may become a democratic confederation, or it may just grow into an anarchic and weak conglomeration of markets for other nations' goods and services.

Democrats need to seek out indigenous democratic impulses. There is always a desire for self-government, always some expression of participation, accountability, consent, and representation, even in traditional hierarchical societies. These need to be identified, tapped, modified, and incorporated into new democratic practices with an indigenous flavor. The tortoises among the democratizers may ultimately outlive or outpace the hares, for they will have the time and patience to explore conditions along the way, and to adapt their gait to changing circumstances. Tragically, democracy in a hurry often looks something like France in 1794 or China in 1989.

It certainly seems possible that the most attractive democratic ideal in the face of the brutal realities of Jihad and the dull realities of McWorld will be a confederal union of semi-autonomous communities smaller than nation-states, tied together into regional economic associations and markets larger than nation-states—participatory and self-determining in local matters at the bottom, representative and accountable at the top. The nation-state would play a diminished role, and sovereignty would lose some of its political potency. The Green movement adage "Think globally, act locally" would actually come to describe the conduct of politics.

This vision reflects only an ideal, however—one that is not terribly likely to be realized. Freedom, Jean-Jacques Rousseau once wrote, is a food easy to eat but hard to digest. Still, democracy has always played itself out against the odds. And democracy remains both a form of coherence as binding as McWorld and a secular faith potentially as inspiring as Jihad.

## A

Abramovitz, Moses, 225–226
access, democracy and, 109
Africa, and democracy, 213
African National Congress (ANC), 175–180
Afro-Asian Conference, of 1955, 166
"Alternative Vote Plus" voting system, 21
anti-Semitism, 159
Asian financial crisis, 170, 189–190, 191–192, 197–203
Asian values, 193–196, 227, 228, 229
Association of South-East Asian Nations (ASEAN), 195
Aubry, Martine, 71
Asnar, Jose Maria, 95–96

## B

Balkans, 144–146
Bandung, Indonesia, and Afro-Asian Conference, 166, 167
Bank of England, 15, 27
Barber, Benjamin, 230, 236–240
Basic Law, of Germany, 37–38, 39
Basques, 112–113
Berlin Wall, 37, 38, 129
Bharatiya Janata Party, 191–192
birthrates: in Latin America, 171; in Third World, 166–167
Blair, Tony, 19, 24, 26–27, 93–94; and Germany, 48, 49; popularity of, 15–17; Third Way and, 16, 30–36, 95–96
Blumenthal, Sydney, 33
Bosnia, 113
Brandt, Willy, 47
Brazil, 168–171
Britain, 22–29, 220, 225; Tony Blair and, 15–17; constitutional reform and, 18–21; European Court of Justice and, 135–136; Germany and, 49; left-of-center politics and, 93–94; the Third Way and, 16, 30–36
Bundesbank, 43, 48, 52

## C

campaign finance reform, 118–119
Canada, parliamentary government in, 114–116
capitalism, democracy and, 111, 219–226
Cardoso, Fernando Henrique, 171
Carter, Jimmy, 115, 116
Catalonia, 112–113
center-left, political parties, 32–33
Central Committee, of China, 184, 185
Charter 88, 19, 20
checks and balances, democracy and, 110
Chernomyrdin, Viktor, 149, 152, 157, 158
Chile, 169

China: and capitalism, 188–190, 218; and Confucianism, 193, 194, 229, 235; and leadership of Jiang Zemin, 182–187
Chirac, Jacques, 64–65
Christian Democratic Party, 96–97; of Germany, 39, 44–45, 47; of Italy, 74, 76–77
Christian values, 96, 145–146
Churchill, Sir Winston, 28–29
citizens, democracy and, 106
civic community, 74–75
civic society, and post-Communist states, 144–146
clash of civilizations, Huntington's theory of, 227–229, 231–235
Clinton, Bill, 50; and campaign finance reform, 118–119; and China, 182; and relations with Russia, 153; and the Third Way, 31–34
Colombia, 209
common agricultural policy (CAP), 45, 49
Communist Party: of China, 183–187; of France, 68, 72, 76–77; of Russia, 151, 152, 156, 159
competition, democracy and, 106
Comprehensive Test Ban Treaty, 191
Confederation of South African Trade Unions (COSATU), 176
Confucianism, 193, 194, 229, 235
congressional model, of legislature, 114–117
consensus, democracy and, 109
Conservative Party, of Britain, 15, 18–21, 33–36
constitutional reform: in Britain, 18–21, 27; in France, 64–65; in Germany, 39
Contract with America, 118
Cook, Robin, 17
cooperation, democracy and, 107
Coreper, 136–137
Council of Ministers, of the European Union, 134–135
Crossed Swords (Ma Licheng and Ling Zhijun), 186
cultural determinism, 145–146
cultural diversity, of Europeans, 125–126, 127
culture, and its influence on international conflict, 228–230, 231–235, 236–240

## D

Dahl, Robert, 108, 109, 208–209, 220–221
D'Alemo, Massimo, 76–77
Day of German Unity, 38
de Gaulle, Charles, 64
de Klerk, F. W., 176
decentralization, of Europe. See devolution
Delors, Jacques, 133, 138

democracy, 105–111; Barber's theory of, 239–240; in Britain, 18–21; and capitalism, 219–226; in China, 182; Europe and, 129; in Germany, 37–43, 44–52; in Italy, 74–75; in Nigeria, 181; and parliamentary or congressional legislature, 114–117; post-Communist states and, 144–146; in Russia, 147, 149–153, 155; in South Africa, 175–180; third wave of, 208–216
Democracy in America (Toqueville), 107
Democratic Party: of Japan, 78–79; and the Third Way, 33
Deng Xiaoping, 183, 187, 188–189
devolution, 112–113; of Scotland and Wales, 15, 18, 19, 20

## E

ecological imperative, globalism and, 238
economic crises: in Latin America, 168–171; in Mexico, 172–174; in Russia, 147–148, 149–153
economic models, 217–218; Chinese, 188, German, 40–42, 55–61; Japanese, 83–87
economic participation, of women, 99, 103
education, differences in European, 125–126
education, in Latin America, 170–171
efficiency, of democracy, 110
elections, democracy and, 106
electoral reform: in Britain, 18, 19, 20, 21, 28–29; in France, 64–65
emerging market fund managers (EMFMs), 200–201
EMILY's List, 101
ethnic cleansing, 145
euro, 97, 139–143; Britain and, 20, 21, 29; Germany and, 37, 43, 47, 51
Europe: Britain's relationship with, 15, 17; trying to define, 127–131; devolution in, 112–113; diversity in, 125–126; left-of-center political parties in, 93–94; right-of-center political parties in, 95–97
Europe, central, 144–146
European Central Bank (ECB), 140. See also euro
European Commission, 46, 133–134, 138
European Community, 20
European Convention on Human Rights, 18, 19–21
European Court of Justice, 135–136
European Monetary Union (EMU), 37, 43, 139–143. See also euro
European Parliament, 132, 136, 138
European Union: Britain and, 23, 130–131; center-left governments of, 93–94; France and, 72, 73; Germany and, 37, 43, 45–46, 49, 53; institutional reform in,

132–137, 138; post-Communist countries and, 146
Eurosceptics, 97, 133, 135

## F

federalism, democracy and, 109, 110
*Federalist Papers, The,* 106
Fischer, Joschka, 50, 51, 53
France, 45, 46, 48, 220; and anti-Americanism, 69–73; constitutional reform in, 64–65; devolution and, 112; economic model of, 217; Germany and, 49; political parties in, 66–68; racism in, 62–63, 64
Free Democratic Party (FDP), of Germany, 39, 44
free market system, 31–32
Freedom House, 210, 211
Freedom of Information Act, in Britain, 18, 19
Friedman, Milton, 223
Fukuyama, Francis, 228, 230, 234

## G

gangs, Russian, 155, 158
GEAR (Growth, Employment, and Redistribution), 176
gender differences, regarding peace and war, 103
Germany, 53–54, 220, 224, 225, 230; democracy in, 37–43; devolution and, 112; economic model of, 40–42, 55–61, 217; left-of-center politics of, 93, 94; Gerhard Schröder and, 44–52
Giddens, Anthony, 21, 33
Gingrich, Newt, 118
Global South, 167
globalism versus tribalism, Barber's theory of, 236–240
Gorbachev, Mikhail, 157
Green Party: of France, 68; of Germany, 39, 44–45, 46, 48, 49, 51–52
Greenspan, Alan, 202–203

## H

Hague, William, 16, 17, 20, 27, 97
"Hapsburg factor," 146
Hashimoto, Ryutaro, 78–79, 80
Honecker, Erich, 38
House of Commons, in Britain, 18
House of Lords, in Britain, 18, 19, 20, 28
Huntington, Samuel, 146, 208, 227–229, 231–235

## I

immigration: Britain and, 25; France and, 62, 72; Germany and, 62, 97

Independent Commission on the Voting System, in England, 19, 20
India, 191–192, 209, 239
Indonesia, 166–167, 195–196, 199, 203
industrial modernization, 220
information–technology imperative, globalism and, 237–238
Inkatha Freedom Party, 175, 176
International Monetary Fund, 150, 153, 166, 191, 192, 198–199, 202
Ireland, 15, 16, 18, 23
Islamic civilization, Huntington's theory of, 228–229, 232, 234, 235
Italy: and the civic community, 74–75; devolution and, 113; economic model of, 217; political parties in, 76–77

## J

Japan, 220, 224; economic model of, 218; elections in, 78–82; financial crisis in, 83–87
Jiang Zemin, 183–187
Jihad versus McWorld, Barber's theory of, 230, 236–240
Jospin, Lionel, 63, 64–65, 66–68, 69–73, 94

## K

keiretsu, 84, 87
Kinnock, Neil, 19, 24
Kohl, Helmut, 40, 44, 47, 53, 55–61
Kovalyov, Sergei, 155
Kurds, 113

## L

Labor Party, of Britain, 15–17, 18–21, 24, 27, 32–36
Labor reform: in France, 70–72; in Germany, 41, 57, 58–61
Lafontaine, Oskar, 47, 48, 51, 54, 56
land reform, in Brazil, 171
Latin America, 168–171, 212–213
law and custom, in Britain, 18
Le Pen, Jean-Marie, 62, 72, 97, 165
Lebed, Aleksander, 152, 154, 157–158
left-of-center political parties, in Europe, 93–94
Liberal Democratic Party: of Britain, 16, 19; of Japan, 78–82, 84–87
Luzhkov, Yuri, 152

## M

Maastricht Treaty, 135, 140, 142, 143; Britain and, 20
Madres de La Plaza de Mayo, 100
Major, John, 16, 17, 18, 23–24
majority rule, 107, 109
*Making Democracy Work: Civic Traditions in Modern Italy* (Putnam), 74–75

Malaysia, 195, 196, 201–202
Mandela, Nelson Rolihlahla, 175–180
Mandelson, Peter, 16, 17, 33, 95
Mao Tse-tung, 184, 188–189
market economy, and post-Communist states, 144–146
market imperative, globalism and, 236–237
Marxism, 221–222, 223; in China, 183, 188, 236
Mbeki, Thabo, 176, 177, 180
Mexico, 169–170, 172–174, 198, 202, 210
*Mibestimmung,* 55
military rulers, 214; in Nigeria, 181
military spending, of the Third World, 167
Mitterrand, François, 46, 71
Myanmar, 195

## N

NAFTA (North American Free Trade Association), 172
National Front Party, of France, 65, 66, 97
National Party, of South Africa, 175, 176
National People's Congress, of China, 184
nationalism, European, 97, 112–113, 238–239
NATO, 42, 45, 48, 50, 128, 130, 146
Nazis, 37, 38
*New Britain* (Blair), 19
New Labor party, of Britain, 15–17, 18–21, 30–36
Nigeria, 181
Noorderhaven, Niels G., 125–126
nuclear weapons, 191, 192

## O

Obasanjo, Olusegun, 181
Obuchi, Keizo, 79, 80, 81
Olson, Mancur, 224
Operation Clean Hands, 74
Organization for Economic Cooperation and Development (OECD), 128, 140, 141
Ortega y Gasset, José, 238, 240

## P

Pakistan, 191, 192
parliamentary model, of legislature, 114–117, 118
participation, democracy and, 109
Party for Democratic Socialism (PDS), of Germany, 39, 44
party list proportional representation, 20
Party of European Socialists (PES), 93–94
Peru, 214
Philippines, 195, 199
Pinochet, Augusto, 169
pluralism, democracy and, 109

post-Communist countries, 129, 144–146, 147–148, 149–153, 154–159
poverty, and the Third World, 165, 166–167, 168–169
presidentialism, democracy and, 110
Primakov, Yevgeny M., 147, 148
privatization: of Chilean economy, 169–170, 173; of Russian economy, 150–151
public funding, of political parties, 118–119
public realm, democracy and, 106
Putnam, Robert, 74–75

**Q**

Qiao Shi, 184, 187
quota system, for women in politics, 102–103

**R**

racism: in Britain, 25; in France, 62–63; in Germany, 62; in South Africa, 175, 178, 179; in the Third World, 165
"Reagan Revolution," 225
red-Green alliance, in Germany, 44, 48, 51–52
representation, democracy and, 107, 108
resource imperative, and globalism, 237
responsiveness, of rulers to citizenry, 109
reunification, of East and West Germany, 37, 38, 42–43, 55, 58
right-of-center political parties, in Europe, 95–97
Rohatyn, Felix, 69, 70
rule of law, democracy and, 108, 145
Russia: change in, 154–159; comparison with China, 188–189, 190; economic crisis in, 149–153; devolution and, 112–113

**S**

Salinas de Gortari, Carlos, 172, 173
Santer, Jacques, 133–134, 138
scandal, in British politics, 16, 17
Scharping, Rudolf, 49, 50
Schmidt, Helmut, 47
Schröder, Gerhard, 44–50, 93–94; red-Green coalition and, 51–52, 53–54

Schumpeter, Joseph, 208–209, 219, 220, 222–223
Scotland, 15, 18, 19, 20, 23, 27, 112
Shenzhen, China, 189
Silva-Herzog, Jesus, 174
Singapore, 195, 196, 199, 218
Single European Act, Britain and, 20
Single Transferable Vote System, 20
Smith, Adam, 219, 220, 223
Smith, John, 19
Social Democratic Party, of Germany (SPD), 38, 39, 44, 47, 48, 51–52, 53
Socialist Party, of France, 68, 71, 72
South Africa, 175–180
South Korea, 203, 218, 229–230
sovereignty, parliamentary, 109
Spain, 45, 95; Basques and Catalans of, 112–113
Sri Lanka, 209
Straw, Jack, 34, 35
suffrage movements, 98–99
Sweden, 225

**T**

Thailand, 195, 196, 199–200, 201, 203
Thatcher, Margaret, 18, 23–24, 25–26, 33, 34, 96
Third Reich, 37–38
third wave, of democratization, 208–216
Third Way, the, 16, 21, 30–36, 95–96
Third World, definition of, 165, 166–167
Tiananmen Square demonstrations, 182, 186, 187, 189
Tito, Marshal, 217–218
Tocqueville, Alexis de, 74, 107
Tory Party, British, 15–17, 23, 27, 34–36
transparency, and Asian business, 198
Truth and Reconciliation Commission (TRC), 177–178
tsars, 156–157
Turkey, 113, 209
two-party system, and congressional government, 115–116, 118–119

**U**

United Democratic Movement (UDM), of South Africa, 178
United States, 220; campaign finance in, 118–119; and China,

185, 187; congressional government in, 114–117; and France, 69–73; and Germany, 50; and India, 191; and Latin America, 170; and Mexico, 173, 202; and Russia, 147, 152–153
United Nations, and women's issues, 99, 101, 104

**V**

Védrine, Hubert, 69–70
Vietnam, 199, 200
violence: in Russia, 155, 158; in South Africa, 178–179

**W**

Wales, 15, 18, 28
Weber, Max, 145–146, 228, 229
Weimar Republic, 37–38
welfare reform; in Britain, 23, 30–31; in Germany, 55–57, 58–59
welfare state, development of, 225–226
Western civilization, Huntington's theory of, 227–230, 231, 235
white papers (intentions to legislate), in Britain, 19
women in politics, 98–104
Women of Russia Party, 102
World Bank, 165, 166, 171, 191, 192

**X**

xenophobia: European, 97; Russian, 155, 159

**Y**

Yeltsin, Boris N., 147, 148, 149, 151, 154, 155, 157–158

**Z**

Zedillo, Ernesto, 173–174
Zhao Ziyang, 185
Zhirinovsky, Vladimir, 151
Zhu Rongji, 185
Zyuganov, Gennadi, 152, 156

# AE Article Review Form

We encourage you to photocopy and use this page as a tool to assess how the articles in **Annual Editions** expand on the information in your textbook. By reflecting on the articles you will gain enhanced text information. You can also access this useful form on a product's book support Web site at **http://www.dushkin.com/online/.**

NAME:                                                                                    DATE:

_____

TITLE AND NUMBER OF ARTICLE:

_____

BRIEFLY STATE THE MAIN IDEA OF THIS ARTICLE:

_____

LIST THREE IMPORTANT FACTS THAT THE AUTHOR USES TO SUPPORT THE MAIN IDEA:




_____

WHAT INFORMATION OR IDEAS DISCUSSED IN THIS ARTICLE ARE ALSO DISCUSSED IN YOUR TEXTBOOK OR OTHER READINGS THAT YOU HAVE DONE? LIST THE TEXTBOOK CHAPTERS AND PAGE NUMBERS:




_____

LIST ANY EXAMPLES OF BIAS OR FAULTY REASONING THAT YOU FOUND IN THE ARTICLE:




_____

LIST ANY NEW TERMS/CONCEPTS THAT WERE DISCUSSED IN THE ARTICLE, AND WRITE A SHORT DEFINITION:




_____

ANNUAL EDITIONS revisions depend on two major opinion sources: one is our Advisory Board, listed in the front of this volume, which works with us in scanning the thousands of articles published in the public press each year; the other is you—the person actually using the book. Please help us and the users of the next edition by completing the prepaid article rating form on this page and returning it to us. Thank you for your help!

## ANNUAL EDITIONS: Comparative Politics 99/00

### ARTICLE RATING FORM

Here is an opportunity for you to have direct input into the next revision of this volume. We would like you to rate each of the 50 articles listed below, using the following scale:

**1. Excellent: should definitely be retained**
**2. Above average: should probably be retained**
**3. Below average: should probably be deleted**
**4. Poor: should definitely be deleted**

Your ratings will play a vital part in the next revision. So please mail this prepaid form to us just as soon as you complete it. Thanks for your help!

**RATING**

**ARTICLE**

1. Tony Blair Rides Triumphant as a Visionary and a Promoter
2. Unwritten Rules: Britain's Constitutional Revolution
3. There Will Always Be an England
4. Perspectives on "New" Labour's "Third Way"
5. From the Bonn to the Berlin Republic: Can a Stable Democracy Continue?
6. Gerhard Schröder's Government
7. Birth of the Berlin Republic
8. Goodbye to All That
9. Perspectives on the German Model
10. Field Victory Colors French View of Themselves
11. Resisting Reform to de Gaulle's Old Constitution
12. Right and Left in France: Two Recent Reports
13. Perspectives on the French Model
14. Tocqueville in Italy
15. Former Communist Installed in Italy
16. The July 1998 Election: Two Reports
17. Japan's Search for a New Path
18. Europe: A Continental Drift—to the Left
19. Europe's Right: Displaced, Defeated and Not Sure What to Do Next
20. Women in Power: From Tokenism to Critical Mass
21. What Democracy Is . . . and Is Not
22. Devolution Can Be Salvation
23. Parliament and Congress: Is the Grass Greener on the Other Side?
24. Campaign and Party Finance: What Americans Might Learn from Abroad
25. The Untied States of Europe

**RATING**

**ARTICLE**

26. What Is Europe? The Changing Idea of a Continent
27. The Institutional Framework of the EU
28. Europe's Censure Motion
29. Europe's New Currency: Gambling on the Euro
30. Eastern Europe a Decade Later: The Postcommunist Divide
31. What Now for Russia?
32. Russia's Summer of Discontent
33. Can Russia Change?
34. Let's Abolish the Third World
35. The 'Third World' Is Dead, but Spirits Linger
36. Latin Economies Soar, Stumble with Reforms
37. Mexico: Sweeping Changes of Last Decade Translate into a Tale of 2 Economies
38. After Mandela's Miracle in South Africa
39. Nigeria's Long Road Back to Democracy
40. Jiang Zemin Takes Command
41. In March toward Capitalism, China Has Avoided Russia's Path
42. What a Difference a Year Can Make
43. Asian Values Revisited: What Would Confucius Say Now?
44. Asia and the "Magic" of the Marketplace
45. Is the Third Wave Over?
46. Serial Utopia
47. Capitalism and Democracy
48. Cultural Explanations: The Man in the Baghdad Cafe
49. A Debate on Cultural Conflicts
50. Jihad vs. McWorld

(Continued on next page)

We Want Your Advice

‖‖‖‖

## BUSINESS REPLY MAIL
FIRST-CLASS MAIL  PERMIT NO. 84  GUILFORD CT

POSTAGE WILL BE PAID BY ADDRESSEE

**Dushkin/McGraw-Hill
Sluice Dock
Guilford, CT 06437-9989**

‖‖‖‖‖‖‖‖‖‖‖‖‖‖‖‖‖‖‖‖‖‖‖‖‖‖‖‖‖‖

## ABOUT YOU

Name                                                                    Date

Are you a teacher? ☐   A student? ☐
Your school's name

Department

Address                                          City                    State      Zip

School telephone #

## YOUR COMMENTS ARE IMPORTANT TO US !

Please fill in the following information:
For which course did you use this book?

Did you use a text with this *ANNUAL EDITION*?  ☐ yes  ☐ no
What was the title of the text?

What are your general reactions to the *Annual Editions* concept?

Have you read any particular articles recently that you think should be included in the next edition?

Are there any articles you feel should be replaced in the next edition? Why?

Are there any World Wide Web sites you feel should be included in the next edition? Please annotate.

May we contact you for editorial input?  ☐ yes  ☐ no
May we quote your comments?  ☐ yes  ☐ no